Early Christ Groups and Greco-Roman Associations

EARLY CHRIST GROUPS AND GRECO-ROMAN ASSOCIATIONS
Organizational Models and Social Practices

Copyright © 2022 Richard S. Ascough. All rights reserved. Except for brief quotations in critical publications or reviews, no part of this book may be reproduced in any manner without prior written permission from the publisher. Write: Permissions, Wipf and Stock Publishers, 199 W. 8th Ave., Suite 3, Eugene, OR 97401.

Cascade Books
An Imprint of Wipf and Stock Publishers
199 W. 8th Ave., Suite 3
Eugene, OR 97401

www.wipfandstock.com

PAPERBACK ISBN: 978-1-6667-0901-8
HARDCOVER ISBN: 978-1-6667-0902-5
EBOOK ISBN: 978-1-6667-0903-2

Cataloguing-in-Publication data:

Names: Ascough, Richard S., author.

Title: Early Christ groups and Greco-Roman associations : organizational models and social pracitces. / Richard S. Ascough.

Description: Eugene, OR: Cascade Books, 2022. | Includes bibliographical references and indexes.

Identifiers: ISBN 978-1-6667-0901-8 (paperback). | ISBN 978-1-6667-0902-5 (hardcover). | ISBN 978-1-6667-0903-2 (ebook).

Subjects: LSCH: Christian communities—Mediterranean Region. | Associations, institutions, etc.—Greece—Sources. | Associations, institutions, etc.—Rome—Sources. | Civilization, Greco-Roman—Sources. | Inscriptions, Greek. | Inscriptions, Latin.

Classification: BL1060 A85 2022 (print). | BL1060 (ebook).

Scripture quotations are taken from the New Revised Standard Version Bible, copyright © 1989 National Council of the Churches of Christ in the United States of America. Used by permission. All rights reserved worldwide.

Early Christ Groups and Greco-Roman Associations

Organizational Models and Social Practices

RICHARD S. ASCOUGH

CASCADE *Books* • Eugene, Oregon

Dedicated to John S. Kloppenborg
in gratitude for mentorship, collegiality, and friendship

Contents

Permissions | ix
Illustrations | xii
Acknowledgments | xiii
Abbreviations | xv

1 Introduction | 1

   ## SECTION I: MODELING CHRIST GROUPS

2 Greco-Roman Philosophic, Religious, and Voluntary Associations | 17
3 Paul, Synagogues, and Associations: Reframing the Question of Models for Pauline Christ Groups | 36
4 Voluntary Associations and the Formation of Pauline Christian Communities: Overcoming the Objections | 57
5 Translocal Relationships among Voluntary Associations and Early Christianity | 89
6 "Map-maker, map-maker, make me a map . . .": Redescribing Greco-Roman "Elective Social Formations" | 106
7 The Thessalonian Christian Community as a Professional Voluntary Association | 122
8 Matthew and Community Formation | 140

   ## SECTION II: RECRUITMENT

9 Redescribing the Thessalonians' "Mission" in Light of Greco-Roman Associations | 169
10 Defining Community-Ethos in Light of the 'Other': Recruitment Rhetoric among Greco-Roman Associations | 191

11 "A Place to Stand, a Place to Grow": Architectural and Epigraphic Evidence for Expansion in Greco-Roman Associations | 208

SECTION III: MEALS AND MEMORIALS

12 Forms of Commensality in Greco-Roman Associations | 233

13 Social and Political Characteristics of Greco-Roman Association Meals | 247

14 The Apostolic Decree of Acts and Greco-Roman Associations: Eating in the Shadow of the Roman Empire | 261

15 A Question of Death: Paul's Community-Building Language in 1 Thessalonians 4:13–18 | 277

16 Of Memories and Meals: Greco-Roman Associations and the Early Jesus-group at Thessalonikē | 299

17 Benefaction Gone Wrong: The "Sin" of Ananias and Sapphira in Context | 319

Bibliography | 335

Index of Ancient Sources | 373

Index of Modern Authors | 387

Index of Subjects | 393

Permissions

Chapter 1: A few paragraphs are adapted from "What Are They *Now* Saying about Christ Groups and Associations?" *Currents in Biblical Research* 13 (2015) 207–44 (https://doi.org/10.1177/1476993X14522900), and are used here with permission of Sage Publishing.

Chapter 2: "Greco-Roman Philosophic, Religious, and Voluntary Associations." This article first appeared in *Community Formation in the Early Church and the Church Today*, edited by Richard N. Longenecker, 3–19. Peabody, MA: Hendrickson, 2002. Used by permission of Baker Academic, a division of Baker Publishing Group.

Chapter 3: "Paul, Synagogues, and Associations: Reframing the Question of Models for Pauline Christ Groups." This article first appeared in *Journal of the Jesus Movement in Its Jewish Setting* 2 (2015) 27–52. Reprinted by permission.

Chapter 4: "Voluntary Associations and the Formation of Pauline Churches: Addressing the Objections." This article first appeared in *Vereine, Synagogen und Gemeinden im kaiserzeitlichen Kleinasien*, edited by Andreas Gutsfeld and Dietrich-Alex Koch, 149–83. STAC 25. Tübingen: Mohr Siebeck, 2006. Reprinted by permission of the publisher.

Chapter 5: "Translocal Relationships among Voluntary Associations and Early Christianity." This article first appeared in *Journal of Early Christian Studies* 5 (1997) 223–41. Copyright © 1997 Johns Hopkins University Press and the North American Patristics Society. Published with permission by Johns Hopkins University Press.

Chapter 6: "'Map-maker, Map-maker, Make me a Map': Re-describing Greco-Roman 'Elective Social Formations.'" This article first appeared in *Introducing Religion: Essays in Honor of Jonathan Z. Smith*, edited by Willi

Braun and Russell T. McCutcheon, 68–84. London: Equinox, 2008. Reproduced with permission of The Licensor through PLSclear.

Chapter 7: "The Thessalonian Christian Community as a Professional Voluntary Association." This article first appeared in *Journal of Biblical Literature* 119 (2000) 311–28. Reprinted by permission of the publisher.

Chapter 8: "Matthew and Community Formation." This article first appeared in *The Gospel of Matthew in Current Study: Studies in Memory of William G. Thompson, SJ*, edited by David E. Aune, 96–126. Grand Rapids: Eerdmans, 2001. Reprinted by permission of the publisher.

Chapter 9: "Redescribing the Thessalonians' 'Mission' in Light of Greco-Roman Associations." This article first appeared in *New Testament Studies* 60 (2014) 61–82. Reprinted by permission.

Chapter 10: "Defining Community-Ethos in Light of the 'Other': Recruitment Rhetoric Among Greco-Roman Religious Groups." This article first appeared in *Annali di Storia dell'Esegesi* 24 (2007) 59–75. Reprinted by permission of the publisher.

Chapter 11: "'A Place to Stand, A Place to Grow': Architectural and Epigraphic Evidence for Expansion in Greco-Roman Associations." This article first appeared in *Identity and Interaction in the Ancient Mediterranean: Jews, Christians and Others. Festschrift for Stephen G. Wilson*, edited by Zeba Crook and Philip A. Harland, 76–98. New Testament Monographs 18. Sheffield: Sheffield Phoenix, 2007. Reprinted by permission of the publisher.

Chapter 12: "Forms of Commensality in Greco-Roman Associations." Copyright © 2008 Classical Association of the Atlantic States, Inc. This article first appeared in *Classical World* 102 (2008) 33–45. Published with permission by Johns Hopkins University Press.

Chapter 13: "Social and Political Characteristics of Greco-Roman Association Meals." This article first appeared in *Meals in the Early Christian World: Social Formation, Experimentation, and Conflict at the Table*, edited by Dennis E. Smith and Hal Taussig, 59–72. New York: Palgrave MacMillan, 2012. Reprinted by permission.

Chapter 14: "The Apostolic Decree of Acts and Greco-Roman Associations: Eating in the Shadow of the Roman Empire." This article first appeared in *Aposteldekret und antike Vereinswesen: Gemeinschaft und ihre Ordnung*, edited by Markus Öhler, 297–316. WUNT 280. Tübingen: Mohr Siebeck, 2011. Reprinted by permission of the publisher.

Chapter 15: "A Question of Death: Paul's Community-Building Language in 1 Thessalonians 4:13–18." This article first appeared in *Journal of Biblical Literature* 123 (2004) 509–30. Reprinted by permission of the publisher.

Chapter 16: "Of Memories and Meals: Greco-Roman Associations and the Early Jesus-group at Thessalonikē." This article first appeared in *From Roman to Early Christian Thessalonikē: Studies in Religion and Archaeology*, edited by Laura Nasrallah, Charalambos Bakirtzis, and Steven J. Friesen, 49–72. HTS 64. Cambridge: Harvard Theological Studies, Harvard Divinity School, 2010. Reprinted by permission.

Chapter 17: "Benefaction Gone Wrong: The 'Sin' of Ananias and Sapphira in Context." This article first appeared in *Text and Artifact in the Religions of Mediterranean Antiquity: Essays in Honour of Peter Richardson*, edited by Stephen G. Wilson and Michel Desjardins, 91–110. ESCJ 9. Waterloo, ON: Wilfrid Laurier University, 2000. Reprinted by permission.

Illustrations

Figure 11.1: Pergamon, Podiensaal, facing SE
 (photo by Richard S. Ascough) | 217

Figure 11.2: Ephesos, Terrace House 2, Residential Unit 6
 (photo by Richard S. Ascough) | 220

Figure 11.3: Ephesos, Terrace House 2, Residential Unit 6, inscription
 (photo by Richard S. Ascough) | 221

Acknowledgments

I AM APPRECIATIVE OF financial support I received for my work on associations from the following agencies: Social Sciences and Humanities Research Council of Canada (SSHRC), Government of Ontario (PREA), Queen's University, Society of Biblical Literature, Catholic Biblical Association, and the Wabash Center. I am particularly grateful to the Alexander von Humboldt Foundation for a Research Fellowship that supported my stay at the Westfälische Wilhelms-Universität, Münster, Germany, in 2003–2004, where I was able to collect most of the material that appears in the annotated bibliography in ARGW, which subsequently fed into much of my research.

As always, I am thankful to Cheryl O'Shea, whose keen editorial eye saved me from many infelicities in formatting, grammar, punctuation, and such, not only with many of the original publications but in the reformatting for this book. This reformatting took place in early 2021 while the entire globe was dealing with the ongoing threat of the COVID-19 pandemic. As my own city moved in and out of various forms of lockdown, I am grateful to have had the support of my running friends, the Running Dragons, and our ancillary sub-groups, the Reading Dragons and the Kayaking Dragons: Suzanne, Alana, Robin, Mark, Bob, Leanne, Pete, Dalton, Steve, Andrea, Sandy, Cami, and Jim. I am particularly thankful to Suzanne and Mark, along with Maddie, Will, Katie, and Desmond, who are exceptionally supportive in so many ways. My constant source of pride is my children, Josiah and Hannah, who, along with Brandon, never cease to amaze me, not only with their own accomplishments but in their deep compassion for other people and for the world we inhabit.

Many colleagues have provided intellectual and social engagement over my career, and I am fortunate enough to have had too many to mention here, save for a few who have gone above and beyond in their support: Bill Arnal, Alicia Batten, Brigidda Bell, Willi Braun, Amy Clanfield, Zeba Crook,

Bob Derrenbacker, Phil Harland, Maia Kotrosits, Sharday Mosurinjohn, Colleen Shantz, Dan Smith, Erin Vearncombe, and Heidi Wendt.

Finally, I want to express my appreciation to John Kloppenborg, who encouraged me to put together this collection of my publications, most recently while we were touring sites related to associations in Pompeii and Ostia. Over the three decades of my academic career, beginning with my MA and PhD degrees in Toronto, John has been a big supporter and champion of my work. I dedicate this book to him, with deep gratitude for his mentorship, collegiality, and friendship.

All of the essays in this volume except the Introduction have been published previously, and I am grateful to the original publishers for giving me permission to republish them here. The content of each essay remains unchanged, and the original pagination is provided in bolded square brackets. There have been some minor formatting changes so that the essays are consistent across this book, including the use of American spelling and consistency in the citation format (last name, short title, page number). The Bibliography covers all of the essays in this volume. A comprehensive bibliography on associations in the ancient world is regularly updated online at http://philipharland.com/greco-roman-associations/welcome/bibliography-on-associations-in-the-greco-roman-world/. Almost all inscriptions have multiple citations based on the various corpora in which they appear. This was one of the most frustrating aspects of our early research endeavors: attempting to find a consistent and commonly accepted citation format. With the publication of AGRW and the GRA volumes we eventually worked out what works best, so I have made slight changes to the citation format of some essays not only for consistency but for ease of reference, particularly with the Index of Ancient Sources.

Abbreviations

EPIGRAPHIC ABBREVIATIONS FOLLOW THOSE used on the AGRW website http://philipharland.com/greco-roman-associations/welcome/how-to-use-the-inscriptions-database/#abbrev, which is based on G. H. R. Horsley and J. A. L. Lee, *A Preliminary Checklist of Abbreviations of Greek Epigraphic Volumes*, in *Epigraphica* 56 (1994) 129–69. Papyrological abbreviations follow J. F. Oates, R. S. Bagnall, and W. H. Willis, *Checklist of Editions of Greek Papyri and Ostraca* (5th ed., BASPSupp 9; Oakville, CT: American Society of Papyrologists, 2001). Abbreviations for ancient authors, including biblical texts, follow *The SBL Handbook of Style*. Volumes not included in the above references, along with commonly cited reference works are abbreviated as follows:

AB	Anchor Bible
ABD	David Noel Freedman, ed., *The Anchor Bible Dictionary*. 6 vols. New York: Doubleday, 1992
AGRW	Richard S. Ascough, Philip A. Harland, and John S. Kloppenborg. *Associations in the Greco-Roman World: A Sourcebook*. Waco: Baylor University Press, 2012
AJEC	Ancient Judaism and Early Christianity
AnBib	Analecta Biblica
ANF	*Ante-Nicene Fathers*
ANTC	Abingdon New Testament Commentaries
ANRW	*Aufstieg und Niedergang der römischen Welt*
ATLA	American Theological Library Association

BAGD		Walter Bauer, Frederick W. Danker, W. F. Arndt, and F. W. Gingrich. *Greek-English Lexicon of the New Testament and Other Early Christian Literature*. 2nd ed. Chicago: University of Chicago Press, 1979
BASOR		*Bulletin of the American Schools of Oriental Research*
BASORSup		*Bulletin of the American Schools of Oriental Research Supplements*
BASPSupp		*Bulletin of the American Society of Papyrologists Supplements*
BCH		*Bulletin de correspondence hellénique*
BEFAR		*Bibliothèque des écoles françaises d'Athènes et de Rome*
BECNT		Baker Exegetical Comentary on the New Testament
BETL		Bibliotheca Ephemeridum theologicarum Lovaniensium
Bib		*Biblica*
BJS		Brown Judaic Studies
BLE		*Bulletin de Littérature Ecclésiastique*
BNTC		Black New Testament Commentaries
BRev		*Bible Review*
BSac		*Bibliotheca Sacra*
BU		Biblische Untersuchungen
BR		*Biblical Research*
BZNW		Beihefte zur Zeitschrift für die neutestamentliche Wissenschaft und die Kunde der älteren Kirche
CBET		Contrubtions to Biblical Exegesis and Theology
ConBNT		Coniectanea biblica. New Testament Series
CBQ		*Catholic Biblical Quarterly*
CJ		*Classical Journal*
ClAnt		*Classical Antinquity*
ConBNT		Coniectanea Biblica: New Testament Series
CNT		Commentaire du Nouveau Testament
CP		*Classical Philology*
CRINT		Compendia rerum Iudaicarum ad Novum Testamentum
CSCT		Columbia Studies in the Classical Tradition

CurrBR	*Currents in Biblical Research*
CW	*Classical World*
EBib	Études Bibliques
ECL	Early Christianity and Its Literature
EKK	Evangelisch-katholischer Kommentar zum Neuen Testament
EPRO	Etudes préliminaires aux religions orientales dans l'Empire romain
ETL	*Ephemerides Theolgicae Lovanienses*
ExpTim	*Expository Times*
FAS	Frankfurter althistorische Studien
FF	Foundations and Facets
GBS	Guides to Biblical Scholarship
GNT	Grundrisse zum Neuen Testament
GRA I	Kloppenborg, John S. and Richard S. Ascough. *Greco-Roman Associations: Texts, Translations, and Commentary. Vol. 1. Attica, Central Greece, Macedonia, Thrace.* BZNW 181. Berlin: de Gruyter, 2011.
GRA II	Harland, Philip A. *Greco-Roman Associations: Texts, Translations, and Commentary. Vol. 2. North Coast of the Black Sea, Asia Minor.* BZNW 204. Berlin: de Gruyter, 2014
GRA III	Kloppenborg, John S. *Greco-Roman Associations: Texts, Translations, and Commentary. Vol. 3, Ptolemaic and Early Roman Egypt.* BZNW 246. Berlin: de Gruyter, 2020
GRBS	*Greek, Roman, and Byzantine Studies*
HvTSt	*Hervormde teologiese studies*
HNT	Handbuch zum Neuen Testament
HTR	*Harvard Theological Review*
HTS	Harvard Theological Studies
IBC	Interpretation: A Bible Commentary for Teaching and Preaching
ICC	International Critical Commentary
IG	Inscriptiones Graecae. Editio Minor. Berlin: de Gruyter, 1924–
Int	*Interpretation*

JAC	Jahrbuch für Antike und Christentum
JAAR	Journal of the American Academy of Religion
JAOS	Journal of the American Oriental Society
JBL	Journal of Biblical Literature
JECS	Journal of Early Christian Studies
JJMJS	Journal of the Jesus Movement in Its Jewish Setting
JRA	Journal of Roman Archaeology
JRS	Journal of Roman Studies
JSNT	Journal for the Study of the New Testament
JSNTSup	Supplement to the Journal of the Study of the New Testament
JSOT	Journal for the Study of the Old Testament
JTS	Journal of Theological Studies
LCL	Loeb Classical Library
LEC	Library Early Christianity
LNTS	Library of New Testament Studies
LSJ	Henry George Liddell, Robert Scott, and Henry Stuart Jones. *A Greek-English Lexicon*. 9th ed. Oxford: Clarendon, 1996.
MNTC	Moffatt New Testament Commentary
MTZ	Münchener theologische Zeitschrift
NAC	New American Commentary
NCB	New Century Bible
NIBC	New International Bible Commentary
NICNT	New International Commentary on the New Testament
NIGTC	New International Greek Testament Commentary
NovT	Novum Testamentum
NovTSup	Supplements to Novum Testamentum
NTAbh	Neutestamentliche Abhandlungen
NTD	Das Neue Testament Deutsch
NTOA	Novum Testamentum et Orbis Antiquus
NTS	New Testament Studies
OECT	Oxford Early Christian Texts

R&T	*Religion & Theology*
RGRW	Religions in the Graeco-Roman World
RTR	*Reformed Theological Review*
SBLMS	Society of Biblical Literature Monograph Series
SBLSP	Society of Biblical Literature Seminar Papers
SBLDS	Society of Biblical Literature Dissertation Series
SBS	Stuttgarter Bibelstudien
SJLA	Studies in Judaism in Late Antiquity
SNTSMS	Society for New Testament Studies Monograph Series
SNTW	Studies in the New Testament and Its World
SP	Sacra Pagina
STDJ	Studies on the Texts of the Desert of Judah
StPB	Studia Post-biblica
SR	*Studies in Religion*
ST	*Studia Theologica*
STAC	Studien und Texte zu Antike und Christentum
STK	*Svensk teologisk kvartalskrift*
SUNT	Studien zur Umwelt des Neuen Testaments
TANZ	Texte und Arbeiten zum neutestamentlichen Zeitalter
TDNT	Gerhard Kittel and Gerhard Friedrich, eds., *Theological Dictionary of the New Testament*. 10 vols. Translated by Geoffrey W. Bromiley. Grand Rapids: Eerdmans, 1964–1976
TNTC	Tyndale New Testament Commentaries
TS	*Theological Studies*
TSK	*Theologische Studien und Kritiken*
TynBul	*Tyndale Bulletin*
WBC	Word Biblical Commentary
WGRW	Writings from the Greco-Roman World
WUNT	Wissenschaftliche Untersuchungen zum Neuen Testament
ZBK NT	Zürcher Bibelkommentare Neue Testament

ZNW	*Zeitschrift für die neutestamentliche Wissenschaft und die Kunde der älteren Kirche*
ZPE	*Zeitschrift für Papyrologie und Epigraphik*
ZWT	*Zeitschrift für wissenschaftliche Theologie*

I

Introduction

FROM AT LEAST THE late fourth century BCE right through the Roman imperial period, there is evidence of persons in the circum-Mediterranean world joining together to form private and semiprivate associations. The basis for such social formations might have been common ethnic background, common cult, common occupation, common residency—or any combination thereof—but these associations provided for their members a shared purpose and identity. By the Roman period, such groups are attested throughout cities and villages, and among the poor through to the elite. The evidence comes primarily from inscriptions and papyri, although there are references to associations in ancient literary texts along with some archaeological evidence of remains of their meeting places.[1] The epigraphic and papyrological evidence is predominantly membership lists, funerary inscriptions, dedications to deities and patrons, and, especially, announcements of honors bestowed upon association members or benefactors. Although found less frequently, also important are the bylaws of associations, petitions and complaints, and civic decrees. Study of such groups continues to provide new insights into social and cultural life in antiquity.[2]

1. See Ascough, Harland, and Kloppenborg, *Associations in the Greco-Roman World* (AGRW).
2. E.g., van Nijf, *Civic World*; Nielsen, *Housing the Chosen*; Borbonus, *Columbarium Tombs*; Gabrielsen and Thomsen, eds., *Private Associations*; Last and Harland, *Group*

2   Early Christ Groups and Greco-Roman Associations

Over the past two and a half decades, there has been an increasing interest in how the data from the associations can help scholars better understand the development of Christ groups in the first and second centuries. The use of the associations as a model met with initial skepticism throughout the 1980s and early 1990s, but as more scholarly work was published there was increasing acceptance, and in the present moment many scholars, particularly those working on Paul, presume rather than argue that the associations are "good to think with" in exploring early Christianity.[3] My own published work was at the forefront of this move from skepticism to acceptance, although more because I stumbled into it than by design and intent, at least at first. But given the interest this topic is now generating, it seemed that this would be a good time to collect some of my contributions to the debate as it developed over the period.

In 1992, just I was finishing my MA, my supervisor, John Kloppenborg, suggested that I be part of an inaugural group that would meet biweekly to translate Greek. This "Hellenistic Texts Seminar" (HTS)—composed of John, me, Leif Vaage, Bradley McLean, Caroline Whelan, and Bill Arnal—rotated among the members' houses to share dinner cooked by the host and tackle previously untranslated Greek texts. I believe it was Bradley who early on suggested that we work our way through Franciszek Sokolowski's *Lois sacrées des cités grecque*. Little did I know at the time that these somewhat obscure inscriptions, sometimes written in Ionic or Doric Greek, would be the gateway to a career-long focus on associations, as we started branching out into other corpora with a focus on association inscriptions. The challenges we faced in attempting to be self-trained epigraphers and the hard lessons we learned in these early days led Bradley to write his comprehensive and eminently useful *Introduction to Greek Epigraphy of the Hellenistic and Roman Periods*.[4]

The HTS focus on inscriptions from associations linked well with another project, begun as a Special Seminar in the Canadian Society of Biblical Studies, that was exploring voluntary associations and early Christianity. This three-year project led to the publication of *Voluntary Associations in the Graeco-Roman World*,[5] the indexes for which I was privileged to compile in my role as a student research assistant. Through a series of graduate seminars, my own work began to focus on Philippi and Thessalonike, and I

Survival.

3. Kloppenborg, "Membership Practices," 187–88; Kloppenborg, "Moralizing of Discourse," 228.

4. McLean, *Introduction to Greek Epigraphy*.

5. Kloppenborg and Wilson, eds., *Voluntary Associations*.

compiled and translated association inscriptions from across Macedonia in order to help me rethink the social composition of the Pauline Christ groups in these two cities. The resulting dissertation was four hundred pages, with an additional two hundred pages of inscriptions. I extracted the dissertation's literature review to be reworked into a little volume called *What Are They Saying about the Formation of Pauline Churches?*, which outlines the strengths and weaknesses of the four scholarly models generally employed for understanding Pauline Christian groups: synagogues, philosophical schools, the mysteries, and associations.

The substantive argument of the dissertation was reworked to appear as *Paul's Macedonian Associations*. In writing the dissertation, I initially thought that the Thessalonian and Philippian Christ groups would resemble one another quite significantly, since they were in close proximity in the same province. The comparative process, both between the social context reflected in the two letters and with the association data, would not sustain that argument. I concluded that both Christ groups resembled associations in community language and practice, and both appeared to outsiders as associations and functioned internally as associations. Nevertheless, the Christ group at Thessalonike shared more traits in common with an occupational association, while the group at Philippi was similar in its characteristics to what at the time we were broadly referring as a religious association. Even as the taxonomy of associations has become more nuanced, these fundamental differences between the two Macedonian Christ groups can, I would argue, be sustained.

Other members of the group went on to publish work in this area, most notably John Kloppenborg himself, who not only has a long list of publications on associations but has recently published what is likely to stand for some time as the definitive guide—*Christ's Associations: Connecting and Belonging in the Ancient City*. Other members of the HTS group who came and went over the years include Philip Harland, Alicia Batten, Richard Last, Sarah Rollens, Ryan Olfert, Patrick Stange, Rebecca Runesson, and Christina Gousopoulos, among others.[6]

One of the great challenges to comparing and contrasting early Christ groups with associations was the availability of data from the associations themselves, beyond the four rather well-known inscriptions often used as evidence: SIG^3 985 (Philadelphia, late II BCE–early I CE = AGRW 121), CIL XIV 2112 (Lanuvium, 136 CE = AGRW 310), ILS 7213 (Rome, 153 CE = AGRW 322), and IG II^2 1368 (Athens, 164/165 CE = AGRW 7). Too

---

6. Harland, *Associations*; and Harland, *Dynamics of Identity*; Batten, "Moral World"; Last, *Pauline Church*.

often these same four texts were used to both support and challenge claims of intersections among Christ groups and associations. This is, however, a very limited data set, and although these particular texts are lengthy and quite interesting in their detail, there is much more extant evidence from associations available.

The three best-known sourcebooks on Greco-Roman associations at the time, however, dated back over one hundred years. Two are written in French and one in German.[7] Two collections published in the last quarter of the twentieth century focus respectively on Roman youth associations[8] and leadership in occupational *collegia* in Italy.[9] More recent collections have also focused on particular types of associations, such as Dionysiac associations[10] and Roman associations of textile dealers.[11] Despite these very helpful resources, many thousands of epigraphic and papyri association texts remain widely distributed across corpora, journals, and books. Unfortunately, most of these texts were untapped, since they are difficult to locate and access and, for the most part, are not translated.

In order to address the problem of access, John Kloppenborg, Philip Harland, and I initiated a multi-volume critical edition of texts and translations of select association inscriptions and papyri. The first volume focuses on Attica, Central Greece, Macedonia, and Thrace (GRA I),[12] the second includes texts from Asia Minor and the Bosphoros (GRA II),[13] and the third volume focuses on Ptolemaic and early Roman Egypt (GRA III).[14] Volume 4, on the Aegean Islands, Syria-Palestine, Egypt, and North Africa, is well underway, while the fifth volume, on the Western Provinces, and the sixth, on Italy, are still a few years from completion.

In order to facilitate broader access to the association data, we published a sourcebook of English translations of inscriptions, papyri, and literary texts, each with a very brief introduction: *Associations in the Greco-Roman World* (AGRW).[15] We also included descriptions of about

---

7. Foucaurt, *Des associations religieuses*; Waltzing, *Étude Historique*; Poland, *Geschichte des griechischen Vereinswesens*.

8. Jaczynowska, *Les associations*.

9. Royden, *Magistrates*.

10. Aneziri, *Die Vereine der dionysischen Techniten*; Jaccottet *Choisir Dionysos*.

11. Liu, *Guilds of Textile Dealers*; Labarre and Le Dinahet, "Le métiers du textile."

12. Kloppenborg and Ascough, *Greco-Roman Associations*.

13. Harland, *Greco-Roman Associations*.

14. Kloppenborg, *Greco-Roman Associations*.

15. Ascough, Harland, and Kloppenborg, *Associations in the Greco-Roman World*, (AGRW).

two-thirds of the extant archaeological remains from association buildings. An annotated bibliography of well over three hundred secondary works on all aspects of associations represents almost all of the major publications in English, German, and French up to 2011. The subject index facilitates connections among the primary and secondary works in the sourcebook. Our goal is to allow scholars and students to read the primary texts and form their own interpretations, connections, and ideas about the nature of associations in the ancient world and their intersections with early Christ groups and Jewish groups.

The original Greek and Latin texts for the inscriptions in the book are available on the companion website at http://philipharland.com/greco-roman-associations, which also now includes a considerable number of other association inscriptions and papyri texts with translation and, wherever possible, photographs, along with a comprehensive bibliography. This website continues to expand as we add new texts to it and make corrections to the texts and translations in the printed volumes as they are drawn to our attention. In a separate but related research trajectory, the Copenhagen Associations Project is developing a database of all attestations of private associations in the Greek-speaking world, from Italy to India (https://copenhagenassociations.saxo.ku.dk). Another project—the Ghent Database of Roman Guilds (https://gdrg.ugent.be)—is documenting occupational associations across the Roman Empire.

As the inscriptional and papyrological evidence for associations continues to be collected and analyzed, the complexity of the associations' social location within urban centers has become increasingly apparent. Interlinked with this, studies of early Christian texts are using the associations to understand how Christ groups negotiated their identity and their connections within the urban environments in which they were growing in the eastern areas of the Roman Empire. Over the past decade and a half, scholars have addressed directly the relationship between the associations and early Christ groups.[16] When one compares the social organization and practices of these groups to the Christ groups, it is clear that the latter would have been identified as, and identified themselves as, a particular manifestation of the same phenomenon. Researchers have taken a specific interest in understanding the social organization of associations, and many scholars

---

16. See particularly Kloppenborg and Wilson, eds., *Voluntary Associations*; Harland, *Associations*; Öhler, "Römisches Vereinsrecht"; Öhler, "Antikes Vereinswesen"; Öhler, "Graeco-Roman Associations"; Ebel, *Attraktivität*; Last, "Communities That Write"; Murray, *Restricted Generosity*; Kloppenborg, *Christ's Associations*. For a comprehensive overview see Ascough, *What Are They Saying about the Formation of Pauline Churches?*, 71–94, with an update in Ascough, "What Are They *Now* Saying about?."

now argue that associations can provide a framework for understanding early Jewish and Christian groups. To date, the majority of the work has focused on linking the data from the study of associations to data found in documents contained in the canon of the New Testament, such as Paul's letters.[17] Other work has studied Jewish and Christian groups more broadly in light of associations.[18]

This research on Christ groups and associations over the past few decades has brought to the fore many similarities and differences between Christ groups and associations, particularly, albeit not limited to, the Pauline Christ groups. Early Christian writings in the New Testament and beyond resonate with the language and practices of associations. There is extensive use of fictive kinship language such as "father" and "brother" alongside an emphasis on friendship and shared property. Although the writings bear the rhetoric of egalitarianism and shared responsibilities, it is also clear that in many Christ groups there was a hierarchical leadership structure, especially from the second century onwards. Christ groups noted a reliance on patronage, and seemed to have held meetings in private residences, although occasionally they could be found in public spaces (e.g., the temple forecourt in Jerusalem or by a riverside). Christ groups looked and sounded like associations in structure and organization, including similar cult practices (particularly ritual meals) and regulations. They were technically illicit but generally tolerated as insignificant (with a few localized exceptions), and by the second century and beyond even self-described as associations. More and more, however, the research is suggesting that this second-century evidence is simply a continuation of the presumed community model adopted by the Christ groups and affirmed by their founders and the later writers who narrated their development.

STRUCTURE OF THE BOOK

The essays included in this book are a selection of those that I have written on the topic of associations. I have organized them thematically rather than chronologically in order to show how patterns developed in my thinking and writing. They are grouped in three sections, the first dealing

---

17. For example, on Paul: Ascough, "Thessalonian Christian Community" (Chapter 7, below); Ascough, "Paul and Associations"; Ascough, "Question of Death" (Chapter 15, below); Harrison, "Paul's House Churches"; Kloppenborg, "Collegia and *Thiasoi*"; Last, *Pauline Church*. On Revelation: Harland, "Honouring the Emperor." On Acts: Öhler, *Aposteldekret und antikes Vereinswesen*. On Gospels: Ascough, "Matthew" (= Chapter 8, below); Kloppenborg, "Disaffiliation"; Last, "Communities That Write."

18. Runesson, *Origins*; Runesson, "Origins of the Synagogue."

with associations as a model for Christ groups, the second focused on how associations and Christ groups compare and contrast in terms of recruitment and rivalry, and the third on two key elements of group life: meals and funerary rites.

The essay that is Chapter 2 comes from early in my career and was commissioned for a conference that dealt, in part, with the historical development of Christ groups within the broader Greco-Roman context. Since Alan Segal contributed a paper on Jewish groups to the conference,[19] my own essay focuses on other types of voluntary membership groups. I provide a brief overview of a few philosophical schools, the mysteries associated with Eleusis and Andania, and private religious associations, summarizing the more detailed presentation in my earlier book.[20] The mysteries, or "mystery religions" as they have been called, were used heavily in the history-of-religions school as the basis for understanding the origins of Christ groups. Wayne Meeks dropped this category in his brief proposal of models for understanding the formation of the *ekklēsia* but added the household alongside synagogues, philosophical schools, and voluntary associations, eventually rejecting all but the synagogues as a viable basis for understanding the foundation of the "church."[21]

Throughout the next decade or so, attempts to use the data from associations continued to garner pushback from those who favored the synagogues as the exclusive model for early Christ groups. In order to attempt to sort through the arguments and put to rest the idea that somehow the modeling is proposing a binary choice between synagogues *or* associations, I wrote "Paul, Synagogues, and Associations: Reframing the Question of Models for Pauline Christ Groups" (Chapter 3). My aim was methodological—to demonstrate how nuanced the approach was—since others had already demonstrated how the data from synagogues aligned with the broad category of "association," making the synagogue a subcategory of "association."[22] Erich Gruen remained unconvinced and took up the argument in a response published a year later.[23] I provided a rejoinder to his paper in the following year, restating my case that

> The issue is not really whether synagogues or Pauline Christ groups were or were not associations. The real issue is whether we learn anything useful by comparing data from a variety of

19. Segal, "Jewish Experience."
20. Ascough, *What Are They Saying about the Formation of Pauline Churches?*
21. Meeks, *First Urban Christians*, 74–84.
22. See Runesson, *Origins*; Runesson "Origins of the Synagogue."
23. Gruen, "Synagogues and Voluntary Associations."

different ancient groups. All indications seem to suggest that much has and will be learned from doing so.[24]

Although many scholars have taken to classifying Judean groups within the broader category of associations, others remain skeptical, and so the debate continues.

The sharp differentiation between *synagogue* and *association* is not the only argument that has been deployed in order to distance early Christ groups from any taint of "paganism." At a conference on associations in Münster, Germany, in 2001, I presented a paper attempting to address many of the objections (Chapter 4). Most of these were first deployed in Meeks's rejection of the associations as a model—differing group terminology and leadership structure, lack of egalitarianism, and translocal connections inherent in Christ groups along with Christian exclusivity[25]—and were repeated, mostly without any reference to any significant data. Using the growing database of association inscriptions and papyri, I show that these objections cannot be sustained since they focus primarily on only four association inscriptions that turn out not to be representative of the vast data available to us.

In an early article on "Translocal Relationships among Voluntary Associations and Early Christianity" (Chapter 5), I tackled the most troubling of these objections in some detail. Analysis of inscriptional data suggests that some associations had translocal links. At the same time, early Christian groups are shown to be more locally based than is often assumed. Thus, despite the common assumption to the contrary (at that time) within New Testament scholarship, both Christian congregations and associations can be seen as locally based groups with limited translocal connections. This conclusion opened the way for the more profitable use of associations as an analogy for understanding the formation and organization of early Christian groups.

Chapter 6 pushes the boundary on this somewhat, and was written for the Festschrift published in honor of Jonathan Z. Smith, whose own work has probably been the most influential on my own, with the exception of John Kloppenborg. Drawing on Smith's "Map Is not Territory,"[26] I attempt to lay out what is at stake in the debate over the redescriptive process of locating Christ groups in the taxon of associations. My aim was to further break down the scholarly barriers between identifying groups as Jewish, Christian, and other, well aware that, as Smith eloquently argued, the

24. Ascough, "Methodological Reflections."
25. Meeks, *First Urban Christians*, 78–80.
26. Smith, *Map Is not Territory*, 289–309.

category of Jewish was too often being deployed prophylactically to prevent contamination of Christ groups by "paganism."[27] Although my suggestion to rename "voluntary association" as "elective social formation" never really caught on, we did mostly drop the adjective "voluntary." More important, however, is the way scholarship has since developed to recognize how essential is Smith's argument for complex comparisons that involve more than two variables.

In order to make more concrete some of the implications of this modelling, I have included two chapters that undertake the comparative process. Chapter 7 demonstrates how data from 1 Thessalonians aligns with data from a variety of occupational associations in such a way that makes it likely that the ancient observer would not have categorized them as significantly different.[28] To be sure, the group to which Paul writes had as their patron deity a god not found in the other groups, but then again, an occupational group devoted to Isis would differ from a group devoted to Zeus in this same regard. But when it comes to composition and structure, all of these groups are remarkably similar and thus not *categorically* differentiated. The case study in Chapter 8 involving the Gospel of Matthew is somewhat different insofar as I attempt to mine the narrative about Jesus for implications for readers being addressed through that narrative. I show how the redactions the author injects into the words and deeds of Jesus reflect a concern with developmental stages of an incipient organization—forming, storming, norming, and performing—and thus indicates that we have here a work written as a story while aiming to move an associated group of people to the next stage of their development.

The three essays in the second section all focus on some form of recruitment. Chapter 9 presumes the argument of Chapter 7—that the Christ group at Thessalonike is an occupational association—and then extrapolates what that means in terms of their supposed "missionary" activity reflected in 1 Thess 1:2–10 and the "sounding forth" of the word of the Lord from them. The text is generally understood to be making reference to the Thessalonians participating in missionary activity in which they proclaim the salvific message of Christ. Read this way, the text presumes that the Thessalonians have evangelized areas even before Paul and his companions. That a newly constituted group of artisans would undertake such an aggressive program seems unlikely. The rhetoric of the passage is better understood in light of the practice of associations in proclaiming honors for their gods and

---

27. Smith, *Drudgery Divine*.

28. For more on the Thessalonians as an association see Ascough, *Paul's Macedonian Associations*, 162–90; Ascough, *1 and 2 Thessalonians*.

their founders and benefactors, the news about which spread via networks of traders, artisans, and other travelers throughout the provinces of Macedonia and Achaia.

This kind of self-promotion through honoring gods and patrons is a form of recruitment rhetoric seen throughout associations, as I argue in Chapter 10.[29] Although seemingly competitive on the surface, it also is an emic mechanism for self-definition, a way a group designates to itself that "we are this and not that," where the "that" is a group that differs perhaps only marginally from them in the etic perspective. Within the Corinthian Christ group, we see this reflected in the (for Paul, irritating) practice of self-designation through founding figure: "I belong to Paul," or "I belong to Apollos," or "I belong to Cephas," or "I belong to Christ" (1 Cor 1:12).

Chapter 11 moves from rhetoric to architectural evidence for group growth in Greco-Roman associations. Like Chapter 9, it pushes back against the presumption that early Christ groups were aggressively evangelistic while associations were not.[30] It summarizes evidence from building expansions and inscriptions recording membership lists (*alba*) to demonstrate that associations could and did undergo some modest growth. This essay anticipates a more detailed investigation published in a Festschrift for John Kloppenborg, in which I survey extant remains of space utilized by associations in locations such as converted houses, temples, guild halls, and dedicated buildings.[31] Here I note that even as groups grew larger over time, they continued to emphasize small, intimate gatherings, usually focused on a cult meal involving no more than a dozen or two dozen members. Growth of any group, Christian or otherwise, beyond this would require great logistical effort to find new meeting places.

The final section of the book contains six essays that focus on meal practices, funerary concerns, or both. Chapter 12 introduces Charles Grignon's typology of commensality to show that association meals cannot be reduced to a single category. While many association meals fit into the classification *segregative*, insofar as the meal is a mechanism for demarcating group membership boundaries, this is not always the case, even within a single association. Other types of commensality—exceptional, transgressive, and extradomestic—are attested in the data. Chapter 13 builds on this argument to show how association meals functioned as a way of assimilating and resisting Roman hegemony, and thus how members negotiated

---

29. On associations and this kind rhetoric see Ascough, "Greco-Roman Religions in Sardis and Smyrna."

30. See also Ascough, "Did the Philippian Christ Group Know."

31. Ascough, "Reimagining."

social relationships and group boundaries.³² This concern with boundary definition at meals can be seen in the narrative of the first Jerusalem Council found in Acts 15 (Chapter 14). What starts as a question about whether non-Judeans need to be circumcised when joining a Christ group ends with a decision regulating the consumption of foodstuffs and sexuality. Gentiles are off the hook for circumcision (Acts 15:19) and Judeans are required only to observe the bare minimum of regulations around meals: avoidance of "sacred" food, meat of improperly sacrificed animals, and postbanquet sexual favors (Acts 15:19–20).³³ In this way, Christ groups are indistinguishable from other associations when it comes to having regulations around meal practices.

Boundary definition is a key part of the argument of the remaining three papers. Chapter 15 shows how a question the Thessalonians posed to Paul about dead members generated his first written foray into the implications of apocalyptic imagery for those who adhere to Christ (1 Thess 4:13–18). For the Thessalonians themselves, however, the question revolves around who is or is not to be included in the group. Whereas normally associations would take care of the burial and memorialization of deceased members, Paul's initial promise of escape from the "coming wrath" (1:9) seems to have triggered the fear that anyone dying before the manifestation of that wrath might miss out on the glory that would attend Christ's return from heaven (1:10). Not so, says Paul, for as with other associations, there is no reason for the Thessalonians to consider their dead as lost to the group; they too will be "caught up" with the living at the coming of Christ (4:16–17).

Chapter 16 merges the topics of meals and memorial for the deceased, again at Thessalonike, but with an examination of the second letter addressed to that group. Here I point to indications in 2 Thessalonians that the group members held a ritualized meal similar to that articulated in 1 Cor 11. Although not necessarily a "Lord's Supper," the meal came with behavioral expectations, which, it seems, some of the members had contravened. As a result, they were prohibited from participation in the ritualized commensality of the group, a practice we find in other associations. The writer of Acts imagines that a more extreme punishment befalls those who betray the group norms in the early Christ group (Chapter 17). When Ananias and Sapphira try to pass themselves off as more benevolent than

---

32. I expand this argument further with respect to meal rituals in Ascough, "Communal Meals."

33. Meals are a central part of early Christ groups, so much so that the author of Acts deploys meal scenes as a structuring device in the overall narrative; see Ascough, "Function of Meals."

they are—presumably in order to garner greater honors as often befall associations patrons—they are struck dead on the spot. While the associations are not invoked explicitly in the text of Acts, their honorific practices are common enough, I argue, to be familiar to the reading audience.

CONCLUSION

One prominent theme that runs through many of the essays in this volume, particularly those published early in my career, is the nature of the comparative process. Our training as New Testament scholars often includes textual criticism, which involves, in part, finding family relationships between texts by determining the earliest witnesses and those that follow. Even today the Institute for New Testament Textual Research (INTF) in Münster deploys the "Coherence-Based Genealogical Method" (CBGM), which assumes all extant copies of New Testament texts can be connected to other extant or posited texts. And redaction criticism too assumes a genealogical relationship between Mark and Matthew and Luke. So when early scholars attempted to make comparisons for Paul's Christ groups, it is no wonder that their default was to ask about genealogical connections: Which type of groups came first, and who copied whom?

Such genealogical connections are, however, a red herring, since they assume a false binary in the comparative process itself.[34] As I argue in a fairly recent overview of the *status quaestionis* on Christ and associations, the scholarly taxonomy that divides groups into three or more distinct categories, such as Jews, Christians, and others, or synagogues, churches, and associations, is not tenable. The research demonstrates that early Christ groups and synagogues cannot be categorized as somehow separate and distinct from the myriad other groups in antiquity. This has not always been the case, and in some sectors this tripart division (of Jews, Christians, and others) persists. Yet, it is clear to many of us that it would make no sense to the ancient person to ask whether such-and-such a group was or was not an association, for that category itself has already been essentialized in scholarly discourse.

As scholars we can and must reclaim the term *association* for what it really is: a broad basket into which most, if not all, antique groups can be placed, including those comprising Judeans, Christ adherents, or both. The category of the association only becomes useful when we add nuance: viz. "a privately organized Zeus association," or "a semipublic Isis association," or "an association of Dionysos devotees," or "an association of Christ

---

34. For the groundbreaking work on this see Smith, *Drudgery Divine*.

followers," and so forth.³⁵ Without this nuance, the category is useless, and thus also is the framing of the question of whether Christ groups were or were not associations. Clearly, they were, since their members associated with one another. Noting their similarities to associations is only the starting point, however, for the much more interesting process of highlighting their distinctions from the myriad of other associations in their geographic locale, including (other) Christ-based and Judean associations extant there.³⁶

---

35. See Ascough, "Map Maker" (= ch. 6); Kloppenborg, "Greco-Roman *Thiasoi*," 189–90, 196.

36. See further Ascough, "Bringing Chaos to Order," where I argue that "The historian of Graeco-Roman antiquity writing in and for the twenty-first century needs to be concerned to describe the Graeco-Roman world in a way that neither highlights, isolates, nor ignores early Jesus-groups any more than other groups in order to see what patterns might emerge within the chaos of the time" (p. 299).

SECTION I

Modeling Christ Groups

2

Greco-Roman Philosophic, Religious, and Voluntary Associations

A GROUP IS GENERALLY defined as a collection of persons with a feeling of common identity, goals, and norms. For example, slaves working the Roman mines in Spain had—whether they liked it or not—a common social identity (slave), a common goal (mining), and shared norms of behavior (work or be punished). Associations, however, are more formal than groups. Associations are composed of persons who not only share common interests and activities but also have deliberately organized for some specific purpose or purposes. Therefore, associations have established rules of organization and procedure and established patterns of leadership.

Associations can be divided into two basic categories—involuntary and voluntary. Involuntary associations have a membership based on birth or compulsion. This was generally the case with the *demes* and *phratries* of ancient Athens. It is also true of a conscripted army. Voluntary associations, however, are formed by persons who freely and deliberately choose to join and who can likewise choose to resign. Examples would be a guild of actors or a gathering of Isis worshipers.

Voluntary associations in the Greco-Roman world have a long history, going back at least to the laws of Solon in sixth-century BCE Athens. Such associations continued to grow through the classical period and were flourishing in the Hellenistic period. During the first century CE their presence was felt throughout the entire Roman Empire, in cities and villages alike—although, of course, there is considerably more attestation for associations in urban centers than in rural areas. A variety of extant sources attest to various voluntary associations in antiquity. These include literary texts, papyri, inscriptions, and archaeological remains. All of these sources are important in an investigation of community formation in Greco-Roman associations.

This article will focus on three types of associations in the Greco-Roman world: (1) philosophical associations, which are sometimes called philosophical [4] schools; (2) public religious associations, which are often called "mystery religions"; and (3) private religious and professional associations, which are usually referred to more generically as "voluntary" associations.

PHILOSOPHICAL ASSOCIATIONS

The word *school* can mean different things in different contexts. When applied to philosophical thought in antiquity it generally refers to persons who follow the same founder and propagate ideas and doctrines similar to those the founder articulated. Schools in this sense generally had as their goal creating a pathway to human flourishing. They focused on intellectual discourse and followed a particular way of life. Philosophical schools, however, were not always *groups* in terms of a sociological definition. That is, members of a school may be considered to be those who held related ideas, but these same persons may not—and generally did not—meet together as a group of one sort or another.

Our focus here, however, is not on the varying ideas of the many philosophical schools of antiquity, such as the Platonists, the Aristotelians, the Stoics, the Epicureans, the Pythagoreans, the Cynics, or the Skeptics. Rather, we want to focus attention on how philosophical associations were organized. In so doing, however, we run into a problem concerning our sources; most of the extant sources for the philosophical schools are interested in their ideas and founders, not in the form and organization of the schools themselves.

Alan Culpepper has set out some of the characteristics that were shared by a number of the philosophical schools of antiquity:

> (1) they were groups of disciples which usually emphasized *philia* and *koinonia*; (2) they gathered around, and traced their origins to, a founder whom they regarded as an exemplary, wise,

or good man; (3) they valued the teachings of their founder and the traditions about him; (4) members of the schools were disciples or students of the founder; (5) teaching, learning, studying, and writing were common activities; (6) most schools observed communal meals, often in memory of their founders; (7) they had rules or practices regarding admission, retention of membership, and advancement within the membership; (8) they often maintained some degree of distance or withdrawal from the rest of society; and (9) they developed organizational means of insuring their perpetuity.[1]

Furthermore, Culpepper notes that the organizational complexity of a school was usually tied to its understanding of the role of fellowship (*koinōnia*): "The more a school emphasized 'fellowship' the more likely it was to have a developed, structured organization and rules governing its communal life."[2]

If we focus our attention on philosophical schools for which evidence from around the first century CE indicates that members formed themselves into associations, we are really limited to two particular groups—the Pythagoreans and the Epicureans, with less evidence for the former than the latter. The Epicureans, in fact, are the only group for which we have direct first-century evidence. The [5] Pythagorean school, however, probably influenced the organization of the other philosophical schools in antiquity and so also deserves attention.

The Pythagorean School

During the sixth century BCE, Pythagoras (died about 497 BCE) founded a closely knit school at Croton in southern Italy in which he emphasized asceticism and ritual purity, with a focus on the deliverance of the soul. It is difficult to determine the exact organizational structure of the Pythagorean school, for membership in it required secrecy, and many of its traditions were passed on by memory alone. Those writers who do discuss the school's structure, such as Diogenes Laertius, Porphyry, and Iamblichus, are late in date (all third to fourth century CE) and somewhat unreliable. It is even unclear whether Pythagoras himself actually intended to found a school at all, since "Pythagoreanism was more of a way of life than a philosophy."[3]

---

1. Culpepper, *Johannine School*, 258–59.
2. Culpepper, *Johannine School*, 254.
3. Culpepper, *Johannine School*, 247, 249.

Nonetheless, the Pythagorean school welcomed candidates for membership. Pythagoras's preaching attracted some adherents by calling people away from a life of luxury to a life of simplicity. According to one report, which may very well have been inflated, two thousand men, plus their wives and children, did not return home after hearing Pythagoras, but pooled their property and built an auditorium (*homakoion*) as large as a city (Iamblichus, *Life of Pythagoras* 6, citing Nicomachus). Other sources, however, suggest that the school was composed mostly of young aristocratic men, some of whom were handpicked by Pythagoras himself. These aristocratic connections provide the most likely reason for the school's political connections as well as for the fact that conflicts seem to have sometimes been a part of the school's life.

A description of the initiation procedure into the Pythagorean school can be found in a number of sources, particularly in Iamblichus, *Life of Pythagoras* 17—although, again, these descriptions may be only later, apocryphal reconstructions. According to our sources, initiation into the school began with a scrutiny of the devotee's family background, their way of life (e.g., leisure time, joys, disappointments), their physique, and their gait. They were then ignored for three years as a means of testing the strength of their desire to learn. Should they pass this testing period, they entered a five-year novitiate during which time they could not speak. At the end of this period, those who were approved underwent rites of purification and were initiated into the association. For those who were rejected, however, a tomb was raised as if they were dead. And if in the future a Pythagorean encountered those rejected, they were treated as if they were strangers.

Once membership was attained, the candidates became disciples (*mathētai*) and were considered to be members of the fellowship (*koinōnia*) or school (*scholē*). According to Diogenes Laertius, Pythagoras "was the first to say 'Friends have all things in common' and 'Friendship is equality'; indeed, his disciples put all their possessions into one common stock" (8.10, citing *Timaeus*). This communal practice may have been short-lived or only applicable to an inner group. [6] But when the policy was operative, property was submitted at the beginning of the five-year silent probationary period. If after five years as a novice a candidate was rejected, double the amount contributed was returned; but if the candidate was accepted, the property was held in common by the group.

Pythagorean communal life was structured around an ordered daily schedule and included common meals. Restrictions were placed on the members' diets (no beans or meat, only uncooked food), their drink (pure water alone), their clothing (no wool), and certain materials (e.g., cypress could not be used in coffins). It is difficult to know all that occurred in the community, simply because the traditions of the school were to be kept secret and those who violated this code were punished or expelled. Control rested with Pythagoras when he was living and his successor after his death. Leadership was passed on through election or by the previous leader's appointment; leadership positions were held for life.

The Pythagoreans memorized the teachings of their founder and were in some ways more interested in commitment to the person and principles of Pythagoras than in acquiring knowledge. Nonetheless, they also studied Homer and perhaps some science and mathematics, and they probably used music for edification. Members were divided into two ranks: the students (*mathēmatiko*), who received the full teachings and participated in debate, and the hearers (*akousmatikoi*), who were given only a summary (Iamblichus, *Life of Pythagoras* 18). Although Iamblichus notes that both of these two groups were recognized as Pythagoreans, those designated students looked down on the so-called hearers as not having received their instruction directly from Pythagoras.

Daily life in the Pythagorean school was fairly routine. Iamblichus describes a typical day of the members, although his description seems to apply most directly to those not living in the community and so probably reflects a later form of the school. Upon waking they took a lonely morning walk and then met together for discussion. Following some exercise they had breakfast of bread and honey. The afternoon was spent fulfilling civic obligations, although in the late afternoon they took another walk—this time in pairs or threesomes in order to review their disciplines. After a bath they met for a meal that began with libations and the burning of incense. Eating ceased before sunset and the meal was closed with libations and a public reading. Moral admonishments concluded the evening before members went to bed (cf. *Life of Pythagoras* 21). Whatever the date of this description, it gives us a sense of the lifestyle of the Pythagoreans generally. And it is not difficult to see how such a regime might have occurred in a communal setting, with instruction replacing political activities in the afternoon.

By the end of the fourth century BCE the Pythagorean school had all but disappeared. There is little evidence for it until the first century BCE at Rome, where Neo-Pythagoreanism continued the traditions of Pythagoras and venerated his name. Eventually, however, both classical Pythagoreanism and Neo-Pythagoreanism were subsumed by Neo-Platonism in the second century CE. [7]

The Epicurean Garden

Epicurus (c. 342 or 341–271 or 270 BCE) formed his garden in Athens during the latter part of the fourth century to the early third century BCE. Sources for understanding this community are better than for many of the other philosophical schools, since Epicurus himself wrote much and some of what he wrote survives. Other extant reports about Epicurus, though less reliable, can help round out our picture of the organization of the Epicurean school—particularly those by Diogenes Laertius, Cicero, and Plutarch.

Epicurus is usually considered to be the first to have intentionally set out to form a philosophical association. Born on the island of Samos, a citizen of Athens by birth, and having studied at Athens as a youth, he returned to Athens in 306 BCE. As an Athenian citizen he was able to purchase both a house and adjacent land for a garden outside the city wall, and it is at his house and garden, rather than the gymnasium, that he established his school. Members lived together in the house and pursued their daily regime in the garden. And although the Epicurean community withdrew from the world to seek a better way of life, it is probable that the house and garden were located within a densely populated, busy quarter of Athens. As such, the school was not particularly well secluded, and the withdrawal of its members from public life led, at times, to disfavor among the general population.

Epicurus's garden "placed more emphasis on community and friendship than any other philosophical school."[4] Epicurean associations were formed as fictive kinship groups and based on a household model. The goal was friendship, and the Epicureans sought to produce love and intimacy among all members. Cicero (106–43 BCE), the Roman orator, philosopher, and statesman, writing in the first century BCE, records that "in just one household—and a small one at that—Epicurus assembled such large congregations of friends which were bound together by a shared feeling of the deepest love. And even now the Epicureans do the same thing" (*On Goals* 1.65).

Eusebius, the fourth-century Christian apologist, church historian, and bishop of Caesarea in Palestine from 313 until his death in 339, cites Numenius as saying: "The school of Epicurus resembles a true commonwealth (*politeia*), altogether free of factionalism, sharing one mind and one disposition, of which they were and are and, it appears, will be followers" (*Praep. ev.* 14.5). Such a close relationship among its members contributed to the overall success of Epicureanism. Nevertheless, goods were not held in common, for Epicurus considered such a practice to imply mistrust. Rather, the simple lifestyle of the Epicureans was supported by wealthier members

---

4. Culpepper, *Johannine School*, 101.

and adherents through patronage. At the same time, Epicurean associations outside Athens paid some form of dues to the Athenian Garden.

The Epicurean schools were dominated by their founder, who provided them with an organizational model and practical wisdom. In some respects, Epicureanism was closer to a sect or cult than a philosophical association, for not only were Epicurus's teachings held in high esteem but he himself was [8] venerated as "father" and "the wise one" by his followers. Seneca (c. 4 BCE–65 CE), the Roman philosopher, tells us that an oath of allegiance to Epicurus was taken by his disciples and suggests that his teachings were followed with vigor: "We will be obedient to Epicurus, according to whom we have made it our choice to live" (*Epistles* 25.5). The Epicureans met for a banquet once a month in honor of their founder and his early disciple, Metrodorus. After Epicurus's death, regular funeral offerings were undertaken for him and his family, and a celebration was made on his birthday. By the first century CE, it appears, Epicurus was worshiped as "a god who had revealed wisdom."[5]

There is some debate over the nature of leadership among the Epicureans. For while there was no official leadership structure; there seems to have been a hierarchy of leadership based largely on the level of attainment in the philosophy of Epicurus. Epicurus, or his successor, held the highest place of honor as "the wise one." Below were "associate leaders" (*kathēgēmones*) who were called "philosophers." These were followed by "assistant leaders" (*kathēgetai*) or "instructors," who each had a group of students over whom they were responsible. A distinction was made between advanced students (*synētheis*) and novices (*kataskeuazomenoi*). Once admitted to the association, a novice was taught full submission to the instructor. Each member was trained to respect and obey the person who was more advanced. "On this principle," as Norman DeWitt observes, "one member could be said to be better than another only so far as he had made more progress."[6] But all members, especially younger members, were subject to admonition and reproof from one another, and all were expected to accept it willingly and learn from the correction. Furthermore, once admitted into the association a person was warned against all other forms of knowledge—such as music, rhetoric, or geometry—which were thought to interfere with the pursuit of happiness.

A clear distinction was made between "friends" (*philoi*), or associate members of the group, and those who were "devotees" (*gnōrimoi*) or part of

---

5. Culpepper, *Johannine School*, 109; cf. DeWitt, *Epicurus and His Philosophy*, 97–101.

6. DeWitt, *Epicurus and His Philosophy*, 100.

the inner circle close to Epicurus or his successors. Membership included both males and females, whether slaves or free. The presence of women is suggestive of the pleasure-seeking goal that formed part of Epicurus's philosophy. There is, however, some evidence that these women were full participants in the lifestyle and teachings of the school. And slaves probably worked as secretaries and copyists for the large-scale publishing endeavors of Epicurus and his followers.

Epicureanism is considered a missionary movement, for Epicurean centers were established throughout the Mediterranean world and attracted many adherents. Epicurus himself maintained contact with these various centers through his letters to them, although no letters are extant. Along with his maxims, he also wrote principles of conduct for his followers in various locations as well as summaries of his teaching. Yet, despite the presence of such groups throughout the Mediterranean world, little is known about Epicureanism beyond the garden in Athens. The house and garden were still operative in the first century BCE, but much in need of repair. The movement finally died out in the second century CE. [9]

PUBLIC RELIGIOUS ASSOCIATIONS

When discussing religious associations the primary focus is usually on the ancient mysteries, which are often misnamed mystery religions. Walter Burkert distinguishes three types of organization around the ancient mysteries: (1) the itinerant practitioner, (2) the sanctuary, and (3) the association of worshipers.[7] In the case of the itinerant, "there was no backing by a corporation or community."[8] The remaining two categories can be characterized as public and private religious associations, respectively. And although they had some similar organizational characteristics, they were dissimilar enough to warrant separate investigation.

Public religious associations were most often found connected to a public sanctuary and fell under the administration of the city (*polis*). Within this realm lies the mystery cults, which themselves were often tied to the *polis*—as was the case of the mysteries of Demeter at Eleusis, near Athens. Other well-known and popular mysteries include those of Dionysos, Demeter, Isis, and Mithras. For the most part these mysteries began as local cult groups but, at least by the first or second century CE, grew to have a broader appeal throughout the Greco-Roman world.

---

7. Burkert, *Ancient Mystery Cults*, 31.
8. Burkert, *Ancient Mystery Cults*, 31.

Initiation into one or another of the mysteries was usually a matter of choice. One participated in a ritual of status transformation that was usually a collective experience. For the most part the ceremonies were tied to the cycle of nature. Otherwise, very little is known about the actual rites themselves, since, as the name implies, their rituals were closely guarded secrets. Apuleius, the second-century CE Roman rhetorician and Platonic sophist, says concerning the mysteries of Isis, "If I were allowed to tell you, and you were allowed to be told, you would soon hear everything; but, as it is, my tongue would suffer for its indiscretion and your ears for their inquisitiveness" (*Metam.* 18). Once initiated, persons could return for special ceremonies or festivals. Noninitiates, however, were barred from participation.

The Mysteries at Eleusis

The Eleusinian mysteries provide an interesting, and somewhat representative, case study of the larger mystery cults, since, as Everett Ferguson points out, they "exercised a formative influence on the mysteries of the eastern cults" and, by at least the first century CE, were open to anyone who wished to join.[9] The group began as a domestic cult at Eleusis. It soon, however, broadened out to include not only citizens of Eleusis, but also of Athens and eventually all Attica. Following Alexander the Great's conquest of Greece, the appeal of the Eleusinian mysteries was broadened still further. For despite the initial expense of initiation into the cult, its benefits—particularly its promise of a happy afterlife—were considered worthy of the cost, and it became popular with many. Initiation into the Eleusinian mysteries was open to all men and women, and sometimes even to children. [10]

Initiates underwent three stages. In or around February or March they were purified through the "lesser mysteries" by fasting, the sacrifice of a pig, a water ritual (either sprinkling or bathing), the singing of hymns, and the bearing of a sacred vessel of some sort—though much of this, admittedly, remains a "mystery" to us. The "greater mysteries" took place over a ten-day period in September and involved a great procession from Athens to Eleusis, along with various rituals involving purification, sacrifices, and rites for the dead. A third level of initiation, "overseer" (*epoptēs*), could be attained one year after initiation into the greater mysteries. At the conclusion of the nocturnal rites in a large hall on the eighth day of the festival, those who were so designated remained behind to be shown some sacred objects called *hiera*—the nature of which is unknown, but perhaps consisted of cut wheat, sacred chests or baskets, and poppy flowers. The central rites of initiation

---

9. Ferguson, *Backgrounds*, 200.

seem to have included "things enacted" (*drōmena*, perhaps a sacred pageant recounting the foundational myth), "things said" (*legomena*), and "things shown" (*deiknymena*). Those initiated then considered one another to be "brothers" (*adelphoi*).

Other mysteries, such as those of Dionysos, Isis, and Mithras, had initiation rituals and levels of adherence similar to those at Eleusis. The Isis mysteries had three classes of adherents: (1) those who attended the daily ceremonies and joined processions, (2) initiates who had the right to enter the temple and participate in the ceremonies, and (3) various levels of priests. The male-only mystery of Mithraism had seven grades of initiation, corresponding to the order of the seven planets in astrology.

There was most often found at the sanctuaries of these mysteries a group of priests or priestesses (or both) who oversaw the administration of the cult. Priesthood could be obtained through inheritance, through election, or through purchase. For the most part, such officials were paid professionals whose numbers would never increase beyond the ability to be funded by the revenues from the cult. Walter Burkert somewhat overstates the case when he says, in comparing public mysteries with private religious associations, that "a corporation of this kind cannot develop into a self-sufficient, alternative religious community in the full sense."[10] Indeed, private religious associations composed of officials from the public mysteries existed in antiquity (as we will discuss below). Nonetheless, Burkert is correct insofar as the public mysteries, like the civic cults, remained less intimately organized than the private religious associations.

The Mysteries of Andania

Before discussing private religious associations in detail, it is worthwhile first to look at a private religious association that gained enough civic importance to become, in effect, a public mystery cult in the city of Andania, which was located in the southwestern part of the Greek Peloponnesus. In fact, the Andanian mystery cult was regarded by Pausanias, a second-century CE geographer and traveler, as second in importance only to the cult of Eleusis (see his *Description of Greece* 4.33.3–6). The lengthy regulations of the Andanian cult are recorded in an inscription that dates from 92/91 BCE (see IG V.1 1390).[11] [11] Little is revealed in the inscription concerning the initiation rituals and sacrifices. Rather, much of the inscription is taken up with regulations to be followed by those participating in the mysteries. In so

---

10. Burkert, *Ancient Mystery Cults*, 4.
11. Translated in Meyer, ed., *Ancient Mysteries*, 51–59.

doing, however, the inscription also reveals the organizational structure of this private religious association that became in southern Greece something of a public mystery cult.

The Andanian mysteries were laden with layers of officials. At the top stood Mnasistratos, with his wife and children, who was the founder (or refounder) of the cult as a result of his having donated a chest and books, and who was duly honored with a crown, the lead position in sacred processions, and portions of the sacrifices. Under Mnasistratos was a supervisory council of ten male citizens, who were to be at least forty years old and appointed by general election. This group was to oversee the administration of the sacred officials. Under the supervisory council were the sacred officials, both male and female, who were appointed on the basis of their capabilities. From among the sacred officials were chosen mystagogues and twenty rod bearers. This latter category of rod bearers designates those who were to enforce the regulations of the association through physical punishment. The entire body of sacred officials was required to swear an oath of purity and of maintenance of the secrets of the mysteries. Once sworn, they received from the previous year's officials the cultic objects. The supervisor of the female sacred officials also was to appoint by lot one woman to oversee a group of sacred virgins to participate in the mysteries.

Other officials are mentioned in the regulations regarding the procession, including the priests and priestesses of the gods of the mysteries (particularly "the Great Mother" Demeter, the divine benefactress of humanity), the director of the games, the mistress of the banquet and her assistants, and various entertainers (i.e., "flute players"). There is a clear distinction between the initiated and the uninitiated, with the latter being banned from certain areas in the sacred grove. Some of the civic officials would continue in a related supervisory role during the time of the festival. Thus the supervisor of the market was in charge of the selling of goods in the area of the sacred grove, and the scribe of the magistrates administered the oath to the sacred officials appointed for the festival. The city treasurer was to oversee and audit five (wealthy) persons elected to manage the funds from the mysteries. These five were responsible for all the revenues and disbursements, and they were to provide a balanced financial account at the end of the festival. For the festival was to be financially self-sustaining, with any extra revenue reverting back to the city.

The sacrificial animals were to be chosen carefully according to specific criteria. Once sacrificed, portions were allotted to various officials and the remainder was consumed as part of a sacred meal. There is a clear concern in the Andanian cult inscription for orderly behavior during the festival—especially during the performance of the sacred rites. Disorderly behavior is regulated through the threat of fines, floggings, and expulsions, as designated by the officials and administered by the rod bearers. In addition, the names of convicted offenders and their offenses were to be permanently inscribed on a building in the sacred area. [12]

Little differentiation is made in the inscription between male and female or slave and free in terms of their participation in the sacred rituals. The sacred area itself is to be treated as a place of refuge for slaves. Differentiation, however, is made in terms of purity regulations (e.g., a female official is to take an additional oath of fidelity to her husband) and punishments (e.g., free persons are fined, whereas slaves are fined double and scourged). The Andanian cult inscription ends with the words: "The rule is to be authoritative for all time."

VOLUNTARY ASSOCIATIONS

Whereas the philosophical associations ("philosophical schools") and public religious associations ("mystery religions") were legal within the Roman Empire, private religious associations and professional associations (usually referred to more generically as "voluntary" associations) were technically barred under various Roman laws enacted as early as 184 BCE. Exceptions were granted to associations considered to have been established for some time—as, for example, the Jewish synagogues, which used this exemption to claim protection from local civic authorities. Yet despite occasional suppression by the authorities, voluntary associations never completely disappeared, and they were always able to reassert themselves as a viable presence in Greco-Roman society.

Private Religious Associations

Private religious associations were groups that met for the primary purpose of religious worship, but did so outside of the larger, civically sanctioned mysteries and cults of the day. Their domain was generally domestic—although a number of associations met in public spaces, and some even met as private religious associations within a larger public cult. Membership in a private religious association was based primarily on the attraction of the particular deity or deities worshiped. Therefore, they tended to draw persons from all strata of Greco-Roman society—although the elites of society were probably not as numerous in such associations as were the urban poor, slaves, and freed persons. Religious associations were generally gender inclusive, at least in admitting to membership both males and females. As one inscription puts it, they are open to "men and women, freeborn and slaves" (SIG³ 985). One even finds instances of the membership of children in Dionysiac religious associations. Nevertheless, there were also religious associations that were gender exclusive—either all male or all female. And in mixed-gender associations positions of leadership tended to be predominantly male, although there were a number of exceptions.

Professional Associations

Professional voluntary associations, or guilds, were made up of artisans or manual laborers. Guilds from a wide range of professions existed throughout the Greco-Roman world. Among laborers there were guilds for almost every profes[13]sion, including leatherworkers, purple-dyers, carpenters, bakers, tanners, silversmiths, and the like. Entertainers had their own guilds; evidence exists for associations of actors ("Dionysiac artists"), gladiators, and athletes. Domestic workers tended to stick together and so formed associations composed exclusively of such. Professional musicians even formed themselves into professional associations, with their members being employed each year for the various cultic celebrations—such as those of the Andanian mysteries. There are, in fact, very few professions not represented in the extant records of the professional voluntary associations of antiquity.

Although the central commonality among members of professional associations was their occupation, the religious aspect of such associations should not be discounted. In every instance professional associations claimed the patronage of a deity or deities, and they took seriously their worship of such deities; and whenever they met, the gods were invoked, and special festivals and rituals were central to their communal life. Often the deity or deities chosen had some connection to the particular profession. Thus, we find such connections as a Delian association of shippers who worshiped Poseidon, the god of the sea, or an association of gardeners dedicated to the earth goddess Demeter. A number of different professions were associated with Dionysos, such as winegrowers, cowherds, actors, and pantomimes.

Professional associations (as well, of course, as private religious associations) were generally small in terms of membership, averaging perhaps fifteen to one hundred—although at times they could reach as high as four hundred or even twelve hundred members. The social status of the members was generally tied to the status of their particular profession within Greco-Roman society. In such a highly structured culture, each profession would have had its place within the social stratification of the day. It is therefore safe to assume that being laborers, the majority of the members of professional associations were of the artisan class, and so generally poor. Within this underclass, however, professional associations could include slaves, freed persons, and free persons. In a number of instances, in fact, recorded members of professional associations have three names, which indicates that they were Roman citizens. Likewise, the professional associations of antiquity had some wealthy members and drew on patrons to sponsor their activities.

Unlike many of the private religious associations, professional associations tended to be gender exclusive. This was due in large part to gender separation in the workforce. Thus professions dominated by males had professional associations composed only of males, and professions dominated by females tended to have all-female associations. What little crossover there was reflects elites of one gender patronizing an association of the opposite gender. For example, in one Roman association we have the case of a woman patron of an all-male association who is publicly thanked in an inscription for her patronage, but who does not herself participate in the banquet that her generosity has funded (cf. CIL 10243; dated 153 CE). [14]

ORGANIZATIONAL STRUCTURE

Professional associations often organized themselves by modeling the civic structures. This can be seen in the variety of civic titles used to designate such associations—for instance the titles *phylē, hetairia, kollēgion, synedrion, synodos, ekklēsia*, and *politeuma*. The terms for "citizenship" (*politeuma* and its cognates), for example, are found in use in two Egyptian associations, one religious and one professional (composed of soldiers), in a Carian association dedicated to Zeus, and in a number of associations formed on the basis of a common homeland by those living outside their home city (e.g., the Tyrian Merchants at Ostia). There are also at least five instances of the use of *ekklēsia* as a community designator, from Samos, Asia Minor, and Delos, all from the second century BCE to the second century CE. In light of this evidence, it is especially interesting to note that Luke, who uses the designation *ekklēsia* for Christian groups, also calls the assembly of professional silversmiths at Ephesos an *ekklēsia* (Acts 19:32).

Community founders played key roles in the maintenance of the association, often presiding over the association or acting as its patron. We find instances of founders dedicating rooms or buildings for the use of the association. But founders could also maintain a high degree of control over the group. Such was the case with Xanthos, who would not allow the sacrifices to be undertaken if he were not present and reserved the right of succession for his designate (cf. IG II² 1366).

Much has been made of the inclusive, egalitarian nature of voluntary associations, and, for the most part, this seems to have been the case at a very general level. Belonging to an association often brought about opportunities to participate in the organizational structure of the association. We also, however, find a degree of hierarchy in associations insofar as there are levels of leadership and honors to which members may aspire. Voluntary associations did not have a uniform organizational structure. This is not to say that they did not have any organizational structure. Indeed, they tend to reflect complex organizational behavior, albeit with local differences in structures and titles.

Voluntary associations were adaptive, well able to transform their structures in order to respond to new situations arising either internally or outside the group. Associations that shared a common designator and common leadership terminology did not always assign similar functions to those titles. This is well illustrated in the cases of eight associations of Sarapiastai found throughout the Greco-Roman world, which show no similarity of organization.

The range of titles found for functionaries within both religious and professional voluntary associations is vast. Some of the more common titles include "priest" and "priestess" (those who were responsible for the cult of the association), "treasurer" (*tamias,* who oversaw the collection and disbursement of funds), "secretary" (*grammateus,* who recorded the minutes of the meeting and insured that inscriptions were commissioned), "manager" (*epimeletēs*), and "examiner" (*exetastēs*). Many other titles are given on the basis of function, such as "water bearer" or "casket bearer" or "bouncer." The leader of the association could go by a number of titles, including *patēr, matēr, archōn,* and *prostatēs*—the [15] latter found only occasionally in the sense of "patron." It is interesting to note that in at least six non-Jewish associations, five of which are in Macedonia, the title *archisynagōgos* is used of a leader. Such leaders would convene and chair meetings, oversee the rites, arrange for banquets and funerals, and enforce the regulations and decrees of the associations. They often also served as patrons or benefactors and were so designated through honorific statements.

Among leadership titles in associations we even find the occasional use of *episkopos* and *diakonos.* Only in some cases can it be determined what such titles indicate. Furthermore, the titles seem to have connoted different job descriptions from association to association. *Episkopos* was used to indicate a financial officer, a cult functionary, and a person who oversaw the honorific matters of the association. *Diakonos* was used of sacral officials, including a priest, and of liturgical functionaries. It is clear that the latter title was not restricted to the role of a table functionary, as is so often assumed.

Positions of leadership could be gained through appointment (particularly by the founder of the association), election, or, in some cases, through purchase, with the position going to the highest bidder. Funds, of course, would go to the administration of the association. Serving as a leader in an association brought with it great status within the association and, if the association was large enough, brought status within the larger social context. At the same time, positions of leadership could be financially burdensome, for cash-flow problems and revenue shortfalls were expected to be alleviated by those in leadership. This is particularly true in the case of the treasurer. An inscription from Kallatis records the situation of a treasurer who had to repay, with interest, association money he had lost in a maritime investment gone sour (cf. SIG^3 1108; dating from the third century BCE).

Patronage was also an important feature of association life, as it was generally in the Greco-Roman world. Wealthy patrons would bestow on a particular association financial donations to be used for operating costs, religious festivals, commemorative events, or social occasions. Such benefaction was recognized through public proclamations and honorary inscriptions. In fact, such benefaction was often encouraged among the membership by setting up some sort of agonistic situation—as witness, for example, an inscription from the Piraeus, which, in the midst of honoring one benefactor, states that the statute was set up "so that also the others shall be zealous for honor among the members, knowing that they will receive thanks from the members deserving of benefaction" (IG II^2 1263; from the third century BCE. Such benefaction could be costly, and those who fell on hard times would have to withdraw their patronage. Among the Egyptian papyri we find the following letter:

> To Thrax, the president, and to the fellow members of the association, from Epiodoros. Since I am impoverished and unable to act as benefactor to the guild, I ask that you accept my resignation. Farewell. (P.Kar. 575; dated 184 CE)

One can certainly feel the pathos of the sender of this letter. [16]

The other primary means for obtaining money for the association was through the collection of membership dues, either on entrance into the association or during attendance at each meeting. Membership into an association located in the Roman city of Lanuvium during the second century CE, for example, was gained through the payment of an initiation fee of one hundred sesterces and an amphora of good wine (CIL XIV

2112). Dues would go toward the association's expenses—although, in most cases, without patronage membership dues were not enough to cover all the group's expenses. Expenses would include the association's banquets, festivals, burial of members, and general expenses. In some cases money might be collected toward the upkeep of buildings or the erection of statues and inscriptions. Occasionally associations used their common funds to help out needy members.

Associations evidenced strong bonds among members. It is common to find kinship language used within the group, with members referred to as "brothers," and leaders and patrons designated as "fathers" or "mothers." These strong bonds were also expressed by the use of such a designation as "friends" for the associates of the group (cf. IG II^2 1369). The communal bond itself is often designated by the term *koinon* and its cognates.

It would be misleading, however, to suggest that internal community relations were completely amicable. We have, in fact, abundant evidence to the contrary. Inscriptions were often set up outlining the internal community regulations of associations. Members were warned against such abuses as "disorderliness" (*akosmeō*), taking another member's seat, insulting another member (or a member's mother), or physically abusing another. In general, failure to meet the moral or communal standards set by the association would result in one or more of any number of the following punishments: fines, flogging, restrictions from the association's rituals, temporary expulsion, or loss of membership. In some cases, a special group of "bouncers" was in place to remove violators of the association's regulations (see IG II^2 1368).

Although sometimes accused of all sorts of vices—not only in antiquity, but also today in scholarly literature—many religious associations included moral codes of conduct for both personal ethics and social morality. In a well-known inscription from Philadelphia in Lydia, for example, men and free women are prohibited from having sexual intercourse with anyone other than their spouse on pain of restricted access to the association's meeting place for the men and "evil curses" for the women (SIG^3 985).

In addition to intragroup tensions, voluntary associations seem to have been also at times in conflict with one another. This is implied in the cry of the Athenian Iobacchoi: "Now we are the first of all the Iobacchoi!" (IG II^2 1368). It is also suggested in the stipulation of a priestess of Dionysos at Thessalonike that when she dies, if the designated association does not carry out her wishes, her bequest is to be transferred to a different association (IG X/2.1 260). To be sure, the latter association will be watching the first group.

Membership in a number of voluntary associations included initiation rites. An Attic inscription dating from the second century CE, for example, de[17]scribes a process whereby a candidate must be examined by a number of officials to see whether he is "holy, pious, and good" before gaining entry into the association (IG II² 1369). Likewise, the fragmented ending of IG X/2.1 255 from Thessalonike seems to indicate that one of the priestesses violated the association's code by involving noninitiates in the sacred rites of the association, which suggests that an initiation was required for full participation.

One particularly illustrative text from Philadelphia, in Egypt, records on papyri the "authoritative" laws of the association (*synodos*) of Zeus Hypsistos (P.Lond. VII 2193; dated about 69–58 BCE). The association met in a public temple and elected a president and his assistant for a one-year term. No other officers seem to exist. The association itself was formed not by a single individual but by the members themselves. A monthly banquet is stipulated at which there are to be libations, prayers, and "other customary rites on behalf of the god." The text then goes on to set forth the association's communal regulations:

> All are to obey the president and his assistant in the matters pertaining to the association (*koinon*), and they shall be present at all command occasions to be prescribed for them and at meetings and assemblies (*synagōgai*) and outings. It shall not be permissible for any one of them to [. . .] or to make factions or to leave the brotherhood of the president to join another brotherhood or for men to enter into one another's pedigrees at the banquet, or to abuse one another at the banquet, or to chatter or to indict or charge another or to resign for the course of the year or again to bring the drinking to nought.[12]

Unfortunately, the text becomes fragmented at this point. The exclusivity clause forbidding the joining of another association is particularly interesting since such a clause is not found in the extant regulations of other associations.

CONCLUSION

Further nuancing of the data regarding the various types of associations in Greco-Roman antiquity is certainly possible and necessary. For example, in

---

12. For text, translation, and commentary see Roberts, Skeat, and Nock, "Guild of Zeus Hypsistos."

addition to the two types of private associations described above—religious and professional—there are other types, some of which overlap with these two broad categories, such as associations based on common ethnic or geographic origin or residence in the same neighborhood.

Furthermore, it is difficult to demarcate the different types of associations as clearly as one might wish. The Pythagorean school, for example, was one of the earliest philosophical schools, yet its organization may have been influenced by Greek political associations (*hetaireiai*) or by Orphic associations (*thiasoi*). Indeed, the philosophical schools of the Pythagoreans and the Epicureans have often been understood as religious associations.[13] An example of a less well-known group comes from Egypt, where we have the following inscription: [18] "The philosophers [honored] Aelius Demetrius, rhetor, after Flavius Hierax their fellow diner dedicated [this statue of] . . . and father" (I.Alex. 98; dating from the second half of the second century CE). The public mysteries often contained within their structures smaller, private religious associations. And private religious associations were sometimes composed entirely of members of the same occupation without formally being professional associations (see SEG 45 [1995] 2074).

One result of treating these usually separated associations together in this article is to underline the necessity of seeing all of them—and I would include here as well Jewish and Christian associations—as somewhat differing manifestations of the same phenomenon: as differing manifestations of voluntary associations. As further explorations of these varieties of voluntary associations are undertaken, we will undoubtedly begin to understand more fully the array of associative models that were operative in antiquity and under whose influence those who worshiped Jesus began to form themselves into associations. In doing so, we will see how much, as Ilias Arnaoutoglou has reminded us, "cultural context influences and shapes the forms of organizational structure."[14]

---

13. Cf. Strabo 17.1.8; Tertullian, *Apol.* 38.1.5; but see Culpepper, *Johannine School*, 248, 252.

14. Arnaoutoglou, "Between *koinon* and *idion*," 75.

3

Paul, Synagogues, and Associations

Reframing the Question of Models for Pauline Christ Groups

IN THE CONTINUING AND growing discourse on how best to understand the social organization of Pauline Christ groups, some approaches continue to advocate for a separation of categories such as synagogue and association while attempting to place the Pauline groups into one or the other of these. Yet, in order to progress further in the analysis, the question should not be whether Christ groups are synagogues or associations, as if these two categories are separate and distinct. In fact, the overlap among Judean groups, Christ groups, and associations breaks down such falsely rigid dichotomies.[1]

In my 1998 volume surveying analogous models used for understanding Pauline Christ groups, I used a modified version of the quadruple division on ancient groups outlined by Wayne Meeks in his book *The First*

---

1. "Associations" in antiquity are groups of men and/or women that are "normally organized around a common ethnic identity, deity or cult, trade or profession, or neighborhood, and are to be distinguished from civic organizations" (Kloppenborg, "Associations, Voluntary," 1062). In antiquity, there was no broad category or even a term "association" that would encompass the variety of groups that are included in this designation by modern scholars. There was, in fact, a large range of terminology used by the ancients themselves to delineate what moderns call "associations." The failure to recognize that the etic category of "association" is a modern construct lies at the heart of much of the problematic attempts to locate Judean groups and Christ groups, an issue to which we return in the conclusion of this article.

Urban Christians[2]: households, philosophical schools, synagogues, and voluntary associations.[3] On the assumption that the household was the foundational [28] structure for many manifestations of the other three,[4] I replaced it with "ancient mysteries" as a separate category. My book summarized scholarship up to that time on each of these models, concluding that "no one model is adequate in and of itself for explaining all aspects of Paul's Christian communities."[5] Any one model, I suggested, might better explain a Pauline Christ group *in a particular location* better than the others, but need not be *the* model that best applies to every group to which Paul writes. Since that time, much work has been done on all the models, although particularly that of the associations.[6] Nevertheless, the sharp distinctive boundary between each has remained firmly in place, as first set out by Meeks and reiterated by my own early work.

According to Meeks's analysis, "synagogue" is a distinct, separate category from "association," and to make a comparison with a Christ group one must choose whether the latter is "more like" a synagogue *or* an association. For Meeks it is the former: "Because Christianity was an offshoot of Judaism, the urban Christian groups obviously had the diaspora synagogue as the nearest and most natural model."[7] Thus, the synagogue is not "other than" the associations; [29]it is "better than." He goes on to say, "The synagogue incorporated features of both the two types of groups we have

2. Meeks, *First Urban Christians*.

3. This fourfold model has antecedents in the work of earlier scholars such as E. A. Judge, Robert Wilken, and L. William Countryman, who explored variously the relationship of Christianity to philosophical schools and *collegia* (cf. Ascough, *What Are They Saying about the Formation of Pauline Churches?*, 38–40, 83–86). L. Michael White referenced the "four models" in his doctoral dissertation, supervised by Meeks, and later made published mention of it in White, "Adolf Harnack," 120 (my thanks to White for pointing me to these references). I start with Meeks, however, since throughout the debate that followed the publication of his book, even until today, he is the most oft-cited source, particularly by those who want to drive a wedge between synagogues and associations (using the same limited data set of four inscriptions that Meeks cites, alongside the same arguments).

4. Although I still see the household as key to the organizational structure of many types of groups, I would not be quite so insistent that it is foundational for all groups.

5. Ascough, *What Are They Saying about the Formation of Pauline Churches?*, 95.

6. See Ascough, "What Are They *Now* Saying." The "voluntary" nomenclature has generally been dropped; cf. Ascough, "'Map-maker,'" 69 (Chapter 6, 107 below).

7. Meeks, *First Urban Christians*, 80. Meeks rejected the association model on the basis of a few key differences, all of which have been directly addressed in Ascough, "Translocal Relationships" (Chapter 5, below); Ascough, "Formation of Pauline Churches" (Chapter 4, below); Ascough, *Paul's Macedonian Associations*, 47–109; Kloppenborg, "Edwin Hatch." Meeks has since then expressed much more openness to using the associations as a model (Meeks, "Taking Stock and Moving On," 141).

already looked at, the association and the household."[8] Despite adopting the collegial structure and being legally construed as *collegia*, these Judean groups "possessed what is most visibly lacking" when the household and association models are compared with Pauline Christianity, namely, "the sense of belonging to a larger entity: Israel, the People of God, concretely represented by the land of Israel and the Temple in Jerusalem."[9] Thus, for Meeks it is this theological construct—a sense of continuity with the traditions of Israel—that governs the choice of "synagogue" as model for Christ groups. It is by no means clear, however, that Paul's groups had such a construct, even when Paul himself might have done so.[10]

My own conclusions tended towards a different direction, with a greater inclination to viewing the early Christ groups as more like associations *than* synagogues. In framing the discussion this way, however, both Meeks and I pit synagogues against associations, like two divorced parents vying for the attention of their only child. Such a division is not, however, correct. I attempted to address this somewhat in an essay published in 2008, in which I challenged the tripartite, taxonomic configuration of "Jews, Christians, and others/pagans" while proposing a complex, and thus more thickly descriptive, approach under the broad rubric of Greco-Roman "elective social formations" that compared all such groups "with respect to" a particular variable (e.g., meal practices, [30] leadership, nomenclature).[11] Nevertheless, the debate about the best analogous model for early Christ groups persists in employing a sharp dichotomy between synagogues and associations, viewing them as competitors, albeit sometimes subtly, as the organizing model of early Christ groups. Indeed, at times, even after noting similarities between synagogues and associations, many scholars insist that ultimately the differences disqualify Christ groups from categorization as associations.

JUDEAN SYNAGOGUES AS ASSOCIATIONS[12]

The idea that Judean synagogues can be classified as associations is by no means new. Both Josephus and Philo point to Judean groups using the

8. Meeks, *First Urban Christians*, 80.

9. Meeks, *First Urban Christians*, 80.

10. Cf. Ascough, "What Are They *Now* Saying." Kloppenborg rightly points out, and calls into question, the scholarly assumption regarding Pauline church order that rests on the premise that Paul laid down the structure and polity of the earliest communities and that one can simply "read off" their social history from Paul's letters (Kloppenborg, "Egalitarianism," 248).

11. Ascough, "'Map-maker'" (Chapter 6, below).

12. Abbreviations for Epigraphic and Papyrological Collections follow those used

terminology of associations. For example, in a document attributed to Julius Caesar from ca. 47–46 BCE, the emperor is quoted as equating the Judean community on Delos with other associations (*thiasoi*). Caesar notes that unlike *other* associations that were banned from meeting, Judean groups were allowed to continue to gather:[13]

> For even Gaius Caesar, our praetor and consul, passed a decree preventing societies (*thiasoi*) from gathering together in the city [of Rome], yet he did not prevent these [Judeans] alone from collecting funds or having common meals. Likewise, when I prevent other societies (*thiasoi*), I permit these [Judeans] alone to gather together according to their [31] ancestral customs and laws, and to feast. (Josephus, *Ant.* 14.213–216 = AGRW L33; cf. *Ant.* 14.235; 259–260)

In his composition of instructions and background for a Judean embassy traveling to see the emperor Gaius in 39 or 40 CE, Philo recalls earlier actions of Augustus, who allowed Judean associations (*synodoi*) to gather even when other types of associations were forbidden from doing so:

> [Augustus] sent a letter to all the governors of the provinces in Asia, because he heard that the sacred first fruits were being treated with disrespect. He ordered them to permit only the Judeans to come together in gatherings (*synagōgia*). For these synods (*synodoi*) were not based on drunkenness and drunken behavior to cause disturbance. Instead, they were schools of temperance and justice, where people practiced virtue and contributed the annual first fruits every year, sending sacred ambassadors to take them to the temple in Jerusalem. (Philo, *Legat.* 311–313 = AGRW L37; cf. *Legat.* 316)

In both Josephus and Philo, what sets apart the Judean gatherings is not their inherent difference in categorization from associations, but that they

---

on the AGRW website (http://philipharland.com/greco-roman-associations/welcome/how-to-use-the-inscriptions-database/#abbrev/), which is based on Horsley and Lee, "Preliminary Checklist"; and Oates, Bagnall, and Willis, *Checklist*.

13. In this article I follow those who translate *Ioudaioi* as "Judean" rather than "Jew": "Adopting this geographic, ethnic, and cultural understanding of the term helps to avoid misunderstandings among modern lay readers and some modern scholars who may tend to separate 'religion' from its ethnic or cultural matrix" (Harland, *Dynamics of Identity*, 15). Harland's entire book "is an argument for approaching Judeans in the diaspora primarily as one among many immigrant and ethnic groups" (15), and convincingly so; see esp. Harland, *Dynamics of Identity*, 14–16.

are of a particular sort of association by virtue of their socially upstanding collective behavior and having a long history of meeting together.[14]

There are some scholars who nevertheless resist the categorization of synagogues as associations, such as Shimon Applebaum,[15] Mary Smallwood,[16] [32] and Margaret Williams,[17] among others. In such cases the rejection of the connection between synagogues and associations draws heavily on the 1914 work of Jean Juster, who viewed the synagogues as sui generis and in no way related to associations.[18] Although there are some similarities, "the resemblances are superficial and the differences fundamental."[19] In 1951, [33] however, Simeon Guterman responded point

---

14. Philo seems rather taken with the alcoholic-infused excesses of non-Judean associations; see *Ebr.* 20–21 and 23 = AGRW L8; *Contempl.* 40, 64, and 83–89 = AGRW L9; *Flacc.* 4–5 = AGRW L36; *Flacc.* 135–37 = AGRW L10. See further Seland, "Philo and the Clubs," esp. 110–17; Fitzpatrick-McKinley, "Synagogue Communities," 79–80.

15. Shimon Applebaum cites Caesar's exemption of Judean communities from the law prohibiting associations, concluding that Judean *politeumata* were not *collegia* ("Organization," 502). Their membership was determined by ethnic status rather than election, and their regulations were predetermined by Torah rather than created upon the formation of the community. That said, Applebaum does accept that in some cities there existed Judean occupational associations that would have been subject to the *Lex Iulia* ("Organization," 476, 481–83; cf. Segal, "Jewish Experience," 27–28). Thus, for Applebaum it is only insofar as synagogues held the status of *politeuma* that they were different from associations; other Judean groups could be thus classified.

16. E. Mary Smallwood views synagogues as having a much broader function than the associations, particularly in the political role that local Judean associations took on in their cities in order to negotiate with Roman authorities (Smallwood, *Jews under Roman Rule*, 133–38).

17. Margaret H. Williams is perhaps one of the clearest opponents of categorizing Judean synagogues as associations, at least in Rome. Her examination of the evidence leads her to conclude that the similarities are superficial and are much outweighed by the differences (Williams, "Structure of the Jewish Community," 216; following Juster, *Les Juifs*, 418–24). For example, the texts usually cited in support of the connection from Josephus (*Ant.* 14.213–216) cannot be authenticated, and the two references in Seutonius (*Jul.* 42.3 = AGRW L32 and *Aug.* 32.1 = AGRW L34), in which Judeans are banned from Rome, neither ban all Judeans nor indicate that those who are banned have fallen afoul of laws pertaining to *collegia*. Williams then gives four kinds of evidence that Judeans in Rome had a central council to which all the various *proseuchē* in the city were accountable, but they were collectively conservative and isolationist, more focused on their own "Jewishness" than any appearance of "Romanness" in form.

18. Juster, *Les Juifs*, 414, 424; see further esp. 413–24.

19. Gruen, *Diaspora*, 121; cf. Applebaum "Organization," 464–65; Smallwood, *Jews under Roman Rule*, 133; Williams, "Structure of the Jewish Community," 216. This approach is generally also followed by Levine (*Ancient Synagogue*, 130–31), who concludes, "For all the engaging comparisons that have been made between the synagogue and comparable Greco-Roman associations (*thiasos, koinon, collegia*, etc.), many of them cogent to some degree, no analogy can do justice to the unique role

by point to Juster's argument, demonstrating that the differences are not so great and that synagogues can and should be classified as associations.

To begin with, "the fact that the Jewish community was always referred to collectively as *universitas* or *corpus*, or by some similar designation suggests to him [Juster] that the Jewish community or synagogue was not commonly regarded as a *collegium*."[20] Yet, as Guterman points out, a diversity of names was used to designate associations, so the lack of evidence among Judean groups "for the use of such familiar terms as *collegium* or *thiasoi* is by no means to be construed as a vital defect."[21] Other claims made by Juster are addressed in turn.[22] Juster's assertion that Judean communities are nationally based falters in the West, where they were not considered to compose part of the Judean nation under Roman law. We might add that other associations are construed similarly in their diaspora locations based primarily on a specific geographic or ethnic identity.[23]

Smallwood makes a similar argument: "Membership was automatic for a Jew by right of birth, without question of admission or enrollment; on the other hand, membership was exclusive to Jews and proselytes, while other *collegia* were corporations with voluntary, open membership."[24] Yet, it [34] is simply not the case that *all* associations had an open admission policy.[25] There are associations whose membership was restricted by one or more factors, such as hereditary succession (e.g., AGRW 322; CIL III 6150; VIII) or social status (e.g., citizen associations [*orgeōnes*] such as GRA I 44; 45). Nor, we might add, was ethnicity an a priori condition for admission to the Judean synagogue, at least if one allows for the early presence of God-fearers and sympathizers in the synagogues. Thus, Juster's (and following him, Smallwood's) contrast of the exclusive conditions for membership among Judean groups with the openness of associations cannot be maintained.

---

of this institution" (Levine, *Ancient Synagogue*, 173; see also Levine, "First-Century Synagogue," 27–28). Yet, as Peter Richardson shows, after having pointed to multiple similarities himself and earlier rejecting sui generis arguments, "in the end [Levine] seems to make a *sui generis* argument of synagogues," thus failing to draw the "obvious conclusion" that early diaspora synagogues borrowed from the model of associations (Richardson, *Building Jewish*, 219).

20. Guterman, *Religious Toleration*, 131.

21. Guterman, *Religious Toleration*, 131–32 (θιασοι is unaccented in original quote); cf. Ascough, *Paul's Macedonian Associations*, 71–78.

22. Guterman, *Religious Toleration*, 136–48.

23. See Schürer, *History of the Jewish People*, 3.1: 107–11 for some detailed comparisons. On associations that are formed on the basis of ethnic identity and/or immigrant status see Harland, *Associations*, 33–36. See further below.

24. Smallwood, *Jews under Roman Rule*, 134.

25. Guterman, *Religious Toleration*, 142–43.

Nor can one highlight groups of Judeans (particularly in Alexandria and Rome) and their synagogues as a "special case" of ethnic associations. They were not so different than other immigrant groups at the time that formed associations based on common ethnic identity. For example, on the island of Delos we find Egyptians (AGRW 221, 230), Tyrians (AGRW 223, II–I BCE), Berytians (AGRW 224–28, II–I BCE), Syrians (AGRW 229, II–I BCE), Italians (AGRW 231–32, 237, II–I BCE), Athenians (AGRW 238, II–I BCE), and Bithynians (AGRW 239, undated). We also have evidence for Pisidians (AGRW 273, early II BCE) and Lycians (AGRW 174, early II BCE) in Sidon, Syria, and in a later period we find Tyrians in Puteoli (AGRW 317, 174 CE), *Asianoi* in Macedonia (IG X/2.1 309, 480, both II–III CE), Thrace (AGRW 64, 196–98 CE), and the Lower Danube area (AGRW 77 [Municipium Montanensium, II CE], 78 [Nikopolis ad Istrum, early III CE], 71 [Dionysopolis, 222–35 CE]), and Alexandrians in Scythia Minor (AGRW 82, 160 CE), Neapolis, Italy (AGRW 312, ca. 100 CE), and Rome (AGRW 319, 146 CE). Understandably, when arriving in a new location, immigrants sought out others who spoke their language, ate the same food, and shared a similar background, and in some cases they formed an association on the basis of such commonalities.

Even in their being granted an exemption from the laws pertaining to *collegia*, it is clear that Judean groups were assumed to be *collegia* by the Romans and thus in need of a special exemption. Yet, despite the supposed general ban on associations, there was tacit acceptance that associations would continue to meet, and, except in cases where they became overtly political, they were simply ignored by the imperial authorities.[26] Neither is it [35] fully clear that Judean groups were actually fully exempt from such laws. Judean groups could be subject to the political heavy-handedness of the rulers when they were deemed to be too disruptive to civic society, just as was the case on occasion with other associations. Whatever might be the details around the potential involvement of Christ adherents, in the view of Suetonius, it is "the Jews" who are the subject of Claudius's ejection from Rome in the mid-first century CE, predicated on their political unrest (*Claud.* 25.4; cf. Cassius Dio 60.6.6–7). Political reasons also may have been the case with the expulsion of the Jews earlier under Tiberius, although here the rationale is less clear (Josephus, *Ant.* 18.3.5; Tacitus, *Ann.* 2.85; Suetonius, *Tib.* 36).[27]

Likewise, it is not the case, as Smallwood argues, that associations were either politically neutral or were embroiled in election shenanigans (about which Cicero so vehemently complains; see AGRW L25, L26, L28), since

26. Cotter, "Collegia and Roman Law."
27. See Rutgers, "Roman Policy," 60–65.

there are cases where associations included civic officials and patrons (e.g., AGRW 7, 74, 108, 109), organized civic events such as festivals (e.g., AGRW 18; *topos* inscriptions from Magnesia ad Maeander[28]), and were involved in the work of the *polis* in a positive manner (e.g., AGRW 162), even holding places of prominence at civic events.[29]

Guterman lists a number of association features within synagogues, such as the possession of a treasury for which funds were collected, banquets and common meals, election of officers, and burial of members.[30] The so-called lack of "statutes" in Judean groups is belied by Juster's own admission that they had the law of Moses, among other binding regulations, in particular Judean groups such as that at Apamea, which possessed a *nomos*.[31] Most significantly, "Jewish communities possessed a juridical personality" and as such had, among [36] other things, "the right to purchase and maintain land, to sell, and to contract obligations, to receive donations and give donations, and the right to send legations to the emperor."[32] Guterman concludes that based both on the evidence from Josephus and the overall similarity in organization, Judean communities can be regarded as *collegia*.[33]

Recent scholarly work on Judean groups and associations has affirmed that the former can be categorized among the latter, especially in the legal setting,[34] but also in their organizational patterns. For example, within his discussion of the similarities among the organizational structures of the Essene community and that of Hellenistic associations, Martin Hengel notes that "the Jewish synagogue communities of the Diaspora had the same legal form" as the associations, and the Jews imitated the associations' pattern of

---

28. See Ascough, "Carving Out Public Space," 93–110.

29. Among other things, this is suggested by the presence of τόπος markers on seats in which associations are given prominence in theaters; see Ascough, "Carving Out Public Space." For further evidence and argumentation of associations' positive participation in civic life see Harland, *Associations*, 101–12.

30. Guterman, *Religious Toleration*, 132–33.

31. Guterman, *Religious Toleration*, 136–37.

32. Guterman, *Religious Toleration*, 133. He notes that after the reign of Marcus Aurelius synagogues, like associations, also had the right to receive legacies, although this seems only to have been the case for Italy, since Caracalla forbade such a legacy in Antioch (Guterman, *Religious Toleration*, 133–35). We avoid the details here, however, since this postdates the time of our immediate interest.

33. Guterman, *Religious Toleration*, 150.

34. See Smallwood, *Jews under Roman Rule*, 133–43; Schürer, *History of the Jewish People*, 3.1: 115–16; Leon, *Jews of Ancient Rome*, 9–11; Cotter, "Collegia and Roman Law," 76–78; Claußen, *Versammlung*, 224–26, 231; Ebner, *Stadt als Lebensraum*, 227–28; and especially Tellbe, *Paul between Synagogue and State*, 24–63.

fostering "patriotic connections and religious interests" among their own *ethnos* ("nation") scattered throughout Egypt.[35] [37]

Two scholars in particular, however, have laid the groundwork for reframing the discourse by showing that synagogues themselves have characteristics of associations and as such are part of a larger comparative category of "Greco-Roman associations" more generally: Peter Richardson and Anders Runesson.[36] Their systematic treatments may finally put to rest such arguments to the contrary. [38]

Richardson argues that "synagogues functioned—and were perceived—as *collegia* in the diaspora."[37] Noting the general legislative ban on associations enacted under Julius Caesar and Augustus, Richardson points out that it was only occasionally that *collegia* were restricted and during such times synagogues were exempted.[38] Although he does not highlight the point, it is important to reiterate, as noted above, the necessity to explicitly exempt Judean groups; presumably they would otherwise have fallen under the laws applying to *collegia*. That is, in the view of the Roman imperial legislature, synagogues fell into the category of *collegia* and thus needed special exemption from the laws applying to such.

Turning to epigraphic, literary, and archaeological data for synagogue buildings in the period prior to the destruction of the temple, Richardson demonstrates a consistency among synagogues' primary focus on multiple communal functions such as meals, education, and civil law.

35. Hengel, *Judaism and Hellenism*, 243–45, 311. Baumgarten expands upon the comparisons of commensality in Philo and Josephus to compare Judean sects such as the Essenes, Pharisees, and Sadducees to associations and philosophical schools ("Graeco-Roman Voluntary Associations," 93–111). The comparison explains why ancient Judean sectarianism flourished at the time it did, since Judean sects and associations were both in similar circumstances, attracting literate urbanites at a time of extreme social disruption. On the similarities between the community associated with the Qumran documents and the Greco-Roman associations see Weinfeld, *Organizational Pattern*; Klinghardt, "Manual of Discipline"; Richardson, *Building Jewish*, 165–85; Herrmann, "Gemeindergel von Qumran"; Harland, *Dynamics of Identity*, esp. 182–85; Gillihan, *Civic Ideology*.

36. Others who conclude that synagogues were organized as associations include White, *Building God's House*, 82–83; Barclay, "Money and Meetings," esp. 114–15, 126; Trebilco, "Jews, Christians and the Associations," 333; Rajak, "Synagogue," 161–73; Harland, *Dynamics of Identity*, 36–42. Mantel enumerates twelve similarities that lead him to conclude that Judean sects in Palestine, including the Great Synagogue in Jerusalem, "were modeled in their organization on the Hellenistic religious and social associations" (Mantel, "Nature," 75); although the similarities are neither "uniform" nor singularly decisive, "taken together" the similarities suggest the influence of the associations (Mantel, "Nature," 91).

37. Richardson, *Building Jewish*, 111.

38. Richardson, *Building Jewish*, 115.

Synagogues looked and behaved like voluntary associations. As they developed first in Diaspora, they shared in this architectural complexity (with communal emphasis, benches, meals, worship, courtyards, ancillary spaces, etc.). Within the life of the *polis*, they adopted patterns of behavior similar to associations, such as reserving seats in the theater (Miletus) or finding a donor to give them a house (Priene, Dura, etc.).[39]

While Richardson recognizes that Judean communities might be differentiated from other associations, he rightly notes that the differences "do not subvert the claim that synagogues were associations, for the variety among associations was wide enough that—architecturally, organizationally, and behaviorally—synagogues fell naturally within those limits."[40] [39]Runesson extends this argument both in range and detail.[41] He argues that synagogues developed in different ways, depending upon their location. In Palestine there were two basic types of institution: "public city/town/village assemblies and (semi-public) voluntary associations."[42] The public assemblies are rooted in the Persian period and included Torah liturgies while also serving as the administrative center of the surrounding population. In contrast, the regulations of the voluntary association type were predominantly inwardly focused, with little concern beyond group boundaries. Similar to their public counterparts, these nonofficial institutions—both denominations (such as the Pharisees, the Essenes, and the Sadducees) and sects (such as the Samaritans, the *Therapeutae*, and the Qumran community)—were engaged in the reading and interpretation of Torah. Yet they came to the fore at a later time, during the Ptolemic period, when conditions were such that there was "a loosened attitude of the Jerusalem authorities to the control of the interpretation of the law" along with the process of canonizing Scripture and "increasing Hellenistic influence, including the Greek organizational forms of the *thiasoi*, or voluntary associations," which could be adopted and adapted.[43]

In the diaspora, synagogues were regarded as associations and generally treated as such under Roman law but were granted special privileges based on their "antiquity" that exempted them from the legal ban on *collegia*. Thus, "the main difference between the Jewish 'synagogues' and other

---

39. Richardson, *Building Jewish*, 204; see further 207–21.

40. Richardson, *Building Jewish*, 218.

41. Runesson, *Origins*. See also his survey of scholarship on the origins of the synagogue, in which he demonstrates the breakdown of the consensus view of the exilic origins of the synagogue in favor of seeing the associations as the model, first in Palestine and subsequently in the diaspora: Runesson, "Origins of the Synagogue."

42. Runesson, *Origins*, 395.

43. Runesson, *Origins*, 398–99.

collegia was the extended privileges granted the Jews; we are thus dealing with a difference in degree rather than in nature between the 'synagogue' and other associations."[44] Liturgical developments, including Torah reading, took place variously in place and time in the diaspora synagogues as Jews from Palestine immigrated westward, although "by the first century Torah reading liturgies were firmly established everywhere."[45] Nevertheless, the social pattern and the [40] temple-like architectural design of Diaspora synagogues resemble the broad organizational form of the *collegia*.[46]

SYNAGOGUES AS THE INTERMEDIARY MODEL FOR CHRIST GROUPS

Notwithstanding the misgivings of some scholars as to whether Judean synagogues were associations, as we have seen, other scholars do accept this categorization. This lays the groundwork for scholars to view Christ groups and synagogues under the same broad umbrella—namely, as associations—since there are a number of group characteristics that are manifest in some associations, synagogues, and Christ groups, such as focus on cult liturgies, common banquets and/or meals, provision of burial for members, rules for admission and exclusion, monetary contributions, written regulations, reliance on patronage, a designated leadership structure, ethical expectations, and translocal connections.[47] Despite these mutual similarities, or

---

44. Runesson, *Origins*, 468–69.

45. Runesson, *Origins*, 470; 480.

46. Runesson, *Origins*, 471. It is important to note that Judean synagogues manifest diverse features, often depending upon locale (as demonstrated by Runesson, *Origins*; Rajak, "Synagogue and Community," 22–38). The category "synagogue" itself should not be rarified into a singular model.

47. For evidence from Christ groups see Ascough, "What Are They *Now* Saying," in which I summarize the substantive work done in this area since 1998. For the synagogues, along with the material summarized above, see the overview in Fitzpatrick-McKinley, "Synagogue Communities," 63–70. On the whole, Fitzpatrick-McKinley recognizes a number of similarities among synagogues and associations, but in the end concludes that "there were a number of differences between the Graeco-Roman clubs and the synagogues of the Jews" (69). Curiously, she cites only three substantive differences, much fewer than the number of similarities she names. The first difference is the exclusiveness of the synagogues, which, we noted above, is somewhat overstated, as Fitzpatrick-McKinley at least recognizes by drawing attention to the possible presence of God-fearers and converts. Second, drawing on Meeks, she notes that to outsiders the synagogue restrictions on conviviality "may have seemed a little too intense" (69). But this is a matter of degree, not of kind; Josephus and Philo cluster Judean groups with associations even when making this distinction. Third, she notes the diaspora sense of belonging was not just to their *polis* of residence but also to Israel, the "land and its

perhaps because of them, there continues to be resistance to claims that Christ groups were modeled on associations. Indeed, when it comes to understanding Christ groups, the [41] associations often take a back seat to the synagogues, with the latter playing an intermediary role. For example, in his popular, and thus influential, introductory textbook, Bart Ehrman writes,

> We are particularly well informed about ancient *trade organizations and funeral societies*. The church in Thessalonica may have been roughly organized like one of these groups.[48]

At this point, he makes reference to a side box on the opposite page that includes the bylaws of the Association of Diana and Antinoüs from Lanuvium (CIL XIV 2112 = AGRW 310; 136 CE). Within the boxed text itself, Ehrman reiterates the importance of the associations, albeit again referencing a "burial society," which belies his claim to be among those "well-informed" about ancient associations, since this category is all but defunct.[49] Yet having made the initial connection of a Christ group with the associations, Ehrman continues,

> On the other hand, given its central commitment to a religious purpose, it may have had some close organizational affinities with the Jewish synagogue as well, although the Jewish community was probably much larger than the Christian group. It appears that some of the local converts became leaders in the Christian congregation and that they organized their meetings, distributed the funds [42] they collected, and guided the thinking of the group about religious matters (5:12–13).[50]

Ehrman thus quickly shifts from the associations to the synagogue as the model for Christian community at Thessalonike. The source for the "local converts" who became leaders is a bit ambiguous in his text but following as it does on the claim about the large Judean community in Thessalonike, Ehrman conveys the idea that leadership in the local Christ group was drawn

---

temple city" (70). Yet, as I have pointed out elsewhere, such feeling cannot have been overly intense, for we have scant evidence of the diaspora Judean communities rallying to the aid of Jerusalem during the siege of 68–70 CE (Ascough, "Translocal Relationships," 236 [Chapter 5, 100 below]). It seems there were limits to their commitment!

48. Ehrman, *Brief Introduction*, 208 (italics original).

49. See especially Ausbüttel, *Untersuchungen*, 20, 29; Kloppenborg, "Collegia and Thiasoi," 20–23; Rebillard, *Care of the Dead*, 38–39. In noting the problems with the special category of "*collegia funeraticia*," Perry rightly comments, "The better approach to the topic is to catalog all instances of a college—of whatever type—acting in a funerary capacity" (Perry, *Roman Collegia*, 32).

50. Ehrman, *Brief Introduction*, 208.

from the synagogue, even while the rank and file were predominantly "pagan," and thus the Christ group itself would naturally follow the synagogue model.[51] He does not reference again the associations.

Although the primary focus of his study is the organizational leadership of the early Christians, the title of James T. Burtchaell's book conveys clearly his fundamental understanding of the lines of influence: *From Synagogue to Church*. Practices found in the Christian churches of both the earliest period and later developments can be linked, through continuity with Judean antecedents, to the Judean synagogue "from which Christians emerged."[52] The synagogues, however, had little to do with associations beyond surface resemblances in the naming offices and the electing and honoring of incumbents to these positions. In the synagogues, officers held positions for much longer time periods and focused their attention "on the entire welfare of the people" rather than on short-term aims of the group.[53] A translocal view created a sense of continuity with Jews elsewhere,[54] while a backward, historic view connected them with the traditions and leaders of Israel, especially Moses. Above all, Jews found the ultimate authority in their God, rather than their elected officials. Thus, despite similarities in titles, the synagogues had little else in common with associations. And, although he does not state it explicitly, this removes any possible influence of the associations on the development of the early Christ groups. For Burtchaell, [43] "the synagogue became the church, not by dint of a new social format, but in view of new convictions within its members."[55] It seems that for Burtchaell, Christian groups thus inherit all that is embedded in the history and organization of the Jews with little or no (corrupting?) influence from outsiders and carry these traditions forward in ways the Jews themselves do not.

In Claußen's comprehensive review of the structure and organization of the ancient synagogues, he considers briefly the influence of associations, although he relies on the work of Meeks and thus ends up discounting their influence on early Christ groups, and arguing that synagogues influenced the structure of early Christian house churches, both in Palestine and in the diaspora: "Vor allem Privathaushalt, Verein, Synagoge und philosophische

---

51. The same rhetorical move is present almost verbatim in Ehrman's more comprehensive introductory textbook; see Ehrman, *New Testament: Historical Introduction* 316–17.

52. Burtchaell, *From Synagogue to Church*, 272.

53. Burtchaell, *From Synagogue to Church*, 272.

54. The argument that associations had no translocal connections in the manner of Judean and Christian groups is addressed in detail in Ascough, "Translocal Relationships"(Chapter 5, below).

55. Burtchaell, *From Synagogue to Church*, 352.

Schule bildeten die vielfach herangezogenen Vorbilder der frühchristlichen Gemeindestruktur, wobei zumindest bei Meeks eine gewisse Neigung auszumachen ist, der Diasporasynagoge die führende vorbildrolle zuzubilligen."[56] Yet, as Runesson points out, Claußen's assumption that the majority of synagogue gatherings were household based is questionable, since there were a variety of institutional forms associated with terms such as *synagōgē* and *proseuchē* at that time.[57]

In some cases, scholars maintain a distinction within the affirmation of synagogues as associations, bracketing out synagogues as, at best, a special kind of association, and ultimately driving a wedge between the two by emphasizing that Christ groups were synagogues *rather than* associations. For example, Mark Nanos cites Smallwood and others in affirming that the synagogues had the legal standing of associations in the ancient world, albeit with special privileges based on their "ancestral customs."[58] Two pages later, he quotes La Piana cautiously but affirmingly to the effect that synagogues were in many respects similar to associations, but in other ways were superior: "In a word, the Jewish associations, taken all together, actually possessed all the essential elements of organization and government pertaining to a city, and not merely [44] showed the semblance of such institutions, as was the case with the collegia."[59] Yet La Piana's work in this particular area needs to be used with caution, since La Piana seems unable to make up his mind whether synagogues can be classified alongside associations. For example, he notes that the diaspora synagogues adopted the "Greek nomenclature of the associations,"[60] yet claims that they were not *collegia*,[61] only to contradict this later with the statement that a number of synagogues "were really Jewish *collegia domestica*"[62]—that is, a particular type of association.

For Nanos, it is the affiliation of the Christian communities with synagogues—as synagogues—rather than associations that protects them from imperial interferences in the middle part of the first century. Citing Suetonius's reference to Julius Caesar dissolving all guilds except those with ancient foundations (*Jul.* 42.3 = AGRW L32), Nanos argues that it is only through their being "subordinate" to the "governing authorities" of the

---

56. Claussen, *Versammlung*, 47, drawing on Meeks, *First Urban Christians*.
57. Runesson, Review of Claußen, 314.
58. Nanos, *Mystery of Romans*, 43–44.
59. La Piana, "Foreign Groups," 349–50; Nanos, *Mystery of Romans*, 47.
60. La Piana, "Foreign Groups," 360.
61. La Piana, "Foreign Groups," 349 and n. 17.
62. La Piana, "Foreign Groups," 355 n. 23.

synagogue that the Christ adherents at Rome to whom Paul writes would have been protected: "Paul *and* the Christian Jews and gentiles of Rome both understood their community(s) as part of the Jewish community(s) when Paul wrote Romans, with Christian gentiles identified as 'righteous gentiles' who were now worshipping in the midst of Israel in fulfillment of the eschatological ingathering of the nations (15:5–12)."[63] Had the Christ adherents been designated as a "private club" they would have had insufficient grounds to practice their religion freely within the city.[64]

Nanos presumes that Christ groups would need to apply to the Roman authorities for "the right to congregate for fellowship and worship, [45] even in their own homes or tenement rooms," and we have no evidence for such taking place.[65] This, he argues, is because their designation as synagogues provided sufficient protection. This claim, however, does not account for the evidence that despite the general ban on associations, there was tacit acceptance that associations would continue to meet, and, except in cases where they became overtly political, they were simply ignored by the imperial authorities.[66] That is, many non-Christ groups in first-century Rome show no evidence of applying for imperial approval and yet continued to meet in private, despite not having protected themselves by subordinating themselves to the synagogue authorities. Furthermore, although Judean groups did seem to have some privileges, Judeans in particular cities were not immune from periods of opposition from local authorities.[67] Thus, even an alliance with a synagogue would provide Christ groups with no guarantee of freedom from interference.

Other scholars have made the same assumption, even while not so explicitly attempting to distance Christ groups from direct affiliation with associations through the buffer of the synagogues. Thus, for Guterman, it is Christianity's identification with Judaism, whose associations had the status "*religio licita*," that protects it from persecution by Roman authorities; once

---

63. Nanos, *Mystery of Romans*, 75 (italics original).

64. Nanos, *Mystery of Romans*, 74–75. He is reacting to suggestions that Christ groups sought protection from the authorities by designating themselves as "funerary associations," a category of which he is rightly skeptical, as it has been called into question as a *taxon*, as noted above (see footnote 49). Most recent work on Christ groups as associations no longer relies on this defunct argument. In his 2002 book, Nanos makes a similar argument for the Galatian Christ groups affiliating with local Judean communities in order to gain safeguards from the Roman legal protections offered to Judean groups (Nanos, *Irony of Galatians*, 257–67, esp. 264).

65. Nanos, *Mystery of Romans*, 74.

66. Cotter, "Collegia and Roman Law," 74–89.

67. Tellbe, *Paul between Synagogue and State*, 63.

separation occurred, Christians were prosecuted under Roman law.[68] Even Runesson follows an explicit claim—"In the Diaspora the Jewish communities were most likely organized and understood by the surrounding community as *collegia*"—by noting, "In the same way, the early Christ-believers were organized as voluntary associations, first within, and later outside the umbrella of Jewish voluntary associations."[69] But it is Roger W. Gehring's summary that perhaps best encapsulates what is at stake when scholars make such claims, whether consciously or subconsciously: [46]

> It is also possible that Hellenistic associations had an *indirect* influence on the early Christian house churches by way of the Jewish synagogue. If the Diaspora synagogue was organized like an association, this would provide an explanation for the fact that elements of the association can be seen in the organization of the house church. One must distinguish between the theological self-understanding of the early Christian house churches, on the one hand, and the sociological and legal form of organization or outward appearance, on the other. It could be that the house churches were organized like a house synagogue (that is, like an association or household) and yet *understood themselves theologically not as an association but as an ecclesia* or the family/house of God, which in turn would suggest a theological connection between the house church and the house synagogue.[70]

While many scholars, myself included, have been arguing that structurally the Christ groups have the organizational form that would categorize them as "associations," as did the synagogues, for some scholars there clearly remains an important distinction insofar as they are concerned that the "theology" of the associations (if one can speak of such) should not be seen to be tainting the self-understanding of Christ groups. For some scholars, Christ groups are protected from such "pagan" influences through the synagogues.

John Kloppenborg has aptly illustrated the issue of theological or ideological concerns interfering with scholarly pursuit of the connections between associations and the early Christian groups in his analysis of the reaction of scholars to the work of Edwin Hatch (and others) at the end

---

68. Guterman, *Religious Toleration*, 157–18. Guterman (like others) is, however, incorrect in asserting the category of *religio licita* as a legally defined category that protected Judeans (or any others) by granting them official status. There is no ancient support for the existence of such a category (see Harland, *Associations*, 222), which originated with Tertullian (*Apol.* 21.1); see further Esler, *Community and Gospel*, 211–15; Rajak, "Was There a Roman Charter."

69. Runesson, Review of Claussen, 314.

70. Gehring, *House Church and Mission*, 21 (italics added).

of the nineteenth century.[71] In the various negative responses that Hatch received to his suggestion that Paul's communities resembled associations and were thus structurally influenced by them, it is clear that much of the polemic is driven by theological considerations rather than an engagement with the data, and expressed as a fundamental opposition to the suggestion that "paganism" had any influence on early Christianity. Moreover, Jonathan Z. Smith's *Drudgery Divine* provides a detailed analysis as to how Judaism was used (mostly by [47] Protestants) to isolate early Christ groups from their "pagan" surroundings (which, for the Protestants, represented Catholicism).[72] It seems to me that framing the question of antecedents for Pauline Christ groups in a manner that pits synagogues against associations falls prey to the same methodological mistake, even if for different reasons. The question itself must be rethought.

REFRAMING THE QUESTION OF ASSOCIATIONS AS A MODEL

There is a game that my children enjoyed playing, called *Apples to Apples*, that involves categorization and definition. In the game, the dealer turns up a card on which there is a word, and each player must submit, facedown, a card with another word on it that they think the dealer will choose as the best match to the upturned card. Hence the name of the game; if the faceup card reads "apple" then a player's best bet is to submit a card that best encapsulates "appleness"—e.g., a card bearing the word *round* or *sweet*, or (even better) the words *Granny Smith*. It strikes me that we are playing a version of this game in the debate about models for early Christ groups, but we are playing it wrong—or at least we are misreading the cards. The *apple* card on the table says "Christ group," and when one player throws down the "synagogue" card as a matching *apple* (that is, as matching "Christ group"), others say, "That's not an apple; it's a banana!" In response, they throw down their own match for *apple*, which reads "association"—to which the other side retorts, "That's not an apple; that's a grapefruit!" We are left, then, with quite a fruit basket, but little way forward in the debate.

What a summary of scholarship shows, however, is that we are not, in fact, dealing with different fruit at all. Our taxonomy is incorrect, which skews our conclusions. If I may be permitted to persist with the fruit game analogy, I think the card faceup on the table says "associations," a decidedly scholarly (etic) category. When one player puts down the "synagogue"

---

71. Kloppenborg, "Edwin Hatch," 226–28.
72. Smith, *Drudgery Divine*, esp. 83.

card, they are indicating a *particular type* of association—perhaps a "Golden Delicious." When another player puts down the "Christ group" card, they too have a match, but again, it is a *particular type* of association, a "Granny Smith." In biological terms, they are different species but of the same genus; different type of apples, but both still of the *malus* genus.

Returning to Gehring, he asks "whether the synthesis between Judaism and Hellenism can be demonstrated in concentrated form here in the synagogue—in other words, patterned after the organization of a voluntary [48] association yet Jewish in self-understanding."[73] On the one hand, it makes sense that the self-understanding of a group of Judeans would be "Jewish." Yet Gehring's statement underlines the fundamental methodological problem in the way the question is often framed in the debate between synagogues and associations—a "Jewish self-understanding" in comparison to what? An "association's self-understanding"? Framed this way, the question is ridiculous, as no ancient group would think like this (nor would they be able to).[74] The taxon "association" as it is used in the scholarly literature is a modern construct—again, an "etic" category; the ancients themselves had numerous words for such groups (the "emic" perspective), which are not entirely synonymous (e.g., *thiasos, eranos, koinon, collegium*). Nor would it even make sense to the majority of ancients to contrast Judean self-understanding with Gentile self-understanding; this is a thoroughly Judean framework in and of itself (and when used by modern scholars, often buys into a Pauline theological framework). As religious studies scholars we need to frame the difference appropriately, such as contrasting Judean self-understanding with other possible emic, ethnic self-understandings such as that of the "*Asianoi*," and then for comparative purposes cite examples of associations of *Asianoi*, which have both ancient traditions and ethnic character traits, and also in some cases include non-*Asianoi* in their group (see, for example, AGRW 64 = GRA I 87, Perinthos, 196–97 CE; IG X/2.1 309, Thessalonike, II–III CE).

Kloppenborg has observed that, "our data about associations is sufficiently fragmentary and scattered that it is difficult to tessellate these data into a coherent picture that would permit systematic comparison to the

---

73. Gehring, *House Church and Mission*, 21 n. 117.

74. Occasionally Judean groups referred to themselves as "associations"; for example, *synodos* in IJO II Nysa 26 (see comments in Harland, *Greco-Roman Associations*, 355), and Josephus *Ant.* 14.235 or *thiasos* in Josephus, *Ant.* 14.213–216 (quoted above), and perhaps IJO I Ach. 41 (see comments there). There is more evidence for groups that held no special ethnic Judean quality employing the term *synagōgē* for their group (e.g., AGRW 63, 95; IPerinthos 59) or *archisynagōgos* for their leader (e.g., AGRW 39, 45, 49, 63; see Kloppenborg and Ascough, *Greco-Roman Associations*, 311–12); cf. Harland, *Dynamics of Identity*, 40–41.

practices [49] of Christ groups."[75] This is correct, to a degree, but seems to assume that we have enough unfragmentary and unscattered data to permit a coherent picture of the Christ groups themselves. In fact, we do not. Although much of the evidence for the early Christ groups is collected into a single volume—the canonical New Testament—which can give the *appearance* of coherence, these texts were written by multiple authors spread over at least the second half of the first century (probably later), and geographically spread around the eastern circum-Mediterranean. It is no more a coherent picture than that acquired by association data. One can extend this to the data for ancient synagogues, which again is fragmentary and scattered.

It is the scattered and fragmentary nature of *all* of this data that makes the comparative process difficult. More to the point, any attempt to tessellate the association data into a coherent picture of what an association was in and of itself would of necessity ignore the various different types of associations.[76] To return to our horticultural metaphor, the genus is association, which has various species based on such factors as kinship, neighborhood, ethnicity, occupation, or cultic practice.[77] Breaking the taxonomy down further, we could suggest there are Dionysos associations, Zeus associations, Hero associations—all of them species designations of the larger genus.

There is not a tripartite division of synagogue, Christ group, and other—there is only associations, with all their various manifestations and permutations.[78] As John Barclay notes with a slightly different emphasis, "To ask, therefore, in what respects the Diaspora synagogues or early churches were like 'associations' is akin to asking whether churches today are like clubs: there [50] are too many different kinds of church, and too many different kinds of club to make this vague and over-generalized comparison of much heuristic value."[79] Once we recognize that synagogue and Christ

---

75. Kloppenborg, "Associations and Their Meals," 48.

76. If there is any justification for using "Greco-Roman associations" in a way that is inclusive of all groupings, including Judeans and Christians, it is that it serves as a quick reference that locates the general topic of scholarly discourse ("association") within the temporal and locative frame designated "Greco-Roman" by scholarly discourse.

77. Kloppenborg, "Associations in the Ancient World," 323–25; Ascough, Harland, and Kloppenborg, *Associations in the Greco-Roman World*, 2.

78. Thus, the recently published critical edition volumes and sourcebook on associations assume that Judean groups are to be categorized as associations, not contrasted with them: GRA I 73, 82; GRA II 95, 106, 113, 139, 150; cf. AGRW 46, 59, 86, 89, 105, 127, 145, 149, 196, 270, 307, 329, and perhaps 283 and 286.

79. Barclay, "Money and Meetings," 114–15. Although she does not expand on her comment, Rajak is quite correct when she observes concerning the similarities between Judean groups, including synagogues, and associations that "it is unwarranted to think in terms of a unitary Graeco-Roman model, as scholars have sometimes been

group are simply two different species of association, we can leave behind arguments about whether or not Christ groups *are* or *are not* synagogues and focus on the more complex, and thus more interesting, comparative investigation across all the apples in the basket (so to speak) to see how their similarities, and their differences, help us understand each species in its own right.[80]

From the ancients' perspective, a group of foreigners meeting in the house down the road—those people who arrived a generation ago from Judea and speak Greek in a funny way—are certainly perceived as different. But in many respects, they are also similar. Despite their accent, they speak Greek. They shop at some of the same stalls, and like us (from the perspective of the neighbor), they meet regularly as a form of social experimentation. And thus, how one frames the comparative question will determine the relationship. Do they meet regularly in a house in the name of a particular deity? Yes. Do they pour out libations to their deity and follow this with a drunken discourse over philosophy? Well, not really—but take out the libation and the drunkenness and they do pursue philosophical-like conversations. Thus, they are at the same time both similar and different.

Yet, when one imposes the scholarly taxa such as "synagogue" and "other"/"pagan" group, one privileges the differences of the synagogues and [51] demeans the differences among the "others" by making them secondary. In the framing of the comparison we are thus already deciding which is the preferred group; as Smith notes, our language, our choice of categories, creates the world we want to study while reflecting the world that we inhabit.[81] No wonder, then, that when we read Philo's comparison of synagogues and associations we readily agree with his assessment and see it as self-evidently historical. To wit, Philo suggests that in contrast to the sobriety and philosophical nature of particular Judean groups (*Therapeutai*

---

over-inclined to do" ("Synagogue and Community," 37). There was, as she notes, a "broad framework of a spectrum of types of Graeco-Roman associations" within which the various Judean groups could adapt and experiment. As I noted, it would thus be unwise to assume that in using the etic association as a comparator we are employing a term that signifies one particular thing.

80. Although my argument has focused on how the category synagogue is used as a buffer between Christ groups and their wider so-called pagan surroundings, the breakdown of the rigid distinctions between the three categories also works the other way, mitigating arguments put forth that would isolate early Christ groups *from* the synagogues (as does Esler), on the basis of architectural distinctions—with Judeans meeting in dedicated buildings termed *proseuchai*, and Christ groups meeting in domestic spaces or rented commercial venues (see Esler, *Conflict and Identity*, 77–107, esp. 106).

81. Smith, *Relating Religion*, 4.

and synagogues), the associations are raucous, drunken feasts—a contrast to which many scholars have given the nod of approval. I hope that my argument has given pause to such assent. Instead, we should see synagogues as a different manifestation of "association," bearing both similarities to and differences from other manifestations of associations. Likewise, Christ groups bear both similarities to and differences from other manifestations of associations, including—but not limited to—synagogues.

Nevertheless, my overarching aim is not an attempt to slot synagogues (or Christ groups, for that matter) into the particular category of association, as if doing so will provide some sort of leverage for better understanding. Rather, my aim is to call into question the categories, and the categorization, themselves. We must drop the dichotomous either/or categorization and reframe the discussion around the comparative exploration of similarities and differences across all types of Greco-Roman associations, including synagogues and Christ groups, in order to move forward in our understanding of the complex interactions reflected in all of our texts, sacred or otherwise.[82]

---

82. Like all metaphors, pushed too far, the fruit metaphor does begin to break down. As Mark Nanos pointed out to me (via email), while one cannot simply take a Granny Smith and call it a Red Delicious, as there is evidence that a Judean group could be identified as both a synagogue and an *ekklesia*. That said, I think a focus on the terminology for group meetings is part of the problem. So while we most commonly associate the word *synagogue* with Judean meetings, there are non-Judean groups that use that term as well. For example, in Perinthos, Thrace, there is a synagogue of barbers dedicated to Zeus, which is clearly not Judean (GRA I 86 = AGRW 63, I–II CE). Similarly, the use of *archisynagōgos* as a leadership term appears in non-Judean groups (see footnote 74 above; cf. Ascough, *Paul's Macedonian Associations*, 79–80, including n. 38). Thus, a focus on nomenclature can only get us so far, which is why I want to push beyond it to formulate comparisons that would be construed something like, "comparing the synagogue of Judeans in Perinthos with the synagogue of barbers with respect to their dedicatory practices." The use of *synagogue* is not the most interesting aspect, nor does it make them "the same." It simply invites the deeper comparison of two "associations." This is something I have advocated more strongly elsewhere; see Ascough, "'Map-maker'" (Chapter 6, below). We should drop either/or bifurcations and essentializing and focus on deeper analysis of "X compared to Y with respect to Z" and on practices (or so-called theologies) reflected in the texts. For example, many groups had meals, so we can identify the similarities in practice (reclining, gathering in small numbers, drinking) in order to highlight the differences, not so we can argue that one type of group is better than another (as does Philo) but simply to show the range of practices. In so doing, it may well be that one particular Judean group differs from another Judean group, especially in a different location, yet both claim the designator *synagogue*.

My thanks to many who read and commented on versions of this paper, including Mark Nanos, Anders Runesson, Richard Last, Erich Gruen, Philip F. Esler, L. Michael White, Cheryl O'Shea, and the anonymous peer reviewers for *JJMJS*.

4

Voluntary Associations and the Formation of Pauline Christian Communities

Overcoming the Objections

INTRODUCTION

As THE TWENTY-FIRST CENTURY opens, increasing attention is being paid to the social contexts of early Christianity.[1] However, as Jonathan Z. Smith has argued, many biblical scholars continue to appeal to the "Jewish roots" of Christianity in order to insulate formative Christianity from its so-called pagan surroundings.[2] He then shows how polemical agendas have been the context of the discussion and have skewed both the presentation of the

---

1. Unfortunately, many studies of the sociocultural context of early Christianity have been reduced to providing "background information," only sometimes deemed significant for understanding the deeper ("more significant") theological truths of the texts (Elliott, *What Is Social-Scientific Criticism?*, 12). Too often exegetes are left to make the transfer from "background" to exegesis (e.g., Ferguson, *Backgrounds*; Barrett, *New Testament Background*). Fortunately, more recent social-scientific studies of the New Testament have advanced beyond this, providing solid exegetical insights based on a thorough understanding of the social world of the text.

2. See Smith, *Drudgery Divine*, 83; also Wiens, "Mystery Concepts," 1251; Kloppenborg, "Edwin Hatch," 226–28.

"facts" and the subsequent analyses and conclusions. These observations extend to the debate over the use of models for understanding early Pauline community organization. Most scholars eschew models other than the synagogue for understanding Pauline Christianity. The model is often applied to all of the Christian communities with very little attempt to understand each of them in their own particular locale. Nor is there any real attempt to consider models other than the synagogue, models such as philosophical schools, mysteries, and voluntary associations.³ While we do not want to [150] disparage the importance of formative Judaism and the synagogues for the understanding of early Christian communities, we do want to suggest that other models of community organization need to be seriously considered as part of the matrix of early Christian community formation.

Behind the reluctance to consider models other than the synagogue, Smith identifies a scholarly predisposition to equate comparison with inheritance. That is, when faced with similarities among two groups, or movements, or even texts, scholars immediately determine that there is a genealogical connection.⁴ They assume that one of the groups being studied must have borrowed from the other. As a result, they seem to fear that an admission that Christian groups have a relationship with something other than Judaism is an admission that it somehow became corrupted.

Smith goes on to suggest that rather than seek, or even assume, such genealogical connections, the process should be one of analogical comparisons. In an analogical investigation the comparative process is not undertaken to find direct relationships. One is not looking for the earlier exemplar, nor is one trying to determine the direction of borrowing.⁵ Rather, one type of association is compared to another in order to highlight both similarities *and* differences. Indeed, what is inherently interesting in the comparative process is not so much the similarities among various groups, although these are important, but the differences.⁶ It is precisely in finding difference that one is invited into "negotiation, classification and comparison."⁷ It is only in defining peculiarities that one is able to note what was distinctive about early Christian groups.

The comparative connections used rest in the mind of the interpreter and help the interpreter understand how things might be reimagined or

---

3. There are exceptions; see Ascough, *What are They Saying about the Formation of Pauline Churches?*
4. Smith, *Drudgery Divine*, 47.
5. Cf. Kloppenborg, "Edwin Hatch," 228–30.
6. Smith, *Drudgery Divine*, 42, 47.
7. Smith, *Drudgery Divine*, 42.

redescribed. The comparison takes place around a set of options that are specified by the interpreter. This approach does not preclude the borrowing of aspects from one religion to another—indeed, we have suggested as much and more in the case of some of the Pauline communities and the associations.[8] However, rather than simply explain origins, Smith proposes that the setting beside one another of various facets of religion will lead to greater insight and awareness of all the groups being studied. It is with this foundational methodological commitment that we turn to an investigation of Pauline Christian communities and the voluntary associations of antiquity. [151]

PIONEERS AND PROPONENTS

The use of "voluntary associations" as a model for understanding early Christian community formation goes back more than a century.[9] Indeed, if one were to include some of the earliest commentators on Christian groups, one could even argue that the use of this model goes back to the patristic period. We find there writers such as Tertullian, Celsus, and Alexander Severus using associations as the point of comparison for Christian groups.[10] However, it was with the studies by Mommsen and de Rossi that the associations were used by critical scholars as a means for understanding Christian origins.[11] From the latter part of the nineteenth century[12] through the early part of the twentieth century[13] associations continued to be profitably explored by New Testament scholars. However, from the twenties through to the sixties

---

8. E.g., Ascough, "Thessalonian Christian Community" (Chapter 7, below).

9. In our investigation we will use the term "voluntary associations" or "associations" rather than the more specific "Roman *collegia*," which generally refers to Latin associations, most of them in the Western part of the empire. This decision is not without problems but reflects the breadth of investigations currently being undertaken in North America. The term "voluntary association" is less than ideal but captures the essence of the type of group that we are discussing. That there was no one term used for associations in antiquity makes it difficult to find an antique name for them. Various attempts at defining the category have been made. In general, a voluntary association can be defined as "a group of men and/or women organized on the basis of freely chosen membership for a common purpose" (Ascough, "Associations, Voluntary," 117).

10. Tertullian, *Apol.* 38–39; Celsus in Origen, *Cels.* 1.1; 8.17, 47; Scriptores Historiae Augustae, Alexander Severus 49.

11. Mommsen, *De collegiis et sodaliciis*; Rossi, *La Roma sotterranea cristiana*.

12. Renan, *Apostles*; Heinrici, "Christengemeinden Korinths"; Hatch, *Organization*; Hatch, *Influence*.

13. Hardy, *Studies in Roman History*; Radin, *Legislation*; Wilson, *St. Paul and Paganism*.

interest in the associations waned. Although it is difficult to document why (since no one seems to explicitly reject the model), I suspect it has much to do with the discovery of Christian and Jewish documents such as Didache and the Dead Sea Scrolls and, to a lesser extent, the Nag Hammadi codices.

Edwin Judge was one of the first scholars in the modern era to bring the associations back into focus by suggesting that despite the differences, Christian groups would have been indistinguishable from other types of voluntary associations, both in their own minds and in the minds of the [152] public.[14] This opinion was confirmed by others such as Robert Wilken, William Countryman, and Marta Sordi.[15] The most influential study of the last quarter of the twentieth century, however, was Wayne Meeks's *The First Urban Christians*. In eleven pages Meeks lays out four possible models for community formation, which have become the reference point in the debate over the appropriate analogy for understanding the early Christian communities: the household, voluntary associations, synagogues, and philosophical schools.[16] Meeks himself favors the synagogue model and offers reasons why the other models are not viable. His persuasiveness is shown in the number of studies that simply adopt his critique, particularly of the voluntary associations model, usually without an examination of the primary evidence.[17]

Although Meeks's study *might* have signaled the end of the use of the associations for understanding early Christian community formation, the issue was taken up as a five-year seminar by members of the Canadian Society of Biblical Studies (CSBS), from 1988 to 1993—the published papers from which were edited by John Kloppenborg and Stephen Wilson as *Voluntary Associations in the Greco-Roman World*.[18] The articles in this volume

14. Judge, *Social Pattern*, 44–45.

15. Wilken, "Collegia," 268–91; Countryman, "Patrons and Officers," 135–43; Sordi, "Christians," 147, 182–86.

16. Meeks, *First Urban Christians*, 74–84. In my own work on this issue (Ascough, *What are They Saying about the Formation of Pauline Churches?*, 7–9) I suggest that the household is not a viable model as distinct from the other models, since the others are often based in the household (but see Kloppenborg, "Collegia and *Thiasoi*," 16–30. I point out that the other analogous model that is often used is that of the ancient mysteries.)

17. For example, Jeffers, *Greco-Roman World*, 79–80; Clarke, *Serve the Community*, 159–60. In both cases they spend considerable time describing the associations but in the end decide against generally adopting them as a model for understanding Christian community by citing Meeks's objections.

18. Kloppenborg and Wilson, eds., *Voluntary Associations*. Two of Kloppenborg's students have also recently completed doctoral dissertations on this topic (Ascough, "Voluntary Associations and Community Formation" [1997]; Harland, "Claiming a Place in Polis and Empire" [1999]).

represent a [153] range of positions, from those who view the associations as an important analogue for understanding ancient Jewish and Christian groups to those who are more reserved in the application of the analogy. Whether as a direct result of the work of the CSBS or not (and in some cases a direct link can be made), a number of articles, both published and unpublished, have continued to investigate the relationship of the voluntary associations to early Christian communities.[19]

PROBLEMS AND POSSIBILITIES[20]

There are a number of areas where the associations are being used as a model for defining and understanding early Christian communities, in particular the Pauline communities.[21] Nevertheless, the analogy has its detract-[154]tors, both those who engage the idea as a possibility, only to reject it, and those who argue against it in detail. Bart Ehrman is one who raises the issue, specifically with respect to the Thessalonian Christian community. In his recent introductory textbook he points to social groups in the Greco-Roman world that "met periodically for worship and socializing" and notes that "we are especially well informed about ancient trade organizations and funeral societies."[22] He even includes the text of CIL XIV 2112 (Lanuvium) as an illustration and claims that "the church in Thessalonica may have been roughly organized like one of these groups."[23] However, he seems to immediately back

---

19. Since for this colloquium I was asked to speak about the North American context, this will be my primary focus. At the same time, I want to recognize at the beginning that this is not to suggest that there are no significant works being published in Europe, for clearly this is not the case. Scholars such as Klauck, *Hausgemeinde als Lebensform*, 1-15; Klauck, *Hausgemeinde und Hauskirche*; Klauck, *Religious Context*; Lampe, "Das korinthische Herrenmahl"; Klinghardt, *Gemeinschaftsmahl*; and Schmeller, *Hierarchie und Egalität*, to name a few, have used the voluntary associations as a lens to understand aspects of early Christian communities. Others such as Pilhofer, *Philippi*; and Bormann, *Philippi*, have used the associations in their studies. However, these scholars fall outside the mandate of the current paper.

20. Abbreviations for collections of inscriptions follow those found in Horsley and Lee, "Checklist." Abbreviations for classical authors and papyrological collections follow those found in Kittel and Friedrich, eds., *TDNT*, 1:xvi-xxxix.

21. Other areas of comparison include Matthew (Ascough, "Matthew [Chapter 8, below]"; Carter, *Matthew and the Margins*, 49), the book of Acts (Ascough, "Benefaction Gone Wrong"[Chapter 17, below]), and the book of Revelation (Harland, "Claiming a Place"; Harland, "Honouring the Emperor").

22. Ehrman, *Brief Introduction* (2nd ed.), 282. His reference to "funeral societies," a category under much dispute of late, also shows that he is unaware of recent studies and suggests that he is, like many, reliant upon Meeks, *First Urban Christians*.

23. Ehrman, *Brief Introduction* (2nd ed.), 282.

away from using the associations as a model by stating, "on the other hand, given its central commitment to a religious purpose, it may have had some close organizational affinities with the Jewish synagogue as well, although the synagogue may have been much larger than the Christian group."[24] Ironically, he himself does not seem to be particularly "well-informed" since he sees the "religious purpose" of the Christian groups as disqualifying them as associations, despite the fact that "religious associations are now seen as one of the primary types of associations."[25] Even more problematic is his appeal to a "large" Jewish synagogue at Thessalonica, despite the lack of any archaeological or literary evidence outside of Acts 17.[26]

In his recent book on early Christian leadership, *Serve the Community of the Church*, Andrew Clarke looks to a number of ancient organizations for leadership models including the civic structures, households, synagogues, and voluntary associations. He shows that the associations were the locus of exercising leadership and receiving honors for those who could not otherwise participate in the more public aristocratic system of honor exchange, namely, artisans, merchants, workers, and slaves.[27] However, when it comes to the use of the associations for understanding how early Christian communities were structured Clarke backs away. He admits [155] that "it is not unreasonable that some of the earliest Christians were formerly, or continued to be, members of associations or at least familiar with such groups," and thus that the associations exerted "direct or indirect" influence on Christian community.[28] However, he thinks it remains "unproven whether the early Christian communities either viewed themselves as associations, or were expressly modeled on such social and religious groups."[29] Yet despite his agnosticism he hints that the "significant differences" between the associations and Christian groups disqualify them as having influence. Clarke concludes his study by arguing that although Paul's communities attempted to reflect the organizational structures of their contexts, Paul's own countercultural stance meant that his pattern of Christian organization was sui generis.[30]

---

24. Ehrman, *Brief Introduction* (2nd ed.), 282.
25. See Kloppenborg, "Collegia and *Thiasoi*."
26. See Ascough, "Thessalonian Christian Community," 313 (Chapter 7, 124, below); and Ascough, "Voluntary Associations."
27. Clarke, *Serve the Community*, 59–77.
28. Clarke, *Serve the Community*, 159.
29. Clarke, *Serve the Community*, 159–60.
30. Clarke, *Serve the Community*, 249–51.

Ehrman and Clarke are representative of other scholars who entertain the use of the associations as an analogy for early Christian groups only to reject it. In many (not all) cases the cause of the rejection is not a fresh investigation of the primary data but a reiteration of the problems raised by Meeks and, to some extent, those raised in an article by Barton and Horsley.[31] The issues they raise go right to the issue of methodology, since claims are made that the evidence does not support, or at least does not support without more serious nuance.[32] With this in mind, it seems best to address some of the major objections directly and bring them into conversation with the data from the voluntary associations.

GROUP TERMINOLOGY

One of the significant differences pointed to between voluntary associations and the Christian groups is the "complete absence" of any common [156] terminology.[33] Two elements need to be addressed in response to this issue: (a) the idea of "common terminology" between the associations and the Christian groups;[34] and (b) the Christian designation *ekklēsia*. First, there is the issue of common terminology. In the associations there is a wide diversity of titles. Once an association was founded it might take on any number of possible names. Often associations were named after their human founders (see IKyme 30; IG XII/1 127.60; XII/3 1098). A group's name might also be taken from the basis of their common association (for example, *Aigyptoioi, Salaminioi, Molpoi,* and *Porphyrobaphon*)[35] or from their patron deity (for example, *Dionysiastai, Herakleistai,* and *Asklepiastoi*).[36]

---

31. Meeks, *First Urban Christians*, 78–80; Barton and Horsley, "Hellenistic Cult Group." In the end, the differences prove too great for Meeks, who looks to the synagogues and the philosophical schools as the best model; Barton and Horsley, "Hellenistic Cult Group," 40 suggest a combination of philosophical school and voluntary association.

32. Recently, Kloppenborg, "Edwin Hatch," 231–37 has argued that Meeks has misread the evidence and effectively takes Meeks to task on a number of these differences, as does Ascough, "Translocal Relationships" (Chapter 5, below). Carter, *Matthew and the Margins*, 568 n. 252 notes Meeks's objections but apparently accepts my "effective refutation" of them (presumably in Ascough, "Matthew"[Chapter 8, below]).

33. Meeks, *First Urban Christians*, 79; also Jeffers, *Greco-Roman World*, 80.

34. "Common terminology" is Meeks's term; we prefer "overlapping terminology."

35. Wilken, *Christians*, 34–35, 44.

36. For a more complete list of guild names that indicate religious activities or divinities see Poland, *Geschichte des griechischen Vereinswesens*, 33–46, 57–62. Inscriptional evidence attests the fact that there is no standard nomenclature for the designation of associations. Even lawyers in ancient Rome used no single, clearly defined name

In Macedonia alone we find a variety of names used in association inscriptions. *Thiasos* is used of six associations (AGRW 54; IG X/2.1 309; 506 for two different associations; 260 for two different associations) and the latinized *thiasus* is used of four associations (CIL III 703; 704; Pilhofer 338; 095). The corresponding Latin word *collegium* is used of two of the associations (SEG 37 (1987) 559; CIL III 633), and the Greek form of the word, *kollēgion*, is used once (CIG 2007f). We also find the use of *synētheia* of four associations (IBeroea 1 [= Tačeve-Hitova, "Hypsistos," no. 13]; Horsley, *New Documents* 4, no. 17; IG X/2.1 291; 933), along with *symposia*. (Pilhofer 697/2), *technē* (SIG³ 1140 of a guild), and *doumos* of an association of merchant marines (GRA I 75; cf. the term used in IG X/2.1 860).

More often an association is named according to its adherents. *Mystai* is the most common name, being used of six different Macedonian associations, four of them devoted to Dionysos (IG X/2.1 259; 260; IMakedD 920; 1104) and two of them associations of Asiani (AGRW 54; IG X/2.1 309, which may have worshiped Dionysos). "Maenads" is used of an association of women worshipers of Dionysos (Pilhofer 338). *Consacrani* is used once (Pilhofer 339), its being the Latin equivalent of *symmystai*.[37] [157] *Synthiasitai* is used once (IMakedD 284). *Thrēskeutai* is used in five inscriptions (GRA I 72; IG X/2.1 192; 220; SIRIS 123; 124) while *cultores* is used in three others (CIL III 633; SIRIS 122; Pilhofer 209).[38] The designation *synklitai* is used of two groups of associates (IG X/2.1 68; 58) while *synētheis* is used of four others (Tačeve-Hitova, "Hypsistos," no. 9; IBeroea 371; IG X/2.1 288; 289). Finally, a number of singular designations are used of an association, indicating either a trade (e.g., purple-dyers, silversmiths, donkey-drivers) or some other form of identification (e.g., *Asiani, prinophoroi*).

This diversity of group designators for voluntary associations suggests that there was no one designation by which all groups could be identified. If Christian groups are to be understood within the matrix of the associations, we would be amiss to demand of them that they adopt a particular title to identify themselves as an association. Such a concern does not seem to be part of the fabric of ancient society. Thus, whatever a group's name, they

---

for an association. In their writings they use synonymous words, particularly the idea *collegium* and *corpus*, to indicate private associations (Ausbüttel, *Untersuchungen*, 16). Sometimes one association had several names; for example, see the *lex collegii* from Lanuvium (CIL XIV 2112; Ausbüttel, *Untersuchungen*, 19). Often the names of associations differed according to geographical location (Ausbüttel, *Untersuchungen*, 33).

37. Collart, "Inscriptions de Philippes," 431.

38. Lemerle, "Inscriptions," 142 suggests that associations of *thrēskeutai* are rare; cf. Poland, *Geschichte des griechischen Vereinswesens*, 36. All of our instances come from the third century CE, which is late for such usage.

could still be understood, both socially and legally, as what modern scholars call voluntary associations. Although it is quite clear that members of an association might consider their own association better or more attractive than another association, it is a difference of degree, not of kind.

The second issue in need of being addressed vis-a-vis association terminology is the use of *ekklēsia*. This referent for the Christian community is widely attested in the New Testament. It is used throughout Acts to refer to the early Christian community. Matthew places it on the lips of Jesus three times in his Gospel (Matt 16:18, 18:17). Paul uses the term in the plural to indicate Christian groups in various locations (e.g., Rom 16:16; 1 Cor 7:17; 11:16; 16:19; 2 Cor 8:1; 11:28; Gal 1:22) and in the singular to indicate the church universal (e.g., 1 Cor 10:32; 15:9; Gal 1:13; Phil 3:6).[39] It is also used to refer to the local Christian community (e.g., Rom 16:1, 5; 1 Cor 1:2; 11:18). This is the sense in 1 Thess 1:1 when Paul addresses *tē ekklēsia Thessalonikeōn*. In Phil 4:15 he writes "no *ekklēsia* entered into partnership with me ... except you only," implying the designation *ekklēsia* for the Philippians. [158]

The Septuagint (LXX) and the Greek civic context are often recognized as background for the use of the term.[40] The word *ekklēsia* is used over one hundred times in the LXX, in most instances as a translation for the Hebrew *qhl*. Few scholars address cogently the issue of why the Christian groups would choose to use *ekklēsia* over *synagōgē*. Most often the LXX background is cited in order to show how the title was derived from the community's roots in Judaism.[41] Duling's comments are representative with reference to Matthew: "Given the Septuagint rendering of Hebrew 'assembly' (*qahal*) as

39. Cf. Meeks, *First Urban Christians*, 42–43; Hainz, "Anfange des Bischofs," is incorrect in suggesting that Paul's use of *ekklēsia* in the plural always refers only to the Jerusalem church (e.g., 1 Cor 11:16) while in the singular it refers to the local congregation.

40. See Schmidt, "ἐκκλησία," 513, 530-31; Cotter, "Women's Authority Roles," 370; McCready, "*Ecclesia* and Voluntary Associations," 60–61.

41. For Paul see, for example, Plummer, *Thessalonians*, 3; Rigaux, *Saint Paul*, 348–49; Schmidt, "ἐκκλησία," 516; Hawthorne, *Philippians*, 134; Holtz, *Thessalonicher*, 38; Wanamaker, *Thessalonians*, 70; O'Brien, *Philippians*, 377; Richard, *Thessalonians*, 38; McCready, "Ekklèsia," 60–61. Campbell, "Origin and Meaning," argues that the term does not come from the Old Testament as a designation for "the true people of God," but he does find the primary source for *Christian* usage in the Psalms and Sirach. Collins, *Studies*, 287, suggests that as a Christian community designator it originated among Jewish Christians in Jerusalem, from whom Paul "borrowed" it, although Collins goes on to suggest that in 1 Thess 1:1 it retains both the civic and the LXX sense. However, he emphasizes the LXX in suggesting "Paul enables us to see that his choice of the term *ekklēsia* was not simply a borrowing of traditional terminology but the deliberate application to the Thessalonians of a biblical model whereby he could interpret their experience. By using the idea of election in reference to this community, composed essentially of Gentiles, Paul inserts them into the context of salvation history."

both *synagōgē* and *ekklēsia* and the relation of these two terms to the 'house-synagogue' and the 'house-church,' it is naturally *the* central option for the Matthean group."[42] However, this assumption will not stand, for Matthew or for Paul, since *ekklēsia* is not the only option; *synagōgē* is also an option. In fact, *synagōgē* is the more frequently chosen word in the LXX as a translation of *qhl* in the Hebrew Bible.[43] [159] Thus, *synagōgē* would seem to be a more obvious choice if the LXX is viewed as the primary background.[44]

The term *ekklēsia* is found in a few instances as a designator for voluntary associations.[45] It is not frequently the group designator. However, it is one of many designations that the associations have taken over from the civic government.[46] Thus, it is difficult not to agree with Kloppenborg that within the context of urban-based Christian communities the term *ekklēsia* would have been heard to be indicative of a voluntary association.[47] This

---

42. Duling, "Matthean Brotherhood," 164 (italics original).

43. McCready, "Ekklēsia," 60; Schmidt, "ἐκκλησία," 513–14, esp. n. 25.

44. Cf. Ascough, "Matthew," 112–14 (Chapter 8, 154–56, below).

45. See Poland, *Geschichte des griechischen Vereinswesens*, 332 (Samos); OGIS 488 (Kastollos near Philadelphia, II CE); IGLAM 1381 (Aspendus [Pamphylia]); IGLAM 1382 (Aspendus); IDelos 1519 (196 BCE). O'Brien, *Philippians*, 377 n. 61 is simply incorrect in stating that *ekklēsia* "did not designate an 'organization' or 'society.'"

46. See Poland, *Geschichte des griechischen Vereinswesens*, 152–68. The term *ekklēsia* is used one hundred eleven times in the New Testament, although only three have the civic sense (Acts 19:32, 39, 41). Only one of these refers to a legal body (*ekklēsia engomos*, Acts 19:39) and is presented in contrast to the *ekklēsia* gathered without official sanction at the theater in Ephesos (Ferguson, *Legal and Governmental Terms*, 54–55).

47. Kloppenborg, "Edwin Hatch," 231. As I have suggested elsewhere (Ascough, "Matthew," 114 [Chapter 8, 154, below]), there is also the possibility that at least in some cases the Jesus-communities wanted to somehow distinguish themselves from the non-Jesus-believing groups through their community designator, and thus chose *ekklēsia* over *synagōgē*. This is likely the case with the Matthean group, who have recently been separated from the synagogue (or are in the process). The Matthean Christians would hear *ekklēsia* as marking them off as distinct from the Jewish *synagōgē* and as designating them as similar in structure to a voluntary association. This contrast is made even stronger through the language of "their/your synagogues" (4:23; 9:35; 10:17; 12:9; 13:54; 23:34; all but the first unique to Matthew) and the synagogues of the "hypocrites" (6:2; cf. 6:5, 23:13–26). In choosing *ekklēsia* Matthew wants the newly founded group to be readily understood as a different type of association than the Jewish associations from which he and his companions have been expelled (perhaps also seen in the placement of "*my* synagogue" on the lips of Jesus in Matt 16:18). According to Dieter Georgi many of those Christians who came to embrace the "Easter experiences" as conveyed by Paul were not themselves Jewish. Undoubtedly some were, but in many cases not even a majority of a particular community were Jewish (i.e., Galatia, Philippi, Thessalonike). In these cases it is unlikely that in working out a self-identity they would have seen themselves in competition with Jewish groups but rather with any other groups in general. Thus, Paul's use of *ekklēsia* becomes more significant than

is also the view of Neumann, who suggests, "It would have [160] needed explanation if Greek Christians had not seen religious fellowships or *thiasoi* in their new associations."⁴⁸

For other overlapping terminology we might look at the term *adelphos*. The word literally means "sons of the same mother."⁴⁹ It is a word that occurs frequently as a fictive kinship term within a variety of Christian communities, especially the Pauline communities.⁵⁰ Although he provides no direct evidence himself, Plummer asserts that *adelphos* is commonly used for members of voluntary associations.⁵¹ As an illustration, we have

---

Georgi allows. Georgi points out that Paul himself never uses the terms "Christian" or "Christianity," suggesting that he did not know these terms (Georgi, "Early Church," 40). However, as Georgi admits, neither does Paul use *synagōgē* or *proseuchē*. Georgi suggests that he uses *ekklēsia* to deliberately compete with the "assembly of free citizens meeting in the local theater" rather than to compete with local Jewish groups ("Early Church," 41). In so doing, however, Paul's groups would also be competing with other small, non-Jewish associations ("voluntary associations") that often took their nomenclature from the civic institutions (and more often not in direct competition but in the sense of "imitation as flattery").

48. Neumann, *Der römische Staat*, 46–54, quoted in Schmidt, "ἐκκλησία," 516 n. 36; Neumann's work was not available to me. Lietzmann, *Korinther*, 4 n. 2, calls the three uses of *ekklēsia* cited by Poland the exceptions that prove the rule ("die drei scheinbaren Ausnahmen . . . bestatigen diese Regel") that the LXX is the source for the Christian use of the term: "Es ist ein in der Christenheit selbst entstandener Name der Gemeinde, der in der LXX seine Quelle hat." However, this view tends both to blur all of the Christian groups and ignore the context of how it would be heard by local recipients of Paul's letters (perhaps differently from place to place). Despite his agreement with Lietzmann, Schmidt, "ἐκκλησία," 514 admits that, "some Gentile Christian circles, which were not so well, or not at all, acquainted with the OT context, might have understood the term in the light of its immediate derivation and possible recollections of Greek fellowships. It is quite possible, and wholly natural, that many matters of organization in Christian congregations should have been regulated according to the pattern of contemporary societies." This is especially the case for the Macedonian context where there is no evidence for a Jewish presence before the end of the second century CE. Klauck, *Religious Context*, 54 notes that since outsiders might have perceived Christian groups as associations, Christians might have called themselves *ekklēsia* in order to clear up the confusion. However, this is predicated on his comment that *ekklēsia* does not occur frequently in association inscriptions as a result of "an awareness of the distinction between the private association and the public assembly" (Klauck, *Religious Context*, 46). However, Klauck leaves two aspects unexplained: (a) why many associations would use other terms from public assembly quite frequently, and (b) why the early Christians thought it better to be perceived as a public, civic assembly rather than a private association (the former most likely to be perceived as a challenge [at least at the level of honor] to the local authorities).

49. LSJ s.v.

50. Meeks, *First Urban Christians*, 86–89; cf. Smith, *Relating Religion*, 336; Bartchy, "Undermining Ancient Patriarchy."

51. Plummer, *1 Thessalonians*, 19. Plummer has probably overstated the case as it

68   Section I: Modeling Christ Groups

[161] an interesting inscription from an association of masons from mid-first-century CE Rough Cilicia that lists the names of a number of unrelated men[52] who have joint shares in a tomb that belongs to a *koinon* (TAMSuppl III 201). Their regulations stipulate:

> If any brother (*adelphos*) should wish to sell his share, the remaining brothers shall buy it. If the brothers (*hoi adelphoi*) do not wish to buy the share, then let them take the aforementioned cash, and let them (all) withdraw from the association.[53]

This is a clear, mid-first-century CE example of *adelphos* used of men in an association. Another example comes from third-century BCE Manshiyeh, where members of an association of Dionysiac artists are named as *adelphoi* (OGIS 51; cf. OGIS 50), although it is clear that they are not relatives.[54] In P.Paris 42 (II BCE) it is used of members of a religious association formed within the Serapeum at Memphis.[55] In Latin inscriptions one also finds reference to members of associations as *fratres*.[56] [162]

LEADERSHIP AND OFFICIALS

Another claim against the analogy of the associations is that the leadership structure of the associations was much different than that found in Christian groups.[57] Again, the evidence does not support such a claim.[58]

---

is not a particularly common designation (cf. Kloppenborg, "Egalitarianism," 259; von Harnack, *Mission and Expansion of Christianity*, 1:405–6 n. 1). Nevertheless, there is evidence for its use in associations; see Poland, *Geschichte des griechischen Vereinswesens*, 56; Bomer, *Religion der Sklaven*, 72–78; Deissmann, *Bible Studies*, 88; Moulton and Milligan, *Vocabulary*, 9; Nock, "Historical Importance," 105.

52. The exceptions are two of the ten, who are named as sons of the same father.

53. The men named earlier in the inscription are not the entire *koinon*, just those who have a share in one particular tomb of the *koinon*. The regulation suggests that should one of these men withdraw, the others must "buy-out" his share unless a replacement can be found. If they do not, they must withdraw (as a group) from the larger *koinon*, each receiving the stated amount of cash. However, the tomb remains the property of the *koinon*, which is not disbanded.

54. The association is dedicated to the Twin Gods (*theous adelphous* = the Dioscuri) as well as Dionysos. The Dioscuri were seen as prime examples of brotherly affection (Kloppenborg, "ΦΙΛΑΔΕΛΦΙΑ," 285, 287).

55. Moulton and Milligan, *Vocabulary*, 9; cf. P.Tor I.Ii.20, II BCE.

56. CIL VI 377, 406, 7487, 10681, 21812; see Kloppenborg, "Edwin Hatch," 216 n. 17, 237.

57. Meeks, *First Urban Christians*, 79–80.

58. For an example from 1 Thessalonians see Ascough, "Thessalonian Christian

For example, in Philippians the leaders of the community are singled out by Paul as *episkopoi kai diakonoi* (1:1).[59] This is Paul's only use of these titles together.[60] The separate designations for the two offices has led most to suggest[61] that the former indicates a supervisory role while the latter is one [163] of service. However, nothing else in the letter indicates what functions these officers might have had.[62]

The verb *episkopein* is common in the LXX as a translation of *bqr* and *pqr*. The noun *episkopos* is used primarily as an official designation for an overseer or inspector of some type. This is a common source appealed to for

Community," 317–18 (Chapter 7, 127–28, below).

59. Although there is no text critical justification for it, some scholars see this as a later gloss; so Schenk, *Philipperbrief*, 78–82. Schenk's argument and the arguments against it are summarized by Peterlin, *Paul's Letter*, 20–21. The assumption that the phrase refers to later church offices and thus cannot be present in a letter written by Paul in the mid-fifties is directly countered by the argument below that these offices represent a local manifestation of leadership titles and do not represent ecclesial offices within the church universal. Some textual witnesses do read *synepiskopos* (B^2 D^c K 22 I 24 I^s 1739 1881 it arm Chrysostom Euthalius Cassiodorus Theophylact) but this makes for an awkward construction and the reading "is to be rejected" as it "arose no doubt from dogmatic or ecclesiastical interests" (Metzger, *Textual Commentary*, 611, who notes that Theodore of Mopsuestia rejected it). These are clearly titles of certain functionaries and not an address to the entire congregation (Dibelius, *Thessalonicher*, 60).

60. The title *episkopos* only occurs in later New Testament documents (1 Tim 3:2; Tit 1:7; Acts 20:28; 1 Pet 2:25). *Diakonos* as a title is used elsewhere for men and women in Christian service; Rom 13:4; 15:8; 16:1; 1 Cor 3:5; 2 Cor 3:6; 6:4; 11:15, 23; Gal 2:17; 1 Thess 3:2; cf. Eph 3:7; 6:21; Col 1:7, 23, 25; 1 Tim 3:8, 12; 4:6. For some methodological cautions in studying ecclesiastical offices in Paul, and especially the fallacy of reading later church practices into the letters, see Reumann, "Church Office," 82–91.

61. Peterlin, *Paul's Letter*, 22. Some suggest that the phrase reflects a single office and should be designated *"episkopoi* who are deacons" or *"episkopoi* who serve" (Collange, *Philippians*, 39; Hawthorne, *Philippians*, 9–10; see critique in O'Brien, *Philippians*, 48–49 n. 21). Moulton and Milligan, *Vocabulary*, 245, suggest that the phrase in Phil 1:1 be translated "with them that have oversight, and them that do service [minister]" so as to reflect a description of function not of office, as in the New Testament the words have a "distinctive use." The use of the terms for offices in the larger cultural context, however, makes this latter claim less likely.

62. Peterlin, *Paul's Letter*, 22. These offices are different than those held in other Pauline Christian communities (cf. Streeter, *Primitive Church*, 53–65; Hainz, "Anfange des Bischofs," 103). Reumann, "Church Office," 89–90, is correct in his assessment that "each congregation seems to develop *ad hoc* and on its own, with what Collins calls in Philippi 'local idiosyncrasy'" (citing Collins, *Diakonia*, 236 who himself refers to von Campenhausen, *Ecclesiastical Authority*, 69). Dibelius, *Thessalonicher*, 62; also hinted at by Beare, *Philippians*, 49; Reumann, "Church Office," 90) attempts to connect these functionaries with the gathering and distribution of funds at Philippi (Phil 4:10–20; see further Hatch, *Organization*, 38–46, who describes the distribution of funds as the task of the *episkopos* in the later Christian church).

70   Section I: Modeling Christ Groups

the use of *episkopos* in Phil 1:1.[63] Other commentators point to the background in the use of *mbqr* in the Damascus Document (IQS 6.12–20) and a few other of the Qumran scrolls.[64] In the Damascus Document the *mbqr* is defined as "shepherding the flock and returning the lost" (CD 13.7–9), which has affinities to the *episkopoi* in Acts 20:28.[65] However, these Jewish analogies are not the most obvious place to find the background for how the predominantly non-Jewish Philippians would understand *episkopos*.[66] [164]

The term *episkopos* is used frequently in classical writings.[67] In such usage it indicates an official title of a man designated to oversee a new colony or serve as inspector in a foreign land. It might also "involve oversight of goods and possessions."[68] However, "the data assembled by Hans Lietzmann in 1914 and subsequently expanded by others make a far better case for *episkopos* as a supervisory office in the state, in various societies, and other groups in the Graeco-Roman world, often with financial responsibilities."[69] A review of the evidence of the associations shows this to be so.

Episkopos is used in an inscription from Thera where it indicates financial officers of an association (*koinon*): "It is resolved that the *episkopoi* Dion and Meleippus shall accept the offer and invest the money" (IG XII/3 329, II BCE).[70] In IGL 1990 (Salkhat [Nabataea]) it is used of the financial officers of a temple,[71] as it is in other similar inscriptions (IGL 1989; 2298).[72]

63. E.g., O'Brien, *Philippians*, 47.

64. See Reicke, "Constitution," 143–56; Braun, *Qumran*, 329–32; Fitzmyer, "Jewish Christianity," 247–48; Jeremias, *Jerusalem*, 260–261; Thiering, "Mebaqqer," 59–74; Hawthorne, *Philippians*, 8.

65. Weinfeld, *Organizational Pattern*, 20.

66. See Ascough, "Voluntary Associations," 176–89; Ascough, "Thessalonian Christian Community," 311–13 (Chapter 7, 122–24, below). See also Hainz, "Anfange des Bischofs," 98–102, who is skeptical of the connection of *mbqr* with *episkopos*, although he judges it more likely than the voluntary associations. In my view, the overall similarities of the Qumran sect with the voluntary associations suggest that there is probably no direct influence of the sect on Christianity or vice versa but that both were influenced by the practices and languages of the voluntary associations, not necessarily in terms of direct borrowing but through a shared milieu with the associations in which the pattern for communal organization was already in place.

67. Lightfoot, *Philippians*, 95.

68. Reumann, "Church Office," 88.

69. Reumann, "Church Office," 88; cf. Best, "Bishops and Deacons," 371.

70. Renan, *Apostles*, 351 n. 35; Hatch, *Organization*, 37 n. 26 (text and translation); Lightfoot, *Philippians*, 95 n. 2 (who notes the accusative plural *-os* is a dialectic form); Poland, *Geschichte des griechischen Vereinswesens*, 375 (B 221); Dibelius, *Thessalonicher*, 60.

71. Noted in Hatch, *Organization*, 37 n. 26; Dibelius, *Thessalonicher*, 60.

72. Dibelius, *Thessalonicher*, 60.

Voluntary Associations and the Formation of Pauline Christian Communities 71

An inscription from Bostra (OGIS II 614) names an *episkopos* as an official, as does one from Kanata (OGIS 611 8f., time of Trajan).[73] From Myconos (Poland, Geschichte des griechischen Vereinswesens, B 186, end II BCE) an *episkopos* of a *synodos* is to transfer the care of an honorary deed, under threat of penalty.[74] In a Thracian inscription (Poland, *Geschicte des griechischen Vereinswesens*, B 79 = Cagnat I no. 682) *episkopos* is used as a title for a cult functionary.[75] An inscription from Delos (IDelos 1522, lines 8, 10, 13, early II CE) attests to a Dionysiac *thiasos* named after its founder Ameinichos, that was headed by an *episkopos* "who was responsible for proclaiming the honours bestowed upon benefactors."[76] Overall, the evidence for the use of *episkopos* in associations is [165] clear, but a specific function attached to it is ambiguous.[77] These officials seemed to have held different job descriptions in different associations.[78]

Turning to *diakonos* we note that the word has a wide range of designations in antiquity. It can mean "servant" and often is used to refer to one who waits on tables. Although there have been many attempts to find support for prototypes in Jewish literature, "these pale for Philippian use in the face of references to *diakonoi* in Greek guilds and societies."[79] It is used within the contexts of both temples and religious associations for those who assist in

---

73. Dibelius, *Thessalonicher*, 60.

74. Poland, *Geschichte des griechischen Vereinswesens*, 375; Dibelius, *Thessalonicher*, 60.

75. Poland, *Geschichte des griechischen Vereinswesens*, 375. Other inscriptions from associations indicate the existence of the title (Dibelius, *Thessalonicher*, 60; cf. Deissmann, *Bible Studies*, 230–31): IG XII/1 49, 50, 731; CIL V 7914, 7870 (Nizza).

76. McLean, "Place of Cult," 225 n. 148.

77. So Dibelius, *Thessalonicher*, 60–61; cf. von Harnack, *Mission and Expansion of Christianity*, 1:339.

78. Foucart, *associations religieuses*, 32, suggests that within the association inscriptions the same general functions were carried out by those titled variously *episkopoi, epimelētai, syndikoi,* or *logistai*. The negative response to Hatch, *Organization*, 26–39, in Salmon, "Christian Ministry," 18–20, and Sanday, "Origin," 98–100, is based more on Hatch's attempt to designate the *episkopoi* as *financial* officers rather than his attempt to understand the associations as a general background for the Christian use of the title. This is also true of the discounting of the associations as an adequate background by Loening, *Gemeindeverfassung*, 47; Rohde, *Urchristliche und frühkatholische Ämter*, 55; and Hainz, "Anfange des Bischofs," 94–96—all of whom point out the difficulty in determining the function of the *episkopoi* in Philippians. Especially telling against the hypothesis that the Philippian *episkopoi* were financial officers is the separation of the title (Phil 1:1) from Paul's thanks for the financial gift (4:10–20) within the structure of the letter; Hainz, "Anfange des Bischofs," 93.

79. Reumann, "Contributions," 448; cf. Reumann, "Church Office," 89.

the cult.⁸⁰ Moulton and Milligan note that "there is now abundant evidence that the way had been prepared for the Christian usage of this word by its technical application to the holders of various offices."⁸¹ It is used of sacral officials in a number of inscriptions including IMagnMai 109 (c. 100 BCE), CIG 1793b, IG IV 774 (Troezen, Argolis, III BCE), 824 (Troezen, Argolis), IG IX/1 486 (1111 BCE). An inscription from Kyzikos names five *diakonoi* among the functionaries at a thank offering to the Great Mother (RIG 1226, I BCE). In IMagnMai 217 (I BCE) *diakonoi* are listed among those who set up a statue of Hermes. [166]

From the private associations we find *to koinon tōn diakonōn* of nine men dedicated to the Egyptian gods, one of whom presided as priest (CIG 1800, Ambrakia),⁸² and an association which includes two male *diakonoi* and a female *diakonos* along with a priest and priestess of the twelve gods (CIG 3037, Metropolis, Lydia).⁸³ Similarly, Μουσεῖον 93 (Kyzikos) lists a female *diakonos* and five male *diakonoi* along with a priest and priestess while another inscription from Kyzikos mentions *diakonoi* (Μουσεῖον 100).⁸⁴ Even Poland, who denies the connection between the Christian use of *episkopos* and the associations, is willing to entertain the idea that the Christian use of *diakonos* was taken over from the associations.⁸⁵ However, he is rightly critical of Hatch's narrower view that their function should be seen as those who distribute food to the others.⁸⁶

In light of this evidence from associations, it seems unnecessary to go to the lengths of Lightfoot to prove that *presbyteros* is a synonym of *episkopos*

80. LSJ s.v.; e.g., Ziebarth, *Das griechische Vereinswesen*, 153; Lietzmann, "Zur altchristlichen Verfassungsgeschichte," 106–7; Dibelius, *Thessalonicher*, 61; Georgi, *Opponents of Paul*, 27.

81. Moulton and Milligan, *Vocabulary*, 149. The following information is presented variously by Moulton and Milligan, *Vocabulary*, 149; Dibelius, *Thessalonicher*, 61; Collins, *Diakonia*, 166–68.

82. Collins, *Diakonia*, 167, following Poland, *Geschichte des griechischen Vereinswesens*, 165 suggests that this is not necessarily a formal association and points to another example of *symporeumenoi* who describe themselves as a *koinon*. However, in both cases it is probably a formally constituted private association within the public cult, not unlike IG X/2.1 58 from Thessalonike.

83. All the priests and priestesses seem to be related; Collins, *Diakonia*, 168.

84. With no evidence Collins, *Diakonia*, 168, simply surmises that in CIG 3037, Μουσεῖον 93, and Μουσεῖον 100 the male and female *diakonoi* are given "an occasional and privileged role" to serve at religious feasts, presumably to underline his earlier point that "there is no reason to see anything more in the word than the designation of a ceremonial waiter" (*Diakonia*, 166; cf. Hatch, *Organization*, 50).

85. Poland, *Geschichte des griechischen Vereinswesens*, 391–92, cf. 377.

86. Poland, *Geschichte des griechischen Vereinswesens*, 392 n. *; cf. 534; cf. Hatch, *Organization*, 49–50.

and that Paul intends the former term in his address to the Philippians, despite only writing *episkopoi kai diakonoi* (Phil 1:1).[87] While Lightfoot is correct in suggesting that in the Jewish synagogues *presbyteros* and *episkopos* go together, the lack of the former term in Philippians is one indication of the lack of a significant Jewish presence in the church and an indication that the titles have resonances elsewhere.[88] In [167] fact, Lightfoot himself suggests that the use of *episkopos* in the voluntary associations would make it the most obvious choice for the "presiding members of the new society."[89] He states that although the infant church would appear to the Jew as a synagogue, to the non-Jew it would appear as a "confraternity."

It is more likely that at Philippi the leadership structure of the Christian community has adopted nomenclature that would immediately be understood in light of use among voluntary associations.[90] That the titles *episkopos*

87. Hatch, *Organization*, 96–99; cf. 194.

88. Lightfoot suggests that the office of *presbyteros* is "essentially Jewish" as distinct from *episkopos*; that is best understood by looking at works "chiefly among heathen nations" (Lightfoot, *Philippians*, 96). However, *presbyteros* is also attested as a title in some associations; see CIG 2221; Poland, *Geschichte des griechischen Vereinswesens*, 98–102; Deissmann, *Light from the Ancient East*, 223–35. Lightfoot's argument also falters by the fact that nowhere in the authentic Pauline letters is *presbyteros* used as a title; it only occurs in 1 Tim 5:1, 2, 17, 19 and Tit 1:5 within the larger Pauline corpus.

89. Lightfoot, *Philippians*, 194.

90. Cf. Reumann, "Church Office," 90: "The Philippians chose their terms for leaders from a world they know, of government, guilds, societies and the *oikos*" (also Reumann, "Contributions," 449). Although Reumann points to the background of the titles in the voluntary associations, he does not expand much on it. Others who allow for the associations as background for this use in Philippians include Vincent, *Philippians*, 45 (with caution; "The process of natural selection, however, would be helped by the familiar employment of the title in the clubs or guilds to designate functions analogous to those of the ecclesiastical administrator."); Fee, *Philippians*, 68 n. 50 ("This may well be so, especially since it would have been a convenient term to adopt."). The connection is denied by many; see the summary in Kloppenborg, "Edwin Hatch," 217–20; Sanday, "Origin," 98–100; Sohm, *Kirchenrecht*, 1:87 n. 13; Ziebarth, *Das griechische Vereinswesen*, 131; Poland, *Geschichte des griechischen Vereinswesens*, 377, who deny the connection regarding *episkopos* and seem to be reacting against the later Christian evidence of a monoepiscopate and a universal application of the title *episkopos*; within Christian churches (this also seems to underlie Rohde's thinking [*Urchristliche und frühkatholische Ämter*, 55–56]). Dassmann, "Hausgemeinde"; and Schöllgen, "Hausgemeinden" move too quickly from positing the *oikos* as the background to Paul's communities to using Ignatius of Antioch to explain the rise of the monoepiscopate and the function of presbyters and deacons, without pausing to discuss the local peculiarities of leadership expressed in Paul's letters (Dassmann, "Hausgemeinde," 89–90 does suggest that the *paterfamilias* of the house-based Christian community would become the leader of the group, but he does not show why this would lead to the titles *presbyteros* and *diakonos* at Philippi). Dibelius, *Thessalonicher*, 61 points out that at the earlier period there does not seem to be consistency in the application of titles within the Pauline churches, citing the titles in 1 Corinthians as

and *diakonos* themselves are not used in all of the voluntary associations, only a few, is not problematic as there is no consistency in the use [168] of titles for officials within the association inscriptions. For example, we can note a mid-second-century CE inscription from a large voluntary association of over four hundred members that was grounded in a single household.[91] It had been moved from Mitylene to the Roman Campagna en masse and there seems to have attracted some new adherents from those who came into contact with the head of the household and his wife (Gallicanus and Agrippinilla). Like the early church, this association was of mixed membership, male and female, slaves, freedmen, and masters. In total, twenty-two different offices, most with titles, are reflected in the inscription, many of them held by women.[92] The association's use of titles was extensive but differed greatly from those used in other associations dedicated to the same deity, Dionysos, reflecting an experimentation with titles found also in the churches.[93]

Overall, within the Christian communities we find no consistency for titles of officials and we might suggest that they were as diverse as those within the associations.[94] In choosing particular titles for their leaders the Philippians are like the associations in a concern for titles; we will look in

---

different than those in Philippians. He also points out (*Thessalonicher*, 62) that Polycarp's letter to the Philippians shows that even in the early second century CE the Philippians do not have a monoepiscopate as do some communities in Asia Minor; Polycarp speaks of *presbyteroi* and *diakonoi* (where *presbyteros* is not synonymous with *episkopos* as the latter are referred to elsewhere in the letter as *hygoumenoi*; see Vincent, *Philippians*, 47).

91. Text and translation McLean, "Agrippinilla Inscription."
92. See McLean, "Agrippinilla Inscription," 262.
93. McLean, "Agrippinilla Inscription," 258–59.
94. Kloppenborg, "Edwin Hatch," 232. Cf. Streeter, *Primitive Church*, 53–65 who points out that Paul's churches did not follow a uniform pattern with regard to church leadership; while the Corinthians regarded "apostles, prophets, and teachers" as leaders, the Philippians were led by *presbyteroi* and *diakonoi*. For the diversity of terms used for officials in the voluntary association inscriptions see the lists in Liebenam, *Geschichte und organisation*, 164–69, 199–220; Poland, *Geschichte des griechischen Vereinswesens*, 337–423; Kloppenborg, "Edwin Hatch," 232; Ellis, *Pauline Theology*, 136; cf. the conclusion of Arnaoutoglou, "ΑΡΧΕΡΑΝΙΣΤΗΣ," 110 on the use of *archeranistēs* in inscriptions from associations in Athens and Rhodes: "Associations were not monolithic groupings, but groups which would adapt to new developments by transforming their structure, or more often, their nomenclature; the semantic variety of the term *archeranistēs* reveals that what is true for one region of the Greek world is not necessarily valid for another."

vain for any standard titles among the associations that we could expect in a specifically Christian association. Nevertheless, the titles chosen for leaders at Philippi reflect those in use within at least some associations.[95] However, the exact nature of these offices remains obscure.[96] [169]

At the same time, we must acknowledge that there are some titles frequently used in associations that do not seem to be evidenced in Pauline Christian groups, titles such as priest or priestess,[97] and civic leadership titles (e.g., president or treasurer). Yet it is unclear whether this is due to a deliberate choice to avoid such titles (Matt 23:6–12),[98] or whether it is only later that such titles come into use within Christianity (see 1 Peter 2:9).

EGALITARIANISM

Another critique of the analogy of the associations is that the Christian groups were more inclusive in terms of social stratification than were the voluntary associations. That is, it is suggested that the associations tended to draw together people who were generally socially homogeneous while the Christian groups allowed for more equality within a group of varying social categories.[99] However, this notion of egalitarianism has been misrepresented on both sides of the argument. Although the associations were *de facto* hierarchical for the most part (usually based on social ranking), they often presented themselves as egalitarian. Schmeller has illustrated that the associations were at the same time hierarchical *and* egalitarian—hierarchical with respect to patrons and offices and egalitarian with respect to the

---

95. Fee, *Philippians*, 67 points out that the use of *syn* indicates that when the leaders are singled out they are "not 'over' the church, but are addressed 'alongside' of the church, as a *distinguishable* part of the whole, but as *part of the whole*, not above or outside it." Ernst, "Von der Ortsgemeinde," 126 is correct in that "die Voraussetzungen für ein entwickeltes Kirchenverständnis waren noch nicht gegeben," but goes too far in suggesting "daß es in der Gemeinde von Philippi neben der Autorität des Paulus keine konkurrierenden 'Ämter' gegeben hat."

96. Cf. Hainz, "Anfänge des Bischofs," 107: "So bleibt auch die Bedeutung dieser Ämter unbestimmbar."

97. But see Rom 15:16.

98. On the relationship of this passage to the use of titles in voluntary associations see Ascough, "Matthew" (Chapter 8, below).

99. Meeks, *First Urban Christians*, 79. So also Schöllgen, "Hausgemeinden," 74–75. Barton and Horsley, "Hellenistic Cult Group," 38–39 use the same principle as Meeks to differentiate Christian groups from the associations, but from a different perspective. They suggest that while both groups aimed at being egalitarian, the egalitarian nature of Christianity was *undermined* by the elevation of some members over others on the basis of their spiritual gifts. Nevertheless, because Christianity aimed at egalitarianism it is still thought to be different than the associations.

general membership.[100] In similar fashion, the Christian communi[170]ties reflect both hierarchy and egalitarianism. Although we have evidence of Christian rhetoric of egalitarianism it often does not match with the actual practices that went on in the Christian communities.[101] For example, one senses that in the Christian groups it is unlikely that a slave who prophesied would be elevated to a higher status than his master who had a gift of hospitality. That the egalitarianism was difficult to sustain in practice can be seen from the divisions that arose in the Corinthian church (1 Cor 1–4) that manifested themselves as debates over meat eating (1 Cor 8–10), discord at the community meal (1 Cor 11:17–34), and trouble over spiritual gifts (1 Cor 11–14).[102]

In a recent essay Kloppenborg examines 1 Cor 6:1–11 in light of the voluntary associations. He shows that Paul's injunction against taking one another to court betrays a problem within the Corinthian congregation that is found within the voluntary associations and suggests that the early Christian communities were not as egalitarian as often claimed. Legal action of the sort described in 1 Cor 6 presupposes that both parties are from the wealthy strata of society. Civil cases were brought to the courts by such people as a means of displaying status; "The courts, as instruments of social control, were one way in which superior social status was displayed and maintained" in a public forum.[103] Paul's charge in 1 Cor 6 aims to curb such displays of competition for honor among the wealthy of the congregation. The regulations of a number of voluntary associations shows that regularly occurring agonistic community interaction required that restrictions be placed on members who were challenging one another's honor, both during the meetings of the association and outside of the meetings. This sometimes manifested itself by members taking one another to court. Thus, we see a marked similarity between the Corinthian Christians and the voluntary associations both in terms of internal conflict among members and in terms of regulated conflict resolution over the issue of honor and equality.[104] This mix of hierarchy and egalitarianism at once reflects the dominant cultural

---

100. See Schmeller, *Hierarchie und Egalität*.

101. Cf. Schmeller, *Hierarchie und Egalität*, 92–93.

102. See further the varying data put forth in Barton and Horsley, "Hellenistic Cult Group," and the response by Kloppenborg, "Edwin Hatch," 234–36 to Meeks that although membership within both types of groups was inclusive to some degree, the "inclusivity" of Paul's churches has been as exaggerated, as has the hierarchical nature of the associations.

103. Kloppenborg, "Egalitarianism," 255–56.

104. In an independent study published about the same time Schmeller, *Hierarchie und Egalität*, 86–87 arrives at a similar conclusion.

milieu of which the associations and Christian groups were a part and also offers some relief from it.

Overall, the relationship of the elite and non-elite in associations is a complex one. There are a number of associations in which the presence of the elite conferred various benefits on the association but also brought [171] about some tensions, much like the mixture of elite and non-elite in the Corinthian community.[105] At the same time, some associations were composed exclusively of non-elite and developed strategies to protect themselves from exploitation, much like rhetoric of the letter of James.[106] Again, positing one single model will not suffice for understanding associations. Using such a reconstructed model as a foil against which to understand early Christian groups is disingenuous at best.

EXCLUSIVITY

Related to the idea of egalitarianism is the claim that Christian groups were exclusive and totalistic in ways not found in pagan associations.[107] Although Meeks offers no evidence to support his claim, there is evidence that membership in one association did not preclude membership in another. For example, in the second century BCE (185/84) an Athenian named Simon of Poros became a charter member of a new *orgeōnes* dedicated to Dionysos (IG XI/2 1325; cf. IG XI/2 1326, 2948) while still a member of another association dedicated to the Mother of the Gods, suggesting that dual membership was allowed (IG XI/1 1327, 1328).[108] In Ephesos a priest served both the *mystai* of Dionysos Pheos and an association devoted to Demeter.[109] Overall, there is evidence for persons belonging to more than one association. In fact, in the second century CE it was even seen by officials as a problem, so much so that "Marcus Aurelius and Lucius Verus re-enacted a law to the effect that it was not lawful to belong to [172] more than one guild."[110] Yet despite this law, its strict enforcement seems to have been unlikely.[111]

According to Meeks, "baptized into Christ" meant that the Christian community was the primary group for the members and demanded primary

---

105. Kloppenborg, "Status und Wohltätigkeit," 135–46.

106. Kloppenborg, "Status und Wohltätigkeit," 146–56.

107. Meeks, *First Urban Christians*, 78.

108. Cf. IG II² 1361; Ferguson, "Attic Orgeones," 105, 117; Jones, "Economic Life," 173; Waltzing, *Étude Historique*, 4:248–51; cf. Kraabel, "Diaspora Synagogue," 85–126.

109. McLean, "Trade Guilds," 31.

110. Cf. *Digest* 47.22.1.2; Harland, "Spheres of Contention," 61.

111. Meiggs, *Roman Ostia*, 321–23; Harland, "Spheres of Contention," 61–62.

allegiance.[112] Similarly, Klauck quotes Philo's criticism of the associations of Alexandria:

> There exist in the city associations [θίασοι] with numerous members, and there is nothing healthy in their fellowship [κοινωνία], which is based on unmixed wine, drunkenness, feasts and the unbridled conduct which results from these.[113]

Klauck writes that

> after such a devastating judgment, need we look around for further testimony? There can be no doubt that the self-assessment of Judaism and Christianity prevented them from simply setting themselves on the same level as private cultic associations.[114]

Klauck's statement is problematic on two accounts. First, he assumes that there is such as thing as "Judaism" or "Christianity" in the first and second century CE that would allow a uniform type of judgment. Clearly, there is evidence to the contrary.[115] Philo's comments certainly indicate that Philo himself opposed Jews participating in associations in Alexandria. However, this is not necessarily the case elsewhere, nor for all people. Second, Klauck is unclear in what is meant by a group setting itself "on the same level" as another group. The inscriptional evidence suggests a high degree of intergroup rivalry among many associations, with claims and challenges around preeminence. Thus, it is unlikely that *any* association would see itself "on the same level" as another group. That is, one's own group will always be perceived as superior (in the same way that Philo sees the Jewish group as superior!).

It is clear that for Paul "baptized into Christ" generally excludes one from full participation in the religious life of other associations, yet this is not how the Corinthians understood it. In 1 Cor 8–10 Paul addresses the [173] "strong" at Corinth, who seem to be attending temple sacrifices and the subsequent banquet (1 Cor 8:10; 10:14), and Paul is cautiously affirming of the practice. Certainly, participation in the civic cult would have been required of Erastus, the city treasurer in Corinth (see Rom 16:23). Thus, for some of the Corinthians, at least, Christianity was not initially understood as demanding exclusive allegiance. Thus, we find that yet again, in order to insulate Christian groups from associations the evidence has been exaggerated.

112. Meeks, *First Urban Christians*, 78–79; so also Jeffers, *Greco-Roman World*, 79–80.
113. *Flacc.* 4.1.36 in Klauck, *Religious Context*, 54.
114. Klauck, *Religious Context*, 54.
115. Ascough, "Translocal Relationships," 234–41 (see Chapter 5, 98–105, below)

A number of factors seem to play into the assumption of nonexclusivity. First, we do have evidence of patrons patronizing more than one association. In this case they may have been honorary members or not even members of the associations patronized.[116] Even if they are members of more than one association, it is a small minority of the general population that can split allegiance this way. Second, an assumption seems to be made that the small, private associations functioned much like the larger, public mysteries: the latter did allow one to be *initiated* into more than just their own group. Yet these public mysteries were different from the small, private associations. Finally, there seems also to be a bias that since these groups were "pagan" they could not be imagined to be as morally rigorous as Judaism and Christianity nor as intellectually demanding as the philosophical schools, and thus would have been lax about membership. This is both a biased and misleading notion.[117]

There are even exceptions to the nonexclusivity of the associations. While we have nothing to suggest that associations generally demanded exclusivity, it is reasonable to assume that, for the most part, they at least de facto received the primary allegiance of their members.[118] A number of reasons can be suggested. First, at least in the case of professional associations, they would gather persons in one particular urban area involved in a particular type of occupation. There would be no need (or opportunity) to join another professional association. Second, joining an association often involved dues and sometimes contributions to banquets. For most persons there would be little extra cash on hand to join a number of associations—only one would be necessary (and affordable) for the social interaction desired. Third, the competition for honor among associations and claims to be the best of the groups would imply that members have no need to join a competing group—to do so would be to join an inferior group. [174]

In Sardis we find a late first- or early second-century CE inscription which delineates that the temple warden *therapeutai* of Zeus the Legislator are not to participate in the mysteries of Sabazios, Agdistis, and Ma.[119]

---

116. Cf. IG X/2.1 506 commemorates Isiodorus, who was a priest of two or more *thiasoi*, but it does not indicate whether he was so simultaneously or successively.

117. See Batten, "Moral World."

118. Cf. Harland, "Spheres of Contention," 64.

119. Horsley, *New Documents* 1, 22. Text in CCCA 1.456; Robert, "Une nouvelle inscription," 306–30; Horsley, *New Documents* 1, 3; Herrmann, "Mystenvereine," 329–35. The following translation is from Horsley, *New Documents* 1, 21–22. See also Herrmann, "Mystenvereine," 321–29, for other inscriptions testifying to the *therapeutai* of Zeus at Sardis, esp. ISardBR 22.

> In the thirty-nine years of Artaxerxes' reign, Droaphernes son of Barakis, governor of Lydia dedicated a statue to Zeus the Legislator. He (Droaphernes) instructs his (Zeus') temple warden devotees who enter the innermost sanctum and who serve and crown the god not to participate in the mysteries of Sabazios with those who bring the burnt offerings and (the mysteries) of Agdistis and Ma. They instruct Dorates the temple-warden to keep away from these mysteries.

This inscription is a Greek rewriting from an earlier Aramaic edict from ca. 365 BCE.[120] The primary deity in the latter inscription is Zeus Baradates ("the Legislator"), the epithet being a Greek translation of the name of a Persian deity (Ahura Mazda).[121] Both Sabazios and Agdistis are also of Persian origin, while Ma is a Cappadocian goddess.[122] That an earlier text is later translated and reinscribed shows the force of the prohibition over a five-hundred-year period.[123] "What we are looking at here is one voluntary religious association in one particular locality which has retained alive—and apparently in not too contaminated a form—Iranian religious traditions long after the Persian Empire had disappeared."[124] In the first or second century CE, a certain Dorates has transgressed the prohibittion, [175] and the recutting of the stone is a means to bring him into line.[125] This entire scenario is interesting because it shows that a notion of religious exclusivity is not confined to Jewish and Christian groups.[126] A further spin-off of this inscription is the conservatism reflected in it. For at least this one association at Sardis, the second century CE was "not a period of syncretism of 'religious creativity' but of conservatism, reinforcing the piety of the past."[127]

---

120. That the text legislates against participation in the mysteries of these deities suggests that their cults also existed at Sardis in the fourth century BCE. Horsley, *New Documents* 1, 22 points out that this is "a product of the breadth of the dominion of the Persian empire."

121. Gschnitzer, "Eine persische Kultstiftung" argues against this interpretation, suggesting that *Baradateō* should be taken as a genitive (it is the normal Ionic form).

122. Horsley, *New Documents* 1, 22.

123. Edwards, *Religion & Power*, 32; cf. Briant, "Les iraniens d'Asie Mineure," 167-95, thinks it is more likely that the text retrojects backwards current concerns; either way, it is the "current" concern that interests us.

124. Horsley, *New Documents* 1, 23.

125. Horsley, *New Documents* 1, 23.

126. Horsley, *New Documents* 1, 23. See further Kraabel, "Paganism and Judaism," 254 in reference to Robert, "Une nouvelle inscription"; Herrmann, "Mystenvereine," 329-35, esp. 334-35.

127. Kraabel, "Paganism and Judaism," 254. This is also true in the case of a column that re-creates the image of a goddess with the essential features from the seventh

Another important text that indicates an exclusive group is the papyrus text found in Philadelphia, Egypt, and dating from the first century BCE (ca. 69–58). The regulations of this association (*koinon*) stipulate that "it shall not be permissible for any one of them . . . to leave the brotherhood (*phratras*) of the president or to join another brotherhood" (P.Lond. 2193, line 14). The text cannot indicate that a person would leave one of the civic *phratriae* into which he was born, nor can it mean membership in another type of association, nor a subgroup of the current association. Rather, as a synonym for *synodos*, the word *phratras* indicates that members could not join with another similar drinking club, of which there were likely many at Philadelphia.[128]

In claiming a difference between the associations and Christian communities based on the latter being exclusive and totalistic, critics not only assume that some associations were not exclusive (a false assumption, as we have just demonstrated), but they also ignore evidence that some Christian groups did participate in aspects of civic life, including cultic activities.[129] As we suggested, at Corinth some Christians seem to have been [**176**] joining with non-Christians at communal meals in various contexts, including meals in pagan temples (1 Cor 8–10). In Asia Minor Christians are encouraged "to adopt the common conventions of praying for or honoring civic or imperial officials and emperors" (1 Pet 2:11–17; 1 Tim 2:1–2; Tit 3:1; Polycarp, *Phil.* 12.3; *Mart. Pol.* 10.2), a view that also is in evidence for the Roman church (Rom 13; 1 Clement 60–61).[130] At least one Christian seems to have also been a member of a shippers' guild at Ostia[131] and thus presumably took part in the cultic life of the association. "This evidence for dual affiliations or 'loyalties' (to use Meeks's term) on the part of Christians should

---

century BCE, an image that is also represented on Sardian coins from the time of Hadrian and beyond; see Hanfmann, and Balmuth, "Image," 254; Kraabel, "Paganism and Judaism," 254. The same image also appears on coins from other Lydian cities at that time; Kraabel, "Paganism and Judaism," 254.

128. Roberts, Skeat, and Nock, "Guild of Zeus Hypsistos," 52.

129. This is also true for Jewish groups for which evidence is emerging that indicates that not all were exclusive; see Seland, "Philo and the Clubs"; Ascough, "Local and Translocal Relationships," 235–36 (Chapter 5, 99–100, below); Harland, "Honouring the Emperor," 108; Harland, "Spheres of Contention," 62–63. See also Wilson, "OI POTE IOUDAIOI" on Jewish defectors.

130. See Harland, "Honouring the Emperor," 115. See his earlier article for the argument that the significance of the imperial cult for the corporate lives of voluntary associations should not be underestimated: Harland, "Honours and Worship."

131. See CIL XIV 251, which lists a M. Curtius Victorinus in its membership list. A man of the same name is listed on a Christian epitaph (CIL XIV 1900), and it is thought to be the same person (Harland, "Honouring the Emperor," 110; Meiggs, *Roman Ostia*, 389).

not be passed off as an exception."¹³² Indeed, "there is a sense in which we should be surprised if a person were to sever all such contacts with fellow-workers once affiliated with another group such as the Christians or the local synagogue; for removing oneself would sever the network connections necessary for business activity, thereby threatening one's means of livelihood."¹³³ We are not here arguing that the associations were exclusive, just that the *assumption* of their nonexclusivity needs to be more careful nuance before a contrast with Christian groups can be made.

TRANSLOCAL LINKS

A prevalent argument against the associations as an analogy for Christian groups is that the associations did not have the "extralocal linkages" which characterize the Christian movement. Rather, it is argued, each association was a self-contained local phenomenon. In fact, it is this difference of the *localized* nature of voluntary associations versus the translocal nature of Christianity that is most often pointed to by scholars as indicative of the [177] vast difference between Christian groups and associations.¹³⁴ However, a close analysis of the literary and inscriptional evidence reveals that some voluntary associations in antiquity had translocal links *and* that Christianity was more locally based than is often assumed.¹³⁵

Evidence for the translocal nature of associations can be found in a number of places. Ethnic associations composed of people living away from their homeland often maintained official links with their native city (e.g., CIG 5853) or country (e.g., IG XII/7 506).¹³⁶ Even the associations' names could suggest a connection with a distant land—in the Piraeus there existed an association of *Aigyptioi*, an association of *Kitieis* (or *hoi emporoi tōn Kitieōn*), a group of Cyprian *Salaminioi*, and a group of *Sidōnioi*.¹³⁷ The guild of Dionysiac artists was one of the longest standing religious associations. It began in Attica around the third century BCE and can be traced to

132. Harland, "Honouring the Emperor," 102.

133. Harland, "Honouring the Emperor," 119.

134. Jeffers, *Greco-Roman World*, 80 follows Meeks in this assertion. In responding to Meeks, Kloppenborg does not address this issue. However, in a later essay he notes his agreement with our arguments that the local-translocal distinction is not always valid (Kloppenborg, "Collegia and *Thiasoi*," 27–28 n. 19); cf. Wilson, "Voluntary Associations," 14–15 n. 5, who also endorses the argument.

135. The case is argued in detail with numerous illustrations from inscriptions in Ascough, "Local and Translocal Relationships" (Chapter 5, below).

136. Cf. Dow, "Egyptian Cults," 230.

137. Cf. Dow, "Egyptian Cults," 230.

the end of the Roman Republic.¹³⁸ During the first and second centuries CE they were known as a universal or worldwide (*tēs oikoumenēs*) guild (BGU 1074; IEph 22).

In the case of Christianity, the translocal link among a number of the various congregations is Paul. However, Paul had trouble enough maintaining the unity of his local congregations (especially Corinth and Galatia), and there is little evidence that there were ties between different locales, with the exception of the missionaries themselves. At least during its formative stage Christianity seems to have been made up of local groups with only very loose translocal connections—much the same as some of the voluntary associations.

MORAL ETHOS

A frequently cited problem with the associations accuses them of disinterest in instructing their members in ethical principles, in contrast to the Christian groups that concerned themselves with the behavior of their [178] members.¹³⁹ Barton and Horsley are somewhat restrained in their claim, pointing out that there are some similarities in the moral code of the Pauline groups and that found in SIG³ 985 (Philadelphia [Lydia], I BCE). However, they go on to suggest that the Christian groups were *more* rigorous in their moral injunctions, focusing not only on the suppression of vices but also on the exhibition of virtues.¹⁴⁰ However, it is questionable whether this distinction would have been recognized by those in antiquity. Some associations did advocate the exhibition of virtues among their members.¹⁴¹ There may have been a difference in rhetoric—Pauline groups adopted the language of sanctification while other groups thought of more static qualifications such as the maintenance of moral purity in order to participate in the rituals. However, this is not a decisive distinction phenomenologically; in both instances maintenance of moral codes was required.¹⁴² Indeed, "moral

138. Tod, "Clubs, Greek," 255.
139. See Meeks, *Moral World*, 114; Jeffers, *Greco-Roman World*, 80.
140. Barton and Horsley, "Hellenistic Cult Group," 37.
141. Members could also be noted for their piety (*eusebeia*, see, for example, IPergamon 485 [I BCE]; IDelos 1016 [172–62 BCE]) although the outward expression of respect for the gods was often tied to financial contributions—either public or private benefaction (Adkins, *Merit and Responsibility*, 135; Batten, "Moral World," 4–5).
142. Barton and Horsley, "Hellenistic Cult Group," 41 also suggest that the cult association at Philadelphia that they examined (SIG³ 965) sought salvation from Zeus in this world, while the Christian groups looked for salvation in the world to come. While this is true for the association they examine, a number of religious associations did look

language was used to promote internal order within the associations, an essential ingredient for their survival."[143]

The regulations of the private association of Zeus (SIG³ 985, Philadelphia, Lydia) is one of the most significant texts in terms of recording moral language. The text results from a dream experienced by the association founder in which Zeus establishes regulations around access to the household-based association dedicated to the savior gods.

> When coming into this *oikos* let men and women, free people and slaves, swear by all the gods neither to know nor make use wittingly of any deceit against a man or a woman, neither poison harmful to men nor harmful spells. They are not themselves to make use of a love potion, abortifacient, contraceptive, or any other thing fatal to children; nor are they to recommend it to, nor connive at it with, another. They are not to refrain in any respect from being well-intentioned toward this *oikos*.

Anyone who knows of any infraction of these regulations is to expose it. A male association member must only have sexual relations with his wife. [179] Failure to follow this will result in severe penalties for both the man and the woman involved:

> Woman and man, whoever does any of the things written above, let him not enter this *oikos*. For great are the gods set up in it: they watch over these things and will not tolerate those who transgress the ordinances.

A free woman who does not restrict her sexual practices to her husband faces even stiffer penalties; not only is she "defiled and full of endemic pollution," but she is "unworthy to reverence this god" and barred from the rituals.[144] Failure to obey brings about

> evil curses from the gods for disregarding these ordinances. For the god does not desire these things to happen at all, nor does he wish it, but he wants obedience. The gods will be gracious to those who obey, and always give them all good things, whatever gods give to men they love.

---

for betterment in the afterlife by choosing a particular patron deity (Burkert, *Ancient Mystery Cults*, 21–23; Burkert, *Greek Religion*, 293–95).

143. Batten, "Moral World," 1.

144. That a free woman is specified is probably a recognition that a female slave would have little control over how her master treated her. The association is open to "men and women, free people and slaves." At the very least, there is a recognition in the regulations that involves moral choice. Although slave women have equal access to the association, they do not have equal choice due to their legal status as nonpersons.

The good things promised probably include some of those things named as the inscription breaks off: "good recompenses, health, salvation, peace, safety on land and sea . . ." The retribution of the gods on those who disobey is similar to (in fact, harsher than) Paul's warnings in 1 Thess 4:6b: ". . . that no one transgress, and wrong his brother in this matter, because the Lord is an avenger in all these things, as we solemnly forewarned you." In the case of both the associations and 1 Thessalonians the concern is not with personal sexual purity in and of itself but with the larger implications for the community to which the transgressor belongs. In the inscription sexual indiscretion seems to affect adversely the rituals (cf. also LSCGSup 91). Although the regulations of this inscription do not focus on morality, "they are not completely severed from it."[145] That is, although the regulations do not aim at conversion or even, necessarily, character transformation, they do reflect attitudes that suggest that certain practices in the culture, although common, "were not universally condoned."

A similar attitude can also be seen in a number of other inscriptions. In IG II² 1366 (Sounion, Attica, II–III CE) there is a concern for purity that requires abstinence from certain practices and activities before participation in the rituals: "No one impure is to enter but let them be purified from garlic and swine and women." Women who want to enter must wash them[180]selves "from head to foot" for seven days after menstruation, ten days after contact with a corpse, and forty days after miscarriage/abortion (the text is somewhat unclear which is indicated). The concern for purity is not the only concern behind these injunctions. There is also a promise that the god, Men Tyrannos, will benefit those who approach him in "sincerity (*haplous*) of soul." Such "sincerity" is expressed with respect to the heart as a moral duty in Eph 6:5 and Col 3:22 (slaves obedience to masters "as to Christ") and in 2 Cor 11:3 in Paul's worry that the Corinthians' thoughts "will be led astray from a sincere and pure devotion to Christ."[146] Although within this association moral impurity can be cleansed through washings, there exists an "unforgivable" sin: "Anyone who meddles with the god's possessions or is a busybody, may they incur sin (*hamartia*) against Men Tyrannos which he certainly cannot expiate."[147]

In P.Mich 243 (I CE) a community regulation stipulates that "if a member ignores someone who is in distress and does not assist in helping him out of his trouble" he shall be fined. This stands out from the more

---

145. Batten, "Moral World," 10.

146. Horsley, *New Documents* 3, 24.

147. The reference to sin in an inscription associated with Men is not unique to this text; see Horsley, *New Documents* 3, 24.

typical regulations pertaining to fights over seating arrangements and failure to place a wreath on a tomb. In the case of mutual assistance, we come close to the charitable impulse that was an important part of early Christian ethics. In IG II² 1343 (Athens, 37/36 BCE) the praise given to a priest resulting from his "not being one who loves money" suggests that "avarice was not admirable."[148]

If one defines the mysteries of Mithras as an association,[149] then one also finds there the expression of moral codes. The initiates into the grade of "lion" are required to

> keep their hands pure of all that which is painful, harmful, or dirty, and since it is an initiate of cathartic fire those hands are being washed, they use appropriate substance and avoid water because it is inimical to fire. They also purify the tongue of sin by means of honey. (Porphyry, *De Antro* 15)

This concern in the initiation process goes beyond simply maintenance of ritual purity and is suggestive of a transformation that includes a moral dimension.[150] [181]

These inscriptions do not prove the case that all voluntary associations were concerned with personal moral codes. Indeed, it seems to be the exception rather than the rule in terms of the current database of association inscriptions. However, even these examples suggest that one cannot simply eliminate the need for taking seriously the associations as an analogue for early Christian groups on the basis of some perceived lack of moral rigor. Poland's observation in the early part of the twentieth century that the immorality of the associations was exaggerated has gone unheeded.[151]

CULTIC ACTIVITIES

A number of cultic activities within the associations have been used to highlight the differences between them and the Christian communities. The concern within the associations with conviviality and cult is highlighted by Barton and Horsley, who suggest that the early Christians' lack of mysteries, purifications and expiations, and sacrifices and the inclusion of prayers, hymns, teaching, and the sharing of a common meal sets them apart from

---

148. Batten, "Moral World," 6.
149. As does Beck, "Mysteries of Mithras," 176–85.
150. Batten, Moral World, 2.
151. Poland, *Geschichte des griechischen Vereinswesens*, 499–501. This is not true of the recent work of Batten, "Moral World."

the associations.[152] This critique is problematic on two accounts. First, Christian groups did include some rituals, particularly baptism and the meal of remembrance (Eucharist). As far as we can tell from early Christian sources, Christian baptism reflects the hallmarks of a ritual. While the New Testament texts themselves say little about the process of baptism, a late first-century document called Didache includes a number of details. Although Didache does not advocate one particular process of baptism (though it signals a clear preference), it does emphasize the proper preparation of the initiates, the use of appropriate overseers, and two ritual symbols: water and a formula invoking the name of God. More importantly, it is clear that all three stages of a ritual of status transformation—separation, liminality, and aggregation—are present in the carrying out of a baptism.[153] Likewise, the Christian eucharistic meal has a cultic function. All three Synoptic Gospels record Jesus's institution of this meal (Matt 26:26–30; Mark 14:22–26; Luke 22:17–20), and Paul gives some formulaic details that are surprisingly similar to Luke's account (1 Cor 11:23–26). In [182] all cases "on the one hand, they give the aetiological reason for the current practice of the church and lead it back to its sustaining foundation; on the other hand, they have received their shape and form from the liturgical practice of the church."[154] The institution of a commemoratory meal probably goes back to the historical Jesus, but soon after his death cultic aspects became a separate rite.[155] Second, we can note that the language of mystery[156] and purification[157] occurs in a number of New Testament texts. Third, it is simply not the case that features such as prayers, hymns, teaching, and meals were not part of the life of associations; quite the contrary is in fact the case.[158]

152. Barton and Horsley, "Hellenistic Cult Group," 39. They note earlier that the deity, while present in both groups, is not represented physically in the Christian groups as it is in the association, giving the Christian groups an unusual "non-cultic" character (Hellenistic Cult Group, 30). This is a similar objection to the one addressed here.

153. For details see Ascough, "Baptismal Ritual."

154. Klauck, "Lord's Supper," 363; cf. Chilton, "Eucharist"; Carpinelli, "Memorial." Acts also seems to include references to a shared meal (e.g., 2:42, 46; 6:1–2), as do Didache (chs. 9–10) and Ignatius (e.g., *Smyrn.* 7:1, 8:9), the latter two being much more explicitly *eucharistia*.

155. Klauck, "Lord's Supper," 371.

156. E.g., Phil 2:17; 4:12; cf. Rom 16:25; 1 Cor 2:1; 4:1; 15:51.

157. E.g., Paul's concern with sexual purity; 1 Cor 5:1–2, 9–13; 6:12–20; cf. Phil 1:1, 1:10; 2 Cor 11:3; 1 Thess 4:1–8; . On expiation see Rom 3:25.

158. For example, see on prayer: IG II² 1343; SIG³ 694; IMagnMai 98; LSAM 19; cf. IG II² 4636, 4637. Hymns: IMagnMai 100 A; IPerg 485; LSAM 28; IG XI/4 1299; there were even professional associations of musicians who took the name *molpoi* (see LSAM 50; 53; LSS 91; IEph 899; 900; 901; 903; 906). Teaching: legislative material in

CONCLUSION

In this paper I have attempted to raise and address a number of problematic areas for using the associations to understand the formation of Christian community, particularly Pauline communities. My intention was to invite discussion at the level of methodology. Of necessity I have overlooked a number of important issues in which the associations can be profitably used for the investigation of Christian community. These would include issues such as internal conflict and conflict resolution, community regulations, benefaction and honor, and finances. In my dissertation I have explored [183] these areas with connection to 1 Thessalonians and Philippians[159] (and elsewhere with reference to Acts and Matthew)[160] and in both cases find the voluntary associations to be helpful in rethinking early Christian community formation. It seems to me, however, that before we can move forward in further exploring these issues, the objections raised to the use of the associations need to be addressed. I hope in this paper at least to have initiated a discussion about how this can be accomplished.

---

association inscriptions is akin to Paul's parenetic sections of his letter; IG XI/4 1299 includes a lengthy hymn in hexameter verse recounting the founding and development of the cult of Sarapis on Delos; an inscription commemorating the founding of an association dedicated to Poseidon celebrates the saving of the city with a hymn (ITralleis 1); these latter two cases seem to function in a didactic fashion similar to Paul's use of a hymn in Phil 2:6–11. Meals: IG II^2 1366; 1368; IPriene 195; 205; LSCG 77; SIG^3 1009; 1024; IG V/1 1390; IG XI/4 1299; IDelos 1520; LSAM 09; IEph 24; P.Mich 243; 244.

159. For details on my comparison between 1 Thessalonians and the associations see Ascough, "Thessalonian Christian Community" (Chapter 7, below).

160. Ascough, "Benefaction Gone Wrong" (Chapter 17, below); Ascough, "Matthew" (Chapter 8, below).

5

Translocal Relationships among Voluntary Associations and Early Christianity

IN THE PAST A number of scholars have used the voluntary associations of Greco-Roman antiquity as an analogy for understanding early Christian groups in urban centers, particularly Paul's churches.[1] However, some of these same scholars have highlighted the differences between the voluntary associations and the Christian communities in order to lessen the

---

1. A standard definition of voluntary associations is provided by Tod ("Clubs, Greek," 254): "voluntary associations of persons [were] more or less permanently organized for the pursuit of a common end, and so distinguishable both from the State and its component elements . . . and . . . from temporary unions for transitory purposes" (see also Roberts, Skeat, and Nock, "Guild of Zeus Hypsistos," 75). Almost all of the Roman voluntary associations were concerned with the worship of a deity and claimed its protection, most were concerned with the burial of members, and many with the importance of a particular trade (Duff, *Personality*, 102, citing Waltzing, *Étude historique*, passim; Daube, "Review of Duff, *Personality*," 91). Words used for voluntary associations are numerous, but the primary Greek words are *orgeōnes*, *eranos*, and *thiasos*, while the primary Latin word is *collegia*. The use of analogy is important. We are not here trying to suggest a genealogical relationship but rather that comparison in terms of analogy is both profitable and warranted. On the use of analogy, see Smith, *Drudgery Divine*, esp. 36–53.

significance of the analogy. Often emphasized is the localized nature of voluntary associations versus the translocal nature of Christianity. [224]

A close analysis of relevant material suggests that some voluntary associations in antiquity had translocal links, and that Christianity was more locally based than is often assumed. Thus both Christian congregations and voluntary associations were locally based groups with limited translocal connections. In establishing this, the way is opened for more fruitful use of the analogy of voluntary associations for understanding the formation and organization of early Christian groups.

Two of the earliest scholars to argue that the Christian groups were *collegia* were Theodore Mommsen and Geovanni De Rossi.[2] Another important and early scholar was Edwin Hatch,[3] although he experienced strong opposition.[4] However, by 1910 Max Radin could write:[225]

> Now, the Christians formed associations everywhere. Indeed, Christian worship of that time, as all worship, was unthinkable except in that form... We must assume then that as societies the Christian collegia were on a par with the vast majority of other collegia, even with those of the privileged Jewish ones.[5]

Most modern New Testament scholars have stopped short in their use of the analogy for a number of reasons, not least of which is the problem with translocal links. E. A. Judge is a bit ambivalent, suggesting that in the mind of the public, Christians would not have been distinguished from other

---

2. Mommsen, *De collegiis et sodaliciis*; and Rossi, *La Roma sotterranea cristiana*. See Wilken, "Collegia," 291 n. 50; cf. Liebenam, *Geschichte und organisation*, 272 n. 4. Other important early scholars include Renan, *Apostles*, 278–89; and Heinrici, "Christengemeinden"; and Heinrici, "Zum genossenschaftlichen Charakter." See the summary of Heinrici's work in Schmeller, *Hierarchie und Egalität*, 11–13.

3. Hatch, *Organization*, esp. 26–39; and Hatch, *Influence*, 283–309. Hatch's position is summarized nicely in Josaitis, *Edwin Hatch*, 35–42.

4. Opposition to Hatch occurred primarily in the areas of church structure and terminology. While some scholars were willing to grant the influence of voluntary associations, they were not willing to accept Hatch's suggestion that church practices (such as baptism) and titles for church officers (such as *episkopos*) were rooted in a non-Jewish context. See further Kloppenborg, "Edwin Hatch," esp. 217–20.

5. Radin, *Legislation*, 127–28. Scholars who used the associations as an analogy for understanding early Christianity were not blind to the possible differences between the groups. Hatch (*Organization*, 36) points out that the Christian groups and the associations differed in their approach to charity. Hardy (*Studies in Roman History*), while maintaining that Christianity was very similar to associations (pp. 131, 133, 141), does highlight some differing features (p. 142). Neither scholar, however, considers the problem of local vs. translocal links to warrant comment. Cf. also Wilson, *Paul and Paganism*, 123–24.

unofficial associations.⁶ Although he maintains that they had "international links" like the Jews, he admits that unlike the Jews they lacked a national seat for their cult. However, Judge goes on to suggest that "the international direction ... may be unusual, but does not seriously qualify the similarity at the local level."⁷ Some seventeen years later William Countryman states that every association, due to the characteristic of being a "strictly local institution," was "firmly enmeshed in the social order of its city" with no outside authority higher than the patron.⁸ In this way, the analogy of associations and Christianity is played down.

In the early 1970s Robert Wilken contrasted associations with the ancient philosophical schools by pointing out that "the *collegia* were [226] local associations seldom exceeding several hundred members."⁹ In a later work he states that the associations were drawn from people living in a specific city and "were not 'international.'"¹⁰ Christianity, for Wilken, is more like the Stoics or Epicureans in reaching beyond local boundaries. He does, however, concede that on the local level Christianity "engaged in much the same activities as other associations."¹¹ This leads him to conclude that Christianity represents a combination of "philosophical school" and "association."¹²

Barton and Horsley use their lengthy analysis of an inscription from Philadelphia (SIG³ 985) to point out some similarities that early Christianity shared with cult groups.¹³ For example, both were characterized by voluntary membership and relied on cooperation and hospitality. Both types of groups were founded by private initiative and attracted members through their offer of security and salvation in an age of uncertainty about traditional institutions. However, the most important difference that Barton and Horsley highlight is the international scope of the Christian groups, in contrast to the localized nature of the associations.¹⁴ While they do note that the character of individual Christian groups is much like that of localized associations, nevertheless, they emphasize the differences in the overall

---

6. Judge, *Social Pattern*, 44.

7. Judge, *Social Pattern*, 46.

8. Countryman, "Patrons and Officers," 138. He cites as an exception to this characteristic the guilds of Dionysiac actors (p. 136), a group to which we will return below.

9. Wilken, "Collegia," 279; Wilken, *Christians as the Romans Saw Them*, 35.

10. Wilken, *Christians as the Romans Saw Them*, 35.

11. Wilken, "Collegia," 287. Also Barton and Horsley, "Hellenistic Cult Group," 40.

12. Wilken, "Collegia," 287.

13. Barton and Horsley, "Hellenistic Cult Group," 28.

14. Barton and Horsley, "Hellenistic Cult Group," 28.

localization of the two groups—that voluntary associations were strictly localized whereas Christ groups, though localized, also fostered translocal links.[15]

Wayne Meeks is much stronger in disassociating the two types of groupings. He points out four differences between Christian groups and voluntary associations: Christian exclusivity towards other deities, Christian "inclusivity" across various levels of society, the lack of overlap in significant terminology, and Christian translocal links.[16] Kloppenborg effectively addresses Meeks directly on the first three issues but is silent on the subject of translocal links.[17]

Thus we see that there has been a major shift throughout the twentieth century in the understanding of the use of voluntary associations as an [227] analogy for early Christianity. It is a shift that needs to be explained, and much of it hinges on the issue of translocal links. It is noteworthy that in all of these modern scholarly works very little primary data is presented in order to substantiate the claim that the associations were local while the Christian groups were "translocal."[18]

Without significant new data, one must ask how this critique of the analogy came about. I would suggest that it occurred as a misreading of the evidence of Tod and soon became incorporated into the modern secondary literature.[19] In 1932 Tod wrote concerning voluntary associations, "In the first place, these ancient societies were almost entirely local: at most they extended over an island or an Egyptian province."[20] However, Tod's comments are given in the context of a discussion about the associations of antiquity and *modern (that is, 1930s) trade unions*. He contrasts them by following the above statement with, "The modern trade-union, on the other hand, is national or even, to some extent, international."[21] If this is the contrast then it is not difficult to agree with Tod.[22] But this is not what is implied in

---

15. Barton and Horsley, "Hellenistic Cult Group," 28.
16. Meeks, *First Urban Christians*, 78–80.
17. Kloppenborg, "Edwin Hatch," 231–37.
18. Meeks presents the most substantial evidence; others simply rely on earlier assertions (for example, Stambaugh and Balch, *New Testament*, 141, who cite Meeks, *First Urban Christians*, 78–80; cf. Schmeller, *Hierarchie und Egalität*, 17).
19. As most scholars do not footnote their assertion, this is conjectural. However, neither do most point to any primary evidence.
20. Tod, *Sidelights*, 81.
21. Tod, *Sidelights*, 81.
22. For example, unlike the modern trade unions, few ancient associations benefitted their members economically (Fisher, "Roman Associations," 1222). By the late Roman Empire some clubs were transformed from voluntary associations into state-controlled

the comments of later writers on the subject, who, as we have seen, indicate that all associations (not just [228] trade associations) were fundamentally different from Christianity in this area of local versus translocal links.

We see, perhaps, in Wilken's work a clearer statement than elsewhere of what is meant by "translocal links" when the term is used by others. Wilken maintains that Christianity is "a 'worldwide' sect whose adherents lived throughout the Mediterranean world and shared a common religious profession and style of life."[23] This is unlike the voluntary associations, which "were not 'international.'"

Using Wilken's descriptions as representative of the position of other scholars, we can investigate the twofold assertion of his statement: that voluntary associations were local in a way that Christian groups were not, *and* that early Christianity was a translocal movement in a way that the voluntary associations were not. With the evidence to be presented below, what is being called into question is both a common modern understanding of voluntary associations and a common modern conception of early Christianity. I would suggest that the evidence is such that we can no longer confidently assert that early Christian groups had, to use Tod's words, "national or even, to some extent, international" links any more than did the voluntary associations. In arguing this, yet another of the obstacles to using the voluntary associations as an analogy to early Christianity can be removed.

EVIDENCE FROM ASSOCIATIONS

An investigation of the evidence from voluntary associations shows that there were in fact stronger translocal links between some associations than is often admitted. The testimony from the voluntary associations is epigraphical, and thus by nature scattered both geographically and temporally, but there is enough evidence to suggest that many associations had a history of translocal links, which had not died out by the first century CE.

The most obvious place to begin when investigating translocal links between associations is to look to groups of "foreigners" (people of one ethnic background living in another locale) in the circum-Mediterranean

---

guilds (Countryman, "Patrons and Officers," 136; Burford, *Craftsmen*, 149–50). On the increase in strikes in the later ᵉmpire (after Hadrian's reign) see MacMullen, "Roman Strikes"; and Baldwin, "Strikes." Buckler ("Labour Disputes") discusses four strikes in the Roman province of Asia, three from the second century CE and one from the fifth century CE; cf. Broughton, "Roman Asia Minor," 4:847–49.

23. Wilken, "Collegia," 287; Wilken, *Christians as the Romans Saw Them*, 35.

world, as they often continued the worship of their homeland.[24] These groups are obvious for two reasons. First, the amount of contact with [229] their native land might enlighten our discussion. Second, "foreigners" were often traders or artisans—precisely those people who are attested in numerous association inscriptions.[25]

Traders were, by definition, "on the move," traveling throughout the then known world. Yet traders from one area who did business elsewhere could be united in one association, as is seen in Athens. An association of Kittian merchants asked for, and received, approval from the Athenian boule to set up a temple to Aphrodite (IG II² 337). In doing so, they cite the precedent set by the granting of the same privilege to the Egyptians in Athens.[26] In the Piraeus the situation seems to have been similar in terms of the formation of associations. The deme of Piraeus had to enact a decree (IG II² 1177) in the mid-fourth century BCE in order to control the unauthorized use of the Thesmophorion (the temple of Demeter) by the newly forming *thiasoi* made up of people from outside of Piraeus.[27]

That a group is composed of foreigners does not necessarily mean that there are translocal connections between this group and another group or another location. However, there does seem to be an implicit translocal element in the existence of such associations, with their inevitable orientation toward the place of origin. This implies other translocal links, even where they are not specifically mentioned.

A number of groups throughout the Mediterranean seem to have maintained ties with another locale.[28] On Delos there was a sizable group of traders called the *Rōmaioi* who had their own agora, temples, and associations (ca. I BCE–I CE). These associations list their members as

---

24. Tod, "Clubs," 254; cf. Fisher, "Greek Associations," 1186–87.

25. A further reason is that Paul himself was an artisan and seems to have worked in his trade as he traveled.

26. The precedent actually goes back to the third century BCE when the Athenian state allowed the Thracians the right to found a sanctuary of their national goddess (IG II² 1283, 261/60 BCE; Ferguson, "Attic Orgeones," 97–98). This was the first instance of an alien group being granted such a privilege.

27. Ferguson, "Attic Orgeones," 96. Other groups were able to look to the Athenian *orgeones* for their name and, probably, structure, even where there was no intervention on the part of the Athenians. Ferguson illustrates this with two inscriptions in which the word *orgeōnes* is used: IG VII 33 (Megara, "before imperial times") and RIG 1307 (Teos, ca. 150 BCE; Ferguson, "Attic Orgeones," 61 n. 1; cf. Poland, *Geschichte des griechischen Vereinswesens*, 15). In both cases the word is partially restored, but Ferguson suggests that the restorations are "not improbable." Thus, we can see "connections" without direct "links," which may also be true for Christianity.

28. Ferguson, "Attic Orgeones," 100 n. 45.

Rōmaioi, but also list their city of origin—many "were Greeks from [230] Southern Italy and Sicily, or natives of Campania and Apulia and other Italian regions."[29] Clearly they felt some connection with the capital city of the empire (probably because they were "citizens"). Also, on Delos the Greek and oriental slaves of the merchants formed an association patterned on the Roman *collegium*,[30] thus using a translocal model for a local organization.[31]

In Rome itself foreign *collegia* probably originated among foreign merchants living in Rome who wanted to celebrate their native cults.[32] Often their religious practices served to give them a sense of cohesion and continuity with their homeland.[33] However much they opened themselves up to other persons, they "did not entirely lose their national character and connections."[34]

Associations of foreign merchants in Rome had an official standing in their city or province of origin and sometimes in Rome itself.[35] An interesting inscription from Puteoli (CIG 5853) reveals the interconnectedness of two associations of Tyrian merchants, both to one another and to their home city. When the Tyrian merchants at Puteoli (the port of Rome) were not able to pay their rent, they wrote a letter to the city of Tyre asking for funding to maintain their *statio* (their business and social headquarters). The Tyrian senate responded by reinstating an old custom of having the Tyrian association in Rome pay the rent of the association at Puteoli. Thus, "between the two stations there was a connection not only of commercial, but of social, moral, and religious interest, involving mutual obligations."[36]

Along with trade associations, the associations of the Egyptian gods present an interesting case study for translocal links.[37] The cult of Isis [231] and Sarapis remained in the control of the Alexandrians and Egyptians even

---

29. La Piana, "Foreign Groups," 251.

30. La Piana, "Foreign Groups," 252.

31. Rhodes also had a large group of Italian merchants, although it is unclear whether they had translocal connections to their homeland.

32. La Piana, "Foreign Groups," 240, 246; cf. 274.

33. La Piana, "Foreign Groups," 321. Cf. Brady ("Reception," 21), who suggests that an association "must have always meant more to the person who was away from home, residing in a city whose citizenship he did not possess."

34. La Piana, "Foreign Groups," 323.

35. La Piana, "Foreign Groups," 245–46.

36. La Piana, "Foreign Groups," 258.

37. On Egyptian guilds see Roberts, Skeat, and Nock, "Guild of Zeus Hypsistos"; Boak, "Organization of Guilds"; and more generally San Nicolò, *Aegyptisches Vereinswesen*; and San Nicolò, "Zur Vereinsgerichtsbarkeit."

during the period of its greatest expansion.[38] It never became Latinized but always retained strong cultic and iconographic links to the temples of the Nile valley.[39] For example, on Delos a third-century BCE cult of Sarapis founded by Apollonius the Elder remained private, and "Egyptian," for more than a century.[40] Throughout that time the association maintained ties to Egypt, as witnessed in the following second-century BCE inscription:

> The priest Apollonios had this engraved according to the command of the god. Our grandfather Apollonios, an Egyptian of the sacerdotal class, having his god brought with him from Egypt, continued to do service (for his god) in accordance with tradition and purportedly lived to ninety-seven years of age. (IG XI/4 1299)

In Athens, when an association of *Sarapiastai* was opened up to Athenians, they took on the administrative roles but the Egyptians maintained the religious aspects.[41] An association in Priene (Asia Minor) stipulates that the priest must provide an Egyptian so that the sacrificial rites will be properly performed (I.Priene 195, *ca.* 200 BCE). This tells us two things: that not all of the priests of this cult of Sarapis and Isis were Egyptian, and that there is nevertheless some connection with Egypt.[42] More significantly, an adherent of the cult of Isis and Sarapis [232] was able to travel throughout the empire and be received by the local Isiac group wherever he or she happened to be.[43]

38. La Piana, "Foreign Groups," 304–5.

39. La Piana, "Foreign Groups," 308. There are also indications that the worship of the Egyptian gods envisioned some links to Egypt, particularly with respect to the water of the Nile. For example, Serapeum A on Delos had an underground crypt that was directly connected to the Inopus River. It was thought that this river had physical links with the Nile; thus the crypt was provided with authentic Nile water (Wild, *Water*, 34–35).

40. IG XII/7 506; cf. Dow, "Egyptian Cults," 230.

41. Brady, "Reception," 21.

42. Mixed ethnic backgrounds are attested in other associations: around 200 BCE three maenads were imported from Thebes to form three separate *thiasoi* of Dionysos at Magnesia ad Maeander (IMagMai 215; McLean, "For the Love of Dionysos," 30–31); an inscription from Thessalonike reads "To Makedon, the *thiasos* of *Asiani*, to their fellow *mystes*, Publius Aelius Alexander being priest" (IG X/2.1 309)—the use of a common Macedonian proper name in an inscription of a *thiasos* of people from Asia (*Asiani*) suggests that the *thiasos* was not limited to persons from Asia (cf. Edson, "Cults of Thessalonica," 155 incl. n. 3, for a similar situation at Dacia [CIL III 870]; see also Nilsson, *Dionysiac Mysteries*, 50, 55 n. 55).

43. La Piana ("Foreign Groups," 337) illustrates this by citing Lucius's move from Africa to Rome after his initiation (according to Apuleius, *Metam.*). Lucius does undergo the initiation rites again in Rome, but this is done because the first initiation was not deemed complete, not as a requirement to join the Roman group. See Nock,

Other inscriptions from associations dedicated to the Egyptian gods stand out as particularly informative for showing translocal links. An inscription from Thessalonike (IG X/2.1 255; I/II CE copy of an earlier text) records that Sarapis appeared twice to Xenainetos in a dream[44] and enjoined him to deliver both a verbal and written message to his political rival, Eurynomos, concerning the establishment of the cult of Sarapis and Isis in Opus, a town in the region of eastern Locris (on the Euboean Gulf).[45] Since this copy of the inscription was found in the sanctuary of Sarapis in Thessalonike, Xenainetos's dream probably took place in Thessalonike.[46] After the cult was established in Opus, the story was inscribed for use by the association there, and a copy was taken to the Thessalonian cult center to become part of its local tradition. The inscription was reinscribed in Thessalonike around the first to mid-second century CE by devotees of the cult in Thessalonike.[47] Clearly [233] there is a connection between the association in Opus and that in Thessalonike, both in the founding of the association in Opus and the memory of that founding in the Thessalonian association.

Another example of foreign connections within the Egyptian associations comes from Magnesia. An inscription records that when a priest of the cult of Sarapis at Magnesia runs afoul of the civic magistrates over the building site of a temple, a tribunal comes to Magnesia from abroad to clear up any misunderstanding (IMagMai 99). This suggests both that the priest was a foreigner[48] and that control of his actions, at the very least, was still governed from outside his current place of residence.

The guild of Dionysiac artists presents another interesting case study of translocal links. This guild was one of the longest-standing religious

---

Conversion, 147–49.

44. Probably during a period of incubation, a time when a person slept in a shrine awaiting healing, advice, a prophecy, or a vision (Horsley, *New Documents* 1, 31). Cf. Acts 12:7–10; 23:11; Horsley, *New Documents* 1, 32; Sellew, "Religious Propaganda," 16. Xenainetos seems to have been in Thessalonike on official business as a representative of the city of Opus.

In the cult of Sarapis and Isis dreams were important in revelations, prophecy, healing (Tinh, "Sarapis and Isis," 111), and initiation (Heyob, *Cult of Isis*, 57, 59; cf. Fraikin, "Sarapis and Isis," 3). The introduction of the cult of Sarapis and Isis to a new location was often inaugurated through a dream in which the god appeared and gave instructions.

45. The ruins of Opus have not been identified with certainty; Fraikin, "Sarapis and Isis," 2.

46. Contra Hanson, "Dream/Visions Report," 5.

47. See Sellew, "Religious Propaganda," 17–19. Cf. the cult of Egyptian gods which came to Cius, in Bithynia, near the end of the third century BCE, probably not directly from Egypt but from its mother city Miletus where Isis was the focus of a *thiasos*.

48. Sokolowski, "Propagation," 446 n. 16.

associations. It began in Attica around the third century BCE, or earlier, and can be traced to the end of the Roman Republic.[49] During that time the guild served not only to unite members of a common profession but was employed by various states in ambassadorial duties because of its members' wide-ranging travel.[50] They may even have had a hand in negotiating a treaty between Rome and Pergamon; the Pergamonian boule and demos honor the Dionysiac artists in an inscription from 129 BCE (SIG³ 694).

By the first century CE it is not uncommon to find this association referred to as *oikoumenēs*, which we might translate as "universal" or "worldwide," as seen in the letter of Claudius from 43 CE and IEph 22 from Nysa (142 CE).[51] This latter text comes from the second century CE when the evidence for the worldwide guild is most plentiful, revealing that there were branches throughout the empire, with the primary group located in Rome.[52] Local Dionysiac associations [234] probably existed alongside the larger, worldwide guild, although eventually most were absorbed into the worldwide guild.[53]

In this section we have raised the issue concerning the meaning of *translocal* when scholars argue that voluntary associations are local as opposed to translocal. The data show that it is not clear that associations had little or no contacts outside of a local group. A number of inscriptions point to the maintenance of contact with the association's place of origin, with its members, or both—as well as to contact between associations in various locales. Thus, there seems to be some translocal connections among some voluntary associations.

EVIDENCE FROM JUDAISM AND CHRISTIANITY

If, as we have seen, some (but not all) voluntary associations had translocal connections, it does not necessarily follow that these, rather than the local groups, should be given priority in a comparison with early Christian groups. Hence, the second part of our argument involves showing that *early*

---

49. Tod, "Clubs," 254.

50. See further Pickard-Cambridge, *Dramatic Festivals*, 281–85; cf. Sifakis, *Hellenistic Drama*, 136–71.

51. Text in Pickard-Cambridge, *Dramatic Festivals*, 319–20; cf. 297–99; partial translation in MacMullen and Lane, eds., *Paganism and Christianity*, 65–66.

52. For example, the members ("world citizens") of the Dionysiac association at Ephesos seem to be linked to the association at Rome (Poland, *Geschichte des griechischen Vereinswesens*, 129, 146); see further Pickard-Cambridge, *Dramatic Festivals*, 297–302).

53. Pickard-Cambridge, *Dramatic Festivals*, 298.

Christianity should be viewed with an emphasis on its "local" character rather than its translocal connections. In this way, we will find a meeting ground between those who contrast solely local associations with translocal Christian congregations.

Before turning to Christianity, however, it is worth a brief detour into the Jewish communities as reflected in the diaspora synagogues and the Dead Sea community. Many scholars who do not accept the analogy of the voluntary associations for Christian groups often suggest that Christian groups had much more in common with Jewish groups, particularly in regard to their requirement of exclusive adherence and their translocal connection to Jerusalem. However, there is a growing body of literature which suggests that in fact the Jewish groups had much in common with voluntary associations. If this is so, then the use of associations as an analogy to Christian groups is strengthened even more.

Studies of diaspora synagogues have noted similarities to Greco-Roman voluntary associations.[54] For example, the diaspora synagogues adopted the "Greek nomenclature of the associations," which "included [235] a great variety of terms in different places."[55] A number of studies have also been produced illustrating the similarities between the Qumran documents, the community associated with them, and the Greco-Roman voluntary associations.[56] Here we might simply note that the Dead Sea community definitely had translocal links, both to Egypt (cf. the Damascus Document found in three of the Qumran caves and the *geniza* of a Cairo synagogue)[57] and various towns in Palestine.[58]

Along with the similarities between Jewish groups and voluntary associations there is some evidence that within Judaism there could exist an openness to participation in other forms of worship. In fact, it is no longer

---

54. See Richardson, "Early Synagogues."

55. La Piana, "Foreign Groups," 360.

56. Bardtke, "Der gegenwärtige Stand der Erforschung"; Schneider, "Problematik des Hellenistischen in den Qumrantexten," 305-9; Dombrowski, "היחד in 1QS"; Hengel, *Judaism and Hellenism*, 1:243-44; Weinfeld, *Organizational Pattern*; cf. Kloppenborg, "Edwin Hatch," 226-28; and Smith, *Drudgery Divine*, 83, on the problematic use of Judaism as a means to isolate Christianity from the Greco-Roman world.

57. Vermes, *Dead Sea Scrolls*, 81.

58. Cf. Vermes, *Dead Sea Scrolls*, 15-18. Private associations in the form of guilds have a long history in Palestine, probably dating from before the Hellenistic period; see Mendelsohn, "Guilds in Ancient Palestine"; cf. Mendelsohn, "Guilds in Babylonia and Assyria," on guilds in Babylonia and Assyria. The *marzeaḥ*, seen by many to be "a *thiasos* dedicated to a particular god in which the memorial rites are characterized by eating and drinking," has a long history at Ugarit, at Palmyra, and in Palestine (Greenfield, "*Marzeaḥ* as a Social Institution," 451).

clear that Judaism was exclusive in a way different than other cult groups.[59] For example, Philo has strong polemic against Jews who joined associations and partook of their social practices, suggesting that a significant number of Jews of Alexandria did so, so much so that Philo [236] felt the need to address the problem.[60] However, for Philo the actual problem with the associations is what goes on at the association meetings, as he goes on to suggest that Jews might join non-Jewish social associations that allow the Jews to keep their own customs and standards of behavior: "As for contributions and club subscriptions, when the object is to share the best of possessions, prudence [*phronēsis*], such payments are praiseworthy and profitable."[61] Yet there are few examples of associations that did not align themselves with any deity at all; it could be that Philo is here suggesting that Jews could be part of an association which had a "pagan" deity as its divine patron.[62] In fact, the rabbinic text *t.Hul.* 2.3 implies that Jews in Caesarea Maritima joined in pagan rituals:

> If one slaughters an animal in order to sprinkle its blood for idolatrous purposes or to offer its fat parts for idolatrous purposes, such meat is considered as sacrifices of the dead. If it had already been slaughtered, and one sprinkled its blood for idolatrous purposes and offered its fat parts for idolatrous purposes ... This happened in Caesarea.[63]

These examples suggest that not all Jews in antiquity were against participation in the voluntary associations and its ritual practices.

The translocal link among diaspora Jews and Jerusalem also had its limitations. During the Palestinian uprising of the mid-first century CE the Jews of Rome (and elsewhere) "seem to have avoided entanglement

---

59. Some polemical writings indicate that many people still required exclusive worship within Judaism, but this tells us more about the actual problems that were being addressed; cf. Bradshaw, *Origins of Christian Worship*, 68–70.

60. See *Ebr.* 14; Borgen, "Participation of Jews," 45; contra La Piana, "Foreign Groups," 343.

61. *Ebr.* 20; translation in Borgen, "Participation of the Jews," 46.

62. One might also note that Erastus, a member of the Corinthian congregation, would have been required to participate in cultic rituals at city council meetings due to his position as city treasurer (Rom 16:13). And when writing to the Corinthians Paul does not limit the participation of Christians in pagan temple meals, except under certain conditions (1 Cor 8:1–13, 10:23–11:1; cf. Borgen, "Participation of the Jews," 57–59).

63. Translation in Borgen, "Participation of the Jews," 42; see also Levine, *Caesarea under Roman Rule*, 45.

in the rebellions and to have remained calm, saving their privileges and traditions."[64] Their links to Jerusalem were not so strong that they felt compelled to take a stand in support of their brethren on the other side of the empire.

In turning to Christianity, we must evaluate what evidence there is that [237] it was a translocal or worldwide religion. The translocal link for many scholars is Paul. He is seen to connect the various congregations. Certainly he himself would like to think that the congregations are connected, but this may not have been the case. For example, the support of the Philippian church went to Paul, not the other congregations with which he worked (Phil 4:14–16; see also 2 Cor 11:9) and may have been based on a reciprocal patron-client relationship.[65]

For the Christian groups themselves their first priority seems to have remained their own local congregations. This is best seen in Paul's attempt to collect money for the Jerusalem church. Meeks points to Paul's collection as indicating translocal obligations to other Christians.[66] However, Paul's troubles with raising the money promised, and his rhetorical strategies in his letters to the Corinthians (2 Cor 8:1–15; 9:1–5), suggest that they, at least, remained unconvinced that they had a social and religious obligation to an otherwise unknown group. What confuses the Corinthians is not necessarily the fact that they have to donate, but that the monies are going to Jerusalem rather than the common fund of the local congregation.[67] Also, the financial support for the Jerusalem church came from the newer, Pauline churches (not the reverse), which would have gone against expectations. In a translocal organization the established center usually supports the struggling, newer organizations.[68]

---

64. La Piana, "Foreign Groups," 374.

65. See further Bormann, *Philippi*.

66. Meeks, *First Urban Christians*, 110.

67. Kloppenborg, "Edwin Hatch," 237. La Piana ("Foreign Groups," 372–73) highlights the willingness of the Jews of the diaspora to contribute to the collection of funds for Jerusalem because of their strong translocal link to Jerusalem. If this is so, then it contrasts with the attitude of the Corinthians who, given Paul's rhetoric and his repeated appeals, did not have such a feeling of obligation—that is to say, they consider themselves to be a localized group, much like the associations.

Priority may also have been placed on smaller groups within one urban center (1 Cor 1:10–17). Voluntary associations could also have more than one local group. Cities with more than one grouping of a larger association include Thessalonike (Dionysiac, early III CE) and Magnesia ad Maeander (Dionysiac, III BCE); see McLean, "Love of Dionysos," 30–31.

68. Townsend, "Missionary Journeys," 437 n. 38.

Concerning both terminology for group designation and terminology for officers, Christian groups have similarities to voluntary associations not in particular usages, but in the diversity of usages among the groups. [238] Local particularities of language can be cited for both Christian groups and associations. Of eight societies of *Sarapiastai* throughout the Greek world "there is no similarity of organization, so far as one can observe, between any two of them."[69] However, the same can be said of Pauline churches, where it would be difficult to show a similar structure between the church at Galatia and the church at Corinth.

> There is no a priori reason to assume that there was uniformity among the Pauline churches, any more than one should assume a uniform organizational structure in associations. On the contrary, titles were highly variable, local particularities abound, and in many instances, we have no indication of how officers were designated.[70]

In the case of Paul, and of the *Sarapiastai*, the differences are due to their differing locations in the circum-Mediterranean world.[71]

Take, for example, the term *ekklēsia*, which is used by Paul as a designation for his churches in both the singular and the plural. Paul's use of the word in the plural shows that in his mind there were connections among Christian groups within one or more provinces rather than simply within a town (i.e., Rom 16:16; 1 Cor 7:17; 11:16; 16:19; 2 Cor 8:1; 11:28; Gal 1:22; 1 Thess 2:14);[72] sometimes he uses the singular to indicate the church universal (i.e., 1 Cor 10:32; 15:9; Gal 1:13; Phil 3:6). However, both Paul and the Christian community used *ekklēsia* in the local sense (i.e., Rom 16:1, 5; 1 Cor 1:2; 11:18), much like some associations who used it as a self-designator.[73] While the term may have been used by Paul on the basis of the LXX,[74] "in the

---

69. Dow, "Egyptian Cults," 191.

70. Kloppenborg, "Edwin Hatch," 232.

71. Dow ("Egyptian Cults," 191) suggests that since it has proven unfruitful to compare various clubs of Sarapiastai throughout the Greek world, we would be better served to compare the Attic Sarapiastai to cult societies of all other kinds within Attica itself, a task which proves to be quite successful (see McLean, "For the Love of Dionysos"). The same could prove to be the case for Pauline churches; more local studies are needed before any solid conclusions are put forward.

72. Cf. Meeks, *First Urban Christians*, 42–43.

73. Liebenam, *Geschichte und organisation*, 272–73; Hardy, *Studies in Roman History*, 141; Poland, *Geschichte des griechischen Vereinswesens*, 332.

74. As Schmidt maintains ("ἐκκλησία," 513–14, esp. n. 25).

environment of Greek cities, the term would almost certainly be understood (by all involved) as one of the names for a voluntary association."[75]

When Countryman suggests that the associations were "strictly local," he goes on to state that "in the church, however, the officers enjoyed [239] life tenure and derived their authority from outside the congregation, either literally or in theory."[76] Yet this assumes much for Pauline churches. The disputes within the Corinthian congregation make it clear that there was no one authority in the church who could oversee all aspects and negotiate between various factions. Paul attempts to take on this role as an external authority, but the letters of 2 Corinthians should show us that he was not always successful.[77] The earliest that we might see some indication of Christianity as a "worldwide" phenomenon with a central seat of authority is the early to mid-second century in the writings of Ignatius and 1 Clement. Even here, however, the idea of the primacy of the bishop of Rome is not entirely clear.[78]

Meeks suggests that Paul and other "missionaries" actively sought to establish a notion of a "universal people of God."[79] "The letters themselves, the messengers who brought them, and the repeated visits to the local assemblies by Paul and his associates all emphasized this interrelatedness."[80] This assumption can be called into question. Townsend's call for a reevaluation of the consideration of Acts as presenting Paul undergoing "missionary journeys" is apropos. He warns about (and illustrates) commentators "reading their own presuppositions back into apostolic times" in this regard.[81] It may be that neither Paul nor, especially, his converts thought of what they were up to as a mission or even as having any more translocal connections than other associations.[82] [240]

---

75. Kloppenborg, "Edwin Hatch," 231.

76. Countryman, "Patrons and Officers," 138.

77. 1 Cor 9; 2 Cor 1:15–2:13; 2 Cor 10–13; cf. Furnish, *2 Corinthians*, 44, 141. Paul never assumes that his own communities were in contact with one another, even in 2 Cor 8, where the reference to the Macedonians is very general. If his aim was to establish a translocal, "worldwide" group, one would think that from the beginning he would have been encouraging local leaders to meet with leaders from other locales or even to go to Jerusalem.

78. See Brown and Meier, *Antioch and Rome*, 164–66, on 1 Clement; Schoedel, "Ignatius," 386, and Chadwick, "Silence of Bishops," 170, on Ignatius.

79. Stemming from Paul's Jewish roots (Meeks, *First Urban Christians*, 108).

80. Meeks, *First Urban Christians*, 109.

81. Townsend, "Missionary Journeys," 436.

82. Certainly Paul refers to his "churches" and the common teaching and practices therein (1 Cor 4:17; 7:17; 11:16), but this does not necessarily represent a monolithic movement. The Corinthians may not have been impressed with Paul's rhetorical strategy; it is unlikely that they moved swiftly and eagerly to "correct" their practices in light

Meeks's claims are again called into question when he states that it is "peculiar" that early Christian groups could emulate the "intimate, close-knit life of the local groups" and still be part of a much larger, worldwide, movement.[83] It is unlikely that Paul's words that others "invoke the name of our Lord Jesus Christ in every place" (1 Cor 1:2) would have been any different than a similar claim of a priest of Isis or of Asclepius, the worship of whom was spread throughout the empire.[84] Meeks simply assumes this indicates "translocal connections"[85] before immediately turning to the "supralocal organization" of Christianity in the time of Constantine.

We see perhaps in the Dionysos artists' association an analogy to what may have occurred in Christianity. Over a period of three of four centuries this association grew from local groups with very loose translocal connections to the "worldwide" guild of artists (see above). Likewise Christianity did become a strong, well-defined global movement, but not until a few centuries beyond the foundations of the original groups. Christianity became a universal religion without national or racial connections only "through a long and painful process of evolution."[86] Thus, the description of formative Christian groups as universal would certainly not be an apt description.

It is also significant that early Christian and non-Christian writers "did not consider it incongruous to speak explicitly of the church as a *thiasos*."[87] When Trajan banned fraternities, Christian groups, at least in Bythinia, gave up their usual practices because they thought that the ban applied to them (that is, they fit the description of fraternities).[88] It is worth noting that Pliny's letter concerning the Christians in Bithynia [241] does not reflect the governor's anxiety that the worldwide phenomenon might lead to rebellion but rather the local merchants' distress over the effect on their trade of the masses joining Christian groups.

---

of Paul's letters.

83. Meeks, *First Urban Christians*, 70.

84. An analogy might be the formula *heis Theos* ("one God"). It is applied not only to the Christian God but also to other deities such as Sarapis—*heis Theos Sarapis* ("one God, Sarapis"); see Bonner, *Studies in Magical Amulets*, 10, 41, 46–47.

85. Although Meeks himself points out that some scholars think that this phrase was added later to the Pauline corpus in order to "catholicize" it (Meeks, *First Urban Christians*, 229 n. 155).

86. La Piana, "Foreign Groups," 339.

87. Malherbe, *Social Aspects*, 89; cf. 88; Hardy, *Studies in Roman History*, 141; Celsus in Origen, *Cels.* 3.2.3; Lucian, *Pergr. mort.* 11; cf. Eusebius, *Hist. eccl.* 6.19, 16; 7.32, 27; 10.1; Tertullian, *Apol* 39 (referring to Christianity as *factio Christiane, corpus, secta Dei*, and other titles used of associations); CIL VIII 9585.

88. Pliny, *Ep.* 10.96; Judge, *Social Pattern*, 48.

CONCLUSION

We have attempted to show through an evaluation of the available data both that some voluntary associations in antiquity had translocal links, *and* that Christian groups were more locally based than is often assumed. There is no doubt that the *primary* basis for associations was local,[89] but, we would argue, this would be equally true for the Christian groups. Christian congregations and voluntary associations were both locally based groups with limited translocal connections. The elimination of the false dichotomy between local associations and translocal Christianity allows for a more profitable use of the voluntary associations as an analogy for understanding the formation and organization of early Christian groups.[90]

---

89. Cf. Fisher, "Roman Associations," 1209.

90. I am grateful for financial support received during the research and writing of this paper from a Social Sciences and Humanities Research Council of Canada Fellowship and a Catholic Biblical Association of America Memorial Stipend.

6

"Map-maker, map-maker, make me a map..."

Redescribing Greco-Roman "Elective Social Formations"

Difference makes a comparative analysis interesting; similarity makes it possible.[1]

Der Ball ist rund. Das Spiel dauert neunzig Minuten. Soviel ist schon mal klar. Alles andere ist Theorie. Und ab![2]

NEITHER ANCIENT WRITERS NOR modern scholars seem able fully to escape their own social locations when attempting to describe groups that are classified as Greco-Roman voluntary associations. The diversity in the various taxonomies offered by scholars raises the issue of whether it is possible, or even desirable, to attempt classification of associations for use in the (re)description of Greco-Roman antiquity. Yet, as Jonathan Z. Smith

---

1. Poole, "Metaphors and Maps," 417.
2. Opening line from *Lola rennt*, 1998, dir. Tom Tykwer.

has so aptly argued and demonstrated, theoretical classification is an essential component of the scholarly enterprise. Nevertheless, as Bruce Lincoln notes, although theory is important, it is preferable "to leave theory embedded in practice whenever possible, so that generalizations may gradually emerge from the detailed analysis of specific materials."[3] This essay takes up this challenge by grounding some of the theoretical implications of Smith's work in the concrete example of Greco-Roman voluntary associations, or what might better be termed "religious formations"[4] or even "elective social formations."[5] It demonstrates that the [69] current paradigms for classifying associations have run their course, and a new mode of comparison that is complex but usable is needed for a broader project of redescribing the religious landscape of Greco-Roman antiquity.[6]

This need is not surprising, since part of the ongoing scholarly endeavor is the interplay between classification and analysis. It is only after having settled on an issue of identity that a taxonomy becomes available—that is, one must identify what one is talking about in order to classify it.[7] This circularity does not undermine the process. It is necessary that we define a thing to be investigated before classifying its variations while at the same time allowing for the classification to refine the definition—the "rectification of categories."[8] We have arrived at this point in the study of ancient religious group formations and their relationship to Jewish and Christian groups. For a long time—too long, I will suggest—scholars have designated the study in terms of "Jews, Christians, and others." It is time to attempt a new configuration which will produce a better understanding of the overall phenomenon while at the same time providing an apparatus for a much more complex and detailed means of talking comparatively across various group boundaries.

    3. Smith, *To Take Place*, 172; Poole, "Metaphors and Maps."

    4. Cf. a phrase from Smith in which he speaks of "Late Antique *religious formations* ranging from voluntary associations to trans-local communication networks" (Smith, *Relating Religion*, 205, italics added).

    5. Following Malina ("Early Christian Groups," 108–9), I think the notion of "elective" is somewhat better than "voluntary" as the adjective. I do think this notion is important to maintain, however, since there is enough data to suggest that in the case of synagogues, churches, and associations persons can "elect" not to be members (no matter their ethnic standing or occupational focus), either by deliberately withdrawing from the group or by transgressing some group boundary or norm and being forcibly withdrawn.

    6. The significance of the comparative process is that it helps us understand how things might be redescribed rather than how things actually are or were (Smith, *Drudgery Divine*, 52; cf. Cameron and Miller, "Introduction," 11).

    7. Cf. Elsner and Rutherford, "Introduction," 8–9.

    8. Cf. Mack, *Christian Myth*, 73–74.

"MAP IS NOT TERRITORY"...
BUT IT IS TERRITORIAL

Smith argues in his seminal essay "Map is not Territory" that value and meaning are imputed to our contexts through "structures of congruity and conformity."[9] That is, we understand our world by organizing it. To be sure, when we assign borders and categorizing elements to our world we act as an "imperial figure"—the very notion of "map" implies ownership, power, and restriction over who/what is "in" and "out." Any taxonomic system "does not simply and idly differentiate the phenomena being classified, but—what is more important—in classifying it also ranks them."[10] Nevertheless, such actions guarantee meaning for those doing the ordering,[11] as can be seen in the study of religion over the past few centuries. [70]

Throughout the early Enlightenment period, into the early decades of the twentieth century, European scholars "had a well-established convention for categorizing the peoples of the world into four parts, rather unequal in size and uneven in specificity, namely, Christians, Jews, Mohammedans (as Muslims were commonly called then), and the rest," the latter of which comprised those "variously termed heathens, pagans, idolaters, or, occasionally, polytheists—terms that could be used more or less interchangeably."[12] This four-way taxonomy remained in use for centuries.[13] Tomoko Masuzawa quotes Vincent Milner, writing in the mid-1800s, who explains that the name *pagan*—drawn from the designation given to those who lived in nonurban areas who continued in their religious practices even after the edicts of Constantine and others—is rooted in a contrast with the so-called great monotheistic religions: "In the middle ages, this name was given to all who were not Jews or Christians, theirs being considered the only true religion and divine revelations; but, in more modern times, Mohammedans, who worship the one supreme God of the Jews and Christians are not called *pagans*."[14]

Such distinctions may be rooted even earlier. The term *polytheism* possibly was coined by the Hellenistic Jewish writer Philo of Alexandria, only to be picked up once again in the 1600s as a replacement for, albeit

---

9. Smith, *Map Is Not Territory*, 292.
10. Lincoln, *Discourse*, 7.
11. Smith, *Map Is Not Territory*, 292.
12. Masuzawa, *Invention*, 47.
13. Masuzawa, *Invention*, 58–59.
14. Milner, *Religious Denominations*, 517, quoted in Masuzawa, *Invention*, 47.

synonymous with, *idolatry*.[15] The net effect is to affirm the prevailing notion that all who inhabited the nonurban landscape and were not much touched "by the civilizing knowledge of Christianity ... did not have a religion in the proper sense of the term."[16] Those not of the three branches of the religion of the Abrahamic family could thus be grouped together as "other," or, in the discourse of nineteenth-century human scientists, as "primitive" religions.[17] The net effect of this fourfold taxonomy was to sustain a seemingly contradictory view that "either there were countless religions or there was only one." However, "the elasticity of the taxonomic system variously and flexibly enabled the demarcation of 'our' sanctified domain from 'their' state of perdition, but it enabled little else."[18]

This prevailing fourfold taxonomic system carries on even today in discussing Greco-Roman religions, with the removal of the category Muslim, since it postdates the period under investigation. Thus, while scholars of antiquity take care to claim not to be privileging Christianity, the very fact that it is separated out, along with Judaism, from the rest perpetuates the status quo of the fourfold taxonomic system. No amount of [71] playing with the title of our studies will eliminate this fact. That is, when we continue to talk about "Christians, Jews, and _____," whatever term we place in the blank will not challenge the system.[19] Thus, while much critique is given to those who would use the word *pagan*, the substitution of *polytheist* or *other* is no less colonialist since the taxonomic formulation itself is what embeds the prevailing Western cultural assumptions of the supremacy of the monotheistic religions. By categorizing ancient religions into three—Judaism, Christianity, and others—scholars were (are) able to legitimate the ascendancy of Christianity from its Jewish roots to reign supreme over its source and its competition.[20]

---

15. See Masuzawa, *Invention*, 47 n. 24.

16. Masuzawa, *Invention*, 48–49.

17. Masuzawa, *Invention*, 49, 44. Although it takes us outside of the purview of this paper, Masuzawa (*Invention*) provides a fascinating picture of the development of the discourse of religious studies and the study of "world religions," well worth reading in its own right.

18. Masuzawa, *Invention*, 60–61.

19. This can be seen in the perpetuation of the singular classification despite the oft-repeated claim that there existed in the first century multiple "Judaisms" and multiple "Christianities." It is interesting that when the supposedly neutral category "Greco-Roman religions" abuts "Christianity" and "Judaism," it is only the former term that carries with it a temporal and locative indication—the implicit assumption being that the latter two transcend, or at least transfer across, time and place.

20. Cf. Smith, *Drudgery Divine*; Masuzawa, *Invention*, 148–78, 301–303.

With the rise of the scientific study of religion the fourfold taxonomy eventually gave way to the current prevailing taxonomy of ten to twelve world religions. Even this taxonomy, however, continued to perpetuate European hegemony, as Masuzawa clearly demonstrates. This should come as no surprise, for taxonomy is

> not only an epistemological instrument (a means for organizing information), but it is also (as it comes to organize the organizers) an instrument for the construction of society. And to the extent that taxonomies are socially determined, hegemonic taxonomies will tend to reproduce the same hierarchic system of which they are themselves a product.[21]

Perhaps such problems are inevitable, since "the writing of history and the constructing of religion are, of course, tied up with power and hence with the social construction of insiders and outsiders."[22]

Nevertheless, as a result of this expanded taxonomy scholars determined the manner in which "a 'religion' was to be recognized, to be identified as such, so that it might be *compared* with another."[23] In the study of Greco-Roman antiquity, however, the old taxonomic system prevailed even when the comparative enterprise was introduced. In large part, this was due to the expanded taxonomic system focusing on so-called "living" religions, and thus the multiple religious groups of the Greco-Roman era could be classified together as "antique" or, sometimes, as "primitive" religions. The assumption embedded herein again is the supremacy of nascent Christianity over its roots in Judaism and over the "others" found in its surrounding culture.[24] [72]

Part of the challenge involved the seeming anomaly of the relationship of Christianity to Judaism, a Semitic religion, and the prevailing notion that all things valued in the West were grounded in the world of the Greeks, namely, "science, art, rationality, democracy, etc."[25] The "modern discourse on religion and religions" was a "discourse on secularization" and, at the same time, "a discourse of othering."[26] As such, the religious discourse played a major role in the forging of "the essential identity of the West."[27] Masuzawa's task, however, is not "to cleanse and purify the science we have

21. Lincoln, *Discourse*, 7–8; cf. Smith, *Relating Religion*, 4.
22. Crossley and Karner, "Writing History," 4.
23. Masuzawa, *Invention*, 64 (italics original).
24. Cf. Smith, "Classification," 41.
25. Masuzawa, *Invention*, 19.
26. Masuzawa, *Invention*, 19.
27. Masuzawa, *Invention*, 20.

inherited—such efforts, in any case, always seem to end up whitewashing our own situation rather than rectifying the past—but rather it is a matter of being historical *differently*."[28] Given that the categorization of Christianity and Judaism as separate religions from the categorization of Greco-Roman religions not only is a core part of that modernist European discourse, but is also prevalent in scholarly conversations within the study of classics and Christian origins, it would seem that we need also to push beyond such categories in order to undertake the rectification of the past, in order to understand *differently*.[29]

Even were we able to define *other* in some acceptable way, one can question what it might mean to speak of "religions" other than Judaism and Christianity in the Greco-Roman period. Religion is generally thought of as "a distinct and broadly coherent system of beliefs and principles," which is "misleading for studying religion in the Roman Empire."[30] Rives cuts to the point accurately, but incompletely:

> The diversity of religion in the Roman world was not that of separate and distinct "religions," each with its own set of core beliefs and principles and its particular scriptures, clergy, shrines, rituals, and customs ... [I]t is almost impossible, *apart from a few exceptions such as Judaism and Christianity*, to identify any coherent or unified systems of religion at all (and even Judaism in this period may fit the model less well than many people would suppose). Instead, the coexistence of religious conceptions and practices that would seem incompatible to people used to the idea of "a religion" was apparently taken for granted in the Roman Empire.[31] [73]

Given Rives's caveat concerning Judaism, it seems that, for him, in antiquity Christianity alone fits the modern definition of religion. Yet elsewhere in the volume Rives rightly challenges the tendency of scholars to read

---

28. Masuzawa, *Invention*, 21 (italics original).

29. Cf. Cameron and Miller, "Introduction," 19: "So long as we resist defamiliarization of our subject area by choosing as our 'normative' paradigm Christian and/or Jewish religious formations, we will be prevented from seeing the unfamiliar, the strange, in the matrix of Greco-Roman group formations."

30. Rives, *Religion*, 5. "It is significant that in neither Greek nor Latin was there a word that really corresponds to the English term 'a religion'" (Rives, *Religion*, 13). Rather than think of Greco-Roman cult, myth, and art as "a religion," we should view the tradition "as a set of approaches to the divine" and, in so doing, we will be "in a much better position to understand it" (Rives, *Religion*, 43). That is to say, Greco-Roman "religion" is about behavior rather than dogmas and creeds (Rives, *Religion*, 89).

31. Rives, *Religion*, 5, (italics added).

Greco-Roman antiquity through the lens of Christian history and theology. Here he needs more care in reading *Christian* history through that same lens. Plenty of studies have demonstrated the wide diversity and multifaceted nature of the movements that coalesce into what becomes known as Christianity (with a capital C). At least during the first and second centuries, however, there was not an independent, single-minded movement that would fit the modern definition of *religion*.[32] This in turn confirms that one cannot legitimately claim to be comparing three distinct *religions* when one looks at ancient Judaism, Christianity, and others.

Those who followed a set of ritualized practices within the framework of a monotheistic worldview, such as the various Jewish groups, including the Jewish-Gentile Jesus followers, were part and parcel of the diversity of the world around them. They fit the general observation that

> on a fundamental level the various religious traditions of the empire had more similarities than differences. As a result, when people from one tradition were confronted with another, they often found much that was familiar and immediately understandable and tended to treat what was unfamiliar simply as a local peculiarity . . . People thought not so much in terms of "different religions," as we might today, but simply of varying local customs with regard to the gods.[33]

True, some were more different than others, but the monotheists were not alone in this noticeable differentiation[34] and cannot be grouped together into a distinct category without considerable difficulty.

> We still do not reckon adequately with the fact that Greek paganism, unlike any modern international religion, is a very radically noncentralized conglomerate, fitting very well into the category of "traditional" religions. Modern scholars, under the influence of "rationalized" religious traditions, still tend to look for overarching and co-ordinated meanings in Greek religion and to overlook its diffuse nature and piecemeal functionality.[35] [74]

---

32. As Rives points out only a few pages later, it is only for Christian writers from Tertullian on that the Latin word *religio* comes to mean something akin to the modern sense of "a religion," and "before that time, the linguistic evidence suggests that most people would have found the modern concept of 'a religion' rather alien" (Rives, *Religion*, 14). It was rather philosophy that was closer to the modern notion of "a religion" in that it presented "a distinctive way of life based on an integrated understanding of the cosmos" (Rives, *Religion*, 38, cf. 41; cf. Horsley, "Paul's Assembly.").

33. Rives, *Religion*, 6.

34. See examples in Rives, *Religion*, 182–93.

35. Scullion, "Pilgrimage," 117, cf. 119. I would argue that the same is also true for

The continuation of variations of Judaism and Christianity and the demise of other groups have led to a situation in which "it is tempting to interpret them in terms of contemporary experience and to assign them more importance that they perhaps had at the time."[36] Instead, we should treat Christianity and Judaism "strictly as historical phenomena, part of the complex pattern of religious life in the Roman Empire."[37]

"CLASSIFY AND CONQUER"[38]

At this point we turn our attention to a specific case to illustrate the problem of classification within a (taxonomically classified) subsection of Greco-Roman religious traditions, namely, those designated as voluntary associations. Many attempts have been made to define nonofficial or semiofficial groups of people that met together regularly in various locations in the Greek and then the Roman world[39] and to classify them according to clear demarcations. There is a clear array of diversity among these ancient groups, whether one looks at ethnic composition, internal organization, legal status, function, and so on.[40] For this reason, scholars have attempted to categorize and classify these associations into some sort of definable order, most often by first separating out "Jews" and "Christians" and then classifying the remaining associations in order to understand the nature of these religious formations.

The range of categories employed in the description of Greco-Roman group formations should not be surprising given the range of terms used for such groups in antiquity,[41] and yet to a large degree the diversity may be explained by the specific focus of the scholars involved. Jonathan S. Perry demonstrates how influential on their scholarship of the associations were the particular religious commitments of such venerable and agenda-setting

---

how scholars frame discourse around early Christian groups and formative Judaism, but space does not allow the development of that argument here.

36. Rives, *Religion*, 7.

37. Rives, *Religion*, 7. Although Rives claims to be doing this, we find throughout this otherwise carefully crafted monograph the frequent singling out of Judaism and of Christianity in their own separate sections in each chapter.

38. F. Max Müller's "somewhat free" translation of "Divide et impera" (see Masuzawa, *Invention*, 216).

39. See Ascough, *Paul's Macedonian Associations*, 3 n. 9. In the following I shall not give a general overview of the historical development of scholarship on associations—for that see Ascough, *Paul's Macedonian Associations*, 3–10. I shall focus my attention on the employment of taxonomies.

40. Belayche, "En quête de marqueurs."

41. See Poland, *Geschichte des griechischen Vereinswesens*, 5–172.

scholars as Theodor Mommsen, Giovanni Battisata de Rossi, and Jean-Pierre Waltzing.[42] His observation about the exchange between the former two could be extended to a study of the lives and commitments of many scholars working in this area: it "is not merely intriguing as biographical narrative; rather, it demonstrates how individual personalities can and do shape scholarly opinion."[43] [75]

It was Mommsen who first propagated the notion that associations that were designated as a *collegium tenuiorum* were exempt from a legal restriction placed upon such associations under the Roman Empire in the early second century CE.[44] Since only one such association was known, the *cultures Dianae et Antinoi* (CIL XIV 2112), Mommsen broadened the taxonomic category: "the *collegia tenuiorum* were, *as a category*, '*collegia funeratica*,' a term Mommsen coined specifically for this description."[45] It was a term that he had created from nowhere and which does not seem to have existed in antiquity.[46] Within scholarship of the ensuing 150 years "the existence of a discrete category of *collegia funeraticia* has been assumed, virtually without question."[47] It is a category that can no longer be sustained, as many types of *collegia* took on some sort of funerary activity.[48]

De Rossi's work on the Christian cemeteries, particularly the Roman catacombs, led him to argue that Christian groups presented themselves to Roman authorities as familial *collegia* whose primary concern was burial of members.[49] Since such associations were tolerated, Christians were able to meet unmolested by officials. Some Christian cemeteries, he suggested, had their origin in the funerary *collegia* of important and influential households.[50] The fundamental problem with this theory is "the utter lack of evidence that the Christians were typically recognized, *by the authorities*, as legitimate claimants to this exemption under the law."[51] Perry summarizes the work of Mommsen and De Rossi, and the conflict that their conclusions engendered between them:

42. Perry, *Roman* Collegia.
43. Perry, *Roman* Collegia, 40.
44. Mommsen, *De collegiis et sodaliciis*.
45. Perry, *Roman* Collegia, 30 (italics original).
46. Perry, *Roman* Collegia, 35.
47. Perry, *Roman* Collegia, 31.
48. Perry, *Roman* Collegia, 32; cf. Ausbüttel *Untersuchungen*, 20, 29; Kloppenborg, "Egalitarianism."
49. Rossi, *La Roma sotterranea cristiana*.
50. This theory persists. See, e.g., Jeffers, *Conflict at Rome*, 88.
51. Perry, *Roman* Collegia, 53 (italics original).

Mommsen "secularized" the *collegia funeraticia*, attempting to discern a group of cultors fundamentally *without* overriding religious commitments. By contrast, De Rossi sought to explain the growth of Christian communities in the Roman Empire by positing the *collegium* as a suitable subterfuge for a persecuted minority. Thus, while one man feigned "classical fastidiousness," rejecting the "magic potions" of religion, the other felt a kinship with his co-religionists, as they dodged official oversight and would eventually triumph over the officials themselves.[52]

Such personal interests continued to mark the work of scholars in the field.

It was Waltzing's context in France at the turn of the twentieth century and his commitment to Christian Democracy that led him to view all associations as, fundamentally, workingmen's associations, which, in turn, produced "a distorted view of lower-class life in the Empire," albeit, one that persisted throughout the discussions of the associations in the early twentieth century.[53] Waltzing was concerned to demonstrate the [76] importance and desirability of corporate action; suppression of workers proved to be counterproductive for the Romans, and "the obvious implication is that present-day 'emperors' ought to follow a more liberal policy regarding corporate action among workers, rather than a policy that would lead to despotism and thereafter to decline."[54] And while Christian groups are similar in many respects to such workers associations, what, for Waltzing, sets the Christians apart and, indeed, places them on the moral high ground above all other associative forms is their charity, their willingness to give aid to those in need.[55]

Not only has Waltzing's fundamental view of the role of the associations, and the superiority of Christianity to it, persisted throughout the twentieth century, it has had huge impact on social and political movements in Europe, particularly Fascist Italy. The work done during this era on the associations of the Roman Empire very much reflects the desires and aspirations of those within the Italian Fascist state and, eventually, to some degree, Hitler's Third Reich. Perry traces in detail this complex and fascinating history in the scholarship of the *collegia* in the remainder of his book. Particularly important in this regard was the work of Giuseppe Bottai, who as Minister of National Education, supported the work of the Institute of Roman Studies (ISR) in Rome while drawing upon their work to support

---

52. Perry, *Roman* Collegia, 60 (italics original).
53. Perry, *Roman* Collegia, 19, 62.
54. Perry, *Roman* Collegia, 83.
55. Waltzing, *Étude Historique*, 2:168, 189; Perry, *Roman* Collegia, 86–87.

Fascist aims of promoting the superiority of Roman (that is, Italian) culture. Largely under his hand, scholarship, particularly that done on associations, "became a tool of a totalitarian state."[56]

The work of Frank M. Ausbüttel[57] represents a move away from older attempts to classify associations based on function or legal standing[58] towards an approach that takes seriously the social interactions among association members and between members and their broader contexts.[59] Ausbüttel focuses on heterogeneous membership bases which allowed for "normal," that is, culturally prescribed, social interactions to take place. Such sociological approaches have continued in work such as that of Kloppenborg,[60] who classifies private, non-elite associations according to three designations: households, common trade, and common cultic interests.[61] To this Harland adds ethnic or geographically based associations and neighborhood or locational associations.[62] Rives maintains a tripartite division, but uses ethnic, occupational, and cultic designations.[63] Clearly, various types of associations intertwined social, religious, behavioral, and funerary dimensions,[64] and "it is not always easy or even appropriate to make sharp divisions between them."[65] [77]

Overall, there seems to be a general consensus developing around a tripartite classification of associations: religious associations (*religiöse Vereine*), groups of one common national background (*landsmannschaftliche Vereine*), and associations whose members have the same profession (*Berufsvereine*).[66] However, this consensus has been challenged by Liu, who notes that a radical disjuncture between the sociological classification and

---

56. Perry, *Roman* Collegia, 162.

57. Ausbüttel, *Untersuchungen*.

58. E.g., De Robertis *Storia delle corporazioni*; Duff, *Personality*, 95–161.

59. Liu, "Occupation," 2.

60. Kloppenborg, "Collegia and *Thiasoi*."

61. In a more recent article Kloppenborg adds a fourth category: "ethnic group" ("Egalitarianism").

62. Harland, *Associations*, 28–52.

63. Rives, *Religion*, 122.

64. Harland, *Associations*, 86–87.

65. Rives, *Religion*, 122.

66. See Öhler "Antikes Vereinswesen." Other taxonomies exist. For example, Bollmann (*Römische Vereinshäuser*, 58–126) attempts a taxonomy of the building remains from associations within three categories: (1) those with an axial entrance, portico court, and cult place; (2) temple structures; and (3) halls and *tabernae* (the most common form). Despite all the attempts to categorize the buildings, however, "all of the identified *scholae* were designed for both social and religious activities, regardless of which categories of *collegia* the *scholae* belonged to" (Liu, "Occupation," 4, 6).

the legal standing of associations is not viable. In light of work such as that of Sirks,[67] she notes "pure sociological classification of the Roman associations based on purpose or membership composition, trendy as the latter is, becomes inadequate for not taking into consideration the gradation and difference of the associations from the perspective of the Roman governing authorities and law."[68]

Progress in understanding the associations has been hindered by the competing taxonomies that have been proffered and the definitions put forth in order to distinguish them. This suggests that the quest for definitions remains "the hallmark of scholasticism."[69] Despite the inherent dangers of classification, however, "the rejection of classificatory interest is . . . a rejection of thought."[70] The challenge is to find a mode of taxonomic classification that is not overly general in its descriptions and allows for identification of similarities and differences among a wide range of phenomena. Linderski notes that "science progresses when it asks how a thing behaves and not what it is,"[71] or, we might add, what it "believes."[72] Thus, we will now turn our attention to a possible way forward in the study of "elective social formations" that focuses on behavior in a manner that will help provide a basis for redescribing Greco-Roman antiquity.

DIGITIZED TOPOGRAPHIES— HERE, THERE, AND EVERYWHERE

Taxonomy is not, first and foremost, about classification but about comparison. And as such, any attempt at a "new" taxonomy is, at heart, a means of doing better comparisons and thus is "a route to redescription and rectification" of categories.[73] The issue is not *whether* we should compare but *how* we shall compare.[74] Thus, "comparisons are not given; they are the result of thought,"[75] [78] and as such, the "disciplined inquiry" of comparison brings together in the mind of the scholar differences that can lead to a redescription of that which is under analysis.

67. Sirks, *Food for Rome*.
68. Liu, "Occupation," 4.
69. Linderski, "Religious Communities," 652.
70. Smith, "Classification," 43.
71. Linderski, "Religious Communities," 652.
72. North, "Réflexions," 344.
73. Smith, *Relating Religion*, 29.
74. Cf. Smith, *Relating Religion*, 9; Poole, "Metaphors and Maps," 414.
75. Smith, *Relating Religion*, 23.

Smith's focus on "'difference,' a complex term which invites negotiation, classification and comparison"[76] means comparison is not a matter of identifying one thing as another in terms of genealogical relationships. Rather, Smith advocates analogical comparison that is not interested in finding direct connections. It aims to highlight similarities and differences among a limited set of options. The analogy rests in the mind of the scholar conducting the investigation and helps one to understand how things might be reimagined or redescribed—"a disciplined exaggeration in the service of knowledge."[77] The comparison takes place around a specific set of options which is specified by the interpreter. In so doing, the investigator can arrive at a deeper analysis than that possible through the simple (and simplistic) postulation (or, I would add, refutation) of genealogical relationships.

The existence of religious formations in Greco-Roman antiquity points us towards what Cameron and Miller have termed "reflexive social experiments."[78] Although Cameron and Miller focus on Christian formations that "were concerned to shape meaningful collective identities in the face of the constraints and challenges of the times," they note that these "can be compared to similar sorts of social experimentation occasioned by the times."[79] Their categories for comparison, derived from *religious* formations as instances of social experimentation,[80] are helpful as a beginning point for possible areas of comparison among all Greco-Roman elective social formations: social locations (ethnic identity, profession, social status, gender), mythmaking (deities recognized, rituals employed, social occasions shared, discursive modes used), and social formations (structures, benefits, dominant practices, attraction, recruitment).

The challenge is to introduce only enough distortion to make a taxonomic model workable for the scholarly enterprise while preserving enough of the distinctive features of the taxa so as to recognize the heuristic nature of the final outcome. Again, Smith has helped us conceive a way forward by suggesting that all comparison should be carried out not in terms of binaries but in terms of, at the very least, a three-way relationship, such as comparing X, Y, and Z with respect to a particular variable (e.g., "*x* resembles *y*

---

76. Smith, *Drudgery Divine*, 42.

77. Smith, *Drudgery Divine*, 52.

78. Cameron and Miller, "Introduction," 17; cf. Mack, *Christian Myth*, 211.

79. Cameron and Miller, "Introduction," 17; Cameron and Miller, "Conclusion," 504.

80. Cf. Cameron and Miller, "Conclusion," 499–505. See also Rives, who demonstrates "that associations tended to engage in much the same types of activities" that one finds in Greco-Roman society as a whole (*Religion*, 122).

more than z with respect to"[81]). While "thick description" is one obvious way in which such comparisons can be achieved, such descriptions are less helpful as heuristic devises for analysis of large bodies of data. The "flatness" of the representation can be construed to imply either hierarchical or genealogical relationships, thus suggesting that X and Y stand in genealogical relationship, or that both together have produced the variable.

It is possible, then, in the method that Smith advocates to slip into the maintenance of binary relationships. The suggestion that X can be compared to Y *with respect to* a variable can be (ab)used to set up a binary opposition between the larger categories. Thus, while we may no longer want to compare, for example, synagogues with churches, Smith's proposal suggests that it is possible to compare synagogues and churches with respect to meals (e.g., to say that churches resemble synagogues more than pagan groups with respect to the ritual meal). However, this assumes coherent groups the members of which can be classified as synagogues or as churches. In antiquity, this is not the case.

More helpful in clarifying the process is to note that "two or more instances of a phenomenon may be compared if, and only if, there exists some variable . . . that is common to each instance."[82] Where this falters as a heuristic device is the caveat that a "variable" carries with it "an identical meaning in all of its occurrences."[83] This seems to beg the question. For, while two texts from separate synagogues might mention a meal practice (= variable), the brevity of the reference or the ambiguity of all that may be involved or implied in a particular meal practice would disqualify the comparison from taking place.

What I am proposing is a way forward that takes account of the broad range of Greco-Roman social formations, in all their individuality, while allowing the specificity of a "variable" to determine the range of Xs, Ys, and Zs, in the comparison. For example, rather than pick or choose a few exemplars of meals from Jewish, Christian, and "other" texts and then extrapolate from them generalized meal practices that will define the broader categories of Christian, Jewish, and other, the scholar would search a broad range of texts to determine all those within which meals are mentioned. One can then look at these data to gather other information about how these various groups, across time and space, look similar and dissimilar, not only with respect to the initial variable (in this case meals), but also with respect to other variables. For example, from a collection of all elective social formations

---

81. Smith, *Drudgery Divine*, 51.
82. Poole, "Metaphors and Maps," 415.
83. Poole, "Metaphors and Maps," 415.

whose texts mention meals one might find that in the first-century groups A, B, C, D, E, F, and G appear. One can then further refine the search to see what, if anything these might hold in common, discovering, for example, that while A, C, and E hold meals in banqueting halls, B, D, and F hold their meals at a graveside, and G does both. From the results of this search one can then extrapolate networks of similarities and differences among the various individual groups. Admittedly, this is not as neat and [80] clean as binary or even triadic comparisons. It will lead, however, to a much thicker and more helpful (re)description of Greco-Roman antiquity.

The major challenge before scholars is accessing the scattered and diverse data. Yet in the electronic age this could be less of a problem than ever before. A desideratum for the progress of the redescription of Greco-Roman antiquity is a computer database that contains as many references as can be found to the wide variety of elective social formations (that is, to the formations of so-called Jews, Christians, and others) and is tagged with dates, locations, medium of composition, and, most importantly, a broad range of key words (the variables). These latter remain the artificial construction of scholars, chosen for the purposes of comparison. While such a database is by no means a perfect solution to the problem of comparison, it will help move the process forward by sidestepping the privileging of Christian or Jewish groups and the positing of binary opposites. At the same time, it will allow for adequate specificity in the terms of reference that are under investigation. At the very least, it will move us away from the a priori notion that Judaism and Christianity stand out as special (and dominant) in the study of Greco-Roman religions.

This proposal does not claim to have solved the issue of how one compares taxa, nor does it absolve the scholar from thick, open-textured description and redescription. Rather, it opens an avenue for broader comparison, while maintaining the nature of the comparative process.[84] As Smith notes of biological classification, "numerical phenetics . . . is self-consciously *polythetic* in that each member of a class possesses a large, but unspecified number of properties, with each property possessed by a large number of individuals in a class, but no single property needs be possessed by every member of the class."[85] What I am suggesting is something similar for mapping Greco-Roman religious formations. Knowing full well that not every individual member classed in the subgroups will have each and every property, the properties themselves can be used to sort and analyze the taxa.

---

84. Cf. Poole, "Metaphors and Maps," 414–15.
85. Smith, "Classification," 37 (italics original).

As with any experiment in which the experimenter sets up the parameters and then steps back to run the experiment, the organization of taxa within a taxonomy rests upon, in fact, requires, the conceit of the experimenter in setting forth the principles by which the experiment will be conducted. Yet having set the environment (Greco-Roman antiquity) and the principles of organization (variables), those conducting the experiment step back to see what, if anything, develops in the ensuing chaotic ordering of the data. It is not the following of the imposed principles, then, that is of interest, but the patterns and networks of relationships that develop once those principles are imposed. [81]

Making concrete the variables in the formulation "with respect to" should not be understood as being more "objective." The very choice of what to insert as the variables reflects the values and the preoccupations of the scholar who employs them.[86] We do not escape the hierarchical nature of the taxonomic process. We do, however, recognize it and employ it for what it is—a tool of analysis in the interest in moving us forward, in this case, moving us forward to a redescription of Greco-Roman group formations. Such an approach will address the desideratum of Smith, who responds to the dichotomy of a diffusionist approach of comparison and to an approach that focuses on patterns at the expense of history, by seeking an approach that addresses "the integration of a complex notion of pattern and system with an equally complex notion of history."[87]

---

86. Cf. Lincoln, *Discourse*, 133.

87. Smith, *Imagining Religion*, 29. Support for the research and writing of this paper has been provided through a Queen's University Chancellor's Research Award, an Ontario Government Premier's Research Excellence Award, and a Social Sciences and Humanities Research Council of Canada Standard Research Grant. I am grateful to my research assistant, Rachel McRae, for her help on this project.

7

The Thessalonian Christian Community as a Professional Voluntary Association

AMONG SCHOLARS OF THE New Testament there is a growing awareness of the importance of studies of early Christianity that take seriously local peculiarities. Exegetes recognize that New Testament texts must be read in the light of the social situation to which each was addressed if they are to be properly understood.[1] In this article we will attempt to do this by investigating the social makeup of the Thessalonian Christian community. Overall, we hope to show that the Thessalonian Christian community founded by Paul was similar in composition and structure to a professional voluntary association.[2]

THE THESSALONIANS AS GENTILES

According to Acts 17:1–9 Paul created the Thessalonian church from Jews and God-fearers whom he "stole away" from the synagogue at Thessalonike.

---

1. Judge, *Social Pattern*, 72; cf. Kloppenborg, "ΦΙΛΑΔΕΛΦΙΑ," 267.

2. This study is limited to an investigation of 1 Thessalonians, since the authenticity of 2 Thessalonians is disputed. For a summary of the debate see Jewett, *Thessalonian Correspondence*, 3–18; Menken, *2 Thessalonians*, 27–43; Wanamaker, *Thessalonians*, 17–28.

The Thessalonian Christian Community as a Professional Voluntary Association 123

Commentaries on 1 Thessalonians generally rely on this account for understanding how the Thessalonian Christian community was formed.[3] However, [312] while there is no denying the connection of early Christianity to first-century Judaism generally, in the specific case of the Thessalonian Christian community,[4] all the evidence suggests that if there were any Jews and "God-fearers" in the congregation, their presence was small enough that their Jewish background does not seem to be a factor in the overall ethos of the congregation.[5]

The primary piece of evidence for the Gentile composition of the Thessalonian Christian community comes from 1 Thess 1:9, which indicates that prior to their conversion the Thessalonians had been involved in "worshiping idols," an unlikely designation for Jews or God-fearers.[6] Elsewhere in the letter Paul gives no special attention to Jewish persons or practices, including synagogue practices,[7] and there is little use of the Hebrew Bible or the LXX.[8] [313]

---

3. For example, Eadie, *Thessalonians*, 12–13; Milligan, *Thessalonians*, xxvi–xxx; Frame, *Thessalonians*, 1–7; Rigaux, *Thessaloniciens*, 3–11, 20; Masson, *Thessaloniciens*, 5–6; Laub, "Paulus als Gemeindegründer," 25; Bruce, *1 & 2 Thessalonians*, xxi–xxviii; less so Best, *Thessalonians*, 2–7; Holtz, *Thessalonicher*, 9–10; Wanamaker, *Thessalonians*, 6–16. Also Hugédé, *Saint Paul*, 67–90.

4. And also the Christian community at Philippi; see Ascough, "Voluntary Associations," 100–103.

5. Despite a reliance on the Acts account of the origins of the Thessalonian Christian community, some commentators acknowledge the predominance of Gentiles in the congregation: Eadie, *Thessalonians*, 12–13; Frame, *Thessalonians*, 3–4; Rigaux, *Thessaloniciens*, 20; Best, *Thessalonians*, 5; Laub, "Gemeindegründer," 18, 20; Bruce, *Thessalonians*, xxii–xxiii. See also Dobschütz, *Thessalonicher-Briefe*, 11; Plummer, *Commentary*, xvi; Jewett, *Thessalonian Correspondence*, 118–19; Wanamaker, *Thessalonians*, 85; Lührmann, "Beginnings of the Church," 239; de Vos, *Church and Community*, 146–47.

6. Paul would not describe Jews (or God-fearers) as turning from idols to God; Plummer, *First Thessalonians*, 13; Neil, *Thessalonians*, 27; Best, *Thessalonians*, 82; Collins, *Studies*, 287; Jewett, *Thessalonian Correspondence*, 118–19; Wanamaker, *Thessalonians*, 85; Williams, *1 and 2 Thessalonians*, 35. Holtz (*Thessalonicher*, 10) suggests that Paul is referring to the time before they became "God-fearers" and attached themselves to the synagogue, but this is an unlikely interpretation that relies on the account of Acts 17:1–4. Note also that if 2:14–16 is taken as authentic, then Paul's distinction between the Thessalonians' persecution by their "own countrymen" (*hypo tōn idiōn symphyletōn*) and the persecution of those in Judea by "the Jews" (*hypo tōn Ioudaiōn*) also suggests that the Thessalonians are not themselves Jewish (nor in conflict with a Jewish group).

7. See Best, *Thessalonians*, 5. 1 Thessalonians 2:13–16 indicates that the Thessalonian Christians imitated the Christian communities in Judea. This passage is thought by many, however, to be an interpolation into Paul's letter. For details see Pearson, "1 Thessalonians," 79–94; Collins, "Integrity," 67–106; Richard, *Thessalonians*, 17–19; Boers, "Form-Critical Study," esp. 151–52.

8. See Plummer, *First Epistle to the Thessalonians*, xx–xxii; also Collins, *Birth of the*

The depiction in Acts 17:1–9 reflects one of the clear concerns of the writer of Acts—to show how closely tied Christianity is to Judaism. Thus, in Acts Paul always goes first to the Jews but is rejected so turns to the Gentiles. This is not the picture of Paul's missionary strategy that emerges from Paul's letters, however, where he clearly identifies himself as the "apostle to the Gentiles" (Rom 11:13).[9]

The primarily Gentile composition of the Thessalonian church is not surprising, given the Macedonian context. A review of ancient literature finds only one clear reference to Jews in Macedonia in the first century CE: Philo's record of a letter from Herod Agrippa (37–44 CE) to Caligula, which notes that most provinces in Rome's control include a Jewish population, listing among them Macedonia *(Legat.* 281–283). Agrippa's point, however, is to indicate how widespread Judaism has become. The comments are so general that Agrippa (or Philo in re-creating the letter) may simply have affirmed a Macedonian Jewish community with little knowledge to the contrary.[10]

Irina Levinskaya provides a more hopeful picture when she concludes that epigraphic evidence from Macedonia "supports the picture we can obtain from the book of Acts."[11] In reality, the epigraphical evidence is only slightly more informative, and Levinskaya is overly optimistic.[12] For the most part, evidence for a Jewish presence is from the third century CE or later.[13] Thus, it is probable that the Thessalonian Christian community was made up of Gentiles. [314]

THE THESSALONIANS AS MANUAL LABORERS

In 1 Thessalonians Paul is particularly concerned to establish his ethos in the *exordium* of the letter (1:2–2:12): "You know what kind of men we

---

New Testament, 105.

9. That Acts reflects Luke's theological and historical concerns rather than a reliable account of factual events has long been recognized; see Haenchen, *Acts of the Apostles,* 90–116, 505–14; Lüdemann, *Early Christianity,* 1–16, 184–88.

10. See Lührmann, "Beginnings," 239.

11. Levinskaya, *Book of Acts,* 195.

12. For a detailed critique of Levinskaya and an analysis of the available epigraphic evidence see Ascough, "Voluntary Associations," 178–89.

13. Despite this, large communities of Jews and God-fearers in Macedonia continue to be affirmed: Lightfoot, "Biblical Essays," 242–45; Nehama, *Histoire des Israelites,* 1:31–44; Schürer, *History of the Jewish People* 3.1:65; Papazoglou, "Macedonia under the Romans," 207. Acts seems to be the basis on which many scholars make the assumption that a substantial Jewish community existed at Thessalonike (and Philippi).

proved to be among you for your sake" (1:5). This is elaborated in 2:1-12, where Paul notes his blameless moral conduct (2:3, 5-6, 9-10; cf. 4:1-7), his accountability toward God (2:5; cf. 4:1), and his encouragement and exhortation (2:7-8, 11-12; cf. 4:1, 18; 5:11).[14] In the midst of this he emphasizes the nature of his ministry among the Thessalonians: *Mnēmoneuete gar, adelphoi, ton kopon hēmōn kai ton mochthon; nyktos kai hēmeras ergazomenoi pros to mē epibarēsai tina hymōn ekēryxamen eis hymas to euangelion tou theou* (2:9). In using the verb *ergazomai*, Paul is clearly indicating manual labor.[15] The combination of *kopos* and *mochthos* indicates that the labor was physically challenging. Used together, they suggest "fatigue and weariness, hardship and distress."[16] Paul does not underplay but in fact highlights his own manual labor in the midst of establishing his ethos. Later Paul encourages the Thessalonians to continue to live in a manner pleasing to God "as you learned from us" (4:1) and exhorts them to "work with your hands" (*ergazesthai tais* [*idias*][17] *chersin hymōn* [4:11]).[18]

Despite the generally negative attitude toward manual labor in antiquity,[19] in 1 Thessalonians Paul's language about work reflects a more positive attitude, a clear indication of where to locate the Thessalonians on the social map of antiquity. Paul's central message in 1 Thessalonians is to reaffirm for the Christians at Thessalonike that they are his "glory" and his "joy" (2:20). Throughout the letter Paul suggests that they share his own social level and are themselves [315] manual workers.[20] To be placed in such a low-ranking category as manual worker, if one occupied a higher

14. See Lyons, *Pauline Autobiography*, 189-201, for a detailed examination.

15. LSJ, *s.v.*

16. Collins, *Birth of the New Testament*, 11. They also suggest that the labor continued for some time, certainly longer than the three-week stay indicated by Acts 17.

17. The word *idias* is omitted in a number of important manuscripts but included in others. The omission in the original would not much affect the meaning of the phrase.

18. In doing so he uses a phrase similar to that of 1 Cor 4:12, where he states that he worked with his own hands (*ergazomenoi tais idiais chersin*). However, there is a difference in the two uses. In 1 Cor 4:12 Paul's handwork is linked to his hardships as an apostle and serves as a contrast to the Corinthians' claim to wisdom and riches. In 1 Thessalonians Paul is not contrasting the recipients with himself.

19. Hock, *Social Context*, 36; cf. Joshel, *Work*, 63-69; Garnsey, "Non-slave Labour," 35; MacMullen, *Roman Social Relations*, 138-41, esp. 114-16; Grant, *Early Christianity*, 81.

20. Those who also understand the Thessalonians to be manual workers include Rigaux, *Thessaloniciens*, 521; Best, *Thessalonians*, 176; Hock, *Social Context*, 42-47; Meeks, *First Urban Christians*, 64-65; Jewett, *Thessalonian Correspondence*, 120-21; Russell, "Idle in 2 Thess 3.6-12," 111-12; Schollgen, "Hausgemeinden," 76; Kloppenborg, "ΦΙΛΑΔΕΛΦΙΑ," 267; Murphy-O'Connor, *Paul*, 117; Fatum, "Brotherhood in Christ," 184; de Vos, *Church and Community Conflicts*, 154. Contra Barclay, "Conflict in Thessalonica," 519.

rank, would represent not praise but denigration and dishonor—certainly it would be grounds to reject Paul and his message. In fact, it would represent a challenge to one's honor that could not go unanswered; Paul would not gain friends but would make enemies with such bold claims if they were being made among the elite. For Paul's rhetoric to work the Thessalonians must be among the lower-ranking persons of ancient society. That Paul does not disparage but rather commends work confirms that the Thessalonians are manual workers.[21]

Presumably Paul and the Thessalonians worked at the same trade, or at least at trades within the same general area, thus facilitating contact between Paul and the Thessalonians. And it was while at work that Paul preached the gospel and presumably made his initial converts. Thus, the core of the Thessalonian community comprised handworkers who shared Paul's trade. Unfortunately, Paul does not state the nature of his manual labor in 1 Thessalonians or elsewhere. Acts 18:3, however, suggests that Paul was a *skēnopoios*.[22] This word has a basic meaning of "tentmaker,"[23] but since tents were made primarily of leather, it could indicate that Paul was more generally a leatherworker.[24] As an itinerant worker, Paul probably worked in one of the local shops at Thessalonike. Since Paul was there "night and day," presumably he would have used the opportunity to share his gospel message with fellow workers and customers, the former being the most likely candidates for proselytizing.[25] Such workers were probably already involved in some form of voluntary association. [316]

THE THESSALONIANS AS A VOLUNTARY ASSOCIATION

Voluntary associations—groups of men, women, or both, who gathered together regularly as a result of some shared interest—were widespread throughout Greco-Roman antiquity.[26] There were two primary types of

---

21. One could also point to Paul's other references to work within the letter: 1:3; 3:2, 5; 5:3, 12; see further Ascough, "Voluntary Associations," 78–81.

22. According to Lüdemann (*Early Christianity*, 198), Acts 18:2–3 and Paul's connection in Corinth with Aquila and Priscilla is "a singular and quite untendentious report" suggesting that the tradition of Paul the *skēnopoios* is fairly reliable.

23. LSJ, *s.v.*

24. Hock, *Social Context*, 20–21, 72. Cf. Forbes, *Ancient Technology*, 58–66.

25. See de Vos, *Church and Community Conflicts*, 153 n. 110. On Paul's use of the workshop in his mission strategy see further Hock, "Workshop," 438–43; also Collins, *Birth of the New Testament*, 13–14.

26. For further details see Ascough, *What Are They Saying about the Formation of*

associations.[27] Religious associations organized themselves around the veneration of a particular deity or deities and attracted adherents from the various strata of society. Professional associations were more homogeneous, attracting members from within a single profession or related professions.[28]

Unlike the paucity of evidence for synagogues, there is significant evidence for voluntary associations in Macedonia during the formative period of early Christianity.[29] Inscriptions concerning voluntary associations have been found ranging from Kalliani and Stobi in the south and north of the western part of the province respectively to Philippi and its surrounding villages in the eastern part of the province. The existence of voluntary associations is not limited to urban areas. Although most of the inscriptions come from cities (especially Thessalonike, Philippi, and Edessa), there are a number of inscriptions from smaller villages, particularly those around Philippi (Reussilova, Proussotchani, Alistrati, Podgora, Kalambaki, Raktcha, and Selian). Most of the inscriptions date to the Common Era, with a number from the first and early second century.[30]

There is quite a diversity in terms of the function of each association, the deity worshiped, the name of either the association or the associates, and the [317] type of officials in the association. The members are generally from the lower ranks of society, and in a number of cases are artisans and merchants.[31] Since this is similar to the social location we suggested for

---

Pauline Churches?, 74–79. For a more detailed overview see Kloppenborg, "Collegia and *Thiasoi*"; or Schmeller, *Hierarchie und Egalität*, 19–53. A survey of the use of associations in understanding Pauline Christian communities can be found in Ascough, *What Are They Saying about the Formation of Pauline Churches?*, 71–94.

27. A third type, funerary associations, is often identified. However, Kloppenborg has cogently argued that associations formed solely for the burial of members did not exist until the second century CE (from the time of Hadrian and beyond); "Collegia and *Thiasoi*," 20–22; cf. Ziebarth, *Das griechische Vereinswesen*, 17; Poland, *Geschichte des griechischen Vereinswesens*, 56, 503–04; Fraser, *Rhodian Funerary Monuments*, 58–70. In fact, even at that time they were a "legal fiction," a way of gaining legal recognition to meet as a group while another purpose (usually social) was the primary interest of the group. Nevertheless, many associations did include the proper burial of their members as one of their benefits (Kloppenborg, "Collegia and *Thiasoi*," 21).

28. Kloppenborg, "Collegia and *Thiasoi*," 24.

29. For details see Ascough, "Voluntary Associations," 297–308 and especially the seventy-five Macedonian voluntary association inscriptions transcribed and translated in Appendix 1.

30. Examples from Thessalonike include IG X/2.1 67; 71; 72; 259; 68; 255; 58; 503; Voutiras, "Berufs-und Kultverein," 87–96.

31. An association of purple-dyers is found at Thessalonike (IG X/2.1 291) and perhaps Philippi (Pilhofer, *Philippi*, 179–82). Also at Thessalonike is an association of yoke makers (Horsley, *New Documents* 4, 215 no. 17). Associations of donkey-drivers are found at Beroea (Woodward, "Inscriptions from Beroea," 155 no. 22), coppersmiths at

the members of the Thessalonian Christian community, we are in a strong position to read 1 Thessalonians in light of the data from the voluntary associations to note similarities and differences between these Macedonian Christian communities and voluntary associations.

Officials and Their Titles

Within the Macedonian voluntary association inscriptions a number of different officials are attested, although there is no consistency in the terms used for these officials.[32] Turning to 1 Thessalonians, we note that there is clearly some leadership in the Thessalonian Christian community. Paul makes reference to unnamed leaders by encouraging the Thessalonians *eidenai tous kopiōntas en hymin kai proïstamenous hymōn en kyriō kai nouthetountas hymas kai hēgeisthai autous hyperekperissou en agapē dia to ergon autōn* (5:12-13). Paul uses a general designation for such leaders as those who are "over" others (*proïstēmi*), indicating a group of persons who have a special function within the congregation.[33] [318]

Paul refers to one of the responsibilities of these leaders by using the cognate verb of *kopos* The noun occurs twice elsewhere in the letter, once for Paul's manual labor among the Thessalonians (2:9) and once for his work at the formative stages of the community (3:5). It is likely that the leaders at Thessalonike continued with both kinds of activity, manual labor alongside community members and the labor of community formation.[34] If so, the leaders of the Thessalonians are like the leaders of many voluntary associations. They are chosen from within the association itself and carry on

---

Amphipolis (SIG³ 1140), and silversmiths at Kalambaki (Salač, "Inscriptions du Pange," 78 no. 39). See further Ascough, "Voluntary Associations," 301-5.

32. For example, *archisynagōgos* (IG X/2.1 288; 289), *grammateus* (IG X/2.1 288; 289), *archimagareus* (IG X/2.1 65), *epimelētēs* (IG X/2.1 288), *archōn* (IG X/2.1 58), *archinakoros* (IG X/2.1 244; 220; 65; 220), *hydroskopos* (IG X/2.1 503), *galaktēphoros* (IG X/2.1 65), *kistaphorēsasan* (IG X/2.1 65). This diversity is typical for associations generally; see Kloppenborg, "Edwin Hatch," 232.

33. Rigaux, *Thessaloniciens*, 576-78; Best, "Bishops and Deacons," 372; cf. Laub, "Gemeindegründer," 33; Hainz, *Ekklesia*, 38-39. Wanamaker's suggestion (*Thessalonians*, 193; also Jewett, *Thessalonian Correspondence*, 103) that they are patrons and exercise authority by virtue of their wealth is unlikely, as they are not named and thus not honored (unlike the other illustrations he uses). Further, such patronage is discouraged in 1 Thess 4:9-12. The designation *ho proestōs* can be used as a title, as is found in an inscription from an association (*symbōsis*) of male worshippers of the Dioscurü:———— *kai tē Dioskouritōn symbiōsei andrōn, prosestōtos Telesphoriōnos, grammateyontos Aklēpaiou* (CIG 3540, Pergamum; Ellis, *Pauline Theology*, 135).

34. Not simply "Christian" *kopos*, as Hainz (*Ekklesia*, 43-44) seems to suggest.

with their everyday tasks as workers while having some authority in official meetings of the association. Referring to these leaders in his letter reflects a willingness on Paul's part to allow his Christian communities to develop locally and without a preconceived notion of church leadership imposed on them.[35] That the leaders in the community are unnamed does not indicate that Paul does not know them so much as that the leadership positions might have rotated on a monthly or yearly basis, as was common in the associations. Paul leaves them unnamed so that the general exhortation will be applicable to any who are in a position of leadership.[36]

Internal Relationships

Locating the Thessalonian Christian community in the context of the voluntary associations helps explain Paul's injunction that the Thessalonians *noutheteite tous ataktous* (5:14).[37] *Ataktos* and its cognates can have various meanings including "moral wrongdoing," "idleness from work," and "disorderliness."[38] Some commentators understand *ataktos* in 1 Thess 5:14 to mean "lazy" or "idle" (that is, those who will not work) based on Paul's injunction in 4:11 and references to the idle in 2 Thess 3:6-11.[39] If this is the case, then it is clear that Paul is writing to those whom others in the group could reasonably expect to be working, namely, other workers. Thus, it fits well within the context of a workers' association, particularly those of the same trade (and perhaps even the same workshop), for whom the lack of a number of fellow workers [319] would require increased output on their behalf and would certainly strain community relations.

A number of scholars, however, understand *ataktos* to indicate undisciplined or disorderly actions or persons.[40] The word was used for "standing

---

35. Laub, "Gemeindegründer," 32.

36. See Laub, who points out that Paul does not address the leaders directly but addresses the entire community ("Gemeindegründer," 32-33); also Hainz, *Ekklesia*, 47.

37. Paul also singles out the "fainthearted" and the "weak" as being in need of special attention.

38. See LSJ, *s.v.*; Moulton and Milligan, *Vocabulary*, 89; cf. Spicq, "Thessaloniciens," 1-8.

39. Milligan, *Thessalonians*, 152-54; Frame, *Thessalonians*, 196-97; Neil, *Thessalonians*, 124; Best, *Thessalonians*, 230 (who seems uncertain); Bruce, *Thessalonians*, 122-23; Wanamaker, *Thessalonians*, 196-97; Williams, *Thessalonians*, 96-97.

40. Plummer, *Second Epistle to the Thessalonians*, 94; Rigaux, *Thessaloniciens*, 582-83; Marshall, *Thessalonians*, 150; Jewett, *Thessalonian Correspondence*, 104-15; Collins, *Birth of the New Testament*, 94; Richard, *Thessalonians*, 270. A close connection was often made between laziness and disorderliness, so the term might indicate both.

against the order or nature of God" and in military contexts of those who would not follow commands or who broke rank.[41] The use in 1 Thessalonians suggests to some commentators that some of the Thessalonian Christians have given up working and are trespassing social boundaries because they perceive the parousia to be near.[42] Robert Jewett suggests that they are "obstinate resisters of authority" and turns to 2 Thess 3:6–15 to suggest that they have also given up their occupations and are relying on other members of the congregation for support.[43] He is correct that "there is no evidence in this passage that the motivation of their behavior was laziness," a false inference, he suggests, from Paul's own example of his self-sufficiency.[44] However, Jewett does not make a strong case that the *ataktoi* are directly challenging the leadership of the Christian community, an inference based on military contexts.[45]

In almost all of the interpretations of this passage the eschatological context of 1 Thess 5:1–11 determines for the interpreter whom Paul addresses as the *ataktoi* in 1 Thess 5:14, although almost universally 2 Thessalonians is immediately introduced into the argument.[46] The context of 1 Thess 5:12–22, however, and the shift in 5:11 from the *probatio* to the *peroratio*, means that Paul's preceding discussion of eschatology need not frame the discussion of the *ataktoi* in 1 Thess 5:14.[47] In fact, 1 Thess 5:12–22 seems to be concerned with internal community relationships, and one cannot simply bracket out the *ataktoi* as a separate problem. They are part of Paul's concern that the mem[320]bers of the community coexist well together, encourage one another (5:11, 14, including the leaders 5:12), are

---

41. Plummer, *Second Epistle to the Thessalonians*, 94; Jewett, *Thessalonian Correspondence*, 104.

42. Marxsen, *Thessalonicher*, 71; Jewett, *Thessalonian Correspondence*, 104–5.

43. Jewett, *Thessalonian Correspondence*, 105.

44. Jewett, *Thessalonian Correspondence*, 105.

45. The best evidence comes from the reference in 5:12 to leaders who admonish the Thessalonians (*nouthetountas hymas*) and the injunction that the Thessalonians admonish (*noutheteite*) the *ataktoi* in 5:14 (not mentioned by Jewett). However, this is tenuous at best, and Paul's words in both verses need to be seen as directed to the congregation as a whole. The first reference need not indicate that the function of the leaders is to admonish the idle.

46. See Richard, *Thessalonians*, 270. For a survey of the various positions see Jewett, *Thessalonian Correspondence*, 135–47. Jewett himself assumes that apocalypticism is the dominant theme not only of the letter but within the congregation. However, this is based more on his reading of 2 Thessalonians, which he understands to be authentic.

47. The same is true of 2 Thess 3:6–13.

considerate of others (the "fainthearted," "weak"), and worship God properly, in a context not of personal piety but of communal piety (5:16–22).

With this communal context in mind, we turn again to the voluntary associations.[48] A number of inscriptions show that the voluntary associations often struggled with the problem of disorderly behavior, so much so that legislation was introduced to limit it, and fines and corporal punishment were used to enforce the legislation. For example, the second-century CE rule of the *Iobacchoi* (IG II^2 1368; Athens) uses the verb *atakteō*, a synonym of *atakteō*,[49] of those who disrupt a meeting:

> If anyone begins a fight or if someone is found disorderly (*eurethē tis akosmōn*), or if someone comes and sits in someone else's seat or is insulting or abuses someone else . . . the one who committed the insult or the abuse shall pay to the association 25 drachmae and the one who was the cause of the fight shall pay the same 25 drachmae or not come to any more meetings of the Iobakchoi until he pays. (lines 72–83)

In lines 136–146 *akosmeō* is used again in a similar context. Anyone who causes a disturbance at a meeting is indicated by an official through the touch of a thyros and is signaled to leave the feast. Should one so designated refuse to leave, a special category of "bouncers" (*hippoi*) was in place to remove such persons physically, who then also became liable to the same punishment stipulated earlier for those who fight.

In the regulations of the mysteries of Andania (IG V/1 1390 [96 BCE]) is a section titled "Concerning the Disorderly" (*akosmountōn*), which reads:

[321]

---

48. De Vos links the use of *ataktoi* to voluntary associations (*Church and Community Conflicts*, 157–73, esp. 166–68), but does so in terms of associations involved in civil disobedience as a response to repression, not in terms of internal disruptions within the group itself. However, the evidence for professional associations undertaking civil action is quite limited; see Fisher, "Roman Associations," 1222; Kloppenborg, "Collegia and *Thiasoi*," 19–20.

49. That *atakteō* and *akosmeō* can be used synonymously can be seen in Suidas's *Lexicon* entry for *akosma*, which lists simply "*aprepē, atakta*." Plutarch uses the cognates synonymously in describing the universe, noting that there is nothing *atakton oud' akatakosmēton* ("unplaced or unorganized") left over to crash into the existing worlds (*Def. Orac.* 424 A [LCL]). In describing one who must evidence repentance, Philo notes that a person must avoid "great gatherings" (*tous tōn pollōn thiasous*) since "a crowd (*ochlos*) is another name for everything that is disorderly (*atakton*), indecorous (*akosmon*), discordant (*plēmmeles*), culpable (*upaition*)" (*Praem. Poen.* 20 [LCL]). When writing of matter and its relationship to God, Origen refers at one point to matter being in a state of confusion and disorder (*hēn de ataktos hē hylē kai akosmētos*, *Philocal.* 24.1), using the words as synonyms.

> And whenever the sacrifices and mysteries are celebrated, let everyone keep silent and listen to the things announced. And let the officers flog the disobedient and those who live indecently and prevent them from (participating) in the mysteries. (lines 39-41)

Such inscriptions give some indication of the type of disturbances that could occur at a meeting (fighting, disruptions of order and ceremony, abuse of others), along with guidance on how to deal with such (fines and floggings).[50] We agree with Jewett and others that *ataktoi* indicates that some in the Thessalonian Christian community are disorderly. However, this is not a challenge to the leadership from a breakaway group but involves disruptions and disturbances in the context of worship.[51] Paul's injunction "see that none of you repays evil for evil, but always seek to do good to one another and to all," following his "be patient with them all" (including the *ataktoi*) indicates that verbal admonishing should suffice to stem disorderliness, rather than fines and flogging.

In 1 Thess 4:11 Paul encourages the Thessalonians *philotimeisthai hēsychazein*. In doing so he uses a term frequent in voluntary association inscriptions, but he gives it a different nuance. The verb *philotimeomai* and the cognate noun *philotimia* are often used in the voluntary association inscriptions in contexts not of "living quietly" but of competition between members. *Philotimeomai* and *philotimia* are most often used for the competition and rivalry for honor within the group itself.[52] [322] The quest for

---

50. See also CIL XIV 2112; P.Mich 243; P.Lond. 2710. In Macedonia gymnasiarchal law from Beroea (Cormack, "Gymnasiarchal Law") legislates against disobedient, unruly behavior using the word *atakteō* (cf. Horsley, *New Documents* 4, 104). From Amphipolis a fragment of a military code from ca. 200 BCE seems to refer to the need to control soldiers who are intent on looting (SEG 40 [1990] no. 524 frag. A, col. 2, lines. 1-3; cf. Spicq, "Thessaloniciens," 6 and nn. 2-3).

51. See Spicq, "Thessaloniciens," 11-12; Reicke, "Thessalonicherbriefe," 851-53. Reicke also connects the *ataktoi* to the associations but does so in the context of their eschatological enthusiasm (*Schwärmerei*), and particularly Paul's reference to "drinking" in 1 Thess 5:7 (Reicke, *Diakonie*, 242-43, 247). He moves quickly to emphasize that the *ataktoi* were also lazy and living the "parasitic" life, drawing almost immediately upon 2 Thess 3:6-16 (pp. 243-44). He concludes, "dass die soziale Unordnung in Thessalonich ein Ausdruck der eschatologischen überspanntheit war, oder der Schwärmerei" (p. 245). Later in the same work Reicke details the community problems encountered in the associations (pp. 321-38) but does not tie it in explicitly to his earlier discussion of Paul's Christian communities ("Zum Teil fällt das Licht rückwärts auf die oben behandelten paulinischen Briefe" [p. 338]).

52. See Klopppenborg, "Egalitarianism," 258. *Philotimia* can also be used to describe the benefaction itself; see IG II², 1292 (Attica, third century BCE), where crowns are awarded to the treasurer and secretary of the association of Sarapistai "so that there will be a rivalry among everyone to strive for honor" ([e]*phamillon hēi to* [*eis a*]*utous philo*[*tieisthai*]); cf. IG II² 1314 (Piraeus, 213/212 BCE); 1315 (Piraeus, 211/210 BCE);

honors was promoted as a means to encourage members to contribute more and more lavishly to the social practices of the association. For example, in IG II² 1263 (Piraeus, 300 BCE) the secretary of an association is honored with the erection of a statue, "so that also the others shall be zealous for honor (*philotimōntai*) among the members, knowing that they will receive thanks from the members deserving of benefaction."[53] In the second century CE at Athens an association of male friends (*eranon synagon philoi andres*) proclaimed, "Let the association increase by zeal for honor" (*auxanetō d[e] ho eranos epi philoteimiais* [IG II² 1369]). For Paul, in contrast, the "quest for honor" is found in a community of mutual coexistence, not a life of competition with one another for honor.[54]

Thus, although there are some similarities between the Thessalonian Christian community and the voluntary associations, Paul also reflects a desire for a community ethos different from that found in the associations. Yet it is still significant that Paul uses voluntary association language to produce this different community ethos. Paul uses association language self-consciously to encourage a different type of social control (without fines or floggings). This suggests that the Thessalonian Christian community shares the same discursive field as the associations and is best placed within that field. That is, despite these differences in community relationships, they are still analogous to the voluntary associations.

FURTHER IMPLICATIONS FOR COMMUNITY STRUCTURE

The context of the voluntary associations raises an intriguing possibility concerning Paul's comments in 1 Thess 1:9b, where he conveys to the Thessalonians the report that he has heard about them from others; *pōs epestrepsate pros ton theon apo tōn eidolon douleuein theō zōnti kai alēthinō*.[55]

IG XII/5, 606 (Ceos, III BCE); IDelos 1519 (153/152 BCE).

53. "*Hopōs an pasin paneron tois boulomenois philotimeisthai peri to hieron hoti ti mēthēsontai kat' axian hekastos hōn an euergetēsei tous thiasōntas*" (lines 27–31; cf. IG II² 1271 [a *thiasos* of Piraeus, 298/297 BCE]; 1273.A [a *thiasos* in Piraeus, 222/221 BCE]; 1277 [a *koinon* in Athens, 278/277 BCE]; 1292 [a *koinon* in Athens, ca. 250 BCE].

54. Contra the usual understanding of 1 Thess 4:11 as referring to individuals who should not rely on the support of others in the church: Milligan, *Thessalonians*, 55; Frame, *Thessalonians*, 163; Plummer, *First Thessalonians*, 66; Neil, *Thessalonians*, 87–88; Best, *Thessalonians*, 177–78; Bruce, *Thessalonians*, 91–93; Wanamaker, *Thessalonians*, 164; Williams, *Thessalonians*, 78.

55. *Pōs* should be taken not as "how" (that is, not as a description of the method of their becoming Christian) but as "that" (indicative of their having done so) (Best,

Most interpreters of 1 Thessalonians seem to understand the second-person plural in 1:9b as a reference to individual conversion experiences initiated by Paul's [323] preaching.[56] *Epistrephō* literally means "to turn" or "to turn back." It can be used with an ethical sense of obligation to do something that one has been asked or required to do (which can be acted upon or ignored)[57] or in the religious sense of turning to a deity.[58] In the LXX it is found particularly in the phrase *epistrephein . . . kyrion* (*theon*). Although it is rare in Paul, he does use it for conversion experiences in 2 Cor 3:16 (turning to the Lord, a citation from Exod 34:34) and in Gal 4:9 (for Christians turning back to idols). The word *epistrephō* "is a suitable word to express the change from one faith to another."[59]

Thus, it is possible that Paul is referring to the collective experience of an already-formed group of Thessalonians.[60] If Paul did preach among workers of the same trade (as we have suggested), they were undoubtedly part of a professional association of handworkers of the same trade and were thus involved in idolatrous worship.[61] Rather than envision a scenario in which a number of individuals were converted by Paul over time, a picture encouraged by the usual reading of Acts, we could imagine that over time Paul manages to persuade the members of the existing professional association to switch their allegiance from their patron deity or deities "to serve a living and true God."[62] In [324] this case 1 Thess 1:9b would be better paraphrased "you all turned (collectively) to God from idols."

Thessalonians, 81–82).

56. I found no instances in which this was explicitly expressed, but it was certainly implied in the comments of many exegetes, esp. Perkins, "1 Thessalonians," 325–34. Some, such as Williams (Thessalonians, 33, 35), suggest that a confirmation of the Acts account can be found here, thus indicating individual conversions. Holtz (Thessalonicher, 62) suggests that one can see behind 1:9 a mission sermon with an emphasis on monotheism like that in Joseph and Aseneth, a text that focuses on the conversion of an individual.

57. See Moulton and Milligan, *Vocabulary*, 246; cf. Bertram, "ἐπιστρέφω," 722–23.

58. Bertram, "ἐπιστρέφω," 722–25; Richard, *Thessalonians*, 53.

59. Best, *Thessalonians*, 82. For individual conversions see, e.g., Acts 3:19; 11:21; 14:15; 15:19; 26:18. A collective conversion might be envisioned in Acts 9:35: "all the residents of Lydda and Sharon saw him, and they turned (*epestrepsan*) to the Lord."

60. Collins notes that in 1 Thess 1:6 [sic, for 1:7] Paul calls the Thessalonians an example (singular) to other churches, indicating that "it is not the believing individuals as such who are cited as examples for the believers of the Grecian provinces, rather it is the belief of the church as such which is exemplary" (Collins, *Studies*, 295).

61. In antiquity the word *idol* does not always carry such a pejorative sense and was used often by Gentiles to describe that upon which they focused their worship as an "image" (LSJ, *s.v.*; Moulton and Milligan, *Vocabulary*, 183; Büchsel, "εἴδωλον," 375–77).

62. The transformation of an existing trade association at Thessalonike is suggested

The introduction of a new deity to a collective, family-based and/or guild-based association is attested in a few cases in antiquity (e.g., SIG^3 985; IG X/2.1 255). However, old allegiances die hard, and it would take some time for former patron deities to be replaced by a new deity, if ever, since in associations there would be no need for an exclusive switch—more than one deity could be worshiped. For this reason there is no clear example of a voluntary association converting to the worship of a new deity accompanied by the disregarding of earlier allegiances. That the Thessalonians have done so stands out as unique—perhaps this is the reason they have been noted among other believers and that they have become a paradigm for imitation (1 Thess 1:7–9).

We may also explain the lack of analogues in antiquity as a result of the aggressive missionary impulse of Pauline Christianity, with its monotheistic demands, being a unique feature in antiquity—other groups were not concerned with converting individuals or groups.[63] Groups that did undertake the worship of another god often broke away from earlier deities slowly, as they were not faced with the same monotheistic demands that Paul's Christianity brought with it. While it is true that the text does not indicate the turning of an entire group to the veneration of Jesus, neither does it indicate what is assumed by most: individual conversions. The possibility of a group conversion should not be discounted too quickly.

Another intriguing possibility arises from the suggestion that the Thessalonian Christian community was formed as a professional association of handworkers, perhaps tentmakers or leatherworkers. If this were the case, we would expect that the group would be composed primarily of males, since women would not be members of an association of artisans in a trade dominated by males,[64] even if they worked in the same occupation.[65] Most

---

by Kloppenborg ("ΦΙΛΑΔΕΛΦΙΑ," 276; cf. Kloppenborg, "Edwin Hatch," 235), although he does not pursue this idea; cf. Evans, "Eschatology and Ethics," 89. Others who assume that the Thessalonians are a voluntary association include Fatum, "Brotherhood in Christ," passim; Ehrman, *New Testament: Historical Introduction* (1997, 1st ed.) 263 (although he also ties the community structure to the synagogue); de Vos, *Church and Community Conflicts*, 164. De Vos suggests that "to the average Thessalonian, the Christian community probably would have resembled a *thiasos*" (*Church and Community Conflicts*, 153 n. 110), but he does not explore the details of the connections outside of civic disruptions by associations. He does allow for Kloppenborg's suggestion of a "converted trade *thiasos*."

63. Goodman, *Mission and Conversion*; McKnight, *Light among the Gentiles*; summarized in Ascough, "Voluntary Associations," 158–61.

64. Waltzing, *Etude Historique*, 1.348; Whelan, "Amica Pauli," 75–76; Schmeller, *Hierarchie und Egalität*, 48; Kloppenborg, "Collegia and *Thiasoi*," 25.

65. Pomeroy, *Goddesses*, 201. Women could serve as patrons of all-male guilds, although they did not participate in them (see Kloppenborg, "Collegia and *Thiasoi*," 25; Whelan, "Arnica Pauli," 76). Honorifics given to a woman patron by an association

inter[325]preters do not read 1 Thessalonians this way, but rather see the group as including both men and women.[66]

However, there are some indications in 1 Thessalonians that the community is made up primarily of men. Clearly, there is no indication of women in the community, and no advice is given to women, children, or families. Most telling, however, is Paul's command to each member of the community: *eidenai hekaston hymōn to eautou skeuos ktasthai en agiasmōn kai timē, mē en pathei epithymias kathaper kai ta ethnē ta mē eidota ton theon, to mē hyperbainein kai pleonektein en tō pragmati ton adelphon autou* (4:4-6). This passage has created much difficulty for commentators. Any interpretation rests on the precise meaning of *skeuos* in the context of this passage.[67] Quite literally the word means "vessel, tool, utensil"[68] but is probably being used euphemistically by Paul. Three suggestions have been put forth: "wife,"[69] "body,"[70] and "male genitalia."

This latter position is summarized by Wanamaker: "It seems better to understand *skeuos* as connoting the human body in its sexual aspect, that is, as [326] a euphemism for the genitalia."[71] This is how it is used as a transla-

---

do not necessarily indicate that she is a member in the association (Waltzing, *Etude Historique*, 1:349).

66. This is particularly obvious in newer works, which tend to translate *adelphos* inclusively as "brothers and sisters"; see NRSV; Hainz, *Ekklesia*, 41 n. 5, 45; McGehee, "Rejoinder"; Richard, *Thessalonians*, 128, and passim; Lührmann, "Beginnings," 247. I have little doubt that Paul elsewhere uses *adelphos* inclusively, and I support such translations; however, for the reasons given below *adelphos* is better translated as "brothers" in 1 Thessalonians.

67. Although this is not the only problem in the passage; see Collins, *Studies*, 299.

68. LSJ, *s.v.*

69. Reading "to take a wife for himself" (RSV). So Best, *Thessalonians*, 161-62; also Frame, *Thessalonians*, 149-50; Maurer, "σκεῦος," 365-67; Meeks, *First Urban Christians*, 228 n. 130; Collins, *Studies*, 313; Yarbrough, *Not Like the Gentiles*, 69-73; Holtz, *Thessalonicher*, 157-58; Malherbe, *Paul and the Thessalonians*, 51. See further those cited in Collins, *Studies*, 311-12. Bassler uses 1 Cor 7:36-38 as background and suggests that in 1 Thess 4:4 *skeuos* refers to a virgin and indicates that the Thessalonians should stay celibate, even if betrothed to another (Bassler, "Modest Proposal," 61).

70. Reading "to gain mastery over his body" (NEB; NIV). So Plummer, *First Thessalonians*, 59-60; Dibelius, *Thessalonicher*, 21; Neil, *Thessalonians*, 79-80; Rigaux, *Thessaloniciens*, 504-6; Morris, *Thessalonians*, 124; Marxsen, *Thessalonicher*, 60-61; Richard, *Thessalonians*, 198 (Morris, Marxsen, and Richard also note the suggestion of sexual control); McGehee, "Rejoinder." See also the list in Collins, *Studies*, 312.

71. Wanamaker, *Thessalonians*, 152. Cf. BAGD, *s.v.* So also Reese, *1 and 2 Thessalonians*, 44; Whitton, "Neglected Meaning," 142-143; Bruce, *Thessalonians*, 83; Marshall, *1 and 2 Thessalonians*, 108-109; Williams, *Thessalonians*, 72 (cautiously); and especially Donfried, "Cults of Thessalonica," 341-42; and Elgvin, "'To Master His Own Vessel,'" who suggests that this interpretation "has not been persuasive."

tion for *kly* in the LXX of 1 Sam 21:5, where David assures the priest of Nob that "the young men's vessels are holy" in response to a question about whether they have kept themselves from women.[72] It is also attested in such uses in nonbiblical Greek.[73]

The passage itself is clearly placed in the context of sexual misconduct, with Paul enclosing his words with references not only to *agiasmos* (4:3, 7) but also to *porneia* (4:3) and *akatharsia* (4:7), the latter two terms often used in contexts of sexual immorality.[74] Karl Paul Donfried places the text within the larger cultic context of Thessalonike:

> All of this suggests that Paul is very deliberately dealing with a situation of grave immorality, not too dissimilar to the cultic temptations of Corinth. Thus, Paul's severe warnings in this section, using the weightiest authorities he possibly can, is intended to distinguish the behavior of the Thessalonian Christians from their former heathen and pagan life which is still much alive in the various cults of the city.[75]

The interpretation of *skeuos* as "genitalia" seems to be the one that best takes account of the textual data.[76] However, one cannot simply assume that although the pronouns used are masculine, the instruction to control (*ktasthai*) the genitalia "would apply equally to women."[77] The understanding of sexuality in antiquity seems to mitigate this. In the understanding of the ancients' "ideology of sexual hierarchy," it was assumed that "at the masculine end of the scale stood strength and control, at the feminine end weakness and vulnerability."[78] As Dale Martin points out with respect to 1 Cor 7:36–38,

> Paul's exclusive address to the young man thus reveals his assumption of the male-female hierarchy of strength. He addresses the one who has power, the [327] man, and delegates to him the responsibility for doing what needs to be done in the woman's best interest (at least according to Paul's point of view).

---

72. See Bruce, *Thessalonians*, 83.

73. See Maurer, "σκεῦος," 359; BAGD, *s.v.*

74. Murphy-O'Connor, *Paul*, 125; Donfried, "Cults of Thessalonica," 341; cf. Fatum, "Brotherhood in Christ," 189.

75. Donfried, "Cults of Thessalonica," 341–42.

76. Yet it is clear that each of the options has problems; see Collins, *Studies*, 299, 314.

77. Wanamaker, *Thessalonians*, 153.

78. Martin, *Corinthian Body*, 226–27.

The weaker of the two, the woman, cannot be relied upon to make a decision for herself.[79]

Women were assumed to be more easily consumed by desire and more willing to give in to it. Control in such situations rested with the male. Because of their own physiology, women lacked the ability to control their own sexual desires.[80] Thus, when Paul speaks of controlling the genitalia (*skeuos*), he would be addressing the males, who physiologically were thought to have the ability to do so.[81]

That the Thessalonian Christian community is primarily a group of males finds some support in a recent essay by Lone Fatum.[82] Fatum begins by noting that both 1 Thessalonians and the audience to which it is addressed are "defined by androcentric values and social conventions and organized in terms of the patriarchal structures so characteristic of urban society in Graeco-Roman Antiquity."[83] She uses 1 Thess 4:3-8 to show how exclusively male is Paul's exhortation in the letter. Although she understands *skeuos* as "wife," she notes that "the power to interpret gender and to administer sexuality" was "generally accepted as a male prerogative."[84]

Fatum draws back from arguing that the community was only males— "Historically we may assume, of course, as stated already, that women were among the converts in Thessalonica." She points to Acts 17:4 but immediately shows that one cannot rely on the veracity of the Acts account.[85] She reasons that women in the community are embedded in the lives of men such that when Paul addresses the Thessalonians "they are not among the brothers of Christ; individually they are not members of the new community." As such, they are "invisible in Christ," and "their socio-sexual presence among the brothers is, virtually, a non-presence."[86]

If it is the case that the Thessalonian Christian community was primarily composed of males, then this particular community was atypical among Christian communities known from Paul's letters, such as those at Corinth, Philippi, and Rome. [328]

---

79. Martin, *Corinthian Body*, 227.

80. See further the discussion in Martin, *Corinthian Body*, 219-28.

81. Dale Martin states: "With the Stoics, Paul shares the belief that the complete extirpation of desire is both possible and preferable, even within sexual relations in marriage" ("Paul without Passion," 207).

82. Fatum, "Brotherhood in Christ," 183-97.

83. Fatum, "Brotherhood in Christ," 184.

84. Fatum, "Brotherhood in Christ," 191.

85. Fatum, "Brotherhood in Christ," 192-93.

86. Fatum, "Brotherhood in Christ," 194.

CONCLUSION

In this article we have argued that the Thessalonian Christian community was similar to a professional voluntary association. To do so, we illustrated some of Paul's language in 1 Thessalonians by reference to the typicalities of association language. We saw that some of the community features of the Thessalonian Christian community find ready analogies in the voluntary associations. Overall, this helps us to understand better, and often in new ways, both Paul and his practices, and the practices and structure of the groups to which he writes. Although there is no single association inscription that has all the features of 1 Thessalonians (and thus no single association that is exactly the same), the comparative process reveals that on the social map of antiquity the type of group structure that the Thessalonians would have assumed, and the type of group that outsiders would have assumed that they were, was that of a voluntary association. That is, the Thessalonian Christians would *appear* to outsiders as a voluntary association, and they would *function* internally as one. Paul's letters show that he is aware of associations and writes within this discursive field. Although he does not disapprove of the way the Macedonian Christian communities are formed, he attempts to make strategic adjustments to how they have configured themselves. In so doing his starting point is voluntary association language.

8

Matthew and Community Formation

INTRODUCTION

DENNIS C. DULING HAS recently argued that "the Matthean *ekklēsia* can be described as a fictive kinship group or fictive brotherhood association"; that is, it is a type of voluntary association.¹ He warns that although the associa[97]tions do not explain every aspect of the Matthean group, "they explain some of its features."² In essence, I think this evaluation is correct. However, the case needs to be argued and illustrated, two tasks that Duling only partially fulfills.³ In fact, despite his description of voluntary associations, ultimately Duling finds the Jewish background and the LXX more informative for understanding the Matthean community.⁴ While it

---

1. Duling, "Matthean Brotherhood," 178, 163; cf. Malina, "Early Christian Groups," 107, 108; Duling, "Social-Scientific Small Group Research," 188.

2. Duling. "Matthean Brotherhood," 159.

3. Duling cites, but does not quote, only IG II² 1368 and CIL XIV 2112. Since the presentation of this paper, Duling has developed part of his argument in detail by showing how the group process of conflict resolution reflected in Matt 18:15–17 has parallels in, among other things, the process in the association of the Iobacchi (IG II² 1368); Duling, "Matthew 18:15–17."

4. In fact, despite suggesting that Jewish groups are voluntary associations, Duling

is true that Duling gives a brief description of Jewish groups as voluntary associations in order to justify his use of the category of association, ultimately he has not really employed the non-Jewish material in understanding the Matthean material.[5] In stating this, I would by no means deny the connection of the Matthean com[98]munity with Judaism. In this way the work of Duling is not only interesting but also compelling. However, his thesis that the Matthean community can be understood as a voluntary association can be strengthened when one takes account of a broader database of material from the associations.[6]

Duling is not the only one to understand the Matthean community as a voluntary association. This is also the assessment of Anthony J. Saldarini, who states that "within Greco-Roman society, Matthew's group would have been understood as a private, voluntary association," and it is within this social context that it must be understood.[7] He understands the Matthean group to be a "deviant association," i.e., an association that has been formed by those who have been rejected by the dominant forces in society and are attempting to defend and restore "respectability to their 'deviant' behavior."[8] He goes on to suggest that

---

still seems tied to the idea that Judaism itself was a closed system when he argues that Matthew's scribes are "marginal scribes" and that the group would be viewed as "marginal" ("Matthean Brotherhood," 178–80). Although he attempts to be more broadly based, all of his examples and arguments are grounded in the Jewish worldview. The marginality of the group is lessened when one sees the Matthean group as *yet* another variation of the voluntary associations of antiquity, no more or less marginal than the others but at the same time understanding themselves as somehow better and set apart from other groups. Even this sense of being better than another group can be seen in voluntary associations—the Iobacchi of Athens proclaim, "now we are the best of all" (IG II^2 1368). Even in his later paper ("Matthew 18:15–17"), Duling emphasizes the group at Qumran, albeit following Weinfeld (*Organizational Pattern*), in understanding the Qumran group as a voluntary association.

5. See Duling, "Matthean Brotherhood," 163–64. E.g., Duling's discussion of the leadership designation of "scribe" (*grammateus*) in Matthew sees their background only in Judaism ("Matthean Brotherhood," 172–80). However, one can also note that scribes were common in non-Jewish associations; see IG II^2 1317, 1328, 1390; LSAM 3; SIG^3 1012; P.Mich. 246, 248. This same limitation is true of his discussion of "brotherhood" where all of his examples come from the synagogues ("Matthean Brotherhood," 166–71). Non-Jewish groups are only mentioned in passing.

6. Cf. Duling's own invitation ("Matthean Brotherhood," 159) for further study: "This hypothesis will have to be eventually tested with other variables in the Gospel." Cf. Duling, "Matthew 18:15–17."

7. Saldarini, *Matthew's Christian-Jewish Community*, 197; cf. 120.

8. Saldarini, *Matthew's Christian-Jewish Community*, 111; cf. Saldarini, "Gospel of Matthew," 54.

> Matthew's community engages in many of the functions of a deviant association. It recruits members, develops a coherent world view and belief system, articulates an ideology and rhetoric to sustain its behavior, and attacks competing social institutions and groups. The formation of such a voluntary association requires adjustment to a new situation, the need to assign new community functions and status rankings, and the creation of new community goals. All of these activities are carried out in the narrative through the sermons and teachings of Jesus.[9]

Yet in his comparison of voluntary associations and the Matthean group, Saldarini fails to note significant differences along with the similarities. [99] For example, he suggests that active membership in an association "depends on feelings of solidarity with other members of the group"[10] and suggests that disputes among members would break down relationships and threaten the survival of the group. Yet, as we shall show below, the inscriptional record reveals that association members were highly agonistic, and competition among members was often encouraged in group legislation, a marked difference from the Matthean group.

A third voice which may be added to this understanding is that of Michael H. Crosby, who argues that household-based, nonhierarchical voluntary associations are reflected in the house church envisioned by Matthew.[11] Crosby provides the most information about how Matthew's group could be understood as a voluntary association although, like Duling and Saldarini, he relies primarily upon secondary works rather than illustrating his points from primary data. Furthermore, he emphasizes the egalitarian nature of the associations and suggests that the Matthean community builds upon this "potential threat to the status quo of patriarchy" by being even more inclusive.[12] While I would affirm the sense that the Matthean community is striving to be more egalitarian in outlook,[13] I would question Crosby's initial assumption about the egalitarian nature of the associations.[14] In fact, with a

---

9. Saldarini, *Matthew's Christian-Jewish Community*, 112; cf. Saldarini, "Gospel of Matthew," 55. It is unclear whether Saldarini means to indicate that all voluntary associations in antiquity were deviant associations or whether this is a subtype of associations. If the former, then this can be called into question. If the latter, he needs to show examples of such from antiquity and how they are defined as "deviant" against their wider Greco-Roman context.

10. Saldarini, *Matthew's Christian-Jewish Community*, 103.

11. Crosby, *House of Disciples*, 104–10; cf. 29–31.

12. Crosby, *House of Disciples*, 106; cf. 108.

13. Cf. Crosby, *House of Disciples*, 110.

14. Crosby's only evidence for this "threat to patriarchy" is his citation of Stambaugh

predominant emphasis on their own leadership structure, associations seem to have reflected *both* egalitarianism and hierarchy at the same time.

Bruce J. Malina has shown that the first three stages of community growth can be designated as community formation, community cohesion, and community regulations—what he calls "forming," "storming," and "norming."[15] Only after these stages have been completed is the group in a position to enter the "performing" stage, when group members work co- [100]operatively towards a particular goal.[16] By using this model as a framework,[17] and supplementing the work of Duling, Saldarini, and Crosby with my own work with voluntary association inscriptions, I intend to illustrate where Matthew reflects typical features of voluntary associations and where there are notable differences. Viewing the Matthean community against a wide background of associations may help us understand more clearly the dynamics of social interaction reflected in the Gospel of Matthew. Seeing some of those dynamics against the background of the associations will also help us better understand what was unique and particular about the Matthean community. In fact, this is what I find missing in the works cited above; in simply stating that the Matthean group is like the voluntary associations, they fail to engage what may be as interesting—namely, how they are distinct from the dominant ethos that pervaded the associations.[18]

Using Malina's categories, we will examine the stages of group formation, which the Matthean group seems to have passed through, and which are reflected in the Gospel text. In Matthew's redactional activity we can

---

and Balch (*New Testament*, 125), which, in my reading, does not frame the issue of egalitarianism in the associations in this way.

15. Malina, "Early Christian Groups," 103–5, drawing on Tuckman, "Development Sequence," 384–99.

16. Malina, "Early Christian Groups," 105.

17. Malina ("Early Christian Groups," 110) calls for a redoing of the Synoptic story line in light of the forming, storming, norming, performing, and adjourning model. My intent is slightly different: to reexamine the group that gave rise to one of these documents in light of the first three stages. Throughout his article, Malina applies his models to the Jesus movement and to the Pauline communities, but does not explicitly apply them to the communities behind the Gospels themselves.

18. Cf. Smith, *Drudgery Divine*, 36–53, esp. 47. This is also true of Weinfeld, *Organizatioal Patterns*, in his well-argued presentation of the similarities between the Qumran community and the voluntary associations. While Saldarini (*Matthew's Christian-Jewish Community*, 120; cf. Saldini, *Pharisees, Scribes and Sadducees*, 68) is correct in his assessment that "no generalizations about Greek associations can be used confidently to describe or define a group," it is still possible to highlight some typical features. In holding up the Matthean group against the association inscriptions, we are not arguing that they are the same as one particular association, but that they have similarities to, and marked differences from, what we can observe in the database of association inscriptions.

also see how the writer attempts to address the needs of the group[19] and thus reflects the group's self-definition and structure.[20] [101]

THE MATTHEAN COMMUNITY AS A VOLUNTARY ASSOCIATION

According to Malina, the first condition for any sort of group formation is "a culture that prepares people for group roles."[21] This indeed we have; during the first and second centuries CE there was a proliferation of smaller groups throughout the Roman Empire, so much so that few people would not have some experience of these in one form or another: philosophical schools, professional associations, religious associations, synagogues.[22] We will focus particularly on the voluntary associations, which can be defined as groups of men, women, or both, organized on the basis of freely chosen membership for a common purpose.[23] The comparison of Christian [102]

19. Barton, "Communal Dimension," 407.

20. By "structure" I imply their sense of group boundaries and means of internal cohesion; cf. Barton, "Communal Dimension," 407. Cf. Saldarini ("Jewish-Christian Conflict," 39): "the story of Jesus in Matthew reflects the experience of Matthew's community and its social situation." But see Jack Dean Kingsbury on the problem of moving from text to social situation ("Conclusion," 262).

Matthew addresses his community through his editing of the traditions that have circulated, in oral and literary form (esp. Mark and the Sayings Gospel Q; cf. LaVerdiere and Thompson, "New Testament Communities," 574). In doing so he arrives at an authoritative text for the community, and one that helps provide community definition—the Gospel of Matthew. On the question of the place of Q and Mark in the Matthean community, M. Eugene Boring suggests that they were "authoritative" texts in the Matthean community, and that the community may have been founded by one (or more) of the members of the Q community, with Mark being brought in by a group who joined at a later stage ("Convergence of Source Analysis," 587–88). This assumes that the Matthean community is distinct from the Jewish synagogues as a separate group from an early period. Yet Boring wants to view a "Yavnian" experience in 70–90 CE as a decisive moment for a breaking away of the Matthean community. This makes little sense if they already have a distinct identity with authoritative texts. My own view is that Q and Mark were used by the Matthean Jewish Christians to recall words and deeds of Jesus. Only when they formed a separate group did they need an authoritative text—the Gospel of Matthew—which incorporated the best of their stories with the community's sense of a distinct identity.

21. Malina, "Early Christian Groups," 103.

22. Cf. Malina, "Early Christian Groups," 101; see also Ascough, *What Are They Saying about the Formation of Pauline Churches?*

23. See further Ascough, *What Are They Saying about the Formation of Pauline Churches?*, 74–79; Kloppenborg, "Collegia and *Thiasoi*"; Schmeller, *Hierarchie und Egalität*, 19–53. A survey of the use of associations in understanding Pauline Christian communities can be found in Ascough, *What Are They Saying about the Formation of*

groups with the voluntary associations is warranted since associations were "concerned with the social well-being of collective selves," as were the Christian groups in antiquity.[24]

Community Formation—Forming

This is the stage in which members of the group first come together and recognize the benefits of mutual interdependence. According to Malina's model, "groups always have a purpose that consists in the perception of some needed and meaningful change."[25] For the Matthean group, the need to organize arose from the perception that the social well-being of those who identified themselves with the Messiah named Jesus was not being enhanced through continued contact with their former small group, i.e., the synagogue. Quite the opposite, in fact.[26]

The exact nature of the break between Matthew's Christian community[27] and the synagogues is a complex problem which others have sum- [103] marized more ably than I can.[28] However one understands the relationship

---

Pauline Churches?, 71–94.

24. Malina, "Early Christian Groups," 107.

25. Malina, "Early Christian Groups," 106.

26. Malina ("Early Christian Groups," 99) attributes the awareness of the need for change within all Christian groups, including Matthew's group, to an experience of the Risen Lord (citing 28:18–20). However, I would suggest that in the case of Matthew, the need for a separate group is a secondary development predicated by the conflictual situations the Jewish Christians are experiencing in the synagogue. The perception was not simply the general thought that "something was amiss with Israel" (Malina, "Early Christian Groups," 101) but the direct, negative experience of something being amiss for Christians in the synagogues.

27. Graham N. Stanton assumes that Matthew is writing to a number of communities, based on his inability to imagine that the trouble and expense of producing a well-crafted document like the Gospel of Matthew would have been deemed necessary for a single, small group: Stanton, "Revisiting Matthew's Communities," 11–12. However, we have no way of knowing the circumstances of the production of Matthew. Moreover, considerable expense went into the production of inscriptions and memorials by members of small, independent voluntary associations. At the same time, I find myself somewhat persuaded by Stanton's suggestion that the lack of specific details in the community regulations in Matthew suggests a document sent generally to a number of communities rather than to one community in a particular situation (Stanton, "Revisiting Matthew's Communities," 12). Thus, I will speak of Matthew's community (singular) but remain open to the possibility that there was a loose confederation of communities. The latter possibility does not undermine my attempt to compare the Matthean situation to the voluntary associations, as associations could have loose translocal connections; see Ascough, "Translocal Relationships" (Chapter 5, above).

28. See Senior, *Gospel of Matthew*, 7–20; Stanton, "Origin and Purpose," 1910–21;

of the *Birkat ha-minim* to early Christianity,[29] it seems certain that "Matthew was actively engaged with Jewish rivals."[30] Matthew, and those to whom he writes, were involved in conflict with members of synagogues which were in relatively close proximity to Matthew's group.[31] [104]

The recounting of the foundational stage of the newly formed Matthean community is retrojected back to the time of Jesus in the narrative. Within the larger (fourth) section of the Gospel (13:53—17:27), Matthew connects the origins of the church to the failure of Israel to accept Jesus as the Messiah.[32] Thus, this section is concerned with the founding of the *ekklēsia*. Matt 16:13-20 is central to the section, and it is here that we find the first of three uses of the term *ekklēsia*. Matthew changes the flow of his Markan source so that Peter's confession is no longer rejected or corrected but serves as a blessing in which "Peter is praised as the recipient of a divine revelation (16:17), called the foundation of the Church (16:18), and given special authority (16:19)."[33]

Stanton, "Communities of Matthew."

29. Of late many are inclined not to see the situation of the rabbis at Yavneh as a large monolithic movement in which the *Birkat ha-minim* was introduced in order to expel Christians en masse from the synagogues throughout Palestine and the Diaspora. Rather, "the Yavnean rabbis were a minority, took a long time to formulate their vision, and an even longer time to impose it, and, as a result, the *Birkat ha-minim* at first had only a marginal effect on Christians and no discernible effect on the Matthean community at all" (Wilson, *Related Strangers*, 47). See van der Horst, "Birkat ha-minim"; Aune, "Origins," 491–93; Stanton, *Studies in Matthew*, 142–45; Wilson, *Related Strangers*, 46–47.

30. Wilson, *Related Strangers*, 47; LaVerdiere and Thompson, "New Testament Communities," 572–73.

31. The synagogues themselves bear striking similarities to voluntary associations and thus can be classified as such; see Ellis, *Pauline Theology*, 122–45; Richardson, "Early Synagogues." Some of the data is briefly summarized in Duling, "Matthean Brotherhood," 163–64. From the time of Julius Caesar, the Romans probably classified synagogues as collegia (Cotter, "Collegia and Roman Law," 76–78). In discussing the Pharisees and scribes as members of a voluntary association, Saldarini (*Pharisees, Scribes and Sadducees*, 67–70; cf. 216–20) suggests that there are only very general similarities (but see 281). Gaston ("Pharisaic Problems," 99–100) moves in a similar direction but even more cautiously. On the rabbis as a collegia see Levey, "Caesarea and the Jews," 65. A number of studies have also been produced illustrating the similarities between the Qumran documents and the community associated with them and the Greco-Roman voluntary associations; see esp. Weinfeld, *Organizational Pattern*; Duling, "Matthew 18:15–17"; Walker-Ramish ("Voluntary Associations") argues against the connection.

32. Davies and Allison, *Matthew*, 2:642, 649. Davies and Allison (*Matthew*, 2:649) note that Matthew's focus on Peter seems to occur in the fourth section of the Gospel due to Matthew's ecclesiology.

33. Harrington, *Matthew*, 250. Matt 16:17-19 is a controversial passage fraught

The verses preceding 16:17-19 begin to move the reader to see Jesus in light of the great heroes of the past such as Elijah, Jeremiah, and John the Baptist. However, "it at once becomes apparent that the contrasts are greater than the similarities."[34] As the "Christ, the Son of the living God, Jesus "stands alone." His connection to God thus moves him out of the simply human realm and into the realm of the divine: a divinized hero. This is further supported by texts that refer to his special status: "he will save his people from their sins" (1:21); he is named Emmanuel, "God with us" (1:23); and a heavenly voice declares at his baptism, "This is my beloved Son, with whom I am well pleased" (3:17). Thus, Jesus is not the *human* founder of the *ekklēsia*. The foundational role belongs to Peter.[35] [105] Jesus is rather the *divine patron* of the *ekklēsia*.[36]

After the record of Peter's confession of Jesus's unique identity, Matthew expands the story by first explaining how Simon also came to be named Peter, a fact he has received from Mark (Mark 3:16). J. Andrew Overman points out that "it is Matthew who finds in this name a message

---

with exegetical difficulties (see bibliog. in Davies and Allison, *Matthew*, 2:643-47). By discussing it here I do not propose to solve all the problems, nor even to discuss each one in detail. Nevertheless, since this passage is unique to Matthew and has thus been understood to reflect specifically Matthean concerns (Gundry, *Matthew*, 330-31), it does warrant some attention.

34. Davies and Allison, *Matthew*, 2:641.

35. Contra Gundry (*Matthew*, 334), who argues that Peter represents all the disciples and thus the superstructure of the Church rather than its foundation (cf. Davies and Allison, *Matthew*, 2:635, who state that Peter is not placed on the same level as the rest of the disciples). Davies and Allison (*Matthew*, 2:642-43) understand Peter as a "new Abraham" who stands at the head of a new people. I agree with their assessment that "he is a man with a unique role in salvation-history," and that "his faith is the means by which God brings a new people into being." However, for the writer of Matthew, Peter represents the one who was chosen as the founder of the unique, separate community to which Matthew writes. J. Andrew Overman uses the sociological analyses of Max Weber as a lens to understand the passing on of the leadership from the charismatic founder (Jesus) to Peter through "designation"(Overman, *Church and Community*, 246-48). Yet surely the context in Matthew, with the climaxing christological confession about Jesus's identity which precedes the "designation," indicates that something more is going on here. Overman (*Church and Community*, 249) rightly notes that "the person and the confession cannot be distinguished here." Peter is thus the human founder of the group. Cf. Crosby (*House of Disciples*, 51), who notes that in 16:18 "the foundational function is transferred to Peter." Also Luz, *Theology*, 94.

36. Jesus is also presented elsewhere in Matthew as the mediator of divine revelation: 11:25-27 ("knowledge of the Father"); 13:3-9 ("secrets of the kingdom"). At both the baptism (3:17) and the transfiguration (17:5), a heavenly voice declares "this is my beloved Son." Peter, James, and John experience a vision at the transfiguration (17:1-8). Cf. in 1:23b Jesus is "Emmanuel . . . God with us." After the resurrection, wherever two or three are gathered, he will be in the midst of them (18:20).

for his church and interprets the name accordingly."[37] Thus, Peter *(Petros)* is played off "rock" *(petra)*—"you are Peter, and upon this 'rock' I will build my *ekklēsia*" (16:18).[38] By playing off another reference to *petra* in the Gospel, it is clear that Matthew intends Peter to be the *foundation* of the church (cf. 7:24-25, the story of two types of foundations).[39]

More significantly, Matthew has Jesus point out that Peter's insight did not come through human means. Rather, it was revealed "by my Father in heaven" (16:7b). Thus, it is a divine revelation. As such, "this adds tremendous weight and authority to Peter's position and claims about Jesus."[40] Thus, in 16:17-19 (unique to Matthew) Peter is presented as the [106] (fictive) founder of the group while Jesus is the deified hero or deity who gives the directives to the founder.[41] In this way, the origins of the group are analogous to the origins of many voluntary associations.

Often the formation and propagation of voluntary associations was given divine sanction. In response to a manifestation of a deity via a dream, vision, or an oracle, an association might be formed to participate in the worship of that deity. An inscription from Philadelphia in Lydia (SIG³ 985) records the ordinances given by Zeus to a certain Dionysius while he slept.

> The ordinances given to Dionysius in his sleep were written up giving access into his *oikos* to men and women, free people and slaves . . . To this man Zeus has given ordinances for the performance of the purifications, the cleansings and the mysteries, in accordance with the ancestral custom and as has now been written. (ll. 4-6, 12-14)

The dream convinces Dionysius either to establish an association in his house *(oikos)* or, more likely, to allow others to have access to an association already existing in his house.

Dreams also play an important part in the expansion of a Delian association of worshippers of Sarapis and Isis (IG XI/4 1299).[42] The cult was

---

37. Overman, *Church and Community*, 240.

38. For the plethora of possible interpretations of this phrase and the meaning of "this rock" see Davies and Allison, *Matthew*, 2:627; e.g., Peter's faith, Peter's confession, Peter's preaching office, the truth revealed to Peter, the twelve apostles, Jesus, Jesus's teaching, God. On the Old Testament background of the images of "rock" and "keys" see Harrington, *Matthew*, 251; Overman, *Church and Community*, 240-42.

39. Davies and Allison, *Matthew*, 2:627, 634; Overman, *Church and Community*, 240.

40. Overman, *Church and Community*, 240.

41. Warren Carter notes how the opening two chapters of Matthew locate the origins of the community in the purposes of God and then in the ministry of Jesus and his call to others to "follow me" (Carter, "Community Definition," 647-50).

42. Franciszek Sokolowski briefly discusses this inscription and describes it as

brought from Egypt by an immigrating devotee. Within two generations, this family cult had outgrown the rented premises where the devotees met. The priest Apollonios records:

> The god (Sarapis) revealed to me in a dream that a Sarapeum must be consecrated to him alone, and that he is no longer to be in rented rooms as before, and further that he (Sarapis) will find the place where it (the temple) should be situated and will indicate the location with a sign. And this happened (as he promised). (ll. 13–18) [107]

We have here the move from a private association to a public cult, although it is probable that the private association continued alongside the public cult.[43] Thus, the divinity intervenes in the significant reconfiguration of the group.

In an inscription from Sounion (IG II² 1366), it is said of the founder, Xanthos, that "the god chose him" (*airetisantos tou theou*; l. 2). Most probably this is a reference to a divine epiphany. The god may have appeared to Xanthos, either in a dream or "in person," commanding him to build the sanctuary.[44]

These examples show that in presenting the foundation of the *ekklēsia* in terms of a directive from the divinized hero to a specific individual, Matthew's depiction fits one of the characteristic means whereby associations were founded. However, whereas the god might appear in a dream or speak through an oracle, in the case of the foundation of Matthew's community, the divine will was revealed at both the supernatural *and* the natural level—supernatural through the revelation of Jesus's true identity to Peter by God (16:17) and natural through the physical presence of the human "Son of the living God" with Peter (16:16).

Community Cohesion—Storming

The storming stage is the painful process of transition from a collection of individuals to a collective. At this stage there is conflict within the group as individual members assert their own needs through argument and criticism

---

recounting the story of a man who, after having Sarapis come to him in his sleep, finds some writing hidden in the frame of the door which instructs him where and how to build the temple (ll. 56–58), which Sokolowski connects to the use of a *Himmelsbriefe*; "Propagation," 443. On the use of dreams in the expansion of the cult of Artemis see IEphesos 24.

43. Nock, *Conversion*, 55.

44. Cf. CMRDM 4.137. For other examples of the use of dreams, visions, and oracles see IG II² 255; IPriene 139; IEph 24; SIG³ 1044.

of the leaders.[45] We see this reflected in Matthew. Challenges were being made to the authority of the community and the demands made for membership. False prophets attempted to attract some away while persecutions by both Jews and the civic magistrates were rife. As a result, some were leaving the community. In describing the persecutions which the group endures, Matthew has divided and edited a single Markan passage (Mark 13:9–13). In 10:17–25 we read of persecution from outside the community and betrayal within. Matthew continues by drawing on Q 12:8–19, emphasizing that endurance is needed. One must stand firm in one's con- [108] victions about Jesus and acknowledge him before others. Failure to do so results in rejection before God (10:32–33).[46] Matthew here inserts another Q passage to which he adds the concluding statement, "one's foes will be those of one's own household" (10:36). This clearly echoes 10:21 (par. Mark 13:12) where brothers and fathers and children are in conflict. Yet in 10:25 Matthew added, "If they have called the master of the house Beelzebul, how much more will they malign those of his household (*tous oikiakous autou*)." Clearly this is a reference to the Matthean community as a (fictive) kin-based relationship. Thus, when Matthew indicates that foes will come from one's own household (10:21, 35–36), it is suggestive not only of divisions among families but divisions within the Christian group itself. Hence, "brother will deliver up brother to death" (*paradōsei de adelphos adelphon eis thanaton*, 10:21).

We see this further in 24:9–14, the other pericope in which Matthew has adapted Mark 13:9–13, where we read:

> Then they will hand you over to be tortured and will put you to death; and you will be hated by all nations because of my name. Then many will fall away, and they will betray one another and hate one another. And many false prophets will arise and lead many astray. And because of the increase of lawlessness, the love of many will grow cold. But the one who endures to the end will be saved. And this good news of the kingdom will be proclaimed throughout the world, as a testimony to all the nations; and then the end will come.

---

45. Malina, "Early Christian Groups," 104.

46. The narrative works on two levels, that of the narrative world and that of the world of the readers. Thus, while the earlier part of the mission instructions (10:5–6) would seem to be confined to Jesus's disciples (remain within the house of Israel), the latter part refers to experiences of the community after the death and resurrection of Jesus (10:16–23). See Senior, *Gospel of Matthew*, 117–18; see also Davies and Allison, *Matthew*, 2:179–80.

Clearly internal tensions have affected the group, indicating that it has experienced what Malina calls the "storming" stage of community formation. This passage was meant to "explain the attrition within the group, and to support those who remained but were nevertheless troubled by the doubts departing members had spawned."[47] This is further confirmed in [109] the regulations concerning forgiveness and reconciliation, which suggest a time when conflict was rife but hope was still held that members would return (18:21–35).

Not only are internal tensions among group members evident in the text, something more sinister is afoot. These texts clearly reflect the Matthean community's experience of physical persecution.[48] The most obvious source of this persecution in the Matthean picture is the Jewish synagogues. The disciples will be delivered (*paradidōmi*) up to "their synagogues" (10:17), clearly indicating a Jewish assembly.[49]

The first few verses of Matthew 24:9-12 read: "Then they will deliver you up to tribulation, and put you to death; and you will be hated by all nations for my name's sake" (24:9-10). This can be connected with 10:18, "you will be dragged before governors (*hēgemonas*) and kings (*basileis*) because of me." This is clearly a reference to the persecution of the Matthean Christians by Roman authorities. Nevertheless, most commentators struggle to determine what exactly the nature of charges against the Matthean Christians would be—"We are not given sufficient information to know how and why the members ended up in court."[50] Various suggestions have been made such as the Christian movement being perceived as "suspect," or "deviant," or "dangerous," or "seditious," or "lawless," but little detail is given to suggest why or how they were so perceived.[51]

---

47. Overman, *Church and Community*, 331. Overman (*Church and Community*, 332) points out that the phrase "hate one another" stands in direct contrast to the love command that was the summation of the Law within the Matthean community.

48. Overman, *Church and Community*, 155; Morris, *Matthew*, 600; Plummer, *Matthew*, 331.

49. *Paradidōmi* is the term used of Jesus being handed over to Pilate by the Jews (27:2, 18), and by Pilate to soldiers for crucifixion (27:26; Overman, *Church and Community*, 154).

50. Overman, *Church and Community*, 156. Often no reason for the persecution is given except a general response to evangelization; see Davies and Allison, *Matthew*, 2:183–84; Blomberg, *Matthew*, 174; Morris, *Matthew*, 254; Harrington, *Matthew*, 333–34; Hagner, *Matthew 1–13*, 277; Gundry, *Matthew*, 478–79. Patte (*Matthew*, 149) assumes that in 10:18 it is the Jews who drag the Matthean Christians before the Roman authorities, but this is not necessarily the case for 24:9–10. Within the eschatological discourse of chapter 24, the persecutions are one of the signs of the coming parousia of Jesus.

51. Overman (*Church and Community*, 156) suggests that they were seen as seditious in the tradition of John the Baptist and Jesus because they emulated similar

I would suggest that it is similar to the official Roman sanctions [110] against voluntary associations. Matthew is often read in light of Christians being singled out by the authorities, but they may have been no more singled out than other association members were at various points in history. Members of voluntary associations often suffered at the hands of others, particularly those in authority. At various points during the Roman period, attempts were made to suppress voluntary associations.[52] As early as 186 BCE the Roman Senate acted against an association of worshipers of Dionysos. The *senate* dissolved the *collegia* in 64 BCE and enacted two further decrees against associations in 56-55 BCE. In 49 BCE a Lex Julia banned all associations, with the exception of those that had been established for a long time.[53]

At the beginning of the first century, the number of associations had grown once again. In an attempt to control the associations, Augustus passed a law that every association had to be sanctioned by the *senate* or emperor.[54] This was continued under successive emperors during the first century but was enforced only sporadically.[55] An exchange between Pliny, governor of Bithynia, and the emperor Trajan over the formation of a firemen's guild (*heraeria*) illustrates that official wariness over such groups continued into the second century (*Ep.* 10.33-34, cf. 10.92).

All of this suggests that during the first and early second centuries care had to be taken by those who regularly gathered as a group for social or cultic purposes. Despite the prohibition against such associations, these measures do not seem to have been uniformly enforced. If Claudius, Nero, and Trajan are seen to suppress the *collegia*, it is because these clubs continued to spring up and grow whenever the political climate allowed them to do so.[56] It is into this general context of official suspicion of associations, alongside their continued existence, that we might view the formation of the Matthean Christian community. Encounters with the authorities are to be avoided at all cost. At 5:25-26 Matthew includes a Q text that advocates

---

behavior, but this is pure speculation. Overman (*Church and Community*, 157) also suggests that the picture of them "on the run" from town to town is perhaps hyperbolic. However, it may reflect their recent recruitment efforts.

52. For details of the following summary see Cotter, "Collegia and Roman Law."

53. Jewish groups gained exemption through this provision (Cotter, "Collegia and Roman Law," 76-78; Richardson, "Synagogues as Collegia," 93), although later they were occasionally disbanded (e.g., temporarily under Claudius; Cotter, "Collegia and Roman Law," 78).

54. See CIL VI 2193 (= ILS 4966); cf. Suetonius, *Aug.* 32.1; CIL VI 2193.

55. Cotter, "Collegia and Roman Law," 88.

56. Cotter, "Collegia and Roman Law," 88.

[111] reconciliation with an accuser before one gets to court. Not to do so will involve imprisonment and fines. Matthew connects this saying to Jesus's advice to reconcile with one's brother even if it means interrupting participation in worship (5:21–24). Divisions within the community itself will not only result in some members leaving but will also be brought to the attention of the civic (Roman) authorities, who are only too eager to suppress such newly forming groups.

The connection of the persecution sayings with apocalyptic visions indicates that for Matthew "betrayal and falling away from the group as a result of this political and civil pressure were seen as an indication that the end was near."[57] However, the storming stage is also the stage at which hope for success and for betterment is instilled within the group for those who are members. We find this hope for the community reflected in the beatitudes (Matt 5:3–12), which reinforce the blessing of God upon them despite their underdog status.

Community Relations—Norming

"The norming stage is marked by interpersonal conflict resolution in favour of mutually agreed upon patterns of behaviour."[58] It "involves group members in the attempt to resolve earlier conflicts, often by negotiating clear guidelines for group behaviour."[59] There are a number of ways in which Matthew evidences a concern with community definition: "by naming, by separation and social organization, by association with a group, by practices and ritual, by invective against opponents, by claims to the exclusive center for revelation, or by claims to be the true heirs and interpreters of a tradition."[60] I want to highlight some of these features of community definition and examine them in light of the voluntary associations to see what light can be shed on the Matthean group's practices. [112]

---

57. Overman, *Church and Community*, 158; cf. 332–33.

58. Malina, "Early Christian Groups," 104.

59. Malina, "Early Christian Groups," 104; cf. Saldarini, *Matthew's Christian-Jewish Community*, 89–90.

60. Carter, "Community Definition," 637.

Section I: Modeling Christ Groups

Community Designations

Most commentators have noted Matthew's distinctive use of the term *ekklēsia* in his Gospel.⁶¹ The term is used three times in two verses:

> 16:18: "And I tell you, you are Peter, and on this rock I will build my *ekklēsia*, and the gates of Hades will not prevail against it."
> 18:17: "If the member refuses to listen to them, tell it to the *ekklēsia*; and if the offender refuses to listen even to the *ekklēsia*, let such a one be to you as a Gentile and a tax collector."

The Matthean use of the term *ekklēsia* is often highlighted in discussions of the Christian community's relationship to Judaism. Most often the LXX background is cited in order to show how the title was derived from the community's roots in Judaism.⁶² The word *ekklēsia* is used more than a hundred [113] times in the LXX, in most instances as a translation for the Hebrew

---

61. Davies and Allison (*Matthew*, 2:629, 635) suggest that Matthew uses two slightly different meanings for *ekklēsia*—the universal church in 16:18 and the local assembly in 18:17. However, they do not show why this is the case, nor do I think it is self-evidently obvious why this would be the case for Matthew's audience. Certainly, it is the predominant way of understanding these verses in later Christian history, but this need not be read back into Matthew (cf. Saldarini, *Matthew's Christian-Jewish Community*, 116, 118).

62. So Filson, *Matthew*, 187; Hill, *Matthew*, 261; Frankemolle, *Jahwebund*, summarized in Senior, *Matthew*, 90–91; Morris, *Matthew*, 424–25; Blomberg, *Matthew*, 252–23; Kilgallen, *Matthew*, 132; Gundry, *Matthew*, 332–33 (on p. 335 he states that Matthew's composition of 16:17–19 in Greek eliminates the quest for the right Semitic word behind his use of *ekklēsia* but does not investigate the background of the word in the Greek world). Davies and Allison (*Matthew*, 2:629) state that "it is doubted whether the background to early Christian usage is to be found in the LXX and it must be conceded that the New Testament uses of *ekklēsia* sometimes lack LXX parallels." Despite this, they only look to Jewish literature for antecedents of early Christian self-identity and never do investigate the background of the term outside of the Jewish world. Alfred Plummer (253) goes so far as to suggest that *ekklēsia* at 18:17 indicates the local Jewish assembly rather than the Christian community.

In a modified assessment of the position, Saldarini argues that Matthew is not using *ekklēsia* as a title for his group (*Matthew's Christian-Jewish Community*, 116, 119–20), but Saldarini still understands the primary referent of *ekklēsia* to lie in the LXX (117). The term is used to indicate that Matthew's community is "the assembly (*ekklēsia*) of Israel according to the teachings of Jesus" as distinct from "the assembly of Israel" (119). Saldarini is quite right in observing that Matthew's use of *ekklēsia* "must be determined from immediate literary and social context and not by usage in other Christian literature" (116, 118; contra Stanton, "Revisiting Matthew's Communities," 16). Yet the use of this term as a title in the civic environment of antiquity makes Saldarini's argument that it has no titular function in Matthew unlikely. The term shows up in Matthew at precisely those places where the later community is in view and one would expect a title to be used.

qhl. However, *synagōgē* is the more frequently chosen word as a translation of *qhl*.[63] Few scholars address cogently the issue of why the Christian groups would choose to use *ekklēsia* over *synagōgē* Duling breezes too quickly over the issue when he notes that "given the Septuagint rendering of Hebrew 'assembly' (*qahal*) as both *synagōgē* and *ekklēsia* and the relation of these two terms to the 'house-synagogue' and the 'house-church,' it is naturally *the* central option for the Matthean group."[64] Yet *ekklēsia* is not *the* central option; *synagōgē* is *also* an option—an option that the Matthean group (and other Christian groups) did *not* adopt. Clearly, the Matthean Christians wanted to "differentiate" themselves from Jewish groups.[65] Thus, the LXX use of the term *ekklēsia* is not necessarily the primary reference for their group designation. If they saw themselves as the true Israel, why not retain the designator *synagōgē*? If they saw themselves as distinct and outside of Judaism, why the need to find antecedents in the LXX?

Again, the voluntary associations can be helpful. Despite McCready's claim that "there is little evidence that voluntary associations or clubs used the word *ekklēsia* as a community designation,"[66] there are a few examples: one from Samos;[67] OGIS 488 (Kastollos near Philadelphia, second century CE); IGLAM 1381 (Aspendus [Pamphylia]); IGLAM 1382 (Aspendus); IDelos 1519 (196 BCE). The most obvious source from which these associations have taken over the term is the civic government (not the LXX!), [114] where the word was commonly used of "an assembly of the citizens of a 'free' city."[68] The use of *ekklēsia* was similar to the use of other civic terms used by the associations, such as *taxis, phylē, hairesis, kollēgion, syllogos, synteleia, synedrion, systēma, synodos,* and *koinon*.[69] "In the environment of Greek cities, the term *ekklēsia* would almost certainly be understood (by all involved) as one of the names for a voluntary association."[70]

63. McCready, "Ekklēsia," 60; Schmidt, "ἐκκλησία," 513–14, esp. n. 25.

64. Duling, "Matthean Brotherhood," 164 (italics original).

65. Cf. Luz (*Theology*, 97): Matthew's group "has a new name—'my congregation,'" as distinct from the "old 'congregation,' Israel." Harrington (*Matthew*, 248, 269) notes that the difference in terminology is for differentiation and suggests that Jewish Christians have adopted the "Greek title" for their communities (251). However, he does not explain what he means by this.

66. McCready, "Ekklēsia," 62.

67. Ziebarth, *Das griechische Vereinswesen*, 116 no. 3.

68. Cotter, "Woman's Authority Roles," 370.

69. See Poland, *Geschichte des griechischen Vereinswesens*, 152–68.

70. Kloppenborg, "Edwin Hatch," 231. Saldarini (*Matthew's Christian-Jewish Community*, 116–17) points out the use of *ekklēsia* by voluntary associations but does not use it as background for Matthew's group. His note (117; cf. 265 n. 135) that it is not a technical term for a cultic group does not subtract from the fact that it was used for

The Matthean Christians would hear *ekklēsia* as marking them off as distinct from the Jewish *synagōgai* and as designating them as similar in structure to a voluntary association.[71] By adopting the title *ekklēsia* for the community, the Matthean Christians are standing in clear *contrast* to the Jewish groups who have used the term *synagōgē*. This contrast is made even stronger through the language of "their/your synagogues" (4:23; 9:35; 10:17; 12:9; 13:54; 23:34)[72] and the synagogues of the "hypocrites" (6:2; cf. 6:5, 23:13–26). In choosing *ekklēsia* Matthew wants the newly founded group to be readily understood as a different *type* of association than the Jewish associations from which he and his companions have been expelled.[73] [115]

Conflict Resolution

It is clear that Matthew's community had experienced a time of internal conflict and division and had created regulations by which such conflict could be resolved. This is seen particularly in the community discourse of chapter 18 but also in the regulations concerning respect for the brethren (5:1—7:29) and elsewhere in the Gospel.[74] In the sayings on forgiveness (18:15–22) instructions are given concerning a community member found to be in sin.[75] A process is to be followed when dealing with an erring mem-

---

associations. There is such a wide variety of terms used of associations in antiquity that it would be difficult to argue that a "technical term" would need to be used in order to identify an association as such.

71. Saldarini (*Matthew's Christian-Jewish Community*, 117) is probably correct in his assessment that both the general Greek usage and the LXX were sources for Matthew's choice of the term.

72. In all but the first case the use of "their/your" is unique to Matthew. Matt 4:23 comes from Mark 1:39, which L. Michael White suggests was the literary prototype for the remainder; White, "Crisis Management," 215 n. 17.

73. This is emphasized by Matthew's placement on Jesus's lips the phrase "my *ekklēsia*" (*mou tēn ekklēsian*, 16:18) in contrast to "their" synagogues (Crosby, *House of Disciples*, 51).

74. Cf. LaVerdiere and Thompson, "New Testament Communities," 579; Thompson, "Historical Perspective," 261.

75. Thompson (*Matthew's Advice*, 258) is clearly correct when he notes that "the narrative introductions situate Mt 17:22—18:35 within Matthew, and its situation implies that this passage was particularly relevant to the Matthean community." He goes on to state that 18:1–20 "reveal a divided community ... sin was disrupting the Matthean community, and the need for fraternal correction was urgent" (259). Where I would disagree is in his suggestion that 17:22—18:35 is to be seen as "proverbial" advice because it is not legal or prescriptive (264). I do think it is meant to function prescriptively within the community—Barton ("Communal Dimension," 407) calls Matthew 18 "a kind of 'community rule' to deal with matters of internal discipline."

ber. If after a confrontation, s/he does not change ways, then the next step is undertaken. The steps are these:

1. an individual approaches the erring member
2. a group of two or three approach the erring member so that they may act as witnesses
3. the erring member's ways are brought before the entire community (*ekklēsia*)
4. the erring member is expelled by the group

If at any point in the process the erring member verbalizes a desire to change and be reintegrated into the group, then those overseeing the process must accept that member back into fellowship. There is no limit on how often such a person may be confronted and ask for forgiveness (this is the import of Jesus advocating forgiveness "seventy times seven" [18:22]).[76]

With this communal context for conflict resolution in mind, we turn again to the voluntary associations. A number of regulations from volun[116]tary associations indicate that agonistic situations were common within such groups.[77] For example, the second-century CE rule of the Iobacchi (IG II² 1368; Athens) states:

> If anyone begins a fight or if someone is found disorderly (*heurethē tis akosmōn*), or if someone comes and sits in someone else's seat or is insulting or abuses someone else ... the one who committed the insult or the abuse shall pay to the association 25 drachmae and the one who was the cause of the fight shall pay the same 25 drachmae or not come to any more meetings of the Iobacchi until he pays. (ll. 72–83)

Anyone singled out by an official for having caused a disturbance is ejected from the meeting, if not voluntarily then by a group of "bouncers" (*hippoi*). If one member strikes another member, the one struck is to file a report with the priest, who in turn convenes a meeting of the entire group who vote on a verdict. The resulting penalty is expulsion "for as long as it seems appropriate" as well as a fine. The same penalty applies to the one who is struck if he takes the matter outside of the group to the public courts.[78]

---

76. Luz, *Theology*, 106.

77. Such regulations seem also to have had legal force. There are instances where members or relatives of members bring a civil suit against the association for not carrying out the contracted duties; see P.Enteuxeis 1.20.

78. Kloppenborg has shown how Paul's injunction against taking one another to court in 1 Cor 6:1–11 betrays a problem within the Corinthian congregation that is

A fourth-century BCE inscription from an Athenian association stipulates that anyone who attempts to introduce legislation which goes against that already agreed upon by the membership is to be fined (IG II² 1361; see also IG II² 1275). In P.Lond 2710 members are forbidden "to make factions . . . to enter into one another's pedigrees at the banquet, or to abuse one another at the banquet or chatter or to indict or charge one another or to resign during the course of the year or to bring the drinking to naught." A section concerning the "disorderly" (*akosmountōn*) in the regulations of the mysteries of Andania (IG V/1 1390; 96 BCE) begins: [117]

> And whenever the sacrifices and mysteries are celebrated, let everyone keep silent and listen to the things announced. And let the officers flog the disobedient and those who live indecently and prevent them from (participating) in the mysteries. (ll. 39–41)

A similar injunction against those who are disorderly in a procession is found in LSAM 9, although the punishment here is a beating with a rod.

In CIL XIV 2112 (II CE) any member who disrupts the banquet or speaks abusively of another or causes an uproar shall be fined. If a complaint is to be made, it is to be brought up at a business meeting rather than at a banquet. P.Cairo.dem 30605 (157/156 BCE) imposes fines for a member who does not provide what is required for the festival. More interestingly, in another set of regulations from the same Egyptian religious association (P.Cairo.dem 30606; 158–157 BCE), a fine is levied upon a member who brings a complaint before the civic authorities before bringing it before the membership of the group. Fines are also imposed for insults (e.g., "you are a leper"), striking another member, or refusing to attend a meeting. In the case of insults, the erring member is expelled from the group. If two members meet on the road and one asks the other for money, presumably out of need, the one asked must give or else be fined by the group. The exception is a clause which states that the one who is reluctant to give must swear an oath before the god that he cannot afford to give anything.

A similar concern for fellow members is expressed in P.Mich 243 (early imperial period; cf. P.Mich 244). The usual financial penalties are levied against members who fail to meet their responsibilities; who misconduct

---

common within the voluntary associations ("Egalitarianism"). Schmeller (*Hierarchie und Egalität*, 86–87) arrives at a similar conclusion. We might also note the similarity with Matt 5:25. The similarity between the statutes concerning an erring member in 18:15–17 and the Iobacchi inscription (and the Qumran community documents) is noted in Weinfeld, *Organizational Pattern*, 49; and expanded in Duling, "Matthew 18:15–17," esp. 263–66; cf. Duling, "Matthean Brotherhood," 167, 168.

themselves in public, at banquets, or during the funerary ceremonies (including failure to shave); or who fail to attend a meeting. It also stipulates that, "If a member ignores someone who is in distress and does not assist in helping him out of his trouble, he shall pay 8 drachmae."

These regulations from voluntary associations give some indication of the type of disturbances that could occur at meetings (fighting, disruptions of order and ceremony, abuse of others) or between members (failure to care), along with guidance on how to deal with such (fines, floggings, and expulsion). In most cases the erring member is brought before the entire group and the punishment proclaimed and exacted publicly. These regulations of a number of voluntary associations also show that regularly occurring agonistic community interaction required that re[118]strictions be placed on members who were in conflict with one another both during the meetings of the association and outside of the meetings. Recalling Matthew's injunctions against an erring member and the number of times one must forgive another, we can assume, I think, that such conflictual situations were regular occurrences within the Matthean Christian community. Thus, we see a similarity between this Christian community and the voluntary associations in terms of both internal conflict among members and regulated conflict resolution.[79]

Other passages might also be indicated in this. In 5:21-24[80] a member (*adelphos*) is warned that bearing anger internally against another member will result in "judgment" (*krisis*) and articulating insults ("says to his brother 'raka'") will result in being brought before the "council." This "council" or *synedrion* is usually thought to be the Jewish Sanhedrin,[81] but it could also indicate the collective membership of the Matthean Christian group.[82] Within the Matthean community, persistence and intensification

---

79. One might also ask whether being handed over to councils (*synedria*, plural) and the "flogging" in the synagogues referred to in 10:17 (a passage unique to Matthew) is meted out upon individual Christians who have remained within the synagogue groups and are punished for seemingly disrupting group cohesion, as is the case with punishments in other voluntary associations. In the current context in Matthew, it applies to the mission commission of the group members as a warning against what to expect as they spread the message.

80. This is unique to Matthew but is joined with a Q text about making amends with one's accuser on the way to court (Q 12:58-59).

81. See Allen, *Matthew*, 48; Lohse, "συνέδριον," 867; Filson, *Matthew*, 85; Davies and Allison, *Matthew* 1:514; Morris, *Matthew*, 115; Hagner, *Matthew*, 116; cf. Gundry, *Matthew*, 85. Keener understands it with reference to a heavenly Sanhedrin ("Matthew 5:22").

82. Others have suggested a smaller group within the Matthean Christian community, responsible for church discipline; so Hill, *Matthew*, 121; Weise, "Mt 5 21f," 117-19. The word *synedrion* is used for non-Jewish voluntary associations (see Poland,

[119] of the insults will result in the council's judgment, the "hell of fire," perhaps a locution for expulsion.[83]

The primary difference between the Matthean Christians and the voluntary associations in terms of conflict resolution is the emphasis within this Christian group on forgiveness—not defending one's honor according to the typical patterns.[84] In fact, the regulations concerning community discipline are prefaced with Jesus's sayings about humility (18:1–5), proper treatment of the defenseless (18:6–9), and the importance of "little ones" in the kingdom (18:10–14).[85] The onus is placed on the one

---

Geschichte des griechischen Vereinswesens, 156–58) and is thus applicable to the Matthean community. Davies and Allison (*Matthew*, 1:514) state that the lack of attestation in New Testament times for *synedrion* as "a church body responsible for discipline of church members" indicates that the reference must be to the Jerusalem high council or a local court; cf. Guelich, *Sermon on the Mount*, 187. However, they overlook the adoption of the term by local voluntary associations. The word *synedrion* is used of the college of presbyters envisioned as part of a three-tiered church organization put forth by Ignatius of Antioch (*Magn.* 6.1; *Phld.* 8.1). The word, like so many used by the voluntary associations, Christian groups, and synagogues, was taken from the civic government.

83. Stanton uses "the very stringent moral requirements (5:20, 48; 18:8–9; 19:11–12) and the strong internal discipline of Christian communities (18:5–19)" as evidence that the Matthean communities were minority, sectarian groups (Stanton, "Communities of Matthew," 386). In light of the evidence from voluntary associations, this statement may need some nuancing. While the sectarian nature of such groups can be shown, their "minority" status might have been overemphasized—there were lots of other groups expressing similar forms of community and experiencing community in similar ways.

84. Kloppenborg ("Egalitarianism," 259) suggests that the primary difference between Christian groups and associations is that the Christians "did not use the blunt instruments of fining or expelling those who threatened the stability of the group," but rather "a rhetoric of belonging based on the language of 'brother- and sisterhood,' was nurtured." In general, this is the case. However, one should note that the language of "brotherhood" can be found in some association inscriptions (contra Kloppenborg, "Egalitarianism," 259; Saldarini, *Mathew's Christian-Jewish Community*, 93). Nevertheless, it is not a particularly common designation (cf. Harnack, *Mission and Expansion of Christianity*, 1:405–6 n. 1). Duling makes clear the emphasis on "brotherhood" in Matthew ("Matthean Brotherhood," 164–72) but makes little reference to the usage in the associations. For evidence for the use of "brothers" in associations see TAMSup III 201; OGTS 51 (cf. OGTS 50); P.Paris 42; see also Poland, *Geschichte des griechischen Vereinswesens*, 56; Bömer, *Untersuchungen*, 72–78; Deissmann, *Bible Studies*, 88; Moulton and Milligan, *Vocabulary*, 9. In Latin inscriptions one also finds reference to members of associations as *fratres* (CIL VI 377, 406, 7487, 10681, 21812; see Kloppenbnrg, "Edwin Hatch," 216 n. 17).

85. Matt 24:9–13 (Matthean additions to Mark) suggests that many will leave the community and join with others. The exclusivity demanded within Christian groups would strike the ancient person as odd, as many joined more than one association. Once the erring Christian was convinced of the need to adhere only to the Matthean group, regulations were in place to bring them back into the community (18:15–17; on these regulations see Thompson, *Matthew's Advice*, 262–63). Thompson (*Matthew's*

[120] who is wronged *not* to act as one would expect; rather s/he should forgive "seventy times seven" (18:22).[86]

As we noted above, when one does confront an erring member, the steps by which one does so insure confidentiality at first and allow the person to change course before being brought before the entire group. By structuring conflict resolution around personal confrontation before recourse to public exposure, honor codes are set off to one side. The dialogue is to be private rather than public.[87] It is only after such steps have been taken that the public pronouncement and expulsion are carried out. The erring member must not persist in his or her ways once s/he becomes aware of the conflictual situation. If one knows one has wronged another member, then one is to stop what one is doing, even if in the midst of ritual, and go and be reconciled (5:24; cf. vv. 25–26). The agonistic claims for honor expressed through the conflictual situations are to be put aside. We see this also in Matthew's adaptation of Q 6:29–30, in which one does not retaliate (5:38–42); in Q 6:37–38, 41–42, where one is warned about trying to correct another without first examining oneself (7:1–5); and Q 6:29b–30, where one is to give beyond what one is asked (5:40, 42).

Egalitarianism

This emphasis on forgiveness and the nondefense of one's honor raises another important issue, that of the hierarchical versus egalitarian nature of the group. As Stephen C. Barton notes, "Potential sources of tension and conflict within the group are addressed by the attempt to encourage an ideal of the community as a nonhierarchical brotherhood (Matt 23:8–10), whose dominant ethos is one of forgiveness and pastoral care for the one who 'goes astray.'"[88] Such egalitarianism may "represent the author's ideology about formal organization,"[89] but the struggle over its implementation is evidenced in the text, particularly in contexts of leadership within the community.[90] [121]

Advice, 263) rightly points out that it is not a specific group that is (or specific groups that are) defecting but individuals.

86. Luz (*Theology*, 106–8) points out the tension within these texts, which indicate a community that exercises discipline and expulsion, yet holds to an ideal of forgiveness.

87. Saldarini (*Matthew's Christian-Jewish Community*, 103) calls the binding relationships of the group "more personal than structured."

88. Barton, "Communal Dimension," 408.

89. Duling, "Small Group Research," 188.

90. For a detailed study of this issue see Duling, "'Egalitarian' Ideology."

Evidence for leadership within the community includes the power to "bind and loose" being conveyed to Peter (16:19), the contrast of "their" scribes (7:29) with scribes "trained for the kingdom of heaven" (13:52),[91] and a possible reference to a "council" (*synedrion*) to which erring members are responsible (5:22). There are also a number of references to people in positions of leadership, such as apostles (10:2), prophets (5:10–12; 11:9; 10:40–42; 13:57; 21:11, 23–27; 23:29–36), teachers (5:19; 28:20), and wise men (23:34).[92] Nevertheless, those in leadership positions are warned against declaring themselves with titles of honor such as rabbi, father, or teacher (23:8–10). There is a clear contrast to the synagogues here.[93] At the same time, "Matthew presents [the community's] governance as a theocracy focusing not on offices and officials but on the community of disciples which does God's will revealed by Jesus (1:21; 11:25–27; 12:46–50)."[94] The process of discipline through which a member must go involves the entire community rather than a single leader or a group of leaders.[95] [122] Carter points to a number of other egalitarian structures evidenced in Matthew:

> Women are not to be objects of male lust and power. The warnings against adultery are severe . . . Children are valued and model important characteristics of the community's existence

---

91. Duling ("Matthean Brotherhood," 172–75) discusses the implications of 8:19; 13:52; and 23:34 for the existence of a scribal leadership in Matthew, although he sees it as "marginal" scribal leadership with respect to the dominant leadership of scribes within the larger society. Stanton ("Revisiting Matthew's Communities," 20) notes his agreement with the traditional view that the "scribe trained for the kingdom" is "the evangelist's own self-portrait"; see Cope, *Matthew*.

92. See Duling, "Matthean Brotherhood," 178–79; Luz, *Theology*, 105. Duling ("Small Group Research," 189) also includes "righteous men" (10:41–42) as a leadership title. Stanton ("Revisiting Matthew's Communities," 19) understands this as a designation for a group within the Matthean communities (likewise "the prophets"). Stanton ("Revisiting Matthew's Communities," 20) also suggests that the "wise men" are the same as "the prophets."

93. Krentz, "Community and Character," 569; Wilson, *Related Strangers*, 52. Krentz ("Community and Character," 569) points out that all of these "are titles of honor for teachers of the Law inside Judaism." But, at least in the case of *pater* and "teacher," they are not exclusive to Judaism.

94. Carter, "Community Definition," 650; cf. Krentz, "Community and Character," 572. We noted earlier that Peter was given authority to "bind and loose" (16:19). However, this authority is also granted to the entire community (18:18). Overman (*Church and Community*, 243) suggests that "this very fact highlights the Matthean ideal that leadership and community coalesce. There were leaders and authoritative roles operative in Matthew's church, but he tried to view the community as the primary focus of attention and the locus of authority and wisdom." Cf. Viviano, "Social World," 16; Carlston, "Christology," 1302–3.

95. Carter, "Community Definition," 652.

(19:13-15; cf. 2:1-23; 18:1-14). Excessive wealth is to be redistributed and used for the poor (19:16-30; 6:19-34). Community members are to live not as masters but slaves (20:17-28).[96]

In sum, the typical Greco-Roman household structures are overturned within the community itself in an attempt at egalitarianism.[97] Yet at the same time, there remain in the community a structure and leadership which in themselves point to a de facto hierarchy.[98]

In these data one can see similarity *and* difference with the voluntary associations. Within many associations there was also both hierarchy and equality.[99] The hierarchy existed among the founder and the officials of the association, many of whom received larger portions of the meat from the sacrifices than the general membership. However, among the members themselves it is not uncommon to find citizens and noncitizens, masters and slaves, and men and women, rich and poor, all fellowshipping together in one association.[100] Thus, in its inclusivity and egalitarianism, the [123] Matthean community is similar to the general egalitarianism of the associations.[101]

The difference between the Matthean group and the associations lies in the emphasis put on titles of honor within the associations. Officials were

---

96. Carter, "Community Definition," 652.

97. Corley, *Private Women, Public Meals*, 178; cf. Carter, "Community Definition," 652. See also Wire, "Gender Roles"; Wainwright, *Feminist Critical Reading*.

98. Stanton, "Revisiting Matthew's Communities," 20-21. Saldarini's assessment is that since Matthew "eschews many, but not all, official roles and titles (23:1-12 versus 23:34), his group must have some formal organization but is not highly institutional" (Saldarini, *Matthew's Christian-Jewish Community*, 86). Krentz ("Community and Character," 572-73) understands there to be a group of Christian leaders in the Matthean community, which Matthew opposes with his vision of an egalitarian community.

99. Cf. Schmeller, *Hierarchie und Egalität*, 42.

100. Professional/trade associations would be the most socially homogeneous (Schmeller, *Hierarchie und Egalität*, 49), other types of associations less so. In comparing Pauline groups to the associations, Wayne A. Meeks suggests that the Christian groups were more inclusive in terms of social stratification than were the voluntary associations (Meeks, *First Urban Christians*, 79); so also Schollgen, "Hausgemeinden," 74-75. However, see Kloppenborg ("Edwin Hatch," 234-36), who argues that although membership within both types of "groups" was inclusive to some degree, the "inclusivity" of Paul's churches has been exaggerated, as has been the exclusivity of associations.

101. Wainwright (*Feminist Critical Reading*, 355) concludes that "the Matthean vision of *ekklēsia* has been shown to be inclusive, legitimating, therefore, structures and practices within the community that allowed for women's participation together with men in a way that was not always possible in the prevailing patriarchal culture." Yet it is precisely within the confines of voluntary (religious) associations that such inclusivity was possible and was often practiced.

common in the associations, and there was a "positive exuberance" with granting titles to functionaries.[102] Officials were responsible for the sacrifices, banquets, and festivals (priests; priestesses), for the collection and disbursement of monies (treasurers), and for the convening and chairing of meetings (presidents). A person might be elected to one of these positions by the members of the association, or in some cases the office would be purchased by the highest bidder. Either way, serving in such a capacity often could bring with it a heavy financial burden as the official was required to expend his or her own money in carrying out the requisite duties. In exchange, of course, he or she received multiple honors (statues, crowns, proclamations, inscriptions) from the association members.[103]

The quest for honors was promoted as a means to encourage members to contribute more and more lavishly to the social practices of the association. It was encouraged within the associations by appeals to *philotimia*. For example, in IG II^2 1263 (Piraeus, 300 BCE) the secretary of an association is honored with the erection of a statue, "so that also the others shall be zealous for honor (*philotimōntai*) among the members, knowing that they will receive thanks from the members deserving of benefaction."[104] In contrast, within the Matthean group not only are titles and leadership positions subdued; one's piety (almsgiving, prayer, fasting) [124] is not to be displayed externally but in secret (6:1–18). Unlike the members of associations, the Matthean Christians are to evidence humility and service (23:11–12).[105]

Cooperative Work—Performing

At the fourth stage of group cohesion there is an ability to look outward, beyond the formative stages of the group towards establishing the vision that first inspired the formation of the group, in Malina's words, the "performing" stage. "Members take social roles that make the group more rewarding

---

102. Meeks, *First Urban Christians*, 134. Often these officials imitated both the titles and functions of civic officials (Meeks, *First Urban Christians*, 31, 134).

103. For example, see IDelos 1521; IG II^2 1263, 1291, 1292, 1317; IKios 22.

104. See also IG II^2 1271, 1273.A, 1277, 1292, 1314, 1315, 1369; IG XII/5 606; IDelos 1519.

105. Saldarini ("Delegitimation," 671) suggests that Matthew's particular type of egalitarianism is typical of sects and reform movements and sees Matthew's group as such within Judaism. However, since it is different than other types of associations, this "sectarian" nature of the group can be broadened to the wider Greco-Roman context. The same can be said of Luz's analysis (*Theology*, 105). Luz understands the Matthean community as having "many structural elements in common with a sect visibly in the process of self-definition." Yet his definition of a "sect" (105 n. 5) also describes many voluntary associations (see esp. SIG^3 985).

to all. They work together cooperatively to achieve mutual goals."[106] This is encapsulated in the Great Commission of 28:19-20. This is the present experience of the Matthean community.[107] It is only when the gospel has been preached to the entire world that the end will come about and the strife and persecutions that the Matthean Christians are suffering will come to an end (24:14).

William G. Thompson noted that Matthew stresses four themes which, I would suggest, are indicative of the performing stage of the Matthean community: emphasis on the Gentile mission rather than simply a mission to Jews, acceptance of an independent identity apart from the developing Yavnian Judaism, community coherence and mutuality as a basis for the Gentile mission, and final judgment at the return of the Son of Man as a motivation for the Gentile mission.[108] The Gospel of Matthew itself repre-
[125] sents the end result of their "forming, storming, and norming" and a movement towards "performing." Nevertheless, Matthew's community is not just outward looking. They are also inwardly focused. Much of Matthew's instructional material is meant not just to record what decisions have been made in the group but is meant to continue to guide relationships within the group for some time to come.[109]

CONCLUSION

Dennis C. Duling suggests that the Matthean group is "beginning to move to a level of assimilation, formal organization, development of norms and style of leadership which suggest that it might be called an 'incipient corporation.'"[110] I have attempted to show, by using Bruce J. Malina's categories, that in fact, the Matthean group has already moved beyond "incipient corporation." By the time the Gospel is written down the group has gone through the first three stages of community definition—community formation, community cohesion, and community regulations. Throughout this process they reflect characteristic features of many voluntary associations of antiquity: a divine patron who speaks to a human founder ("forming"); internal divisions and external pressures ("storming"); and community designations and regulations ("norming"). The Gospel concludes by turning the

---

106. Malina, "Early Christian Groups," 105.
107. Perkins, "Matthew 28:16-20," 587.
108. LaVerdiere and Thompson, "New Testament Communities," 574-82.
109. Cf. Overman, *Church and Community*, 337-411.
110. Duling, "Matthean Brotherhood," 159; cf. 161.

group to the "performing" stage, when group members work cooperatively towards a particular goal.[111]

The Gospel of Matthew reflects the group's manifesto—it sets the [126] agenda and defines the parameters of belonging to the group.[112] This is why both the Sayings Gospel Q and the Gospel of Mark are inadequate—they are not tailored for the specific needs of the newly forming group. In setting this agenda within a narrative framework, the Gospel of Matthew conveys the past history of the group and offers hope for success for the members. It tells the story of the one to whom the group is devoted, one who faced difficult odds and overcame even death, and it promises that those who belong to the group will do likewise.[113]

---

111. Malina, "Early Christian Groups," 105. "Our New Testament documents come from storming and norming situations for the most part" (Malina, "Early Christian Groups," 106: cf. 110 113 n. 8). Others have noted the "community building" function of the Gospels; see Carter, "Community Definition," 637. Carter examines how Matthew uses encomia in his attempt at community definition and building. He notes three types of concerns evidenced in writers of *bioi* (which he suggests is the genre of Matthew), which are loosely similar to the three stages identified by Malina: the "community's origin, accomplishments or institutions, and deeds and virtues" (647). Matthew's Gospel can be generically a *bios* and at the same time a "foundation document"; see Stanton, "Revisiting Matthew's Communities," 10. It is also an apologetic work, providing "legitimating answers" for the membership; Stanton, "Communities of Matthew," 388. At the time of the writing of the Gospel of Matthew, the community had not undergone the fifth and final stage—"adjourning."

112. As Barton ("Communal Dimension," 407) points out, there are two aspects to the editing of the Jesus traditions that meet the needs of the community: "community self-definition, and the maintenance of group boundaries and internal cohesion." As "second-generation" literature, the Gospels are "community forming literature" (see Overman, *Church and Community*, 246–48).

113. I did not have the opportunity to meet Bill Thompson, and this I regret. However, it has become increasingly clear to me that Bill Thompson's presence still very much pervades the corridors and the ethos of the Institute of Pastoral Studies at Loyola University Chicago—a presence that has been pointed out to me on many occasions. His contributions to biblical scholarship have been significant, and his continued input will be missed. His concern for the pastoral application of biblical texts was well received by many who might otherwise have failed to grasp the implications of academic scholarship for pastoral ministry. (See Thompson, *Matthew's Advice*; Thompson, *Matthew's Story*; LaVerdiere and Thompson, "New Testament Communities," 593–97.) I feel it a great honor to participate in this symposium in memory of Bill Thompson, and to have been asked to contribute on a topic which launched Prof. Thompson's academic career—community in Matthew. (*Matthew's Advice to a Divided Community*, Thompson's doctoral dissertation, examines the composition of Matt 17:22—18:35, texts which have enjoyed privileged status among those examining Matthew's ecclesiology.)

SECTION II

Recruitment

9

Redescribing the Thessalonians' "Mission" in Light of Greco-Roman Associations

IN THE THANKSGIVING SECTION of 1 Thessalonians (1:2–10), the writers of the letter—Paul, Silvanus, and Timothy—assure the Christ *ekklēsia* members that they are the persistent focus of prayer and remembrance. The writers draw attention to the group's faith, hope, and love (1:3), recalling the manner in which the gospel (*euangelion*) came to the people of this bustling commercial port city (1:5). In the latter part of the thanksgiving, the writers note their reception by those that would form the core of the Thessalonian Christ group:

> And you became imitators of us and of the Lord, for in spite of persecution (*thlipsis*) you received the word (*dexamenoi ton logon*) with joy inspired by the Holy Spirit, so that you became an example (*typon*) to all the believers in Macedonia and in Achaia. For the word of the Lord has sounded forth from you not only in Macedonia and Achaia, but in every place your faith in God has become known, so that we have no need to speak about it. For the people of those regions report about us what kind of welcome (*eisodos*) we had among you, and how you turned to God from idols, to serve a living and true God, and to wait for his Son from heaven, whom he raised from the [**62**] dead—Jesus, who rescues us from the wrath that is coming. (1 Thess 1:6–10)

Clearly, the writers are pleased that the Thessalonians have been proactive in spreading news of some sort as a result of their encounter with the Paul party.[1]

There is a clear trend among commentators in understanding the text as referring to the Thessalonians participating in some form of missionary activity. While most scholars recognize the text is ambiguous as to the nature of that activity, they assume that it primarily, if not exclusively, involves the proclamation of the salvific message that the Thessalonians themselves heard from Paul (cf. 1 Thess 2:1–12). The model of behavior underlying this understanding seems to be based on the narrative description of the work of individuals or groups of individuals described in the book of Acts. Nowhere in Acts, however, do we have an entire Christ group such as that at Thessalonike, engaging in such recruitment activities. Rather, representatives are dispatched to do so, but rarely from non-Judean-based groups. It is likewise difficult to find exemplars of group missionary activities in the Greco-Roman world.

The current paradigm for understanding 1 Thess 1:6–10 fails to engage fully the reality of life in the Greco-Roman world and is limited by perceptions garnered through the narrative worlds of the Gospels and Acts along with modern experiences of missionary movements. In order to redescribe the context and rectify the current paradigm, we need to understand what the Thessalonians themselves imagined they were doing by contextualizing their frame of reference for hearing Paul's words. In light of typical practices of ancient associations, the Thessalonian Christ group's activities referred to in 1 Thess 1:6–10 can be understood as proclaiming honors for their founders and benefactors, alongside praise for their deity. News about these honorifics then spread through networks of traders, artisans, and other travelers throughout the provinces of Macedonia and Achaia. Such reports included information about the Paul party and about the God they proclaimed but cannot be categorized as *missionizing* in the modern sense of having recruitment as the primary aim of the proclamation.

---

1. Although often reference is made simply to "Paul" as if he worked alone at Thessalonike and was the sole writer of the letter, this is patently not the case. The other common referent is "the missionaries," a term I am deliberately attempting to avoid for reasons that I hope will become clear. Thus, I will refer to the group that arrived in Thessalonike and established the *ekklēsia* there as "the Paul party," singling out Paul as their leader, but not as sole proprietor of the message.

THESSALONIANS AS A "MISSIONARY" GROUP

A number of recent commentators interpret 1 Thess 1:2–10 as reflecting active proclamation of the message of salvation through the death and [63] resurrection of Jesus. Malherbe, for example, interprets the phrase "work of faith and labor of love and steadfastness of hope" (1:3) as using "traditional terms" referencing "the Thessalonians' preaching."[2] Verse 8 builds on this "because he wishes to say something further about the Thessalonians' faith that caused them to preach (v 3) and made them an example to other believers (v 7)."[3] Malherbe's rationale for understanding the words as references to preaching is stated up front: "prudence dictates that the focus be on the context in which they are used. The context here (1:2–10) deals with the preaching and reception of the word, and the three terms stressing the effort of the Thessalonians describe the strenuousness with which they preach."[4] The argument is, however, circular, since the later verses are only linked to preaching through Malherbe's particular interpretation of v. 3. That is, v. 3 cannot be understood as referring to preaching on the basis of an interpretation of vv. 8–9 being references to preaching on the basis of v. 3!

Other commentators similarly interpret the text as referring to missionary activity. Frame cannot imagine that the Thessalonian believers are not involved in oral proclamation and recruitment to Christ groups, although in his comments on vv. 8–9, he leaves somewhat obscure whether the Thessalonians themselves are witnesses or whether that role falls to their appointees.[5] Best notes that despite the Thessalonians' tribulations, their acceptance of the gospel message was accompanied by joy as they set about to "encourage believers in other areas and also encourage outsiders to become believers."[6] Without much elaboration, Bruce assumes verbal proclamation on the part of the Thessalonians.[7] Laub notes the Paul party's role as a model for the Thessalonians' activity.[8] Richard [64] merges his emphasis on the Thessalonian community's reputation as the content and the missionary

---

2. Malherbe, *Paul and the Thessalonians*, 117.
3. Malherbe, *Paul and the Thessalonians*, 117.
4. Malherbe, *Paul and the Thessalonians*, 108.
5. Frame, *Thessalonians*, 76.
6. Best, *Thessalonians*, 80.
7. Bruce, *Thessalonians*, 15–16.
8. Laub, "Paulus als Gemeindegründer," 31. Others who understand this text as referring to the Thessalonians undertaking missionary proclamation, both at home and abroad, include Henneken, *Verkündigung und Prophetie*, 63; Trevijano Etcheverría, "La mision en Tesalonica," 279; Fee, *Thessalonians*, 43–44; Lambrecht, "Call to Witness," 324–25; Plummer, *Paul's Understanding*, 59–64; Witherington, *Thessalonians*, 73.

practice of proclamation when he notes, "the Thessalonian community was an example or model *in missionary terms* to others on the Greek mainland."[9] He then clarifies that "in missionary terms" indicates that Paul's gospel message of salvation came to the Thessalonians first, "and then from that dynamic community rang out loudly to all parts of Greece."[10]

Perhaps the most pervasively cited argument in this regard comes from an article by James Ware, who contends that 1 Thess 1:5–8 points to the Thessalonians not only receiving the message from Paul but actively communicating it to others.[11] When the writers refer to the Thessalonians as a *typos* to believers in Macedonia and Achaia, they are signaling that the Christ group imitated the Paul party's evangelistic efforts. Ware claims, "Paul regarded the Thessalonians' successful imitation of him as bound up in their participation with him in the extension of the gospel."[12] Ware has to admit, however, that the grammar does not easily lend itself to the Thessalonians actively spreading the word, noting that it only allows for them as the word's point of departure.[13] Yet despite his reading of v. 8, Ware easily slides into the conclusion that the Thessalonian believers imitated Paul by the active communication of the gospel, although he does note that they may not have undertaken such in quite the same way as Paul.[14] Thus, he insists that the Thessalonians were a "missionary congregation" spreading an idea, but concedes that we have no means of knowing the nature of their evangelizing.

Dickson has recently engaged Ware's arguments in detail, pointing to five problematic aspects. Most convincing among them is Dickson's close reading of how the Thessalonians function as a *typos*: "The γάρ, therefore, explains the *means* by which the Thessalonians became a τύπος throughout Macedonia and Achaia, not the manner in which they did."[15] He adds that the Thessalonians are singled out as agents of the "word of the Lord," for which one would expect the writers to note *di'* [65] *hymōn* ("through you") or *hyph' hymōn* ("by you") rather than *aph' hymōn* ("from you").[16] Their emphasis clearly lies with the initial visit of the Paul party to the Thessalonians, which is the substance of news that has spread among Christ groups in Macedonia and Achaia ("all the believers," 1 Thess 1:7) rather than among

---

9. Richard, *Thessalonians*, 70 (italics original).
10. Richard, *Thessalonians*, 71.
11. Ware, "Missionary Congregation," 127.
12. Ware, "Missionary Congregation," 128.
13. Ware, "Missionary Congregation," 128.
14. Ware, "Missionary Congregation," 130.
15. Dickson, *Mission-Commitment*, 97 (italics original).
16. Dickson, *Mission-Commitment*, 97.

nonbelievers.[17] The Thessalonians' reception of the Paul party and their message "thunders forth" throughout the regions.[18]

Dickson correctly concludes that 1 Thess 1:8 does not reflect an active missionary congregation: "Paul's point throughout 1:6–10 is simply to encourage the Thessalonians in the knowledge that their faithful response to the powerful apostolic gospel has been reported throughout Macedonia, Achaia and beyond, and that as a result they have become an example to all the believers of those regions."[19] Dickson is rather vague, however, on the details of how this took place, resorting to the passive "has been reported." This is also the case with Reinmuth, who is clear that the Thessalonians themselves were not involved in missionary work but is vague on the nature of his presumed "rege Austausch unter den jungen Gemeinden" that contributed to the promulgation of the Thessalonian Christ group's reputation.[20] Coulot likewise suggests that the Thessalonians are not likely to have undertaken evangelism, per se, as this was a difficult endeavor, by Paul's own admission.[21] Rather, it is news of their "journey of faith" that has gone out along with a report about their reception of the Paul party. Coulot does not, however, indicate how this might have taken place. All of this begs the question of how and by whom did "news" spread and of what nature was the "news"? Data from similar small groups from that time provide insight into what this might be.

ASSOCIATIONS "SOUNDING FORTH"

There is not any single, uniform description that encompasses all associations during the Greco-Roman period. They varied in their size and composition as much as in their rituals and the deities they worshiped. The manifestation of a Dionysos group in one locale might bear some similarities to [66] an Isis group in a distant Roman province, and yet differ in significant aspects from a second Dionysos group in its home city. Yet for all this differentiation, such groups are classed together, since they manifest similar patterns of behavior and social organization.[22] Three decades ago, associations were summarily discounted as a viable analogue

17. Dickson, *Mission-Commitment*, 99.
18. Dickson, *Mission-Commitment*, 102.
19. Dickson, *Mission-Commitment*, 103. So also Bowers, "Church and Mission," 99.
20. Reinmuth, "Thessalonicher," 121; cf. Reinmuth, *Die Thessalonicher*, 52, esp. n. 138.
21. Coulot, "Les Thessaloniciens," 38–39.
22. For general descriptions of associations see Harland, *Associations*, 25–87.

for understanding groups of Christ believers (and other Judean groups) in the first few centuries of the Common Era. Yet, through recent work on a vast array of association inscriptions, papyri, and literary texts, along with archaeological building remains, data from Greco-Roman associations are now well recognized as analogous for understanding how Christ groups were founded and organized.[23] I have argued the case elsewhere for the Thessalonike Christ group having a number of affinities with associations and build on those arguments here to suggest yet another link between the Thessalonike Christ group and the practices of associations in antiquity.[24] Exploring how associations "sounded forth" about their deities, their founders, and themselves can help us better understand the referents to which the Thessalonians themselves might look when they hear the words of 1 Thess 1:2–10. [67]

Honoring Deities

Many decrees, regulations, honors, and dedications set up by associations draw attention to the patron deity or deities of the group. Some do so explicitly by invoking the deity directly, particularly in the opening lines of the inscription, as does an association of initiates at Thessalonike: "For the good fortune of Zeus Dionysos Gongylos" (AGRW 50, I CE) or the dedication to "Highest God" (*Theos Hypsistos*) by a Thessalonian association of banqueters (AGRW 51, late-I CE).[25] Other associations are broader in their openings by referencing Tyche—e.g., "to good fortune"—or more generally "gods."[26] Slightly less direct is the inclusion of a relief of the deity, as is the

---

23. On Christ groups and associations see particularly Kloppenborg, "Edwin Hatch"; Ascough, "Addressing the Objections"; Harland, *Dynamics of Identity*, esp. 25–46. Wayne Meeks has retracted his earlier suggestion that the associations are not a useful analogy for understanding early Christ groups (Meeks, "Taking Stock and Moving On," 141).

24. See particularly Ascough, "Thessalonian Christian Community" (Chapter 7, above); Ascough, *Paul's Macedonian Associations*, 162–90; Ascough, "Of Memories and Meals" (Chapter 16, below); Ascough, "Question of Death" (Chapter 15, below); Ascough, "Paul's 'Apocalypticism,'"; cf. Hardin, "Decrees and Drachmas."

25. Inscriptions and papyri are referenced by their entry number in two new collections of association texts; see Ascough, Harland, and Kloppenborg, *Associations in the Greco-Roman World* (AGRW). The Greek and Latin texts and select translations are also available online at http://philipharland.com/greco-roman-associations.

26. The invocation "ΘΕΟΙ" is particularly frequent in Athenian inscriptions (see AGRW 2, 10, 12, 18, 20, 21) and indicates that the matter related in the following inscribed text has been discussed after the proper religious rites had been completed; see Kloppenborg and Ascough, *Greco-Roman Associations*, 28.

case of Anubis in the inscribed honorifics granted to a benefactor by sacred-object bearers at Thessalonike (AGRW 47, I BCE–I CE). The incorporation of a deity's name into the group self-designation also conveys the allegiance of members, such as *Asklepiastai* (GRA I 54), *Dionysiastai* (GRA I 33, 36, 58), *Bakchoi* (AGRW 7, 65, 80, 193, 218), *Aphrodisiasts* (AGRW 258), or *Sarapiastai* (GRA I 26, 27) (this is also the case, one might add, in the designation, *Christian*). In many cases, an epithet is added to the name of the deity; for example, Aphrodite Ourania ("Heavenly," AGRW 85), Artemis Kalliste ("Most Beautiful," GRA I 24), Zeus Hypsistos ("Highest," AGRW 36, 38, 45, 110, 295), Dionysos Kathegemon ("the Leader," AGRW 115, 116, 148, 251, 327). Such are the means whereby the patron deity is proclaimed and honored by association members.

In 1 Thess 1:9–10, the writers note the reports about how the Thessalonians "turned to God from idols, to serve a living and true God, and to wait for his Son from heaven, whom he raised from the dead—Jesus, who rescues us from the wrath that is coming." Although this does not make explicit claims about the Thessalonians' core beliefs, it suggests that their change of allegiance from one or more deities to an exclusive commitment to the "living and true" God of Jesus forms part of the message that is spreading about them. Also announced is the power of this God to bring about wrath on earth, and to provide escape for those who align themselves with this deity. As with the associations noted above, the Thessalonians are likely to have been keen to show their new God [68] expressions of their devotion, and as such would narrate to themselves and to others the story of how they came to know of this God (through the agency of the Paul party) and why they chose to appropriate this God above all others.

Whether or not the language the writers use here is that of the Thessalonians themselves is quite a different issue. Commentators have noted the clearly Jewish monotheistic expressions in this statement, while recognizing that a "turning from idols" hardly presupposes a predominantly Jewish community.[27] At the very least, the framing of this statement has been influenced by the Paul party and as such may not fully reflect how the Thessalonians themselves would convey the narrative of their change of allegiance. This is not to suggest that it is antithetical to their convictions of monotheism or of a coming apocalyptic conflagration; both are presumed for the audience at various points throughout the rest of the letter. Nevertheless, in this statement the situation (including the reports of it) is refracted through the lens of

---

27. Fee, *Thessalonians*, 48–49; Ascough, *Paul's Macedonian Associations*, 202.

the letter writers and may well reflect their attempt to help the Thessalonians shape their narrative into the broader Jewish monotheistic framework.[28]

Thus, while the Thessalonians' recognition of the one God who stands over and above all other gods (1:9–10) is an important aspect of what is being announced about them, too often the discussion of the Thessalonians' "missionizing" ends with the assumption that this theological conviction is the sole basis of any proclamation and that all other details feed into attempts to evangelize and recruit new believers. It is this latter assumption that proves problematic in light of the association data, for the associations did not limit proclamations to narratives and honors for deities but extended beyond to include honors for founders and benefactors along with praise for the association itself. There is evidence in 1 Thessalonians that such is also the case with the Christ group. In this regard, public pronouncements serve as a mechanism for self-promotion and claims of preeminence, a by-product of which may well be evangelism and recruitment, but such is not the primary aim.[29] [69]

Honoring Founders

The writers of 1 Thessalonians note that the Thessalonian Christ group knows "what we became among you for you" (*oidate hoioi egenēthēmen [en] hymin di' hymas*, 1:5b). Despite this knowledge, however, the writers provide details in chapter 2 of "what kind of entrance" (*hopoian eisodon*, 1:9a) the Paul party had among the Thessalonians. These details make it abundantly clear that Paul and the others were foundational in establishing the group of Christ believers—they worked alongside them in a trade while they proclaimed the message that caused them to turn from idols to God (2:9; 1:9b).

Among associations, group dynamics are such that founders and benefactors are duly recognized for their work with the group, often through the

---

28. Some commentators have suggested that the expressions in 1:9–10 come from a pre-Pauline creedal formulation of some sort; see Best, *Thessalonians*, 81–87. Others find that this is not at all clear; see the discussion in Holtz, *Thessalonicher*, 54–64; Wanamaker, *Thessalonians*, 84–86; Malherbe, *Thessalonians*, 118–19, all of whom find arguments for some kind of creedal formulation behind the text to be weak, while Fee sees the issue as not particularly relevant to understanding the text (*Thessalonians*, 50).

29. Such claims for preeminence, rather than attempts to recruit new members, are more likely to draw negative responses from other groups at Thessalonike, which might lie behind the *thlipsis* the Thessalonians are experiencing. In 1:10, the promise to Christ adherents is twofold: salvation from wrath, but also wrath on those not inside the group (Fee, *Thessalonians*, 50). The Thessalonians cannot have missed the implications here that whomever is behind the *thlipsis* is destined to suffer the wrath of God.

dedication of honorary inscriptions. For example, in Argos, Peloponnessos, during the Roman period, an association of leather-dressers (*spatolēastai*) set up a monument for their founder and hero Marcus Antonius Aristokrates, son of Anaxion (AGRW 24). In Lindos on the island of Rhodes, a group devoted to the Dioskouri gods, Kastor and Pollux, took their name from their founder, Philokrates: the *koinon* of Philokrateian Dioskouriasts. They dedicated a statue to the gods on behalf of another man who had served them well, noting "his piety, goodwill, and benefaction towards them" (AGRW 252; 93 BCE). On the same island, in the town of Rhodes, a list of contest victories is followed by a list of the names of the male and female benefactors of the *koinon* of immigrants from cities in Asia Minor, Alexandria (Egypt or Asia Minor), Antioch (Syria or Asia Minor), and Amphipolis (Thracia). Among them the first named is the founder: "Nikasion of Kyzikos to whom the right of residency was granted, founder of the association" (AGRW 257, early II BCE).[30]

In Thessalonike itself, an association of "sport-lovers" (*sythnētheis philopaiktorōn*) set up an honorary dedication for a man, although the reason for doing so is not clear (AGRW 53, ca. 100–150 CE). Their self-designation, however, embeds a name: "The members of the association around Lucius Rusticilius Agathopous" (*hoi peri L. Rousteikeilion Agathopodan synētheis*). The use of *hoi peri* with the accusative suggests Lucius is the founder and/or organizer of the association.[31]

Other associations honor founders of meeting places, such as the small association of a dozen "sacred-object bearers (*hieraphoroi*) and fellow-banqueters (*synklitai*)" affiliated with the Egyptian gods in Thessalonike, who honor Aulus Papius Chilon for establishing an *oikos* (AGRW 47, I BCE—I CE). A decree of the [70] Dionysiasts of Piraeus recognizes a benefactor upon his death by honoring him with a statue in the temple (AGRW 21; 176/5 BCE). Dionysios is commended for displaying

> in many things the goodwill that he had and continued to have toward all who brought the synod (*synodos*) together for the god. Also, when he was asked he was always the cause of some good thing, both for individuals and for the common good, being a benefactor (*philanthrōpos*) at all times.

Among these good things was the provision of a sacrificial site for the members, who also take the designation *orgeōnes* or "sacrificing associates." A record of all the things that Dionysios has done for the association is

---

30. See also AGRW 285 (Kanopus [Nile Delta, Lower Egypt], 29/28 BCE); AGRW 310 (Lanuvium [Campania, Italy], 136 CE).

31. Nigdelis, "Voluntary Associations," 28.

"registered in the archives for all time," including his funding of a statue of Dionysos erected in the temple "in accordance with the oracle of the god." Such were his benefactions that the honors are decreed to continue to his children (with, of course, the expectation that they will continue the family munificence!).

The regulations for an association devoted to the god Men Tyrannos (AGRW 22; Laurion [Attica], late II or early III CE) are recorded twice, with the second version expanding upon the first. The initial inscription opened with "Xanthos the Lycian consecrated the sanctuary of Men—the god having chosen him," which was elaborated in the opening of version two to include an epithet of the deity and the servile status of the founder: "Xanthos the Lycian slave of Gaius Orbius, consecrated the sanctuary of Men Tyrannos—the god having chosen him." The founder of this cult group, Xanthos, is an immigrant from the region of Lycia, south of Phrygia. Both versions of the inscription preserve the rights of Xanthos to govern the sacrifices and limit the right of appointment to him alone and ensure he retains direct control over the group and its activities.

Xanthos's concern to retain control over the group he founded differs from the Paul party's less direct guidance of their groups, although calls for imitation elsewhere might suggest a somewhat heavy-handed presence (1 Cor 4:16, 11:1; cf. Eph 5:1; 2 Thess 3:7, 9). Xanthos retains the right to appoint leaders in his absence, a practice not fully clear from the authentic Pauline letters but certainly affirmed in the Pastoral Epistles. That there are persons exercising leadership within the Thessalonian group is nevertheless clear from the writers' instructions to respect and esteem "those laboring among you" (1 Thess 5:12–13). Finally, we can note the reference to the deity "having chosen" Xanthos (*hairetisantos tou theou*). The writers use a similar metaphor in reference to the Thessalonians—"we know your calling" (*eidotes tēn eklogēn*, 1:4). Although the object of the selection differs—the founder in the inscription, membership in the epistle—the sentiment is similar. The group is formed by the will of the deity rather than on human terms alone. [71]

Promoting Reputation and Growth

Concern for enhancing the reputation of an association ripples throughout the data. Associations set up inscriptions to draw attention to themselves, noting in elaborate language the achievements of their founders, patrons, and leaders with hopes of inspiring other members to undertake actions that would likewise enhance the association's reputation and perhaps even attract new members. Such dedications draw attention to what has been done for the group and what, in return, the group has done for the individuals or members. The association might record the manner in which they were founded and benefacted or their own role in recognizing such deeds. Sometimes both are noted. For example, a late first-century BCE inscription from Athens records a decree of the *Soteriastai* for their founder, Diodoros son of Sokrates (GRA I 48; 37/36 or 36/35 BCE), who has been "well-disposed" to the *koinon*, acting in a beneficial manner in both word and deed (*kai logo kai ergōi*, line 9). He not only shared responsibility for the initial gathering and created the *synodos*, but he also served as its treasurer and then priest. The sixty-member association resolves unanimously to recognize Diodoros's "zeal" by crowning him annually with an olive wreath and proclaiming that "the *koinon* of the Soterastai crowns Diodoros in accordance with this decision" (ll. 37–39). Next is noted the decision by the association to proclaim these resolutions in a more permanent fashion by inscribing them on a stele to be set up in the sacred enclosure. The overarching goal of these resolutions is stated towards the end: "so that when these things have been completed, all members might be zealous to enhance the *synodos*, seeing that its founder obtained a fitting token of goodwill and memorial" (ll. 39–43).[32]

Not unlike this inscription concerning Diodorus, the writers of 1 Thessalonians comment "our *euangelion* came to you not only in word (*logos*) but also in power (*dynamis*), and in the Holy Spirit, and with full conviction" (1 Thess 1:5).[33] While this is taken to indicate what the writers have observed about the Thessalonians, it may be recalling the manner in which the Thessalonians themselves have reported the visitors' time among them, a report noted in 1:9. The view [72] that the Thessalonians are dispatching "missionaries" who precede the Paul party and proclaim a complex theological message which they themselves have only just heard

---

32. In a second-century BCE inscription from Delos, members resolve to honor a benefactor in order to prompt future benefactions and engender admiration and competition from outsiders, who will likewise seek to benefact the association (AGRW 223; 153/152 BCE). See also AGRW 255 (Rhodes, II BCE); AGRW 98 (Bithynia, late Hellenistic or early imperial period); AGRW 8 (Liopesi [Attica], II BCE). For examples of association inscriptions from Athens and Piraeus, both in Achaia, recognizing the *philotimia* ("zeal," "ambition") of members see GRA I 2, 5, 9, 12, 15, 17, 18, 19, 21, 22, 25, 27, 28, 29, 32, 35, 37, 39, 45; AGRW 7.

33. Alongside the role of the Holy Spirit, the writers draw attention to "power" and "conviction" (1:5), suggesting that the writers' understanding of "mission" (to use the modern term) is not at all restricted to verbal proclamation of the message *about* Christ—it also entails embodiment. In the case of the Thessalonians, they are embodying it by carrying out the usual practices of associations in honoring founders/patrons—*viz*. Paul and company—but in so doing, they draw attention to Paul's God and Paul's message.

and barely had time to absorb seems rather fanciful. The wider context of association behavior suggests it is more likely that the Thessalonians have been proclaiming in their city the role the Paul party has played in establishing the group. As a major transportation hub, this news would not spread by virtue of the overwhelming theological power of the message. Rather, the merchants, artisans, sailors, and others that move through the Thessalonians' interconnected networks would hear and talk about the honors being proclaimed for a party of travelers who offer escape from a coming conflagration in exchange for allegiance to a new deity (1:10).

Narrating Reception

In recounting their time among the Thessalonians, the letter writers note, "So deeply do we care for you that we are determined to share with you not only the gospel of God but also our own selves, because you have become very dear to us" (2:8). The use of a correlative construction here "is not so much contrasting the proclamation of the gospel over against the sharing of his own life with the Thessalonians . . . Rather, the emphasis lies with the latter half of the verse and especially focuses on Paul's heavy personal investment and sacrificial living while he was among the Thessalonians."[34] This, it seems, is the content of the news that is spreading through the provinces of Macedonia and Achaia, as the writers have already noted that "people in those regions report about us what kind of entrance (*eisodos*) we had among you" (1:9). The frequent references to their time among the Thessalonians in the first three chapters, and particularly formulations "concerning his *eisodos* and its effect upon the readers make it unmistakable that his *eisodos* and the readers' faith is a, if not *the*, main concern of Paul's in the first part of the epistle."[35] Once again we can turn to the association data to discover how groups at that time portrayed the impact that individuals had on their group.[36] [73]

---

34. Burke, "Holy Spirit," 145–46.

35. Kim, "Paul's Entry," 523 (italics added). Although Paul only uses *eisodos* twice in 1 Thessalonians (and in no other letter), he directly connects his success among them to this "entrance."

36. Winter draws on the *eisodos* conventions of orators to explain the background of Paul's self-presentation in 1 Thess 2, arguing that Paul is denying that he embodied the vices usually associated with sophists while at the same time claiming virtues for himself ("Entries and Ethics," 57–64; see also vom Brocke, *Thessaloniki*, 143–51). Winter rightly links the spread of Paul's reputation noted in 1:8–9a to the Thessalonians' honoring Paul, but his examples involve citizens of cities honoring orators for speeches they delivered. The writers of 1 Thessalonians, however, place emphasis on the Paul party's conduct

An association of ship owners and merchants in second-century BCE Athens recorded the approach they made to the Athenian city council requesting permission to erect a statue of a man who served as the city official in charge of welcoming visitors (AGRW 5; 112/111 BCE). Not only does the text indicate a close relationship between this association, composed mostly of foreigners, and a city official and the city council, it also demonstrates the high regard for hospitality. Such hospitality would go well beyond making the association members feel welcome; it would involve helping them establish network connections in both the social and, especially, business arenas.[37]

Berytian immigrants on Delos record in a lengthy inscription the honors bestowed on a Roman banker named Marcus Minatius, who contributed generously to the operations of the association (*koinon*) as a whole and to individual members therein (AGRW 224; post-153/152 BCE). He is granted a statue, a portrait, and an annual daylong festival, including a banquet at which he is seated in the place of honor. Along with his financial contributions, the inscription notes his hospitality: "He also invited all of us to the sacrifice, which he prepared for the gods to be accomplished for the *synodos*, and he invited us to the banquet." Furthermore, he promised to continue in the same hospitable fashion towards the group, for which they will continue to honor him. Their motivation for doing so (aside from the obvious insurance that he will indeed continue as a benefactor) is to demonstrate that the association "may appear to be honoring good men, never neglecting any opportunity to return favor." The honors cannot be altered for all time, on pain of death, a clear encouragement to others who might emulate the honoree and benefact the association (ll. 53–69).

The well-known story of the foundation of a household Sarapis association in Opus, Macedonia, illustrates how a deity and its emissary might be received (AGRW 52; Thessalonike, I–II CE copy of I BCE text). While sleeping in a shrine (*oikos*), Xenainetos is visited in a dream by Sarapis and commanded to deliver a letter that has miraculously appeared under his pillow. Upon returning to Opus, he takes the letter to his political rival, Eurynomos, who, upon reading the letter, establishes an association devoted to Sarapis and Isis, who are received among the gods in the household of Sosinike. The inscribed text seems to come from a later time, as it presumes a couple of generations of female leadership in [74] the association and a more developed administrative structure. What stands out, however, is the

---

among a small group of coworkers rather than words delivered in public. In this regard, the honors bestowed by small associations seem the better analogy than civic honors for understanding how the Thessalonians acted to promote the Paul party's *eisodos*.

37. As Bollmann notes, informal networking was probably a primary concern of associations (Bollmann, *Römische Vereinshäuser*, 38).

initial entrance of the gods into the household of Sosinike, which the inscription makes clear was preceded by "hospitality" funded by Eurynomos.

Returning to 1 Thessalonians, we note that despite having "no need to say anything" about the type of "entrance" (*eisodos*) of the Paul party among the Thessalonians (1:8), the writers nevertheless narrate their version of events. They begin by stating that the Thessalonians already know about their *eisodos* (2:1), although their insistence makes one wonder whether the Thessalonians would indeed agree with the writers' version. Nevertheless, by their own admission, the writers are happy with the way events unfolded. They note that they "proclaimed" the gospel message, but did not ask for anything in return in the form of money (2:5) or honors (2:6). They "shared themselves" with the Thessalonians (2:8) by working alongside them as artisans, keeping the same hours and undertaking the same labor (2:9), all the while maintaining paternal oversight (2:11).[38]

After summarizing their time among the Thessalonians, the writers note, "For what is our hope or joy or crown of boasting before our Lord Jesus at his coming? Is it not you? Yes, you are our glory and joy!" (2:19–20). This serves as a contrast (or reciprocation) of the Thessalonians' boasting about the Paul party. They will note later in the letter that they have heard through Timothy that the Thessalonians "always remember us kindly and long to see us" (3.6). As Kim notes, "Paul connects the Thessalonians' faith (the successful outcome of his mission) with their happy memory of and positive disposition toward him (an expression of their appreciation of his *eisodos*)."[39] Again, this kindly remembrance resonates with the honorifics we have seen in association inscriptions.

Public Proclamations

In most of the above examples, associations inscribed on a rather impermeable medium the honors they bestow upon their founders and benefactors. These inscriptions functioned in a similar fashion to modern-day billboards, attracting attention to the association as well as to the honoree. Although many, if not most, of those passing by could not or would not read the inscription, for those paying attention, the association's existence, affiliation with deities, and bestowing of honors would be expounded. Perhaps as insurance against movement of the inscription to another, less

---

38. Although the authenticity of the next few verses is disputed, we can note that they recount how the Thessalonians received the message through action (2:13), manifested in their imitation of believers elsewhere (2:14).

39. Kim, "Paul's Entry," 522.

conspicuous location, some associations inscribed very clearly on the stone itself where it was to be placed: e.g., in temples (AGRW 7, 16, 20, 21, 39, 123, 221; GRA I 21, 28, 48), outside sanctuary enclosures (GRA I 27, 29, 33), below or beside statues (AGRW 138, 168, 170, 188, 243, 247, 248, 284, 287; GRA I 32), on altars (AGRW 139, 164, 165, 198), on [75] monuments and graves (AGRW 125, 160, 235, 240, 325), and within civic buildings and spaces (AGRW 6, 139, 298, 306).

Proclaiming the honors granted was an important supplement to the erection of such monuments. For example, the Dionysiac Worldwide Performers (*technitai*) honor a man who benefacted a number of their associations (AGRW 184; Nysa [Ionia/Caria], ca. 142 CE). The Ephesian association votes "to honor him publicly with a gold crown in services and libations during the contest." They also decree that during each meeting "they will make a public announcement and honor him." Furthermore, they ensure that the honors are not only proclaimed at home but also abroad by voting that copies of the decree be sent to the benefactor's home city of Nysa and that copies of the inscription be sent by an "embassy of elders" to the Emperor and to the association (*synodos*) of *technitai* at Rome, who also benefitted from the largess of the honoree. Slightly earlier, a decree from the same type of association, this time in Galatia, records a vote bestowing honors upon a benefactor of the *technitai* who put on the competitions and for whom a statue will be set up in "the most noticeable place in the metropolis," another in the theater, and a third in the city of Neapolis (AGRW 212; 128 CE). All of this is done to "display the greatness of the man and the proper thanksgiving of the *synodos* to the greatest emperor Caesar Trajan Hadrian Augustus and the greatest governor Trebius Sergianus."[40]

Proclamations functioned to make known to nonmembers both the deity that was the focus of the association's devotion and the commitment of the group's membership not only to that deity but also to one another. Together, inscriptions and proclamations functioned in part as a recruitment strategy, since advertising the benefits of membership such as financial help granted to members through loans or gifts (e.g., AGRW 9, 243, 281, 304) could attract new members.[41] The announcement of honors on benefactors

40. See also GRA I 24 (Athens, 236/5 BCE); GRA I 29 (Piraeus, 211/10 BCE); AGRW 251 (Lindos, Rhodes, ca. 125–100 BCE). Associations did not limit their public demonstrations to erecting inscriptions and proclaiming honors, however. Some associations also took part in processions; see, for example, AGRW 18 (Piraeus, 240/239 BCE).

41. For evidence that associations were involved in recruitment see Ascough, "'Place to Stand'" (Chapter 11, below). For some indication of their recruitment rhetoric in which they promoted their own group as more desirable in terms of membership see Ascough, "Defining Community-Ethos" (Chapter 10, below). For examples of

would serve to entice new patrons, who might be convinced to make financial donations to the association. [76]

REDESCRIBING THE THESSALONIAN "MISSION"

The association data illuminate the context within which news from and about the Thessalonian Christ group spread; inscriptions abound recording honors for patron deities and for founders and benefactors, alongside public proclamations of such. This challenges some assumptions that are often made in the discussion of 1 Thess 1:2–10. Commentators seem to ground their understanding of the text by consciously or, more often, unconsciously, drawing on the depiction in the book of Acts in which Paul and his colleagues declaim the message of Christ. Placed alongside the Gospel portrayals of Jesus's disciples hearing Jesus and immediately dropping everything, including their livelihood, in order to go out and preach from town to town, it seems missionaries were the norm. Whatever the historicity of these depictions, they reflect actions that are hardly sustainable for most people. While it is true that philosophers lived such a lifestyle, and thus are an interesting analogy for some early Christ-believing individuals such as Paul, one can hardly think of the hand-working artisans in Thessalonike quickly turning into philosophical preachers—they would lack both training and resources.

In the text of 1 Thessalonians there is little that would suggest that this is the scenario that the letter writers imagine. In 1:8 *exēcheomai* does not suggest that the Thessalonians immediately undertook their own missionary work; it suggests, "little more than that the report of their faith went forth."[42] In addition, "the phrase 'from you' is not to be taken as a form of 'agency'—as though the Thessalonian believers themselves had preceded Paul in proclaiming Christ elsewhere—but in its ordinary sense of 'the point from which something begins.'"[43] The bulk of the Thessalonians do not preach; they are the source of the reports, the content of which are to be found in vv. 9–10.[44] The emphasis in this text lies on the *actions* of the Thessalonians: hospitality ("what kind of entrance"), cult ("turned to God from idols"), and "waiting" (for Jesus's return). Indeed, that the content of the

---

inscriptions addressing issues of adding new members see AGRW 3, 6, 41, 310.

42. Wanamaker, *Thessalonians*, 83. Although a similar sentiment occurs in Rom 1:8, it is more clearly tied to the act of oral proclamation (*hē pistis hymōn katangelletai en holō tō kosmō*).

43. Fee, *Thessalonians*, 43.

44. Fee, *Thessalonians*, 44.

reports would focus not predominantly on the message of salvation but on the proclamation of what the Thessalonian group has done makes sense in the context of the discursive strategies of associations in the Greco-Roman world.

This is not to deny that the Thessalonians were linking their honoring of the original messengers with some announcement of the arrival of God into their midst—that is, the message that the Paul party brought to Thessalonike. Certainly, the phrase *ho logos tou kyriou* ("word of the Lord"; 1:8) has some [77] indication of message content.[45] The primary focus, however, is on actions, either the manner in which the *logos* was brought (accompanied by power, the Holy Spirit, and conviction; 1:5) or the manner in which it was received (with affliction and joy; 1:6b). In vv. 4-6a the clause "we know your election" is the main point. The evidentiary basis of "knowing" comes from two types of data, as indicated by *hoti*: the manner in which the gospel "came" (*egenēthē*) (1:5), and that the Thessalonians became (*egenēthēte*) imitators of the messengers (1:6a) in their behavior.

The emphasis on actions is also indicated in the Thessalonians becoming a *typos* ("example") for other believers (1:7). The word is singular because the writers indicate the experience of the community as a whole rather than as separate individuals within the group.[46] Had the Thessalonians commissioned "missionaries," one might expect that they would be acknowledged in some manner in the letter. Many commentators simply assume the imitation referred to in v. 6 is referencing preaching and missionary work, since this is what Paul is most remembered for in the Christian tradition. Yet oral proclamation and subsequent teaching are only part of the activities for which Paul and his companions would have been known at Thessalonike. Working daily with their hands was another model activity, as would be their cult observances—or, more precisely, their failure to participate in regular cult to the gods and (presumably) their insistence on resting from work on one day of the week. Hence, the writers can note, "you know what we became (*egenēthēmen*) among you for you" (1:5b, my translation).

The report that is spreading through the regions concerning the Thessalonians "faith" (1:8) is the distribution of the news *about the Thessalonians*, not their preaching of (Paul's) good news. This "faith" element would include a report of the divine agency in establishing this new cult among them, but the emphasis is on their actions: their hospitality, their rituals, and their *waiting* for God to act (cf. the "hope" of 1:3). All three aspects of v. 3

---

45. Understanding the phrase here as an objective genitive that references the message about what Christ is doing for the Thessalonians rather than a subjective genitive indicating a message originating with Christ himself (Fee, *Thessalonians*, 43-44).

46. Wannamaker, *Thessalonians*, 82.

are community-based, not outreach-based. The letter writers are referencing the Thessalonians' manual labor (cf. 2:9) rather than any missionary preaching on the part of the Thessalonians; it is their communal care for one another that motivates them.[47] On the few occasions elsewhere that Paul's letters note *euangelion hymōn*, the emphasis is on oral proclamation (Rom 2:16; 16:25; 2 Cor 4:3–5; cf. 2 Thess 2:14). In the case of 1 Thess 1:5, however, this oral element is much subdued, almost subsumed by the quick succession of modifications—not only orally, but in power, in the Spirit, and with conviction (1:5). In 1 Thess 1:9, the letter writers note [78] that the content of the reports circulating in the wider region are "about us" (*peri hēmōn*) and about the activities of Thessalonians; they do not reference the salvific work of Christ. The end of v. 5 and beginning of v. 6 likewise place the emphasis squarely on Paul and his companions rather than the content of their message.[48]

Networking

Having demonstrated that proclaiming honorifics for deities, founders, and patrons is rather typical association behavior, and having argued that the text of 1 Thess 1:2–10 places emphasis on the behavior of the Thessalonians rather than their beliefs, we are now in a position to suggest an alternative explication of the situation, one that better fits with behavior patterns in antiquity.[49] Once the Thessalonian Christ group had formed in the city, they would continue to come into daily contact with others, either through social or, more likely, business contacts. Small merchants played key roles in the spread of commerce in the circum-Mediterranean.[50] As artisan (leather?) workers,[51] the Thessalonian Christ adherents would have had

---

47. Fee, *Thessalonians*, 26.

48. Other than indications of travel plans (1 Cor 16:5; 2 Cor 1:16; 2:13; 7:5; 1 Tim 1:3), Paul's only references to believers in Macedonia highlight their financial contributions, not their preaching or their morality (Rom 15:26; 2 Cor 8:1–7; 9:1–5, 11:9), suggesting that it is for internal community behaviors that the Thessalonians are known at Corinth and elsewhere.

49. Despite their otherwise rather idiosyncratic reading of the text, Malina and Plich are likely correct to limit the audience in Macedonia and Achaia to "members of Christ groups who are attuned to the gossip network following Paul's activity. The information is ingroup information that ingroup members share, as opposed to outgroups who know little, if anything, about the honorable behavior of the Thessalonian Christ group members" (*Letters of Paul*, 38).

50. Rathbone, "Merchant Networks."

51. See Ascough, *Paul's Macedonian Associations*, 169–76; Hock, *Social Context*, 42–47.

frequent contact with a wide swath of traders using the land and sea routes for dispersing goods. Moreover, Thessalonike was a focal point on the Via Egnatia, the major east-west artery that "facilitated and renewed commercial activities, encouraged cultural interactions, became a venue of imperial propaganda, and ultimately, contributed to the reshaping of the human and natural landscape."[52] It is along this road network, and the sea networks (Thessalonike to Kenchreae in particular), that reports of the Thessalonian Christ group's honoring of their founders and their deity would travel. [79]

We need not assume that the travelers preached nor even proclaimed the gospel message widely, but only that they related their observations of the Thessalonians' behavior to other groups and persons with whom they were networked. As they moved through the existing networks, travelers would speak about the recognition that a particular (and peculiar?) small group in Thessalonike was bestowing upon some recent visitors who founded their association, or at least reframed the group's focus towards a new deity. As we have seen, such reporting was expected and promoted by associations. Since Paul worked among the artisan class, such would be his first point of contact in each new city. We should not mistake letter writers' hyperbole concerning the reports spreading "in all places" (*en panti topō*, 1:8) as indicating anything more than "everywhere that we happened to go." That is, it can seem to the Paul party that "everyone" is talking about them, but that simply reflects the particular network circuits within which they traveled.

Recent work in network analysis supports this scenario. Networks of people, goods, and ideas in the circum-Mediterranean were weblike, spreading out in multiple directions, with persons traveling not only back and forth along one path, but diverting through other paths as well. Yet the movement is not random or chaotic—a "structural environment" is created, and it is through these paths "that information and ideas, resources and services can be transmitted through groups."[53] The interactions do not generally occur among complete strangers but take place because of some relationship, whether remote or close. For example, in our imagined scenario the network for transference of information takes place when one merchant speaks with a supplier, or another merchant, or a ship captain, or perhaps through friends and social contacts, including those forged

---

52. Lolos, "Via Egnatia after Egnatius," 277. For a broader description but with a focus on Thessalonike see vom Brocke, *Thessaloniki*, 108–12, who presents good evidence for the routes by which the "word of the Lord" "sounded forth" from Thessalonike, but who gives no indication as to the content or the means.

53. Malkin, Constantakopoulou, and Panagopoulou, "Introduction," 4.

through membership in associations.[54] As noted, physical networks on the land and sea facilitated such contacts. [80]

Those who traveled along these networked paths presumably included some of the Thessalonian Christ believers themselves, but would not have been limited to such, and these would likely not make up the bulk of the travelers. Those who heard these reports—the *autoi* of 1:9—included (but were not necessarily limited to) those who had responded positively to the subsequent message brought to them by the Paul party (namely, the "believers" mentioned in 1:7). The writers do not claim that such people became believers through the witness of the Thessalonians themselves, only that those who (now) believe had heard of the proclamations and the actions of the Thessalonian Christ group prior to the visit of the Paul party. The Paul party had "no need to speak about" *the Thessalonians*' "faith in God" (*hē pistis hymōn hē pros*, 1:8), a very different claim than that the Paul party had no need to proclaim the salvific message of God through Christ.

CONCLUSION

Association inscriptions and papyri indicate that many groups publicly proclaimed their accolades for honorees, sometimes on a regular basis. In general, however, association declarations of honors began verbally and were only later more formally ratified through group processes and subsequently recorded on more permanent media. These texts, however, are meant to record the primary means by which honors are conveyed publicly, namely, through proclamations. As far as we know, the first-generation Thessalonian Christ group did not erect any inscriptions. Nevertheless, the thanksgiving section of 1 Thessalonians includes details that suggest that Thessalonians were similar in their actions to other associations.

At first, members of the Thessalonike Christ group talked among themselves and with friends, family, and business associates about how their group came to be formed. This included both the actions of the visitors and

---

54. Cf. Malkin, Constantakopoulou, and Panagopoulou, "Introduction," 6. Gabrielsen demonstrates that network theory is applicable to nonpublic associations in the Greek world, particularly during Hellenistic times (Gabrielsen, "Brotherhoods of Faith"). Bendlin demonstrates that a large number of the aristocratic and nonaristocratic male population of Roman society was part of *collegia*, *sodalitates*, or other communities, which had their own "internal public space" (*innere Öffentlichkeit*) that provided for alternative political, social, and religious networking to the networks forged in public spaces (Bendlin, "Gemeinschaft, Öffentlichkeit," 28–34). Networks of associations of Dionysos artists eventually forged translocal connections that transcended local civic boundaries, as can be seen in their issuing their own coinage that they used within their own network (Psoma, "Profitable Networks.").

the responses of the group members, along with the divine guidance of the process. These conversations reflected their developing narrative of group formation. Even as these conversations continued, however, the pattern from other associations and details in 1 Thess 1:2–10 suggest that the Thessalonians began more public proclamations of honors for God and for those who founded their group (the Paul party). These proclamations advertise the benefits of group membership and as such can serve as a recruitment mechanism, but this is not the only, or even the primary, reason for the proclamations, which typically focuses on the overall reputation of the group. [81]

Those who heard the stories about the Thessalonians' actions and the proclamations of honors for God and founders included merchants who travelled along the trade networks of the region, a large group that would include native Thessalonians as well as persons from throughout the Roman Empire. In traveling to other places these merchants had considerable time to talk with one another about events in recently visited locales, conversations that would continue with their contacts in each new city they visited. Thus, the "reports" referred to by the letter writers (1:9) may be little more than what could be deemed "gossip." There is no reason to suppose these groups of travellers did not include some Christ believers from Thessalonike itself, but the latter's primary purpose in travel was business rather than evangelism.

The initial public oral declamations within Thessalonike are likely among the reasons the Thessalonians seem to have drawn the ire of other groups in the city itself—the *thlipsis* to which the letter writers refer. It need not have been caused by theological debates alone but could just as easily be grounded in competition for preeminence with other groups.[55] Neither would the Thessalonians be "surprised"[56] that groups elsewhere in the province and beyond had heard of their reputation—they would more likely be pleased, for such is the aim of group proclamation. The letter writers affirm that what the Thessalonians are doing locally is indeed effective.

If one were to ask the Thessalonians whether they were doing something new or different, I suspect they would answer in the negative—they were doing what associations did: proclaiming honors for their patrons and their God. On the one hand, the letter writers are pleased about the manner the Thessalonians are celebrating the coming of the Paul party to Thessalonike. On the other hand, the writers also clearly articulate their own

---

55. Cf. Ascough, "Completion of a Religious Duty"; Harland, "Spheres of Contention."

56. So Frame, *Thessalonians*, 84.

spurning of glory, suggesting that unlike so many association founders and benefactors, they did not request that they be recognized publicly for their work on behalf of the Thessalonians (*oute zētountes ex anthrōpōn doxan oute aph' hymōn oute ap' allōn*, 1 Thess 2:6).

Given patterns of recruitment rhetoric, it is likely that other groups and individuals are impressed by reports about the honors that the Thessalonians have bestowed upon their God and upon Paul and the others. The modern commentary emphasis on the oral proclamation of a message of divine intervention, rather than the embodiment of that message in the practical outworking of a particular group misconstrues the Greco-Roman context within which small Christ [82] groups formed. Data from the associations help us better understand how the work of the gods (such as Christ) would stand alongside the work of individuals (such as Paul) and the actions of an association (such as the Thessalonian *ekklēsia*) to embody the full message (*euangelion*) of the group. Understanding networks among merchants and associations as the avenue for dissemination of news about the actions and proclamations of the Thessalonians fits better with group behavioral patterns in antiquity than does presuming the Thessalonian handworkers quickly became evangelistic preachers in the same way as participants in later church missionary movements did.[57]

---

57. I am grateful to John Kloppenborg, Jeffrey Weima, and John Barclay for their helpful comments and suggestions concerning drafts of this article.

10

Defining Community-Ethos in Light of the 'Other'

Recruitment Rhetoric among Greco-Roman Associations

WOLFGANG STEGEMANN IS CORRECT in pointing to definitions of religion as inherently anachronistic and linked to essentialist, Euro-American, post-Enlightenment thinking.[1] He is also quite correct in looking for religion not as a separate entity unto itself, but as embedded within society and culture.[2] As he states, "If we understand ancient Judaism and early Christianity as religions, we unavoidably treat them according to the model of modern Christianity."[3] Instead, suggests Stegemann, we need to locate adherents' statements about "the newly formed associations later called 'Christian'" in the sphere of discourse in which their contemporaries would have located such statements.[4] In doing so, we must recognize that such statements were inseparable from "other dimensions of social life experiences within Mediterranean cultures."[5]

1. Stegemann, "Emergence."
2. Stegemann, "Emergence," 84.
3. Stegemann, "Emergence," 85.
4. Stegemann, "Emergence," 86.
5. Stegemann, "Emergence," 86.

Stegemann, drawing on the work of Bruce Malina, seeks to locate "religion" in polity and kinship in ancient Mediterranean societies, noting words that signal the political and familial nature of "embedded religion."[6] He illustrates this from Paul, noting that "we can find numerous expressions which show that, for example, the Pauline communities understood their discursive as well as nondiscursive practices [60] within the contexts of the social institution which we call the family (*oikos, adelphoi, i.a.*)."[7] To this observation I would add the voluntary associations of antiquity. Indeed, it is in the latter that I find myself disagreeing somewhat with Stegemann's emphasis on ethnicity as the particular sphere of discourse for Paul and his contemporaries.[8] He quotes affirmatively Rowan Williams, but, I think, misses a crucial point Williams makes: "The 'religion' of classical Greece or Rome... is simply the totality of cultic practices, mythology and speculation about the gods current among the people of a specific area or ethnic-linguistic unit or network of such units."[9] Rather than dispute Stegemann's use of ethnicity, I would broaden it to take seriously specific areas that include multiple ethnic groupings, linguistic units that transgress ethic boundaries (e.g., Greek as the lingua franca of the Roman Empire), and, especially, the notion of networks of various units.[10]

It is precisely in the Greco-Roman associations of antiquity that we find the networking of these units in many different ways. In identifying, describing, and analyzing texts of self-promotion over others—those that can be identified as employing recruitment rhetoric—we can see that their polemical exchanges with (real or imagined) others reflects primarily an attempt to provide the group with a self-identity and, in so doing, to retain, and perhaps gain, members.[11] When the rhetoric found among Christian

6. Stegemann, "Emergence," 87.
7. Stegemann, "Emergence," 87.
8. Stegemann, "Emergence," 87–91.
9. Williams, "Does It Make Sense," 5, quoted in Stegemann, "Emergence," 87–88.

10. Cf. Manuel Castells whose summary of studies of African Americans in the United States reveals that their cultural-political identity is "actually organized around principles of self-identification that are *not* ethnic but religious (Islam, black churches), and strongly gendered (male pride, male responsibility, subordination of females)" (Castells, *Power of Identity*, 58, italics added). Castells goes on to challenge the notion of ethnicity as the basis for community, at least in the modern age, suggesting that ethnic concerns are integrated into other forms of cultural identity; "Race matters, but it hardly constructs meaning any longer" (*Power of Identity*, 59, cf. 53). I contend that the same was true in the Roman Empire of the first century CE.

11. On the strategy of defining oneself or one's group against others see Aasgaard, "Among Gentiles, Jews, and Christians," 156; cf. Neufeld, "Christian Communities," 38–39.

Defining Community-Ethos in Light of the 'Other' 193

and Jewish groups is placed within this larger cultural matrix, we find that their rhetoric of contrasting their superiority with other groups has a similar function to that of other Greco-Roman associations.

GROUP FORMATION AND SOCIAL IDENTITY [61]

Manuel Castells opens the second volume of his sociological study of the information age by defining social movements as being "purposive collective actions whose outcome, in victory as in defeat, transforms the values and institutions of society."[12] His study in this second volume, *The Power of Identity*, focuses on large-scale social movements in the late twentieth-century global context. However, his typology for the construction of identity can be adapted to the study of the ancient Greco-Roman associations.[13] His theoretical framework provides a means by which we can contextualize what I will call the "rhetoric of recruitment" as a means of group self-identification.

Castells defines "identity" as "people's source of meaning and experience," and as such it is constructed by both individuals and communities.[14] In terms of group identity, groups come into existence when members name themselves as belonging to some collective entity (that is, they claim a social identity) and are named by outsiders as belonging to such. To have a social group in a community context, both criteria must be met. Persons must not only identify themselves as a group but also be recognized by others as being a group. Group identity has both an internal and external context.

Castells identifies three forms of identity building: "legitimating identity," "resistance identity," and "project identity."[15] "Legitimating identity" is "introduced by the dominant institutions of society to extend and rationalize their domination vis-à-vis social actors."[16] Within society, groups generated under this form tend to support the status quo of the organizations and institutions of the society itself. In terms of our study of associations in antiquity, it is the public and semipublic associations that fit most naturally into this category. Groups of priests formally affiliated with a temple cult

---

12. Castells, *Power of Identity*, 3.

13. As Castells points out, "How, and by whom, different types of identities are constructed, and with what outcomes, cannot be addressed in general, abstract terms: it is a matter of social context" (*Power of Identity*, 10). It must, he asserts, be situated historically.

14. Castells, *Power of Identity*, 6–7.

15. Castells, *Power of Identity*, 8.

16. Castells, *Power of Identity*, 8.

and sanctioned by local or state governments serve a legitimating role in a particular locale. The same might also be argued for semipublic associations such as the Augustales of Rome, who functioned to broker the emperor cult to the general population.

"Resistance identity" is "generated by those actors that are in positions/conditions devalued and/or stigmatized by the logic of domination, thus building trenches of resistance and survival on the basis of [62] principles different from, or opposed to, those permeating the institutions of society."[17] Although most apparent in contexts of unbearable oppression, the building of resistance identity includes the setting of clear boundaries between insiders and outsiders and seeks to exclude those who support the dominant institutions. An obvious illustration from antiquity comes in the form of rebels organized to fight against the Roman Empire, such as the Zealots in Palestine. Another example is the group that withdrew from participation in the Jerusalem temple, as seems to be the case of those living at Qumran. This is also the category to which most voluntary associations in Greco-Roman antiquity might naturally fit. While not necessarily actively resisting the dominant institutions, they continue to meet regularly despite their official status as illegal institutions.[18] As long as they remain nonpolitical, there is a level of tolerance for them among the Roman elite. However, at any sign of disturbance to the organizations and institutions of society, such groups are repressed. Nevertheless, many of these groups persist in their resistance identity by transgressing societal conventions through such practices as egalitarian leadership, political discourses, and the inclusion of women. Castells suggests that resistance to social isolation, among other factors, leads people to "cluster in community organizations" through which they come to form a cultural, communal identity.[19] In contexts of social mobilization, as was the case in the Roman Empire, people engage in social movements that while not necessarily revolutionary, do lead people to discover common interests, share life, and produce new meaning.[20]

Castells's third form of identity building is "project identity," when social actors, on the basis of whichever cultural materials are available to them, build a new identity that redefines their position in society and, by so doing, seek the transformation of the overall social structure.[21] Indeed, it is at this

---

17. Castells, *Power of Identity*, 8.

18. Ascough, *Paul's Macedonian Associations*, 42–46. But see Harland, *Associations*, 162–69.

19. Castells, *Power of Identity*, 60.

20. Castells, *Power of Identity*, 60.

21. Castells, *Power of Identity*, 8.

point that, in the context of Greco-Roman antiquity, we find the associations on the boundary between resistance identity and project identity. In the very process of re-creating a microcosm of the status quo in which the powerless have a voice and, in many ways, the conventions of society are transgressed, these groups present a view, often linked to a divinity and particular ritual acts, that imagines a world much different from that of the status quo. The most [63] obvious way this is done is in replicating the civic structures of government while allowing the poor and even noncitizens the means to attain positions of power and authority in the group. In this replication, the associations imagine a world in which all of their members, at the very least, will have positions of recognized authority—a very different view from those who control the dominant institutions of society. In some cases, we have examples of groups that seek legal (or quasi-legal) recognition by those in power, as is the case in Philo's attempt to argue that Jews be exempt from the laws governing private associations because Jewish groups fit the exception clause of having been established long ago (Philo, *Legat.* 40.311–316; cf. Josephus, *Ant.* 16.6.160–165).[22]

Castells makes it clear that while a particular snapshot of time might allow for the categorization of a group in one of these identity movements, through time a single group can take on multiple forms of identity building. He states, "Naturally, identities that start as resistance may induce projects, and may also, along the course of history, become dominant in the institutions of society, thus becoming legitimizing identities to rationalize their domination."[23] One need only recall the challenge of understanding the rise to dominance of Christianity. However, the ultimate dominance of Christianity over others should not be read back into the historical record as the inevitable aim of the rhetorical flourishes of early generations of Christians. Understanding the rhetoric within the wider social context of how various ancient associations located themselves in terms of resistance and project identity by asserting their superiority over other groups suggests that Christian groups were engaged in the process of identity formation, and its ancillary recruitment rhetoric, in much the same manner as other Greco-Roman groups.

22. Richardson, *Building Jewish*, 113–15. Cf. Harland, *Associations*, 160.
23. Castells, *Power of Identity*, 8, cf. 67.

THE RHETORIC OF RECRUITMENT

In the classical world the primary understanding of epideictic rhetoric was in its function as commendation for a person's qualities or deeds.[24] It is clear, however, that ancient writers also recognized the [64] ideological persuasiveness of epideictic rhetoric. Praise is never given for its own sake. Quintilian notes, "Really, all of praise resembles exercises in persuasion, since for the most part the same things that are praised in the one case are advised in the other" (*Inst.* 3.7.28, LCL).[25] And Aristotle remarks, "To praise a man is in one respect akin to urging a course of action" (*Rhet.* 1.9.35).[26] Thus, he counsels, "Whenever you want to praise anyone, think what you would urge people to do; and when you want to urge the doing of anything, think what you would praise a man for having done" (*Rhet.* 1.9.36). Although Aristotle's examples are always drawn from applications to male persons, he provides the caveat in the opening that praise is not "always of a human or divine being but often of inanimate things" (*Rhet.* 1.9.2). It is my contention that this would also include "objects" such as cities, civic bodies, and groups of people.[27] Thus, what Aristotle applies to praise of humans can likewise apply to praise of institutions. Since epideictic rhetoric urges action through increasing adherence to values,[28] it is somewhat akin to propaganda.

Epideictic rhetoric thus serves as a useful category for exploring texts from various types of ancient associations that announce the praiseworthiness of the group, particularly in contrast to other groups. Rather than the usual assumption that epideictic rhetoric functions only to entertain and impress the audience, we can understand the employment of classical forms of epideictic rhetoric as serving an ideological purpose. We find modern analogies in advertising, which traffics in commonly held values in the same way ancient epideictic rhetoric reinforced particular values.[29] The function of many modern advertisements seems less about providing product information and more about entertainment. Yet, they are not simply providing

---

24. See Aristotle, *Ad Rhetorica* 1.9. The rhetorical handbooks point to stereotypical *topoi* that can be used to honor or to blame a certain person, distinguishing between "external circumstances, physical attributes and personal qualities of character"; see Smit, "Epideictic Rhetoric," 187, who points particularly to Aristotle, *Ad Rhetorica* 1.9, *Rhetorica ad Alexandrum* 35, and *Rhetorica ad Herennium* 3.6–8.

25. Habinek, *Ancient Rhetoric*, 57; Perelman and Olbrechts-Tyteca, *New Rhetoric*, 10.

26. English translations of Aristotle's *Ad Rhetorica* 1.9 are by Roberts in Aristotle, *Aristotle's Rhetoric and Poetics*.

27. On cities see Ascough, "Completion of a Religious Duty."

28. Perelman and Olbrechts-Tyteca, *New Rhetoric*, 50. Habineck, *Ancient Rhetoric*, 54.

29. Cf. Perelman and Olbrechts-Tyteca, *New Rhetoric*, 50; Walker, *Rhetoric*, 168.

entertainment but portraying values and loosely associating them with a product.[30] In so doing, ads make us disposed to the action of buying without directly arguing that we should buy and without giving any factual information about the product or its functional use. Their persuasiveness rests not [65] only in reinforcing commonly held views but by influencing the audience to act positively towards that which is promoted—in this case, to purchase a particular product.[31]

We can see this ideologically driven function in much of the language of the groups of antiquity. While this often functions to reinforce the group identity, it also functions to advocate to outsiders that this particular group is worthy, not only of praise and honor, but also of adherence. That is, the epideictic rhetoric argues with the outsider that they should join the group. In this way, it can be labeled the "rhetoric of recruitment." Such recruitment rhetoric aims to attract people into a group or to solidify group boundaries in order to promote adherence to a group. We would be amiss if we were to suggest that this recruitment rhetoric reflects actual conversions. Rather, recruitment rhetoric must be understood as a means to identify group identity and cohesion. It is the means of persuasion that a particular group, or at least a member of a particular group, thought would be persuasive in gaining new members or providing legitimacy to current members. Although often these are presented in a rational way, their function can be otherwise. As Bryant notes,

> The entire effort to explicate religious conflict and change in terms of rationality thus appears misguided, seeing as sacred beliefs and rituals are only minimally zweckrational, or grounded in an objective means-ends practicality, and maximally wertrational, and so indicative of identities taken and of values upheld. Religious discourses, in other words, are fundamentally performative, expressive, not empirical; they register no autonomous or demonstrable "facts" about the numinous or supernatural, but only the groping efforts of localized human groups to impart meaning to their existence, and to make sense of—and so

---

30. Mark Garrett Longaker, course notes for RHE 330E Of Rhetoric and Advertising, http://www.cwrl.utexas.edu/~longaker/rhe330e/presentations/prl.ppt.

31. We find another contemporary analogy in the world of scientific investigation and publication in Kathryn Northcut's examination of a paleornithological dispute in scientific publications as a means to highlight the "epideictic nature of some of the discourse produced in this complex and contentious rhetorical context" ("Unexpected Ceremony," 6).

manage—the natural, biological, social, and psychological realities they experience.[32]

Thus, in our examination of particular texts we will focus on how these texts attempt to make sense of the world, and the gods, for actual and potential group members, and thus how these texts are examples of epideictic rhetoric and, as such, function as recruitment rhetoric in resistance and project identity formation. [66]

As we turn our attention to the various types of associations of antiquity, I will contend that the course of action urged by the self-congratulatory praise of a group is the giving of one's adherence to that group in terms of stronger allegiance of members or of joining of nonmembers. Groups can refer to a range of *topoi*, such as their own heritage of founding, and past deeds as a basis to bolster their credibility for their claims to honor and glory. For example, the honoring of founders or leaders fits what Aristotle says about the highlighting of noble birth as a means of bringing honor and praise in the context of an encomium: "Now good birth in a race or a state means that its members are indigenous or ancient: that its earliest leaders were distinguished men, and that from them have sprung many who were distinguished for qualities that we admire" (*Rhet.* 1.5.5). With this in mind, we now turn our attention to examine some specific examples of associations that employ the rhetoric of recruitment.

VOLUNTARY ASSOCIATIONS

An inscription from Lanuvium, Italy, and dating to 136 CE, records the bylaws of an association established under the guise of a commitment to burial of members. What is quickly apparent from these bylaws is that the primary concern of this association is the banquet that accompanies the monthly gatherings. The bulk of the bylaws, ten of the fifteen, are concerned with issues surrounding the holding of banquets and the provision of wine and food. Four of the remaining five bylaws concern burial. The first bylaw addresses the issue of membership: "It was voted unanimously that whoever wants to enter this society shall pay an initiation fee of 100 sesterces and an amphora of good wine and shall pay monthly dues of five *asses*." Through this inscription the association invites the inquirer to consider taking up membership. Immediately before the bylaws, the stone reads, "You, who wish to join this association as a new member should first read the by-laws carefully before entering, so as not to find cause for complaint later

---

32. Bryant, "Beware the Gift of Theory," 27; cf. Bryant, "Cost-Benefit Accounting."

or bequeath a lawsuit to your heir." The bylaws themselves promise that due care will be taken to ensure the proper burial of members when they die, even if they die away from home. It is also clear, however, that the banquets will be a place of commensality and a place where those in positions of leadership, inside and outside the association, will receive honors.

The association links itself to the imperial household through the honoring (via more banquets, naturally) of the emperor Hadrian and, especially, his young lover Antinoüs; to the *polis* through the honoring of the town patron Caesennius Rufus; and to the divine realm [67] through the honoring of the goddess Diana. The reiteration of these connections would serve to indicate, and thus promote, the high status that any (paid-up) member will enjoy. Lest questions be raised about the legality of joining what naturally seems to be a type of group that is under imperial prohibition, the inscription cites the text of a clause from the *senatus consultum* of the Roman people that shows that monthly meetings made in the name of collecting contributions for the burial of the dead have been sanctioned. The overall message is clear; this is an honorable, legal group (unlike so many others?), that has a fun time, is socially and politically connected, and will take care of its own (as long as they have paid their dues). Given both the invitation to outsiders to consider carefully the bylaws before joining, and given that the first of those bylaws concerns the initiation fee for new members, this inscription seems to function, at least in part, as a billboard advertising the association in order to recruit new members.

In the well-known inscription of the Athenian adherents of Dionysos—the Iobacchoi (IG II² 1368), dating to c. 164–165 CE—we find the statutes of the group and the process whereby they were ratified. The inscription opens by celebrating the adoption of the statutes by the association. Recalling their foundation some years ago, they note that their statutes were drawn up earlier by their priests but are now being presented to the group. Upon approval by their priest, leader (*archbacchos*), and patron, the inscription records the "spontaneous" celebration of the membership:

> We will use these forever! Bravo for the priest! Revive the statutes! . . . Health and good order to the Bacheion!

There follows a ratification by the general membership, passed unanimously, and followed by more celebration, recorded verbatim in the inscription: "Now you have good fortune; now we are the best of all Bacchic societies." This claim to preeminence is important to note. It is, of course, a form of self-praise, and while not formally constructed as an epideictic speech, it serves the same function. It follows Aristotle's advice concerning heightening the effect of praise: "We must, for instance, point out that a man is the only one, or the first, or almost the only one who has done something, or that he has done it *better* than anyone else" (*Rhet.* 1.9.38, italics added).[33] By comparing themselves with others, they highlight their own outstanding qualities. The Iobacchoi claim to have surpassed all other groups of Iobacchoi in their ratification of these statutes. [68]

We need also recall that the goal of praise, according to Aristotle, is the urging of a course of action. It is striking then, that in the statutes recorded immediately following the self-praise and claim of preeminence, the opening concern is with the qualifications for becoming a member: "Let it not be lawful for anyone to be an Iobacchos unless he was first enlisted on the customary list in the presence of the priest and was approved by a vote of the Iobacchoi as to whether he appears to be worthy and suitable for the Baccheion." I would suggest that the self-praise serves to advertise the group to outsiders and sends a not-so-subtle message that it is a group worthy of adherence. Having raised this possibility, then, the inscription immediately names the process whereby one can join. Of course, not all may join, and due process must be followed. The goal is only to accept those who are "worthy and suitable," again a means of bolstering the durability of membership in the group to those both on the inside and on the outside. This is an exclusive group—to be part of it is to be part of the honorable and praiseworthy members of society.

After receiving approval, and paying the requisite entrance fees, one becomes a card-carrying member of the group: "Let the priest give to everyone who has been enlisted and approved by vote a letter indicating that he is an Iobacchos." Presumably, this letter functions as one's ticket into privileged circles in the *polis*, allowing one access to persons, places, and events reserved for this preeminent group of Iobacchoi. Again, this text clearly conveys a message of the desirability of belonging to *this* particular group of Iobacchoi rather than any other group of Iobacchoi or, for that matter, any other group in Athens.

We find other examples of this sense of pride in group membership. Van Nijf points out that the *collegia* of *fabri*, *centonarii*, and *dendrophori* "routinely accepted members of varying occupational backgrounds, despite the concerns of the authorities that outsiders should not be admitted."[34] Many men belonged to more than one of these associations (even after the ban on dual memberships in the mid-second century CE), and advertised that fact in a manner that suggests a "sense of pride."[35] Indeed, the *collegia*

---

33. Cf. Malina and Neyrey, *Portraits of Paul*, 24.
34. Van Nijf, "Collegia and Civic Guards," 314.
35. Van Nijf, "Collegia and Civic Guards," 315.

themselves "do not seem to have limited themselves to a membership from one profession, but recruited their members among a wider group of successful traders and businessmen."[36] [69]

Van Nijf focuses on the associations' use of language of preeminence as a means to promote their public image but overlooks the implications for recruitment practices.[37] The evidence is interesting in light of our previous analysis of the functionality of rhetoric, particularly epideictic rhetoric, in promotional advertising that seeks to recruit brand loyalty. Indeed, we find numerous inscriptions that list associations with adjectival designations such as *splendidissimum, dignissimum, honestissimum, megas*, and others (e.g., *splendidissima collegia fabrum et centonariorum* [CIL XI 1230, Placentia], *dignissimum corpus pistorum siliginariorum* [CIL VI 22], *honestissimum corpus dendrophororum* [CIL X 1786, Puteoli], *hē Gerousia tou megaloud synergiou* [ISide 102]).[38] Also instructive along these lines are the associations that refer to themselves with respect to their position within the city, such as the *collegia principalia*.[39]

JEWISH GROUPS

Aristotle notes that when praise for a person (or institution) cannot be found, one may pit him against others (*Rhet.* 1.9.39). The ideal is to make the comparison with famous persons, in so far as surpassing the greatness of others bolsters one's case.[40] However, "if you cannot compare your hero with famous men, you should at least compare him with other people generally" (*Rhet.* 1.9.39). We find this type of comparative praise in the intergroup rivalries among associations. In noting this we should not lose sight of the fact that, according to Aristotle, all of this should be urging some course of action. Again, one possible course of action urged here, I contend, is the adherence of new members to the association involved.

It is particularly interesting that Jewish writers should choose to compare and, especially, contrast themselves with associations, a factor we can also note in Christian rhetoric (below). As Harland notes, "That they [Philo, Tertullian, and others] chose associations as the object of their rather

36. Van Nijf, "Collegia and Civic Guards," 315.
37. Van Nijf, "Collegia and Civic Guards," 315; so also Harland, "Spheres of Contention."
38. See further Waltzing, *Étude Historique*, 4:574–75.
39. Van Nijf, "Collegia and Civic Guards," 316; cf. Ausbüttel, *Untersuchungen*, 75–76.
40. Malina and Neyrey, *Portraits of Paul*, 24.

one-sided comparison ... shows how both Jews and [70] Christians (as well as outsiders) could express their identities in terms of association life,"[41] as did the Iobacchi who proclaimed themselves to be the "best of all" bacchic groups (IG II² 1368, discussed above).

In the writings of Philo, we find numerous sections in which the right of assembly of the Jews is defended. However, in defending this right, the praise upon the Jewish groups and the blame placed upon the non-Jewish groups indicates the superiority of the former. While not explicitly aimed at recruiting persons into these groups, the rhetoric does attempt to compel others to recognize that the Jewish groups are better than all those around them. It is striking that were it not for texts such as these, texts from "insiders," much of what we know to be distinctive about Jews in the Greco-Roman world would be absent. As Goodman notes:

> If knowledge of Judaism was not greatly augmented by the survival of much internal literature preserved for special reasons by later Jews and Christians, historians would still be aware of Jews as a distinct ethnic and religious group, but Jews would not seem anything like as marginal in the Graeco-Roman world as they do when their own, often jaundiced, views of the outside provide the basis for understanding them. Jews lived alongside non-Jews even in many parts of their homeland to a much greater degree than scholars tend to allow.[42]

It seems, then, that the rhetoric of texts by Jewish writers such as Philo (and Josephus) are aimed to create an ethos of self-identity in which Jews (and any outsiders who care to listen) understand themselves as *different* from others with whom they live and mingle.

Take, for example, Philo's text *On the Embassy to Gaius* in which he recollects his arguments before the emperor. Recalling the good feeling of Augustus towards the Jews, he notes that Augustus commanded the provincial governors in Asia "to permit the Jews alone to assemble together in the synagogues for these assemblies were not revels, which from drunkenness and intoxication proceeded to violence, so as to disturb the peaceful condition of the country but were rather schools of temperance and justice" (*Legat.* 40.311–312). The rhetoric both praises the Jewish groups for what they are ("schools of temperance and justice") and contrasts them with other groups in order to drive home the point. Indeed, these other associations were disturbers of the peace and as such had no place within the Pax Romana.

---

41. Harland, *Associations*, 74.
42. Goodman, "Jews, Greeks, and Romans," 13.

The contrast is more pointed, and the praise for a Jewish group more clear, in Philo's treatise *On the Contemplative Life*. Philo spends [71] some of his time comparing and, especially, contrasting the Jewish *therapeutai* with Greco-Roman associations. The latter, he makes clear, participate regularly in drunken banquets that result in property destruction and physical violence (5.40). The meetings of the *therapeutai* are quite the opposite, marked by cheerfulness and conviviality (5.40). Although the *therapeutai* join both men and women together for celebrations "like persons in the bacchanalian revels," they are "drinking the pure wine of the love of God" (11.85). By incidentally raising the bacchanalian revelries Philo again drives home the similarities and differences between the *therapeutai* and other groups. The *therapeutai* are intoxicated not on strong drink but with beautiful singing, ideas, and expressions (11.88–89). If in outward form there is any similarity with other associations, for Philo that is where it ends (cf. Paul in 1 Cor 12–14).

It is striking, however, that in order to assert the true nature of the Jewish groups, synagogues, and the *therapeutai*, Philo relies on *contrast* with other types of associations. This suggests that he perceives a similarity in the composition of these groups. While clearly the Jewish groups are ethnically Jewish, in terms of social location in antiquity—social status and economic standing—the associations and the Jewish groups draw from the same strata. In order to make clear the distinctive features of the Jewish groups, Philo relies on contrasting them with those to whom they might otherwise be favorably compared, both in composition and in actions.

CHRISTIAN GROUPS

Philip Harland has undertaken a comparative study of the language of Christ bearers and fellow initiates in the letters of Ignatius and similar language in ancient mysteries and associations, showing how early Christian authors like Ignatius could express Christian identity in terms familiar from local social and cultural life, particularly association life.[43] He is quite right, and we can profitably explore further not only how the language is similar and contrastive, but what the rhetorical function of such language implies for recruitment. As Harland notes, "from an (ancient) Christian perspective, describing oneself in terms drawn from the world of associations might simultaneously establish a sense of place within local culture or society while also forming a basis from which to assert distinctiveness and even pre-eminence [72] (for the group or its God)."[44] Yet, as I suggested earlier,

43. Harland, "Christ-Bearers," 483.
44. Harland, "Christ-Bearers," 499.

the concern for preeminence is not only a matter of promoting the group's public image but can also be linked to a concern for self-definition ("we are better than *them*"), recruitment ("so come join *us*"), and maintenance ("and *stay with* us").

We will begin with Paul and his self-recommendation in Philippians 3:2–21. Paul introduces his encomium (3:2–3) by censuring his opponents and praising his audience. The repetition of the imperative form of "beware" (*blepete*) introduces three negative characteristics of his opponents: "dogs,"[45] "evil workers," and "mutilators of the flesh." The use of invective and ridicule (3:2; cf. 3:19) to castigate one's enemies is both natural and conventional in Greco-Roman society.[46] Comparison is also an essential component of an encomium, either comparison with heroes or comparison with other notable persons as a means of showing the one praised to be better than the others (Aristotle, *Rhet.* 1.9.38–41). For Paul the comparison is made in Phil 3 with the group of Judaizing Christians he anticipates coming to Philippi. These persons are a negative example that will serve as a contrast to Paul's own positive example.[47] Paul and the Philippians are the "true circumcision" (3:3).

In the narration of the encomium (3:4–5a) Paul gives the details of his background, prefacing it with "if anyone else has reason to be confident in the flesh, I have more" (3:4). This is followed by a recounting of his own Jewish qualifications ascribed through birth: circumcised on the eighth day, membership in the people of Israel, of the tribe of Benjamin, a Hebrew born of Hebrews (3:5). Given his own Jewish background, the opponents could, at best, only equal his own background, and they probably did not. Given the set of standards advocated by the agitators (circumcision as representative of membership in the covenant community and of greater obedience to Torah), his audience would find it difficult to emulate Paul's life. If anyone in his audience becomes circumcised, it will be as an adult, not as an eight-day-old [73] child, as Torah requires. This fits well into Paul's recommendation of himself. His point here is precisely, "You cannot imitate this!"

Paul's final comments before his call to imitation also reinforce his own character within the encomium. By referring to those who agree with him as "perfect" (3:15), Paul again appeals to the sensibilities of his audience.

---

45. The dog was a negative image in antiquity. For Jews, it was synonymous with uncleanness and used of those outside the covenant (O'Brien, *Philippians*, 354–55). In a Gentile context, the dog was proverbial for its unpleasant characteristics such as greed, fawning, and shamelessness. Clearly, this is strong invective aimed not to describe Paul's opponents but to insult them: Koester, "Purpose of Polemic," 320.

46. Marshall, *Enmity*, 35–69.

47. Cf. Fiore, *Function of Personal Example*, 185.

To those who still are not convinced, Paul asserts that God will intervene directly to convince them that Paul's way is the correct one (3:15). One final assertion is used by Paul to keep the Philippians on his side—"let us hold fast to what we have attained" (3:16). A move towards the agitators is, for Paul, a move away from the achievements of the Philippians themselves, and thus dishonorable. This sets up the conclusion of his encomium with its call to imitation: "become fellow-imitators of me" (3:17). In contrast to the *impossibility* of imitating Paul in his achievements within Judaism, Paul now asserts the *possibility* of imitating him in his Christian achievements.[48]

Having recommended himself and enjoined the Philippians to imitate his life,[49] Paul turns to another immediate concern. In vv. 18–21, Paul addresses a challenge to the Philippian Christian community that, unlike the Judaizers, is resident in the city.[50] These "enemies of the cross of Christ" are described in terms of practices of many of the associations of antiquity: indulgence in food and drink.[51] Paul ends the encomium by reminding the Philippians that by imitating his way, they too will share in the achievements, which he outlines for himself, particularly the resurrection (3:21). The honor/memorial held out to the Philippians is the promise of future resurrection. In describing his own achievement of establishing a relationship with Christ (3:10) and in outlining the results of the Philippians' relationship with Christ (3:21), Paul draws on resurrection language. In both cases the contrast is made with those who seek honor in this lifetime (3:3–19). Honor for Paul is the imitation of his life by the Philippians; honor for the Philippians is [74] the transformation of their "body of humiliation" to a "body of his [Christ's] glory" (3:21).

Tertullian, in his *Apology*, likewise uses epideictic rhetoric insofar as he contrasts the Christians with other groups, particularly voluntary

---

48. This is Paul's most extensive argument for imitation. He does make similar recommendations elsewhere. In 1 Cor 4:16 he writes, "I urge you, then, be imitators of me" and in 1 Cor 11:1, "Be imitators of me, as I am of Christ." In 1 Thess 1:6 he recognizes that they "became imitators of us and of the Lord." Cf. Gal 4:12: "Become as I am, for I also have become as you are." See Castelli, *Imitating Paul*, 89–117; cf. Fiore, *Function of Personal Example*, 164–90 for more on Paul's use of example.

49. In fact, they may already have done so in part by vicariously sharing in God's grace with Paul in his sufferings (Phil 1:7); they have followed their founder in his experiences of the deity. Certainly, Paul indicates that some present at Philippi are already imitating him and are to be counted for imitation along with him: "and mark those thus walking (in imitation of me), since you have an example in us (them and me)" (3:17b, my translation).

50. The following is a summary of my argument published elsewhere (Ascough, *Paul's Macedonian Associations*, 146–49).

51. Cf. Ascough, *Paul's Macedonian Associations*, 149.

associations. His primary point with which he begins chapter 38 is that Christians should receive a proper place among the law-tolerant associations. Like the associations, the Christians meet together as an assembly (*Apol.* 39). However, unlike the associations, claims Tertullian, the Christians do not require of their members financial donations (*Apol.* 39). Money that is collected is given to support and bury people, help the destitute, the housebound, and those who have suffered misfortune. The money is not "spent on feasts, and drinking-bouts, and eating-houses" (*Apol.* 39)—namely, those very things that the associations are reputed to have focused on and for which they have received various imperial sanctions.[52]

For Tertullian, praise for the Christians is gained by placing blame on the associations and making the contrast clear. And while the primary aim of his rhetoric is to convince the authorities that Christians are innocent of many of the charges against them, his text lavishes such great praise on the Christian groups and such vitriolic arguments against not only the associations but all forms of Greco-Roman religion and philosophy that it is clearly also a form of recruitment. In Tertullian's presentation, all other forms of religion are rendered base and empty in comparison to the superiority of the Christian religion. His call is not only for leniency but for adherence. He concludes this section by claiming, "When the upright, when the virtuous meet together, when the pious, when the pure assemble in congregation, you ought not to call that a faction, but a curia" (*Apol.* 39). A Christian group is not on par with the associations but with the civic assembly, the courthouse, to which all elite Romans aspire to membership. Here, Tertullian seems to be engaged in rhetoric that would fit Castells's category of "project identity" insofar as he seeks to locate the Christian groups within the mainstream organizations of society. In this case, the *curia* is, in fact, the courthouse of God (cf. the striking similarity with Paul's claim in Phil 3:20 that the Christian's *politeuma* is in heaven). [75]

CONCLUSION

In the foregoing brief overview of just a few examples of the "rhetoric of recruitment" from different types of associations in the Greco-Roman world we find that they are engaged in a polemical exchange with their respective surrounding cultures. However, often the rhetoric is not primarily a matter of competition but rather reflects the language of self-definition aimed at attracting and maintaining members. The groups are engaged in resistance

---

52. Cotter, "Collegia and Roman Law." English translations of Tertullian are by Thelwall, *Tertullian*.

identity formation and project identity formation and are often on the fuzzy edge around the boundary between the two. When we examine Christian groups within this mix, we find that they too reflect a similar process of self-definition and recruitment. Yet it is clear that it is not Christian groups alone that are engaged in this process (as if Christianity is, as is often supposed, a missionary religion *unlike* other groups). All kinds of "embedded" associations in antiquity are employing the rhetoric of superiority, including the othering of those not among "us," and in this way are involved in self-definition as well as persuasion for recruitment and adherence to their own particular group.[53]

---

53. Support for the research and writing of this paper has been provided through an Alexander von Humboldt Research Fellowship, a Queen's University Chancellor's Research Award, an Ontario Government Premier's Research Excellence Award, and a Social Sciences and Humanities Research Council of Canada Standard Research Grant.

11

"A Place to Stand, a Place to Grow"

Architectural and Epigraphic Evidence for Expansion in Greco-Roman Associations

THERE IS A RECENT resurgence in interest in the growth and development of Greco-Roman elective social formations such as Christian and Jewish groups, in part due to the insightful work of Stephen Wilson on the voluntary associations of antiquity,[1] the relationships among Jewish and Christian groups,[2] and the phenomenon of apostasy among all types of groups.[3] On this latter topic Wilson notes that a more neutral term is "defection," which is "sociologically descriptive rather than theologically judgmental."[4] Despite the lack of evidence for defections from one group to another—clearly understandable insofar as groups do not seek to demonstrate that they are not attractive—Wilson has shown that in Jewish, Christian, and even "pagan"[5] groups, there is evidence for apostasy or defection. Among the latter category, although the bulk of the evidence comes from the philosophical schools, "the

---

1. Wilson, "Voluntary Associations."
2. Wilson, *Related Strangers*.
3. Wilson, *Leaving the Fold*.
4. Wilson, *Leaving the Fold*, 3.
5. Although I dislike this tripart taxonomy and argue against it elsewhere, I use it here both for convenience and to reference easily the manner in which it is laid out in much of the secondary literature. See Ascough, "'Map-maker'"(Chapter 6, above).

scraps of evidence suggest that the concept of defection was not unknown in connection with religious cults or *collegia*."[6] [77]

Most often this aspect of defection from "pagan" groups is framed in terms of conversion *to* other groups, specifically Jewish and, more dominantly, Christian. It is these groups that are thought to have been actively recruiting new members from one another and from the pagans. In the focus on the similarities and differences between Christian and Jewish mission in the first two centuries of the Common Era, the other elective social formations of antiquity (the pagans) are often left to the sidelines. The assumption is made that these groups were not involved in mission. However, this is largely a matter of how one understands "mission," and thus what evidence one allows into the discussion. In this essay I will argue that while the broader Christian concept of mission does not apply to such groups as the voluntary associations, there is good evidence to suggest that these groups were nevertheless interested in and successful in expanding their membership base. Since I have argued elsewhere that there is evidence for the rhetoric of recruitment among the texts and inscriptions from these groups,[7] in this essay I will present evidence from archaeological data that suggest group growth indeed took place.

MISSION AND EXPANSION

In the past, many attempts have been made to explain Christian expansion within the Roman Empire, one of the best-known of which is the seminal work by Adolf von Harnack, *The Expansion of Christianity in the First Three Centuries*.[8] Harnack framed the question in a manner that lingers into current discussions that seek to explain the "expansion," "success," and "triumph" of Christianity over other religions. Although it remains a classic study, Harnack's many methodological flaws and theological presuppositions have been the subject of numerous critical studies.[9] Most problematic is Harnack's focus on the superiority of the Christian message over other religious views, all the while maintaining its isolation from its polytheistic surroundings [78] despite the ways in which the environment was prepared for the message of the gospel.

Harnack's two-volume work does provide a great service in documenting the spread of Christianity to the time of Constantine (albeit from

---

6. Wilson, *Leaving the Fold*, 103.
7. Ascough, "Defining Community-Ethos" (Chapter 10, above).
8. Harnack, *Mission and Expansion of Christianity*.
9. White, "Adolf Harnack," 97–104; Vaage, "Ancient Religious Rivalries."

a biased viewpoint), but it does not give much attention to the question of how or, especially, why Christianity spread other than to point to the "very essence of the religion" and to its versatility and amazing power of adaptation.[10] Methodologically, Harnack assumes Christians were different than others and therefore made an "impression" on outsiders.[11] But one might ask whether this is just an accident of the historical record—namely, Christians preserved their letters so Christian letters are well-testified.

Since the influential work of Harnack, many scholars have assumed that the propagation of religions during the Greco-Roman period, especially during the Roman imperial period, was due to a widespread sense of dissatisfaction with the traditional deities, an anxiety brought on by massive dislocation and a yearning for monotheism and salvation.[12] Particularly effective in meeting such needs, it was thought, were the recently imported religions of the East—mystery cults, Judaism, and Christianity. Stephen Neill aptly illustrates the usual position of earlier studies on the "success" of early Christian missions:

> The strict monotheism of the Jewish faith, and the high moral standards inculcated by their law, had attracted many to at least a partial acceptance of the Jewish faith, and this served for some as a preparation for the Christian gospel. In that hard and often cruel world, a fellowship of people who really loved one another and cared for one another's needs clearly had attractive power. The fervent expectations of the Christians, both for the world and for the individual, must have come as a message of hope to those who had none. Jesus became known as the Savior of the world.[13]

In his seminal work on conversion, A. D. Nock seems to have "Christianized" all ancient groups—that is, he assumes an approach to recruitment for non-Christian groups that seems to read too much of the Christian practice into the evidence.[14] This allowed Nock to conclude that in polytheistic religion, members adhered rather than converted.[15] Later studies have revealed the flaws in this approach. For example, Goodman rightly questions [79] the notion that adherents to polytheistic groups were only marginally attached, pointing out that "devotees of a small number of optional cults

10. Harnack, *Mission and Expansion of Christianity*, 2:467.
11. Cf. Harnack, *Mission and Expansion of Christianity*, 1:470.
12. See, for example, Dodds, *Pagan and Christian*.
13. Neil, "Christian Missions," 574.
14. Nock, *Conversion*.
15. Nock, *Conversion*, 15.

in the early Roman empire do seem sometimes to have developed a sense of social identity which drew them together with their fellow-worshippers in contrast to the outside world."[16] As evidence he points to Mithraism, although one can argue that this is also true for many of the voluntary associations in antiquity.

Scholarly consensus on this issue has shifted dramatically in the last twenty years or so—"generalizations like 'an age of anxiety' win few scholarly adherents, while explanations based on 'messages' or 'ideas' alone remain easy to claim but have become more difficult to maintain."[17] Nevertheless, many discussions about mission and evangelism are based, knowingly or not, on the work of Harnack and Nock. As Peerbolte points out concerning the influence of Harnack's two-volume book, "As important and thorough as his work may still be, it set the course for an interpretation of Paul as a 19th-century protestant, or even better: Lutheran missionary spreading his gospel of grace and faith by his many travels through the Eastern part of the Mediterranean."[18]

In his *Mission and Conversion: Proselytizing in the Religious History of the Roman Empire*, Martin Goodman attempts to bring some structure to the discussion. Goodman distinguishes four types of "mission": informational, educational, apologetic, and proselytizing.[19] The first, informational, intends to impart a general message to others without necessarily wanting to change their behavior or status. The second, educational, does intend to change people into more moral or more contented beings, but does not require the auditor to shift fundamental belief systems. Apologetic "mission" intends to protect the legitimacy of a particular cult and beliefs without necessarily demanding that the audience take up those beliefs. Finally, proselytizing mission aims "to encourage outsiders not only to change their way of life but also to be [[80]] incorporated within their group."[20] Goodman recognizes that these are ideal types and that the boundaries between are blurred in practice.[21]

Goodman's aim in his book is to investigate whether any group in antiquity had a notion of "universal proselytizing mission."[22] In adding the ad-

---

16. Goodman, *Mission and Conversion*, 27.

17. Walters, "Coincidence," 320. Some scholars, however, still assert variations of this understanding; see, for example, Baumgarten, "Greco-Roman Voluntary Associations," 109–10.

18. Peerbolte, "Romans 15:14–29," 144.

19. Goodman, *Mission and Conversion*, 3–6.

20. Goodman, *Mission and Conversion*, 4.

21. Goodman, *Mission and Conversion*, 4.

22. Goodman, *Mission and Conversion*, 7.

jective "universal" and in focusing primarily on "proselytizing," Goodman has, as he well recognizes, "clearly stacked the odds against finding evidence for it."[23] In his investigation, then, it is not surprising that he finds little evidence outside of early Christianity for "mission and conversion." He notes that while very early on some Christians were engaged in proselytizing mission work, it was not an activity taken up in imitation of an already existing Jewish activity[24] and may not have extended much past the crucifixion of Jesus, a position that Vaage pushes further by suggesting that it may not have taken place at all during the first two centuries CE.[25] It is only when one gets to the time of the third-century CE Manicheans that one finds "a missionary religion *par excellence*."[26]

When other scholars draw on Goodman's work, they often drop Goodman's important nuances concerning the range and nature of "universal" proselytizing, and they claim that Christian groups are alone in attempting to attract new members. That is, they assume that there were no attempts to recruit new members among other types of groups, particularly among non-Jewish groups.[27] This assumption ignores some critical archaeological evidence for growth among such groups, evidence that might indeed suggest that they undertook some form of recruitment.[28] One can observe the overlooking of [81] evidence from voluntary association in the recent work of Stephen Chester, who suggests that

> Without implying that all or even most members of cult associations qualify as converts, it may be that their "voluntary" aspect makes these associations a particularly suitable comparative

---

23. Goodman, *Mission and Conversion*, 15.

24. Goodman, *Mission and Conversion*, 84–85, 106, 161; cf. Peerbolte, *Paul the Missionary*, 4; Vaage, "Ancient Religious Rivalries," 15.

25. Goodman, *Mission and Conversion*, 106, 174; Vaage, "Ancient Religious Rivalries," 16.

26. Goodman, *Mission and Conversion*, 157.

27. Many follow Goodman in accepting that Jews were engaged in "an apologetic mission to win gentile sympathizers" but not "new Jews" (*Mission and Conversion*, 85, 92; see also the independent but similar conclusion in McKnight, *Light among the Gentiles*, 116–17). It is only later in antiquity that one finds evidence, mainly Talmudic, that suggests at least some Jews may have engaged in proselytizing (Goodman, *Mission and Conversion*, 148).

28. Goodman himself points out that there was some form of "mission" among members of pagan cults, but that "when it occurred, [it] was usually apologetic and propagandistic" (*Mission and Conversion*, 32; see also Beck, "Becoming a Mithraist," 177). The evidence for "universal proselytizing" among the members of the pagan cults is "ambiguous at best" (*Mission and Conversion*, 154; cf. Peerbolte, *Paul the Missionary*, 6; Vaage, "Ancient Religious Rivalries," 13).

tool for probing questions related to conversion. They "fit" this task particularly well.[29]

He goes on to discuss how the Corinthian Christians' actions, customs, and practical arrangements are instinctively drawn "on patterns of behavior familiar from the voluntary associations."[30] In particular, he examines issues of patronage, meals, litigation, and finances. Despite this work, however, he rarely, if ever, returns to the data from the associations. Indeed, in his conclusion to the book he notes:

> In terms of further research, these conclusions suggest the possibility of other comparative studies which move beyond the boundaries of early Christianity. Obvious candidates for inclusion would be the mystery cults, considered this time in their own right, the philosophical schools, and Judaism.[31]

Strikingly missing from this list is the voluntary associations, despite their supposed "fit."

Chester fails to appreciate what his own investigation has hinted at in his observation that there were "considerable differences in expectation between Paul and the Corinthians as to the consequences of conversion."[32] He does not consider that the Corinthians did not view their new alliance with Jesus to be a "conversion" (in the Pauline sense) at all. Indeed, despite Paul's best intentions, the Corinthian house groups continued to conduct their communal life much in the same manner as the associations precisely because that is what they considered themselves to be. By exposing the differences with Paul's view, Chester supports precisely that which he claims to argue against—a striking similarity between a particular Christian community and the generalized pattern of associative behaviors in the Greco-Roman world. The problem, in my view, is that despite his best efforts not to do so, Chester is working with an implicit Christian, one might say "Pauline," view of conversion that he seeks to find in his supposed analogous forms of community. [82] When this particular view of conversion is not found in the groups he investigates, he then eliminates them from consideration, without first considering other forms of recruitment and growth that fall outside of the (assumed) Pauline pattern. In this way, Chester has fallen into much the same mistake as Nock did seventy years earlier.

---

29. Chester, *Conversion at Corinth*, 232.
30. Chester, *Conversion at Corinth*, 233.
31. Chester, *Conversion at Corinth*, 321.
32. Chester, *Conversion at Corinth*, 263.

In order to begin to rectify this scholarly tendency, this essay will present archaeological and epigraphic evidence from the meeting places of Greco-Roman associations and show that these groups *did* undergo some, albeit limited, group expansion and growth. While "conversion" or "evangelism" are not the correct descriptors of the recruitment practices of ancient associations, these groups should not be ignored in broad-based studies of how religious groups interacted with their urban environments in attracting new members. Furthermore, they should not be quickly put aside in discussions of the growth of early Christian groups as they may well prove to have important analogical information for our understanding of early Christian growth.

ASSOCIATION BUILDINGS

Before considering the details of the archaeological evidence from association buildings that indicate an increase in group membership, we do well to note L. Michael White's distillation of five important categories to consider when examining archaeological evidence for architectural adaptation:[33]

1. Pragmatic considerations such as numerical growth, property boundaries, limitations of existing buildings, and destruction of an existing building.

2. Cultural influences such as the common practice of adapting private structures for religious usage.

3. Socioeconomic and political factors such as patronage or change in social, financial, or legal status.

4. Attitudinal factors within the community towards the building, outsiders, or the sense of self-identity.

5. Factors within the cultic life of the community such as relationships within the assembly, rituals, organization, and leadership.

For the purpose of this study, I am particularly interested in the first category—pragmatic considerations—especially "numerical growth." White's list is important in terms of examining archaeological evidence of building adaptation; not all adaptations were a result of growth, and other factors must be considered. Thus, in gathering some exemplars of growth in associations [83], I have been cautious only to include those instances where numerical growth seems to be the primary reason for the adaptation. When

---

33. White, *Social Origins*, 2:22.

"A Place to Stand, a Place to Grow"   215

turning to other types of evidence, such as epigraphic or literary, we need to be equally cautious, employing a "hermeneutic of suspicion" about claims made around recruitment. Nevertheless, when we have considered these factors, there remains evidence for group growth among a variety of associations in antiquity.

Early attestation for recruitment among associations is difficult to find but not entirely absent. For example, an inscription from Phaleron (Attica) dating to c. 365–330 BCE (IG II² 2345) provides a list of one hundred and fifty male names (eighty-five of which are legible), divided according to seven or eight *thiasoi* that vary in size from as low as ten members to as high as fifty to sixty members.[34] Although once thought to be an Athenian phratry list, a recent reexamination of the inscription by Stephen Lambert has provided convincing, if not conclusive, evidence that the list contains the names of members of various *thiasoi* of Herakles, the majority of whose members came from the town of Alopeke, but at least some of whom can be linked the Athenian community on Salamis in the sixth to fourth centuries. The list reflects the full membership of the *thiasoi*,[35] but up to four names were "added to the bottom of some *thiasoi* after the initial inscription of the stone,"[36] only one of whom is identifiable as the son of a man listed earlier. *Thiasoi* of Herakles were normally hereditary or quasi-hereditary,[37] and the unsure nature of the names suggests due caution is necessary. However, that there are a few names added, and if only one is a hereditary new member, then perhaps this inscription is indicative of some slight growth in the association through the addition of new members from outside families.[38] That is, new families have been incorporated into the association.

Another tantalizing early piece of information comes from an inscription from Rhodes in which a number of associations [84] (*koina*) honor Dionysodoros of Alexandria for his services as a member and as a leader (IG

---

34. See Lambert, "*IG* II²," 119. The normal *thiasos* size in the fourth century BCE might be linked to the number of people that could be fed from the meat of one animal; see Lambert, "*IG* II²," 128 n. 57.

35. Lambert, "*IG* II²," 120.

36. Lambert, "*IG* II²," 120.

37. Lambert, "*IG* II²," 125.

38. It is interesting to observe that we have testimony here to multiple *thiasoi* in association with one another (Lambert, "*IG* II²," 127) and there is perhaps a slight suggestion here that membership in the Heraklean *thiasoi* entailed travel around Attica, and one wonders if, rather like some modern types of dining club, there was an association of clubs with reciprocal rights or common membership (Lambert, "*IG* II²," 128). This is further evidence for the existence of translocal links among some associations (cf. Ascough, "Translocal Relationships" [Chapater 5, above]).

XII/1 155).³⁹ The inscription itself seems to be a dossier of sorts, compiling a number of independent inscriptions or extracts of inscriptions concerning Dionysodoros.⁴⁰ In section C (IV, lines 108–109), the *koinon* of Haliadai and Haliastai honor Dionysodoros for his twenty-three consecutive years as *archeranistas* (he was a member for a total of thirty-five years) during which time he "enlarged" the size of the association (*epauxēsas ton eranon*).

The expansion of the Egyptian cult of Sarapis on Delos proves instructive for the Hellenistic period. After two generations of growth, the household association, under its third priest Apollonius, finally undertook the building of a new Sarapeion (Sarapeion A; IG XI/4 1299, late-third to early-second century BCE).⁴¹ The Sarapeion was constructed by the extension of an existing *insula* of private buildings.⁴² In defending the choice to build at this location, the inscription claims that the land was a "dung-heap," although this cannot be taken literally, since it seems to have been a residential neighborhood. White interprets the claim as defending the building of the Sarapeion near a sacred spring.⁴³ In response to the charge that doing so has defiled the land, Apollonius claims that the land was already defiled, perhaps indicting the hereditary guardian of the spring for not maintaining it. The Sarapeion has served, then, to sanctify the land anew.⁴⁴

White goes on to suggest that the domestic property that formed the basis for the architectural expansion into the Sarapeion was none other than the rented property used previously for the association's meetings and recently purchased by the priest Apollonius.⁴⁵ If this interpretation is correct, then clearly the growth of the association not only necessitated expanded premises but also brought about enough revenue (either by subscription or patronage, or both) to allow for the purchase of the rented property.⁴⁶ [85]

---

39. The inscription gives clear evidence for a person being a participating member of more than one association at one time; see Gabrielsen, "Rhodian Associations," 152. Contrary to the current opinion, it was not unusual at all for a person to be simultaneously a member of, and hold office in, more than one *koinon*; the stele alone bears testimony to Dionysodoros's multiple memberships in at least four associations.

40. Gabrielsen, "Rhodian Associations," 138.

41. See White, *Building God's House*, 1:33.

42. See the description in White, *Building God's House*, 1:36.

43. White, *Building God's House*, 1:36.

44. White, *Social Origins*, 1:36.

45. White, *Social Origins*, 1:36–37.

46. Competition to the association that built Sarapeion A came from another Sarapeion (deemed Sarapeion C), which provided greater accommodation to Roman tastes and ultimately triumphed socially on Delos (White, *Social Origins*, 1:38).

The meeting place of an association of Dionysiac *Bukoloi* ("cowherds") has been located on the middle acropolis at Pergamon. This building has been designated as the Podiensaal ("Podium Hall") due to its design.[47] The long side of the rectangular building lies east-west along the main street. The hall itself is about 24 m x 10 m, with a paved yard in front. It did not front the main street but was set back behind a row of stores and workshops.[48] Access to the yard was through a small alley to the east. Behind the hall was a well, probably linked to the Dionysos cult. On the south side a doorway opens from the paved yard, while the cult niche lies directly across from the doorway. On either side of the doorway and the cult niche, set against the walls, is a *pi*-shaped podium, 1 m high and 2 m wide where participants in the cult banquet would have reclined. As Pilhofer points out, the function of the podium is clear; the association members lie on it in such a way that the head of each is oriented to the middle of the hall.[49] Set slightly lower is a marble shelf where food and drink would be set down.

Fig. 11.1: Pergamon, Podiensaal, facing southeast
(photo by Richard S. Ascough) [86]

---

47. See figure 79 in Radt, *Pergamon*, 136–37.

48. Radt, *Pergamon*, 196. Radt gives a description of the excavations on pages 196–99; see also Schwarzer, "Vereinslokale," 231–35.

49. Pilhofer, *Die frühen Christen*, 135.

Two small altars were found near the podium hall in a Byzantine wall, one of which bears a relief of a wine cup and garland and a dedication to "Dionysos Kathegemon" (see Jaccottet no. 92), and the other of which has a relief of an oak garland and a goat-fish with a cornucopia (symbols of the birth sign of the emperor, Capricorn) and is dedicated to Caesar Augustus (Jaccottet no. 93).[50] Both were set up by a chief priest (*archiboukolos*) named Herodes. These altars, along with a number of inscriptions from the Boukoloi at Pergamon, give us a picture of this group from around 27 BCE to the time of Hadrian.[51] The altar inscriptions attest to the presence of an *archibukolos* in the late first century BCE. The dedication to the emperor not only indicates that the Boukoloi were honoring Augustus at this time but may also be linked to an earlier inscription in which an association of Baccants (worshipers of Dionysos) at Pergamon honor King Eumenes II (Jaccottet no. 91, 159 BCE). Whether consciously or not, the members of the latter association stand in the tradition of the bacchants that honors Eumenes II at Pergamon.[52] By the time of the first century, there is epigraphic attestation to the functionaries and cult of the association (Jaccottet nos. 94 and 97), while inscriptions from the end of the first century show the continuation of the association (Jaccottet nos. 95 and 96).

Radt points out that archaeological excavations of the hall indicated that the present form was not the original design, but that the hall developed "nach und nach" from the second to the fourth century CE.[53] He suggests that the western podium was built earlier, perhaps in the second century CE, while the eastern podium was added later. This indicates that the group doubled in size over the two centuries. Since the current layout indicates that the hall can accommodate about seventy participants,[54] then the earlier group was probably about thirty-five members.

Pilohofer finds an analogy in the (international) Asiani association at Thessalonike (IG X/2.1 185) that had a priest but no temple, in continuity with their forbearers in Italy.[55] Both associations are from the time of the empire, and both have no need for a temple.[56] Much like Jewish and [87]

---

50. Jaccottet, *Choisir Dionysos*. Volume 1 contains the inscriptions while volume 2 contains commentary.

51. Jaccottet, *Choisir Dionysos*, 2:99 (cf. 174–75; Radt, *Pergamon*, 198). IPerg 485 (=94), 222 (=95), 488 (=96), 487 (=97), 486 (=99), 319 (=100), 320 (=101), and IGR IV 386 (=98). Numbers in parentheses refer to Jaccottet, *Choisir Dionysos*, I.

52. Jaccottet, *Choisir Dionysos*, 2:99.

53. Radt, *Pergamon*, 196.

54. Radt, *Pergamon*, 197.

55. Pilhofer, *Die frühen Christen*, 127–30.

56. Pilhofer points out that although there is a temple to Dionysos down the road

Christian groups, both these associations look to a savior in the here-and-now (Dionysos) and have eschatological hopes for the future, symbolized in their sharing of wine and meat. Jaccottet attributes the extraordinary success of Dionysiac associations from the third century BCE through fourth century CE to the "ubiquitous, enigmatic" nature of the god that "allowed the Bacchic associations to assemble so freely, with no model, no recurring formalities—a series of unique circles created by and for the persons that constituted them."[57] The associations were "closely linked to the people and their desires" and "enabled an individual approach to the Bacchic phenomenon."[58]

We find more evidence for growth in associations in the city of Ephesos where there is clearly an expansion of Egyptian religions during the Roman imperial period. Although evidence before the second century CE is scant, inscriptional evidence from that century and beyond points to "a well-established cult with clergy and a temple."[59] Excavators found in the harbor area an inscription dedicated to Artemis (although the statue is of Isis), the emperor, and the city, along with "those conducting business at the customs house (*telōnion*) for fishing toll" (IEph 1503 = SIRIS 301, dated to the time of Antoniums Pius).[60] Walters, following Dunand, suggests that the customs house for fishing toll "was an association which gathered under the patronage of Isis," although the members need not have been initiates of the Isis cult.[61] Although Walters affirms the expansion of the Egyptian cults, he does not offer any concrete evidence that they did indeed expand during these centuries.[62] Rather, he shows that the lack of evidence in the republican period and the robust nature of the cult of the Egyptian gods by the second century and beyond suggest that there *was* an expansion of this association. Finding analogies from elsewhere, including the evidence of Sarapion A on Delos (discussed above), Walters claims, "The expansion

---

from this meeting hall, there is no relationship between the temple and the Podiensaal association (*Die frühen Christen*, 137). We have, he suggests, an example of a community without a temple. This is supported by the work of Schwarzer, who compares the podium hall to other buildings of a similar style in Pergamon. He argues that during the Hellenistic period, associations in the city preferred private pubs to public sanctuaries (Schwarzer, "Vereinslokale," 244).

57. Jaccottet, *Choisir Dionysos*, 2:337.
58. Jaccottet, *Choisir Dionysos*, 2:337.
59. Walters, "Coincidence," 316.
60. Walters, "Coincidence," 317.
61. Walters, "Coincidence," 317; Dunand, *Le culte d'Isis*, 71; cf. Horsley, *New Documents* 5, 95–114.
62. Cf. Walters, "Coincidence," 322.

of the cult of the two Egyptians as well as that of the Christians depended most fundamentally [88] on private initiative" rather than on ideology and psychological factors.⁶³ This is supported by Takács who notes, "While Romanization and urbanization made the propagation of the cult of Isis and Sarapis possible, personal interest and ideology as well as local conditions were decisive undercurrents that could enable and facilitate an introduction of Isis and Sarapis and the construction of a temple."⁶⁴

Fig. 11.2: Ephesos, Terrace House 2, Residential Unit 6
(photo by Richard S. Ascough) [89]

---

63. Walters, "Coincidence," 322.

64. Takács, *Isis and Sarapis*, 136; cf. Nilsson, who points to fear of death as the primary motivation for the popularity of, and thus we might add the reason for growth in, the Dionysiac mysteries: "Death is a mighty source of religion and religious belief. Man fears death instinctively and wonders what will befall him after death . . . The Bacchic mysteries owed their popularity in the Roman age to the answer they gave to this deep-seated anxiety. They calmed the fears and smoothed over the anxiety, they promised the bliss of an eternal banquet. They were convenient for easy-going people who wanted to be freed from qualms" (Nilsson, "Bacchic Mysteries," 195). While this might represent *some* of the reasoning, perhaps equally important, if not more so, were the tangible, this-worldly benefits for which people joined the Dionysiac associations.

Fig. 11.3: Ephesos, Terrace House 2, Residential Unit 6, inscription
(photo by Richard S. Ascough)

There is little other evidence for association buildings at Ephesos, although some does exist. In the terrace housing complexes thus far excavated, there are at least two possible association meeting rooms. In the complex designated Terrace House 2, there exists a large room arrangement (950 m²) most notable for its two-story peristyle court, marble-paneled room (H2/31), and a barrel-vaulted *basilica privata*.[65] An inscription from the end of the second century CE names the presumed owner: Gaius Flavius Furius Aptus, a leading citizen of Ephesos.[66] The inscription clearly links him with the cult of Dionysos, as do the artistic themes in the small room adjoining the basilica (H2/8). I would suggest that the elaborate room decorations and the prominence of the leader point to this as a private cult association that operated outside the official cult of Dionysos in the city.

This *oikos*-based association might well have followed the pattern of development of another set of rooms in the Terrace House 1 complex. There, a large peristyle house dating from the first century BCE was adapted at the beginning of the second century CE to serve another function, one that "may be interpreted as a meeting-house of an association, serving especially for banquets."[67] The new structure took over about half the *insula* and was lavishly decorated, suggesting an association that was rather well-off at that time. It was refurbished again in the second half of the second century CE, "in keeping with a desire for increased ceremonial function, especially in the banqueting house."[68] However, by the end of the third century, workshops

65. See diagram in Scherrer, *Ephesus*, 104–5.
66. The full dedicatory inscription reads, "Dionysos Oreios Bakchios before the city. Set up by heratai Gaius Flavius Furius Aptus."
67. Scherrer, *Ephesus*, 100.
68. Scherrer, *Ephesus*, 102.

and small businesses appear fronting Curetes Street, reflecting poorer living [90] standards as a result of earthquake damage and worsening economic conditions. If the second-century rooms are interpreted correctly as a banqueting hall of an association, the property would have belonged to the association itself. One possible explanation, then, for the appearance of the shops would be that members of a workers' association have relocated their workshops to property owned by the association itself, in part to help the struggling members and in part to offset costs within the association through rent. Of course, much of this is conjectural and still awaits further excavation at the site itself.

ASSOCIATION MEMBERSHIP LISTS

One interesting place to look for evidence for growth in associations is the inscribed membership lists, or *alba*, which correctly have been deemed "group portraits in words."[69] These must be used with caution, however, as there are multiple ways to interpret the data. Take, for example, the *alba* of the *collegium lenunculariorum tabulariorum auxiliariorum* of Ostia, a professional association of owners and operators of oar-powered tugboats who would be employed to help large cargo ships maneuver within the harbor.[70] The first album dates from 152 CE (CIL XIV 250) while the second comes from forty years later, 192 CE (CIL XIV 251). Royden mentions three other fragmentary *alba* from this association: CIL XIV 4567 and 4568, both dated to shortly after 152 CE, and Bloch no. 42,[71] which dates to 213 CE.[72] To these can be added a sixth album from this association, dating to 256 CE.[73]

Between the first and the second complete *alba*, there is an increase in the total number of names—from about 125 names to 258 names, while the inscription from 213 CE indicates about 290 names.[74] The two earlier, [91] complete *alba* (CIL XIV 250 and 251) were not inscribed at one time

---

69. Van Nijf, "Collegia and Civic Guards," 333.

70. See Royden, *Magistrates*, 38; also Meiggs, *Roman Ostia*, 297–98. Ostia is rich in evidence for professional associations, with about forty different associations attested (Hermansen, *Ostia*, 55).

71. Bloch, "Ostia," 280.

72. Royden, *Magistrates*, 38.

73. See *AE* (1987), 198; Purcell, Review of Royden, *Magistrates*, 182.

74. Meiggs (*Roman Ostia*, 331) assumes that the presence of only one ex-magistrate suggests that the *album* dates to shortly after the founding of the association. Royden (*Magistrates*, 38) disputes this, pointing out that it merely suggests that the *album* was not in use for a long period and that the association may date to the middle of the first century CE.

but were continually updated. This is indicated on CIL XIV 251 by two clear changes in the lettering, suggesting a different engraver, and by the fact that column 8 was not originally planned for the inscription and has been squeezed in.[75] Also, some of the men listed separately as magistrates also appear in the list of *plebs*, suggesting that when the *album* was first engraved they were not in leadership and that their names were added to the magistrates list later, when they attained that position. Thus, "the *alba* were used to keep a continuous record of the magistrates and the members of the *collegium*."[76]

Royden is rightly cautious of earlier opinions (i.e., Meiggs's) of the "tremendous growth" of this *collegium*.[77] He estimates that the *overall* size of the *collegium* grew by only about twenty to thirty percent between 152 and 213 CE, from about one hundred members to 120 or 130.[78] This would make sense in light of the difficulty involved in substantially increasing the number of tugboats operating in the harbor. Yet, in that time, "roughly 138 men must have joined the *collegium* over the twenty-one-year period, which is roughly equivalent to about seven men per year."[79] Thus, while Royden's skepticism over Meiggs's assumption of the doubling in size of this association is well-taken, these inscriptions still testify to the fact that the association was not at all static but was constantly adding new members that led to an increase, albeit small, of their total membership.

In the second inscription (CIL XIV 251), many names from the earlier inscription (CIL XIV 250) have been dropped (probably due to death) while others reappear, sometimes with indications of a higher social status.[80] Among the new members there are clear indications that sons have entered into their father's *collegium*, some at a very early age.[81] Nevertheless, the evidence "does not imply the existence of legislation mandating the heredity of membership in a *collegium*,"[82] and the subscription of a son does not explain the entirety of the growth of the membership list. It is, however, suggestive of one particular form of recruitment in associations—familial, [92] particularly fathers bringing sons into the association. The inclusion of

---

75. Royden, *Magistrates*, 38.
76. Royden, *Magistrates*, 39, cf. p. 46.
77. Royden, *Magistrates*, 47.
78. Royden, *Magistrates*, 47.
79. Royden, *Magistrates*, 47 n. 100.
80. Royden, *Magistrates*, 238.
81. Royden, *Magistrates*, 238.
82. Royden, *Magistrates*, 238.

freedmen in the *alba*[83] further strengthens the larger familial connections in the association, suggesting that the paterfamilias was a key component in the recruitment of new members. Father-son or *dominus-libertus* (*liberti*) connections are the primary means that the group grew.[84]

Herz feels that Royden is too cautious in his estimations about the overall growth of the group. He points out that in the forty years between the two inscriptions almost the entire membership has been replaced.[85] Overall, however, the increase in names also suggests an increase in the prosperity of Ostia itself, and the increasing fortunes of some of the families represented in the inscription.[86] This being so, then it is possible that the number of tugboats operating in the port did increase, opening up room for more operators to be members of this association. For our purposes, however, it is important to note that the association grows not only through familial connections but also through the addition of non-relatives to the group.

Another interesting *alba* found in Torre Nova (Campagna, near Rome) and dated to the second century CE provides a lengthy list of the names of those who have made financial donations to a Dionysiac association—402 names in total, eighty percent of them Greek and the remainder Latin. Since this is a list of donors to a statue of the high priestess and wife of Marcus Squilla, Agrippinilla, it is quite likely that the actual membership of the association was much higher.[87]

This association was grounded in the household of the senatorial family of Marcus Gavius Squilla Gallicanus. It is probable that the association was founded by Agrippinilla during her husband's single-year term as proconsul of Asia (c. 165 CE), when they lived in Mytilene on the island of Lesbos.[88] Although based on the senator's *familia*, the association is much larger, reflecting the desire of those outside the family, such as Roman administrative staff, freedmen, tradesmen, and new immigrants from Asia Minor, to be affiliated with a person of great influence and power.[89] It is probable that [93] some of these joined the association after it had been moved to Torra Nova.[90] Nevertheless, the majority of the members have

83. Royden, *Magistrates*, 48.
84. Herz, "Kollegien in Ostia," 312–14.
85. Herz, "Kollegien in Ostia," 296.
86. Herz, "Kollegien in Ostia," 324.
87. McLean, "Agrippinilla Inscription," 246.
88. McLean, "Agrippinilla Inscription," 268, 269.
89. McLean, "Agrippinilla Inscription," 268, 269.
90. McLean, "Agrippinilla Inscription," 257.

Greek names, indicating their possible origins in Asia Minor and subsequent move to Italy.[91]

The *familia* structure of the association proved no impediment to the growth and portability of the association.[92] "Membership was not determined by ideological attachment to Dionysos (over against some other god), but rather by the preexisting social bonds and networks. Under the patronage of Dionysos, material benefits were realized by his followers when the social network of the association mediated and nurtured other social networks such as employer/employee, patron/recipient, creditor/debtor."[93]

Some interesting evidence arises from an inscription from the *collegium* of the Augustales at the port city of Misenum, dating to 147–149 CE.[94] One of ten marble statue bases (base 9) contains the testamentary legacy of Q. Cominius Abascantus and his wife to the local Augustales.[95] Most interesting is the inscription on face A, which records the commemoration of Abascantus by his wife through the erection of a statue, presumably on this base. The text not only records the civic achievements of this freedman, but also notes his acts of philanthropy, including that to the *Augustales corporati*, members of the Augustales.[96] [94]

Important for our study is an odd phrase that occurs in the inscription on face A. The benefactions of the deceased are given to the Augustales *corporati*, members of the Augustales, to the tune of twelve sesterces each per year.[97] There then occurs note of benefactions to Augustales *qui in corpore non sunt* (lines 8–9), a designation not known from any other

---

91. In Torre Nova the association seems to have had a meeting hall for symposia, as indicated by the two Keepers of the Cave; see Nilsson ("Bacchic Mysteries," 185), who also points out that many Bacchic associations had halls, sometimes formed as artificial caves. Unfortunately, the location of this meeting hall is no longer known.

92. McLean, "Agrippinilla Inscription," 257.

93. McLean, "Agrippinilla Inscription," 270.

94. Although often considered to be an official, civic, thus not voluntary, association, the Augustales were probably semi-official; see de Ligt, "Governmental Attitudes"; and de Ligt, "Semi-Public Collegia"; Bollmann, *Römische Verinshäuser*, 39–46. At Misenum they can be viewed less as a priestly grouping focused on maintaining the imperial cult, and more as constituting an *ordo* next in status to that of *decuriones*, a middle layer in the social and economic fabric of towns in the Roman West, the *libertina nobilitas* (D'Arms, "Memory, Money, and Status," 129, cf. 131).

95. This is one of two bases from the Augustales, the other being Base 10, dedicated by C. Iulius Phoebus, *curator perp(etuus)*.

96. For the guild building of the Augustales in Ostia and the stages of development of the building see Hermansen, *Ostia*, 111–13.

97. D'Arms, "Memory, Money, and Status," 133.

inscription.[98] This group "constituted a 'reserve tank' for Augustales who qualified, financially and otherwise, for membership in the *corpus*, but who were blocked owing to the enforcement of a strict *numerus clausus*, which can be established beyond reasonable doubt as having consisted of one hundred."[99] Whether or not they actively recruited is difficult to say from this inscription. However, what is striking is that the association proved attractive enough to maintain a waiting list of those who desired to become full members—a list probably numbering about one hundred.[100] It is from this group that the inner circle of full members could draw new recruits when positions opened up,[101] presumably through the death or departure of one of the members. Each of these "members in waiting" are to receive a yearly sum of eight sesterces.[102]

We need also to consider briefly some evidence from the cult of Mithras. Associations dedicated to Mithras were spread throughout the circum-Mediterranean world from at least the second century CE and are considered by many to be an interesting analogy for early Christian groups. Although often labeled as mystery religions, the Mithras groups are more accurately classified as a form of private religious (voluntary) association. As White notes, "Mithraic organizations followed more on the lines of *collegia*."[103] Its voluntary nature is summarized by Gordon:

> "Mithraism" is of course not only a system of teaching about a god and the experience of the individual soul, but an organization, a social teaching, a cultural system that not only explains experience but patterns it. It is this aspect of the cult which transforms it from a mere series of "mystery ideas" into a meaningful personal choice.[104] [95]

In Rome and Ostia one finds "Mithraea established within preexisting structures, including warehouses, baths, cryptoportici (of all sorts), vaulted

98. D'Arms, "Memory, Money, and Status," 131.
99. D'Arms, "Memory, Money, and Status," 128.
100. D'Arms, "Memory, Money, and Status," 134.
101. D'Arms, "Memory, Money, and Status," 132.
102. D'Arms, "Memory, Money, and Status," 134. Interestingly, face C of the inscription indicates that the widow of the benefactor, Nymphidia Monime, was voted into the inner-membership, probably to replace her husband and likely motivated by the association's hope for further benefactions from the childless couple. This unprecedented honor might have been motivated by a desire to make this freedwoman even better disposed to make additional gifts, benefactions, and a legacy (D'Arms, "Memory, Money, and Status," 143).
103. White, *Social Origins*, 1:57; Beck, "Mysteries of Mithras"; Beck, "Mithras Cult."
104. Gordon, "Mithraism and Roman Society," 112.

"A Place to Stand, a Place to Grow" 227

subterranean storage chambers, and (of course) private homes."[105] In fact, "all fourteen sites at Ostia and seven at Rome" reflect such architectural adaptation.[106] Although it was popular among members of the Roman army, the expansion of the cult of Mithras seems not to be linked to the direct influence of the military, particularly in such places as Rome, Ostia, and provinces such as Pannonia and Gaul.[107] Mithras proved attractive to a wide range of persons.

We see this attraction reflected in the Mithras association located in Virunum, in the province of Nordicum.[108] Despite not publicly advertising or engaging in widespread proselytizing, two late-second- and early-third-century CE *alba* from the Mithraists in Virunum suggest that the group both anticipated and realized the addition of new members to their ranks. A bronze plaque originally had more than fifty percent of its usable space left free for the addition of the names of future initiates in the ensuing years.[109] The list of names from the second third of the second column and on reflects a number of different hands (up to sixteen) and suggests that names of new members were added to the plaque annually.[110]

While this evidence indicates that the Mithraic group regularly "topped up" its membership on account of mortality or attrition, further evidence suggests that there was an overall net increase in the membership. A marble *album* from Virunum suggests that there was a "translocation of a number of members of the original Mithraism and the foundation of a new Mithraism built from the ground up."[111] The names on this *album* suggest that the steady increase in the membership through kin and social networks led to the group being oversubscribed for the space in the old Mithraism.[112] This evidence is all the more interesting because it reflects a well-established Mithraic group [96] rather than one in the initial stage of the cult's spread across the Roman world.

Turning attention to Dura-Europos, we find that over time there was a "process of gradual appropriation and adaptation" in the local religious

---

105. White, *Social Origins*, 1:48.

106. White, *Social Origins*, 1:48.

107. White, *Social Origins*, 1:56.

108. I am grateful to Roger Beck for pointing me to this Mithras group and to the work of Piccottini, *Mithrastempel in Virunum*. Beck also discusses this group in some detail in "On Becoming a Mithraist."

109. Beck, "Becoming a Mithraist," 184.

110. Piccottini, *Mithrastempel*, 44–49.

111. Beck, "On Becoming a Mithraist," 187; Piccottini, *Mithrastempel*, 50–51.

112. Beck, "On Becoming a Mithraist," 187, 192–93.

landscape.¹¹³ For example, a professional guild of scribes renovated two houses into a meeting hall.¹¹⁴ In close proximity one also finds evidence for a house renovated as a synagogue, the renovated *domus ecclesiae* of a Christian group, and another house renovated as a Mithraism. The Mithraism originated as a specially decorated single room of a private house. Founded by two military *strategoi* (168–171 CE), it seems to have served mostly upper- or middle-rank military personnel.¹¹⁵ However, during a major renovation (209–211 CE) that included the destruction of much of the domestic space, the Mithraism was expanded to accommodate more members, a reflection of this time of "vigorous growth and activity."¹¹⁶

That this growth coincided with the influx of new soldiers should not cause one to conclude that it necessarily *would* grow—the Mithraic association still needed to attract members, which they did, not only among upper- and middle-rank military personnel but among all military ranks (Roman and foreign) and even among Roman administrative officials.¹¹⁷ The final expansion of the Mithraism occurred after 240 CE, and included an expansion of the seating capacity and enlargement and artistic elaboration of the *tauroctone* niche—indicative of "further growth and greater wealth and public recognition."¹¹⁸

After examining the evidence for architectural adaptation among a variety of groups at Dura-Europos, White concludes,

> In case after case, year after year, these small religious associations adapted private domestic structures for public religious or collegial use. The ability to acquire such property and adapt it for special use through architectural renovation had significant impact on the social fabric of the city.¹¹⁹

We might further point out that what remains understated in White's comments is that they reveal that many groups, not just Christian groups, were experiencing numerical growth and financial stability such that they were able to undertake the renovation of domestic spaces, turning them into sacred meeting halls. White later claims that "growth and adaptation was [97] predicated more on individual acts of patronage and benefaction than

---

113. White, *Social Origins*, 1:43–44.
114. White, *Social Origins*, 1:44.
115. White, *Social Origins*, 1:50.
116. White, *Social Origins*, 1:53.
117. White, *Social Origins*, 1:171 n. 112.
118. White, *Social Origins*, 1:53.
119. White, *Social Origins*, 1:44.

on patterns of conversion or recruitment."[120] But while this is true in terms of the ability to expand a meeting place, the *necessity* to expand a meeting place is in fact predicated on a pattern of numerical growth that presumes at least implicit, if not explicit, recruitment, albeit not a "conversion."[121]

Finally, the evidence from a few other Italian associations might also be briefly considered. The brotherhood of the Arvals, a Roman association of powerful aristocrats who were operative from the time of Augustus to 304 CE, actively recruited into their membership, particularly from among prominent senators.[122] Although they had a limited number of positions, at least during the Julio-Claudian period they filled empty seats with friends, and even opponents, of the emperor.[123] Despite their public character and connections to the emperor, this association may be instructive for understanding recruitment in other religions, particular since "we do not have such detail for any cult in the ancient world save perhaps Christianity and Judaism."[124] Furthermore, an inscription from Cumae shows that the local civic authorities "vetted the admission of new members" for an association of *fabri/centonarii/dendrophori*.[125] While evidence for growth or recruitment in and of itself, it also suggests that other groups were adding new members but did not need the approval of the authorities.

CONCLUSION

By focusing our attention on evidence for growth in associations, I have ignored evidence for their reduction in size. Clearly, there were many cases in which an association remained static or entered into a period of decline.[126] What I [98] have attempted to do in this study is collect some of the primary archaeological and epigraphic evidence for growth among Greco-Roman associations. It is by no means complete, but I hope that it might be taken as representative and provide at least enough evidence to help dispel the notion

120. White, *Social Origins*, 1:57.
121. But see Beck, "On Becoming a Mithraist," 187–88.
122. Scheid, *Romulus et ses Frères*, 184.
123. Scheid, *Romulus et ses Frères*, 284.
124. Slater, Review of Scheid, *Romulus et ses Frères*.
125. Van Nijf, "Collegia and Civic Guards," 315; see CIL X 3699; cf. Waltzing, *Étude Historique*, 1:247.
126. Take, for example, the Tyrian merchants association at Puteoli, which did not grow and expand over a century, remaining in their rented accommodation and relying on their native city for financial help (White, *Social Origins*, 1:32; OGIS 595 = IGRR I 420). The decline of the association membership is a large topic that deserves its own treatment.

that Greco-Roman associations other than Jewish and Christian groups did not undergo any sort of expansion in their membership in antiquity.[127]

---

127. Support for the research and writing of this paper has been provided through an Alexander von Humboldt Research Fellowship, a Queen's University Chancellor's Research Award, an Ontario Government Premier's Research Excellence Award, and a Social Sciences and Humanities Research Council of Canada Standard Research Grant. I am grateful for work done on this topic for me by my research assistants Rachel McRae and David Malone.

SECTION III

Meals and Memorials

12

Forms of Commensality in Greco-Roman Associations

INTRODUCTION

THE DEGREE TO WHICH Greco-Roman associations held banquets as a mainstay of their communal life is clear from literary, architectural, and epigraphic evidence. Literary texts point to regularly occurring meals among association members, even if somewhat exaggerated charges are laid concerning the raucous behavior at such meals.[1] Despite a lack of architectural form to which association buildings conformed,[2] archeological remains of identifiable association meeting places demonstrate that some associations constructed spaces

---

1. Associations were often repudiated for their indulgence in food and drink. See, for example, Philo's claim concerning the associations that "you could find no sound elements but only liquor, tippling, drunkenness and the outrageous conduct they lead to" (*Flacc.* 136; see also Philo, *Legat.* 10.311–12; *Flacc.* 4; Seland, "Philo and the Clubs." See further Ascough, *Paul's Macedonian Associations*, 85–87).

2. There is no common terminology and associations varied in size and function and many owned more than one building; see Bollmann, *Römische Verinshäuser*, 47; van Nijf, *Civic World*, 107; Waltzing, *Étude Historique*, 4:437–43.

for explicit use as banqueting facilities, most often in the form of triclinia.³ Other association buildings include large multipurpose rooms, in which in times of meals "couches could be set out in the main hall, side rooms, the porticoes, or the court itself."⁴ Other [34] associations held meals in the open air using movable equipment or in rented spaces such as *tabernae*.⁵

Turning to epigraphic evidence, one finds some associations defining themselves by reference to banqueting practices, such as the "college of messmates" (*collegium comestorum*), "drinking buddies" (*sodales ex symposia*), and "table companions who customarily share banquets together" (*convictor[es] qui una epula vesci solent*), or "diners" (*comestores*).⁶ In many associations, officials are named for their roles at meals; for example, *klinarchos* ("presider at the table"), *archieranistes* ("head of the feast"), *hesitator* ("host"), and the "Late Drinkers" (*seribibbi*) of Pompeii.⁷ Such evidence suggests that "communal dining was beyond doubt one of the primary functions of the majority of *collegia*, whatever their official *raison d'être*"⁸ and that "to eat and drink well among pleasant company seemed to strike at the very essence of what a collegium was all about."⁹

This widespread literary, architectural, and epigraphic evidence for banqueting leads to the question of how meals functioned within the

---

3. Thorough analyses are offered in Bollmann, *Römische Vereinshäuser*, and in various essays within Egelhaaf-Gaiser and Schäfer, eds., *Religiöse Vereine*. For more on the archaeological evidence of the association banquet room, or triclinium, in houses in Ostia, Porta Marina, Sufetula, North Africa, Pompeii, and Pergamum see Richardson, "Building"; see also Harland, *Associations*, 77–80.

4. Dunbabin, *Roman Banquet*, 94. For example, in Theadelphia an association of weavers received a dining room (*deipnētērion*) from a benefactor (IFayum 2 122; time of Trajan). Before having received this benefaction, they most likely held banquets in houses or temporary facilities.

5. Dunbabin, *Roman Banquet*, 92–93. D. E. Smith points out that while there is no standardization as to where an association's meeting place might be found, "quite often meeting locations would correspond to the predominant aim or identity of the club—thus a funerary club met at a cemetery site, a religious club at a temple, a professional club at the forum" (*From Symposium to Eucharist*, 104–05).

6. Donahue, *Roman Community*, 126; Dunbabin, *Roman Banquet*, 99; cf. Waltzing 1.323 n. 2; Ausbüttel, *Untersuchungen*, 55.

7. For a much fuller list of such association names and functionaries see Smith, *From Symposium to Eucharist*, 90, 96.

8. Dunbabin, *Roman Banquet*, 94.

9. Donahue, *Roman Community*, 85, also 128–38 and table 5.7 on pages 137–38. On association meals in general see further Poland, *Geschichte des griechischen Vereinswesens*, 258–67, 392–95; Ausbüttel, *Untersuchungen*, 55–59; Klauck, *Herrenmahl und hellenistischer Kult*, 68–76; Patterson, "Collegia and the Transformation"; Klinghardt, *Gemeinschaftsmahl*, 21–173. For a brief description of associations see Ascough, *What Are They Saying about the Formation of Pauline Churches?*, 74–78.

associations. This question is helped by a recent essay by French sociologist Claude Grignon, who presents a typology of commensality. In the essay, he defines *commensality* as "a gathering aimed to accomplish in a collective way some material tasks and symbolic obligations linked to the satisfaction of a biological individual need."[10] In other words, people eat because they have to do so; people eat [35] *with other people* because they choose to do so. In many cases, however, the choice of with whom one eats is linked to membership in preexisting social groups and the obligations that come with membership in such groups. Since "commensality is one of the techniques by which identity . . . can be defined and maintained,"[11] the application of a taxonomy of meals allows scholars to compare and contrast the types of social relationships being negotiated within a particular group.

Grignon presents his taxonomy as a set of three contrasting pairs: domestic and institutional commensality, everyday and exceptional commensality, and segregative and transgressive commensality. Domestic commensality represents times when members of a family are together for meals due to the coordination of their respective schedules and reflects a degree of cohesion within a family group. Institutional commensality tends to be situated among those involved in common occupational pursuits for whom regular meals must be taken but for whom there is an existing hierarchy that determines who eats where and with whom. A school lunch hour illustrates this insofar as teachers eat together in one location while students eat together elsewhere. Exceptional commensality marks particular periods in either the annual calendar (e.g., birthday parties) or the life cycle (e.g., wedding feasts). In contrast, everyday commensality is that which takes place as part of day-to-day living. While this latter category is an understandable contrast to "exceptional" commensality, it does not work well as one of the taxa since "everyday" commensality is likely to fall into one of the other categories, particularly domestic or institutional commensality. Grignon's final pairing—segregative and transgressive commensality—demarcates meals used to strengthen social cohesion and meals that allow for the crossing of social boundaries.

Grignon himself suggests that his "essay of clarification" is limited, and that "it is up to my colleagues in other disciplines, historians and anthropologists, to criticize and broaden it."[12] John Donahue takes up this challenge by applying Grignon's typology to describe and analyze the meal practices of the Greco-Roman world.[13] Of the six taxa outlined by Grignon, Donahue finds

10. Grignon, "Commensality."
11. Grignon, "Commensality," 31.
12. Grignon, "Commensality," 25.
13. Donahue, "Typology."

that three have analogues in the Roman world: (1) exceptional commensality, (2) transgressive commensality, and (3) segregative commensality. Surprisingly, Donahue limits his discussion of Roman associations (*collegia*) to the category "segregative commensality," noting that *collegia* meals provided a means "for a group to gain self-identity, to keep tabs on its members, and even to confirm internal divisions or hierarchies."[14] Certainly this is the case for many associations of [36] the Roman period, but Donahue takes a somewhat limited view that blurs numerous facets of the associations in order to fit them into one taxonomic category. Donahue tips his hand in this regard when he notes concerning the associations, "In all these instances, we can suppose that the administrative procedures were similar, as was the simple desire for fellowship and escape from the tedium of daily life through the sharing of food and drink."[15] While the latter comment may reflect part of the attraction of associations, there were much more complex systems of support and networking involved.[16] Donahue's categorization needs to be revisited in light of the evidence for commensality among associations.

Analysis of a broad range of association inscriptions and papyri suggests that some associations may have had more than one type of meal, as is the case with an association in Egypt whose ordinances reference at least two types of banquets (P.Mich V 243; time of Tiberius). All members are expected to contribute to and attend a regular (monthly) banquet, and failure to do so results in fines being levied, as does misconduct during the banquet (e.g., drunken behavior). Such governance points towards the banquets as times of segregative commensality in which a group's ethos is reinscribed. This same association, however, also holds a daylong funeral banquet for a member who dies. Such ritualized meals fit better the category of "exceptional commensality." Thus, within the same association, within a single document, we have two types of commensality represented.[17]

Such an example suggests that the evidence from Greco-Roman associations cannot easily be reduced to a single category. While it is the case that some association meal practices can be classified as involving segregative commensality, other association meals can be located elsewhere within Grignon's typology, reflecting a broader diversity in association commensality.[18] Donahue is to be thanked for pointing a way forward in under-

---

14. Donahue, "Typology," 104.
15. Donahue, "Typology," 106.
16. See Harland, *Associations*; Ascough, *Paul's Macedonian Associations*.
17. This is also the case for the association attested in P.Mich V 244 (Tebtunis, 43 CE).
18. What Arnaoutoglou claims for the linguistic evidence for leadership titles in Greek associations is true also for Greco-Roman association meal practices, namely,

standing the types of Greco-Roman meals and pointing out broad evidence in antiquity for instances of segregative, exceptional, and transgressive commensality. He is, however, overly reductive in limiting the associations to only the segregative category. The picture that emerges from a broad examination of the data demonstrates that three of the taxa can be applied to the meal practices of the associations: segregative commensality, exceptional commensality, and transgressive commensality, as can the subcategory of extradomestic commensality.

According to Grignon, studying commensality allows one to see the way in which "society organizes itself by dividing" and provides [37] insight into "social morphology."[19] Applying his taxonomy to the full range of meal practices of Greco-Roman associations grants insight into how various forms of commensality served as locations of social interaction and group definition. Although this is a more complex picture of association meals than that presented by Donahue, its nuances broaden our understanding of the complexity of social life in the Greco-Roman period.

SEGREGATIVE COMMENSALITY

Segregative commensality brings together members of a group around eating and drinking as a means to assert group boundaries, demarcating who is in and who is outside. According to Grignon, it is "a way to assert or to strengthen the 'We' by pointing out and rejecting, as symbols of otherness, the 'not We,' strangers, rivals, enemies, superiors or inferiors."[20] Through eating with one another, the group becomes 'visible' to itself by limiting its membership to certain individuals (e.g., members, recruits) and excluding others (e.g., defectors). Grignon suggests that strong and ideal types of segregative commensality are found in societies where hierarchy is "the very principle of structure and social life."[21] Segregative commensality is not limited to those in the upper ranks—its strength lies in the ability of groups to be (self-)selective about who can join in the eating and drinking.[22]

Donahue places the Roman collegia into this category, since among them eating was one of the markers of the "strong desire for exclusivity in

---

that the variability and adaptability of the associations makes it difficult to make general, sweeping claims (Arnaoutoglou, "ΑΡΧΕΡΑΝΙΣΤΗΣ," 110).

19. Grignon, "Commensality," 24–25.
20. Grignon, "Commensality," 29; Donahue, "Typology," 104.
21. Grignon, "Commensality," 29.
22. Grignon, "Commensality," 30.

Roman society among the lower orders."[23] Donahue gives a few examples, such as the bylaws of an association in Lanuvium, Italy, which records regulations governing times and procedures for banquets (CIL XIV 2112; 136 CE), and the private association of Aesclepius and Hygia on the Campus Martius in Rome (CIL VI 10234; 153 CE), which receives benefaction to enable the construction of buildings on the Via Appia, one of which is to be used for banquets. This latter inscription records seven special opportunities for meals, although it is likely that there were more, such as those accompanying the monthly meetings or occasional banquets celebrating the birthday of a patron or benefactor.[24] The numerical restriction to sixty members emphasizes the "set apartness" of this association's membership and their mealtimes can thus be typed as "segregative commensality."

Donahue cites other Roman *collegia*, but the investigation could be broadened to include other associations concerned with segregative commensality, including that of the well-known and oft-discussed inscription of the Iobacchoi (IG II² 1368; Athens, c. 164/165 CE),[25] the association of Zeus Hypsistos in Philadelphia, Egypt (P.Lond VII 2193; 69–58 BCE), and an association dedicated to the god Men Tyrannos (IG II² 1366; Sounion, second–third century CE). It is not surprising to find within such regulations restrictions on unruly behavior during banquets, which reflects, at the very least, group discord in the past.[26] Grignon notes that in contexts of segregative commensality, despite (or perhaps because of) an emphasis on conviviality, group members "let down their guard," and in so doing, "the group shows itself freely to itself only because it is out of sight of strangers."[27] The regulations concerning disruptive behavior suggest that association members understand their group life as providing a place of belonging and acceptance rather than a place where the agonistic exchanges typical of the Greco-Roman culture took place. While the regulations do suggest that the ideal was not always met, for taxonomic purposes it is clear that group meals aimed to provide an occasion for group solidarity. Nevertheless, this is not the meals' only function, as

---

23. Donahue, "Typology," 105; cf. Garnsey and Saller, *Roman Empire*, 107–25.

24. Donahue, *Roman Community*, 88. Other associations also had multiple special-occasion banquets; the association of ebony and ivory workers in Rome celebrated seven, the fish-workers association of Rome celebrated five, the association of Diana and Antinous in Lanuvium held six, the association of Silanus at Lucania celebrated five (Donahue, *Roman Community*, 89).

25. The meal practices of this association are discussed in detail in Smith, *From Symposium to Eucharist*, 111–23; cf. Ebel, *Attraktivität früher christlicher Gemeinden*, 76–142.

26. So Donahue, "Typology," 106.

27. Grignon, "Commensality," 29.

Donahue's presentation might suggest, and evidence from other associations suggest that other types of commensality were at work.

EXCEPTIONAL COMMENSALITY

The above examples represent some of the better-known evidence from the Greco-Roman associations. Since they can be categorized as segregative commensality, it is understandable to assume, as does Donahue, that association meals generally best fit this type. There is, however, evidence from other association banqueting practices that fit Grignon's description of "exceptional commensality."[28] In contrast to everyday commensality, exceptional commensality recognizes special dates, events, or both, in the annual calendar (e.g., birthdays) or in the life cycle (e.g., birth, marriage, or death). Such commensality can also correspond to professional life by recognizing events such as graduations, promotions, and retirements.

In applying this category to antiquity, Donahue puts the emphasis on public ceremonies such as those sponsored by the emperor or a wealthy civic patron. He also includes in this category religious ceremonial celebrations linked to the annual calendar like the Saturnalia [39] and the Compitalia. Yet not all of his examples are fully public banquets, since he mentions in this category a number of feasts restricted to certain political or social groups.[29] The association meals, however, are not included, despite Donahue's earlier recognition that the *collegium* of Diana and Antinous at Lanuvium was involved in funerary practices (CIL XIV 2112; 136 CE).[30]

Despite the (rightful) discontinuance of the category funerary association as separate from other types of associations,[31] it is the case that many associations were involved with meals and memorials marking death, which is, as Grignon points out, a form of exceptional commensality. In some associations, a benefit of membership included the guarantee of a decent burial and an annual commemoration of one's death, often in the form of a memorial banquet.[32] Often an already-existing association was endowed with a bequest of money or property (e.g., vineyards or land), the income of which was to be used for a memorial at the tomb of the deceased.[33] Oc-

---

28. Grignon, "Commensality," 27–28.
29. Donahue, "Typology," 101.
30. Donahue, "Typology," 106.
31. See Kloppenborg, "Collegia and *Thiasoi*," 20–22.
32. Dunbabin concludes that from the Hellenistic period on "the interrelationship of dining and death has become a cliché of funerary art" (*Roman Banquet*, 139).
33. The remainder of the income, however, went to the association for their own

casionally an association was formed in order to keep an annual memorial for the deceased, as is the case with CIL III 656 (Selian, n.d.). A number of tombs contained dining facilities (triclinia and sometimes hearths) in order to facilitate the memorial banquets of family or association members.[34] Many associations were involved in funerary festivals known as the *Rosalia* and the *Parentalia*.[35] These annual festivals entailed a commemoration of the deceased and a joyous celebration of the return of spring and summer, with an emphasis on banqueting and fun.[36]

Of particular interest with regard to exceptional commensality is the private or familial foundation whereby an association is formed (or an existing one endowed) in order to establish a memorial at the family tomb.[37] Foundations set up through the benefaction of an [40] association brought honor not only to the person(s) memorialized but also to the association: "Collegia entrusted with tasks which might ideally have gone to such organizations as the *boule* or the *gerousia* had to be regarded as trustworthy and respectable organizations."[38] It represented a claim on the part of the association of belonging to the *polis* and functioned as a means of establishing status in the hierarchical order of the *polis*, regardless of whether those outside of the association noticed.[39] That is, it was a method of demonstrating, if only to themselves, where the members belonged in the larger social order. This is also the case for those who were specific in naming the type of memorial celebration to be held—"self-commemorators who introduced *Rosalia* into their funerary arrangements were thus making a deliberate statement of (assumed) Roman cultural identity."[40] That such meals can be distinguished from segregative commensality is also supported by the fact that while sometimes all

---

use, probably for social gatherings like banquets (see IG X/2.1 259).

34. Dunbabin, *Roman Banquet*, 127–30.

35. The *Rosalia* was popular throughout the Roman Empire, including among associations. See further Toynbee, *Death and Burial*, 63–64; Donahue, *Roman Community*, 132–35, including table 5.6, and on page 129, table 5.5; Ascough, *Paul's Macedonian Associations*, 26–28; Trebilco, *Jewish Communities*, 80. On the *Rosalia* generally see Poland, *Geschichte des griechischen Vereinswesens*, 511–13; and Hoey, "Rosaliae Signorum."

36. Hoey, "Rosaliae Signorum," 22.

37. See discussion in Jones, "Deed of Foundation." An interesting example of a foundation that benefits extant private associations and the city (IEph 3803) is discussed in Drew-Bear, "Act of Foundation." A private citizen of Hypaipa benefacts the wool sellers and the linen weavers with a sum of money and gives to these two guilds and four others the use of a vineyard that he donates to the city.

38. Van Nijf, *Civic World*, 66.

39. Van Nijf, *Civic World*, 66.

40. Van Nijf, *Civic World*, 64.

of the association members would participate in the memorial meal, at other times the number of participants was restricted to select members.[41]

An inscription from third-century Hierapolis illustrates the employment of associations in events of exceptional commensality around burial (IHierapP 305; third century CE). After the usual notes of ownership and warnings not to inter anyone else in the location or to open the sarcophagus, the inscription stipulates that interest from a bequest by the deceased is to be used for a banquet at the tomb. All members of this guild of purple-dyers are eligible, although participants in the annual commemorative banquet are to be chosen by lot each year.[42]

Other forms of exceptional commensality beyond funerary meals can be cited. For example, a banquet could mark the dedication of an association's banqueting hall (see CIL VI 253, 349; CIL IX 5177). This, of course, would be a one-time event, but would commemorate an important occasion in the life of the association. Evidence exists for substantial amounts donated to associations for the purpose of banquets marking special occasions such as birthdays, with some gifts to an association equaling that which might be given as a civic benefaction.[43] At the same time, a bequest to an association to enable it to participate in exceptional commensality need not be lavish, as with the example of a woman who donated two hundred sesterces in order that a local association could hold a banquet on her son's birthday (CIL V 7906, Cemenelum, n.d.). [41]

Some interesting papyri from Egyptian private associations of Sarapis give rise to speculation over the nature of their banqueting activities. That they held banquets is clear from the dozen or so extant invitations.[44] The wording among the invitations is similar insofar as "the formula employed is notably similar to those of invitations to weddings."[45] Nothing else is known about these banquets outside of the invitations, although there is growing consensus that they "had a fundamentally religious character" and involved sacrifices.[46] One might speculate, however, that in formulating the invitations to represent formal wedding invitations, the hosts perceived the banquets as representing a ritual ceremony marking a critical event in the life cycle of the association, and thus are an example of exceptional commensality. This supposition might

---

41. Van Nijf, *Civic World*, 63 and n. 162.

42. There is much evidence for association funerary banquets, but two other interesting examples are IIasos 245–46 (Imperial Period) and IEph 3216.

43. Donahue, *Roman Community*, 135–36.

44. For the text and translation of three of these see Horsley, *New Documents* 1, 5–9.

45. Horsley, *New Documents* 1, 5.

46. Horsley, *New Documents* 1, 6.

be further supported by the evidence of Aelius Aristides, who describes the participation of Sarapis in a banquet held in his honor.[47]

Occasions of exceptional commensality could also bring together more than one association, as is the case of associations of hymn singers who gathered annually at Pergamum for a provincial celebration of Roma (IEph 3801; time of Claudius).[48] Although the association at Pergamum is one of the most prominent of the hymn-singer associations, other groups are known from places like Ephesos and Smyrna, and it is likely that these are among the groups that gathered for the birthday celebrations.[49]

TRANSGRESSIVE COMMENSALITY

Transgressive commensality "plays upon oppositions between social groups and the borders which separate them."[50] It is characterized by temporal, porous group boundaries in which there is "a relationship of exchange between parties of a different social or economic status."[51] Although the boundaries are recognized, they are "temporarily and symbolically transgressed"[52] and thus establish, in the context of a meal, a relation of exchange. Yet, "it is by transgressing them that it contributes to recognizing and maintaining" social distinctions.[53] [42] In such meals, the presence of the distinguished guest is essential to the commensality—even more so than the food—and he or she must convey a sense in which there is identification with those with whom they eat.

According to Donahue, transgressive commensality finds its fullest expression in the Roman world in the *cena*, a formal dinner sponsored by the emperor in which persons from various social ranks mix together. Yet once again it is surprising that Donahue does not include the associations in this category, since he admits that the "social differentiation reinforced by the manipulation of food" that occurs at the emperor's table during the *cena* is "much as we witnessed earlier in the instance of *collegia*."[54] We see this displayed in the honorary banquets held by associations for their patrons and benefactors.

---

47. Aelius Aristides, *Orationes* 45.27–28; translated by Behr, *Aristides*, noted in Harland, "Spheres of Contention," 62; cf. MacMullen, *Paganism*, 38–39.
48. On the hymn singers at Pergamum and their banquets see IPerg 374 (c. 110 CE).
49. So Harland, *Associations*, 125.
50. Grignon, "Commensality," 30.
51. Donahue, "Typology," 106.
52. Grignon, "Commensality," 30.
53. Grignon, "Commensality," 31.
54. Donahue, "Typology," 109.

When associations used banquets as occasions to announce honors awarded to benefactors, the occasions functioned to reinforce social hierarchies that existed outside the group between the elite and those who composed the membership. As Grignon notes concerning such transgressive commensality,

> The dissymmetry of the relationship appears in the initiative of the invitation, which always belongs to the dominant (whether the inferior is guest or host; in the latter case, the invitation of the superior is always an auto-invitation, which the honored hosts are not able to refuse).[55]

Associations are patronized with the expectation on the part of the patron and the understanding on the part of the association that the association will reciprocate through honoring the patron, which included meals.[56]

Take, as an example, IDelos 1520 (153/2 BCE), in which the Berytian Poseidoniastai, an association of merchants, shippers, and warehousemen on Delos, honor their benefactor, a Roman banker named Marcus Minatos, son of Sextus, who has provided substantial funds towards the building of the association headquarters (*oikos*). He is further honored for inviting the association members to a sacrifice he prepared on behalf of the *synodos* and a public dinner, the latter of which Marcus Minatos intends as a regular event that will not only be a benefit for the members but will honor those who patronize the association. Much of the ensuing inscription delineates the honors to be bestowed upon Marcus Minatos, including the erection of a statue [43] and a painted bust, both with an honorary inscription. He will occupy the place of honor at the banquet, and an annual day of honor will be set aside for him, complete with a procession, a gold wreath, and public proclamations. This inscription indicates that a regularly occurring banquet be instituted in order that the social expectation for associations to honor benefactors can take place. Of note is that the social superior has initiated the banquet at which he will be honored while in attendance.

We find another interesting example of associations involved in transgressive commensality in the invitation of members of professional

---

55. Grignon, "Commensality," 31.

56. Not surprisingly, such association meals reinforce the social system, even while transgressing it (Grignon, "Commensality," 31). As Neyrey points out, meals are not rituals but ceremonies that "attend, not to change, but to stability; they are concerned, not with newness, but with continuity" (Neyrey, "Ceremonies in Luke-Acts," 363). Meals-as-ceremonies "replicate the group's basic social system, its values, lines, classifications, and its symbolic world." As such, they can serve to reinforce the "map of persons" in which social positions and status are demarcated by position at meals and food received (Neyrey, "Ceremonies in Luke-Acts," 365–66).

associations to take part in public, civic-sponsored banquets and distributions.[57] Often it was the case that professional associations affiliated with a festival—groups such as the performing artists (e.g., IStratonikeia 309, 684, 685) or athletes (e.g., IPriene 111, 112, 118)—were invited to take part in the public banquets.[58] This might be particularly the case with the somewhat prestigious worldwide association of Dionysiac artists.[59] In such cases where priests or public magistrates have invited artists to meals, it is clear that the normal social boundaries are being crossed. It is very unlikely that these groups would mix during the course of the year, save perhaps were it the case that one of the elite benefacted the professional association.

EXTRADOMESTIC COMMENSALITY

Grignon's category of domestic commensality is quickly discounted in Donahue's application of the taxonomy to public feasting in the Roman world, with good reason.[60] Domestic commensality describes those times when families are together for meals and is referring to private meals within households.[61] In the case of the Greco-Roman associations, there is very little overlap with this type of commensality.[62] Grignon contrasts domestic commensality with institutional commensality. Such commensality is "characterized by the occlusion of the group, which is all the more severe as the enclosure of the institutions to which the partners belong is hermetic."[63] This also would seem not, by definition, to fit with a discussion of voluntary associations, as Donahue assumes.[64] [44]

Grignon, however, finds within the broader designations of "domestic and institutional commensality" a subcategory he terms "extra-domestic commensality," in which he further distinguishes between "commensality at

57. See van Nijf, *Civic World*, 185.
58. Van Nijf, *Civic World*, 185.
59. See van Nijf, *Civic World*, 185.
60. Donahue, "Typology," 98.
61. Grignon, "Commensality," 25. Gignon does allow that "the forms of domestic commensality themselves vary a lot, being sometimes very far from the contemporary pattern of the nuclear family."
62. Here one might consider the example of the foundation deed of Epicteta (IG XII/3 330; Thera, 210–195 BCE), in which a substantial sum of money is given in order to establish an association of relatives (*to koinon*) who are to hold a three-day festival of sacrifices, libations, and banquets to honor the memory of Epicteta, her husband, and her two sons.
63. Grignon, "Commensality," 26.
64. Donahue, "Typology," 98.

work and leisure commensality."[65] Leisure commensality reflects the demands of the wider culture by being concerned "not only to keep or to spread a strategic network of acquaintances, but to 'keep up one's position' by sharing in a system of mutual invitations which approves and attests membership of the same level and in the same social world (the same 'society')."[66] This seems very much to be part of the underlying ethos of banqueting practices in the Greco-Roman period, and Grignon's general description of leisure commensality is apropos for the Roman period: "the position held by some depends on the position of the guests and the invitations he may expect, on the position of those he invites and those who invite him."[67]

The second subcategory of extradomestic commensality is perhaps more applicable to a study of the associations. Grignon describes "commensality at work" as "semi-institutional," since it results from the demands of one's position and the expectations of the larger society that result in one eating meals with those with whom one shares an institutional affiliation— for example, meals taken in corporate restaurants, university cafeterias, or school refectories.[68] Such commensality can be seen in the diverse evidence from the professional associations of the Greco-Roman period; for example, many of the professional associations at Ostia included within their buildings one or more triclinium rooms in which to hold their banquets.[69]

An interesting case of extradomestic "commensality at work" among a professional association can be found in the associations of Augustales, which are attested widely across the Roman Empire.[70]

> Although their formal purpose was the celebration of imperial cult, their most important function seems to have been to provide wealthy freedmen, who were barred by their status from holding municipal magistracies, with an opportunity to acquire public prestige.[71]

Past scholarship assumed that the Augustales were an official civic group and thus not a *voluntary* association. A more recent evaluation has challenged this notion. Although their development was likely encouraged by the emperor, particularly their rapid dissemination [45] throughout the

65. Grignon, "Commensality," 26.
66. Grignon, "Commensality," 26–27.
67. Grignon, "Commensality," 27; see Garnsey and Saller, *Roman Empire*, 122, 157.
68. Grignon, "Commensality," 26.
69. See Hermansen, *Ostia*, 55–89; Meiggs, *Roman Ostia*, 324. For an example from Pergamum see Radt, *Pergamon*, 136–37.
70. Rives, "Epigraphic Evidence," 133.
71. Rives, "Epigraphic Evidence," 133.

empire, "the degree of local variations in their structures suggests that it was not necessary to direct their formation from the center."[72] In some cases, the Augustales acted outside of any civic restrictions.[73]

As part of their mandate, the Augustales regularly participated in banquets.[74] When they are named as recipients of municipal *sportulae*, they "typically occupied the position immediately below that of decurions," signaling to the general public the high standing that they held as an association.[75] The nature of their affiliation and the tasks that they were expected to perform demanded that their meals, in certain instances, be taken together—what Grignon has termed extradomestic, work-related commensality.

CONCLUSION

While Donahue's application of Grignon's taxonomy of commensality to the meal practices of the Roman world is helpful for an understanding of public meals, it is not sufficient to group together all forms of association meals under the single category segregative commensality. In labeling association meals as segregative comensiality, Donahue has overlooked a diverse range of data for the meal practices of a broad collection of Greco-Roman associations across the geographic and temporal span of the Roman Empire and thus paints a rather reductive portrait of commensality within associations. The evidence examined above demonstrates that association meals can be classified as segregative, exceptional, or transgressive commensality, and in some instances might be considered work-related commensality. This application of Grignon's taxonomy provides a window on the variety of ways that associations used commensality to negotiate self-definition and inscribe community boundaries.[76]

---

72. Fisher, "Greek Associations," 1220.

73. D'Arms, "Memory, Money, and Status"; de Ligt, "Semi-Public Collegia," 350–52, 356–58; Bollmann, *Römische Vereinshäuser*, 39–46.

74. See Donahue, *Roman Community*, 124–25, including table 5.3.

75. Donahue, *Roman Community*, 125.

76. Support for the research and writing of this paper has been provided through an Alexander von Humboldt Research Fellowship, a Queen's University Chancellor's Research Award, an Ontario Government Premier's Research Excellence Award, and a Social Sciences and Humanities Research Council of Canada Standard Research Grant. I am grateful for work done on this topic for me by two of my research assistants, most recently Rachel McRae and in the past Erin Vearncombe.

13

Social and Political Characteristics of Greco-Roman Association Meals

"For the Roman aristocracy, banquets are of the essence."[1] Not just the elite, however, held banquets. Among the lower orders, many banquets were attended often through membership in one or more of the associations ubiquitous at that time. Greek and Roman associations brought together men or, occasionally, women for some shared purpose, generally with a membership of ten to fifty, although a few associations were much larger (sometimes in the hundreds).[2] In antiquity, a good portion of the urban population were members of one or more such associations.[3]

Communal meals and banquets were a key part of Greco-Roman associations as is clear from literary, architectural, and epigraphic evidence.[4]

1. Rüpke, *Religion of the Romans*, 143.

2. For a brief description of associations see Kloppenborg and Ascough, *Greco-Roman Associations*, 1–13. For a translation of association texts, including inscriptions, papyri, and literary texts see the entries in Ascough, Harland, and Kloppenborg, *Associations in the Greco-Roman World* (AGRW).

3. MacMullen (*Enemies of the Roman Order*, 174) suggests a figure of one-quarter to one-third for Rome in the second century CE, although it is probably similar for other large urban centers at the time. It is perhaps lower during the first century, although still a significant portion of the population.

4. Dill, *Roman Society*, 278; Dunbabin, *Roman Banquet*, 85, 94; Donahue, *Roman*

Meals were held at regular intervals, with special meals at points of celebration or bereavement among members. Often wealthy members or patrons were honored through banquets, festivals, and *sportulae* of food or money. One's portion at these meals depended on one's rank, while rules for behavior and penalties for their contravention were recorded in inscriptions and enforced as a means of social control. Occasions for banquets and the place and manner of dining were regulated through association bylaws.[5]

As a community of individuals gathered as a collective, the organization of an ancient association is analogous to the political organization of a state, having its own properties, finances, and an internal hierarchy of offices.[6] The association has been viewed as a "petit cite" that equally allows [60] citizens of all social groups to participate in a state-like entity with its own hierarchy and social structures.[7] Analysis of their meals, rituals, and other collective activities and values suggests that associations were autonomous in their structure and had their own internal public space. At the same time, they were part of the urban structure of Roman society. As networking groups they played a role as alternative space for political, social, and religious networking.[8]

Various types of associations evolved from the ancient political clubs (*thiasoi, orgeōnes*) of banqueting citizens and came to include socioeconomic support groups with alien and noncitizen members by the late fourth and third centuries BCE. At this time, associations focused predominantly on fellowship (*synousia*), brokered by common meals and social, judicial, and financial support.[9] By Roman times, there exists evidence of a diversity of professional and nonprofessional (social and/or religious) associations. Throughout their evolution, associations morph from political groups to social groups back to political groups and so on, all the time carrying with them characteristics of both social gatherings and (potentially) politically active groups (it is this latter aspect that most troubled the Romans). Due to this evolutionary yet cyclical morphology between the social and political,

---

Community, 85, also 128–38 and table 5.7 on pages 137–38. Rüpke, *Religion of the Romans*, 208; Ascough, "Forms of Commensality" (Chapter 12, above); Harland, *Associations*, 74–85; Smith, *From Symposium to Eucharist*, 87–125; Taussig, *In the Beginning*, 91. See further Donahue, *Roman Community*, 126–38. On association meals in general see further Poland, *Geschichte des griechischen Vereinswesens*, 258–67, 392–95; Ausbüttel, *Untersuchungen*, 55–59; Klinghardt, *Gemeinschaftsmahl*, 21–173.

5. Liu, *Guilds of Textile Dealers*, 248.
6. Bendlin, "Gemeinschaft," 10.
7. Bendlin, "Gemeinschaft," 11, citing Waltzing, *Ètude Historique*, 1:513.
8. Bendlin, "Gemeinschaft," 15–18.
9. Leiwo, "Religion, or Other Reasons?," 116.

it remains difficult for scholars clearly to classify associations as either one or the other.[10] Because meals play a part in both the socioreligious aspects of associations and the politicoeconomic aspects, we will explore each in turn below.

SOCIAL CHARACTERISTICS OF ASSOCIATION MEALS

In his short book on associations in Greco-Roman Egypt, William Brashaer uses anthropological studies to argue that humans have an instinctive need to form associations that goes back long before Greco-Roman times.[11] As they turned from hunting in groups to settling communities, humans continued to fill their need for group identity by forming associations, albeit of various types (professional, self-help, religious). Examination of group behavior in AGRW 28 (5 BCE) and in other texts leads Brasher to conclude that the formation of associations primarily for social purposes within the cults of Egypt marks their secularization in Greco-Roman times.[12] This, however, drives an anachronistic wedge between two inseparable aspects of ancient group life—social activities and religious devotion. This division cannot be sustained.[13] For example, the *kline*, or dining fraternity, of Sarapis in the third-century CE Egypt offered opportunities for socializing and dancing, commemoration of events such as marriage or coming of age, and worship.[14] As Jinyu Liu has ably argued, [61]

> Feasts were occasions when religion and social life closely intertwined. Religious rituals, including sacrifices, often preceded or accompanied the banquets. In fact, in many cases, religious rituals and banquets were simply different stages of the same events.[15]

Commensality has been defined as "a gathering aimed to accomplish in a collective way some material tasks and symbolic obligations linked to

---

10. Cf. Liu, *Guilds of Textile Dealers*, 248 and n. 8.

11. Brashaer, *Vereine im griechisch-römischen Ägypten*, 19–22. Such groups often excluded women and children.

12. Brashaer, *Vereine im griechisch-römischen Ägypten*, 24.

13. See also Slater's critique ("Scholae," 497) of Bollmann's attempt to mount a similar argument (*Römische Vereinshäuser*, 204–12). Cenival ("Associations dans les Temples") is similarly guilty.

14. Youtie, "Kline of Sarapis."

15. Liu, *Guilds of Textile Dealers*, 250, citing CIL V 7906 and CIL XIV 2112.

the satisfaction of a biological individual need."[16] Although all human beings are constrained to eat by biological necessity, eating in the company of others represents a social choice. "Like sex, the taking of food has a social component, as well as a biological one. Food categories therefore encode social events."[17] The range of company available for meal companionship is most often linked to the preexisting social groups within which an individual is located, and often the subgroups within a group will require particular obligations around meals. Put another way, meals become a way of defining the group's boundaries—who is inside a group and who is on the outside.[18]

At a meal, the food itself becomes part of the "hidden transcript" and encodes particular messages, most notably the "pattern of social relations being expressed."[19]

> Drinks are for strangers, acquaintances, workmen, and family. Meals are for family, close friends, honored guests. The grand operator of the system is the line between intimacy and distance.[20]

In particular, dietary restrictions play a part in this encoding. When one examines the classifications of Leviticus,

> a very strong analogy between table and altar stares us in the face ... At the bottom end of the scale some animals are abominable, not to be touched or eaten. Others are fit for the table, but not for the altar.[21]

This is extended to other rules against mixtures. What one is willing to eat signals whom one is willing to marry. Food thus sends strong signals about social relations. Since most marriages in Greco-Roman society tended to be endogamous, between close-knit families from the same social strata,[22] eating with someone meant that one was willing to accept that person as family.

---

16. Grignon, "Commensality." The following summarizes in part Ascough, "Forms of Commensality" (Chapter 12, above).

17. Douglas, *Implicit Meanings*, 231.

18. Grignon, "Commensality," 31. Nevertheless, in the Roman banquet, differences among participants were signaled by seating position and size of portion (van Nijf, *Civic World*, 152–53; Donahue, "Typology," 97.

19. Douglas, *Implicit Meanings*, 231. For an exploration of "hidden transcripts," see Scott, *Domination*.

20. Douglas, *Implicit Meanings*, 236.

21. Douglas, *Implicit Meanings*, 249.

22. Rowlandson and Bagnall, *Women and Society*, 85.

Likewise, a group's acceptance of culturally dominant meal patterns signaled that it saw itself firmly located within that culture. At the narrower internal level among small social groupings such as associations, epigraphic data from Greco-Roman antiquity suggest that no matter how basic the [62] fare, a strong sense of conviviality was created that allowed the members to bond with one another.[23] For example, members could rely on one another for support in times of crisis; "if a member should be wronged, they and all the friends shall come to his assistance, so that everyone might know that we show piety to the gods and to our friends" (IG II^2 1275 = AGRW 13; Piraeus, late-III–II BCE).

During the Roman period, meals functioned as a form of community building where boundaries were established and maintained.

> The emperor could have his banquets and the social recognition associated with them, but so too on a much more modest scale could the poor workman. It was a convenient and effective way to confirm one's place, especially since food, by its very nature as a critical commodity in pre-industrial society, could be manipulated to underscore more effectively than any other substance the social difference between one person and the next.[24]

The assertion of group boundaries through eating and drinking with one another is a form of "segregative commensality."[25] Clear directives are in place to demarcate "insiders" and "outsiders," and at times of commensality the group becomes visible to itself through those who can attend (generally members and recruits) and those who are excluded (nonmembers and defectors).

The Greco-Roman associations reflect the predilection for segregative commensality.[26] For example, the bylaws of an association in Lanuvium, Italy, records regulations governing times and procedures for banquets that are limited in attendance to members only (CIL XIV 2112 = AGRW 310, 136 CE). The restriction to sixty members in the private association of Aesclepius and Hygia on the Campus Martius in Rome (CIL VI 10234 = AGRW 322, 153 CE), which had dedicated building space for banquets, emphasizes the "set apartness" of this association's members and their mealtimes. Other examples of segregative commensality include the well-known and oft-discussed inscription of the Iobacchoi (IG II^2 1368 = AGRW 7; Athens, c. 164/165 CE), the association of Zeus Hypsistos in Philadelphia, Egypt

---

23. Dunbabin, *Roman Banquet*, 99.
24. Donahue, *Roman Community*, 89.
25. Grignon, "Commensality"; Donahue "Typology."
26. Donahue, "Typology," 105; cf. Garnsey and Saller, *Roman Empire*, 107–25.

(P.Lond VII 2193 = AGRW 295, 69–58 BCE), and an association dedicated to the god Men Tyrannos (IG II² 1366 = AGRW 22; Sounion, second to third century CE).[27] In each case it is clear that group meals aimed at providing an occasion for building and affirming group solidarity, although the regulations around proper behavior and decorum at meals do suggest that this ideal was not always met.[28] In contexts of segregative commensality, group members often "let down their guard."[29] Nevertheless, the regulations [63] restricting such disruptive behavior reflect a group ideal that makes meetings the locus of belonging and acceptance.

The important social role of association meals can be seen by examining evidence from association meeting places, with the caveat that it is difficult to generalize concerning the physical setting of association meals as we do not have specific locations that accompany our inscriptional evidence that they had meals.[30] In many cases, particularly with funerary banquets, the meal would have been held in the open air using movable equipment or in rented spaces such as *taberna*.[31] At the same time, there is no standard architectural form to which association buildings conform, and thus the identification of buildings as belonging to an association must be based on inscriptions or on contents.[32] Such buildings do not always have specific dining areas; in many cases space was generally multipurpose, and at mealtimes "couches could be set out in the main hall, side rooms, the porticoes, or the court itself."[33]

---

27. See Ascough, "Forms of Commensality" (Chapter 12, above). The meal practices of the Iobacchoi association are discussed in detail by Smith, *From Symposium to Eucharist*, 111–23.

28. Donahue, "Typology," 106.

29. Grignon, "Commensality," 29.

30. Smith points out that while there is no standardization as to where an association's meeting place might be found, that location can be linked to the aim or identity of the association (*From Symposium to Eucharist*, 104–5).

31. Dunbabin, *Roman Banquet*, 92–93.

32. There is no common terminology, and associations varied in size and function and many owned more than one building (Bollmann, *Römische Vereinshäuser*, 47). In general, an association's building was called an *aedes* or *schola* in the West and an *oikos*, *station*, or *ergon* in the East (van Nijf, *Civic World*, 107; cf. Waltzing, *Étude Historique*, 4:437–43 for a survey of the Western terminology).

33. Dunbabin, *Roman Banquet*, 94. For example, in Theadelphia an association of weavers received a dining room *(deipneterion)* from a benefactor (IFayum 2 122, time of Trajan). Presumably, before having received this benefaction, they were in the habit of holding banquets, most likely in houses or temporary facilities.

There are, however, some association halls that have clear evidence of banqueting facilities.[34] In Pergamon, for example, there are the remains of the meeting place of an association of Dionysiac *Bukoloi* ("cowherds") in use from the second to fourth century CE (AGRW B6). The hall is divided in half by a cult-niche on the northeast wall and the doorway on the northwest. Permanent stone *triclinia* about one meter high and two meters wide are set along each wall. Together these *triclinia* could accommodate about seventy participants, who would recline with their head oriented toward the middle of the hall. A marble shelf sits slightly below the podium and most likely served as the place for food and drink to be set down. Access to the podium was gained via small sets of steps set against the podium base. Small, irregularly placed openings below the podium probably served for the storage of cultic or dining items. Bones found below the cement floor indicate that a large quantity of meat—beef, ham, and poultry—was consumed.[35] It is difficult to imagine any purpose for the association's use of this hall other than banqueting, indicating a central aspect of their communal practice.

In what appears to be a building belonging to a wealthy association of traders and financial dealers in Pompeii (regia I = AGRW B23; mid-first century CE), there remain five separate rooms, each containing a marble-faced *triclinium* and decorated with elaborate wall paintings of mythological scenes and Dionysiac figures, along with a system for water effects (an example of conspicuous luxury). In total, the building could accommodate up to one hundred diners. As Dunbabin points out, "Whatever their other activities, dining must have played a central role if they needed a special building for this purpose."[36] [64]

In Ostia there exists a large building that housed the wealthy association of carpenters (*fabri tignuari*) that contains four dining rooms in its east wing (building I.xii.1 = AGRW B14; second to fourth century CE). Each room could accommodate up to a dozen diners, indicating that forty to fifty participants were expected on a regular basis.[37] The proximity of this and other association clubhouses to the main forum in Ostia suggests that "these

---

34. I highlight a few examples; more thorough analyses are offered in Bollmann, *Römische Vereinshäuser*, and various essays in Egelhaaf-Gaiser and Schafer, eds., *Religiöse Vereine*. See also various association building descriptions in AGRW B1–B28.

35. Radt, *Pergamon*, 197.

36. Dunbabin, *Roman Banquet*, 97.

37. More diners could be accommodated if temporary structures were set up in the central portico; so Dunbabin, *Roman Banquet*, 97–98. Smith (*From Symposium to Eucharist*, 104) sets the number lower, at thirty-six, but also notes that more could be accommodated.

types of clubs had some connection with the political leaders of the city."[38] This may be too generalized a conclusion to draw, however, as other professional associations in Ostia had shops that probably included their meeting place adjacent to a different, much smaller forum located near the port (the "Forum of the Corporations").[39] The proximity to one or other fora is most likely explained as a desire of a trade-based association to be located near the primary hub of related commercial activity. Although this would give them a public face and may indicate an interest in political activity, this activity would be restricted to honoring the elite, as we will note below.

Drawing on archeological and epigraphic information for meeting locations of associations in Roman imperial Italy, Bollmann provides a taxonomy of the building remains there along three categories: (1) those with an axial entrance, portico court, and cult place, (2) temple structures, and (3) halls and *tabernae*.[40] The third type, halls and *tabernae*, is the most common form of association building remains. When Bollmann examines the civic context of the *collegia* in Rome and Ostia, she finds that the most important consideration for locating a meeting place was its proximity to the center of the city, leading her to conclude that the *collegia* were more concerned with social than religious functions. Although Slater rightly calls this distinction "anachronistic,"[41] it should not detract from the overall conclusion that the predominant physical space that can be identified as having been used and/or owned by associations reflects a clear emphasis on socialization, with banquet space often bearing positions of prominence in the buildings.

The problem of the limited evidence for the banqueting halls pales in comparison to the lack of evidence for the form that the association banquets took. "Since *collegia* seldom put up inscriptions in commemoration of such routine celebrations and none of the collegial bylaws of the *collegia centonariorum* have survived, we do not know the details of these regular convivial events."[42] This observation could be extended to include all types of associations. Nevertheless, there exists an interesting inscription in the British Museum dedicated to Zeus Hypsistos that depicts an association banquet (AGRW 110 [and fig. 9]; from Panormos, near Kyzikos in Asia Minor).[43]

---

38. Smith, *From Symposium to Eucharist*, 104.

39. Dunbabin (*Roman Banquet*, 99; cf. 79–82) notes that unlike the wealthy associations described above, many associations were small and poor and would have met in simple structures in which diners sat to dine, a clear mark of low status. Her argument, however, is not supported by any specific examples.

40. Bollmann, *Römische Vereinshäuser*.

41. Slater, "Scholae," 497.

42. Liu, *Guilds of Textile Dealers*, 249.

43. A similar relief can be seen on AGRW 95 (Apamea Myrleia area, Bithynia, 119

Underneath a relief of three gods (Zeus, Artemis, and Apollo), there is a shallow relief depicting the members of an association holding a banquet. The participants are reclining on their left, [65] watching a female dancing to a flautist and percussionist. To the right of the scene, a man makes preparations over an amphora of wine, probably for the symposium.[44] All in all, this rare piece of epigraphic evidence suggests that associations held their meals in the manner customary for Greco-Roman banquets, as we shall see below.[45]

POLITICAL CHARACTERISTICS OF ASSOCIATION MEALS

Jinyu Liu rightly points out that "the central importance of convivial activities in the collective life of the *collegia* might be demonstrated by the inclusion of (elaborate) rules concerning banquets in the *collegium* bylaws, the presence of dining rooms in the collegial meeting-places (*scholae*), and the attention that convivial activities received from outsiders, especially Christian writers."[46] That the demonstration of the importance of meals for associations is manifest in a public or semipublic manner—through inscriptions, through dedicated physical space, and by being noticed by outsiders—suggests that for the mostly nonelite association members, much was to be gained, and little to be lost, through the public display of convivial activity within the wider cultural context. Cult, funerary practices, and conviviality are "forms of socialization, and manifestations of both collegial solidarity and a means to negotiate such solidarity. Solidarity, however, does not necessarily mean equality."[47] Since these activities took place in public to one degree or another, they also functioned "as important occasions for each group's image-building."[48] Below we will explore briefly some key aspects of the public display by focusing on how banquets functioned to demonstrate group identity to insiders and to outsiders.

Banquets served a variety of purposes for benefactors and participants at the same time. Benefactors increasingly funded banquets in the Roman East, using them as vehicles to recognize, honor, and confirm publicly the

---

or 104 CE).

44. The typical banquet format seems to be assumed; the first part, the meal (*deipnon*) is to be followed by the *symposium,* the drinking part (Smith, *From Symposium to Eucharist,* 9; Klinghardt, *Gemeinschaftsmahl,* 1–2).

45. Cf. Smith, *From Symposium to Eucharist,* 5; Klinghardt, *Gemeinschaftsmahl,* 1.

46. Liu, *Guilds of Textile Dealers,* 248.

47. Liu, *Guilds of Textile Dealers,* 276.

48. Liu, *Guilds of Textile Dealers,* 276.

hierarchical status of groups within their society. While there does not seem to be a fixed empire-wide social hierarchy as in the West, associations were given a place above the plebeians. Banquets gave the associations opportunities to develop a "festive identity." The wealthier members of collegia were able to adopt "status association" with the civic government and the recognized elite.[49]

In this regard, association meals are a type of "transgressive commensality," in which there is "a relationship of exchange between parties of a different social or economic status."[50] Although recognized, boundaries are transgressed, albeit temporarily and symbolically. Yet, "it is by transgressing them that it [transgressive commensality] contributes to recognizing and maintaining" social distinctions.[51] This type of commensality is evidenced through banquets in which [66] associations honor their patrons and benefactors. Occasions where the elite are recognized for their benefaction serve to reinforce social differentiation among the elite and the group members. Yet, by honoring elite men and women as patrons, and even as members of an otherwise nonelite group, the association presents a challenge to the status quo itself, which eschews such porous boundaries in the Roman *ordo*.

The evidence indicates that various association meals can be classified as segregative or transgressive commensality. These classifications allow us also to note how association meals functioned politically as a means for both assimilation and resistance to dominant cultural mores. The rules and regulations within associations represent an attempt to maintain cohesion and peace *(pax)* during meetings in order to minimize the disruptive behavior that so often caused the associations to come under suspicion of local authorities. The ability to expel errant members represents the strongest sanction available to *collegia* under Roman law.[52] Thus, there is collusion with imperial authorities through the maintenance of order in the meetings and banquets.

Harland's study of inscriptions from Roman Asia concerning the involvement of associations in imperial dimensions of civic life confirms the complexity of group-society relations, reflecting the groups' acculturation, adaptation, and selection of cultural traditions while still maintaining community identity.[53] Associations were positively involved in imperial facets of civic life, sociocultural civic activities, and benefactions, maintaining, for

---

49. See van Nijf, *Civic World*, 171, 168, 187.
50. Donahue, "Typology," 106.
51. Grignon, "Commensality," 31.
52. Rüpke, *Religion of the Romans*, 211.
53. Harland, "Honouring the Emperor"; cf. Harland, *Associations*, 177–264.

the most part, positive relationships with imperial officials and honoring the imperial cult. At the same time, the transgressive commensality noted above, along with the general suspicion of associations as verging on the cusp of political action that threatened the state, meant there was always a chance that associations of any sort could be censured or dissolved by local authorities or imperial edict. Thus, associations had to play up their ability to assimilate into the wider culture while carefully negotiating those places where they might be perceived to be expressing resistance to the dominance of imperial rule.

During the Augustan and post-Augustan periods, Roman cultural values spread from Rome into Italy and then to the western and eastern parts of the Roman Empire in a process that many scholars refer to as "Romanization."[54] This process was a complex mixture of "cultural assimilation, hybridization, and resistance."[55] Many factors such as preexisting cultural elements, local elite practices, and social competition affected both the processes and outcomes. The strong cultural ties between earlier Greek culture and the Roman culture that adopted it made it possible for Augustan values to be accepted and adapted easily in the empire's eastern regions, since the new [67] values were often couched in the clothing of the traditional values. This "cultural bricolage"[56] bestowed new functions and meanings on preexisting cultural elements in the context of Roman rule.

One of the key components of Romanization was the development of urban centers, either through postconquest revitalization or the settling of veteran soldiers in "new" colonies. "Armies pacified Rome's opponents, but cities integrated them into its empire, and urban amenities seduced them into complicity."[57] Roman propaganda perpetuated the ideology of the center, while elite Roman men and women set the cultural standards whenever they were abroad. Of particular note is the deployment of the elite men and their families to urban centers in the empire in order to have them spend a term ruling non-Romans as preparation for a return to the political scene in Rome itself. Colonial experience leads to promotion through the ranks. Once resident in the cities, these elite Romans would woo the general population through stages of "good works" (*euergetism*) aimed to placate and pacify the locals—"the building of roads and ports, the widespread distribution of statues and temples, and the spread of urban facilities

---

54. The following is adapted from Ascough, *Lydia*, 55–57.
55. Champion, ed., *Roman Imperialism*, 214.
56. Roth, *Styling Romanisation*, 39.
57. Crossan and Reed, *In Search of Paul*, 184.

of aqueducts and baths."[58] These public displays not only functioned as billboards for the supremacy of Rome, but they also provided the model to which the general populace could aspire.

This Romanization impacted all aspects of life, including religious life. New choices arose for the inhabitants, particularly as "new cults opened themselves up, adopted Roman forms of organization, so that born Romans could participate in them, relate to other members, and not be put off by completely strange customs and roles. It was this institutional assimilation that made real freedom of choice possible, enabling individuals to concentrate on the symbolic level, on ideas of god and notions of salvation."[59] In terms of the impact on commensality, no matter the context, whether "Greek *symposia*, Roman *convivia*, philosophical banquets, sacrificial meals, communal meals of clubs, and Jewish and Christian meals" by the first century all had a common form in which slaves served those who reclined for the meal.[60] This elite form of dining became the norm for all inhabitants of Romanized urban centers and signaled to the Roman authorities that their former enemies were in compliance. Ironically, reclining at meals was not a particularly Roman invention as they themselves had adopted it from their Greek neighbors. Nevertheless, it marked for the Romans a confirmation that civilized society reigned supreme and the Pax Romana would be maintained.

From the Roman elite perspective, it was necessary for banquets to maintain proper decorum, for the sake of those gathered and for the overall well-being of the city. Athenaeus complains, [68]

> People who gather for dinner-parties today, especially if they come from fair Alexandria, shout, bawl, and objurgate the wine-pourer, the waiter, and the chef; the slaves are in tears, being buffeted by knuckles right and left. To say nothing of the guests, who thus dine in complete embarrassment; if the occasion happens to be a religious festival, even the god will cover his face and depart, abandoning not only the house but also the entire city.[61]

This elite expectation for proper decorum at meals seems also to be an expectation within association meals. For many associations, raucous

---

58. Crossan and Reed, *In Search of Paul*, 187–90.

59. Rüpke, *Religion of the Romans*, 214.

60. Balch, "Paul, Families, and Households," 273; cf. also the observation that Judean meal practices imitate Hellenistic practices, which means that they too are "Romanized"; see Smith, *From Symposium to Eucharist*, 14–18.

61. *Deipn.* 420, II–III CE, LCL. Marcus Varro (116–27 BCE) complains about the numerous banquets, which he links directly to the rise in food prices (*Rust*.3.2.16).

behavior was prohibited by explicit regulations forbidding physical and verbal exchanges, including name-calling, which could detract from the honor of other guests or the flow of the celebration itself. For example, one association warns that a member will be fined if, while taking his seat at a banquet, he shoves in front of another member (P.Mich V 243 = AGRW 300; Tebtynis, 14–37 CE). In the Lanuvium association, members who use any abusive or insolent language toward the leaders during a banquet are fined (CIL XIV 2112 = AGRW 310, 136 CE).

That such regulations were necessary, and appear in more than one association inscription, indicates that the type of behavior about which Athenaeus complains among the elite occurred within the nonelite association banquets. Despite such regulations, however, associations were still repudiated for their indulgence in food and drink. For example, Philo of Alexandria claims of the associations that "you could find no sound elements but only liquor, tippling, drunkenness and the outrageous conduct they lead to" (*Flacc.* 136 = AGRW L10). When he compares the Greco-Roman associations with the *Therapeutae* of Alexandria, he deplores the former for behavior leading to idolatry and apostasy, rather than "the joys and sweet comforts of the intellect."[62]

Despite this reputation, associations in the Roman Empire had an overall stabilizing effect. For example, they organized public gatherings within accepted political rhetoric as well as ceremonies for the emperor.[63] Cities likewise benefitted from the existence of associations. They offered many advantages to the urban community such as financial support for public projects and members' knowledge of building techniques. On the individual level, associations played an important role in everyday life. By way of example, Kolb argues that three rare inscriptions describe cooperation between representatives of three associations (probably all unionizations of workers on imperial estates) and the imperial administration.[64] All three inscriptions report similar (successful) requests: associations, represented by a chosen member, ask the imperial administration for a plot on the emperor's [69] private territory for the construction of a cult site or building. The

---

62. Seland, "Philo and the Clubs," 125; also Philo, *Legat.* 10.311–12 (= AGRW L37); *Flacc.* 4 (= AGRW L36); see further Seland, "Philo and the Clubs," 110–27; Ascough, *Paul's Macedonian Associations*, 85–87.

63. The political significance of associations is emphasized in Clauss, "Zur Integrationsleistung."

64. Kolb, "Vereine." The inscriptions are CIL VI 30983 (Monte Testaccio, Rome, middle or end of the second century CE); CIL XIV 4570 (marble table from Ostia, 205 CE), and a fragmentary Roman inscription from 168 CE, today stored in the convent of San Paolo *foori le mura*.

inscriptions emphasize the imperial power with its links to the "ordinary people," which is meant to symbolize the association's prestige. For ordinary people, becoming a member of a professional or religious association was an opportunity to take part in public life as well as to benefit from the social prestige of the associations that was established in a public, ostentatious way through the contact between representatives of associations and the ruling power represented by members of the imperial administration.[65]

CONCLUSION

Meal practices provide only a snapshot of association activity. Nevertheless, the conviviality of the association gives us a picture of how members negotiated key social relationships, both internal and external, through which they integrated into the social fabric of society. Although members were not drawn from the elite, their banqueting practices and the social actions reflected therein allowed the association as a whole, and its individual members, to maintain a sense of belonging, both together and within the wider social contexts of which they were a part. Group boundaries were defined and maintained for insiders while the relationship with outsiders was carefully negotiated through the public display of connections with the civic elite. This gave associations a public presence even while they carefully negotiated a role that would support rather than disrupt the political stability of the rulers. Despite some official opposition to the very existence of associations, during the Roman period associations continued to flourish and in so doing held banquets modeled on the dominant cultural practices. Through these banquets they negotiated their presence in the sociopolitical fabric of the empire.

---

65. For Egypt see San Nicolò, "Zur Vereinsgerichtsbarkeit im hellenistischen Ägypten"; also San Nicolo, *Agyptisches Vereinswesen*, 2.16–22.

14

The Apostolic Decree of Acts and Greco-Roman Associations

Eating in the Shadow of the Roman Empire[1]

ACCORDING TO ACTS, THE influx of non-Judean believers into the Jesus groups caused the Jerusalem cohort, who early on seemed to possess the ways and means of drawing together the various leaders, to hold a meeting to discuss some pressing issues of Torah that the non-Judean influx had caused to surface: the necessity of circumcision, dietary restrictions, and perhaps some ancillary moral obligations. This meeting, which has come to be referred to as the Jerusalem Council or even the First Ecumenical Council, is presented in Acts 15 as addressing these concerns. On the issue of Gentile circumcision, Peter defends the nonnecessity of the ritual process noting, oddly enough, that neither the Jewish ancestors nor his contemporaries could bear this "yoke" (15:10), by which he means the full Torah, as circumcision itself seems not to have been a particular problem for the Judeans. After hearing testimony from Barnabas and Paul, James, the de facto leader of the meeting, addresses the other aspects of Torah. At this

---

1. Support for the research and writing of this paper has been provided through an Ontario Government Premier's Research Excellence Award and a Social Sciences and Humanities Research Council of Canada Standard Research Grant. My thanks to two Research Assistants, Mary Smida and Rachel McRae, for their helpful feedback on this essay.

point, the narrative reads as a formal document in which a culinary answer is provided for a question of circumcision.

James suggests that the Jerusalem leaders write to the Gentile believers advising them "to abstain only from things polluted by idols (*tōn alisgēmatōn*) and from fornication (*tēs porneias*) and from whatever has been strangled (*tou pniktou*) and from blood (*tou haimatos*)" (Acts 15:20). Curiously, when Luke records the letter there is a change in one of the designations as well as in the order of the prohibitions: "abstain from what has been sacrificed to idols (*eidōlothyton*) and from blood and from what is strangled and from fornication" (Acts 15:29). This latter ordering and word change is reflected in the later summary of the letter's content in Acts 21:25.[2] These changes, however, are not significant and in themselves do [298] not present the most pressing exegetical problem. Rather, the problem lies in understanding the overall intent of the Decree as it is framed in Acts.

Indeed, the broad stroke by which the Acts account is quickly assumed to be historical and universal has led to misinterpretations of the text and leaves a number of unanswered questions. One might ask why, if circumcision is the *problem*, meal regulations are the *solution*? Why is food more important than circumcision, when the latter is what demarcates one as part of the covenant, part of the chosen people of God? How is it that merely by having similar menu items, Judeans and non-Judeans are seen to be in communion, despite the very physical thing—circumcision—that sets apart the Judeans? Furthermore, why did Paul, in Galatians, think that the solution was grounded in his collection of money, with the food issue already solved before Cephas even arrived at Antioch? In the following essay, I will contextualize the details of the decree as presented in the book of Acts within the wider Roman world in order to argue that Luke's presentation allows for all Judean-Jesus-groups and non-Judean-Jesus groups to be understood as doing nothing more or less than any good Romanized association would do when it comes to meal practices, including the prohibition against *porneia*. In so doing, I want to be clear at the outset that my chief concern is with how the author of Acts frames the event, not the historicity of the event itself or the veracity of the Acts account.[3] [299]

---

2. The curious aspect of this latter text is that the Jerusalem leaders tell Paul this as if he has not yet been made aware of this letter and its contents. Yet, according to Acts 15, he was there at its composition.

3. Scholars are divided over the historicity of the Jerusalem Council. On the one hand, there are those who think that there was a Jerusalem meeting, which resulted in some form of the Apostolic Decree as a means "to facilitate table fellowship between gentile believers and more law-conscious Jews" (Matson, *Household Conversion Narratives*, 189; also Johnson, *Acts*, 270; Lüdemann, *Early Christianity*, 172; Fitzmyer, *Acts*, 552–23). Ben Witherington takes a somewhat different approach by attempting

THE SOCIOPOLITICAL CONTEXT OF ACTS

There is widespread agreement that Luke is writing in the aftermath of the Jewish War of 66–70 CE, a direct and violent encounter between Rome and the Judeans. During that time, there was "special concern about security, particularly with regard to movements deeply rooted in Judean history and heritage."[4] In the aftermath of the conflict, in which the Judeans suffered greatly and their holy temple and their key city were destroyed, the newly formed Flavian dynasty used the Roman propaganda machinery to spread the word about how the new emperor, Vespasian, and his son Titus had saved the world from the violent threat of these dangerous and uncontrolled "terrorists" living in the border areas of the eastern part of the empire. Fear, prompted by fear-mongering, allowed Romans to look to their new emperor as the savior who had delivered them from this threat.

Although the physical conflict was limited to the geographic area of Judea/Palestine and was rather one-sided when it came to the actual fighting, there was an imperial tendency to expand and maximize the threat. Judeans from other places in the empire were not at all involved in the conflict, nor the punishments of its aftermath, and yet the imperial propaganda did not allow for much differentiation. The widespread dissemination of *Judaea Capta* coins depicting Roman victory and domination over Judea served the Flavians in this regard.[5] Numismatic images of Vespasian reigning over a cowering Judean would indict all people associated with this *ethne*. Similarly, the construction of the Arch of Titus (built c. 81–82 CE under Domitian) captures the sentiments of the earlier decade. When one sees the arch relief of the temple menorah being carried off from Jerusalem along with captured Judean terrorists, it would be difficult *not* to think of one's neighbors, who themselves associate with these very same symbols. Within

---

to link the Decree with the frequent banquets of temple worship and Greco-Roman associations (*Acts*, 461 n. 415). On the other side of the historicity debate, Esler notes that within the narrative, the presumably Aramaic-speaking James "cites" the LXX rather than the Hebrew Bible, showing "quite conclusively that Luke was not using some source originating in the *ipsissima verba* of James, and may easily have drafted the whole speech himself" (Esler, *Community*, 98). Although willing to maintain the general historicity of the account, Matson makes the geographic limitations or implementation more specific: "The places designated at 15:23 as the recipients of the Decrees (Antioch, Syria, and Cilicia) preclude the Decrees from having universal scope. Apart from 16:4, no evidence exists in Acts that Paul ever implements the decision of the Jerusalem Council" (Matson, *Household Conversion Narratives*, 127).

4. Kahl, "Acts," 147.
5. See Lopez, *Apostle to the Conquered*, 35–38.

such a climate, it would not be a particularly good time to self-identify as a descendent of the Judeans.⁶ [300]

Given the context of Vespasian and Titus using the Judean uprising as a focal point for their own grand role in bringing peace and security to the land, it is unlikely that Luke is concerned to tie Jesus groups to Judaism as a way of *protecting* the Jesus groups by having them pass as a *religio licitum*—a legal religion. To do so would be ill-advised, if not dangerous, in the post-70 era. Whatever happened at the pre-70 CE council in Jerusalem, Luke must surely be reworking the tradition (as he does with so much of his source material) in order to fit it into his own agenda. If that agenda includes political accommodation, as seems to be the scholarly consensus, then Luke would not be concerned to protect Jesus believers by merging them with Judeans. Rather, of more concern would be protecting Jewish believers by tying them more to the non-Judean branch of the Jesus movement.⁷

In order to understand how Luke does this, we can draw upon the data from the so-called voluntary associations of antiquity. Markus Öhler has cogently demonstrated similarities between Luke's depiction of the initial

---

6. Also pertinent is the Sebasteion at Aphrodisias. The Sebasteion is a rectangular integration of two long buildings that frame a processional space leading to a temple, which provides the focal point and is dedicated to Aphrodite and the Julio-Claudian emperors. Construction was begun under Tiberius and completed during Nero's time; thus it was extant during the composition of Acts. It is likely based on a similar monument in Rome. The façades of the long north and south buildings were decorated with about two hundred marble panel reliefs depicting a range of scenes. The lower level of the north building depicted the subjugation of conquered peoples within the Roman Empire. Each *ethne* was given its own inscribed base, with a female figure standing upon it. One of these bases reads ETHNOUS IODAIŌN, indicating the Judeans among those conquered and subjugated by Rome.

7. Kahl correctly notes, "It seems more likely that Luke is working hard to make Paul's politically most controversial project appear less subversive to the Roman imperial order" ("Acts," 154). She goes on to claim, "Luke achieves this by presenting it as a properly Jewish venture supported by the full weight of the ancient tradition and law of the Jews." While I would agree that Luke draws heavily from the Judaic past, he presents it as a precursor to what is now a new "way." Within Luke's narrative, initial acceptance of Jesus within Judaism gives way to rejection by many of the *Ioudaioi*, a problem that has proven difficult for modern interpreters to explain fully; see Tannehill, "Story of Israel"; Tyson, "Jewish Public"; Ascough, "Rejection and Repentance"; Johnson, *Acts*, 7-9; Witherington, *Acts*, 73–76. In Acts, there is not wholesale rejection, as there is still promise for Israel, but Luke presents it as an invitation to join something new that God is doing, rather than presenting Christianity as the same thing as what God has done with Israel in the past. For any Roman reader (if there should happen to be any), the Judeans have revolted in Judea and are now suspect, but the Jesus believers at the Jerusalem council, according to Luke, had decades earlier already brokered a way of distinguishing Judean Jesus believers from other Judeans by having them compromise their food regulations.

Jesus group in Jerusalem in the early chapters of Acts and the Greco-Roman associations, noting in particular some clear parallels: an inner structure, the use of *adelphoi,* an ideal of friendship, shared attitudes towards property, shared meal celebrations, meeting places, and equality of membership status alongside [301] hierarchical leadership structures.[8] It is likely, suggests Öhler, that insiders and outsiders considered the early Jerusalem community to be an association. This invites a reading of the Apostolic Decree in light of the data from the associations' legal standing and meal practices.

POLITICAL ACCOMMODATION AMONG ASSOCIATIONS

The formal relationship between associations and the state has a long and complex history of scholarship, often tied up as much with juristic debates on the nature of the Roman legal system as it is with the social position of associations at that time.[9] What does seem clear, however, is that the associations shared an uneasy relationship with representatives of the Roman republic that extended into the imperial era. On the one hand, the associations were the loci of imitation in that they replicated structures, nomenclature, and practices of official governance. On the other hand, they were perceived as having the potential to foster resistance to that governance by taking political action in order to allow the non-elite to gain elite privileges.

During the republic, new associations had to provide public benefit, although they generally fell into suspicion and were legislated against in the *lex Licinia de sodaliciis,* the *lex Julia,* and the decisions of the Senate from the years 64 and 56 BCE. In the Late Republic, *collegia* were heavily involved in political agitation and street violence, which prompted Julius Caesar's ban on them (between 49 and 46 BCE) with exception granted to "old" associations (*collegia antiqua;* Suetonius, *Aug.* 32, I).[10] Jewish communities, for example, were granted privileges by Caesar as they were perceived as *collegia antiqua.* All others, namely those groups that emerged under e or later, were considered to be potential sources of political unrest.

The *Lex Julia* under Augustus sanctioned professional and religious associations, but their political activities were limited, and overtly political associations may have been banned outright.[11] No explicit regulations are

8. Öhler, "Jerusalemer Urgemeinde."
9. See Gutsfeld, "Ita radices."
10. Rüpke, *Religion of the Romans,* 209.
11. Öhler, "Römisches Vereinsrecht," 51–61. Andreas Bendlin has called into question the linking of "legalization" and "'legitimization," the latter not being a

[302] documented for the time under Tiberius, but many new associations were founded under Gaius Caligula. Claudius prohibited the gathering of Jewish communities because he suspected political activities. Nero prohibited some *collegia* that were found responsible for tumults after gladiator games in 59 CE, and in the second century Trajan was again rather skeptical towards associations. In sum, although official suppression of associations was maintained during the Roman era, no specific instance appears to have had any lasting effect.[12]

Despite the general distrust of associations, in practice there were two types of *collegia illicita:* the seditious collegia (*hetaeria*), which were sanctioned, and the innocently illegal, which were ignored by the State likely because of their contributions to society.[13] Indeed, Gutsfeld demonstrates that associations (*Vereinigungen*) might have been the most important form of social unity in terms of urban integration.[14] He distinguishes two forms of integration: (1) normative, the promotion of values and objectives that are binding (*verbindlich*) for the urban community, and (2) functional, the integration of the individual in certain positions and functions within the urban community. Associations were an integral part of the public sphere of a city; their buildings were an essential part of a cityscape, and public funerals of members drew attention to the associations. As such, they were a replication of the urban community, as seen in their [303] promotion of the principle of equality (*Egalität*) in associations as well as in cities, and in the correspondence between the internal organization of an association and the organization of the city. Social hierarchies within the society of a city reappear within associations.

Overall, associations in the Roman Empire had a stabilizing effect.[15] For example, they organized public gatherings within accepted political

---

precondition of the former; in fact, in the first and second centuries CE, suggests Bendlin, it is not clear that the associations were given any sort of official legal standing ("Eine Zusammenkunft um der *religio* willen ist erlaubt . . . ?"; in "politischen und rechtlichen Konstruktionen," 68–77). Examples of punitive actions against associations represent instances when nominal law becomes real law at moments of political crisis (pages 70–71). Earlier scholars such as Hardy argued that the Lex Iulia of Augustus demanded that associations seek Senate approval (a *senatus consultum*) for the right to exist (Hardy, *Studies in Roman History*, 129–31). This position has been called into question by recent scholarship and it seems unlikely that such a demand existed until well into the second century CE, if at all; see Kloppenborg, "Collegia and *Thiasoi*."

12. Kloppenborg, "Associations in the Ancient World," 326–27. On the banning of collegia see Cotter, "Collegia and Roman Law."

13. Duff, *Personality*.

14. Gutsfeld, "Das römisch Vereinigungswesen," 18.

15. For details see Clauss, "Zur Integrationsleistung."

rhetoric as well as ceremonies for the emperor. Within urban centers, associations offered many advantages to the community such as financial support for public projects, members' know-how for constructing public buildings, and such. On the individual level, associations played an important role in everyday life.[16] For ordinary people, becoming a member of a professional or religious association was an opportunity to take part in public life as well as to benefit from the social prestige of the associations that was established in a public, ostentatious way through the contact between representatives of associations and the ruling power represented by members of the imperial administration.

Although scholars dispute whether, or to what actual extent, Roman associations were politically active in a negative sense, the difficult living conditions of tradespeople alone served as a potential source of social unrest and political actions.[17] As noted above, using a number of laws and regulations over different periods of time, the authorities attempted to prevent associations from becoming politically involved. Clearly not all associations were fully dissolved because of political activities, probably because Rome was dependent on the work of at least some of the associations. Increasingly the government granted associations privileges [304] in exchange for loyal service.[18] However, in order to avoid abuse of the privileges by individual members, as well as to prevent associations from becoming too powerful within the state, the concession of privileges was accompanied by an increasing control of the associations by the state. The overall "effect of all this was that *collegia* were presented as respectable organizations, as first-level status groups for ambitious members of the *plebs* that were seen as an integral part of local social hierarchies."[19]

Philip Harland's study of inscriptions from Roman Asia concerning the involvement of associations in imperial dimensions of civic life illustrates the complexity of group-society relations, reflecting the groups' acculturation, adaptation, and selection of cultural traditions while still maintaining

---

16. See Kolb, "Vereine." For Egypt, San Nicolò demonstrates that the statutes of associations there existed parallel to public jurisdiction and did not interfere with or compete against public justice, giving them full autonomy over their statutes as long as they were in accordance with the *ius cogens* ("Zur Vereinsgerichtsbarkeit"; see also San Nicolò, *Ägyptisches Vereinswesen* 2.16–22). On the legal standing of *collegia* in the province of Egypt in the first century CE see further Arnaoutoglou, "Collegia in the Province of Egypt."

17. Schulz-Falkenthal, "Zur politischen Aktivität."

18. In a separate article, Schulz-Falkenthal argues that members of Roman *collegia opificum* were granted privileges from Rome in exchange for their services for the community, such as their work as a fire brigade ("Römische Handwerkerkollegien").

19. Van Nijf, *Civic World*, 155, 166–68; Clauss, "Zur lntegrationsleistung."

community identity.[20] Associations were positively involved in imperial facets of civic life, sociocultural civic activities, and benefactions, maintaining, for the most part, positive relationships with imperial officials and honoring the imperial cult. At the same time, the suspicion of associations as political flash points meant there was always a chance that associations of any sort could be sanctioned or dissolved by local authorities or imperial edict. Thus, associations had to play up their ability to assimilate with the wider culture while carefully negotiating those places where they might be perceived to be expressing resistance to the dominance of imperial rule. Jesus groups would be no different in needing to carefully steer this course.

As it was impossible for the Roman Empire to control fully the founding of new associations within its territory, it granted a general concession to new groups unless they obviously interfered with the state's interests.[21] The Jesus groups were first tolerated under this general concession, before their belief in another god was thought to be proof of their incompatibility with the law and order of the Roman Empire, which occurred generally in [305] the second century although sporadically in the first.[22] Like most associations after Augustus's *Lex Julia,* Jesus groups were technically illicit but were tolerated as insignificant as long as they maintained the *pax*.[23]

One obvious time for illicit political activity within associations was during their meetings, most of which included some sort of banquet practices. The primary function of many associations centered on sharing meals among members, as is clear from literary, architectural, and epigraphic evidence.[24] Rigid regulations about the public sale of meat made it difficult for people to get together for meals, and associations could serve as a meeting

20. Harland, "Honouring the Emperor"; see also Harland, *Associations,* 89–112.

21. Heinrici, "Zur Geschichte der Anfänge."

22. Two obvious first-century examples were the expulsion of Judeans and Jesus believers in 49 CE under Claudius (if indeed this did involve Jesus believers), and the punishment of Jesus believers in Rome when they became Nero's scapegoat for the great fire in that city.

23. Hardy, *Studies in Roman History* 141–43.

24. Dill, *Roman Society,* 278; Rüpke, *Religion of the Romans,* 208; Ascough, "Forms of Commensality" (Chapter 12, above). Associations were often repudiated for their indulgence in food and drink. See, for example, Philo's claim concerning the associations that "you could find no sound elements but only liquor, tippling, drunkenness and the outrageous conduct they lead to" (*Flacc.* 136; see also Philo, *Legat.* 10, 311–312; *Flacc.* 4; Seland, "Philo and the Clubs." See further Ascough, *Paul's Macedonian Associations,* 85–87). Matthias Klinghardt (*Gemeinschaftsmahl,* 11–12), in particular, has been concerned for some time for a clearer understanding of early Christian meal practices in light of the meal practices of the voluntary associations, despite the opposition to making such connection and the difficulty with the sources. He addresses the topic in detail in the first section of the book (*Gemeinschaftsmahl,* 21–174).

point where group members could gather and eat together. Although Roman associations participated seriously in civic and cultic activities and had a benefactory role in society, we should not allow the latter aspects to mask the importance of the observation that the primary raison d'etre of these associations was conviviality.[25] Nevertheless, "collegia did not hold banquets whenever they wanted. Rather, the occasion [306] and the organization of banquets, as well as the manner of dining, were carefully regulated by the collegium bylaws."[26]

Various association meals can be classified as segregative or transgressive commensality in which social relationships are negotiated within a particular group.[27] Meals are used to strengthen social cohesion within the group while allowing for the crossing of social boundaries by bringing together people from different social strata. Thus, association commensality functions as a means for both assimilation and resistance to dominant cultural mores. The rules and regulations within associations represent an attempt to maintain cohesion and peace *(pax)* during meetings in order to minimize the disruptive behavior that so often caused the associations to come under suspicion by local authorities. The ability to expel errant members represents the strongest sanction available to associations under Roman law.[28] Thus, there is collusion with imperial authorities in maintenance of order in association meetings and banquets.

THE APOSTOLIC DECREE AS POLITICAL ACCOMMODATION

The issue of circumcision is raised directly by the believers "who belonged to the sect of the Pharisees" as a key part of the observance of Torah (Acts 15:5). Thus, it is striking that it is not addressed directly in any of the responses given by Peter, or Barnabas and Paul, or James. While it does seem to be the case that a non-Judean believer need not be circumcised, it is "a decision that can only be inferred from the text" in so far as James notes,

25. Dunbabin, *Roman Banquet*, 94; Donahue, *Roman Community*, 85, also 128–38 and table 5.7 on 137–38; Leiwo, "Religion, or Other Reasons?" On association meals in general see further Poland, *Geschichte des griechischen Vereinswesens*, 258–67, 392–95; Ausbüttel, *Untersuchungen*, 55–59; Klauck, *Herrenmahl und hellenistischer Kult*, 68–76; Klinghardt, *Gemeinschaftsmahl* 21–173.

26. Liu, "Occupation," 361. Nevertheless, the lack of epigraphic commemoration of such routine banquets leaves us with a dearth of evidence for much of the convivial times of the associations (Liu, "Occupation," 362).

27. See Ascough, "Forms of Commensality" (Chapter 12, above).

28. Rüpke, *Religion of the Romans*, 211.

"they are not to be 'troubled'" (Acts 15:19).[29] Thus, Luke avoids having James directly address the issue of circumcision, which suggests that for Luke the issue is no longer a pressing one. Instead, meal restrictions become the issue in the narrative, suggesting that Luke, his readers, or both, are facing dietary challenges.

The dominant interpretive trend understands the prohibitions in light of relations between Judeans and non-Judeans as an attempt to broker closer [307] ties between the two through minimal table fellowship requirements.[30] Johnson notes that table fellowship reflected spiritual fellowship and thus asks, "How could *Jews* eat with those whose practices fundamentally defiled themselves and the land and the people? These requirements of the Gentiles therefore enabled Jews to remain in communion with them, since the Gentiles would not be engaging in practices in radical disharmony with the Jewish *ethos,* and the Gentiles would be 'keeping the Torah' as it was spelled out for 'proselytes and sojourners in the land.'"[31] According to Matson, it is James's attempt to mitigate the indiscriminate eating, arising through Peter's abrogation of dietary laws in Acts 10–11, by the imposition of certain restrictions.[32] This is rather myopic, however, as there are many other restrictions that Judeans would place on eating for which James does not allow. According to the Decree, non-Judean Jesus believers are not prohibited from eating pork, yet it is highly unlikely that a Judean Jesus believer would partake of such meat at the house of a non-Judean Jesus believer, and nothing in James's statement mitigates this (unlike the story of Peter's vision earlier in chapter 11).

Also curious is the lack of any sanctions that are to be applied if there is a failure to meet the terms of the Apostolic Decree. That is, unlike the Torah guidelines of Leviticus and Numbers, and equally unlike the social prohibition of the associations, there is no fine, flogging, expulsion, or death associated with noncompliance. In this regard, the Decree has no bite in order to ensure it is enforced. It is quite distinct from Jewish Torah and more akin to an invitation to commensality.

A closer look at the terms of the invitation reveals that rather than place Torah-like prohibitions on the Gentiles, the prescriptions present nothing more than many Romanized inhabitants of the empire would expect to take place at a civilized banquet held by an association. The Apostolic Decree is framed in such a way as to lay out for Luke's time the means whereby Gentiles

---

29. Walaskay, *Acts,* 146–245, 119; Matson, *Household Conversion Narratives,* 126.
30. Savelle, "Reexamination," 462–65.
31. Johnson, *Acts,* 273 (italics original). See also Conzelmann, *Acts,* 119.
32. Matson, *Household Conversion Narratives,* 127.

and Judeans can join together for common meals in a manner that is indistinguishable from other licit associations in the post-70 CE Roman world.

We begin with the idea that Luke would include a text that would separate food into "sacred" and "profane" categories (that is, pure versus ritually tainted). This goes against the strong indications in Luke's Gospel that Jesus resisted just such separations. More so than Mark (or Matthew), Luke highlights the full availability of food for everyone, no matter the [308] particular day it is harvested (Luke 6:1-5), the state of the hands that touch it (Luke 11:37-40), or the company in which it is eaten (Luke 7:36-47; cf. Luke 14:1-24). Thus, Luke's inclusion of the Acts 15 Decree does not reflect a concern with the actual state of the food but with the social practices that surround the eating.[33] Likewise, the usual placing of the onus on the integration of non-Judeans into a Judean context fails to wrestle with the post-70 CE context of the composition of Acts noted above and the rather unsympathetic portrayal of Judeans and Judaism throughout the book of Acts.[34]

The vexing question in Acts 15:20 is to what the prohibitions refer and whether or not they are interrelated or identifying separate issues. In the first instance, non-Judeans are "to abstain from the defilement of idols" (*tou apachesthai tōn alisgēmatōn tōn eidōlōn*), which is a rather vague reference.[35] In the later iteration of the prohibition, this "defilement" is specified as "idol-food" (*eidōlothyton*, 15:29; cf. 21:25), although this does not help bring clarity as the word *eidōlothyton* has little attestation outside of early Christian writings.[36] It is worth pausing here in order to get a better under-

---

33. It is particularly striking that Luke has Jesus claim of the wine "this is my blood . . ." (Luke 22:19-20) and then have it offered as drink, a seeming contradiction to the injunction to avoid blood in Acts 15, if this latter prohibition simply means blood in and of itself. Furthermore, it is significant that Acts nowhere has the believers celebrating the Lord's Supper explicitly even when they do break bread together, suggesting that Luke repudiates a literal interpretation of the words of the Last Supper.

34. Brawley, *Luke-Acts and the Jews*.

35. Other possible translations include "the pollution of idols," "things polluted by idols," and "the contamination of idols." "The verb ἀπέχω (*apechō*) means 'avoid contact' with something" (Bock, *Acts*, 505). Few scholars ask how the earliest non-Judean Jesus believers would have understood the word "idol." Instead, it is simply assumed that there is already buy-in to the notion that an image of a deity is equated with that deity, and that it is the image that is worshiped. This is not, however, congruent with polytheistic rituals.

36. Witherington, *Acts*, 461. The change in nomenclature may be nothing more than a stylistic shift, and many commentators conclude, "the prohibition therefore pertains to the issue discussed at such great length by Paul in 1 Cor 8-10" (see Johnson, *Acts*, 266); Conzelmann, *Acts*, 117-18; Barrett, *Acts*, 731. Some commentators contrast this idol food with the Jewish sense of *corban*, which indicates something dedicated to

standing of how the non-Judeans of Luke's audience might have heard this prohibition. [309]

Jean-Pierre Waltzing notes that during an association meeting, the sacrifice and the banquet were inseparable from each other.[37] This seems not to fit, however, with more recent understandings of the process of ritual sacrifice and the practices around consumption in the postmortem banquet. According to Cicero, Roman religious practice (*religio*) can be understood as the sum of three parts: ritual (*sacra*), auspices (*auspicia*), and prophetic warnings, each one of which is central to the maintenance of the state.[38] The rituals were carefully maintained in order to preserve not only the integrity of the performance but the divine favor over the state and over those sacrificing. Thus, everything was carefully scripted.

Usual (Christian) interpretations merge two separate parts of the ritual: the animal sacrificed to the gods and the subsequent consumption of the leftover meat at the banquet by humans. This merger seems not to have been the understanding within the ancient context. The animal was made sacred through the ritual butchering, and parts of it were offered to the god(s) by being burnt on an altar.[39] "When the offering had been consumed in the flames or placed on the ground, the rest of the victim was 'rendered profane,' that is to say the celebrant 'seized' it by laying his hand upon it, thereby making it suitable for human consumption . . . In this way, the celebrant *did not consume sacred food but* food that the deity had somehow agreed to let him have."[40] The postritual banquet "was far more akin to a gift (*sportula*) given to a client by his patron."[41]

The key part to notice is the separation of the ritual offering into two types: the profane and the sacred. That which is rendered profane is no longer considered part of the sacrifice and is no longer dedicated to the gods.[42]

God in the temple, yet even in pointing this out, Witherington has to admit that the parallels to *corban* "in the Greek realm are θεοθυτον, which means something offered/dedicated to a god, and ειδωλοθυτον, which means something offered/dedicated in a temple" (Witherington, *Acts*, 461; no accents are used in the original quotation).

37. Waltzing, *Étude Historique*, 1:231.
38. Cicero, *De nat.* 3.5, quoted in Warrior, *Roman Religion*, 16.
39. Warrior, *Roman Religion*, 23; Scheid, *Roman Religion*, 84.
40. Scheid, *Roman Religion*, 85–86 (italics added).
41. Scheid, *Roman Religion*, 86.
42. For example, Dio Chrysostom (40–120 CE) writes: "What festivity could please unless the most important thing of all [i.e., friends] were at hand, what symposium could delight you if you lacked the goodwill of the guests? What sacrifice is acceptable to the gods without the participants in the feast? (*Orations* 3.97, LCL). Although not his specific focus, Dio does seem to indicate a difference between the actual sacrifice and the banqueting that follows. That is, he is concerned not with the presence of

"To sacrifice was—in the course of a feast to which the gods were invited—to divide the food into two parts, one part for the deities, the [310] other for the human beings."[43] Thus, it is unlikely that a non-Judean would reference the *profane* portions of the feast as "idol-food" or "meat sacrificed to idols." Had it remained sacred—that is, sacrificed—it still belonged to the god(s). To eat it, even for a non-Judean, would be to profane that which belonged to the gods. When it had undergone the process of being made profane as part of the ritual, it no longer carried that taboo.

The second prohibition in the initial formulation of the Apostolic Decree warns against *porneia*, most often translated as "fornication." There is some disagreement, however, over the nature of this *porneia*. Its most obvious referent is to prostitution, or perhaps "any act of sexual immorality."[44] Ben Witherington is more limited in his interpretation, noting that *porneia* is "the right term to be used if James is thinking of the sort of thing that sometimes accompanied, or at least was believed to accompany, the pagan rites and feasts in pagan temples."[45] Yet this is a rather vague reference, and little evidence is given to support the view of widespread sacred prostitution in antiquity (even in Corinth).[46] What can be demonstrated, however, is the presence of female entertainers at banquets, including banquets following sacrifice rituals. These entertainers were sometimes viewed as a means to sexual pleasure, although some "pagans" saw this as an aberration of etiquette.[47]

The third and fourth prohibitions James raises in Acts 15:20 are sometimes treated separately and sometimes read together: "from that which is

---

participants in the ritual (the sacrifice) but with the aftermath (the banquet).

43. "More recent examinations of the place of sacrifice in public ritual have stressed the meal elements in sacrifice [as opposed to earlier emphasis on the violence], which appear not only in the choice of offering (edible animals) and the mode of 'rendering sacred' (through cooking and burning), but also the use of the remains: shared and eaten or, for gods, sprinkled as ashes or blood at a sacred location . . . Sacrifices essentially constituted meals that the human community shared with gods" (Frankfurter, "Traditional Cult," 558).

44. Johnson, *Acts*, 266; see also Fitzmyer, *Acts* 557.

45. Witherington, *Acts*, 463; so too Bock, *Acts*, 505.

46. Fotopoulos, *Food Offered to Idols*, 173.

47. Fotopoulos, *Food Offered to Idols*, 170. There is also the further challenge not to import our modern sense of what *porneia* encompasses into the ancient prohibitions. That other Decrees needed to spell out what sexual practices were prohibited would suggest that there was no commonly accepted, or at least broadly accepted, view of what "sexual immorality" might entail. For example, the association inscription from Philadelphia (SIG³ 985) prohibits what would otherwise be tolerated (if not fully accepted) sexual practices in order that members might enter into the rituals associated with the god.

strangled" (*tou pniktou*) and "from blood" (*tou haimatos*). Beverly Roberts Gavanta suggests, "This likely is a description of what happens with sacrifices or meals among Gentiles. The result of this form of death is that blood often [311] is not drained from the animal."[48] Bock adds the note that "Philo (*Spec. Laws* 4.23.122–23) describes such a practice," but Bock does not mention that in Philo it is an extreme case rather than normative practice.[49] Johnson connects the terms *haima* and *pniktos* as "a single ritual prohibition: to abstain from 'strangled things' and 'from blood' is equivalent, since when something is strangled and then eaten, the blood remains within it."[50] Witherington, supported by Bock, suggests that the Gentile priest tasting the sacrificial blood was particularly offensive.[51] Neither scholar provides much concrete evidence for the practice in Roman times, other than all too brief and rare instances in the magical papyri and literature and in the Jewish Wisdom of Solomon 12:2–5.[52]

Such interpretations falter on the redundancy of specifying avoidance of sacrificial meat resulting from strangulation or sacrificial meat with blood remaining in it. In both cases, it is simply a restatement or extrapolation of these interpreters' understanding of the first prohibition to avoid any sacrificial food at all.[53] Thus, it is not the means of the sacrifice but the type

---

48. Gaventa, *Acts*, 222.

49. Bock, *Acts*, 506. Mary Douglas notes for Lev 17:17, but applicable to other religious traditions, that "meat for the table must be drained of its blood. No man eats flesh with blood in it. Blood belongs to God alone, for life is in the blood . . . The draining of blood from meat is a ritual act which figures the bloody sacrifice at the altar. Meat is thus transformed from a living creature into a food item" (*Implicit Meanings*, 248).

50. Johnson, *Acts*, 267, citing "the 'sin' attributed to the people in 1 Sam 14:33."

51. Witherington, *Acts*, 464; Bock, *Acts*, 506.

52. On the non-Jewish references see Witherington, *Acts*, 464. Savelle ("Reexamination," 455–56) notes a few instances, but all of them occur in Jewish literature before and after the New Testament period.

53. See Barrett, *Acts*, 733. Although many scholars link these prohibitions with Levitical regulations and the Noahic commands, particularly the regulations around blood and unclean animals, the lack of mention of specific animals such as swine and the lack of reference to shellfish and such remains problematic. On the unlikelihood of the referent here being the Noahic commands or Levitical laws see Witherington, *Acts*, 464–65. Others, however, maintain these links. On Leviticus see Malina and Plich, *Book of Acts*, 109; Johnson, *Acts*, 273; Conzelman, *Acts*, 117–18; Bock, *Acts*, 505; Fitzmyer, *Acts*, 557; Callan, "Apostolic Decree"; Taylor, "Jerusalem Decrees," 377–79. On the Noahic connection see Smith, *From Symposium to Eucharist*, 166; Taylor, "Jerusalem Decrees," 374–77. Wilson (*Luke and the Law*, 84–102) argues against the case that the laws of Leviticus 17–18 are behind Acts 15, as does Klinghardt, *Gesetz und Volk Gottes*, 185–86. Wedderburn ("Apostolic Decree," 369) supports Wilson's arguments against the use of the Levitical and Noahic laws as background to the Apostolic Decree, but distances himself from Wilson's explanation of the text.

of [312] resulting meal that is of concern. In this regard, *what* is eaten does not differentiate Judeans or Jesus believers from the Romans, since Romans did not, as a rule, eat strangled animals or bloody meat.

From this brief analysis of the prohibitions of the Decree, it becomes clear that the prohibitions focus not on moral purity or on minimalist Torah obedience but on banquet etiquette—"The question of table-fellowship between Jew and Gentile is not explicitly raised in Acts 15, but its presence is everywhere implied."[54] This is clearest in the second iteration of the prohibitions—namely the ones scribed for widespread distribution. Here we find the clearer reference to "idol-food" (food properly belonging to the gods due to being sacred) and the placing of *porneia* at the conclusion of the list. The reversal of strangulation and blood to read blood and strangulation is also important. Thus, in its formalized expression the Decree prohibits:

- food dedicated to the gods that has not been profaned within the ritual,
- food that has been improperly slaughtered (namely, strangled),[55]
- food that has been improperly drained of the blood (the life source) during the ritual,
- postbanquet sexual favors.

All four prohibitions are concerned with how a group banquets together and attempts to show that the early Jesus believers upheld strict moral behavior that would be no cause for alarm among Roman authorities.

CONCLUSION

Given the highly charged political use of "Judeans" within the Flavian political propaganda, it is unlikely that Luke is concerned to reconcile Gentiles *to* Judeans. In Acts 15:20, Luke is reconciling Judeans to Gentiles by showing any potential Roman readers that the Judean Jesus believers are willing to accommodate a much less observant state of being than their nonbelieving counterparts when it comes to the meal practices. Through their allegiance to Jesus, these Judeans are not required to keep Torah fully. In fact, they do nothing more than what any self-respecting Roman would do at a ritual—avoiding still-sacred food, not consuming improperly [313] slaughtered and drained meat, and rejecting postbanquet sexual favors. For Luke's post-70 CE readers of Acts 15, the Apostolic Decree lays out the practices that the non-Judeans (Gentiles) are willing to follow in order to provide an

---

54. Esler, *Community*, 98.
55. Barrett, *Acts*, 733.

entrance for the Judean Jesus believers to join with them. The Jesus believers are presented as good Romanized members of society whose association poses no threat to the established Roman *ordo*.[56]

---

56. Despite these compromises, Luke "never even comes close to accepting Caesar's divine status celebrated in the imperial religion and public propaganda" (Kahl, "Acts," 150). As with the other associations, when we probe into the nature of the early Jesus communities as depicted by Luke, we can see that there is an uneasy balance between assimilation and resistance as they negotiate their place within the wider social fabric of life in the Roman Empire.

15

A Question of Death

Paul's Community-Building Language in 1 Thessalonians 4:13–18

IN ANCIENT VOLUNTARY ASSOCIATIONS, death, burial, and memorial figured prominently in the collective lives of their members.[1] In light of this prominence, it is interesting to note, with Jonathan Z. Smith, that questions concerning the status of dead members of the community trigger Paul's most extensive and earliest discussions of the resurrection of the dead (1 Thessalonians and 1 Corinthians).[2] In an attempt to explore further in this article the nature of the Christian community at Thessalonike, I examine here the social context of Paul's eschatological description in 1 Thess 4:13–18. Paul's comments to this community and the social practices lurking behind his words are brought into contact with the larger database of group discourses and practices pertaining to the dead as found among voluntary associations. In particular, I will develop Burton Mack's suggestion that the Thessalonians' question to Paul concerning dead members was a question, not about personal salvation, but about belonging.[3] [510]

---

1. Ancient voluntary associations were not formed solely for the purpose of burial of their members; see Kloppenborg, "Collegia and *Thiasoi*," 20–23.

2. Smith, *Drudgery Divine*, 131 n. 33.

3. Mack, *Who Wrote the New Testament?*, 110.

Voluntary associations are well attested in Macedonia, and the city of Thessalonike provides the richest evidence of them, with at least twenty-six Greek inscriptions dating from the first century to the third century CE, showing a diversity of associations and deities worshiped. The best-attested groups are that of Dionysos and a number of professional associations, although there is also evidence for other types of associations.[4] Epigraphic and papyrological evidence suggests that within associations, death was not simply a matter of not living, nor was the primary concern about death the personal salvation of the individual. Death was inevitable but provided the opportunity for community definition. One did not cease to be a member of an association at death; rather, death was the point at which the association celebrated a person's membership. From among the many members, the deceased individual would be isolated and celebrated as a member of the community. We will explore the nature of the issue that Paul responds to in 1 Thess 4:13–18 in light of the pervasiveness of death in the community-building discourse of the living members of associations.[5]

BURIAL IN ASSOCIATIONS

In antiquity many people were members of one or more voluntary associations. Ramsay MacMullen estimates that one-third of the inhabitants of Rome in the second century CE were members of associations.[6] This figure is likely reflected across the empire at that time, perhaps only slightly less at an earlier time. Modern scholarship usually identifies three broad categories of associations: religious associations, professional associations, and funerary associations.[7] The funerary associations (or *collegia tenuiorum/funeraticia*) were organized to ensure the proper burial of their deceased members. Members paid entrance fees or regular dues, or both, that were used for the burial of [511] members. However, associations formed solely for the burial of members did not exist until the second century CE (from the time of Hadrian and beyond).[8] Even at that time they were a legal fic-

    4. See Ascough, "Voluntary Associations and Community Formation," 297–307. Appendix 1 of the dissertation includes the texts and translations of seventy-five Macedonian inscriptions that are associated with voluntary associations.

    5. I have argued elsewhere that the Thessalonian community was construed as a professional voluntary association; see Ascough, "Thessalonian Christian Community" (Chapter 7, above); also Ascough, *Paul's Macedonian Associations*, 162–90.

    6. MacMullen, *Enemies of the Roman Order*, 174.

    7. Ascough, "Associations, Voluntary," 117–18.

    8. Kloppenborg, "Collegia and *Thiasoi*," 20–22. Cf. Ziebarth (*Das griechische Vereinswesen*, 17) and Poland (*Geschichte des griechischen Vereinswesens*, 56, 503–4), both

tion, a way of gaining legal recognition to meet as a group while another purpose (usually social) was the primary interest of the group.

The frequent mention of associations in burial contexts indicates that associations formed for professional or religious reasons also handled the burial of their own members. In some cases, nonmembers commissioned an association to carry out certain rites at their tomb, although this was not the principal raison d'être of the association. Nevertheless, the extent to which many associations were involved in activities around death is striking:

> About one-third of the total epigraphic production of Roman associations in the eastern provinces records funerary activities of some sort, some inscriptions commemorating the burial of a collegium member by the association, while others mention collegia in recording the funerary arrangements of (wealthy) outsiders. It has been estimated that about one-fifth of all known Italian associations were directly involved in the funerals of their members.[9]

The activities of associations involved in the burial of their members often included setting up inscriptions in memory of their deceased.[10] In this regard, Macedonia is similar to places elsewhere in the empire: for example, the professional association of donkey-drivers from Beroea set up a memorial to one of its members,[11] as did the associates of Poseidonios (set up in conjunction with the deceased's wife and son).[12] Purple-dyers in Thessalonike commemorated [512] their deceased in a similar manner (IG X/2.1 291; II CE), as did the worshipers of Dionysos (IG X/2.1 503; 132 CE), Herakles (IG X/2.1 288 and 289; both 155 CE), the Asiani (IG X/2.1 309 and 480; both II–III CE),[13] and a Hero cult (IG X/2.1 821; II–III CE). A more elaborate funerary practice is described in the epigram of a tomb from Amphipolis, where the dances of the Bacchants are described in detail.[14] Some associations may have been involved in the actual burial of these

---

of whom point out the lack of evidence for the existence of associations devoted exclusively to the burial of members. Also see Fraser, *Rhodian Funerary Monuments*, 58–70; and Kloppenborg, "Collegia and *Thiasoi*," 22, 29 nn. 41–42.

9. Van Nijf, *Civic World*, 31.

10. Kloppenborg, "Collegia and *Thiasoi*," 21; Wilson, "Voluntary Associations," 13. For regulations pertaining to the actual rites associated with burial see LSCG 77 (Delphi, IV BCE) and IG XII/5 593 (Ceos, V BCE).

11. Woodward, "Inscriptions from Beroea," 155 no. 22 (n.d.).

12. Horsley, *New Documents* 4, 215 no. 19 (dated to the imperial period).

13. See also Voutiras, "Berufs-und Kultverein."

14. Paton, *Greek Anthology*, 2:264–65.

members, as was the case with SEG 37 (1987) 559 (Kassandreia, n.d.) and CIG 2000f (Hagios Mamas, II CE). The extensive evidence for the connections between associations and the deceased in Philippi (and Macedonia more generally) led Francis W. Beare to conclude that, "when Paul came to Philippi, he would find ready hearers for a gospel of resurrection from the dead, and life eternal."[15]

Finances were closely connected to the provision of burials and memorials. Dues collected could be designated for burial.[16] In the case of some associations, members could be fined or banished, or both, from the rituals for a set time if they failed to attend the funeral of a member or if they failed to follow the etiquette of the funeral procedures.[17]

The commitment of an association to the burial of its deceased members went beyond informal agreement. In a number of cases inscriptions show that the arrangement was formalized and binding, and grievances were subject to the proceedings of a court of law. For example, an inscription from Lanuvium shows that when the burial of a member took place in a different town, the documents pertaining to the reimbursement of funeral arrangements required the seals of seven Roman citizens (CIL XIV 2112; 136 CE). In the case of suicide, the Lanuvium inscription stipulates that the right to burial has been forfeited.

A papyrus from Egypt preserves the following letter from a woman appealing to King Ptolemaios on behalf of her dead brother: [513]

> I, Krateia, from Alexandrou Nesos, have been wronged by Philip and Dionysius in the following way. My brother Apolodotos was a fellow member of the association with them . . . When my brother died, not only did they not provide a funeral for him or accompany him to the burial site, in violation of the association's rule, but they did not reimburse me for the expenses for his funeral. (P.Enteuxeis 20; 221 BCE)

---

15. Beare, *Philippians*, 9. Beare calls these associations "burial-clubs," as does Paul Perdrizet, who notes the large number of funerary associations at Philippi, the first European city in which Christianity took root (Perdrizet, "Inscriptions de Philippes," 318). Both cases indicate that the associations at Philippi are similar to the Roman *collegia funeriticia*.

16. See IG II^2 1278 (Athens, 277/76 BCE); CIL XIV 2112 (Lanuvium, 136 CE); TAMS III 201(Rough Cilicia, mid–I CE); Livy 2.33.11; Pliny, *Nat.* 21.10; 33.138; Val. Max. 4.4.2; 5.2.3; 5.6.8; Rauh, *Sacred Bonds of Commerce*, 273 and n. 66.

17. See IG XII/1 155 (Rhodes, II BCE); IG II^2 1368 (Athens, II CE); IG II^2 1275 (Pireus, III–II BCE); P.Cairo.Dem. 30605 (Tebtunis, 157/56 BCE), 30606 (Tebtunis, 158/57 BCE); P.Mich.243 (Tebtunis, early I CE), 244 (Tebtunis, 43 CE).

Written on the papyrus in a different handwriting is this response: "After examining the association's rule, compel them to make good and if they contest, send them to me." In another instance, a man files a similar complaint on behalf of his sister, whose family was not reimbursed for the funeral expenses, even though she was a member and a priestess of the association (P.Enteuxeis 21; 218 BCE). In each case, despite the deceased's being a member of an association, the association did not pay for the funeral, which, in the eyes of the complainant, was a breach of contract.

Another significant connection between associations and funerary practices is evidenced in a number of associations that patrons founded or endowed for the purpose of commemorating the anniversary of his or her death at the family tomb. Often association membership included not only the guarantee of a decent burial but also the possibility of the annual commemoration of one's death.[18] A significant number of association inscriptions indicate funerary practices of some sort, particularly memorials for the deceased. Often an already-existing association was endowed with a bequest of money or property (for example, vineyards or land), the income of which was to be used for a memorial at the tomb of the deceased. The remainder of the income went to the association for its own use, probably for social gatherings such as banquets (see IG X/2.1 259; Thessalonike, I CE). Occasionally an association was formed in order to keep an annual memorial for the deceased, as was the case with CIL III 656 (Selian, n.d.).

Many of the Macedonian association inscriptions with funerary contexts indicate that the association was involved in a festival known as the *rosalia*:[19] from Philippi and its surrounding area, we have CIL III 703, 704, 707 (all n.d.); [514] IMakedD 920 (n.d.); Pilhofer 133 (II–III CE), 029/1 (n.d.).[20] Many *viciani* (associations formed of members of a particular village) participated in the celebration of the *rosalia* or *parentalia* at the tomb of the deceased.[21] The *rosalia* is mentioned in a Thessalonian inscription,

---

18. See Renan, *Apostles*, 285–86.

19. On the *rosalia* see Perdrizet, "Inscriptions de Philippes"; Poland, *Geschichte des griechischen Vereinswesens*, 511–13; Collart, *Philippes*, 474–85; Hoey, "Rosaliae Signorum," 22–30; Picard and Avezou, "Le testament de la prêtresse," 53–62. The festival was popular throughout the Roman empire (Phillips, "Rosalia or Rosaria," 1335). Poland notes that the evidence for associations involved with the *rosalia* comes primarily from Bithynia in Asia Minor and around Thessalonike and Philippi "in Thrace" [*sic*] (see *griechischen Vereinswesens*, 511).

20. The abbreviation "Pilhofer" refers to Pilhofer, *Philippi*, vol. 2.

21. The *parentalia* occurred for nine days in February (13–21). Temples were closed and marriages did not take place. The days were taken up with private celebrations for the family dead. The final day was a public ceremony called the *Feralia*, in which a household made offerings at the graves of its deceased members (see further Rose,

IG X/2.1 260 (III CE), where a priestess of a *thiasos* bequeaths two *plethra* of grapevines to ensure that festivities involving rose crowns are conducted.[22]

Rosalia, or "day of roses," was also the name of the Italian feast of the dead, in which the rose played a significant role in the funeral cult.[23] The *rosalia* had two aspects: the commemoration of the deceased and the joyous celebration of the return of spring and summer with an emphasis on banqueting and fun.[24] Since there is little evidence that the connection between roses and funerary practices was indigenous to Macedonia or Thrace before the coming of the Romans, it is probable that when the Italian colonists came to Macedonia they brought many of their own practices and beliefs with them, including the *rosalia*. Since Macedonia was famous for its roses,[25] it is no surprise that Italian settlers imported the *rosalia*.[26] It seems that "self-commemorators who introduced *rosalia* into their funerary arrangements were thus making a deliberate statement of (assumed) Roman cultural identity."[27] [515]

Foundations set up through the benefaction of an association brought honor not only to the person memorialized but also to the association: "Collegia entrusted with tasks which might ideally have gone to such organizations as the *boule* or the *gerousia* had to be regarded as trustworthy and respectable organizations."[28] This trust represented a claim on the part

---

"Feralia," 434; Rose, "Parentalia," 781; Davies, *Death, Burial and Rebirth*, 145–46). For benefaction to ensure that guild members hold a banquet at a tomb of a deceased member on the day of the *parentalia* see CIL XI 5047 (Ocriculum, n.d.). An example of the *parentalia* in Macedonia is found in CIL III 656 from Selian (n.d.); see also Collart, *Philippes*, 474–75 n. 3 no. 7 and pages 479–80.

22. Perdrizet ("Inscriptions de Philippes," 323) points to a large sarcophagus from Thessalonike (now in the Louvre) on the lid of which a man and wife are shown in repose. The wife holds in her hand a crown of roses. See further bibliography in Perdrizet, "Inscriptions de Philippes," 323 nn. 1 and 2.

23. The roses symbolized the return of *la belle saison,* when the earth seems to burst into life.

24. Hoey, "Rosaliae Signorum," 22.

25. Edson, "Cults of Thessalonica," 169; Picard and Avezou, "Testament de la prêtresse," 53–54. On the making of rose crowns in Macedonia see Theophrastus, *De Causis Plant.* 1.13.11 (Dion); *Hist. Plant.* 6.6.4 (the region around Philippi); and Herodotus 8.138.1 (below the eastern slopes of the Bermion range).

26. It is interesting to note that although the Italian *rosalia* is celebrated, the Thracian Horseman often decorates the tombstones in Macedonian villages (Perdrizet, "Inscriptions de Philippes," 320), obviously suggesting synchronistic funerary practices; see Pilhofer 029/1 (Philippi, n.d.), IMakedD 920 (Podgora, n.d.), and CIL III 704 (Reussilova, n.d.).

27. Van Nijf, *Civic World,* 64.

28. Van Nijf, *Civic World,* 66.

A Question of Death   283

of the association of belonging to the *polis* and functioned as a means of establishing status in the hierarchical order of the *polis*, regardless of whether those outside the association noticed.[29] In other words, it was a method of showing where they belonged in the larger social order.

Thus, we see a wide range of practices concerning the dead within associations, from carrying out the funeral of a member or paying the expenses for a family funeral to setting up epitaphs and maintaining tombs, burial grounds, and *columbaria* (collective tombs made up of niches for individual urns). In many associations a major part of the commitment of the association to its membership would include the provision of burial or memorial, or at least a contribution toward the expenses of burial. Members of some associations were expected to bequeath property to the association.[30]

THE SOCIAL IMPLICATIONS OF BURIAL WITHIN ASSOCIATIONS

At this point we need to examine why the burial function of associations was so pervasive in the Greco-Roman period, particularly from the first century CE. Without doubt, the burial activities of associations were linked to the larger social context of the time. A number of studies have investigated why associations assumed the tasks of burial and memorial. For the most part, the explanation asserts the need of the destitute for an assurance of burial.[31] Scholars then link the needs of the destitute to the high mortality rates and the population distribution in the empire, concluding that many persons died without a surviving family member to perform the requisite burial rites. Thus, they had to rely on an association to perform traditional funerary rites.[32] [516]

While this analysis has some merit, it does not present the full picture. Burial by an association was a "relatively expensive privilege,"[33] and the expense of association dues would have kept the really destitute from

29. Van Nijf, *Civic World*, 66.

30. Rauh, *Sacred Bonds*, 255, citing CIL XIV 2112 and Waltzing, *Étude historique*, 4:440–44.

31. E.g., Hopkins, *Death and Renewal*, 214.

32. For descriptions of these positions see van Nijf, *Civic World*, 33. Hopkins describes the problems surrounding the disposal of a large number of bodies every year and cites a first-century BCE boundary stone that stipulates "No burning of corpses beyond this marker in the direction of the city. No dumping of ordure or of corpses." Underneath is written in red letters "Take shit further on, if you want to avoid trouble" (CIL VI 31615 [Rome, n.d.]; *Death and Renewal*, 210).

33. Van Nijf, *Civic World*, 33.

joining. The breakdown of family connections is not a satisfactory explanation, because associations in small, relatively stable villages were just as likely to bury members as those in the city. Thus, Onno M. van Nijf points out, "being buried by a collegium was less a necessity than a conscious choice."[34] There must be other reasons for the choice to be buried by an association and the emphasis given to the deceased's membership in an association.

Van Nijf's investigation of the social context of association burial practices is instructive.[35] Monuments to the dead were the first things a visitor to Rome would see.[36] The presence of burial places around the outskirts of a city, and the intermingling of these with roads, garden plots, sanctuaries, workshops, and homes, reveals a mixing of the living and the dead. "The city of the dead was in many ways an extension of the city of the living, and the 'publicity' provided by a tomb and its inscription was intended for a wider purpose than merely mortuary use; that is, it was intended to have an effect upon the wider community of citizens."[37] For this reason, the display of inscriptions, tombs, and monuments became an extension of the zeal for honor seen among the living in the Greco-Roman world. Burial places were the locus for continued affirmation of one's wealth, social status, and identity. Indeed, given the proclivity to elaboration, one's identity, and that of one's compatriots, might even be somewhat enhanced with one's death.[38] As van Nijf so nicely summarizes, "Elites can use conspicuous consumption in death as a source of symbolic capital," although the potential for social status "was also recognized by individuals lower down the social scale."[39] [517]

Funerary monuments, including inscriptions, "seem to speak the language of belonging."[40] Funerary practices reveal a "strategy of social differentiation" insofar as the type and extravagance of one's memorial reflect one's status. They are also a means of "cultural integration," since they function as symbols of one's place within the larger social context. Mausolea, tombs, and gravestones are examples of "conspicuous consumption in

---

34. Van Nijf, *Civic World*, 33.

35. The following is summarized from van Nijf, *Civic World*, 34–38.

36. Hopkins, *Death and Renewal*, 205. In some Greek cities, some heroes and important individuals were buried in front of public buildings; see Garland, *Greek Way of Death*, 88.

37. Van Nijf, *Civic World*, 35; cf. Joshel, *Work, Identity, and Legal Status*, 7–8. Epitaphs also allow the dead to speak to the living from beyond the grave; Davies, *Death, Burial, and Rebirth*, 153–54.

38. See van Nijf, *Civic World*, 35–36; Meyer, "Explaining the Epigraphic Habit," 74–96.

39. Van Nijf, *Civic World*, 36–37.

40. Van Nijf, *Civic World*, 38.

death," something "the poor attempted, in relative terms, to imitate through membership of a *collegium funeraticium*."[41] During the imperial period, a marked increase in funerary epitaphs that identified the occupation of the deceased suggests

> some change in the sense of community which made it more socially acceptable to construct one's identity primarily in terms of occupation. Indications of collegium membership suggest that this was not just a matter for the individual; it helped to locate the deceased within a wider community of men who, like him, defined themselves in terms of shared occupation.[42]

The evidence takes us beyond the individual, allowing us to see that associations could use monuments "to assert a group identity in the face of others."[43]

As an illustration of the social sense of belonging that arises through funerary practices, van Nijf points to an association inscription from Thessalonike, IG X/2.1 824 (III CE), in which there seems to be competition over whose remains would occupy a particular niche in the association's *columbarium*. The epitaph reads, in part:

> For Tyche. I have made this niche in commemoration of my own partner out of joint efforts. If one of my brothers dares to open this niche, he shall pay . . .[44]

This epitaph suggests a practice in which desirable places within the *columbarium* might be opened in order to replace the remains of the one interred there with the remains of another. This desire for an honorable place within the association even in death suggests that burial practices continued to reinforce the negotiation for a sense of place within an association, expressed in the honorific practices and competitions of the living members. It is probable, then, that the more general prohibition among association inscriptions against disturbing tombs may be directed to other association members rather than to outsiders.[45] [518]

41. Gordon, Beard, Reynolds, and Roueché, "Roman Inscriptions," 151.
42. Van Nijf, *Civic World*, 42.
43. Van Nijf, *Civic World*, 49.
44. Translation in van Nijf, *Civic World*, 46. I follow van Nijf here in taking *adelphos* as a reference to a guild member rather than an actual familial relationship (46 n. 73).
45. Van Nijf, *Civic World*, 46. For the more general prohibition see *Tituli Asiae Minoris Supplements* III 197 and 201 (both Rough Cilicia, mid-first century CE). For the more general regulations around association responsibility for a tomb and fines for desecration going to an association see IEph 2212 (silversmiths; mid-I CE); IHierapJ 227 (purple-dyers; Hierapolis, 200–250 CE); Pennacchietti 07 (water-mill owners and

Other studies support the contention that burial and group belonging cannot be separated. In describing the associations, Nicholas Rauh notes that "by providing opportunities for men with common interests or backgrounds to join together in festival and camaraderie, and to share with one another peak moments of human experience (i.e., births, marriages, festivals, and funerals), they allowed for the development of commonly shared values, friendship, and familial bonds essential to the formation of ancient trade."[46] From his analysis of the burial and commemoration practices of voluntary associations on Rhodes, Peter M. Fraser notes that the "commemorative reunions at the tomb were certainly not only calculated to keep alive the memory of the departed 'friend' or 'brother,' but also in general to cement the bonds which linked the members of the *koinon* to each other."[47]

It seems that Philip A. Harland is correct in asserting that "the cultic, social and burial functions of associations were very much interconnected."[48] The role associations played in the burial and memorial of their members cannot be separated from their sense of group identity, nor from the sense of identity that individuals would gain within the group. This connection can be seen in the honors given to a treasurer of an association in Piraeus for, among other things, paying for some members' tombs from his own pocket "so that even though they have died they might remain noble" (IG II² 1327; 178/77 BCE). Here a living member of the association is concerned that the deceased members be properly honored. Doing so, however, reflects not only on his own honor but also the honor of the deceased individuals and the overall honor of the group of living members (insofar as they take care of their own). Again, van Nijf nicely summarizes the point: "Craftsmen and traders, just like other groups in society, used funerary epigraphy to make statements about their own identity and about their acquired or desired status in civic life."[49]

The concern for group identity links well with numerous studies that have suggested that the first century CE was a time of social disruption. The burgeoning merchant class and the need for artisans across the empire caused many [519] to migrate to new places in order to best employ their skills. It was, to use Jonathan Z. Smith's words, a time of "a new geography."[50]

---

operators; Hierapolis, n.d.); Pennacchietti 25 (gardeners; Hierapolis, n.d.).

46. Rauh, *Sacred Bonds*, 40–41, citing Waltzing, *Étude historique*, 1:322.

47. Fraser, *Rhodian Funerary Monuments*, 63. This should not overlook the importance placed on the desire to have oneself remembered by others; see Davies, *Death, Burial, and Rebirth*, 140.

48. Harland, "Claiming a Place," 66.

49. Van Nijf, *Civic World*, 68.

50. Smith, "Here, There, and Anywhere," 330.

As a result, the usual expressions and experiences of religion became detached from their roots in domestic religion, since "the extended family, the home place, as well as the burial place of the honored dead [were] no longer coextensive *topoi*." Smith goes on to suggest that to overcome this situation, the domestic religion transmuted. An association became the "socially constructed replacement for the family," which was overlaid with a new myth: a true home is imagined "above" and replaces the longed-for home "down here."[51] Through such mythmaking, the religion of the domestic sphere becomes the religion of any sphere, transportable to new locales precisely because a person's true connection is "on high" (cf. Paul's claim that the Philippians' *politeuma* is "in heaven" [Phil 3:20]). Smith states: "Locale, having been displaced, is now replaced."[52]

Burial becomes an important aspect of this social construction. For example, in imperial Rome patrons would often "construct a large tomb complex to house the remains not only of their natural families but also of their household slaves, ex-slaves and *their* families."[53] John R. Patterson attributes the central place of the *collegia* in the burial practices in imperial Rome to the association's "humanizing" of the city by providing opportunities for social interaction as "a remedy against the anonymity of life in a city of a million people."[54] More interesting for our study is his analysis of the burial of individuals, in which cooperation is exhibited between an association and the deceased's family members. This cooperation was worked out in both financial and social terms:

> The clubs therefore provided a double form of insurance. If a member died without leaving a family, he would be buried by the club and saved from the ignominy and anonymity of a pauper's burial. If on the other hand an heir did exist at the time of his death, the club would provide a sum of money for the heir to pay for the funeral (which would otherwise be the first charge on the estate) or perhaps in some cases a niche in the club's *columbarium*. The clubs provided an institution which could in normal circumstances be relied upon [520] to provide a cash sum to pay for a funeral without (much) danger of misappropriation or loss.[55]

---

51. Smith, "Here, There, and Anywhere," 330.
52. Smith, "Here, There, and Anywhere," 331; cf. Smith, *Map Is Not Territory*, xii–xv.
53. Patterson, "Patronage, Collegia and Burial," 18 (italics original).
54. Patterson, "Patronage, Collegia, and Burial," 22–23.
55. Patterson, "Patronage, Collegia and Burial," 23.

Thus, the associations became an aspect of familial funerary duties within the social fabric of the time.[56]

Certainly, voluntary associations are implicated in the social construction of fictive kinship. Fictive kin language, such as that of "brotherhood," can be found in associations. For example, a monument from Sinope, Pontus, refers to *hoi adelphoi euxamenoi* ("the brothers have made a vow"),[57] and another in Tanais refers to itself as *isopoiētoi adelphoi sebomenoi theon hypsiston* ("the adopted brothers worshiping god—Hypsistos").[58] Associations in Rome "tended to have a *columbarium* together with a portico or garden where funeral feasts could be eaten."[59] Such associative practices replace the more traditional custom of having a family meal. Outside of Rome, associations often had a field or enclosure that they used as a burial ground and a place for the communal meal. Such communal, postfunerary meals served "to reunite all the surviving members of the group with each other, and sometimes also with the deceased, in the same way that a chain which has been broken by the disappearance of one of its links must be rejoined."[60]

SOCIAL ISSUES BEHIND 1 THESSALONIANS 4:13–18

We have examined how the burial of association members functioned as a means of community formation and an affirmation of social belonging. We now turn our attention to the issue of the dead in 1 Thess 4:13–18. When Paul writes to the Thessalonians, he is aware of at least two questions under discussion among them: a question of proper conduct for Christians (4:1–12) and a question about "those who had died" (4:13). Burton Mack suggests that "the exhortation to a life of holiness was Paul's answer to the question about proper conduct. The apocalyptic instruction was Paul's answer to the question about those who had died."[61] However, Paul's answer is more than theological. All four units of this section of the body of 1 Thessalonians (4:1–8; 4:9–12; 4:13–18; [521] 5:1–11) not only provide the

---

56. Cf. Davies, *Death, Burial, and Rebirth*, 142.

57. Doublet, "Inscriptions de Paphlagonie," 303–4, no. 7.

58. IPontEux II 449–52, 456 (Bosphorus, third century CE); Harland, "Claiming a Place," 33. See further Ascough, "Voluntary Associations and Community Formation," 324–25; Bartchy, "Undermining Ancient Patriarchy," 68–71.

59. Patterson, "Patronage, Collegia and Burial," 21.

60. Van Gennep, *Rites of Passage*, 164, quoted in Garland, *Greek Way of Death*, 39.

61. Mack, *Who Wrote the New Testament?*, 108.

Thessalonians with indications for their life of faith but serve as opportunities for Paul to prove what he states earlier, that their faithfulness in the life of belief will be the source of *his* honor at Jesus's parousia (1 Thess 2:19–20). Thus, Paul links questions of faith and belief to his own status in the community, and he links the translation of that status to something greater at a future, divine event. His concern is a matter not of his credibility but of his honor as founder and (spiritual) representative of the community. At the same time, Paul uses his eschatological thoughts as the basis for hope, which determines the nature of corporate life for those who worship Jesus. The apocalyptic instruction is as much a part of community building as is the exhortation to a life of holiness.

Paul begins his comments by linking the death of individuals to the broader community issue of grief. Paul is not simply addressing one or two individuals who are grieving the loss of a loved one. Paul's use of fictive kinship terminology (*adelphoi*) to appeal to the Thessalonians emphasizes the corporate nature of the issue. Yet Paul is not reiterating preestablished teachings; this issue is new territory for Paul, and "we can almost see Paul working it out on the spot, desperately trying to find a way to answer the question about those who have died."[62] Some scholars suggest that Paul failed to convey to the Thessalonians that some of their members might die before the parousia of Jesus and that he must now face that issue in light of the death of some.[63] However, "it is unlikely that Paul had failed to encountered [sic] Christians who had experienced the death of fellow believers" during the course of his ministry.[64] Thus, another concern must lie behind the question of grieving over dead members.[65] We suggest that it is a concern over belonging in the community.

In his opening remark in 1 Thess 4:13–18, Paul seems to contrast Christian and pagan grief, expressing his hope that the Thessalonians "may not grieve as others do who have no hope" (4:13). This "grief without hope"

---

62. Mack, *Who Wrote the New Testament*, 111.

63. Other scholars suggest that "Gnostic interlopers" have infiltrated the community, although, as Charles A. Wanamaker points out, such suggestions caricature Gnosticism and do not recognize the absence of anti-Gnostic polemic in the letter (Wanamaker, *Thessalonians*, 165). At the same time, an alternative suggestion that some of the Thessalonians lost confidence in the parousia "runs up against the fact that Paul nowhere in the letter seeks to reassure, let alone prove, that the parousia would take place" (Wanamaker, *Thessalonians*, 165.) Some scholars suggest that the Thessalonians did not fully understand Paul's view of the parousia and believed it to be only for the living, not the dead.

64. Wanamaker, *Thessalonians*, 165.

65. For a discussion of the various proposals that have been put forth by scholars see Richard, *Thessalonians*, 232; Malherbe, *Thessalonians*, 264; Wanamaker, *Thessalonians*, 164–66.

is expressed in [522] the many ancient tombstones from across the Roman Empire that attest to the notion that death was simply the cessation of life, and that with death there was little hope for the future. For example, a Latin inscription from Beneventum, Italy, reads, "If you want to know who I am, the answer is ash and burnt embers" (CIL IX 1837; n.d.).[66] Another records this statement:

> We are nothing.
> See, reader, how quickly
> we mortals return
> from nothing to nothing. (CIL VI 26003; Rome, n.d.)

There is the more perfunctory, "I didn't exist, I existed, I don't exist, I don't care" (CIL V 2283; Altinum, n.d.),[67] while other inscriptions offer practical advice for living:

> Friends, who read this, listen to my advice: mix wine, tie the garlands around your head, drink deep. And do not deny pretty girls the sweets of love. When death comes, earth and fire consume everything. (CIL VI 17985a; Rome, n.d.)

However, not all pagans had "no hope."[68] For example, a father expresses grief for his nine-year-old daughter along with hope of reunion in the afterlife:

> The cruel Fates have left me a sad old age. I shall always be searching for you, my darling Asiatica. Sadly shall I often imagine your face to comfort myself. My consolation will be that soon I shall see you, when my own life is done, and my shadow is joined with yours. (CIL XI 3711; Phrygia, time of Severus)

Survival after death is indicated in the many goods that were buried with an individual, which were intended to make the person's life after death more pleasant.[69] In some cases, pipes were built into the tombs so that food and drink could be delivered to the dead.[70]

---

66. Translations of these Latin epitaphs are found in Hopkins, *Death and Renewal*, 227–30.

67. Hopkins (*Death and Renewal*, 230) notes that this is so common that it is sometimes expressed simply by the initials *nf f ns nc* (*non fui, fui, non sum, non curo*).

68. For examples of epitaphs that reflect a belief in the future life see Lattimore, *Themes*, 45–74, 208–9.

69. Hopkins, *Death and Renewal*, 229.

70. Hopkins, *Death and Renewal*, 234; Davies, *Death, Burial, and Rebirth*, 152.

We see, then, that it would be incorrect simply to assume that in 1 Thess 4:13, Paul's injunction against grieving like those who have no hope is contrasting Christians with all non-Christians. Some non-Christians did hold onto a hope for postmortem reunion with loved ones. Mack raises some important considerations for determining the context of the Thessalonians' questions around those who have died. He places these questions into the context of the [523] Thessalonians' joining a new "family," suggesting that they are struggling with their responsibilities toward those who have died. They are wrestling with whether the dead members of the family are incorporated into the larger family of God and God's kingdom. As Mack writes, "they were asking, do our dead still belong to us and we to them?"[71]

Similarly, Earl Richard states, "Careful reading of 4:13–18 suggests that it is not the resurrection of the dead which is at issue, but the status of those who die before the Lord's return," particularly "the status of the Christian dead and living vis-à-vis the returning Lord."[72] Abraham Malherbe likewise locates the underlying issue of the passage in terms of how living and dead Christians would each participate in the events marking the end of this world, and "how their experience would affect their relationship with each other."[73] Mack poses some other important questions including:

> What if joining the Christ cult exacerbated the problem instead of solving it? What if joining the Christ cult had inadvertently threatened one's sense of belonging to the ancestral traditions lodged in the local cult of the dead? Could that have been the occasion for the question in Thessalonike about those who had died?

From our earlier investigation of burial practices within associations, other questions can be raised, such as, "What if adherence to the Christ-deliverer disrupted a pattern of burial practices without offering anything in its stead?" or "What impact did the death of members have on the social cohesion of the Thessalonian Christian community?"[74]

When Paul first began speaking with those living and working in Thessalonike, he probably brought them a message that defined death as the

---

71. Mack, *Who Wrote the New Testament?*, 110.
72. Richard, *Thessalonians*, 231–32.
73. Malherbe, *Paul and the Thessalonians*, 275.
74. I have argued elsewhere that there is evidence that the Thessalonians' turning to God from idols (1 Thess 1:9) was a collective experience (Ascough, "Thessalonian Christian Community," 322–24 [Chapter 7, 132–35, above]). If this is the case, the prevailing issue for the Thessalonians is a matter of how an already existing group would redefine itself through its alliance with this new patron deity named Jesus Christ.

"enemy" of the living. We know from 1 Cor 15:21–22 that Paul linked death to the result of sin, brought into this world through Adam. It is death that will be overcome in the triumphal return of Jesus (1 Cor 15:54–55). Death is the last enemy to be destroyed (1 Cor 15:26) in the conflagration that is the coming wrath (1 Thess 1:10, cf. 4:6; see also Phil 3:20).[75] [524]

Having accepted Paul's preaching about deliverance from the coming wrath,[76] the Thessalonians may have felt some consternation, even betrayal, that some of their members died before that deliverance arrived. Normally, the living members of an association would have ensured both a proper burial and a pattern of commemoration for the deceased. However, such practices would need no planning in light of the imminent appearance of the deity.[77] The Thessalonians' question to Paul over the dead members may be linked to a practice that they thought could be suspended: the practice of burial and memorial.

Paul's words on this issue indicate that the Thessalonians are not engaging in unacceptable practices (as were the Galatians) or engaging in inner-group disputes (as were the Corinthians). Rather, Paul treats the issue as one of ignorance on the part of the Thessalonians—*ou thelomen de hymas agnoein* (1 Thess 4:13). Their thinking has led to an attitude of grieving (*lypeō*). Paul links their thinking to "those who have no hope." As we have seen, however, the category of those without hope does not include all pagans. Many persons in antiquity did hold out hope for an afterlife for the dead, a hope that was expressed in their funerary practices.

The context of Paul's comments in 1 Thess 4:13–18 is Paul's response to a number of issues raised by the Thessalonians, including brotherly love

---

75. See Hill, "Establishing the Church," 177: "While it is unlikely that Paul elaborated greatly on eschatology to unbelievers in Thessalonike, his message to prospective converts did include mention of a coming judgment (1 Thess. 1:10; 5:9), a distinct part of apocalyptic writings. The message of impending wrath had to be given by Paul in order to differentiate his God from others and to prepare the Thessalonians to make a commitment to the true and living God, who provided a Deliverer (1 Thess. 1:9–10). Yet among the Gentile population Paul did not highlight any aspects of apocalypticism that gave predominance to the Jews or that might have had offensive overtones."

76. Malherbe, *Paul and the Thessalonians*, 30; Barclay, "Thessalonica and Corinth," 50; Barclay, "Conflict in Thessalonica," 516; Wanamaker, "'Like a Father Treats His Own Children,'" 52.

77. Pushing the historical imagination further, it may be that they have also ceased their practice of collecting regular dues that go into the common chest in order to pay for burial. Indeed, perhaps the funds were even diverted to Paul, since he acknowledges the financial support of the Macedonians (2 Cor 8:1–3), although I think he is specifying the Philippians. Perhaps the grumbling over his hasty departure with these funds is behind his self-defense in 1 Thess 2:1–12.

(4:9–11) and the timing of Jesus's return (5:1–11).[78] That they are concerned over their deceased members, and that they may be aligned with the hopeless suggest that in their former belief system, they did have hope for those who died. Their thinking has changed as a result of their acceptance of Jesus as their patron deity. [525] Such a change in thinking would naturally result in a change of practice—in this case, a cessation of the usual commemorative rituals. Doing so, however, results in a greater feeling of loss for the Thessalonian community members.

Thus, underlying the Thessalonians' question to Paul seems to be the issue of whether the dead members can still be considered part of the community—clearly an issue of belonging and identity. The Thessalonians' cessation of the forum of funerary epigraphy and commemoration, resulting from Paul's preaching, is perceived by them to indicate that any member who dies is no longer part of the association. For the Thessalonians, the dead no longer have hope for the salvation found in Jesus's return.

In his response to the Thessalonians' concern, Paul makes an interesting choice of words to describe the state of deceased Christians. For Paul, these Christians have not died; rather, they have "fallen asleep" (*koimaomai*, 1 Thess 4:13).[79] Whereas his initial preaching about sin causing death might have led the Thessalonians to conclude that those who have died are no longer qualified to be with Jesus when he returns, Paul carefully refers to the dead Christians as "sleeping." In such a state they are still very much a part of the community. For Paul, their death does not indicate that they have "sinned." Thus, there is no need for the living Christians to dissociate themselves from the dead members. Rather, it is their state of sleeping that requires the Thessalonians to include them in their definition of community. As Wayne Meeks puts it,

> Paul is not offering any general theodicy, any general "solution" to the problem of death. It is not the problem of death as a universal phenomenon that is addressed here, but just the power of death to shatter the unique bonds of intimate new community.[80]

78. Paul's opening *peri de* constructions in 4:9 and 5:1 suggest that Paul is responding to questions posed by the Thessalonians, either in writing or through Timothy, and thus the section in between these two verses, 4:13–18, is also a response to the Thessalonians' questions; see Malherbe, "Did the Thessalonians Write to Paul?"

79. It is in contexts of speaking about Christians who have died that Paul uses the verb *koimaomai* (1 Cor 7:39; 11:30; 15:6, 18, 20, 51; 1 Thess 4:13, 14, 15). Paul uses *thanatoō* in contexts where death is metaphorical (Rom 7:4; 8:13, 36; 2 Cor 6:9) and "the dead" (*nekroi*) include Christians and non-Christians. I am not suggesting that Paul coins the metaphor *koimaomai* for death, as the word *koimaomai* was used for death before Paul. However, we do want to note his interesting word choice.

80. Meeks, "Social Functions," 693.

The Thessalonian Christian community can continue to include their dead members who, according to Paul, not only are considered members of the association but also will hold a privileged position at the *parousia* of Jesus—"we who are alive, who are left until the coming of the Lord, will by no means precede those who have died" (1 Thess 4:15).[81] [526]

Having assured the Thessalonians that those who have died are still members of Christ's community, Paul turns his attention to how the dead will take priority over the living at the return of Christ (1 Thess 4:16–17). Paul turns to the language and imagery familiar to him through Jewish apocalyptic literature. Numerous studies have examined the background of Paul's thinking in these verses. For example, in his survey of views on the origins of the parousia, final judgment, and the Day of the Lord in Paul's writings, Larry Kreitzer emphasizes the Hebrew Bible and Jewish pseudepigrapha as the originating point for Paul's ideas.[82] There has been little attention paid, however, to how Paul's audiences would have understood these images.

---

81. For the Corinthians, the presenting situation—the membership of dead members—is the same as for the Thessalonians; however, their response is different. Whereas the Thessalonians grieved and worried about the status of dead members, for the Corinthians the dead members were not considered lost but were still to be included in the larger associative community. This belief works itself out in the practice of the Corinthians being baptized on behalf of the dead (1 Cor 15:29). Since at least some of the Corinthians were already moving toward a philosophy that would later become Gnosticism, they were able to incorporate the recently departed into their larger mythic framework. Paul's response to the Corinthians, on the other hand, represents an alternative process of mythmaking, one that builds on a process already employed in addressing a similar situation at Thessalonike. He affirms a bodily resurrection of the dead Christians as a means of affirming their continued inclusion in the association. In 1 Thessalonians and 1 Corinthians we see the reflection of two similar situations concerning the question of the status of dead members. It is most likely that the questions arose from a similar sociocultural milieu. Although each community has a somewhat different response, Paul's own response is consistent but develops as part of his own mythmaking for each community.

82. Kreitzer, *Jesus and God*, 93–129; see also de Boer, *Defeat of Death*, 181–83. After a detailed study of "echoes" of LXX texts in the words of Paul, particularly the text of Psalm 46 (LXX), Craig A. Evans asserts that "it is clear that Paul has pulled together a variety of traditions in forming 1 Thess. 4.13–5.11" (Evans, "Ascending and Descending," 251). He then suggests that the material had taken shape before Paul's usage: "it is not necessary, therefore, to suppose that Paul was conscious of the precise biblical origin of each tradition." Evans concludes that Paul "may or may not have been conscious" of the inherited biblical material. This being so, one might then ask, what difference does it make to know the precise origin of the texts (the "echoes")? Is it not more informative to examine how the text functions in its context for the intended audience?

The Thessalonian Christians were predominantly Gentile[83] and thus not likely to be familiar with Jewish apocalypticism. Nor is it likely that they were thoroughly taught it by Paul while he lived and worked among them, since Paul seems to be introducing new concepts in 1 Thessalonians. Therefore, rather than explore the theology of Jewish apocalyptic literature, we are better served [527] to focus attention on how Paul employed apocalyptic images in support of social practices at Thessalonike.[84] We need to examine how the Thessalonians might have heard Paul's apocalyptic language in light of their shared community practices. To do so, we turn again to the wider social context of the Greco-Roman world.[85]

Despite frequent claims to the contrary, eschatological and apocalyptic ideas were not limited to Jews in the first century CE. As Hubert Cancik documents, "eschatological ideas appear in various forms and genres," not only in Judaism but also "in the fine literature of the Greeks—their epics, their wisdom, and their natural philosophy."[86] Nevertheless, "discussions of Jewish and then Christian cosmic, universal eschatology have mostly ignored contemporary pagan ideas, or mentioned them only in contrast."[87] This notion needs rectification through attention to the pagan ideas.

In some philosophical traditions, particularly those of the Epicureans and the Stoics, there was a belief that this world would come to an end.[88] Pliny the Elder echoed an Epicurean view when he wrote, "You can almost

83. See Ascough, "Thessalonian Christian Community," 311–13 (Chapter 7, 122–24, above); Ascough, *Paul's Macedonian Associations*, 191–212.

84. Although Christianity and its myths have much in common with the Hebrew Bible and other Jewish writings, Jonathan Z. Smith, in his book *Drudgery Divine*, has adequately documented the extent to which this reality is used to insulate Christianity from its pagan surroundings. Nevertheless, many scholars still maintain that all things Christian originate in things Jewish. For example, Martin Hengel argued recently that "early Christianity grew entirely out of Jewish soil" and that "whatever pagan influences have been suspected in the origins of Christianity were mediated without exception by Judaism" even in the diaspora ("Early Christianity," 1–3, 14).

85. John S. Kloppenborg has framed well the context when he writes, "Much of the conceptual apparatus employed in the description of Pauline communities derives either from Acts, according to which Pauline groups are offshoots of synagogues, or from Paul's own rhetoric, according to which Paul 'founded' churches and claimed responsibility for their organization and orientation. This is to confuse rhetorical statement and its persuasive goals with a description of Pauline communities and assumes, implausibly, that peoples in the cities of the Empire, who had been organizing themselves as *thiasotai, eranistai, orgeōnes, collegia,* and *syssitoi* for more than four centuries were somehow at a loss when it came to organizing a cult group devoted to Christ" ("Critical Histories," 282–83).

86. Cancik, "End of the World," 84–85.

87. Downing, "Common Strands," 170.

88. The following examples can be found in Downing, "Common Strands," 174.

see that the stature of the whole human race is decreasing daily, with few men taller than [528] their fathers, as the crucial conflagration which our age is approaching exhausts the fertility of human semen" (*Nat.* 7.16.73). A similar idea is found in Lucretius: "Even now, indeed, the power of life is broken, and earth, exhausted, scarce produces tiny creatures, she who once produced all kinds, and gave birth to the huge bodies of wild beasts" (*De rerum natura* 2.1150–52). Such sentiments reflect a belief not only in the decline of the natural world but also in the expectation of a cataclysmic ending. Other writers of the time, such as Pliny the Younger and Seneca, had similar notions.[89] F. Gerald Downing concludes, "The way the end, the final destruction, is pictured, seems very similar in various pagan, Jewish and Christian writings." More to the point, "much of the same range of views as were available to Jews in Palestine were readily available and current and certainly comprehensible in the Greco-Roman world cultural context— where a fair number of them probably originated, anyway."[90]

In the face of such an ending, the gods were not marginalized. Cancik notes:

> The proliferation of signs of misfortune gives rise to fear that "eternal night" will darken the world and the hope for a savior: "do not prevent this young man from coming to the aid of the overthrown world" (Virgil, *Georgica* 1.500f., 468ff., 493). In the schema of question and answer and with an instruction discourse, Apollo answers the question whether the soul endures after death or is dissolved. The visionary women of Dodona, as the first women, say: "Zeus was, Zeus is, Zeus will be, O great Zeus!" (Pausanias 10.12.5).[91]

An inscription from Asia Minor records an oracle of the foundation of a cult of Poseidon in Tralles: "Gentle Earth-shaker, enwreathed by a seawater altar, set us free from the wrath (*mēnima*) of Father Zeus for one thousand years" (ITralleis 1; II or III CE). It seems that there was an earthquake that the city escaped. Since Poseidon himself was given the epithet of "earth-shaker" (Seisichton), he was given thanks for protecting the city from the wrath of Zeus, which was manifested in the earthquake.

In pagan eschatology the world, or parts of it, comes under threat, even threat of annihilation, and it is the gods who can either provoke it or prevent it. Neither Jewish nor Christian apocalyptic thinking influenced the

---

89. Downing, "Common Strands," 177. See further Lattimore, *Greek and Latin Epitaphs*, 44–48.

90. Downing, "Common Strands," 180, 185.

91. Cancik, "End of the World," 91.

philosophers and epigraphers who discuss eschatology. This is not to say that Paul was not influenced by Jewish apocalypticism—it is likely that he was. The point is that the Thessalonians need not have been aware of Jewish apocalyptic thought for Paul's words to make sense. [529]

Paul's first preaching at Thessalonike did not arise out of a communal feeling of isolation and oppression,[92] as is often the case with apocalyptic. However, to convince the Thessalonians to "turn" from their gods, Paul needed a rhetorical device to convince them of their need. It is unlikely that Paul's device was the sheer attraction of monotheism or the attraction of "Judaism *sans* circumcision," which are the usual suggestions, bolstered by the Acts account. Rather, Paul needed to convince his audience of the superiority of his God. How better to instill superiority than to threaten destruction? When one announces a coming cataclysmic destruction and then promises deliverance only to those who align themselves with this God, and this God alone, it plays well in a community already used to such discussions. This does not make them "apocalyptic" or millenarian, just scared of destruction. No matter where Paul derived the seeds of this fledgling myth (i.e., Jewish apocalyptic), it plays in a unique way for his Thessalonian audience.

The pagan context provides enough evidence that belief in an afterlife and fear of a divinely mandated cataclysm were widely known. However, the problem is not that "the Greek Thessalonians found it difficult to bring the apocalyptic expectations of resurrection and parousia together into a systematic whole."[93] Rather, it is the death of some members *before* the expected wrath that causes them to raise social questions, not theological questions, about who is considered a member of the association.[94]

CONCLUSION

For many people in the Greco-Roman world, associations provided opportunities for seeking personal and corporate meaning for one's life. Paul's contribution to the formative stages of this social grouping includes both his

---

92. Mack, *Who Wrote the New Testament?*, 109; contra the thesis in Still, *Conflict at Thessalonica*.

93. Malherbe, *Paul and the Thessalonians*, 284. He suggests that although both concepts are Jewish apocalyptic ideas that were present in pre-Pauline Christianity, "they were brought together for the first time in 1 Thess 4:13–18."

94. Meeks seems to link Paul's use of apocalyptic to moral admonition for the overall health of the community by pointing to the parenetic section of 5:13–22 ("Social Functions," 694). However, this latter section takes up a new issue within the letter and thus need not be linked. It is not clear how Meeks thinks "internal discipline" and "obedience of leaders" can be linked to questions about those who have died.

assurance of deliverance from the wrath of God and his words on the place that the dead members will have in the events unfolding around the return of Jesus. [530]

Paul reassures the Thessalonians that the dead members of the Christian association still belong to the community and will have a part in the anticipated return of their patron deity. There is no reason for them to give up hope, any more than there is reason for them to give up burial practices. The burial practices reaffirm, as they always did within associations, the continuing membership of the deceased in the community of the living. They, too, will participate in the return of Jesus. Thus, Paul can exhort the Thessalonians to "encourage one another with these words" (1 Thess 4:18).[95]

---

95. An earlier version of this paper was presented at the Ancient Myths and Modern Theories of Christian Origins Seminar at the annual meeting of the Society of Biblical Literature, Denver, Colorado, November 19, 2001. I am grateful to the members of the seminar for the stimulating and helpful discussion around this paper. Part of the research for this paper was supported by funds from Queen's University and from the Social Sciences and Humanities Research Council of Canada.

16

Of Memories and Meals

Greco-Roman Associations and the Early Jesus Group at Thessalonikē

INTRODUCTION

IN EXAMINING THE INSCRIPTIONAL evidence from antiquity and the canonical texts of the New Testament, it is striking that the two things that seemed to preoccupy Greco-Roman voluntary associations—eating and dying—seem also to be predominant preoccupations of early Jesus believers.[1] The Gospel writers, understandably, focus on Jesus's death and resurrection, although there are frequent references to contexts of eating, particularly in Luke's Gospel. Three of the four Gospel writers also include a ritualized meal that Jesus undertook with his closest followers. In 1 Corinthians, we find Paul reiterating as a tradition handed down the ritual formulation of this reputed last meal of Jesus and doing so in language similar to that found in Luke (1 Cor 11:23–26; cf. Luke 22:19–20). While Paul often focuses on

---

1. Throughout this essay, I avoid the usual designation of "Christian" in favor of "Jesus believer" or "Jesus group." The term "Christian," although commonly used for groups in the first century, conveys a much more developed sense of theology, community, and translocal connections than the evidence would permit, especially for the groups to which Paul writes.

Jesus's death, references to the death of the followers of Jesus are not absent from his writings (e.g., 1 Cor [50] 15:12–19, 29; 2 Cor 4:11; 1 Thess 4:13–18; Phil 1:21–23; Eph 5:14). Neither are meals absent from the discussion, as we find references to eating in Paul's letters: 1 Cor 8:1–11:1, 11:17–22; Gal 2:11–13; Rom 14:17; and perhaps Rom 13:8–10.[2]

An emphasis on dying and on eating should come as no surprise. These are basic to human existence—without the one, the other is hastened, but in all cases dying is inevitable. What is striking, however, is how closely these are linked both in Jesus groups and in various voluntary associations. Admittedly, the link between death and meals is not limited to these two broad groups. Many other types of groups had similar emphases and linkages. For the sake of this investigation, however, I want to single out these particular taxonomic categories and examine what light one group might shed upon the other when they are compared and contrasted, in this case with the intention of showing how the associations illuminate the structure and practices of the Jesus groups.

ASSOCIATIONS AT THESSALONIKE

Within the Roman province of Macedonia, voluntary associations are attested through inscriptions found from Kalliani and Stobi in the south and north of the western part of the province respectively to Philippi and its surrounding villages in the eastern part of the province. The majority of the inscriptions come from urban areas, with sixty-five of eighty-eight known inscriptions from Edessa, Philippi, or Thessalonike, the latter having forty-four inscriptions.[3] Most of the associations attested in Macedonia indicate a dedication to a particular deity. There also exists some evidence among the inscriptions for workers' associations; a guild of purple-dyers is found at Thessalonike (IG X/2.1 291), as is an association of yoke-makers (BE [1972] no. 263). Associations of merchants (Asianoi) are also attested at Thessalonike (Rhomiopoulou 1981, no. 6; IG X/2.1 309, 480), as are an association of donkey-drivers (Nigdelis II.10) and another of wreath-sellers

---

2. Jewett, "Allusions." Elsewhere in the New Testament we find references to the deaths of believers (2 Peter 1:14) and to meals (Jas 2:15–16; Jude 1:12). Such concerns continue to be manifest in extracanonical material and even archaeological evidence. On the latter see Snyder, *Ante Pacem*, 64–65.

3. Although not complete, a preliminary database of seventy-five voluntary association inscriptions from Macedonia found as an appendix in my 1997 dissertation is certainly representative (Ascough, "Voluntary Associations and Community Formation" 297–307). Nigdelis, Ἐπιγραφικὰ Θεσσαλονίκεια adds another thirteen association inscriptions from Thessalonike to my database.

[51] (Nigdelis II.11).[4] Although many inscriptions are simply membership lists (e.g., IG X/2.1 244), a good number of inscriptions are dedications or votives to a deity.[5] Some inscriptions bestow honor on a founder (e.g., IG X/2.1 58) or a patron (e.g., IG X/2.1 192, 220).

The membership base of the Macedonian voluntary associations comes predominantly from the lower ranks of society, although in some cases upper-rank or wealthy persons are patrons and/or members. Indeed, in the Thessalonian associations all social levels are represented.[6] For example, IG X/2.1 192 (III CE) attests to the erection of an honorific stele for their patron by the association of Sarapidai, with the consent of the council and the "sacred *dēmos*" of Thessalonike. Poplius Aelius Nicanor is named as a *Macedoniarch*, which indicates that he is an important official of the Synhedrion, the provincial council.[7] The inscription indicates that at least some of the members belonged to the municipal aristocracy.[8] We have no way, however, of determining whether all of the members of this association were of the same status.

Of fourteen persons named in IG X/2.1 58, at least six were likely slaves or freedmen, as indicated by their names—Felix, Primus, Secundus—although at least two Roman citizens are also members. In IG X/2.1 288 at least two of the members were slaves: Demas and Primitas,[9] although they both served as secretaries within the association alongside a citizen, Marcus Cassius Hermonus. Isidorus, named as the deceased in IG X/2.1 506 (209 CE), was a modest civic official, a *curialis*, of the civic council. His family was of limited economic means, as indicated by his commemoration by a *bomos* rather than a sarcophagus.[10] The text indicates that he was a priest of at least two *thiasoi*, although it does not indicate whether it was simultaneously or successively. In contrast to most of the previous inscriptions mentioned, the inscription of IG X/2.1 220 [52] is poorly executed, with a semiliterate text, suggesting a membership from the lower ranks of society.[11]

4. The abbreviation "Rhomiopoulou" refers to Rhomiopoulou, "New Inscriptions," 299–305; the abbreviation "Nigdelis II" refers the inscriptions numbered in chapter 2 of Nigdelis, Ἐπιγραφικά Θεσσαλονίκεια, 101–216.

5. Deities attested in the inscriptions include: Zeus Hypsistos, Theos Hypsistos, Dionysos, Herakles, Sarapis, Isis, Anubis, and Aphrodite.

6. Nigdelis: "in den Vereinen Thessalonikis alle sozialen Schichten vertreten sind" (Ἐπιγραφικά Θεσσαλονίκεια, 507).

7. Edson, "Cults of Thessalonica," 187.

8. Edson, "Cults of Thessalonica," 187.

9. Bömer, *Untersuchungen*, 4:238.

10. Edson, "Cults of Thessalonica," 160.

11. Edson, "Cults of Thessalonica," 187.

The funerary dedication to a fellow *mystes* named Makedon was inscribed by the *thiasos* of Asiani (IG X/2.1 309) and names their high priest, Publius Aelius Alexander.[12] His name indicates status as a Roman citizen and he is at least a freedman.[13] This name and the careful work on the monument suggest that the social standing of some of the members was higher than that of laborer.[14] The dedication, however, is to a common person (as is the case with Rhomiopoulou 1981, no. 6), suggesting that the Asiani at Thessalonike was a mixed group of higher-status and lower-status persons.[15] The name Makedon, used in the same inscription (IG X/2.1 309), was a common proper name in Macedonia, indicating that this particular person was a native of Macedonia. Thus, "the Asiani of Thessalonica did not limit membership in their *thiasos* to persons of Asianic origin."[16] We can conclude that the Asiani of Thessalonike were a doubly mixed group that included both higher- and lower-status people and those from Asia Minor along with native Macedonians.[17]

THE THESSALONIAN JESUS-GROUP AND THE ASSOCIATIONS

In an earlier article I argued that the Jesus group at Thessalonike appeared to outsiders as a voluntary association and functioned internally as such.[18] Paul's concerns and Paul's language in 1 Thessalonians are similar to concerns and language found in inscriptions set up by associations. Thus, for example, it is possible to see in his instructions about leaders (5:12–13) a suggestion of a rotating leadership structure among the members. The mention of disruptions and disturbances (*ataktoi*, 5:13b–14) can be read in light of the context of religious rites [53] that take place within associations, and his injunction for noncompetition for honor among members (4:11) contrasts with the usual practices among association members. Vom Brocke furthermore argues that

---

12. This may also be the case on the fragmentary IG X/2.1 480, where a certain Cassia Antigona Memone is named.

13. Edson, "Cults of Thessalonica," 157.

14. Edson, "Cults of Thessalonica," 157.

15. See Edson, "Cults of Thessalonica," 157.

16. Edson, "Cults of Thessalonica," 155. An association of Asiani at Napoca in Dacia (CIL III 870) also admitted natives (see Edson, "Cults of Thessalonica," 155 n. 3).

17. IG X/2.1 480 also suggests that the deceased was a member of both the Asiani and an association of Asklepiastai.

18. Ascough, "Thessalonian Christian Community" (Chapter 7, above); Ascough, *Paul's Macedonian Associations*, 162–90.

the proliferation of Dionysos associations at Thessalonike provides the appropriate background for understanding Paul's references to nighttime drinking and drunkenness in 1 Thess 5:5b–8. Here Paul is drawing upon the Thessalonians' experiences of Dionysos associations prior to their belief in Jesus as a contrast to the behavior expected of the Thessalonian Jesus believers—unlike the Dionysos supporters, the Jesus believers do not belong to the night and the activities usually associated with nighttime revelries.[19]

While many would agree that Paul's note that the Thessalonians "turned from idols to God" (1:9) indicates a predominantly Gentile group, I have suggested that a preexisting workers' association turned to worship Jesus en masse. This helps make sense of Paul's claim that he and his coworkers labored while recruiting. Thus, I understand 1 Thess 2:9 to indicate that Paul worked at his trade and became friendly with those working with him, eventually convincing their social organization (their professional association) to replace their patron deities with Jesus. More controversial is my suggestion that the Thessalonian Jesus group was composed at its inception primarily of males, as suggested by, among other things, the ethical injunction that they are to *skeuos ktasthai* (4:4).[20]

Overall, while there are similarities between the Thessalonian Jesus-group community and the voluntary associations, Paul also reflects a desire for a distinctive community ethos. Yet in attempting to manufacture this *ethos*, Paul draws on, and contrasts, the practices and structure of the groups with which the Thessalonians were no doubt familiar—the associations. Although, like so many of the different associations in antiquity, they would have distinguished themselves from all other groups, from a modern perspective they are in appearance and function much more like than unlike such associations. This allows modern scholars to investigate the Thessalonian [54] Jesus group through the lens of the information available from associations in antiquity, particularly those at Thessalonike.

This conclusion led me to give attention both to the Thessalonians' concern with the death of some members and to Paul's response to them in 1 Thess 4:13—5:11.[21] The extent to which many associations were involved

---

19. "Christen gehörten eben nicht wie die Dionysos Anhänger der Nacht an, sondern dem Tage" (vom Brocke, *Thessaloniki*, 129). Reicke argues that "at times an overly realized eschatology in some of the *agape*-meals led to Christian forms of the Saturnalia in Thessalonica" (Reicke, *Diakonie*, 244–45, cited in Jewett "Tenement Churches and Communal Meals," 33). One can see this disorderly meal behavior also in places like Corinth and even in Rome, where Paul notes the "carousings and drunkenness" there in Rom 13:13 (Jewett, "Gospel and Commensality," 242).

20. For a well-reasoned challenge to this last argument see the essay by Johnson-DeBaufre, "'Gazing upon the Invisible.'"

21. Ascough, "Question of Death" (Chapter 15, above).

in activities around death is striking. Many types of associations often ensured burial of their members[22] and offered the possibility of the annual commemoration of their death,[23] particularly in the form of banquets,[24] although the taxonomic category of *collegia funeraticia* has rightly been called into question.[25]

Of the forty-four association inscriptions identified as belonging to Thessalonike, at least eighteen are associated with funerary practices of some sort. Some associations seem to have set up inscriptions in memory of their deceased members, such as the purple-dyers (IG X/2.1 291); the donkey-drivers (Nigdelis II.10); the worshipers of Dionysos (IG X/2.1 503), Herakles (IG X/2.1 288 and 289), and Nemesis (Nigdelis II.9); the Asiani (SEG 42 (1992) 625, IG X/2.1 309 and 480); and a hero cult (IG X/2.1 821). In some cases, an already-existing association is endowed with a bequest of money or property (i.e., vineyards or land), the income of which is to be used for a memorial at the tomb of the deceased. The remainder of the income, however, goes to the association for their own use, probably in social gatherings and banquets (see IG X/2.1 259). An annual commemoration known as the *rosalia* is indicated in a number of Macedonian association inscriptions, including IG X/2.1 260 from Thessalonike, in which a priestess of a *thiasos* bequeaths two *plethra* (one *plethron* is a measure of 100 feet) of grapevines to an association to insure that the *rosalia* is conducted in her memory.[26] As [55] Reinhold Merkelbach notes, "the lost part of the inscription undoubtedly noted that a time of banqueting was intended."[27]

---

22. Van Nijf, *Civic World*, 31. Van Nijf suggests that about one-third of all inscriptions produced by associations in the Roman East indicate some funerary activity. Ausbüttel (*Untersuchungen*, 59) indicates that one-fifth of known Italian associations were involved in their members' funerals. For a collection of 298 association inscriptions found among nearly four thousand gravestones and dedicatory inscriptions in the West see Perry, "Death in the *Familia*."

23. Klauck, *Herrenmahl und hellenistischer Kult*, 83–86.

24. See Dunbabin, *Roman Banquet*, 127–30.

25. Perry, *Roman* Collegia, 32; Ausbüttel, *Untersuchungen*, 20, 29; Kloppenborg, "Collegia and *Thiasoi*," 18–23.

26. On the *rosalia* see Ascough, *Paul's Macedonian Associations*, 26–28. A sarcophagus from the western necropolis of Thessalonike depicts a Dionysiac *thiasos* (Pandermalis, "Monuments and Art," 216–17 and fig. 148). Whether these represent a *thiasos* in the sense of "voluntary association" that we are using here, or whether they represent simply "a band or company marching through the streets with dance and song, esp. in honor of Bacchus, a band of revelers," as the word is defined by LSJ is unclear. The latter seems more likely in the case of the Thessalonian sarcophagus, which has a depiction of satyrs and maenads, Cupids and children, along with panthers and goats carved into three of its sides.

27. Merkelbach, *Die Hirten des Dionysos*, 116: "Auf dem verlorenen Teil der Inschrift

Funerary reliefs from Thessalonike are formulaic, both in their iconography and in their inscriptions, although there is some attempt at personalizing the features of those depicted.[28] The custom of heroizing the deceased "was a widely disseminated custom in the imperial period" and in many cases was "made even clearer by the visual representation."[29] Of particular interest are the stelae in which the deceased is represented "in heroic roles, participating in a banquet of the dead or in the shape of the 'Thracian horseman' or even of Hermes or Aphrodite."[30] Such hero worship is found elsewhere among Macedonian association inscriptions, in places such as Hagios Mamas,[31] the Strymon valley,[32] Philippi,[33] and Sandanski.[34] [56]

This wider context sheds light on the issue behind Paul's reassurances in 1 Thess 4:13-18. In talking to others in Thessalonike, Paul is more likely to have proclaimed that belief in Jesus provides escape from wrath and death rather than promise of eternal life, as suggested by his passing reference, with no explanation, that the Thessalonians await the return of Jesus, who will rescue them "from the wrath that is coming" (1 Thess 1:10). Subsequent to Paul's departure, however, the death of a few members has

---

has zweifellos gestanden, dass auch eine Festmahlzeit vorgesehen war" (quoted in vom Brocke, *Thessaloniki*, 126).

28. Pandermalis, "Monuments and Art," 215.

29. Pandermalis, "Monuments and Art," 216.

30. Pandermalis, "Monuments and Art," 216.

31 CIG 2007f. Robinson ("Inscriptions from Macedonia," 62-63) thinks that the hero is more likely to have been the Thracian rider hero but does not give reasons. However, the mention of an *archisynagogos* in this inscription is also found in two second-century inscriptions of the association (*synētheia*) of Herakles from Thessalonike (IG X/2.1 288 and 289), suggesting that there might be a connection with Herakles (Robinson, "Inscriptions from Macedonia," 63).

32. Papazoglou, "Macedonia under the Romans," 205. A relief from the region of Strymon even represents Dionysos on horseback in the manner of the Thracian Horseman; see also Düll, *Die Götterkulte*, 77-85 and fig. 34; see IG X/2.1 259.

33. At Philippi archaeological excavation has revealed that the *phialē* of the octagon church is connected on the east by three compartments. The first compartment was probably used by the Christians to worship a saint, the name of whom is lost to us; see Koukouli-Chrysantaki, "Colonia Iulia Augusta Philippensis," 42-45; White, *Social Origins*, 1:134-35. This room was taken over from a Hellenistic sanctuary; under the room a vaulted tomb was found containing the sarcophagus of the hero. Often the Christians took over the worship of a hero as the worship of a saint (Pelekanidis, "Kultproblemeim").

34. See Mihailov, "Deux inscriptions." The term *neoi* in the inscription is probably not being used in the technical sense of "youth group" although such groups did exist in Macedonia. The inscription appears inside one of two crowns in relief on the stele, which measures 0.43 x 0.65 x 0.06 m. Two of the five lines inside the second crown are almost illegible, but the name *Pieriōnos Apollōniou* appears on the final three lines.

caused cognitive dissonance among the living, who have become unsure of the status of their dead and whether they are still to be considered part of the community. The issue is sociological, not simply theological, and was framed around the appropriateness of continuing to memorialize the members who have died (presumably, not having escaped the consequences against which Paul warned). In his response, Paul explains that the "sleeping" (*koimaomai*) are still part of the community, and they will be given priority at Jesus's return.[35]

Returning to the associations themselves, clearly the social activities of the group were of more importance than funerary activities; it would not be correct to think that worry about dying took up the whole energy of the associations.[36] While meals could be linked to funerals, a number of social aspects are reflected in the record of the associations at Thessalonike that have nothing to do with a funerary context, including drinking parties and attendance at performances in the arena.[37] At Thessalonike in the first century CE, an association of *mystai* (initiates) dedicated to Zeus Dionysos Gongulos is endowed with a vineyard measuring one-third of five *plethra* (IG X/2.1 259).[38] Conditions are given to the "present and future *mystai*," who are the beneficiaries of the largesse as long as they remain full members of the association. The first, and seemingly primary, condition is that a banquet (*karpēan*) is to be held when the vineyard produces fruit. Three separate occasions are predetermined "according to what was handed over and [57] bequeathed" (*kata to paradedomenon kai tēn dosin*).[39] The banquets are to take place in the shrine (*oikos*) dedicated to Dionysos. During each of the banquets, the *mystai* participate in rituals (*orgia*) that involve a midnight oath to maintain the shrine, which seems to be located on the vineyard

---

35. See further Ascough, "Paul's 'Apocalypticism.'"

36. "Es wäre jedoch falsch zu glauben, dass die Sorge um das Dahinscheiden aus dem Leben die ganze Tatkraft der Vereine aufgesogen habe" (Nigdelis, Επιγραφικά Θεσσαλονίκεια, 506).

37. Nigdelis, Επιγραφικά Θεσσαλονίκεια, 506; vom Brocke, *Thessaloniki*, 128. Within the Dionysiac associations, meals were most likely held reflecting general revelry found in Dionysos parties, in which there was eating, dancing, music and, naturally, much wine flowing (vom Brocke, *Thessaloniki*, 128; Nigdelis, Επιγραφικά Θεσσαλονίκεια, 506; cf. Merkelbach, *Hirten des Dionysos*, 83).

38. This association is likely the same as the one indicated in a membership list from the mid-second century CE (IG X/2.1 244) and may also be connected with a third inscription, dated to 155–56 CE (IG X/2.1 60).

39. Cf. Paul's use of *paradidōmi* with respect to the institution of the Lord's Supper in 1 Cor 11:23.

property itself, and a banquet, as indicated by the phrase "midnight bread" (*mesanyktion artou*).[40]

Another example is seen in an early second-century CE inscription recording the establishment of a meeting place (*oikos*) of the *hoi hieraphoroi synklitai*—"the table-fellowship of bearers of sacred vessels" (IG X/2.1 58). Little else is recorded of this association save a list of thirteen male members who seem to be of lower rank, the last of whom is named as president (*archōn*) of the association.[41] A similar listing of association members is found on a late first-century inscription dedicated to Theos Hypsistos by the son of a man who is designated as *trikliniarchos* (IG X/2.1 68). Although there is no direct link between his functionary title and this association, the lack of other designations regarding when or where he would have served in such a capacity suggests that the office was held within the association itself, and thus they did engage in meals together.

Such commensality has a social dimension that is linked to wider issues of community building. Meals are times of solidifying social bonds, networking, mourning and rejoicing, and establishing the *koinonia* that is to mark the association.[42] It is also the locus where boundaries around that *koinonia* are maintained and regulations are implemented to sustain it. It is to this aspect of the associations that we shall next turn when we explore commensality in 2 Thessalonians.

EVIDENCE FOR COMMENSALITY IN 2 THESSALONIANS

Very little has been written about meals, in particular the Eucharist or Lord's Supper, among the early Pauline Jesus group(s) at Thessalonike. What little there is draws heavily from [58] the practices known to us from Corinth. There is an assumption, explicit or implicit, that Corinth is the paradigm for other Pauline communities. Despite the obvious methodological flaws with such an assumption, it is somewhat ironic in light of Paul's claim in 1 Thessalonians that the Thessalonians themselves "became an example to all the believers in Macedonia and in Achaia" (1:7). Whether or not meal

---

40. Vom Brocke, *Thessaloniki*, 126.

41. The tutelary deity of the association is Anubis. According to Edson ("Cults of Thessalonica," 184), there is only one other example in the Aegean of a private association worshiping Anubis not in conjunction with Sarapis and Isis (the *Synanoubiastai* of Smyrna: RIG 1223; III BCE).

42. On the wider social issues embedded in association life see Ascough, "Question of Death," 515–20 (Chapter 15, 282–88, above); and Ascough, "Paul's 'Apocalypticism.'"

practices are part of the exemplar the Thessalonians provided is difficult to determine—Paul's comment seems to refer more generally to overall behavior rather than to specific practices.

Nevertheless, the two letters ostensibly addressed to the Jesus group at Thessalonike do contain some possible hints about meal practices, albeit more so 2 Thessalonians, whose authenticity and provenance scholars highly contest. Whatever one decides with respect to authorship, with regard to context I am inclined to agree with scholars who maintain that despite 2 Thessalonians being pseudonymous (written as part of a so-called Pauline school), it still must be read in the context of the specific situation at Thessalonike.[43] Thus, it warrants examination for information regarding the practices of the Jesus believers at Thessalonike.

In an earlier work I suggested in a footnote that the cognates of *ataktos* in 2 Thess 3:6–12 could be taken to indicate laziness.[44] In doing so, however, my concern was to differentiate the use of *ataktos* in 1 Thess 5:14 from its usual understanding as "laziness," which I argued was based on reading the context from 2 Thessalonians into 1 Thessalonians. An alternative is to use the evidence from the life of associations to see how and in what contexts they dealt with behavior that might be considered *ataktōs*. I now want to challenge my own assumption, not in terms of my understanding of 1 Thess 5:14 but in my acceptance that 2 Thess 3:6–16 is referring to laziness.[45] I would now suggest that it may well be a reference to disorderly behavior, and that the setting for such behavior would most likely be meal settings, which would then [59] allow for the enforceability of Paul's injunction in 2 Thess 3:10: "Let him not eat" (*mēde esthietō*)."[46]

---

43. Donfried, *Paul*, 66, cf. 50, 53; so also Malherbe, *Paul and the Thessalonians*, 373; Still, *Conflict at Thessalonica*, 58.

44. Ascough, *Paul's Macedonian Associations*, 177–78 n. 63. On the possible renderings of *atakton* see Jewett, *Thessalonian Correspondence*, 104. In the New Testament, the verb *atakteō* only occurs in 2 Thess 3:7 and the adverb *ataktōs* only in 2 Thess 3:6 and 11.

45. Gaventa cites Didache 12:4–5 in support of the reading of 2 Thess 3:6–12 as referencing the "idle": "No Christian shall live idle in idleness. But if anyone will not do so [i.e., work], that person is making Christ into a cheap trade; watch out for such people" (Gaventa, *Thessalonians*, 130). However, this text is set within the context of instructions warning against itinerant preachers who would take advantage of those living in urban centers by demanding of them payment. Such persons are not to receive more than a day's wage and, should they request more, they are "false prophets" (Didache 11.1–21).

46. Those who understand *ataktōs*/*atakteō* in 2 Thess 3:6–12 as "disorderly" include Rigaux, *Thessaloniciens*, 704–5; Bruce, *Thessalonians*, 205; Jewett, *Thessalonian Correspondence*, 104–5; Collins, *Birth of the New Testament*, 94; Menken, *Thessalonians*, 130–33; Russell, "The Idle in 2 Thess," 107–8; Donfried, "2 Thessalonians and the Church

Since the predominant theme of the preceding passage in 2 Thessalonians has focused on apocalyptic events (2:1-12), it has led some commentators to think that those who are referred to as *ataktōs peripatoutos* (usually translated as "living in idleness" in 2 Thess 3:6 and 11) have ceased working and are lazy due to eschatological fervor.[47] The apocalyptic passage, however, is separated from the exhortation against the *ataktōs peripatoutos* through the rhetoric and the epistolary structure of the letter.[48] The body of the letter includes the *probatio*, which effectively ends at 2:12 as the writer turns his attention to other matters. In so doing, he includes a *peroratio* (2:13—3:5) that serves to end the preceding section and segue into what will be the *exhortatio* of 3:6-15. This *peroratio* focuses on the primary theme of the letter, God's faithfulness, and includes a thanksgiving, benediction, and prayer request, all of which serve to distance the apocalyptic *probatio* from the *exhortatio*. This latter piece is framed as a community concern.[49] Paul appeals to his authority to "command" the Thessalonians and invokes fictive kinship language (*adelphoi*) to address a community problem—adherents who *ataktos peripatountos*.[50] The opening recommendation that such persons be avoided is then extended to be a punishment on the transgressors themselves: "Anyone unwilling to work should not eat" (3:10). This is, Paul reminds them, a command that was given while he was among them. [60]

There seem to be two activities that demarcate the *ataktos peripatountos*: they refuse to work and instead participate in activities that single them out as "busybodies" (*periergazomai*, 3:11).[51] As a result, they are to be

---

of Thessalonica," 141-42. Williams (*Thessalonians*, 144) uses "idle" and "disorderly" interchangeably. Malherbe (*Thessalonians*, 450, 456) maintains that the disorderly "are those who willfully reject the accepted norms by which the church is expected to live." Few commentators link the disorderly to a meal context.

47. Jewett, *Thessalonian Correspondence*, 104-5; Bruce, *Thessalonians*, 209; Marshall, *Thessalonians*, 218-19; Cf. Martin, *Thessalonians*, 274.

48. The same situation applies to 1 Thess 5:14 and the use of *tous ataktous* ("the disorderly") there; Ascough, "Thessalonian Christian Community," 319-20 (Chapter 7, 129-31, above).

49. See Malherbe who notes, "Paul's interest in this section is not primarily in the economic policy of the church. It is, rather, in mutual responsibility within the church, which some Thessalonians were threatening by being disorderly and meddlesome. His own behavior was exemplary for its orderliness and self-giving concern for others, and constituted the tradition by which they were to conduct themselves" (*Thessalonians*, 457).

50. On the problems of reading 2 Thess 3:6-12 as a problem of eschatology see further Nicholl, *From Hope to Despair*, 158-63.

51. A number of different suggestions have been made as to the reasons the Thessalonian believers might have ceased working, all of them based on the authenticity of 2 Thessalonians: they have become cynic preachers (Malherbe, *Paul and the Thessalonians*, 101); there is unemployment at Thessalonike (Russell, "Social Problem," 108);

avoided (*stellesthai*, 3:6) and are not allowed to eat (3:10). The example of Paul and his companions being employed in manual labor while in Thessalonike is held up as a contrast to those who have ceased working. The text, however, "provides the community with advice and motivation rather than with detailed disciplinary procedures."[52] It is not clear from the text itself how such advice might be put into practice, nor even in what context(s) it might make sense to give such advice.[53] The question becomes how we envision the Thessalonian Jesus group being able to enforce such an injunction.

A number of inscriptions demonstrates that voluntary associations often struggled with the problem of disorderly behavior at community gatherings, including meals, sacrifices, and processions, so much so that legislation was introduced to limit it, and fines and corporal punishment were used to enforce the legislation.[54] Such inscriptions give an indication of the type of disturbances that could occur at a meeting (fighting, disruptions of order and ceremony, abuse of others), along with guidance on how to deal with such disturbances (fines and floggings). I have argued elsewhere that Paul's use of *ataktoi* indicates that some among the Thessalonian Jesus-believers are disorderly. This is not a challenge to the leadership from a breakaway group, but involves disruptions and disturbances within the context of worship.[55] Paul's injunction, "See that none of you repays evil for evil, but always seek to [61] do good to one another and to all," following his "be patient with them all" (including the *ataktoi*), indicates that in 1 Thess 5:14-15 Paul thinks that verbal admonishing, rather than fines and flogging, should suffice to stem disorderliness. In 2 Thessalonians the author still does not resort to fines and floggings. He does, however, advocate for physical separation from those who are acting disorderly: "Now we command you, beloved, in the name of our Lord Jesus Christ, to keep away from

---

they have come to disdain manual labor (Marshall, *Thessalonians*, 223); they are relying on benefaction (Winter, "'If Any Man Does Not Wish to Work,'" 312); they are undertaking aggressive evangelism (Barclay, "Conflict in Thessalonica," 522-24).

52. Richard, *Thessalonians*, 392.

53. Winter (*Seek the Welfare of the City*, 57-60) suggests that it concerns the patronage system, where one could rely upon a benefactor to supply a meal and one could move from one benefactor to another in order to insure one was fed well. Perhaps this is also what is implied when Paul exhorts the Thessalonians to work quietly and not be reliant upon anyone (1 Thess 4:11). This is how Richard (*Thessalonians*, 390) takes the critique of those who are acting as busybodies—they are involved in the lives of others where they should not be.

54. See Ascough, "Thessalonian Christian Community," 318-21 (Chapter 7, 128-32, above); Ascough, *Paul's Macedonian Associations*, 177-83.

55. Ascough, "Thessalonian Christian Community," 321 (Chapter 7, 132, above).

(*stellesthai*) believers who are walking about disruptively and not according to the tradition that they received from us" (3:6).

There are few other uses of *stellō* in the New Testament. One use occurs with the prefix *hypo-* but the word is similar in meaning. Interestingly enough, it is used with reference to a meal situation. Paul recounts for the Galatians his confrontation with Cephas, noting that it stemmed from Cephas's decision to withdraw from sharing meals with Gentiles, despite having eaten with them for some time:

> For until certain people came from James, he used to eat with the Gentiles. But after they came, he drew back (*hypestellen*) and kept himself separate (*aphōrizen heauton*) for fear of the circumcision faction. (Gal 2:12)

In this case Paul uses two verbs to describe the action: withdrawal *and* separation. This raises the interesting notion that it was possible to withdraw (that is, not eat) without separating (that is, without leaving the dining facility).

Perhaps in 2 Thess 3:6 Paul is suggesting that those acting in a disruptive manner are to withdraw from sharing in the meal but are allowed to remain in the presence of those eating.[56] They could watch while others ate; thus their punishment for acting disorderly and for not working would be nonparticipation in the meal—"let them not eat"—which is enforceable so long as they are actually present at the meal setting. Paul reiterates the notion of separation at the conclusion of the argument, stating generally, "Take note of those who do not obey what we say in this letter; have nothing to do with him (*mē synanamignysthai autō*), so that he may be ashamed" (3:14).

The only other uses of *synanamignymi* in the New Testament are both found in close proximity to one another in 1 Cor 5:9 and 11:

> I wrote to you in my letter not to associate with (*mē synanamignysthai*) sexually immoral persons . . . But now I am writing to you not to [62] associate with (*mē synanamignysthai*) anyone who bears the name of brother or sister who is sexually immoral or greedy, or is an idolater, reviler, drunkard, or robber. Do not even eat with such a one (*tō toioutō mēde synesthiōn*).

Paul seeks to clarify what he meant by his command to disassociate from "immoral" persons (as he communicated in an "earlier" letter, 5:9). His intention in writing "not to associate" really meant not to tolerate immoral persons *within* the community itself. His clarification of his actual meaning is framed beforehand with a clear directive to expel an immoral person

56. Similarly, Best, *Thessalonians*, 333–34.

(5:4–5) and afterwards with the more general admonition to drive the wicked from among them (5:13, quoting Deut 17:7, LXX).

The writer's use of *synanamignymi* in 2 Thess 3:14 has an equally ambiguous reference point. Although literally it indicates avoidance, what the writer may intend is the expulsion of the person(s) from the communal settings (i.e., meetings and meals). This certainly would fit with the earlier injunction in 3:6 to "withdraw" from the disorderly, and together 3:6 and 3:14–15 frame the passage with indications of the separation of some persons from the group. Although 3:6 and 3:14 might mean that the non-disorderly would actively leave the gathering, a more natural expectation is for the "withdrawal" to take the form of the expulsion of the perpetrators of the trouble from the community gatherings. Certainly, this would be a way of ensuring that they "do not eat" (2 Thess 3:10): they are not to be present at the table (if at all) during meals.

Support for placing this command in the context of community meals comes from the work of Robert Jewett, who argues that 2 Thess 3:10 reflects "a communal situation of shared resources, involving regularly eating together and relying on the support of members rather than on a patron."[57] He argues that it might "refer to the Lord's Supper, embedded in a practice of communal meals."[58] Drawing on the work of Peter Lampe, Jewett suggests that the most likely setting for the Thessalonian Jesus group is in tenement buildings, or *insula*, that housed lower-rank handworkers such as those that seem to have composed the group.[59] These meals, suggests Jewett, are *agapē* meals, or love-feasts. [63]

Jewett finds corroborating evidence for Jesus believers' commensality in another letter of Paul. Turing his attention to Gal 2:14, Jewett suggests that Paul's rebuke of Cephas concerning the "truth of the gospel" (*hē alētheia tou euangeliou*) had less to do with doctrine than it did with the social dimensions—"'gospel' in this passage entails a social system requiring 'fellowship,'

---

57. Jewett, "Tenement Churches and Pauline Love Feasts," 44; Jewett, "Tenement Churches and Communal Meals," 23–43.

58. Jewett, "Tenement Churches and Pauline Love Feasts," 44. We find direct reference to a common meal held within Jesus groups from evidence spanning the first through fourth century. In his examination of such evidence, Reicke (*Diakonie*, 14) argues that there was a "single Christian sacrament of table fellowship" that was demarcated as a love-feast.

59. See also Jewett, "Tenement Churches and Communal Meals." Jewett does not disagree with those who envision Jesus groups meeting in the houses of patrons and practicing a form of "love-patriarchalism" wherein the patron-patriarch of the household cares for the others, but he thinks that this is only one possible model, more appropriate to some communities, such as those at Corinth, than to others.

including cross-cultural eating."[60] Cephas was participating with Gentiles in ordinary meals as well as the sacramental meal, since "the love-feast constituted the sacramental meal."[61] Paul was willing to challenge Cephas publicly over his withdrawal because "Paul understood the gospel to be the message that instituted a new form of commensality, in which converted Jews and Gentiles overcame their cultural traditions of separation into distinct and irreconcilable groups in order to participate together in sacramental love-feasts."[62] The inability to reconcile the two positions represented by Cephas and Paul led to a "separation into culturally limited love-feasts," which Paul understood "as a violation of the gospel."[63]

In a later article Jewett develops his thesis to include the Jesus groups at Rome, arguing that in Romans we find reference to a system of self-supporting love-feasts.[64] He looks in detail at Rom 13:10—"the *agape* does no evil to the neighbor; law's fulfillment is therefore the *agape*," arguing that the articular use of *agapē* indicates not "love" generally construed but the *agapē*-meal, or "love-feast," of the early church.[65] The wider context in Romans suggests to Jewett that ideological and cultural conflicts had led to separation from one another for sacramental meals, a development that Paul aims to correct with these words, along with the admonitions in Rom 14:1 and 15:7.[66] Despite earlier scholarly assumptions, then, Romans does, as Jewett suggests, contain a reference to the Jesus group's meal sacrament.[67]

Smit has also found evidence for meal practices among the early Roman Jesus groups, in this case from Rom 14:17: "For the kingdom of God is not food and drink but righteousness and peace and joy in the Holy Spirit." [64] "The association of Rom. 14:17 with symposiastic ideology suggests itself because of the occurrence of terminology central to contemporary symposiastic thought within the context of a conflict precisely about meal fellowship."[68] Drawing largely upon Greco-Roman philosophical literature, Smit shows how central were meals to social interactions and the creation of community, and, as such, the maintenance of orderly behavior was key: "many writings in the 'meal-centered' first century Mediterranean world

---

60. Jewett, "Gospel and Commensality," 240.
61. Jewett, "Gospel and Commensality," 248.
62. Jewett, "Gospel and Commensality," 241.
63. Jewett, "Gospel and Commensality," 249.
64. Jewett, "Allusions."
65. Jewett, "Gospel and Commensality," 274.
66. Jewett, "Gospel and Commensality," 276–77.
67. Jewett, "Gospel and Commensality," 276–77.
68. Smit, "Symposium," 41.

were extremely concerned about having well-ordered and well-organized dinner parties (the early Christians are here no exception), giving them the enjoyment of full *koinōnia*."[69] Within the context in which Rom 14:17 falls, one finds three characteristics of the kingdom of God that are also values maintained in the setting of the symposium: righteousness, peace, and joy (*dikaiosynē*, *eirēnē*, and *chara*). The concept of peace is particularly noteworthy, for "the image of the peaceful symposium is the counterpart of war, and *fights and drunkenness at the symposium*."[70] Yet behind all of this is a concern for fellowship. Eating is not the same as a "meal";[71] the latter involves close fellowship.

One can extend this concern about meals to 2 Thessalonians, where the reluctance to contribute to the meal might well be the sign not of "laziness" per se but of an unwillingness to engage in the true fellowship that is to characterize the meal setting among the Jesus believers. As with Rom 14:17, where Paul calls "upon the Romans to preserve meal fellowship, and not to disrupt their community by disrupting the meal fellowship through disapproving of each other's diet,"[72] we might also suggest that in 2 Thess 3:6-12 the call to contribute goes to the heart of what is *philadelphia* (cf. 1 Thess 4:9-12).

According to Jewett, Paul's command to the Thessalonians in 2 Thess 3:10 is a "typical" example of casuistic law in which the nature of the offense is outlined in the first half and the legal remedy or consequence is given in the second. "Since the sanction implies communal discipline rather than some judicial punishment enacted by an official agency, this saying should be classified as a community regulation."[73] That is, for the law to be effective there must be some way for the noneating of the perpetrator to be enforced. [65] It is because the community shares common meals, suggests Jewett, that it becomes enforceable in the Jesus group.

Returning to 2 Thess 3:10, Jewett suggests that the strength of the command—*mēde esthietō*, "let him not eat"—indicates deprivation of food rather than simply an exclusion from a particular meal or a sacramental celebration.[74] Jewett finds it unlikely that Paul has simply composed this

---

69. Smit, "Symposium," 47.

70. Smit, "Symposium," 49 (italics added). Smit cites the helpful but brief article by Slater, "Peace, the Symposium and the Poet."

71. Smit, "Symposium," 46.

72. Smit, "Symposium," 52.

73. Jewett, "Tenement Churches and Pauline Love Feasts," 52.

74. Jewett, "Tenement Churches and Pauline Love Feasts," 53. Nicholl (*From Hope to Despair*, 167) raises a meal setting as one of two possible scenarios within which the command to "keep away from" might be relevant, the other setting being temporary

instruction; rather, it is a community rule negotiated within the community itself, about which Paul reminds them, as he did when he was among them (thus, the imperfect verbs in 3:10a).[75] Paul's statement in 2 Thess 3:10b "relates to the unwillingness to work, not to the ability or availability of employment" and as such reflect a situation in which the communal nature of the love-feasts was threatened.

To illustrate his point, Jewett invokes some general evidence from "Hellenistic guilds," which, he points out, "prescribe penalties of exclusion from the common meal or from the guild itself for certain offenses, though the payment of fines is a more usual punishment."[76] He slips quickly, however, to blending this with evidence that comes from Qumran, in which expulsion from the table, from the community, or both, is prescribed for infractions (1QS 6.24–7.24). Yet the Qumran community is much more "communalistic" than the associations insofar as the Qumran group seems to have lived together in relative seclusion from the outside world and thus shared much in common besides meals.[77] It is not the case, as Jewett supposes, that the association inscriptions "reflect settings in which communities are eating their meals together."[78] He is correct, however, [66] that they do "presuppose a communal or familial system of some kind."[79] It is the "of some kind" that is in question. The association texts to which Jewett alludes or cites reflect communal settings of occasional, prescribed commensality, often grounded in the language of fictive kinship.[80] As such, they do provide an alternative model of community relations to that which Jewett

---

excommunication. He maintains that deciding between the two options is "difficult" and "for our purposes unnecessary." We do, however, think it is possible to negotiate some evidence in favor of a meal setting, a setting that Nicholl all but ignores after having raised it as a possibility. Overall, few commentators have favored understanding Paul's command in 2 Thess 3:6 as being set within the wider context of love-feasts and/or communion: see Forkman, *Limits of the Religious Community*, 135; Jewett, "Tenement Churches and Communal Meals"; and Jewett, "Gospel and Commensality."

75. Jewett, "Tenement Churches and Pauline Love Feasts," 54.

76. Jewett, "Tenement Churches and Pauline Love Feasts," 52; Jewett, "Tenement Churches and Communal Meals," 35–36.

77. Jewett's blending of the association practices with the Qumran practices seems to have originated by his reliance on the very good work of Weinfeld, *Organizational Pattern*, in which he undertakes a comparison of these groups (much more evident in Jewett's 1993 article "Tenement Churches and Communal Meals"). Jewett, however, skips over some of Weinfeld's nuances.

78. Jewett, "Tenement Churches and Communal Meals," 36.

79. Jewett, "Tenement Churches and Communal Meals," 36.

80. See Harland, *Associations*, 30–33; Harland, "Familial Dimensions"; Ascough, *Paul's Macedonian Associations*, 76–77.

imagines as being grounded in communalism and love.[81] They suggest that it is appropriate to set up sanctions around ritual meals whereby a person is prevented from participation because s/he refuses to adhere to community regulations.

My alternative reading, predicated not on tenement living but on comparison with association practices,[82] suggests that the injunction *mēde esthietō* in 2 Thess 3:10 pertains to a ban of the disorderly from ritualized commensality, the kind of commensality that takes place periodically (perhaps at set times) and provides participants with a means for individual and collective identity.[83] The Pauline prohibition on participation would thus not deprive the offender(s) from ever eating, which would, over time, become a death-sentence. As such, it is unlikely that they would starve themselves. If such an extreme sanction were invoked, [67] the one punished would more likely find food elsewhere than starve, with the net effect being expulsion from the group (as is the case in 1 Cor 5:2). If understood as a ban from full participation in the ritualized commensality of the group, however, the prohibition is enforceable since it causes the one sanctioned to question his or her identity and whether or not s/he wants to continue to find that

---

81. Nicholl (*From Hope to Despair*, 173–74) notes recent moves to expand love patriarchalism to "transformative love-patriarchalism" rooted in Christian love, which the poor are abusing by looking to Christian patrons to replace their old patrons, who needed to be replaced when these manual laborers converted.

82. What is not clear from Jewett's scenario is where such groups would meet, or why the inhabitants of an entire tenement building would be inclined towards belonging to a Jesus group, if indeed this is the location in which the meals took place. Jewett suggests that "a kind of Christian commune or cooperative is required" (Jewett, "Tenement Churches and Communal Meals," 38) but does not show how or even why persons in tenement buildings chose to eat together. Apart from some rurally based groups such as the Qumran inhabitants or the *Therapeutai*, there is little evidence for such groups, particularly in urban areas such as Thessalonike. The exception might be the philosophical schools such as those of Plato or Epicurus, but these seem to be located in Athens in their own day and do not seem to have been exported to other urban areas. As Wilkins and Hill note, "The Urban poor, in Rome at least, lived in tenements without cooking facilities and must of necessity have used the equivalent of fast food from street vendors for a sizeable part of their diet" (Wilkins and Hill, *Food in the Ancient World*, 39). Lampe ("Das korinthische Herrenmahl," 192–96) argues that participants in community meals would bring their own food, akin to a potluck banquet. He finds such practices from earlier times in groups termed *eranos* ("a meal to which each participant contributed a share"), although these groups are quite early in the classical period and it is rare to find evidence for such bringing of provisions in association inscriptions from the first and second century CE.

83. Banquets were markers of class and status and provided those invited with a sense of belonging and identity; see Clarke, *Art in the Lives of Ordinary Romans*, 223–27. In general, meals express patterns of social relations (Douglas, *Implicit Meanings*, 231).

identity through membership in the group (and hence to continue being referred to as *adelphos* ["brother"]). This identity is not individualized but is rather linked to issues of familial connections (fictive or otherwise),[84] social networking, and communication with the gods ("religion"). What I am suggesting here is that the meal context of 2 Thess 3:10 is not ordinary meals but ritual commensality, which comes to light for modern interpreters through the examination of commensality in the life of Greco-Roman associations.[85]

CONCLUSION

For the historian of earliest Jesus groups, the problem at Thessalonike is the paucity of archaeological and literary evidence for religious life in the first few centuries CE.[86] It is striking, however, that, as Pantelis M. Nigdelis demonstrates,[87] there is an increasingly rich and abundant body of evidence for associations. Since our data is still limited, the best we can hope for is to make connections and abstractions based on our data in order to construct a picture of the earliest Jesus group(s) in the city. [68]

In this chapter, I have summarized arguments that I have made elsewhere on the makeup of the Thessalonian Jesus group and the question behind Paul's response to them concerning dead believers (1 Thess 4:13–18), arguments drawn largely from the use of comparative data from

---

84. The references to "brother" or "brotherly love" in the Thessalonian letters are not references to communistic terms of endearment as Jewett seems to suppose but the mechanism by which fictive kinship was created (Jewett, "Tenement Churches and Communal Meals," 38–40).

85. On meals in associations generally see Klauck, *Herrenmahl und hellenistischer Kult*, 68–71; Klinghardt, *Gemeinschaftsmahl*, 29–44.

86. Very little is known about the Jesus group at Thessalonike beyond the letter(s) Paul sent until the fourth century, when Thessalonike is a large and important center of Christianity; see Tsitouridou, "Early Christian Art," 230–32 and Spieser, *Thessalonique*. There is a mention in Melito's *Apology* which notes that the mid-second-century emperor Antoninus Pius "had written a letter to the people of Thessalonica, among other places, telling them to take no new steps against the Christians" (Lightfoot, *Biblical Essays*, 267). In the early third century Tertullian mentions both Thessalonike and Philippi as places "where the letters of the Apostles are read in the original" (Lightfoot, *Biblical Essays*, 267–68). There are also two early bishops mentioned: Aristarchus and Gaius (Lightfoot, *Biblical Essays*, 268). In the fourth century there were martyrdoms in Thessalonike after the edicts of Diocletian, most notably that of Demetrius (whose cult did not develop until after the time of Theodosius), and of three women (and perhaps their companions) who were killed in 304 CE for refusing to participate in cult practices, including the eating of sacrificial meat (Musurillo, ed., *Acts of the Christian Martyrs*, no. 22).

87. Nigdelis, "Voluntary Associations."

Greco-Roman associations. The connection I proposed between this passage and the ritualized memorial of the dead, particularly a dead hero such as Jesus, is suggested by the many connections made in the associations at Thessalonike and beyond between meals and dead heroes, and the interest in the death and eventual return of Jesus among the Jesus believers. I then pushed the comparison further to suggest that in 2 Thessalonians there are indications that the Jesus believers shared a ritualized meal. While this has been assumed by many, the assumption is based on evidence from 1 Corinthians. Such geographic dislocation is unnecessary. Evidence from associations at Thessalonike reveals that they held common meals around which a number of regulatory behaviors were invoked. Comparison with 2 Thess 3:6–14 shows similar concerns, suggesting that the Jesus group at Thessalonike was involved in similar meal practices.[88]

---

88. Support for the research and writing of this paper has been provided through a Queen's University Chancellor's Research Award, an Ontario Government Premier's Research Excellence Award, and a Social Sciences and Humanities Research Council of Canada Standard Research Grant. I am grateful to my research assistants, Rachel McRae and David Malone, for their help on this project.

17

Benefaction Gone Wrong

The "Sin" of Ananias and Sapphira in Context

IN THE EARLY CHAPTERS of Acts, Luke describes the early Christians in Jerusalem as holding all things in common (*apanta koina*) and selling property and possessions to meet the needs of others (Acts 2:41–47; 4:32–35).[1] Two specific examples of those who have sold property are recorded—one positive and one negative. Barnabas lays the proceeds from the sale of a field (*agros*) at the feet of the apostles (Acts 4:36–37). Ananias and Sapphira likewise lay a sum at their feet from the sale of a piece of property (*ktēma*, Acts 5:1–11). In their case, however, they do not turn over the entire proceeds from the sale of the land. When the discovery of their deception is brought to their attention, each in turn dies on the spot.

This negative example has been both puzzling and troublesome for many scholars.[2] Most recognize that the addition in 5:11 of *holēn tēn ekklēsian* to the twice-repeated notation of great fear (5:5b, 11) probably indicates that the story bears an important message for Luke's community.[3]

---

1. The practice quickly seems to have been abandoned within the Acts narrative. By Acts 11:27–30 the Judean churches are impoverished and in need of help, a situation seemingly confirmed by Paul's collection for the poor of Jerusalem (see esp. Rom 15:25–26; 2 Cor 8–9). There are no other New Testament texts that confirm Luke's depiction of the community of goods in Jerusalem.

2. Cf. Bruce, *Acts*, 103; Haenchen, *Acts*, 237.

3. Lüdemann, *Early Christianity*, 64.

Yet, since an explicit description of the motivation is missing from the text, the theories vary as to what that message might be. In order to determine the full import of Luke's inclusion of the story, we must consider what Luke's audience might have assumed to be the motivating factors behind the sin of Ananias and Sapphira, given the larger sociocultural context. To do so we must set our text among [92] the realia we have from antiquity, as Peter Richardson has championed. In this case our artifacts will be inscriptions.

PAST INTERPRETATIONS OF THE STORY

The text of Acts indicates that the sin for which Ananias and Sapphira are condemned is the attempt to deceive the Holy Spirit (Acts 5:3, 9). Many scholars see the lie itself as adequate explanation for the punishment.[4] In no instance do these scholars give an explanation as to why the couple withheld some of the proceeds, or why, in doing so, they felt it necessary to lie to the apostles and the community. While Luke would probably confirm the condemnation of lying both to others (Exod 20:16; Lev 6:2; 19:11) and to God (cf. Ezek 13:1-10; Isa 28:17),[5] it is doubtful whether this is an adequate explanation of this passage.

For this reason, other scholars suggest that the precise nature of the sin lies elsewhere, particularly in the motivation for the lie. A number of commentators focus on the issue of the money retained. For example, Ernst Haenchen suggests that the couple wanted to ensure their future security but felt it necessary to conform to the practice of others within the Christian community.[6] Gerd Lüdemann is harsher in charging them with "dealing selfishly with material possessions."[7]

When ascribing the motivation for the lie to a desire simply to keep back money, most commentators assume that Ananias and Sapphira will be impoverished by the donation of the proceeds from the sale of this property.

---

4. For instance, Marshall, *Acts*, 112; Schmithals, *Apostelgeschichte*, 56; Bruce, *Acts* 102; Barrett, *Acts*, 262; Havelaar, "Hellenistic Parallels," 65; Dunn, *Acts*, 63; Walaskay, *Acts*, 61; Klinghardt, "Manual of Discipline," 255. Forkman (*Limits of the Religious Commnity*, 173–74) attempts to connect their actions with the sin against the Holy Spirit mentioned in Luke 12:10. This explanation is inadequate, however, since the context of Luke 12:8–12, unlike that of Acts 5, places the sin against the Holy Spirit in situations of christological confession before others, particularly those in authority outside the Christian community.

5. Punishment for lying to the gods is also attested in the non-Jewish world; for examples see Havelaar, "Hellenistic Parallels," 70–72.

6. Haenchen, *Acts*, 240.

7. Lüdemann, *Early Christianity*, 64.

Ananias and Sapphira, however, sell *a* parcel of land (*epōlēsen ktēma*), not necessarily *all* of their land and possessions.[8] Simple concern for the money does not explain the lie. As Peter in the story points out (Acts 5:4), the money, or any part of it, was theirs to keep [93] without lying. Their motivation must include something they would gain through the lie.

A number of commentators see behind Acts 5:1–11 the story of Achan's sin in Joshua 7, where Achan keeps some of the spoils that were devoted to God.[9] Certainly there are parallels. In both Acts 5:2–3 and the LXX of Joshua 7:1, the word *nosphizomai* is used of the primary action. Ananias, like Achan before him, seems to have kept something that belongs to God, and he and his family are punished with death. The differences between the stories, however, are greater. In the Acts story, "it is not a question of booty consecrated to Yahweh, but of a voluntary gift of money to the community, and Ananias is not stoned by the community, but Peter's accusation causes him to fall dead."[10] Also, the Christian community does not suffer loss as did the Hebrew people when they attacked Ai while under God's judgment for Achan's actions. Achan presumably took the goods in order to make himself wealthy, whereas Ananias and Sapphira have given over part, but not all, of their own goods. Even with the money they kept back, they are poorer than they were to begin with.

Another approach to the story of Ananias and Sapphira is to set the sin within its community context. Some scholars do so very generally, suggesting that the couple has disrupted the unity of the community[11] or undermined its practices,[12] even to the point of discrediting their testimony to outsiders.[13] Ben Witherington suggests that since the description of Ananias in Acts 5:2 is similar to the description of Judas in Luke 22:3, Ananias's sin is perceived as a "violation of the integrity and *koinōnia* of the community," and the story is not simply "about human greed and duplicitous acstions but

---

8. Cf. Witherington, *Acts*, 215–16.

9. Williams, *Acts*, 88; Munck, *Acts*, 40; Forkman, *Limits*, 172; Neil, *Acts*, 95; Bruce, *Acts*, 102–3, 132; Schmithals, *Apostelgeschichte*, 56; Lüdemann, *Early Christianity*, 65, with reservations; Boismard and Lamouille, *Actes*, 164–65, with reservations; Johnson, *Acts*, 88, 91–92; Sterling, "Athletes of Virtue," 683 n. 12; Walaskay, *Acts*, 61; Witherington, *Acts*, 214–15, with reservations. Some suggest a typological resemblance: Marshall, *Acts*, 111; O'Toole, "You Did not Lie," 200, 209; Talbert, *Reading Acts*, 66.

10. Haenchen, *Acts*, 239, see also 240–41; cf. Johnson, *Literary Function*, 205–6; Pesch, *Apostelgeschichte*, 1:198 n. 11.

11. Johnson, *Literary Function*, 206 and n.3; *Acts*, 87–88; Talbert, *Reading Acts*, 66.

12. Cassidy, *Society and Politics*, 27; O'Toole, "You Did Not Lie," 191, 199.

13. Pesch, *Apostelgeschichte*, 1:198.

about an invasion of the community of the Spirit by the powers of darkness, by means of Ananias."[14] [94]

Other scholars suggest that the sin is the withholding of something that has been vowed to God.[15] Duncan Derrett states that they have retained Sapphira's *ktwbh* or dowry, and in doing so they violate an actual or implied vow to the community. In fact, Derrett goes so far as to claim that this was done at Sapphira's behest, and he compares her role to that of Eve in the garden of Eden.[16] In both aspects, Derrett conjectures far beyond the textual data.[17]

Brian Capper suggests that Ananias's sin lies in not turning over the full amount to the safekeeping of the community during his period of candidacy for membership in the Christian community (the "novitiate phase").[18] It is a "transgression against an accepted norm in his community,"[19] which required the submission of the full amount from the sale of one's property.[20] Thus, Ananias must have broken a prior commitment to hand over the full proceeds from the sale of the land.[21] Furthermore, he has "expressed mistrust of the Church and a selfishness which opposed the whole ethic of the group."[22] In a slightly later article, Capper describes the scenario "as a kind of fall of the first community from innocence (thereafter irretrievable)."[23]

The type of structure that Capper thinks is operative in the Jerusalem Christian community is similar to that described in the Dead Sea Scrolls, particularly the "Community Rule," in which community members are exhorted to share their property.[24] Ananias's action in handing over the money is compared to the procedure at Qumran wherein the prospective member's property was held separately from the community's common

---

14. Witherington, *Acts*, 215.
15. Jeremias, *Jerusalem*, 130 n. 19; Talbert, *Reading Acts*, 65–66.
16. Derrett, "Ananias," 227–29; cf. Marguerat, "La mort," 222–25.
17. Cf. Capper, "Community of Goods," 1743–44; Witherington, *Acts*, 215.
18. Capper, "Interpretation," 124–28; Capper, "In der Hand des Ananias," 223–36.
19. Capper, "Community of Goods," 1742–43.
20. Capper, "Interpretation," 122.
21. Capper, "Interpretation," 123–24; "Community of Goods," 1743.
22. Capper, "Community of Goods," 1747.
23. Capper, "Reciprocity," 503.
24. See Capper, "Interpretation"; Capper, "In der Hand des Ananias"; Capper, "Community of Goods"; Capper, "Palestinian Cultural Context"; Capper, "Reciprocity." Other scholars look to the later rabbinic account of the *qwph* and the *tmhwy*, a weekly and daily collection of money for the poor of the town (Jeremias, *Jerusalem*; Lake, "Communism of Acts," 140–51; cf. m. Peah 8. 7). There is some question whether this was practiced in the first century CE (Seccombe, "Organized Charity").

fund for the duration of his candidacy.²⁵ It was in the physical control of the community but not in the community's possession. In so transferring his property, Capper argues, Ananias still maintained full control over it, and either he would receive it back were his [95] candidacy rejected, or it would pass into the common fund of the community when he was accepted.

There are some difficulties with this view, not least of which is the lack of evidence for such a probationary period in the early church. Furthermore, the penalty for deceiving the community meted out on Ananias and Sapphira was dissimilar to that at Qumran: 1QS 6 stipulates one year's exclusion from the fellowship meal and a reduction of food rations by one quarter.²⁶ Capper's assumption about the probationary period is also called into question by the character of Barnabas, whom we meet again in Acts 9:27 as Paul's advocate before the disciples and in 11:22–26 as the Jerusalem community's envoy to Antioch. In neither case is there any indication that he is serving a probationary period, and he is soon sent out as coevangelist with Paul (beginning at Acts 13:1). Capper attempts to circumvent this problem by suggesting that at the time of Barnabas's contribution he is "being seconded to the leading class of the community."²⁷ This is unlikely since the references in the text to the sale of land and to the actions of laying the proceeds at the feet of the apostles in both the Barnabas and the Ananias and Sapphira accounts seem to highlight a contrast in motivation in performing the same actions.

More problematic is Capper's need to resort to the postulation of an "inner group" of disciples within the Jerusalem community which held things in common and to which Ananias and Sapphira were applying for admission.²⁸ The designation that "all the believers were of one heart and mind" and that "not one of them" claimed personal possessions (4:32) suggests conformity within the entire group, not a two-tiered level of adherence in which the couple are novices.²⁹ Finally, the arguments put forth by Klinghardt³⁰ show that, even in the case of the Dead Sea Scrolls communities (and those of the Pythagoreans to which Capper also appeals), it is not clear that an initiate

---

25. Capper, "Interpretation," 126–28; Capper, "Community of Goods," 1744–47; Capper, "Palestinian Cultural Context," 338.

26. On the differences between the Jerusalem Christian and Qumran communities see Bruce, *Acts* 105 n. 15; Haenchen, *Acts*, 241; Forkman, *Limits of the Religious Community*, 173; Johnson, *Literary Function*, 3–4. Recently Havelaar has defended Capper's position (Havelaar, "Hellenistic Parallels," 75–77).

27. Capper, "Palestinian Cultural Context," 340–41.

28. Capper, "Palestinian Cultural Context," 337–38.

29. Cf. Witherington, *Acts*, 215 n. 74.

30. Klinghardt, "Manual of Discipline," 254–56.

had to submit all possessions "because otherwise the regulation about financial liability for damages (1QS 7.6–8) would make no sense at all."[31] [96]

Within the range of scholarly discussions of Acts 5:1–11, it is surprising that very few make reference to an aspect of life in antiquity that was of fundamental importance: benefaction. There are some vague references. For example, F. F. Bruce notes that Ananias was attempting to "gain a reputation for greater generosity than he had actually earned," and Marshall suggests that Ananias and Sapphira are attempting "to gain credit for a greater personal sacrifice than they had actually made."[32] Richard Rackham thinks that Ananias "desired the praise of the community for the sacrifice of his goods, and at the same time to enjoy the money."[33] In one sentence Halvor Moxnes suggests that the sale of lands and distribution of the proceeds in Acts 2 and 4 is the Lukan ideal of benefaction, which is "dramatically contrasted with the story of Ananias and Sapphira."[34]

The most explicit connection is made by Scott Bartchy, who views Barnabas and Ananias and Sapphira as patrons of the Jerusalem Christian community.[35] In making the claim to have contributed the entire amount of the selling price, the errant couple "openly were seeking the honor appropriate to a truthful and faithful patron, honor appropriate to one who functioned as a flowing river of life for his or her clients." He goes on to suggest that the lie dishonors and shames them and "seriously violated the honor of the group,"[36] hence explaining their punishment. Although Bartchy discusses the texts in the context of "fictive kin groups," he makes no attempt to connect this category with the voluntary associations of antiquity, which themselves were fictive kin groups.[37]

In the remainder of this essay I want to set the story of Ananias and Sapphira within the context of benefaction to voluntary associations in antiquity in order to discern more clearly what Luke's audience might have assumed about Ananias's and Sapphira's motivation. In turn, the wider context of benefaction may provide an explanation for this particular story in Luke's narrative.

31. Klinghardt, "Manual of Discipline," 255.
32. Bruce, *Acts*, 105; Marshall, *Acts*, 110.
33. Rackham, *Acts*, 65, quoted in Capper, "Community of Goods," 1741.
34. Moxnes, "Patron-Client Relations," 265.
35. Bartchy, "Community of Goods," 315–18.
36. Bartchy, "Community of Goods," 316.
37. Duling, "Matthean Brotherhood," 162–63; Duling, "Small Group Research"; Malina, "Early Christian Groups," 108.

BENEFACTION IN ASSOCIATIONS

In Greco-Roman antiquity the practice of benefaction was pervasive in both the public and private sectors.[38] Benefaction was bestowed and in exchange the recipient would "acknowledge and advertise his [97] benefactor's generosity and power."[39] Thus, benefaction was a matter of gaining more honor for oneself.

Benefaction could take many forms.[40] The emperor himself could act as a benefactor to his subjects, who would reciprocate with their loyalty. Among the elite, benefaction was a means by which to gain public favor when running for public office.[41] Wealthy patrons could use benefactions to gain for themselves a large and loyal group that would, quite literally, accompany them throughout the day in order to shower praise upon them. Up-and-coming political players might find themselves the protegé of an influential patron. Even among friends, benefaction could take place with men of equal standing helping one another in times of financial crisis. In this case, the benefaction would be understood in terms of reciprocity and the ideal that friends share things in common, rather than in terms of a patron-client relationship between two unequal parties. In this way honor was maintained on both sides.

Finally, benefaction could occur within a group setting. A wealthy patron (male or female) might choose to fund a particular voluntary association and in exchange would receive public recognition and honor for his or her benefaction.[42] Within the association itself regulations were often put in place in order to ensure that the members' basic needs were met.[43] John Kloppenborg effectively summarizes this particular situation:

> Lacking a bureaucratic mechanism for the redistribution of wealth and benefits, both Greek and Roman rulers relied upon the social networks defined by elites and their extended circles of family, friends, and clients as means both of social control and of redistribution. Cultic associations, *collegia domestica*, and trade guilds served these functions eminently well, for they represented social networks spanning various levels or sectors

---

38. Elliott, "Patronage," 144.
39. Garnsey and Saller, *Roman Empire*, 149.
40. The following is summarized from Garnsey and Saller, *Roman Empire*, 149–59.
41. Moxnes, "Patron-Client Relations," 249.
42. Kloppenborg, "Collegia and *Thiasoi*," 27; Uhlhorn, *Christian Charity*, 23.
43. Garnsey and Saller, *Roman Empire*, 156–57.

of society and providing relatively stable systems through which power was channeled and various benefits disbursed.[44] [98]

It is the latter two aspects of benefaction, among friends and within voluntary associations, that hold particular interest for our understanding of Acts 5:1–11.[45]

Luke's presentation of the foundational stage of the early Christian community at Jerusalem is couched in the language of friendship. The believers are said to hold "all things in common" (*eichon hapanta koina*; Acts 2:44), which would bring to mind for the Greco-Roman reader the Hellenistic *topos* of friendship.[46] For the most part, this "community of goods" was not a legal arrangement, but a knowledge that affection for one's friends would move one to put one's goods at their disposal when the need arose.[47] In some cases the epigraphic record suggests that the strong bond of friendship could lead to the establishing of a voluntary association. An example

---

44. Kloppenborg, "Status and Conflict Resolution," 10–11. Capper ("Reciprocity," 514) is incorrect in suggesting that voluntary associations are never oriented toward ensuring the well-being of their members. On the Romans' use of patronage as social control that maintained the dependence of the poor on the elite see Wallace-Hadrill, "Patronage," 71–78.

45. Cf. Klinghardt, "Manual of Discipline," 255. Within this category of "associations" we can also include Jewish synagogues, as Richardson ("Early Synagogues") has cogently shown, and even the Qumran community (Klinghardt, "Manual of Discipline"). Capper ("Community of Goods," 1752–60; "Palestinian Cultural Context," 341–50) spends considerable energy showing the existence of Essene communities in Jerusalem during the first century CE. Yet he (esp. in "Interpretation" and "Palestinian Cultural Context") is influenced too much by his assumption of the historicity of the Lukan accounts, and thus a search for a genealogical antecedent within Jerusalem in the thirties CE. Furthermore, since Luke was writing at a time when the Qumran/Essene communities had vanished and/or Luke's community was located outside Palestine, where these Jewish groups were relatively unknown, the Essenes cannot be seen as the best analogy for Luke's audience. Yet, even if one were to grant Capper's general assertion of the relevance of the Essene community for understanding the early Jerusalem Christian community (Capper "Interpretation"; "Community of Goods"; "Palestinian Cultural Context"), Klinghardt's argument ("Manual of Discipline," 252) that "the closest parallels to the Manual of Discipline in regard to genre and contents are statutes of *Hellenistic associations*" ultimately points toward the voluntary associations (italics original). The similarities make it more likely that the group behind the documents "was a religious association, rather than a cenobitic 'sect'" (Klinghardt, "Manual of Discipline," 252; see also Weinfeld, *Organizational Pattern*).

46. This is also true of Luke's comment that the believers "were of one heart and soul" (Acts 4:32). See further Dupont, *Salvation of the Gentiles*, 85–102; Johnson, *Literary Function*, 187; Capper, "Palestinian Cultural Context," 324–25; Sterling, "Athletes of Virtue."

47. In antiquity friendship was based more on social and political reciprocity than on emotional attachment (Moxnes, "Patron-Client Relations," 245).

of this can be found in the regulations of an association in Athens during the imperial period (IG II² 1369, probably the second century CE). The inscription [99] notes that "male friends convened a club and by common council established an ordinance of friendship."[48] Then follows the "law of the *eranistōn*":

> It is not lawful for anyone to enter this most holy assembly without being first examined as to whether he is holy and pious and good. Let the patron (*prostatēs*) and the chief eranistes, and the secretary, and the treasurers and the syndics examine [the candidate]. And let these be chosen by lot each year except the patron . . . And let the club increase by zeal for honor.

The inscription becomes fragmented shortly after this point, but the next few lines record the punishments faced by those who cause disturbances within the association meetings (expulsion, fines, and "blows").

Interest in honor is characteristic of most voluntary associations. An inscription from Piraeus (178–177 BCE) is typical of many set up by associations to honor benefactors. Hermes, the treasurer of the association, is honored by the group for having

> proved himself beneficent both to the general membership and to the individual members, putting himself at the disposal of each, and being both eager that the appropriate sacrifices to the gods be made and paying for these frequently, generously, and often from his own resources, and also for [100] some who had died, when the association had no money, he paid for the tomb so that even though they have died they might remain noble, and (he) made expenditures for repairs and he was the one who organized the original collection of the common fund, and he continually talks about and advises what is best and in all things shows himself to be high-minded. (IG II² 1327, lines 5–16; cf. IG II² 1343)

In another inscription from Piraeus (IG II² 1263), the members of an association (*koinon*) of *thiasōtai* honor one of their members, Demitrios, who has acted as secretary, by granting him a crown, a statue, and public proclamation of his worthiness. Among the deeds for which Demitrios is praised is the proper administration of the association's funds (much of which would

---

48. For "friends" (*philoi*) as members of an association see also ISmyrna 720; IG VII 3224; IG XII/9 39 (Boeotia, I CE); SEG 29 1188; SEG 29 1195; SEG 31 1038; *Denkschriften der Österreichischen Akademie der Wissenschaften, Philologisch-historische Klasse* 80 (1962) 59; ZPE 44 (1981) 89 no. 19; perhaps IG II² 1275; cf. Kloppenborg, "Status and Conflict Resolution," 15.

have been out-of-pocket expenses for Demitrios) and, notably, the return of a financial reward given to him by the association from its common fund. The public record of the benefaction of Demitrios and the honors granted to him are meant to goad others, that they too "shall be zealous for honor [*philotimōntai*] among the members, knowing that they will receive thanks from the members deserving of the benefaction" (ll. 27–32).[49] These inscriptions suggest that the receipt of honor was one of the primary motivations for benefaction within associations.[50]

Such benefaction could take many forms. For example, a benefaction of cash is widely attested.[51] Property could be used for a benefaction to an association, through either a gift of land[52] or the donation of all or part of a building.[53] Benefaction to an association could also be done by a husband and wife together. In a first- or second-century BCE inscription from Citium (Cyprus), we have an example of an entire family honored for their benefaction to an association of Artemis:

> With good fortune, Soanteion and the thiasos of Artemis honored Timocrates, son of Stasioikos, and his wife Timagion and their daughter [101] Timas and her daughter Aristion and his sons Stasioikos, Boïskon, Aristokreon, and Aristolochos; and Stasioikos, son of Timocrates, his daughter Karion, Boïskon's son Timokrates, on account of the high-mindedness that they have shown to them [the *thiasos*].[54]

In a similar fashion, an undated inscription from the Gulf of Syme records honors set up by a number of associations for at least two couples: Alexander and his wife Nysa are honored with a golden crown by the Adonistai, the Aphrodistiastai, and the Asclepiastai; Epaphrodite and his wife are likewise honored with a golden crown by the Heroïsts and the Oiaciasts.[55] A first-century BCE inscription records that a man and his wife are to be honored

---

49. See also IG II² 1292, 1297, 1301 (Piraeus, III BCE).

50. For other examples of honorary inscriptions set up by associations see OGIS 50, 51 (Egypt, III BCE); IG XI/4 1061 (Delos, II BCE); IG II² 1343 (Athens, 37–36 BCE); IG XII/1 155 (Rhodes, I BCE); IAlex(K) 91 (Alexandria, IV–V CE); IDelos 1522 (II CE); Foucart, *Des associations religieuses*, 59 (Tralles); IKios 22.

51. For example, IDelos 1519, 1520, 1521; LSAM 9; IEph 2212; IMagnMai 117; CIL III 633; CIL XIV 2112; Collart, *Philippes*, 374–75 n. 3, no. 8.

52. For example, IG X/2.1 259, 260; IG XII/1 736; CIL III 659; CBP 455.

53. IG XII/1 937; MAMA 6 239; CIJ 1 694, 1404, 1432; DFSJ 33; cf. the building of a vaulted tomb for association members in ISmyrna 218.

54. Foucart, *Des associations religieuses*, 55.

55. Foucart, *Des associations religieuses*, 56.

"for all time" by a *koinon* for contributions directed toward the association's buildings and furnishings (IG XII/1 937).

The list goes on. An inscription set up to commemorate those who "freely chose to assist the association [*thiasos*]" includes among its honorees Euhemeros and his wife, who contributed 10 drachmae (the smallest of the sums listed, which range from 10 to 300 drachmae; IKnidos 23, II BCE). IG XII/7 58 (Amorgos, undated) notes the boundaries of the lands, along with the house and gardens, that Xenokles pledged, with the concurrence of his wife and her *kyrios*, to an association (*eranos*). At Philippi a Latin inscription records the dedication of a sanctuary to Liber and Libera and Hercules by Gaius Valerius Fortunatus and his wife Marronia Eutycia.[56] Such husband-and-wife benefaction was also known within Jewish circles. For example, a building in first- or second-century BCE Egypt is dedicated as a *proseuchē*: "Papous constructed this *proseuchē* on his own behalf and on that of his wife and his children."[57]

In light of similar evidence, Uhlhorn suggests that it is within the Greco-Roman associations that one finds "for the first time anything approaching to the life of a Christian community."[58] "Houses, pieces of land, capital sums were either presented or bequeathed to them [the associations], in order that, on appointed days, a *sportula*, a distribution of bread, wine, or money, might be made amongst their members."[59] He argues that the system of charity in Christianity goes beyond that of the [102] associations insofar as it is completely voluntary and that distributions are made more deliberately to the poor and needy, rather than expended on banquets and burials.[60] Nevertheless, the associations still form an analogous backdrop for understanding the early Christian community in Jerusalem.[61]

The widespread practice of associations setting up honors for their benefactors makes it reasonable for Ananias and Sapphira to expect that in return for their benefaction they would have received the honors due to them. In an attempt to extract more honor than they are due, however, they claim to have given over the entire proceeds of the sale of their land. To

---

56. Collart, *Philippes*, 414 n. 1.

57. Fox, "Greek Inscriptions," 411–12. For other examples of husbands and wives involved in benefacting associations see Collart, *Philippes*, 174–75 n. 3, no. 8; IMakedD 920; cf. CIL 1707, IG X/2.1 506.

58. Uhlhorn, *Christian Charity*, 31, 28.

59. Uhlhorn, *Christian Charity*, 24.

60. Uhlhorn, *Christian Charity*, 32, 23–25.

61. Cf. Uhlhorn, *Christian Charity*, 24, 27.

have done so would be deemed more generous, and thus deserving of more honor, than to have given only a portion.

Capper suggests that Ananias and Sapphira would garner "a degree of admiration" only in the case that benefaction through the selling of property was rare.[62] He suggests that since it was not rare within the Christian community, admiration would *not* follow—"the more common such property-donations were, the less fame and reputation there was to be gained from an affected self-elevation into the limelight."[63] Thus, Ananias was not "motivated by a desire for special praise."[64] As our inscriptions show, however, benefaction was commonplace and yet accorded great honor, and it was often accompanied by the suggestion that others should follow suit in supporting the group. It is precisely because dispersing one's wealth was commonplace that we should read this text in the context of benefaction.

LUKE'S VIEW OF BENEFACTION

This understanding of the story of Ananias and Sapphira in light of benefaction fits within Luke's larger view of benefaction throughout the Gospel and Acts. It is clear from the outset that Luke and his community rely on patronage. Luke opens his Gospel by addressing his patron by using an honorific: "It seemed good to me . . . to write an orderly account for you, most excellent Theophilus" (Luke 1:3).[65] The honorific *kratistos* is used three other times by Luke, each case in an address to a Roman official (Acts 23:26; 24:3; 26:25), indicative of the high regard accorded Theophilus. Elsewhere in Luke we find women who support Jesus's ministry by providing from their own resources (Luke 8:1–3). On two [103] separate occasions, centurions are noted for their benefaction to the Jewish people, and both receive God's blessing upon them in turn (Luke 7:1–10; Acts 10:1–8, 31, 44–48). Benefaction within the Christian *ekklēsia* is suggested through the use of houses for meetings (12:12; 16:40; cf. 20:6–8).

Luke uses the term "benefactor" (*euergetēs*) in only one passage, Luke 22:24–27.[66] Jesus responds to a dispute among the disciples as to who would be the greatest with an emphasis on service and humility, unlike the power structures in the Greco-Roman world, where the "kings of the Gentiles

62. Capper, "Community of Goods," 1742.
63. Capper, "Community of Goods," 1742.
64. Capper, "Community of Goods," 1743.
65. Cf. Acts 1:1; Moxnes, "Patron-Client Relations," 267; Fitzmyer, *Luke*, 1:300.
66. Luke also uses *euergesia* for Peter's good deed of healing a lame man (Acts 4:9), and *eueryeteō* in recalling the deeds of Jesus (Acts 10:38).

exercise lordship over them; and those in authority over them are called benefactors" (Luke 22:25). Luke has taken this passage from Mark 10:41-45 and relocated it in the Last Supper discourse. In doing so he has nuanced it differently. Most significantly, Mark's initial indication of "the supposed rulers (*hoi dokountes archein*) over the Gentiles" has been changed to "the kings (*hoi basileis*) of the Gentiles," and then Luke has added the note that these kings are called benefactors (*euergetai kalountai*). In contrast, the disciples are not to claim such titles or authority for themselves, despite their privileged place within the kingdom (Luke 22:28-30). Although they perform a service, they do not receive status or honor in exchange.[67] For Luke, Jesus overturns the usual categories of benefaction and honor.[68] Jesus himself states that he is among others "as one who serves" (Luke 22:27). Through his miracles he seems to broker God's patronage for the people.[69] Nevertheless, he never claims the honor due him.

A point of contrast with the actions of Ananias and Sapphira can be found in the Gospel story of Zacchaeus (Luke 19:1-10). Like Ananias and Sapphira, Zacchaeus has a secret about his personal finances. His secret, however, is the fact that he distributes it to others. When pushed by the criticism of the crowds, he announces that he "already" gives half of his possessions to the poor and [104] repays fourfold anyone he may have defrauded (Luke 19:8).[70] Despite his marginal status as tax collector, and thus a "sinner," Zacchaeus's encounter with Jesus is seemingly the first time he has articulated his actions publicly. Despite his obvious benefaction, he has not sought out the honors that were due him.[71] The significant contrast with Ananias and Sapphira lies in that which is received for one's actions.

67. Moxnes, "Patron-Client Relations," 261.

68. On the importance of benefaction to the writer of Luke-Acts see Danker (*Luke*, esp. 6-17; Danker, *Jesus and the New Age*, esp. 5-10). Yet despite Danker's recognition of the importance of benefaction to Luke in his study of epigraphic texts and the New Testament, he makes no connection between benefaction and the actions of Ananias and Sapphira (*Benefaction*). This is particularly odd in light of the fact that Danker sees in Acts 2:44 and 4:32 clear evidence for Luke viewing as benefactors those who contribute to the holding of all things in common within the community (Danker, *Benefaction*, 333). Capper ("Reciprocity," 516-18) also notes Luke's interest in shifting the boundaries of benefaction but does not link Acts 5:1-11 to this concern.

69. Moxnes, "Patron-Client Relations," 258-60.

70. The verb tenses are in the present rather than the future, and thus should be taken to refer to actions already in progress; see Fitzmyer, *Luke*, 2:1220-21, 1225; Malina and Rohrbaugh, *Social-Science Commentary*, 387.

71. In one regard Moxnes is correct in stating that Zacchaeus "is never portrayed as a patron" insofar as he never receives the requisite honor due a patron. In his use of money, however, he is acting as a benefactor to those who receive his largesse ("Patron-Client Relations," 255).

Whereas Ananias and Sapphira fall dead, Zacchaeus receives praise from Jesus in the pronouncement that "salvation" (*sōtēria*) has arrived, a declaration that also serves to restore him to his place within the community.[72]

Other passages likewise suggest a countercultural view of benefaction, not in terms of the cessation of the practice, but in terms of the expectation of rewards or honors. For example, in Luke 12:33–34 disciples are urged:

> Sell your possessions, and give alms; provide yourselves with purses that do not grow old, with a treasure in the heavens that does not fail, where no thief approaches and no moth destroys. For where your treasure is, there will your heart be also.

This is followed up later by the injunction to the rich ruler to "sell all that you have and distribute to the poor, and you will have treasure in heaven" (Luke 18:22), an invitation too difficult for the man to accept. It is only when we get to Acts 2–5 that we find the attempt being made to fulfil this command in full, at least within the Christian community.

The suggested expectation for one who has sold everything is "treasure in heaven" rather than honor on earth. In lying about the extent of their donation to the Christian community, Ananias and Sapphira were attempting to gain for themselves not only honor on earth, but greater honor on earth than they deserved. For Luke they serve as an example of worldly benefaction, wherein honors are received here and now. This motivation, however, causes them to lie about the extent of their benefaction and they are struck down. [105] The story serves as a warning to those who would be benefactors in Luke's own Christian community, but who might expect honors in exchange. The message is not "give everything or else," but "do not seek recognition for more than you have contributed." One might act as benefactor without having to donate the complete amount of land or property to the association. For example, when Polycharmos donates a portion of his house to the local synagogue in Stobi, the dedicatory inscription makes it very clear that the rights to part of the property are to be retained by Polycharmos and his heirs (CIJ I 694; cf. CIL III 659).

CONCLUSION

Through these passages we see that Luke is presenting for his audience a message about benefaction. In fact, these passages seem to indicate that Luke is attempting to transform the culturally defined pattern of

---

72. Cf. Malina and Rohrbaugh, *Social-Science Commentary*, 387.

patron-client relationships and benefaction within his community.[73] While benefaction remains a necessary part of Christian communal existence, Luke wants to warn any potential benefactors that they should not expect praise.[74] Set within the larger context of both Luke-Acts and the world of the voluntary associations, the story of Ananias and Sapphira is a cautionary tale about wanting honors for benefaction, and a warning against those who act according to human conventions rather than divine conventions.[75] While their "sin" is their lie, their motivation is the desire for greater worldly honor. Their reward for holding back part of the proceeds while claiming to give them all was death. Clearly this is a case of benefaction gone wrong.

---

73. Moxnes, "Patron-Client Relations," 257, 265.

74. Cf. Moxnes, "Patron-Client Relations," 266.

75. Moxnes suggests that Luke's presentation of the people placing the proceeds from the sale of land at the feet of the apostles turns the apostles into brokers of the benefaction of others. In distributing the goods on behalf of others, the apostles disallow the necessity for honor to be passed back onto the benefactors ("Patron-Client Relations," 264–65).

Bibliography

Aasgaard, Reidar. "Among Gentiles, Jews, and Christians: Formation of Christian Identity in Melito of Sardis." In *Religious Rivalries and the Struggle for Success in Sardis and Smyrna*, edited by Richard S. Ascough, 156–74. Studies in Christianity and Judaism 14. Waterloo, ON: Wilfrid Laurier University Press, 2005.

Adkins, A. W. H. *Merit and Responsibility: A Study in Greek Values*. Oxford: Clarendon, 1960.

Allen, W. C. *A Critical and Exegetical Commentary on the Gospel according to St. Matthew*. 3rd ed. ICC. Edinburgh: T. & T. Clark, 1912.

Aneziri, Sophia. *Die Vereine der dionysischen Techniten im Kontext der hellenistischen Gesellschaft: Untersuchungen zur Geschichte, Organisation und Wirkung der hellenistischen Technitenvereine*. Historia Einzelschriften 163. Stuttgart: Steiner, 2003.

Arnaoutoglou, Ilias N. "Collegia in the Province of Egypt in the First Century AD." *Ancient Society* 35 (2005) 197–216.

Applebaum, Shimon. "The Organization of the Jewish Communities in the Diaspora." In *The Jewish People in the First Century: Historical Geography, Political History, Social, Cultural and Religious Life and Institutions*, edited by S. Safrai and M. Stern, 464–503. CRINT 1. Assen: VanGorcum, 1974.

Aristotle. *The Rhetoric and Poetics of Aristotle*. Translated by W. Rhys Roberts and Ingram Bywater. New York: Random House, 1954.

Arnaoutoglou, Ilias N. "ΑΡΧΕΡΑΝΙΣΤΗΣ and Its Meaning in Inscriptions." *ZPE* 104 (1994) 107–10.

——. "Between *koinon* and *idion*: Legal and Social Dimensions of Religious Associations in Ancient Athens." In *Kosmos: Essays in Order, Conflict and Community in Classical Athens*, edited by Paul Cartledge, Paul Millett, and Sitta von Reden, 68–83. Cambridge: Cambridge University Press, 1998.

Ascough, Richard S. "An Analysis of the Baptismal Ritual of the Didache." *Studia Liturgica* 24 (1994) 201–13.

——. "The Apostolic Decree of Acts and Greco-Roman Associations: Eating in the Shadow of the Roman Empire." In *Aposteldekret und antikes Vereinswesen:*

Gemeinschaft und ihre Ordnung, edited by Markus Öhler, 297–316. WUNT 280. Tübingen: Mohr Siebeck, 2011. = **Chapter 14**

———. "Associations, Voluntary." In *Eerdmans Dictionary of the Bible*, edited by David Noel Freedman, 117–18. Grand Rapids: Eerdmans, 2000.

———. "Benefaction Gone Wrong: The 'Sin' of Ananias and Sapphira in Context." In *Text and Artifact in the Religions of Mediterranean Antiquity: Essays in Honour of Peter Richardson*, edited by Stephen G. Wilson and Michel Desjardins, 91–110. Studies in Christianity and Judaism 9. Waterloo, ON: Wilfrid Laurier University Press, 2000. = **Chapter 17**

———. "Bringing Chaos to Order: Historical Memory and the Manipulation of History." *R&T* 15 (2008) 280–303.

———. "Carving Out Public Space: τόπος Inscriptions and Early Christ Groups." In *Epigraphik und Neues Testament*, edited by Joseph Verheyden, Markus Öhler and Thomas Corsten, 93–110. WUNT 365. Tübingen: Mohr Siebeck, 2015.

———. "Communal Meals." In *The Oxford Handbook of Early Christian Ritual*, edited by Risto Uro, Juliette Day, Rikard Roitto, and Richard DeMaris, 204–19. Oxford Handbooks. Oxford: Oxford University Press, 2019.

———. "The Completion of a Religious Duty: The Background of 2 Cor 8:1–15." *NTS* 42 (1996) 584–99.

———. "Defining Community-Ethos in Light of the 'Other': Recruitment Rhetoric among Greco-Roman Religious Groups." *Annali di storia dell'esegesi* 24 (2007) 59–75. = **Chapater 10**

———. "Did the Philippian Christ Group Know They Were a 'Missionary' Group?" In *The First Urban Churches*. Vol. 4, *Philippi*, edited by James Harrison and Lawrence Welborne, 189–220. 4 vols. WGRW Supplement Series 13. Atlanta: SBL, 2018.

———. *1 & 2 Thessalonians: An Introduction and Study Guide; Encountering the Christ Group at Thessalonike*. Sheffield: Sheffield Phoenix, 2014. Reprint, T. & T. Clark Guides to the New Testament. London: Bloomsbury T. & T. Clark, 2017.

———. *1 and 2 Thessalonians: Encountering the Christ Group at Thessalonike*. Phoenix Guides to the New Testament 13. Sheffield: Sheffield Phoenix, 2014.

———. "Forms of Commensality in Greco-Roman Associations." *CW* 102 (2008) 33–46. = **Chapter 12**

———. "The Function of Meals in Forging Early Christian Identity according to the Book of Acts." In *Mahl und religiöse Identität im frühen Christentum—Meals and Religious Identity in Early Christianity*, edited by Matthias Klinghardt and Hal Taussig, 207–39. TANZ 56. Tübingen: Francke, 2012.

———. "Greco-Roman Philosophic, Religious, and Voluntary Associations." In *Community Formation in the Early Church and in the Church Today*, edited by Richard N. Longenecker, 3–19. Peabody, MA: Hendrickson, 2002. = **Chapter 2**

———. "Greco-Roman Religions in Sardis and Smyrna." In *Religious Rivalries and the Struggle for Success in Sardis and Smyrna*, edited by Richard S. Ascough, 40–52. Studies in Christianity and Judaism 14. Waterloo, ON: Wilfrid Laurier University Press, 2005.

———. *Lydia: Paul's Cosmopolitan Hostess*. Paul's Social Network. Collegeville, MN: Liturgical Press, 2009.

———. "'Map-maker, Map-maker, Make Me a Map': Re-describing Greco-Roman 'Elective Social Formations.'" In *Introducing Religion: Essays in Honor of Jonathan*

Z. *Smith*, edited by Willi Braun and Russell T. McCutcheon, 68–84. London: Equinox, 2008. = **Chapter 6**

———. "Matthew and Community Formation." In *The Gospel of Matthew in Current Study: Studies in Memory of William G. Thompson, SJ*, edited by David E. Aune, 96–126. Grand Rapids: Eerdmans, 2001. = **Chapter 8**

———. "Methodological Reflections on Synagogues and Christ Groups as 'Associations': A Response to Erich Gruen." *JJMJS* 4 (2017) 118–26.

———. "Of Memories and Meals: Greco-Roman Associations and the Early Jesus-Group at Thessalonikē." In *From Roman to Early Christian Thessalonikē: Studies in Religion and Archaeology*, edited by Laura Nasrallah, Charalambos Bakirtzis, and Steven J. Friesen, 49–72. Harvard Theological Studies, Harvard Divinity School. Distributed by Harvard University Press, 2010. = **Chapter 16**

———. "Paul and Associations." In *Paul in the Greco-Roman World: A Handbook*, edited by J. Paul Sampley, 1:68–89. 2 vols. Rev. ed. London: Bloomsbury, 2016.

———. "Paul, Synagogues and Associations: Reframing the Question of Models for Pauline Christ Groups." *JJMJS* 2 (2015) 27–52. = **Chapter 3**

———. "Paul's 'Apocalypticism' and the Jesus-Associations at Thessalonica and Corinth." In *Redescribing Paul and the Corinthians*, edited by Ron Cameron and Merrill P. Miller, 151–86. ECL 5. Atlanta: SBL, 2011.

———. *Paul's Macedonian Associations: The Social Context of Philippians and 1 Thessalonians*. WUNT 2/161. Tübingen: Mohr Siebeck, 2003. Reprint, Eugene, OR: Wipf & Stock, 2020.

———. "'A Place to Stand, a Place to Grow': Architectural and Epigraphic Evidence for Expansion in Greco-Roman Associations." In *Identity and Interaction in the Ancient Mediterranean: Jews, Christians and Others*, edited by Zeba A. Crook and Philip A. Harland, 76–98. New Testament Monographs 18. Sheffield: Sheffield Phoenix, 2007. = **Chapter 11**

———. "A Question of Death: Paul's Community-Building Language in 1 Thessalonians 4:13–18." *JBL* 123 (2004) 509–30. = **Chapter 15**

———. "Redescribing the Thessalonians' 'Mission' in Light of Graeco-Roman Associations." *NTS* 60 (2014) 61–82. = **Chapter 9**

———. "Reimagining the Size of Pauline Christ Groups in Light of Association Meeting Places." In *Scribal Practices and Social Structures among Jesus Adherents: Essays in Honour of John S. Kloppenborg*, edited by William E. Arnal, Richard S. Ascough, Robert A. Derrenbacker Jr., and Philip A. Harland, 547–65. BETL 285. Leuven: Peeters, 2016.

———. "Rejection and Repentance: Peter and the People in Luke's Passion Narrative." *Bib* 74 (1993) 349–65.

———. "The Thessalonian Christian Community as a Professional Voluntary Association." *JBL* 119 (2000) 311–28. = **Chapter 7**

———. "Social and Political Characteristics of Greco-Roman Association Meals." In *Meals in the Early Christian World: Social Formation, Experimentation, and Conflict at the Table*, edited by Dennis E. Smith and Hal Taussig, 59–72. New York: Palgrave MacMillan, 2012. = **Chapter 13**

———. "Translocal Relationships among Voluntary Associations and Early Christianity." *JECS* 5 (1997) 223–41. = **Chapter 5**

———. "Voluntary Associations and the Formation of Pauline Churches: Addressing the Objections." In *Vereine, Synagogen und Gemeinden im kaiserzeitlichen*

Kleinasien, edited by Andreas Gutsfeld and Dietrich-Alex Koch, 149–83. STAC 25. Tübingen: Mohr Siebeck, 2006. = **Chapter 4**

———. "Voluntary Associations and Community Formation: Paul's Macedonian Christian Communities in Context." PhD diss., University of St. Michael's College, Toronto School of Theology, 1997.

———. "What Are They *Now* Saying about Christ Groups and Associations?" *CurrBR* 13 (2015) 207–44.

———. *What Are They Saying about the Formation of Pauline Churches?* New York: Paulist, 1998.

Ascough, Richard S., Philip A. Harland, and John S. Kloppenborg. *Associations in the Greco-Roman World: A Sourcebook*. Waco, TX: Baylor University Press, 2012. = AGRW

Ausbüttel, Frank M. *Untersuchungen zu den Vereinen im Westen des römischen Reiches*. FAS 11. Kallmünz: Lassieben, 1982.

Balch, David L. "Paul, Families, and Households." In *Paul in the Greco-Roman World: A Handbook*, edited by J. Paul Sampley, 258–92. Harrisburg, PA: Trinity, 2003.

Baldwin, Barry H. "Strikes in the Roman Empire." *CJ* 59 (1964) 75–76.

Barclay, John M. G. "Conflict in Thessalonica." *CBQ* 55 (1993) 512–30.

———. "Money and Meetings: Group Formation among Diaspora Jews and Early Christians." In *Vereine, Synagogen und Gemeinden im kaiserzeitlichen Kleinasien*, edited by Andreas Gutsfeld and Dietrich-Alex Koch, 113–28. STAC 25. Tübingen: Mohr Siebeck, 2006.

———. "Thessalonica and Corinth: Social Contrasts in Pauline Christianity." *JSNT* 47 (1992) 49–74.

Bardtke, Hans. "Der gegenwärtige Stand der Erforschung der in Palästina neu gefundenen hebräischen Handschriften, 44: Die Rechtsstellung der Qumran-Gemeinde." *Theologische Literaturzeitung* 86 (1961) 93–104.

Barrett, C. K. *The Acts of the Apostles*. ICC. Edinburgh: T. & T. Clark, 1994.

———. *The New Testament Background: Selected Documents*. London: SPCK, 1987.

Bartchy, S. Scott. "Community of Goods in Acts: Idealization or Social Reality?" In *The Future of Early Christianity: Essays in Honor of Helmut Koester*, edited by Birger A. Pearson, in collaboration with A. Thomas Kraabel et al., 309–18. Minneapolis: Fortress, 1991.

———. "Undermining Ancient Patriarchy: The Apostle Paul's Vision of a Society of Siblings." *BTB* 29 (1999) 68–78.

Barton, S. C. "The Communal Dimension of Earliest Christianity: A Critical Survey of the Field." *JTS* 43 (1992) 399–427.

Barton, S. C., and G. H. R. Horsley. "A Hellenistic Cult Group and the New Testament Churches." *Jahrbuch für Antike und Christentum* 24 (1981) 7–41.

Bassler, Jouette M. "Σκεῦος: A Modest Proposal for Illuminating Paul's Use of Metaphor in 1 Thessalonians 4:4." In *The Social World of the First Christians: Essays in Honor of Wayne A. Meeks*, edited by L. Michael White and O. Larry Yarbrough, 53–66. Minneapolis: Fortress, 1995.

Batten, Alicia. "The Moral World of Greco-Roman Associations." *SR* 36 (2007) 135–51.

Baumgarten, Albert. "Graeco-Roman Voluntary Associations and Ancient Jewish Sects." In *Jews in a Graeco-Roman World*, edited by Martin Goodman, 93–111. Oxford: Clarendon, 1998.

Beare, F. W. *A Commentary on the Epistle to the Philippians.* BNTC. London: Black, 1959.
Beck, Roger. "The Mithras Cult as Association." *SR* 21 (1992) 3–13.
———. "The Mysteries of Mithras." In *Voluntary Associations in the Graeco-Roman World*, edited by John S. Kloppenborg and Stephen G. Wilson, 176–85. London: Routledge, 1996.
———. "On Becoming a Mithraist: New Evidence for the Propagation of the Mysteries." In *Religious Rivalries in the Early Roman Empire and the Rise of Christianity*, edited by Leif E. Vaage, 175–94. Studies in Christianity and Judaism 18. Waterloo, ON: Wilfrid Laurier University Press, 2006.
Behr, Charles A., trans. *P. Aelius Aristides: The Complete Works.* 2 vols. Leiden: Brill Academic, 1981–1986.
Belayche, Nicole. "En quête de marqueurs des communautés 'religieuses' gréco-romaines." In *Les communautés religieuses dans le monde Gréco-Romain: Essais de definition*, edited by Nicole Belayche and Simon C. Mimouni, 9–20. Bibliothèque de l'École des Hautes Études sciences religieuses 117. Turnhout, Belgium: Brepols, 2003.
Belayche, Nicole and Simon C. Mimouni, eds. *Les communautés religieuses dans le monde Gréco-Romain: Essais de definition.* Bibliothèque de l'École des Hautes Études sciences religieuses 117. Turnhout, Belgium: Brepols, 2003.
Bendlin, Andreas. "Gemeinschaft, Öffentlichkeit und Identität: Forschungsgeschichtliche Anmerkungen zu den Mustern sozialer Ordnung in Rom." In *Religiöse Vereine in der römischen Antike: Untersuchungen zu Organisation, Ritual und Raumordnung*, edited by Ulrike Egelhaaf-Gaiser and Alfred Schäfer, 9–40. STAC 13. Tübingen: Mohr Siebeck, 2002.
———. "'Eine Zusammenkunft um der religio willen ist erlaubt . . .'? Zu den politischen und rechtlichen Konstruktionen von (religiöser) Vergemeinschaftung in der römischen Kaiserzeit." In *Die verrechtlichte Religion: Der Öffentlichkeitsstatus von Religionsgemeinschaften*, edited by Hans G. Kippenberg and Gunnar Folke Schuppert, 65–107. Tübingen: Mohr Siebeck, 2005.
Bernand, Etienne., ed. *Recueil des inscriptions grecques du Fayoum.* Institut Français d'Archéologie Orientale. Bibliothèque d'étude. Leiden: Brill, 1975–81.
Bertram, Georg. "ἐπιστρέφω, κτλ." In *TDNT* 7:722–29.
Best, Ernest. "Bishops and Deacons: Philippians 1,1." *Studia evangelica* 4 (1968) 371–76.
———. *The First and Second Epistles to the Thessalonians.* BNTC. London: Black, 1972.
Bloch, Herbert. "Ostia. Iscrizioni rinvenute tra il 1930 e il 1939." *Notizie degli Scavi di Antichità* 7 (1953) 239–306.
Blomberg, Craig C. *Matthew.* NAC 22. Nashville: Broadman, 1992.
Boak, A. E. R. "The Organization of Guilds in Greco-Roman Egypt." *Transactions of the American Philological Association* 68 (1937) 212–20.
———. *Papyri from Tebtunis, Part 1.* University of Michigan Studies. Humanistic Series 28. Michigan Papyri 2. Ann Arbor: University of Michigan Press, 1933.
Bock, Darrell L. *Acts.* BECNT. Grand Rapids: Baker, 2007.
Boer, Martinus C. de. *The Defeat of Death: Apocalyptic Eschatology in 1 Corinthians 15 and Romans 5.* JSNTSup 22. Sheffield: Sheffield Academic, 1988.
Boers, Hendrikus. "The Form-Critical Study of Paul's Letters: 1 Thessalonians as a Case Study." *NTS* 22 (1976) 140–58.

Boismard, M-E., and A. Lamouille. *Les Actes des deux apôtres*. 6 vols. EBib, n.s. 12–14, 23, 30, 41. Paris: Lecoffre, 1990–.

Bollmann, Beate. *Römische Vereinshäuser: Untersuchungen zu den Scholae der römischen Berufs-, Kult- und Augustalen-Kollegien in Italien*. Mainz: von Zabern, 1998.

Bömer, Franz. *Untersuchungen über die Religion der Sklaven in Griechenland und Rom*. 2nd ed. Abhandlungen der Geistes- und Sozialwissenschaftlichen Klasse 10.4. Wiesbaden: Verlag der Akademie der Wissenschaften und der Literatur, 1981.

Bonner, Campbell. *Studies in Magical Amulets, Chiefly Graeco-Egyptian*. University of Michigan Studies. Humanistic Series 49. Ann Arbor: University of Michigan Press, 1950.

Borbonus, Dorian. *Columbarium Tombs and Collective Identity in Augustan Rome*. Cambridge: Cambridge University Press, 2014.

Borgen, Peder. "'Yes,' 'No,' 'How Far?': The Participation of Jews and Christians in Pagan Cults." In *Paul in His Hellenistic Context*, edited by Troles Engberg-Pedersen, 30–59. Minneapolis: Fortress, 1995.

Boring, M. Eugene. "The Convergence of Source Analysis, Social History, and Literary Structure in the Gospel of Matthew." In *SBL 1994 Seminar Papers*, edited by Eugene H. Lovering, 587–611. SBLSP 33. Atlanta: Scholars, 1994.

Bormann, Lukas. *Philippi: Staat und Christengemeinde zur Zeit des Paulus*. NovTSup 78. Leiden: Brill, 1995.

Bowers, Paul. "Church and Mission in Paul." *JSNT* 44 (1991) 89–111.

Bradshaw, Paul F. *The Search for the Origins of Christian Worship: Sources and Methods for the Study of Early Liturgy*. London: SPCK, 1992.

Brady, Thomas A. "The Reception of the Egyptian Cults by the Greeks (330–30 B.C.)." In *Sarapis and Isis: Collected Essays*, 9–33. Chicago: Ares, 1978.

Brashaer, William. *Vereine im griechisch-römischen Ägypten*. Zenia. Konstanzer Althistorische Vorträge und Forschungen 7. Konstanz: Universitätsverlag Konstanz, 1993.

Braun, Herbert. *Qumran und das neue Testament*. 2 Vols. Tübingen: Mohr Siebeck, 1966.

Brawley, Robert L. *Luke-Acts and the Jews: Conflict, Apology, and Conciliation*. SBLMS 33. Atlanta: Scholars, 1987.

Briant, Pierre. "Les iraniens d'Asie Mineure apres 1a chute de l'empire archemeide." *Dialogues d'histoire ancienne* 11 (1985) 167–95.

Broughton, T. R. S. "Roman Asia Minor." In *An Economic Survey of Ancient Rome*, edited by Tenny Frank, in collaboration with T. R. S. Broughton et al., 4:499–918. 6 vols. Baltimore: Johns Hopkins Press, 1938.

Brown, Raymond E., and John P. Meier. *Antioch and Rome: New Testament Cradles of Catholic Christianity*. New York: Paulist, 1983.

Bruce, F. F. *The Book of Acts*. Rev. ed. NICNT. Grand Rapids: Eerdmans, 1988.

———. *1 & 2 Thessalonians*. WBC 45. Nashville: Nelson, 1982.

Bryant, Joseph M. "Beware the Gift of Theory: A Historical-Sociological Critique of Rodney Stark's *The Rise of Christianity*." Unpublished paper.

———. "Cost-Benefit Accounting and the Piety Business: Is *Homo Religiosus*, at Bottom, a *Homo Economicus*?" *Method & Theory in the Study of Religion* 12 (2000) 520–48.

Büchsel, F. "εἴδωλον, κτλ." In *TDNT* 2:375–80.

Buckler, W. H. "Labour Disputes in the Province of Asia." In *Anatolian Studies, Presented to Sir William Mitchell Ramsay*, edited by William H. Buckler and W. M. Calder, 27–50. Manchester: Manchester University Press, 1923.

Burford, Alison. *Craftsmen in Greek and Roman Society. Aspects of Greek and Roman Life*. London: Thames & Hudson, 1972.

Burke, Trevor J. "The Holy Spirit as the Controlling Dynamic in Paul's Role as Missionary to the Thessalonians." In *Paul as Missionary: Identity, Activity, Theology, and Practice*, edited by Trevor J. Burke and Brian S. Rosner, 142–57. LNTS 420. London: T. & T. Clark, 2011.

Burkert, Walter. *Ancient Mystery Cults*. Cambridge: Harvard University Press, 1987.

———. *Greek Religion*. Translated by John Raffan. Cambridge: Harvard University Press, 1985.

Burtchaell, James Tunstead. *From Synagogue to Church: Public Services and Offices in the Earliest Christian Communities*. Cambridge: Cambridge University Press, 1992.

Callan, Terrance. "The Background of the Apostolic Decree (Acts 15:20, 29; 21:25)." *CBQ* 55 (1993) 284–97.

Cameron, Ron, and Merrill P. Miller. "Introduction: Ancient Myths and Modern Theories of Christian Origins." In *Redescribing Christian Origins*, edited by Ron Cameron and Merrill P. Miller, 1–30. SBLSymS 28. Atlanta: SBL, 2004.

———. "Conclusion: Redescribing Christian Origins." In *Redescribing Christian Origins*, edited by Ron Cameron and Merrill P. Miller, 497–516. SBLSymS 28. Atlanta: SBL, 2004.

Campbell, J. Y. "The Origin and Meaning of the Christian Use of the Word 'Ekklēsia.'" *JTS* 49 (1948) 130–43.

Campenhausen, Hans von. *Ecclesiastical Authority and Spiritual Power in the Church of the First Three Centuries*. Translated from the German by J. A. Baker. London: Black, 1969.

Cancik, Hubert. "The End of the World, of History, and of the Individual in Greek and Roman Antiquity." In *The Encyclopedia of Apocalypticism*. Vol. 1, *The Origins of Apocalypticism in Judaism and Christianity*, edited by John J. Collins, 84–125. 3 vols. New York: Continuum, 2000.

Capper, Brian J. "Community of Goods in the Early Jerusalem Church." In *ANRW* II. Teilband Religion 26/2. *Vorkonstantinisches Christentum: Neues Testament*, edited by Wolfgang Haase, 1730–74. Berlin: de Gruyter, 1995.

———. "'In der Hand des Ananias': Erwägungen zu 1QS VI, 20 und der urchristlichen Gütergemeinschaft." *Revue de Qumran* 12 (1986) 223–36.

———. "The Interpretation of Acts 5.4." *JSNT* 19 (1983) 117–31.

———. "The Palestinian Cultural Context of Earliest Christian Community of Goods." In *The Book of Acts in Its First-Century Setting*. Vol. 4, *The Book of Acts in Its Palestinian Setting*, edited by Richard Bauckham, 323–56. Grand Rapids: Eerdmans, 1995.

———. "Reciprocity and the Ethic of Acts." In *Witness to the Gospel: The Theology of Acts*, edited by I. Howard Marshall and David Peterson, 499–518. Grand Rapids: Eerdmans, 1998.

Carlston, C. E. "Christology and Church in Matthew." In *The Four Gospels 1992: Festschrift Frans Neirynck*, edited by Frans van Segbroeck, C. M. Tucker, G. Van Belle, and J. Verheyden, 1283–304. 3 vols. BETL 100. Leuven: Leuven University Press, 1992.

Carpinelli, Francis Giordano. "'Do This as My Memorial' (Luke 22:19): Lucan Soteriology of Atonement." *CBQ* 61 (1999) 74–91.
Carter, Warren. "Community Definition and Matthew's Gospel." In *SBL 1997 Seminar Papers*, 637–63. SBLSP 36. Atlanta: Scholars, 1997.
———. *Matthew and the Margins: A Sociopolitical and Religious Reading*. Bible & Liberation Series. Maryknoll. NY: Orbis, 2000.
Cassidy, Richard J. *Society and Politics in the Acts of the Apostles*. Maryknoll, NY: Orbis, 1987.
Castelli, Elisabeth A. *Imitating Paul: A Discourse of Power*. Literary Currents in Biblical Interpretation. Louisville: Westminster John Knox, 1991.
Castells, Manuel. *The Power of Identity*. The Information Age: Economy, Society and Culture 2. Oxford: Blackwell, 1997.
Cenival, Francis de. "Les Associations dans les Temples Égyptiens d'après les Données Fournies par les Papyrus Démotique." In *Religions en Égypte hellénistique et romaine. Colloque de Strasbourg, 15-18 mai 1967*, 5–19. Bibliothèque des centres d'études supérieures spécialisés. Travaux du Centre d'études supérieures spécialisé d'histoire des religions de Strasbourg Paris: Presses Universitaires de France, 1969.
Chadwick, Henry. "The Silence of Bishops in Ignatius." *HTR* 43 (1950) 169–72.
Champion, Craige B., ed. *Roman Imperialism: Readings and Sources*. Interpreting Ancient History 3. Oxford: Blackwell, 2004.
Chester, Stephen J. *Conversion at Corinth: Perspectives on Conversion in Paul's Theology and the Corinthian Church*. SNTW. London: T. & T. Clark, 2003.
Chilton, Bruce. "The Eucharist: Exploring Its Origins." *BRev* 10/6 (1994) 36–43.
Clarke, Andrew D. *Serve the Community of the Church: Christians as Leaders and Ministers*. First-Century Christians in the Graeco-Roman World. Grand Rapids: Eerdmans, 2000.
Clarke, John R. *Art in the Lives of Ordinary Romans: Visual Representation and Non-elite Viewers in Italy, 100 B.C.—A.D. 315*. The Joan Palevsky Imprint in Classical Literature. Berkeley: University of California Press, 2003.
Clauss, Manfred. "Zur Integrationsleistung der römischen Vereinigungen—Ein Kommentar." In *Gesellschaften im Vergleich: Forschungen aus Sozial- und Geschichtswissenschaften*, edited by Hartmut Kaelble and Jürgen Schriewer, 35–38. Comparative Studies Series 9. Frankfurt: Lang, 1999.
Claussen, Carsten. *Versammlung, Gemeinde, Synagoge: Das hellenistisch-jüdische Umfeld der frühchristlichen Gemeinden*. SUNT 27. Göttingen: Vandenhoeck & Ruprecht, 2002.
Collange, Jean-François. *The Epistle of Saint Paul to the Philippians*. Translated by A. W. Heathcote. London: Epworth, 1979.
Collart, Paul. "Inscriptions de Philippes." *BCH* 62 (1938) 409–32.
———. *Philippes, ville de Macédonia, depuis ses origines jusqu'à la fin de la l'époque romaine*. (Thèse, Université de Genève 85.) Paris: Boccard, 1937.
Collins, John N. *Diakonia: Re-interpreting the Ancient Sources*. New York: Oxford University Press, 1990.
Collins, Raymond F. "A propos the Integrity of I Thes." *ETL* 55 (1979) 67–106.
———. *The Birth of the New Testament: The Origin and Development of the First Christian Generation*. New York: Crossroad, 1993.
———. *Studies on the First Letter to the Thessalonians*. BETL 66. Leuven: Leuven University Press, 1984.

Conzelmann, Hans. *Acts of the Apostles*. Hermeneia. Philadelphia: Fortress, 1987.
Cope, O. Lamar. *Matthew: A Scribe Trained for the Kingdom of Heaven*. CBQMS 5. Washington, DC: Catholic Biblical Association of America, 1976.
Corley, Kathleen E. *Private Women, Public Meals: Social Conflict in the Synoptic Tradition*. Peabody, MA: Hendrickson, 1993.
Cormack, James M. R. "The Gymnasiarchal Law of Beroea." In *Ancient Macedonia 2: Papers*, edited by Basil Laourdas and Ch. Makaronas, 139–50. Institute for Balkan Studies 155. Thessalonica: Institute for Balkan Studies, 1977.
Cotter, Wendy J. "The Collegia and Roman Law: State Restrictions on Voluntary Associations, 64 BCE–200 CE." In *Voluntary Associations in the Graeco-Roman World*, edited by John S. Kloppenborg and Stephen G. Wilson, 74–89. London: Routledge, 1996.
———. "Women's Authority Roles in Paul's Churches: Countercultural or Conventional?" *NovT* 36 (1994) 350–72.
Coulot, Claude. "Les Thessaloniciens accueillent l'évangile: Un premier bilan (1Th 1,2–10)." *BLE* 112 (2011) 29–40.
Countryman, William L. "Patrons and Officers in Club and Church." In *Society of Biblical Literature 1977 Seminar Papers*, edited by Paul J. Achtemeier, 135–43. SBLSP 11. Missoula, MT: Scholars, 1977.
Crosby, Michael H. *House of Disciples: Church, Economics, and Justice in Matthew*. Maryknoll, NY: Orbis, 1988.
Crossan, John Dominic, and Jonathan L. Reed. *In Search of Paul: How Jesus's Apostles Opposed Rome's Empire with God's Kingdom*. San Francisco: Harper, 2004.
Crossley, James G., and Christian Karner. "Writing History, Constructing Religion." In *Writing History, Constructing Religion*, edited by James G. Crossley and Christian Karner, 3–8. Aldershot, UK: Ashgate, 2005.
Culpepper, R. Alan. *The Johannine School: An Evaluation of the Johannine-School Hypothesis Based on an Investigation of the Nature of Ancient Schools*. SBLDS 26. Missoula, MT: Scholars, 1975.
D'Arms, John H. "Memory, Money, and Status at Misenum: Three New Inscriptions from the Collegium of the Augustales." *JRS* 90 (2000) 126–44.
Danker, Frederick W. *Benefactor: Epigraphic Study of a Graeco-Roman and New Testament Semantic Field*. St. Louis: Clayton, 1982.
———. *Jesus and the New Age: A Commentary on St. Luke's Gospel*. Completely revised and expanded. Philadelphia: Fortress, 1988.
———. *Luke*. Proclamation Commentaries. Philadelphia: Fortress, 1976.
Dassmann, Ernst. "Hausgemeinde und Bischofsamt." In *Vivarium: Festschrift Theodor Klausner zum 90. Geburtstag*, edited by Ernst Dassmann and Klaus Thraede, 82–97. JAC 11. Münster: Aschendorffsche, 1984.
Daube, David. Review of P. W. Duff, *Personality in Roman Private Law* in *JRS* 33 (1943) 86–93; and 34 (1944) 125–35.
Davies, Jon. *Death, Burial, and Rebirth in the Religions of Antiquity*. Religion in the First Christian Centuries. London: Routledge, 1999.
Davies, W. D., and Dale C. Allison. *The Gospel according to Saint Matthew*. 3 vols. ICC. Edinburgh: T. & T. Clark, 1988–1997.
Deissmann, G. Adolf. *Bible Studies: Contributions Chiefly from Papyri and Inscriptions to the History of the Language, the Literature, and the Religion of Hellenistic Judaism*

and Primitive Christianity. Translated by Alexander Grieve. Edinburgh: T. & T. Clark, 1901. Reprint, Eugene, OR: Wipf & Stock, 2004.

———. Light from the Ancient East: The New Testament Illustrated by Recently Discovered Texts of the Greco Roman World. New and completely revised edition. New York: Doran, 1927. Reprint, Eugene, OR: Wipf & Stock, 2004.

De Robertis, Francesco Maria Storia delle corporazioni e del regime associativo nel mondo romano. 2 vols. Bari, Italy: Adriatica, 1973.

Derrett, J. Duncan M. "Ananias, Sapphira, and the Right of Property." Downside Review 89 (1971) 225–32.

De Vos, Craig Steven. Church and Community Conflicts: The Relationships of the Thessalonian, Corinthian and Philippian Churches. SBLDS 168. Atlanta: Scholars, 1999.

DeWitt, Norman W. Epicurus and His Philosophy. Minneapolis: University of Minnesota Press, 1954.

Dibelius, Martin. An die Thessalonicher I, II. An die Philipper. 3rd ed. HNT 11. Tübingen: Mohr Siebeck, 1937.

Dickson, J. P. Mission-Commitment in Ancient Judaism and in the Pauline Communities: The Shape, Extent and Background of Early Christian Mission. WUNT 2/159. Tübingen: Mohr Siebeck, 2003.

Dill, Samuel. Roman Society from Nero to Marcus Aurelius. London: Macmillan, 1904.

Dobschütz, Ernst von. Die Thessalonicher-Briefe. ATLA Monograph Preservation Program. Göttingen: Vandenhoeck & Ruprecht, 1909.

Dodds, E. R. Pagan and Christian in an Age of Anxiety. Wiles Lectures 1963. New York: Norton, 1965.

Dombrowski, B. W. "היחד in 1QS and τό κοινόν: An Instance of Early Greek and Jewish Synthesis." HTR 59 (1966) 293–307.

Donahue, John F. The Roman Community at Table During the Principate. Ann Arbor: University of Michigan Press, 2004.

———. "Toward a Typology of Roman Public Feasting." In Roman Dining: A Special Issue of American Journal of Philology, edited by Barbara K. Gold and John F. Donahue, 95–113. Baltimore: Johns Hopkins University Press, 2005.

Donfried, Karl Paul. "2 Thessalonians and the Church of Thessalonica." In Origins and Method: Towards a New Understanding of Judaism and Christianity. Essays in Honour of John C. Hurd, edited by Bradley H. McLean, 128–44. JSNTSup 86. Sheffield: JSOT Press, 1993.

———. "The Cults of Thessalonica and the Thessalonian Correspondence." NTS 31 (1985) 336–56.

———. Paul, Thessalonica, and Early Christianity. Grand Rapids: Eerdmans, 2002.

Doublet, Georges. "Inscriptions de Paphlagonie." BCH 13 (1889) 293–319.

Douglas, Mary, ed. Constructive Drinking: Perspectives on Drink from Anthropology. Cambridge: Cambridge University Press, 1987.

———. Implicit Meanings: Selected Essays in Anthropology. 2nd ed. London: Routledge, 1999.

Dow, Sterling. "The Egyptian Cults in Athens." HTR 20 (1937) 183–232.

Downing, F. Gerald. "Common Strands in Pagan, Jewish and Christian Eschatologies in the First Christian Centuries." In Making Sense in (and of) the First Christian Century, edited by F. Gerald Downing, 169–87. JSNTSup 197. Sheffield: Sheffield Academic, 2000.

Drew-Bear, Thomas. "An Act of Foundation from Hypaipa." *Chiron* 10 (1980) 509–36.
Duff, P. W. *Personality in Roman Private Law*. Cambridge: Cambridge University Press, 1938.
Duling, Dennis C. "'Egalitarian' Ideology, Leadership, and Factional Conflict within the Matthean Group." *BTB* 27 (1997) 124–37.
——. "The Matthean Brotherhood and Marginal Scribal Leadership." In *Modelling Early Christianity: Social-Scientific Studies of the New Testament in Its Context*, edited by Philip F. Esler, 159–82. London: Routledge, 1995.
——. "Matthew 18:15–17: Conflict, Confrontation, and Conflict Resolution in a 'Fictive Kin' Association." In *SBL 1998 Seminar Papers*, edited by Eugene H. Lovering, 253–95. SBLSP 37. Atlanta: Scholars, 1998.
——. "Social-Scientific Small Group Research and Second Testament Study." *BTB* 25 (1995) 179–93.
Düll, Siegrid. *Die Götterkulte Nordmakedoniens in römischer Zeit*. Münchener archëologische Studien 7. Munich: Fink, 1977.
Dunand, Françoise. *Le culte d'Isis dans le bassin oriental de la Méditerranée*. EPRO 26. Leiden: Brill, 1973.
Dunbabin, Katherine M. D. *The Roman Banquet: Images of Conviviality*. Cambridge: Cambridge University Press, 2003.
Dunn, James D. G. *The Acts of the Apostles*. Narrative Commentaries. Valley Forge, PA: Trinity, 1996.
Dupont, Jacques. *The Salvation of the Gentiles: Essays in the Acts of the Apostles*. Translated by John R. Keating. An Exploration Book. New York: Paulist, 1979.
Eadie, John. *Commentary on the Greek Text of the Epistles of Paul to the Thessalonians*. ATLA Monograph Preservation Program. London: Macmillan, 1877.
Ebel, Eva. *Die Attraktivität früher christlicher Gemeinden: Die Gemeinde von Korinth im Spiegel griechisch-römischer Vereine*. WUNT 2/178. Tübingen: Mohr Siebeck, 2004.
Ebner, Martin. *Das Urchristentum in seiner Umwelt*. Vol. 1, *Die Stadt als Lebensraum der ersten Christen*. GNT 1/1. Göttingen: Vandenhoeck & Ruprecht, 2012.
Edson, Charles. "Cults of Thessalonica (Macedonica III)." *HTR* 41 (1948) 153–204.
——, ed. *Inscriptiones Thessalonicae et viciniae*. IG X/2.1. Berlin: de Gruyter, 1972.
Edwards, Douglas R. *Religion & Power: Pagans, Jews and Christians in the Greek East*. Oxford: Oxford University Press, 1996.
Egelhaaf-Gaiser, Ulrike, and Alfred Schäfer, eds. *Religiöse Vereine in der römischen Antike: Untersuchungen zu Organisation, Ritual und Raumordnung*. STAC 13. Tübingen: Mohr Siebeck, 2002.
Ehrman, Bart D. *A Brief Introduction to the New Testament*. 2nd ed. Oxford: Oxford University Press, 2009.
——. *The New Testament: A Historical Introduction to the Early Christian Writings*. 1st ed. Oxford: Oxford University Press, 1997.
——. *The New Testament: A Historical Introduction to the Early Christian Writings*. 4th ed. Oxford: Oxford University Press, 2008.
Elgvin, T. "'To Master His Own Vessel': 1 Thess 4.4 in Light of New Qumran Evidence." *NTS* 43 (1997) 604–19.
Elliott, John H. "Patronage and Clientage." In *The Social Sciences and New Testament Interpretation*, edited by Richard L. Rohrbaugh, 144–56. Peabody, MA: Hendrickson, 1996.

———. *What Is Social-Scientific Criticism?* GBS: New Testament Series. Minneapolis: Fortress, 1993.
Ellis, E. Earle. *Pauline Theology: Ministry and Society*. Grand Rapids: Eerdmans, 1989.
Elsner, Jaś, and Ian Rutherford. "Introduction." In *Pilgrimage in Graeco-Roman & Early Christian Antiquity: Seeing the Gods*, edited by Jaś Elsner and Ian Rutherford, 1–38. Oxford: Oxford University Press, 2005.
Ernst, Josef. "Von der Ortsgemeinde zur Grosskirche dargestellt an den Kirchenmodellen des Philipper- und Epheserbriefes." In *Kirche im Werden: Studien zum Thema Amt und Gemeinde im Neuen Testament*, edited by Josef Hainz, 123–42. Munich: Paderborn, 1976.
Esler, Philip F. *Community and Gospel in Luke-Acts: The Social and Political Motivations of Lucan Theology*. SNTSMS 57. Cambridge: Cambridge University Press, 1987.
———. *Conflict and Identity in Romans: The Social Setting of Paul's Letter*. Minneapolis: Fortress, 2003.
Evans, Craig A. "Ascending and Descending with a Shout: Psalm 47.6 and 1 Thessalonians 4.16." In *Paul and the Scriptures of Israel*, edited by Craig A. Evans and James A. Sanders, 238–53. Studies in Scripture in Early Judaism and Christianity 1. JSOTSup 83. Sheffield: JSOT Press, 1993.
Evans, Robert M. "Eschatology and Ethics: A Study of Thessalonica and Paul's Letters to the Thessalonians." ThD diss., University of Basel, 1967.
Fatum, Lone. "Brotherhood in Christ: A Gender Hermeneutical Reading of 1 Thessalonians." In *Constructing Early Christian Families: Family as Social Reality and Metaphor*, edited by Halvor Moxnes, 183–215. London: Routledge, 1997.
Fee, Gordon D. *The First and Second Letters to the Thessalonians*. NICNT. Grand Rapids: Eerdmans, 2009.
———. *Paul's Letter to the Philippians*. NICNT. Grand Rapids: Eerdmans, 1995.
Ferguson, Everett. *Backgrounds of Early Christianity*. Grand Rapids: Eerdmans, 1987.
Ferguson, William Scott. "The Attic Orgeones." *HTR* 37 (1944) 61–140.
Ferguson, W. O. *The Legal and Governmental Terms Common to the Macedonian Greek Inscriptions and the New Testament*. Historical and Linguistic Studies, 2nd ser., 2/3. Chicago: University of Chicago Press, 1913.
Fiore, Benjamin. *The Function of Personal Example in the Socratic and Pastoral Epistles*. AnBib 105. Rome: Biblical Institute Press, 1986.
Fisher, Nicholas R. E. "Greek Associations, Symposia, and Clubs." In *Civilization of the Ancient Mediterranean: Greece and Rome*, edited by Michael Grant and Rachel Kitzinger, 2:1167–97. 3 vols. New York: Scribner, 1988.
———. "Roman Associations, Dinner Parties, and Clubs." In *Civilization of the Ancient Mediterranean: Greece and Rome*, edited by Michael Grant and Rachel Kitzinger, 2:1199–1225. New York: Scribner, 1988.
Fitzmyer, Joseph A. *The Acts of the Apostles*. AB 31. New York: Doubleday, 1998.
———. *The Gospel according to Luke*. 2 vols. AB 28–28A. Garden City, NY: Doubleday, 1981–1985.
———. "Jewish Christianity in Acts in the Light of the Qumran Scrolls." In *Studies in Luke-Acts*, edited by Leander E. Keck and J. Louis Martyn, 233–57. Nashville: Abingdon, 1966.
Fitzpatrick-McKinley, Anne. "Synagogue Communities in the Graeco-Roman Cities." In *Jews in the Hellenistic and Roman Cities*, edited by John R. Barlett, 55–87. London: Routledge, 2002.

Filson, Floyd V. *A Commentary on the Gospel according to St. Matthew*. 2nd ed. BNTC. London: Black, 1971.
Forbes, R. J. *Studies in Ancient Technology*. Vol. 5. 2nd ed. Leiden: Brill, 1966.
Forkman, Goran. *The Limits of the Religious Community: Expulsion from the Religious Community within the Qumran Sect, within Rabbinic Judaism, and within Primitive Christianity*. ConBNT 5. Lund: Gleerup, 1972.
Fotopoulos, John. *Food Offered to Idols in Roman Corinth: A Social-Rhetorical Reconsideration of 1 Corinthians 8:1–11:1*. WUNT 2/151. Tübingen: Mohr Siebeck, 2001.
Foucart, Paul. *Des associations religieuses chez les Grecs: Thiases, èranes, orgéons, avec le texte des inscriptions relatives à ces associations*. Paris: Klincksieck, 1873. Reprint, Ancient Religion and Mythology. New York: Arno, 1975.
Fox, W. S. "Greek Inscriptions in the Royal Ontario Museum." *American Journal of Philology* 38 (1917) 411–12.
Fraikin, Daniel. "Introduction of Sarapis and Isis in Opus." *Numina Aegaea* 1 (1974) 1–3.
Frame, James E. *A Critical and Exegetical Commentary on the Epistles of St. Paul to the Thessalonians*. ICC. Edinburgh: T. & T. Clark, 1912.
Frankemölle, Hubert. *Jahwebund und Kirche Christi*. NTAbh 10. Münster: Aschendorff, 1974.
Frankfurter, David. "Traditional Cult." In *A Companion to the Roman Empire*, edited by D. Potter, 544–64. Blackwell Companions to the Ancient World. Oxford: Blackwell, 2006.
Fraser, P. M. *Rhodian Funerary Monuments*. Oxford: Clarendon, 1977.
Furnish, Victor Paul. *II Corinthians: A New Translation with Introduction and Commentary*. AB 32A. Garden City, NY: Doubleday, 1984.
Gabrielsen, Vincent. "Brotherhoods of Faith and Provident Planning: The Non-Public Associations of the Greek World." In *Greek and Roman Networks in the Mediterranean*, edited by Irad Malkin, Christy Constantakopoulou, and Katerina Panagopoulou, 176–203. London: Routledge, 2009.
———. "The Rhodian Associations Honouring Dionysodoros from Alexandria." *Classica et mediaevalia* 45 (1994) 137–60.
Gabrielsen, Vincent, and Christian A. Thomsen, eds. *Private Associations and the Public Sphere. Proceedings of a Symposium Held at the Royal Danish Academy of Sciences and Letters, 9–11 September 2010*. Scientia Danica. Series H, Humanistica 8, vol. 9. Copenhagen: Det Kongelige Danske Videnskabernes Selskab, 2015.
Garland, Robert. *The Greek Way of Death*. London: Duckworth, 1985.
Garnsey, Peter. "Non-slave Labour in the Roman World." In *Non-slave Labour in the Greco-Roman World*, edited by Peter Garnsey, 34–47. Rev. ed. Cambridge Philological Society Supplement 6. Cambridge: Cambridge Philological Society, 1980.
Garnsey, Peter, and Richard Saller. *The Roman Empire: Economy, Society and Culture*. London: Duckworth, 1987.
Gaston, Lloyd. "Pharisaic Problems." In *Approaches to Ancient Judaism, New Series*. Vol. 3, *Historical and Literary Studies*, edited by Jacob Neusner, 85–100. South Florida Studies in the History of Judaism 56. Atlanta: Scholars, 1993.
Gaventa, Beverly Roberts. *The Acts of the Apostles*. ANTC. Nashville: Abingdon, 2003.
———. *First and Second Thessalonians*. IBC. Louisville: Westminster John Knox, 1998.

Gehring, Roger W. *House Church and Mission: The Importance of Household Structures in Early Christianity*. Peabody, MA: Hendrickson, 2004.
Gennep, Arnold van. *The Rites of Passage*. Translated by Monika B. Vizedom and Gabrielle L. Caffe. London: Routledge & Paul, 1960.
Georgi, Dieter. "The Early Church: Internal Jewish Migration or New Religion. *HTR* 88 (1995) 35–68.
———. *The Opponents of Paul in Second Corinthians: A Study of Religious Propaganda in Late Antiquity*. Philadelphia: Fortress, 1986.
Gillihan, Yonder Moynihan. *Civic Ideology, Organization, and Law in the Rule Scrolls: A Comparative Study of the Covenanters' Sect and Contemporary Voluntary Associations in Political Context*. STDJ 97. Leiden: Brill, 2012.
Goodman, Martin. "Jews, Greeks, and Romans." In *Jews in a Graeco-Roman World*, edited by Martin Goodman, 3–14. Oxford: Clarendon, 1998.
———. *Mission and Conversion: Proselytizing in the Religious History of the Roman Empire*. Oxford: Clarendon, 1994.
Gordon, R. L. "Mithraism and Roman Society: Social Factors in the Explanation of Religious Change in the Roman Empire." *Religion* 2 (1972) 92–121.
Gordon, Richard, Mary Beard, Joyce Reynolds, and Charlotte Roueché. "Roman Inscriptions 1986–90." *JRS* 83 (1993) 131–58.
Grant, Robert M. *Early Christianity and Society: Seven Studies*. New York: Harper & Row, 1977.
Greenfield, Jonas. "The *Marzeaḥ* as a Social Institution." *Acta Antiqua Academiae Hungaricae* 22 (1974) 451–55.
Grignon, Charles. "Commensality and Social Morphology: An Essay of Typology." In *Food, Drink and Identity: Cooking, Eating and Drinking in Europe since the Middle Ages*, edited by Peter Scholliers, 23–33. Oxford: Bert, 2001.
Gruen, Erich S. *Diaspora: Jews amidst Greeks and Romans*. Cambridge: Harvard University Press, 2002.
———. "Synagogues and Voluntary Associations as Institutional Models: A Response to Richard Ascough and Ralph Korner." *JJMJS* 3 (2016) 125–31.
Gschnitzer, F. "Eine persische Kultstiftung in Sardeis und die 'Sippengotter' Vorderasiens" In *Im Bannkreis des Alten Orients: Studien zur Sprach- und Kulturgeschichte des Alten Orients und seines Ausstrahlungsraumes*, edited by W. Medi and H. Trenkwalder, 45–54. Innsbrucker Beitriige zur Kulturwissenschaft 24. Innsbruck: Institut für Sprachwissenschaft, 1986.
Guelich, Robert A. *The Sermon on the Mount: A Foundation for Understanding*. Waco: Word, 1982.
Gundry, Robert H. *Matthew: A Commentary on His Handbook for a Mixed Church under Persecution*. 2nd ed. Grand Rapids: Eerdmans, 1994.
Guterman, Simeon L. *Religious Toleration and Persecution in Ancient Rome*. London: Aiglon, 1951.
Gutsfeld, Andreas. "Ita radices egit res sodaliciaria in totam rem Romanam: Das romisch Vereinigungswesen und die Alte Geschichte im 19. und beginnenden 20. Jahrhundert." Unpublished paper presented at Collegia—Synagōgai—Ekklēsiai: Probleme und Schwerpunkte von Gruppenbildungen im Osten des römischen Kaiserreiches, Westfälische Wilhelms-Universität, Münster, Germany, June 15, 2001.

———. "Das römisch Vereinigungswesen und die Alte Geschichte im 19. und beginnenden 20. Jahrhundert." Unpublished paper presented at Collegia—Synagōgai—Ekklēsiai: Probleme und Schwerpunkte von Gruppenbildungen im Osten des römischen Kaiserreiches, Westfälische Wilhelms-Universität, Münster, Germany, June 15, 2001.

Habinek, Thomas. *Ancient Rhetoric and Oratory*. Blackwell Introductions to the Classical World. Oxford: Blackwell, 2005.

Haenchen, Ernst. *The Acts of the Apostles: A Commentary*. Translated by Bernard Noble and Gerald Shinn, under the supervision of Hugh Anderson, and revised by R. McL. Wilson Philadelphia: Westminter, 1971.

Hagner, Donald A. *Matthew*. 2 vols. WBC 33-33A. Nashville: Nelson, 1993.

Hainz, Josef. "Die Anfange des Bischofs- und Diakonenamtes." In *Kirche und Werden: Studien zum Thema Amt und Gemeinde im Neuen Testament*, edited by Josef Hainz, 91-107. Munich: Schöningh, 1976.

———. *Ekklesia: Strukturen paulinischer Gemeinde-Theologie und Gemeinde-Ordnung*. BU 9. Regensburg: Pustet, 1972.

Hanfmann, G. M. A., and M. Balmuth. "The Image of an Anatolian Goddess at Sardis." In *In Memoriam Helmut Theodor Bossert*, edited by U. B. Alkim, 252-69. Jahrbuch für kleinasiatische Forschung 2. Istanbul: Winter, 1965.

Hanson, John S. "The Dream/Visions Report and Acts 10.1—11.18." PhD diss., Harvard University, 1978.

Hardin, Justin K. "Decrees and Drachmas at Thessalonica: Illegal Assembly in Jason's House (Acts 17.1-10a)." *NTS* 52 (2006) 29-49.

Hardy, E. G. *Studies in Roman History*. ATLA Monograph Preservation Program. London: Macmillan, 1906.

Harland, Philip A. *Associations, Synagogues, and Congregations: Claiming a Place in Ancient Mediterranean Society*. Minneapolis: Fortress, 2003.

———. "Christ-Bearers and Fellow-Initiates: Local Cultural Life and Christian Identity in Ignatius' Letters." *JECS* 11 (2003) 481-99.

———. "Claiming a Place in Polis and Empire: The Significance of Imperial Cults and Connections among Associations, Synagogues and Christian Groups in Roman Asia (c. 27 BCE-138 CE). PhD diss., University of Toronto, 1999.

———. *Dynamics of Identity in the World of the Early Christians: Associations, Judeans, and Cultural Minorities*. New York: T. & T. Clark, 2009.

———. "Familial Dimensions of Group Identity: 'Brothers' (ἀδελφοί)) in Associations of the Greek East." *JBL* 124 (2005) 491-513.

———, ed. *Greco-Roman Associations: Texts, Translations, and Commentary*. Vol. 2, *North Coast of the Black Sea, Asia Minor*. BZNW 204. Berlin: de Gruyter, 2014. = GRA II

———. "Honouring the Emperor or Assailing the Beast: Participation in Civic Life among Associations (Jewish, Christian and Other) in Asia Minor and the Apocalypse of John." *JSNT* 77 (2000) 99-121.

———. "Honours and Worship: Emperors, Imperial Cults and Associations at Ephesus (First to Third Centuries C.E.)." *SR* 25 (1996) 319-34.

———. "Spheres of Contention, Claims of Pre-Eminence: Rivalries among Associations in Sardis and Smyrna." In *Religious Rivalries and the Struggle for Success in Sardis and Smyrna*, edited by Richard S. Ascough, 53-63. Studies in Christianity and Judaism 14. Waterloo, ON: Wilfrid Laurier University Press, 2005.

Harnack, Adolf von. *The Mission and Expansion of Christianity in the First Three Centuries*. 2 vols. London: Williams & Norgate, 1908.

Harrington, Daniel J. *The Gospel of Matthew*. SP 1. Collegeville: Liturgical, 1991.

Harrison, James. "Paul's House Churches and the Cultic Associations." *RTR* 58 (1999) 31–47.

Hatch, Edwin. *The Organization of Early Christian Churches: Eight Lectures*. Bampton Lectures. 1881. Reprint, Eugene, OR: Wipf & Stock, 1999.

———. *The Influence of Greek Ideas on Christianity*. The Hibbert Lectures 1888. 1890. Reprint, Peabody, MA: Hendrickson, 1995.

Havelaar, Henriette. "Hellenistic Parallels to Acts 5:1–11 and the Problem of Conflicting Interpretations." *JSNT* 67 (1997) 63–82.

Hawthorne, Gerald F. *Philippians*. WBC 43. Waco, TX: Word Books, 1983.

Heinrici, Georg. "Die Christengemeinden Korinths und die religiösen Genossenschaften der Griechen." *ZWT* 19 (1876) 465–526.

———. "Zum genossenschaftlichen Charakter der paulinischen Christengemeinden." *TSK* 54 (1881) 505-524.

———. "Zur Geschichte der Anfänge paulinischer Gemeinden." *ZWT* 20 (1877) 89–130.

Hengel, Martin. "Early Christianity as a Jewish-Messianic, Universalistic Movement." In *Conflicts and Challenges in Early Christianity*, edited by Donald A. Hagner, 1–41. Harrisburg, PA: Trinity, 1999.

———. *Judaism and Hellenism: Studies in their Encounter in Palestine during the Early Hellenistic Period*. Translated by John Bowden. 2 vols. Philadelphia: Fortress, 1974.

Henneken, Bartholomäus. *Verkündigung und Prophetie im Ersten Thessalonicherbrief: Ein Beitrag zur Theologie des Wortes Gottes*. SBS 29. Stuttgart: Katholisches Bibelwerk, 1969.

Herrmann, Peter. "Mystenvereine in Sardeis." *Chiron* 26 (1996) 315–48.

Herrmann, Randolf. "Die Gemeindergel von Qumran und das antike Vereinswesen." In *Jewish Identity in the Greco-Roman World*, edited by Jörg Frey Daniel R. Schwartz, and Stephanie Gripentrog, 161–203. AJEC 71. Leiden: Brill, 2007.

Hermansen, Gustav. *Ostia: Aspects of Roman City Life*. Edmonton: University of Alberta Press, 1982.

Herz, Peter. "Kollegien in Ostia: Gedanken zu den Inschriften *CIL* XIV 250 und 251." In *E fontibus haurire: Beiträge zur römischen Geschichte und zu ihren Hilfswissenschaften*, 295–325. Studien zur Geschichte und Kultur des Altertums 8. Paderborn: Schöningh, 1994.

Heyob, Sharon Kelly. *The Cult of Isis among Women in the Graeco-Roman World*. EPRO 51. Leiden: Brill, 1975.

Hill, David. *The Gospel of Matthew*. NCB. London: Oliphants, 1972.

Hill, Judith L. "Establishing the Church in Thessalonica." PhD diss., Duke University, 1990.

Hock, Ronald F. *The Social Context of Paul's Ministry: Tentmaking and Apostleship*. Philadelphia: Fortress, 1980.

———. "The Workshop as a Social Setting for Paul's Missionary Preaching." *CBQ* 41 (1979) 438–50.

Hoey, A. S. "Rosaliae Signorum." *HTR* 30 (1937) 22–30.

Holtz, Traugott. *Der erste Brief an die Thessalonicher*. EKK 13. Zurich: Benziger, 1986.

Hopkins, Keith. *Death and Renewal*. Sociological Studies in Roman History 2. Cambridge: Cambridge University Press, 1983.

Horsley, G. H. R. *New Documents Illustrating Early Christianity: A Review of the Greek Inscriptions and Papyri Published in 1976*. New Documents Illustrating Early Christianity 1. North Ryde, Australia: Ancient History Documentary Research Centre, Macquarie University, 1981.

———. *New Documents Illustrating Early Christianity: A Review of the Greek Inscriptions and Papyri, Published in 1978*. New Documents Illustrating Early Christianity 3. North Ryde, Australia: Ancient History Documentary Research Centre, Macquarie University, 1983.

———. *New Documents Illustrating Early Christianity: A Review of the Greek Inscriptions and Papyri Published in 1979*. New Dcouments Illustrating Early Chistianity 4. North Ryde, Australia: Ancient History Documentary Research Centre, Macquarie University, 1987.

———. *New Documents Illustrating Early Christianity: A Review of the Greek Inscriptions and Papyri: Linguistic Essays; With Cumulative Indexes to vols. 1–5*. New Dcouments Illustrating Early Chistianity 5. North Ryde, Australia: Ancient History Documentary Research Centre, Macquarie University, 1989.

Horsley, G. H. R., and J. A. L. Lee. "A Preliminary Checklist of Abbreviations of Greek Epigraphic Volumes." *Epigraphica* 56 (1994) 129–69.

Horsley, Richard A. "Paul's Assembly in Corinth: An Alternative Society." In *Religion in Roman Corinth: Interdisciplinary Approaches*, edited by Daniel Schowalter and Steven J. Friesen, 371–95. HTS. Cambridge: Harvard University Press, 2005.

Horst, Pieter W. van der. "The Birkat ha-minim in Recent Research." In *Hellenism—Judaism—Christianity: Essays on Their Interaction*. Vol. 2., edited by Pieter W. van der Horst, 99–111. CBET 6. Kampen: Kok Pharos, 1994.

Hugédé, Norbert. *Saint Paul et la Grèce*. Monde hellénique. Paris: Les Belles Lettres, 1982.

Husselman, Elinor Mullet, et al. *Papyri from Tebtunis, Part 2*. University of Michigan Studies. Humanistic Series 29. Michigan Papyri 5. Ann Arbor: University of Michigan Press, 1944.

Jaccottet, Anne-Françoise. *Choisir Dionysos. Les associations dionysiaques ou la face cachée du donysisme*. Vol. 1, *Texte*. 2 vols. Akanthus Crescens 6. Zurich: Akanthus, 2003.

———. *Choisir Dionysos. Les associations dionysiaques ou la face cachée du dionysisme* Vol. 2, *Documents*. 2 vols. Akanthus Crescens 6. Zurich: Akanthus, 2003.

Jaczynowska, Maria. *Les associations de la jeunesse romaine sous le haut-Empire*. Archiwum Filologiczne 136. Wroclaw: Zaklad Narodowy imienia Ossolinskisch, 1978.

Jeffers, James S. *Conflict at Rome: Social Order and Hierarchy in Early Christianity*. Minneapolis: Fortress, 1991.

———. *The Greco-Roman World of the New Testament Era: Exploring the Background of Early Christianity*. Downers Grove, IL: InterVarsity, 1999.

Jeremias, Joachim. *Jerusalem in the Time of Jesus: An Investigation into Economic and Social Conditions during the New Testament Period*. Philadelphia: Fortress, 1969.

Jewett, Robert. "Are There Allusions to the Love Feast in Rom 13:8–10?" In *Common Life in the Early Church: Essays Honoring Graydon F. Snyder*, edited by Julian V. Hill, 265–78. Valley Forge, PA: Trinity, 1998.

———. "Gospel and Commensality: Social and Theological Implications of Galatians 2.14." In *Gospel in Paul: Studies on Corinthians, Galatians and Romans for Richard N. Longenecker*, edited by L. Ann Jervis and Peter Richardson, 240–52. JSNTSup 108. Sheffield: Sheffield Academic, 1994.

———. "Tenement Churches and Communal Meals in the Early Church: The Implications of a Form-Critical Analysis of 2 Thessalonians 3:10." *BR* 38 (1993) 23–43.

———. "Tenement Churches and Pauline Love Feasts." *Quarterly Review* 14 (1994) 43–58.

———. *The Thessalonian Correspondence: Pauline Rhetoric and Millenarian Piety*. FF. New Testament. Philadelphia: Fortress, 1986.

Johnson, Luke Timothy. *The Acts of the Apostles*. SP 5. Collegeville, MN: Liturgical, 1992.

———. *The Literary Function of Possessions in Luke–Acts*. SBLDS 39. Missoula: Scholars, 1977.

Johnson-DeBaufre, Melanie. "'Gazing upon the Invisible': Archaeology, Historiography, and the Elusive Women of 1 Thessalonians." In *From Roman to Early Christian Thessalonikē: Studies in Religion and Archaeology*, edited by Laura Nasrallah, Charalambos Bakirtzis and Steven J. Friesen, 73–108. HTS 64. Cambridge: Harvard University Press, 2010.

Jones, A. H. M. "The Economic Life of the Towns of the Roman Empire." In *La Ville: Deuxième partie: Institutions économiques et sociales*. Vol 2., edited by Jean Firenne, 161–94. Recueils de la Société Jean Bodin 7. Brussels: Editions de la Libraire Éncyclopédique, 1955.

Jones, C. P. "A Deed of Foundation from the Territory of Ephesos." *JRS* 73 (1983) 116–25.

Josaitis, Norman F. *Edwin Hatch and Early Church Order*. Recherches et synthèses. Section d'Histoire 3. Gembloux: Duculot, 1971.

Joshel, Sandra R. *Work, Identity, and Legal Status at Rome: A Study of the Occupational Inscriptions*. Oklahoma Series in Classical Culture. Norman: University of Oklahoma Press, 1992.

Judge, E. A. *The Social Pattern of Christian Groups in the First Century: Some Prolegomena to the Study of New Testament Ideas of Social Obligation*. Christ and Culture Collection. London: Tyndale, 1960.

Juster, Jean. *Les Juifs dans l'empire romain: Leur condition juridique, économique et sociale*. 2 vols. Paris: Geuthner, 1914.

Kahl, Brigitte. "Acts of the Apostles: Pro(to)-Imperial Script and Hidden Transcript. In *In the Shadow of Empire: Reclaiming the Bible as a History of Faithful Resistance*, edited by Richard Horsley, 137–56. Louisville: Westminster John Knox, 2008.

Keener, Craig S. "Matthew 5:22 and the Heavenly Court." *ExpTim* 99 (1987) 46.

Kilgallen, J. J. *A Brief Commentary on the Gospel of Matthew*. Lewiston, NY: Mellen Biblical, 1992.

Kim, Seyoon. "Paul's Entry (εἴσοδος) and the Thessalonians' Faith (1 Thessalonians 1–3)." *NTS* 51 (2005) 519–42.

Kingsbury, Jack Dean. "Conclusion: Analysis of a Conversation." In *Social History of the Matthean Community*, edited by David L. Balch, 259–69. Minneapolis: Fortress, 1991.

Klauck, Hans-Josef. "Die Hausgemeinde als Lebensform im Urchristentum." *MTZ* 32 (1981) 1–15.

———. *Hausgemeinde und Hauskirche im frühen Christentum*. SBS 103. Stuttgart: Katholisches Bibelwerk, 1981.

———. *Herrenmahl und hellenistischer Kult: Eine religionsgeschichtliche Untersuchung zum ersten Korintherbrief*. NTAbh 15. Münster: Aschendorff, 1982.

———. "Lord's Supper." *ABD* 4:362–72.

———. *The Religious Context of Early Christianity: A Guide to Graeco-Roman Religions*. SNTW. Edinburgh: T. & T. Clark, 2000.

Klinghardt, Mattias. *Gesetz und Volk Gottes: Das lukanische Verständnis des Gesetzes nach Herkunft, Funktion und seinem Ort in der Geschichte des Urchristentums*. WUNT 32. Tübingen: Mohr Siebeck, 1988.

———. *Gemeinschaftsmahl und Mahlgemeinschaft. Soziologie und Liturgie fri. ihchristlicher Mahlfeiern*. TANZ 13. Basel: Franke, 1996.

———. "The Manual of Discipline in the Light of Statutes of Hellenistic Associations." In *Methods of Investigation of the Dead Sea Scrolls and the Khirbet Qumran Site: Present Realities and Future Prospects*, edited by John J. Collins, Michael O. Wise, Norman Golb, and Dennis Pardee, 251–70. Annals of the New York Academy of Sciences 722. New York: New York Academy of Sciences, 1994.

Kloppenborg, John S. "Associations and Their Meals." Unpublished paper presented at the Greco-Roman Meals Seminar, Annual Meeting of the Society of Biblical Literature, Chicago, November 19, 2012.

———. "Associations in the Ancient World." In *The Historical Jesus In Context*, edited by Amy Jill Levine, Dale C. Allison, and John Dominic Crossan, 323–38. Princeton Readings in Religions. Princeton: Princeton University Press, 2006.

———. "Associations, Voluntary." In *Encyclopedia of the Bible and Its Reception*, vol. 2, *Anim–Atheism*, edited by Dale C. Allison and Hans-Joseph Klauck, 2:1062–69. 16 vols. Berlin: de Gruyter, 2009–2018.

———. *Christ's Associations: Connecting and Belonging in the Ancient City*. New Haven: Yale University Press, 2019.

———. "*Collegia* and *Thiasoi*: Issues in Function, Taxonomy and Membership." In *Voluntary Associations in the Graeco-Roman World*, edited by John S. Kloppenborg and Stephen G. Wilson, 16–30. London: Routledge, 1996.

———. "Critical Histories and Theories of Religion: A Response to Ron Cameron and Burton Mack." *Method and Theory in the Study of Religion* 8 (1996) 279–89.

———. "Disaffiliation in Associations and the ἀποσυναγωγός of John." *HvTSt* 67 (2011) 159–74.

———. "Edwin Hatch, Churches and *Collegia*." In *Origins and Method: Towards a New Understanding of Judaism and Christianity. Essays in Honour of John C. Hurd*, edited by Bradley H. McLean, 212–38. JSNTSup 86. Sheffield: JSOT Press, 1993.

———. "Egalitarianism in the Myth and Rhetoric of Pauline Churches." In *Reimagining Christian Origins: A Colloquium Honoring Burton L. Mack*, edited by Elizabeth A. Castelli and Hal Taussig, 247–63. Valley Forge, PA: Trinity, 1996.

———. *Greco-Roman Associations: Texts, Translations, and Commentary*. Vol. 3. *Ptolemaic and Early Roman Egypt*. BZNW 246. Berlin: de Gruyter, 2020. = **GRA III**

———. "Greco-Roman *Thiasoi*, the *Ekklēsia* at Corinth, and Conflict Management." In *Redescribing Paul and the Corinthians*, edited by Ron Cameron and Merrill P. Miller, 186–218. ECL 5. Atlanta: Scholars, 2011.

———. "Membership Practices in Pauline Christ Groups." *Early Christianity* 4 (2013) 183–215.

———. "The Moralizing of Discourse in Greco-Roman Associations." In *"The One Who Sows Bountifully": Essays in Honor of Stanley K. Stowers*, edited by Caroline Johnson Hodge, Saul M. Olyan, Daniel Ullucci, and Emma Wasserman, 215–28. BJS 356. Providence, RI: Brown Judaic Studies, 2013.

———. "ΦΙΛΑΔΕΛΦΙΑ, ΘΕΟΔΙΔΑΚΤΟΣ, and the Dioscuri: Rhetorical Engagement in 1 Thessalonians 4.9–12." *NTS* 39 (1993) 265–89.

———. "Status and Conflict Resolution in Early Christian Groups." Unpublished paper presented at the Toronto School of Theology Biblical Department Seminar, September, 1995.

———. "Status und Wohltätigkeit bei Paulus und Jakobus." In *Von Jesus zum Christus: christologische Studien*, edited by Rudolf Hoppe and Ulrich Busse, 127–54. BZNW 93. Berlin: de Gruyter, 1998.

Kloppenborg, John S., and Richard S. Ascough. *Greco-Roman Associations: Texts, Translations, and Commentary*. Vol. 1, *Attica, Central Greece, Macedonia, Thrace*. 3 vols. BZNW 181. Berlin: de Gruyter, 2011. = **GRA I**

Kloppenborg, John S., and Stephen G. Wilson, eds. *Voluntary Associations in the Graeco-Roman World*. London: Routledge, 1996.

Koester, Helmut. "The Purpose of the Polemic of a Pauline Fragment (Philippians III)." *NTS* 8 (1961–62) 317–32.

Kolb, Anne. "Vereine 'kleiner Leute' und die kaiserliche Verwaltung." *ZPE* 107 (1995) 201–12.

Koukouli-Chrysantaki, Chaido. "Colonia Iulia Augusta Philippensis." In *Philippi at the Time of Paul and after His Death*, edited by by Charalambos Bakirtzis and Helmut Koester, 5–35. Harrisburg, PA: Trinity, 1998.

Kraabel, A. Thomas. "The Diaspora Synagogue: Archaeological and Epigraphic Evidence Since Sukenik." In *Ancient Synagogues: Historical Analysis and Archaeological Discovery*, edited by Dan Urman and Paul V. M. Flesher, 1:95–126. 2 vols. StPB 47. Leiden: Brill, 1995.

———. "Paganism and Judaism: The Sardis Evidence." In *Diaspora Jews and Judaism: Essays in Honor of, and in Dialogue with, A. Thomas Kraabel*, edited by J. Andrew Overman and Robert S. MacLennan, 237–55. South Florida Studies in the History of Judaism 41. Atlanta: Scholars, 1992.

Kreitzer, L. Joseph. *Jesus and God in Paul's Eschatology*. JSNTSup 19. Sheffield: Sheffield Academic, 1987.

Krentz, Edgar. "Community and Character: Matthew's Vision of the Church." In *SBL 1987 Seminar Papers*, edited by Kent H. Richards, 565–73. SBLSP 26. Atlanta: Scholars, 1987.

Labarre, Guy, and M.-Th. Le Dinahet. "Le métiers du textile in Asie Mineure de l'époque hellénistique a l'époque impériale." In *Aspects de l'artisanat du textile dans le monde méditerranée (Égypte, Grèce, Monde romain)*, 49–115. Collection de l'Institut d'archéologie et d'histoire de l'antiquité 2. Paris: Boccard, 1996.

Lake, Kirsopp. "The Communism of Acts II. and IV–VI and the Appointment of the Seven." In *The Acts of the Apostles*, edited by F. J. Foakes Jackson and Kirsopp Lake, 5:14–151. 5 vols. Additional notes to the commentary, edited by Kirsopp Lake and H. J. Cadbury. The Beginnings of Christianity. Part 1. London: Macmillan, 1922.

Lambert, Stephen D. "*IG* II² 2345, Thiasoi of Herakles and the Salaminioi Again." *ZPE* 125 (1999) 93–130.
Lambrecht, Jan. "A Call to Witness by All: Evangelisation in 1 Thessalonians." In *Teologie in Konteks*, edited by J. H. Roberts, W. S. Vorster, J. N. Vorster, and J. G. van der Watt, 343–61. Pretoria: Orion, 1991.
Lampe, Peter. "Das korinthische Herrenmahl im Schnittpunkt hellenistisch-römischer Mahlpraxis und paulinischer Theologia Crucis (I Kor 11, 17–34)." *ZNW* 82 (1991) 183–213.
La Piana, George. "Foreign Groups in Rome during the First Century of the Empire." *HTR* 20 (1927) 183–403.
Last, Richard. "Communities That Write: Christ-Groups, Associations, and Gospel Communities." *NTS* 58 (2012) 173–98.
———. *The Pauline Church and the Corinthian Ekklēsia: Greco-Roman Associations in Comparative Context*. SNTSMS 164. Cambridge: Cambridge University Press, 2016.
Last, Richard, and Philip A. Harland. *Group Survival in the Ancient Mediterranean: Rethinking Material Conditions in the Landscape of Jews and Christians*. London: T. & T. Clark, 2020.
Lattimore, Richmond. *Themes in Greek and Latin Epitaphs*. Illinois Studies in Language and Literature. Urbana: University of Illinois Press, 1942.
Laub, Franz. "Paulus als Gemeindegründer (1 Thess)." In *Kirche im Werden: Studien zum Thema Amt und Gemeinde im Neuen Testament*, edited by Josef Hainz, 17–38. Munich: Schöningh, 1976.
LaVerdiere, E. A., and William G. Thompson. "New Testament Communities in Transition: A Study of Matthew and Luke." *TS* 37 (1976) 567–97.
Leiwo, Martti. "Religion, or Other Reasons? Private Associations in Athens." In *Early Hellenistic Athens: Symptoms of Change*, edited by Jaakko Frösén, 103–17. Papers and Monographs of the Finnish Institute at Athens. Helsinki: Finish Institute at Athens, 1997.
Lemerle, Paul. "Inscriptions latines et grecques de Philippes." *BCH* 59 (1935) 126–65.
Leon, Harry J. *The Jews of Ancient Rome*. Updated ed, with a new introduction by Carolyn Osiek. Peabody, MA: Hendrickson, 1995.
Levey, I. M. "Caesarea and the Jews." In *The Joint Expedition to Caesarea Maritima*. Vol. 1, *Studies in the History of Caesarea Maritima*, edited by Charles T. Fritsch, 43–78. BASORSup 19. Missoula, MT: Scholars, 1975.
Levine, Lee I. *The Ancient Synagogue: The First Thousand Years*. New Haven: Yale University Press, 2000.
———. *Caesarea under Roman Rule*. SJLA 7. Leiden: Brill, 1975.
———. "The First-Century Synagogue: New Perspectives." *STK* 77 (2001) 22–30.
Levinskaya, Irina. *The Book of Acts in Its Diaspora Setting*. The Book of Acts in Its First Century Setting 1. Grand Rapids: Eerdmans, 1996.
Liebenam, W. *Zur Geschichte und organisation des römischen Vereinswesens: Drei Untersuchungen*. Leipzig: Teubner, 1890.
Lietzmann, Hans. "Zur altchristlichen Verfassungsgeschichte." *ZWT* 55 (1914) 97–153.
———. *An die Korinther I/11*. 5th ed, revised by Werner Georg Kümmel. HNT 9. Tübingen: Mohr Siebeck, 1969.
Lightfoot, J. B. *Biblical Essays*. London: Macmillan, 1893. Reprint, Peabody, MA: Hendrickson, MA, 1994.

———. *Saint Paul's Epistle to the Philippians*. 6th ed. London: Macmillan, 1881.
Ligt, Luuk de. "Governmental Attitudes Towards Markets and Collegia." In *Mercati permanenti emercati periodici nel mondo romano: Atti degli incontri capresi di storia dell'economiaantica, Capri 13-15 ottobre 1997*, edited by Elio Lo Cascio, 237-52. Bari, Italy: Edipuglia, 2000.
———. "D. 47,22,1,pr.-1 and the Formation of Semi-Public Collegia." *Latomus* 60 (2001) 345-58.
Lincoln, Bruce. *Discourse and the Construction of Society: Comparative Studies of Myth, Ritual, and Classification*. Oxford: Oxford University Press, 1989.
Linderski, J. "Religious Communities." Review of Belayche and Mimouni, *Les communautés religieuses*. *Classical Review* 55 (2005) 651-52.
Liu, Jinyu. Collegia Centonariorum: *The Guilds of Textile Dealers in the Roman West*. CSCT. Leiden: Brill, 2009.
———. "Occupation, Social Organization, and Public Service in the *collegia centonariorum* in the Roman Empire (First Century BC—Fourth Century AD)." PhD diss., Columbia University, 2004.
Loening, Edgar. *Die Gemeindeverfassung des urchristentums: Eine Kirchenrechtliche Untersuchung*. Halle: Niemeyer, 1888.
Lohse, E. "συνέδριον." In *TDNT* 7:860-71.
Lolos, Yannis. "Via Egnatia after Egnatius: Imperial Policy and Inter-regional Contacts." In *Greek and Roman Networks in the Mediterranean*, edited by Irad Malkin, Christy Constantakopoulou, and Katerina Panagopoulou, 264-84. London: Routledge, 2009.
Lopez, Davina C. *Apostle to the Conquered: Reimagining Paul's Mission*. Paul in Critical Contexts. Minneapolis: Fortress, 2008.
Lüdemann, Gerd. *Early Christianity according to the Traditions in Acts: A Commentary*. Translated by John Bowden. Minneapolis: Fortress, 1987.
Lührmann, Dieter. "The Beginnings of the Church at Thessalonica." In *Greeks, Romans, and Christians: Essays in Honor of Abraham J. Malherbe*, edited by David L. Balch, Everett Ferguson, and Wayne A. Meeks, 237-49. Minneapolis: Fortress, 1990.
Luz, Ulrich. *The Theology of the Gospel of Matthew*. Translated by J. Bradford Robinson. New Testament Theology. Cambridge: Cambridge University Press, 1995.
Lyons, George. *Pauline Autobiography: Towards a New Understanding*. SBLDS 73. Atlanta: Scholars, 1985.
Mack, Burton L. *The Christian Myth: Origins, Logic, and Legacy*. New York: Continuum, 2001.
———. *Who Wrote the New Testament? The Making of the Christian Myth*. San Francisco: HarperSanFrancisco, 1995.
MacMullen, Ramsay. *Enemies of the Roman Order: Treason, Unrest, and Alienation in the Empire*. London: Routledge, 1966. Reprint, 1992.
———. "A Note on Roman Strikes." *CJ* 58 (1963) 269-71.
———. *Paganism in the Roman Empire*. New Haven: Yale University Press, 1981.
———. *Roman Social Relations 50 B.C. to A.D. 284*. New Haven: Yale University Press, 1974.
MacMullen, Ramsay, and Eugene N. Lane, eds. *Paganism and Christianity, 100-425 CE: A Sourcebook*. Minneapolis: Fortress, 1992.

Malherbe, Abraham J. "Did the Thessalonians Write to Paul?" In *The Conversation Continues: Studies in Paul & John in Honor of J. Louis Martyn*, edited by Robert T. Fortna and Beverly Roberts Gaventa, 246–57. Nashville: Abingdon, 1990.

———. *Paul and the Thessalonians: The Philosophic Tradition of Pastoral Care*. Philadelphia: Fortress, 1987. Reprint, Eugene, OR: Wipf & Stock, 2011.

———. *Social Aspects of Early Christianity*. 2nd, enlarged ed. Philadelphia: Fortress, 1983.

Malina, Bruce J. "Early Christian Groups: Using Small Group Formation Theory to Explain Christian Organizations." In *Modelling Early Christianity: Social-Scientific Studies of the New Testament in its Context*, edited by Philip F. Esler, 96–113. London: Routledge, 1995.

Malina, Bruce J., and Jerome H. Neyrey. *Portraits of Paul: An Archaeology of Ancient Personality*. Louisville: Westminster John Knox, 1996.

Malina, Bruce J., and John J. Pilch. *Social-Science Commentary on the Book of Acts*. Minneapolis: Fortress, 2008.

———. *Social-Science Commentary on the Letters of Paul*. Minneapolis: Fortress, 2006.

Malina, Bruce J., and Richard L. Rohrbaugh. *Social-Science Commentary on the Synoptic Gospels*. Minneapolis: Fortress, 1992.

———. *Social-Science Commentary on the Synoptic Gospels*. 2nd ed. Minneapolis: Fortress, 2003.

Malkin, Irad, Christy Constantakopoulou, and Katerina Panagopoulou. "Introduction." In *Greek and Roman Networks in the Mediterranean*, edited by Irad Malkin, Christy Constantakopoulou, and Katerina Panagopoulou, 1–11. London: Routledge, 2009.

Mantel, Hugo. "The Nature of the Great Synagogue." *HTR* 60 (1967) 69–91.

Marguerat, Daniel. "La mort d'Ananias et Saphira (Ac 5.1–11) dans la stratégie narrative de Luc." *NTS* 39 (1993) 209–26.

Marshall, I. Howard. *The Acts of the Apostles: An Introduction and Commentary*. TNTC. Grand Rapids: Eerdmans, 1980.

———. *1 and 2 Thessalonians*. NCB. Grand Rapids: Eerdmans, 1983.

Marshall, Peter. *Enmity in Corinth: Social Conventions in Paul's Relations with the Corinthians*. WUNT 2/23. Tübingen: Mohr Siebeck, 1987.

Martin, Dale B. *The Corinthian Body*. New Haven: Yale University Press, 1995.

———. "Paul without Passion: On Paul's Rejection of Desire in Sex and Marriage." In *Constructing Early Christian Families: Family as Social Reality and Metaphor*, edited by Halvor Moxnes, 201–15. London: Routledge, 1997.

Marxsen, Willi. *Der erste Brief an die Thessalonicher*. ZBK NT 11/1. Zurich: Theologischer Verlag, 1979.

Masson, Charles. *Les Deux Épîtres de Saint Paul aux Thessaloniciens*. CNT 11a. Paris: Delachaux & Niestle, 1957.

Masuzawa, Tomoko. *The Invention of World Religions: Or, How European Universalism Was Preserved in the Language of Pluralism*. Chicago: University of Chicago Press, 2005.

Matson, David Lertis. *Household Conversion Narratives in Acts: Pattern and Interpretation*. JSNTSup 123. Sheffield: Sheffield Academic, 1996.

Maurer, C. "σκεῦος." In *TDNT* 7:359–67.

McCready, Wayne O. "Ekklēsia and Voluntary Associations." In *Voluntary Associations in the Graeco-Roman World*, edited by John S. Kloppenborg and Stephen G. Wilson, 59–73. London: Routledge, 1996.

McGehee, Michael. "A Rejoinder to Two Recent Studies Dealing with 1 Thessalonians 4:4." *CBQ* 51 (1989) 82-89.

McKnight, Scot. *A Light among the Gentiles: Jewish Missionary Activity in the Second Temple Period*. Minneapolis: Fortress, 1991.

McLean, Bradley H. "The Agrippinilla Inscription: Religious Associations and Early Church Formation." In *Origins and Method: Towards a New Understanding of Judaism and Christianity; Essays in Honour of John C. Hurd*, edited by Bradley H. McLean, 239-70. JSNTSup 86. Sheffield: JSOT Press, 1993.

———. "For the Love of Dionysos: Five Forms of Dionysias Devotion." Unpublished paper, 1995.

———. *An Introduction to Greek Epigraphy of the Hellenistic and Roman Periods from Alexander the Great down to the Reign of Constantine (323 B.C.–A.D. 337)*. Ann Arbor: University of Michigan Press, 2002.

———. "The Place of Cult in Voluntary Associations and Christian Churches on Delos." In *Voluntary Associations in the Graeco-Roman World*, edited by John S. Kloppenborg and Stephen G. Wilson, 186-225. London: Routledge, 1996.

———. "Trade Guilds of Lydia and Phrygia." Unpublished paper, 1995.

Meeks, Wayne A. *The First Urban Christians: The Social World of the Apostle Paul*. New Haven: Yale University Press, 1983.

———. *The First Urban Christians: The Social World of the Apostle Paul*. 2nd ed. New Haven: Yale University Press, 2003.

———. *The Moral World of the First Christians*. LEC 6. Philadelphia: Westminster John Knox, 1986.

———. "Social Functions of Apocalyptic Language in Pauline Christianity." In *Apocalypticism in the Mediterranean World and the Near East: Proceedings of the International Colloquium on Apocalypticism, Uppsala, August 12-17, 1979*, edited by David Hellholm, 687-705. Tübingen: Mohr Siebeck, 1983.

———. "Taking Stock and Moving On." In *After the First Urban Christians: The Social-Scientific Study of Pauline Christianity Twenty-Five Years Later*, edited by Todd D. Still and David G. Horrell, 134-46. London: T. & T. Clark, 2009.

Meiggs, Russell. *Roman Ostia*. 2nd ed. Oxford: Clarendon, 1960.

Mendelsohn, I. "Guilds in Ancient Palestine." *BASOR* 80/4 (1940) 17-21.

———. "Guilds in Babylonia and Assyria." *JAOS* 60 (1940) 68-72.

Menken, Maarten J. J. *2 Thessalonians*. New Testament Readings. London: Routledge, 1994.

Merkelbach, Reinhold. *Die Hirten des Dionysos: Die Dionysos-Mysterien der römischen Kaiserzeit und der bukolische Roman des Longus*. Stuttgart:. Teubner, 1988.

Metzger, Bruce M. *A Textual Commentary on the Greek New Testament*. London: United Bible Societies, 1971.

Meyer, Elizabeth A. "Explaining the Epigraphic Habit in the Roman Empire: The Evidence of Epitaphs." *JRS* 80 (1990) 74-96.

Meyer, Marvin W., ed. *The Ancient Mysteries: A Sourcebook*. New York: Harper & Row, 1987.

Mihailov, Gorgi. "Deux inscriptions de la province romaine de Macédoine." In *Ancient Macedonian Studies in Honor of Charles F. Edson*, edited by Harry J. Dell, 259-62. Thessaloniki: Institute for Balkan Studies, 1981.

Milligan, George. *St. Paul's Epistles to the Thessalonians: The Greek Text with Introduction and Notes*. London: Macmillan, 1908. Reprint, Eugene, OR: Wipf & Stock, 2005.

Milner, Vincent L. *Religious Denominations of the World*. Philadelphia: Bradley, Garretson, 1872.
Mommsen, Theodor. *De collegiis et sodaliciis Romanorum. Accedit inscriptio lanuvina*. Kiel: Libraria Schwersiana, 1843.
Morris, Leon. *The First and Second Epistles to the Thessalonians*. NICNT. Grand Rapids: Eerdmans, 1959.
———. *The Gospel according to Matthew*. Grand Rapids: Eerdmans, 1992.
Moulton, J. H., and G. Milligan. *The Vocabulary of the Greek New Testament Illustrated from the Papyri and Other Non-literary Sources*. London: Hodder & Stoughton, 1914.
Moxnes, Halvor. "Patron-Client Relations and the New Community in Luke–Acts. In *The Social World of Luke–Acts: Models for Interpretation*, edited by Jerome H. Neyrey, 241–68. Peabody, MA: Hendrickson.
Munck, Johannes. *The Acts of the Apostles: A New Translation with Introduction and Commentary*. Revised by William F. Albright and C. S. Mann Garden City, NY: Doubleday, 1967.
Murphy-O'Connor, Jerome. *Paul: A Critical Life*. Oxford: Clarendon, 1996.
Murray, Timothy J. *Restricted Generosity in the New Testament*. WUNT 2/480. Tübingen: Mohr Siebeck, 2018.
Musurillo, Herbert Anthony, ed. *The Acts of the Christian Martyrs*. OECT. Oxford: Oxford University Press, 1972.
Nanos, Mark D. *The Irony of Galatians: Paul's Letter in First-Century Context*. Minneapolis: Fortress, 2002.
———. *The Mystery of Romans: The Jewish Context of Paul's Letter*. Minneapolis: Fortress, 1996.
Nehama, Joseph. *Histoire des Israélites de Salonique*. Vol. 1, *La Communaute Romaniote—Les Sefaradis et leur Dispersion*. 5 vols. Thessalonica: Molho, 1935.
Neil, William. *The Acts of the Apostles*. NCB. Grand Rapids: Eerdmans, 1973.
———. *The Epistle of Paul to the Thessalonians*. MNTC. London: Hodder & Stoughton, 1950.
Neill, Stephen. "Christian Missions." *Encyclopedia of Religion*, edited by Mircea Eliade et al., 9:573–75. 16 vols. New York: Macmillan, 1987.
Nielsen, Inge. *Housing the Chosen: The Architectural Context of Mystery Groups and Religious Associations in the Ancient World*. Contextualizing the Sacred. Turnhout, Belgium: Brepols, 2014.
Neumann, K. J. *Der römische Staat und die allgemeine Kirche bis auf Diocletian*. ATLA Monograph Preservation Program. Leipzig: Veit, 1890.
Neyrey, Jerome H. "Ceremonies in Luke–Acts: The Case of Meals and Table Fellowship." In *The Social World of Luke–Acts: Models for Interpretation*, edited by Jerome H. Neyrey, 361–87. Peabody, MA: Hendrickson, 1991.
Nicholl, Colin R. *From Hope to Despair in Thessalonica: Situating 1 and 2 Thessalonians*. SNTSMS 126. Cambridge: Cambridge University Press, 2004.
Nigdelis, Pantelis M. Επιγραφικά Θεσσαλονίκεια. Συμβολή στην πολιτική και κοινωνική ιστορία της αρχαίας Θεσσαλονίκης. Thessaloniki: University Studio, 2006.
———. "Voluntary Associations in Roman Thessalonikē: In Search of Identity and Support in a Cosmopolitan Society." In *From Roman to Early Christian Thessalonikē: Studies in Religion and Archaeology*, edited by Laura Nasrallah,

Charalambos Bakirtzis, and Steven J. Friesen, 13-47. HTS 64. Cambridge: Harvard University Press, 2010.

Nijf, Onno M. van. *The Civic World of Professional Associations in the Roman East*. Dutch Monographs on Ancient History and Archaeology 17. Amsterdam: Gieben, 1997.

———. "Collegia and Civic Guards. Two Chapters in the History of Sociability." In *After the Past: Essays in Ancient History in Honour of H. W. Pleket*, edited by Willem Jongman and Marc Kleijwegt, 305-40. Mnemosyne Supplement 233. Leiden: Brill, 2000.

Nilsson, Martin P. "The Bacchic Mysteries of the Roman Age." *HTR* 46 (1953) 175-202.

———. *The Dionysiac Mysteries of the Hellenistic and Roman Age*. Ancient Religion and Mythology. Lund: Gleerup, 1957.

Nock, A. D. *Conversion: The Old and the New in Religion from Alexander the Great to Augustine of Hippo*. Oxford: Oxford University Press, 1933.

———. "The Historical Importance of Cult Associations." *Classical Review* 38 (1924) 105-9.

North, John A. "Réflexions autour des communautés religieuses du monde gréco-romain." In *Les communautés religieuses dans le monde Gréco-Romain: Essais de définition*, edited by N. Belayche and S. C. Mimouni, 337-47. Bibliothèque de l'École des Hautes Études sciences religieuses 117. Turnhout, Belgium: Brepols, 2003.

Northcut, Kathryn. "Unexpected Ceremony: Epideictic Rhetoric in Paleornithology Discourse." Unpublished paper presented at for 2003 Hawaii International Conference on Arts and Humanities, Honolulu, January 12-13, 2003.

Neufeld, Dietmar. "Christian Communities in Sardis and Smyrna." In *Religious Rivalries and the Struggle for Success in Sardis and Smyrna*, edited by Richard S. Ascough, 25-39. Studies in Christianity and Judaism 14. Waterloo, ON: Wilfrid Laurier University Press, 2005.

Oates, J. F., R. S. Bagnall, and W. H. Willis. *Checklist of Editions of Greek and Latin Papyri, Ostraca and Tablets*. 5th ed. BASPSupp 9. Oakville, CT: American Society of Papyrologists, 2001.

O'Brien, Peter T. *The Epistle to the Philippians: A Commentary on the Greek Text*. NIGTC. Grand Rapids: Eerdmans, 1991.

Öhler, Markus. "Antikes Vereinswesen." In *Neues Testament und Antike Kultur*, vol. 2, *Familie, Gesellschaft, Wirtschaft*, edited by K. Scherberich, 79-86. 5 vols. Neukirchen-Vluyn: Neukirchener, 2005.

———, ed. *Aposteldekret und antikes Vereinswesen: Gemeinschaft und ihre Ordnung*. WUNT 280. Tübingen: Mohr Siebeck, 2011.

———. "Graeco-Roman Associations, Judean Synagogues, and Early Christianity in Bithynia-Pontus." In *Authority and Identity in Emerging Christianities in Asia Minor and Greece*, edited by Cilliers Breytenbach and Julien Ogereau, 62-88. AJEC 103. Leiden: Brill, 2018.

———. "Die Jerusalemer Urgemeinde im Spiegel des antiken Vereinswesens." *NTS* 51 (2005) 393-415.

———. "Römisches Vereinsrecht und Christliche Gemeinden." In *Zwischen den Reichen: Neues Testament und Römische Herrschaft: Vortrage auf der Ersten Konferenz der European Association for Biblical Studies*, edited by M. Labahn and J. Zangenberg, 51-71. TANZ 36. Basel: Francke, 2002.

O'Toole, Robert F. "'You Did not Lie to Us (Human Beings) but to God' (Acts 5,4c)." *Bib* 76 (1995) 182–209.
Overman J. Andrew. *Church and Community in Crisis: The Gospel according to Matthew*. The New Testament Context. Valley Forge, PA: Trinity, 1996.
Pandermalis, D. "Monuments and Art in the Roman Period." In *Macedonia: 4000 Years of Greek History and Civilization*, edited by M. B. Sakellariou, 208–21. Historikoi Hellēnikoi chōroi. English. Athens: Athenon, 1988.
Papazoglou, Fanoula. "Macedonia under the Romans." In *Macedonia: 4000 Years of Greek History and Civilization*, edited by M. B. Sakellariou, 192–207. Hellēnikoi chōroi. English. Athens: Athenon, 1988.
Paton, W. R. *The Greek Anthology*. LCL. Cambridge: Harvard University Press, 1916–1918.
Patte, Daniel. *The Gospel according to Matthew: A Structural Commentary on Matthew's Faith*. Philadelphia: Fortress, 1987.
Patterson, John R. "The Collegia and the Transformation of the Towns of Italy in the Second Century AD." In *L'Italie d'Auguste à Dioclétien*, 227–38. Collection de l'École française de Rome 198. Rome: École française de Rome, 1994.
———. "Patronage, Collegia and Burial in Imperial Rome." In *Death in Towns: Urban Responses to the Dying and the Dead, 100–1600*, edited by Steven Bassett, 15–27. Leicester: Leicester University Press, 1992.
Pearson, B. A. "1 Thessalonians 2:13–16: A Deutero-Pauline Interpolation." *HTR* (1971) 79–94.
Peerbolte, L. J. Lietaert. *Paul the Missionary*. CBET 34. Leuven: Peeters, 2003.
———. "Romans 15:14–29 and Paul's Missionary Agenda." In *Persuasion and Dissuasion in Early Christianity, Ancient Judaism, and Hellenism*, edited by Pieter W. van der Horst, Maarten J. J. Menken, Joop F. M. Smit, and Geert van Oyen, 143–59. CBET 33. Leuven: Peeters, 2003.
Pelekanidis, Stylianos. "Kultproblemeim Apostel-Paulus Octagonon von Philippi im Zusammenhang mit einem älteren Heroenkult." In *Atti del IX Congresso Internazionale di Archeologia Cristiana, Roma 21–27 Settembre 1975*, 2:393–97. 2 vols. Studi di Antichità Cristiana 32. Vatican City: Pontificio Istituto di Archeologia Cristiana, 1978.
Perdrizet, Paul. "Inscriptions de Philippes: Les Rosalies." *BCH* 24 (1900) 299–333.
Perelman, Chaïm, and Lucie Olbrechts-Tyteca. *The New Rhetoric: A Treatise on Argumentation*. Translated by John Wilkinson and Purcell Weaver. Notre Dame, IN: University of Notre Dame Press, 1971.
Perkins, Pheme. "1 Thessalonians and Hellenistic Religious Practices." In *To Touch the Text: Biblical and Related Studies in Honor of Joseph A. Fitzmyer, SJ*, edited by Maurya P. Horgan and Paul J. Kobelski, 509–20. New York: Crossroad, 1989.
———. "Matthew 28:16–20, Resurrection, Ecclesiology and Mission." In *SBL 1993 Seminar Papers*, edited by Eugene H. Lovering, 574–88. SBLSP 32. Atlanta: Scholars, 1993.
Perry, Jonathan S. "A Death in the *Familia*: The Funerary Colleges of the Roman Empire." PhD diss., University of North Carolina at Chapel Hill, 1999.
———. *The Roman* Collegia: *The Modern Evolution of an Ancient Concept*. Mnemosyne Supplements / History and Archaeology of Classical Antiquity 277. Leiden: Brill, 2006.
Pesch, Rudolf. *Die Apostelgeschichte*. 2 vols. EKK 5. Zurich: Benzinger, 1986.

Peterlin, Davorin. *Paul's Letter to the Philippians in the Light of Disunity in the Church.* NovTSup 79. Leiden: Brill, 1995.

Phillips, C. Robert. "Rosalia or Rosaria." In *Oxford Classical Dictionary*, edited by Simon Hornblower and Antony Spawforth, 1335. 3rd ed. Oxford: Oxford University Press, 1996.

Picard, Charles, and Charles Avezou. "Le testament de la prêtresse Thessalonicienne." *BCH* 38 (1914) 53–62.

Piccottini, Gernot. *Mithrastempel in Virunum.* Aus Forschung und Kunst 28. Klagenfurt: Geschichtsvereines für Kärnten, 1994.

Pickard-Cambridge, Arthur W. *The Dramatic Festivals of Athens.* 2nd ed. Revised by John Gould and D. M. Lewis. Oxford: Clarendon, 1968.

Pilhofer, Peter. *Die frühen Christen und ihre Welt: Greifswalder Aufsätze 1996–2001.* WUNT 145. Tübingen: Mohr Siebeck, 2002.

———. *Philippi.* Vol. 1, *Die erste christliche Gemeinde Europas.* WUNT 87. Tübingen: Mohr Siebeck, 1995.

———. *Philippi.* Vol. 2, *Katalog der Inschriften von Philippi.* WUNT 119. Tübingen: Mohr Siebeck, 2001.

Plummer, Alfred. *A Commentary on St. Paul's First Epistle to the Thessalonians.* London: Roxburghe, 1918.

———. *A Commentary on St. Paul's Second Epistle to the Thessalonians.* London: Roxburghe, 1918. Reprint, Eugene, OR: Wipf & Stock, 2001.

———. *An Exegetical Commentary on The Gospel according to St. Matthew.* London: Elliot Stock, 1915. Reprint, Thornapple Commentaries. Grand Rapids: Baker, 1982.

Plummer, Robert L. *Paul's Understanding of the Church's Mission: Did the Apostle Paul Expect the Early Christian Communities to Evangelize?* Paternoster Biblical Monographs. Milton Keynes, UK: Paternoster, 2006.

Poland, Franz. *Geschichte des griechischen Vereinswesens.* Leipzig: Teubner, 1909.

Pomeroy, Sarah B. *Goddesses, Whores, Wives, and Slaves: Women in Classical Antiquity.* New York: Schocken, 1975.

Poole, Fitz John Porter. "Metaphors and Maps: Towards Comparison in the Anthropology of Religion." *JAAR* 54 (1986) 411–57.

Psoma, Selene. "Profitable Networks: Coinages, Panegyris and Dionysiac Artists." In *Greek and Roman Networks in the Mediterranean*, edited by Irad Malkin, Christy Constantakopoulou, and Katerina Panagopoulou, 230–48. London: Routledge, 2009.

Purcell, Nocolas. Review of *The Magistrates of the Roman Professional Collegia in Italy from the First to the Third Century A.D.*, by Halsey L. Royden. *CP* 87/2(1992) 178–82.

Rackham, Richard Belward. *The Acts of the Apostles: An Exposition.* London: Methuen, 1901.

Radin, Max. *Legislation of the Greeks and Romans on Corporations.* New York: Tuttle, Morehouse & Taylor, 1910.

Radt, Wolfgang. *Pergamon: Geschichte und Bauten einer antiken Metropole.* Darmstadt: Primus, 1999.

Rajak, Tessa. "Synagogue and Community in the Graeco-Roman Diaspora." In *Jews in the Hellenistic and Roman Cities*, edited by John R. Barlett, 22–38. London: Routledge, 2002.

---. "The Synagogue within the Graeco-Roman City." In *Jews, Christians and Polytheists in the Ancient Synagogue: Cultural Interaction during the Graeco-Roman Period*, edited by Steven Fine, 161-73. Baltimore Studies in the History of Judaism. London: Routledge, 1999.

---. "Was There a Roman Charter for the Jews?" *JRS* 74 (1984) 107-23.

Rathbone, Dominic. "Merchant Networks in the Greek World: The Impact of Rome." In *Greek and Roman Networks in the Mediterranean*, edited by Irad Malkin, Christy Constantakopoulou, and Katerina Panagopoulou, 299-310. London: Routledge, 2009.

Rauh, Nicholas K. *The Sacred Bonds of Commerce: Religion, Economy, and Trade Society at Hellenistic Roman Delos*. Amsterdam: Gieben, 1993.

Rebillard, Éric. *The Care of the Dead in Late Antiquity*. Cornell Studies in Classical Philology. Ithaca, NY: Cornell University Press, 2009.

Reese, James M. *1 and 2 Thessalonians*. New Testament Message 16. Wilmington, DE: Glazier, 1979.

Reicke, Bo. "Constitution of the Primitive Church." In *The Scrolls and the New Testament*, edited by Kirster Stehdahl, 143-56. New York: Harper, 1957.

---. *Diakonie, Festfreude, und Zelos in Verbindung mit der altchristlichen Agapenfeier*. Uppsala Universitets Årsskrift 1951, 5. Uppsala: Lundequist, 1951.

---. "Thessalonicherbriefe." In *Religion in Geschichte und Gegenwart*, edited by Kurt Galling, vol. 6, cols. 851-53. 3rd ed. Tübingen: Mohr Siebeck, 1962.

Reinmuth, Eckart. "Der erste Brief an die Thessalonicher." In *Die Briefe an die Philipper, Thessalonicher und an Philemon*, edited by Nikolaus Walter, Eckart Reinmuth, and Peter Lampe, 102-202. NTD 8/2. Göttingen: Vandenhoeck & Ruprecht, 1998.

Renan, Ernest. *The Apostles: Including the Period from the Death of Jesus until the Greater Mission of Paul*. Translated by Joseph Henry Allen. London: Watts, 1905.

Reumann, John. "Church Office in Paul, Especially in Philippians." In *Origins and Method: Towards a New Understanding of Judaism and Christianity; Essays in Honour of John C. Hurd*, edited by Bradley H. McLean, 82-91. JSNTSup 86. Sheffield: JSOT Press, 1993.

---. "Contributions of the Philippian Community to Paul and to Earliest Christianity." *NTS* 39 (1993) 438-57.

Rhomiopoulou, Katerina. "New Inscriptions in the Archaeological Museum, Thessaloniki." In *Ancient Macedonian Studies in Honor of Charles F. Edson*, edited by Harry J. Dell, 299-305. Thessaloniki: Institute for Balkan Studies, 1981.

Richard, Earl J. *First and Second Thessalonians*. SP 11. Collegeville, MN: Liturgical, 1995.

Richardson, Peter. "Building 'an Association (*Synodos*) . . . and a Place of Their Own.'" In *Community Formation in the Early Church and in the Church Today*, edited by Richard N. Longenecker, 36-56. Peabody, MA: Hendrickson, 2002.

---. *Building Jewish in the Roman East*. Waco, TX: Baylor University Press, 2004.

---. "Early Synagogues as Collegia in the Diaspora and Palestine." In *Voluntary Associations in the Graeco-Roman World*, edited by John S. Kloppenborg and Stephen G. Wilson, 90-109. London: Routledge, 1996.

Rigaux, Béda. *Saint Paul: les épîtres aux Thessaloniciens*. EBib. Paris: Lecoffre, 1956.

Rives, James B. "Epigraphic Evidence: Civic and Religious Life." In *Epigraphic Evidence: Ancient History from Inscriptions*, edited by John Bodel, 118-36. Approaching the Ancient World. London: Routledge, 2001.

———. *Religion in the Roman Empire*. Blackwell Ancient Religions. Oxford: Blackwell, 2007.

Robert, Louis. "Une nouvelle inscription grecque de Sardes: Reglement de l'autorite perse relatif a un culte de Zeus." *Comptes rendus de l'Académie des inscriptions et belles-lettres* 119 (1975) 306–30.

Roberts, Colin, T. C. Skeat, and Arthur Darby Nock. "The Guild of Zeus Hypsistos." *HTR* 29 (1936) 39–88.

Robinson, David M. "Inscriptions from Macedonia." *Transactions of the American Philological Association* 69 (1938) 43–76.

Rohde, Joachim. *Urchristliche und frühkatholische Ämter: Eine Untersuchung zur früchristlichen Amtsentwicklung im Neuen Testament und bei den apostolischen Vätern*. Theologische Arbeiten 33. Berlin: Evangelische Verlagsanstalt, 1976.

Rose, Herbert J. "Feralia." In *Oxford Classical Dictionary*, edited by Nicholas Hammond, 434. 2nd ed. Oxford: Oxford University Press, 1970.

———. "Parentalia." In *Oxford Classical Dictionary*, edited by Nicholas Hammond, 781. 2nd ed. Oxford: Oxford University Press, 1970.

Rossi, Giovanni Battista de. *La Roma sotterranea cristiana*. 4 vols. Rome: Cromolitografia Pontificia, 1864–77.

Roth, Roman. *Styling Romanisation: Pottery and Society in Central Italy*. Cambridge Classical Studies. Cambridge: Cambridge University Press, 2007.

Rowlandson, Jane, and Roger S. Bagnall. *Women and Society in Greek and Roman Egypt*. Cambridge: Cambridge University Prqqess, 1998.

Royden, Halsey L. *The Magistrates of the Roman Professional Collegia in Italy from the First to the Third Century A.D.* Biblioteca di studi antichi 61. Pisa: Giardini, 1988.

Runesson, Anders. *The Origins of the Synagogue: A Socio-Historical Study*. ConBNT 37. Stockholm: Almquest & Wiksell, 2001.

———. "The Origins of the Synagogue in Past and Present Research—Some Comments on Definitions, Theories, and Sources." *ST* 58 (2003) 60–76.

———. Review of *Versammlung*, by Carsten Claussen in *STK* 79 (2003) 62–63.

Rüpke, Jörg. *Religion of the Romans*. Translated and edited by Richard Gordon. Cambridge: Polity, 2007.

Russell, Ronald. "The Idle in 2 Thess 3.6–12: An Eschatological or a Social Problem?" *NTS* 34 (1988) 105–19.

Rutgers, Leonard Victor. "Romana Policy Towards the Jews: Expulsions from the City of Rome During the First Century CE." *ClAnt* 13 (1994) 56–74.

Salač, A. "Inscriptions du Pangée de la région Drama-Cavalla et de Philippes." *BCH* 47 (1923) 49–96.

Saldarini, Anthony J. "Delegitimation of Leaders in Matthew 23." *CBQ* 54 (1992) 659–80.

———. "The Gospel of Matthew and Jewish-Christian Conflict." In *Social History of the Matthean Community: Cross-Disciplinary Approaches*, edited by David L. Balch, 38–61. Minneapolis: Fortress, 1991.

———. *Matthew's Christian-Jewish Community*. Chicago Studies in the History of Judaism. Chicago: University of Chicago Press, 1994.

———. *Pharisees, Scribes and Sadducees in Palestinian Society: A Sociological Approach*. Wilmington, DE: Glazier, 1988.

Salmon, George. "The Christian Ministry." *Expositor* (3rd ser.) 4 (1887) 2–27.

San Nicolò, Mariano. *Ägyptisches Vereinswesen zur Zeit der Ptolemäer und Römer*. 2 vols. Münchener Beiträge zur Papyrusforschung und Antiken Rechtsgeschichte. Munich: Beck, 1913-1915.

———. "Zur Vereinsgerichtsbarkeit im hellenistischen Ägypten." In ΕΠΙΤΥΜΒΙΟΝ *Heinrich Swoboda dargstellt*, 255-99. Reichenberg: Stiepel, 1927.

Sanday, W. "The Origin of Christian Ministry. II. Criticism of Recent Theories." *Expositor* (3rd ser.) 5 (1887) 97-114.

Savelle, Charles H. "A Reexamination of the Prohibitions in Acts 15." *BSac* 161 (2004) 449-68.

Scheid, John. *An Introduction to Roman Religion*. Translated by Janet Lloyd. Bloomington: Indiana University Press, 2003.

———. *Romulus et ses frères: Le collège des frères arvales: Modèle du culte public dans la Rome des empereurs*. BEFAR 275, 806. Paris: Boccard, 1990.

Schenk, Wolfgang. *Der Philipperbrief des Paulus: Kommentar*. Stuttgart: Kohlhammer, 1984.

Scherrer, Peter. *Ephesus*. Istanbul: Österreichisches Archäologisches Institut, 2000.

Schmeller, Thomas. *Hierarchie und Egalität: Eine sozialgeschichtliche Untersuchung paulinischer Gemeinden und griechisch-römischer Vereine*. SBS 162. Stuttgart: Katholisches Bibelwerk, 1995.

Schmidt, Karl L. "ἐκκλησία." In *TDNT* 3:501-36.

Schmithals, Walter. *Die Apostelgeschichte des Lukas*. ZBK NT 3/2. Zürich: Theologischer Verlag, 1982.

Schneider, C. "Zur Problematik des Hellenistischen in den Qumrantexten." In *Qumranprobleme, Vorträge des Leipziger Symposions über Qumranprobleme vom 9 bis 14 Oktober 1961*, edited by Hans Bardtke, 299-314. Berlin: Akademie, 1963.

Schoedel, William R. "Ignatius, Epistles of." *ABD* 3:384-87.

Schöllgen, Georg. "Hausgemeinden, oikos-Ekklesiologie, und monarchischer Episcopat." *JAC* 31 (1988) 74-90.

Schulz-Falkenthal, Heinz. "Zur politischen Aktivität der römischen Handwerkerkollegien." *Wissenschaftliche Zeitschrift der Martin-Luthers Universität. Gesellsachatliche und Sprachwissenschaftliche Reihe* 21 (1972) 79-99.

———. "Römische Handwerkerkollegien im Dienst der städtischen Gemeinschaft und ihre Begünstigung durch staatliche Privilegien." *Wissenschaftliche Zeitschrift der Martin-Luthers Universität: Gesellsachatliche und Sprachwissenschaftliche Reihe* 22 (1973) 21-35.

Schürer, Emil. *The History of the Jewish People in the Age of Jesus Christ (175 B.C.-A.D. 135): A New English Version*. Revised and edited by Geza Vermes, Fergus Millar, and Martin Goodman. 4 vols. Edinburgh: T. & T. Clark, 1986.

Schwarzer, Holger "Vereinslokale im hellenistischen und römischen Pergamon." In *Religiöse Vereine in der römischen Antike. Untersuchungen zu Organisation, Ritual und Raumordnung*, edited by Ulrike Egelhaaf-Gaiser and Alfred Schäfer, 221-60. STAC 13. Tübingen: Mohr Siebeck, 2003.

Scott, James C. *Domination and the Arts of Resistance: Hidden Transcripts*. New Haven: Yale University Press, 1990.

Scullion, Scott. "'Pilgrimage' and Greek Religion: Sacred and Secular in the Pagan Polis." In *Pilgrimage in Graeco-Roman and Early Christian Antiquity: Seeing the Gods*, edited by Jaś Elsner and Ian Rutherford, 111-30. Oxford: Oxford University Press, 2005.

Seccombe, David P. "Was There Organized Charity in Jerusalem Before the Christians?" *JTS* 29 (1978) 140–43.

Segal, Alan F. "The Jewish Experience: Temple, Synagogue, Home, and Fraternal Groups." In *Community Formation in the Early Church and in the Church Today*, edited by Richard N. Longenecker, 20–35. Peabody, MA: Hendrickson, 2002.

Seland, Torrey. "Philo and the Clubs and Associations of Alexandria." In *Voluntary Associations in the Graeco-Roman World*, edited by John S. Kloppenborg and Stephen G. Wilson, 110–27. London: Routledge, 1996.

Sellew, Philip. "Religious Propaganda in Antiquity: A Case from the Sarapeum at Thessaloniki." *Numina Aegaea* 3 (1980) 15–20.

Senior, Donald. *The Gospel of Matthew*. Interpreting Biblical Texts. Nashville: Abingdon, 1997.

———. *What Are They Saying about Matthew?* Rev. ed. Mahwah. NJ: Paulist, 1996.

Sifakis, G. M. *Studies in the History of Hellenistic Drama*. University of London Classical Studies 4. London: Athlone, 1967.

Sirks, Boudewijn. *Food for Rome: The Legal Structure of the Transportation and Processing of Supplies for the Imperial Distributions in Rome and Constantinople*. Studia Amstelodamensia ad epigraphicam, ius antiquum et papyrologicam pertinent 31. Amsterdam: Gieben, 1991.

Slater, William J. "Peace, the Symposium and the Poet." *Illinois Classical Studies* 6 (1981) 205–14.

———. Review of Scheid, *Romulus et ses Frères*. *Bryn Mawr Classical Review* 03.05.19 (1992). http://ccat.sas.upenn.edu/bmcr/1992/03.05.19.html.

———. "The Scholae of Roman Collegia." *JRA* 13 (2000) 493–97.

Smallwood, E. Mary. *The Jews under Roman Rule: From Pompey to Diocletian*. SJLA 20. Leiden: Brill, 1976.

Smit, Joop F. M. "Epideictic Rhetoric in Paul's First Letter to the Corinthians 1–4." *Bib* 84 (2003) 184–201.

Smit, Peter-Ben. "A Symposium in Rom. 14:17? A Note on Paul's Terminology." *NovT* 49 (2007) 40–53.

Smith, Dennis E. *From Symposium to Eucharist: The Banquet in the Early Christian World*. Minneapolis: Fortress, 2003.

Smith, Jonathan Z. "Classification." In *Guide to the Study of Religion*, edited by Willi Braun and Russel T. McCutcheon, 35–43. London: Cassell, 2000.

———. *Drudgery Divine: On the Comparison of Early Christianities and the Religions of Late Antiquity*. Jordan Lectures in Comparative Religion 14. Chicago Studies in the History of Judaism. Chicago: University of Chicago Press, 1990.

———. "Here, There, and Anywhere." In *Relating Religion: Essays in the Study of Religion*, 323–39. Chicago: University of Chicago Press, 2004.

———. *Imagining Religion: From Babylon to Jonestown*. Chicago Studies in the History of Judaism 1. Chicago: University of Chicago Press, 1982.

———. *Map Is not Territory: Studies in the History of Religion*. SJLA 23. Leiden: Brill, 1978.

———. *Relating Religion: Essays in the Study of Religion*. Chicago: University of Chicago Press, 2004.

———. *To Take Place: Toward a Theory in Ritual*. Chicago Studies in the History of Judaism. Chicago: University of Chicago Press, 1989.

Snyder, Graydon F. *Ante Pacem: Archaeological Evidence of Church Life before Constantine.* Macon: Mercer University Press, 1985.

Sohm, Rudolph. *Kirchenrecht.* 2 vols. Berlin: Von Duncker & Humblot, 1923.

Sokolowski, Franciszek. *Lois sacrées des cités grecques. Ecole française d'Athènes.* Travaux et mémoires 18. Paris: Boccard, 1969.

———. "Propagation of the Cult of Sarapis and Isis in Greece." *GRBS* 15 (1974) 441–48.

Sordi, Marta. *The Christians and the Roman Empire.* Translated by Annabel Bedini London: Croom Helm, 1983.

Spieser, Jean-Michel. *Thessalonique et ses monuments du IVe au VIe siècle; Contribution à l'étude d'une ville paléochrétienne.* Bibliothèque des Écoles Françaises d'Athènes et de Rome 254. Athens: École Française d'Athènes, 1984.

Spicq, C. "Les Thessaloniciens 'inquiets' étaient-ils des paresseux?" *ST* 10 (1956) 1–13.

Stambaugh, John E., and David L. Balch. *The New Testament in Its Social Environment.* LEC 2. Philadelphia: Westminster, 1986.

Stanton, Graham N. "The Communities of Matthew." *Int* 46 (1992) 379–91.

———. "The Origin and Purpose of Matthew's Gospel: Matthean Scholarship from 1945–1980." In *ANRW* II. Teilband Religion 25/3. *Vorkonstantinisches Christentum: Leben und Umwelt Jesu; Neues Testament,* edited by Wolfgang Haase, 1889–1951. Berlin: de Gruyter, 1985.

———. "Revisiting Matthew's Communities." In *SBL 1994 Seminar Papers,* edited by Eugene H. Lovering, 9–23. SBLSP 33. Atlanta: Scholars, 1994.

Stegemann, Wolfgang. "The Emergence of God's New People: The Beginnings of Christianity Reconsidered." In *Come è nato il cristianesimo?* Edited by Mauro Pesce Special issue, *Annali di storia dell'esegisi* 21/2 (2004) 76–92. https://asejournal.net/2013/05/04/ase-vol-212-2004/.

Sterling, Gregory E. "'Athletes of Virtue': An Analysis of the Summaries in Acts (2:41–47, 4:32–35; 5:12–16)." *JBL* 113 (1994) 679–96.

Still, Todd D. *Conflict at Thessalonica: A Pauline Church and Its Neighbours.* JSNTSup 183. Sheffield: Sheffield Academic, 1999.

Streeter, B. H. *The Primitive Church: Studied with Special Reference to the Origins of Christian Ministry.* Hewlett Lectures 1928. London: Macmillan, 1929.

Tačeve-Hitova, Margarita. "Dem Hypsistos geweihte Denkmäler in den Balkanländern." *Balkan Studies* 19 (1978) 59–75.

Takács, Sarolta A. *Isis and Sarapis in the Roman World.* RGRW 124. Leiden: Brill, 1995.

Talbert, Charles H. *Reading Acts: A Literary and Theological Commentary on the Acts of the Apostles.* Reading the New Testament Series. New York: Crossroad, 1997.

Tannehill, Robert C. "The Story of Israel within the Lukan Narrative." In *Jesus and the Heritage of Israel: Luke's Narrative Claim upon Israel's Legacy,* edited by David P. Moessner, 325–39. Luke the Interpreter of Israel 1. Harrisburg, PA: Trinity, 1999.

Taussig, Hal. *In the Beginning Was the Meal: Social Experimentation and Early Christian Identity.* Minneapolis: Fortress, 2009.

Taylor, Justin. "The Jerusalem Decrees (Acts 15.20, 29 and 21.25) and the Incident at Antioch (Gal 2.11–14)." *NTS* 46 (2001) 372–80.

Tellbe, Mikael. *Paul between Synagogue and State, Christians, Jews, and Civic Authorities in 1 Thessalonians, Romans, and Philippians.* ConBNT 34. Stockholm: Almqvist & Wiksell, 2001.

Thiering, Barbara E. "Mebaqqer and Episkopos in Light of the Temple Scroll." *JBL* 100 (1981) 59–74.

Thelwall, Sidney. *Tertullian*. ANF 3. Edinburgh: T. & T. Clark, 1976.
Thompson, William G. "An Historical Perspective in the Gospel of Matthew." *JBL* 93 (1974) 243–62.
———. *Matthew's Advice to a Divided Community (Mt. 17,22—18,35)*. AnBib 44. Rome: Biblical Institute Press, 1970.
———. *Matthew's Story: Good News for Uncertain Times*. Mahwah, NJ: Paulist, 1989.
Tinh, Tran Tam. "Sarapis and Isis." In *Jewish and Christian Self-Definition*. Vol. 3. *Self-Definition in the Greco-Roman World*, edited by Ben F. Meyer and E. P. Sanders, 101-17. Philadelphia: Fortress, 1982.
Tod, Marcus N. "Clubs, Greek." In *Oxford Classical Dictionary*, edited by Nicholas G. L. Hammond and H. H. Scullard, 254–55. 2nd ed. Oxford: Oxford University Press, 1970.
———. *Sidelights on Greek History: Three Lectures on the Light Thrown by Greek Inscriptions on the Life and Thought of the Ancient World*. Oxford: Blackwell, 1932.
Townsend, John T. "Missionary Journeys in Acts and European Missionary Societies." In *SBL 1985 Seminar Papers*, edited by Kent H. Richards, 433–37. SBLSP 24. Atlanta: Scholars, 1985.
Toynbee, J. M. C. *Death and Burial in the Roman World*. Aspects of Greek and Roman Life. Ithaca: Cornell University Press, 1971.
Trebilco, Paul R. *Jewish Communities in Asia Minor*. SNTSMS 69. Cambridge: Cambridge University Press, 1991.
———. "Jews, Christians and the Associations in Ephesos: A Comparative Study of Group Structures." In *100 Jahre Österreichische forschungen in Ephesos. Akten des symposions Wien 1995*, edited by Barbara Brandt and Karl R. Krierer, 325–34. Österreichischen Akademie der Wissenschaften Philosophisch-Historische Klasse Denkschriften 260. Vienna: Österreichischen Akademie der Wissenschaften, 1999.
Trevijano Etcheverría, Ramón M. "La mision en Tesalonica (1 Tes 1, 1–2, 16)." *Salmanticensis* 32 (1985) 263–91.
Tsitouridou, Anna. "Early Christian Art." In *Macedonia: 4000 Years of Greek History and Civilization*, edited by M. B. Sakellariou, 238–49. Athens: Athenon, 1988.
———. "Political History." In *Macedonia: 4000 Years of Greek History and Civilization*, edited by M. B. Sakellariou, 224–32. Athens: Athenon, 1988.
Tuckman, B. W. "Development Sequence in Small Groups." *Psychological Bulletin* 63 (1965) 384–99.
Tyson, Joseph B. "The Jewish Public in Luke-Acts." *NTS* 30 (1984) 574–83.
Uhlhorn, Gerhard. *Christian Charity in the Ancient Church*. ATLA Historical Monographs Collection, Series 1. Edinburgh: T. & T. Clark, 1883.
Vaage, Leif E. "Ancient Religious Rivalries and the Struggle for Success: Christians, Jews, and Others in the Early Roman Empire." In *Religious Rivalries in the Early Roman Empire and the Rise of Christianity*, edited by Leif E. Vaage, 3–19. Studies in Christianity and Judaism 18. Waterloo, ON: Wilfrid Laurier University Press, 2006.
Vermes, Geza. *The Dead Sea Scrolls in English*. 3rd ed. London: Penguin, 1987.
Vincent, M. R. *The Epistles to the Philippians and to Philemon*. ICC. Edinburgh: T. & T. Clark, 1897.
Viviano, Benedict T. "Social World and Community Leadership: The Case of Matthew 23:1–12, 34." *JSNT* 39 (1990) 3–21.

Vom Brocke, Christoph. *Thessaloniki—Stadt des Kassander und Gemeinde des Paulus.* WUNT 2/125. Tübingen: Mohr Siebeck, 2001.

Voutiras, Emmanuel. "Berufs- und Kultverein: Ein ΔΟΥΜΟΣ in Thessalonike." *ZPE* 90 (1992) 87-96.

Wainwright, Elaine Mary. *Towards a Feminist Critical Reading of the Gospel according to Matthew.* BZNW 60. Berlin: de Gruyter, 1991.

Walaskay, Paul W. *Acts.* Westminster Bible Companions. Louisville: Westminster John Knox, 1998.

Walker, Jeffrey. *Rhetoric and Poetics in Antiquity.* Oxford: Oxford University Press, 2000.

Walker-Ramish, Sandra. "Graeco-Roman Voluntary Associations and the Damascus Document: A Sociological Analysis." In *Voluntary Associations in the Graeco-Roman World*, edited by John S. Kloppenborg and Stephen G. Wilson, 128-45. London: Routledge, 1996.

Wallace-Hadrill, Andrew. "Patronage in Roman Society: From Republic to Empire." In *Patronage in Ancient Society*, edited by Andrew Wallace-Hadrill, 63-87. Leicester-Nottingham Studies in Ancient Society 1. London: Routledge, 1989.

Walters, James. "The Coincidence of the Expansion of Christianity and the Egyptian Cults in Imperial Ephesos." In *100 Jahre Österreichische Forschungen in Ephesos: Akten des symposions Wien 1995*, edited by Barbara Brandt and Karl R. Krierer, 315-24. Vienna: Österreichischen Akademie der Wissenschaften, 1999.

Waltzing, Jean-Pierre. *Étude Historique sur les corporations Professionnelles chez les Romains depuis les origines jusqu'à la chute de l'Empire d'Occident.* 4 vols. Mémoire couronne par l'Academie royale des Sciences, des Lettres et des Beaux-Arts de Belgique. Leuven: Peeters, 1895-1900.

Wanamaker, Charles A. *The Epistles to the Thessalonians: A Commentary on the Greek Text.* NIGTC. Grand Rapids: Eerdmans, 1990.

———. "'Like a Father Treats His Own Children': Paul and the Conversion of the Thessalonians." *JTS* 92 (1995) 46-55.

Ware, James. "The Thessalonians as a Missionary Congregation: 1 Thessalonians 1,5-8." *ZNW* 83 (1992) 126-31.

Warrior, Valerie M. *Roman Religion.* Cambridge Introduction to Roman Civilization. Cambridge: Cambridge University Press, 2006.

Wedderburn, A. J. M. "The 'Apostolic Decree': Tradition and Redaction." *NovT* 35 (1993) 362-89.

Weinfeld, Moshe. *The Organizational Pattern and the Penal Code of the Qumran Sect: A Comparison with Guilds and Religious Associations of the Hellenistic Period.* NTOA 2. Fribourg, Switzerland: Éditions Universitaires, 1986.

Weise, Manfred. "Mt 5 21f—ein Zeugnis sakraler Rechtsprechung in der Urgemeinde." *ZNW* 49 (1958) 116-23.

Whelan, Caroline F. "Amica Pauli: The Role of Phoebe in the Early Church." *JSNT* 49 (1993) 67-85.

White, L. Michael. "Adolf Harnack and the 'Expansion' of Early Christianity: A Reappraisal of Social History." *Second Century* (1985/86) 97-127.

———. "Crisis Management and Boundary Maintenance: The Social Location of the Matthean Community." In *Social History of the Matthean Community: Cross-Disciplinary Approaches*, edited by David L. Balch, 211-47. Minneapolis: Fortress, 1991.

———. *The Social Origins of Christian Architecture*. Vol. 1, *Building God's House in the Roman World: Architectural Adaptation among Pagans, Jews, and Christians*. HTS 42. Valley Forge, PA: Trinity, 1996.

———. *The Social Origins of Christian Architecture*. Vol. 2, *Texts and Monuments for the Christian Domus Ecclesiae in Its Environment*. Valley Forge, PA: Trinity, 1997.

Whitton, J. "A Neglected Meaning for *skeuos* in 1 Thessalonians 4.4." *NTS* 28 (1982) 142–43.

Wiens, Devon H. "Mystery Concepts in Primitive Christianity and in its Environment." In *ANRW* II. Halbband Religion 23/2. *Vorkonstantinisches Christentum: Verhältnis zu römischem Staat und heidnischer Religion, Fortsetzung*, edited by Hildegaard Temporini, 1248–284. Berlin: de Gruyter, 1980.

Wild, Robert A. *Water in the Cultic Worship of Isis and Sarapis*. EPRO 87. Leiden: Brill, 1981.

Wilken, Robert L. "Collegia, Philosophical Schools, and Theology." In *The Catacombs and the Colosseum: The Roman Empire as the Setting of Primitive Christianity*, edited by Stephen Benko and John J. O'Rourke, 268–91. Valley Forge, PA: Judson, 1971.

———. *The Christians as the Romans Saw Them*. New Haven: Yale University Press, 1984.

Wilkins, John M., and Shaun Hill. *Food in the Ancient World*. Ancient Cultures. Oxford: Blackwell, 2006.

Williams, C. S. C. *A Commentary on the Acts of the Apostles*. 2nd ed. BNTC. London: Black, 1964.

Williams, David John. *1 and 2 Thessalonians*. NIBC 12. Peabody, MA: Hendrickson, 1992.

———. *Acts*. A Good News Commentary. San Francisco: Harper & Row, 1985.

Williams, Margaret H. "The Structure of the Jewish Community at Rome." In *Jews in a Graeco-Roman World*, edited by Martin Goodman, 215–28. Oxford: Clarendon, 1998.

Williams, Rowan. "Does It Make Sense to Speak of Pre-Nicene Orthodoxy?" In *The Making of Orthodoxy: Essays in Honour of Henry Chadwick*, edited by Rowan Williams, 1–23. Cambridge: Cambridge University Press, 1989.

Wilson, Stephen G. *Leaving the Fold: Apostates and Defectors in Antiquity*. Minneapolis: Fortress, 2004.

———. *Luke and the Law*. SNTSMS 50. Cambridge: Cambridge University Press, 1983.

———. "OI POTE IOUDAIOI: Epigraphic Evidence for Jewish Defectors." In *Text and Artifact in the Religions of Mediterranean Antiquity: Essays in Honour of Peter Richardson*, edited by Stephen G. Wilson and Michel Desjardins, 354–71. Studies in Christianity and Judaism 9. Waterloo, ON: Wilfred Laurier University Press, 2000.

———. *Related Strangers: Jewish-Christian Relations 70–170 C.E.* Minneapolis: Fortress, 1995.

———. "Voluntary Associations: An Overview." In *Voluntary Associations in the Graeco-Roman World*, edited by John S. Kloppenborg and Stephen G. Wilson, 1–15. London: Routledge, 1996.

Wilson, Thomas Wilkie. *St. Paul and Paganism*. The Gunning Lectures 1926. Edinburgh: T. & T. Clark, 1927.

Winter, Bruce W. "The Entries and Ethics of the Orators and Paul (1 Thessalonians 2.1–12)." *TynBul* 44 (1993) 55–74.

———. "'If a Man Does Not Wish to Work . . .': A Cultural and Historical Setting for 2 Thessalonians 3:6–16." *TynBul* 40 (1989) 303–15.

———. *Seek the Welfare of the City: Christians as Benefactors and Citizens*. First-Century Christians in the Graeco-Roman World. Grand Rapids: Eerdmans, 1994.

Wire, Antoinette C. "Gender Roles in a Scribal Community." In *Social History of the Matthean Community*, edited by David L. Balch, 87–121. Minneapolis: Fortress, 1991.

Witherington, Ben, III. *The Acts of the Apostles: A Socio-Rhetorical Commentary*. Grand Rapids: Eerdmans, 1998.

———. *1 and 2 Thessalonians: A Socio-Rhetorical Commentary*. Grand Rapids: Eerdmans, 2006.

Woodward, A. M. "Inscriptions from Beroea in Macedonia." *Annual of the British School at Athens* 18 (1911–1912) 133–65.

Yarbrough, O. Larry *Not Like the Gentiles: Marriage Rules in the Letters of Paul*. SBLDS 80. Atlanta: Scholars, 1985.

Youtie, Herbert Chayyim. "The Kline of Sarapis." *HTR* 41 (1948) 9–29.

Ziebarth, Erich Gustav Ludwig. *Das griechische Vereinswesen*. Stuttgart: Hirzel, 1896.

Index of Ancient Sources

HEBREW BIBLE
Exodus
20:16	320

Leviticus
6: 2	320
17:17	274
19:11	320

Joshua
7:1	321

1 Samuel
21:5	136–37

APOCRYPHA
Wisdom of Solomon
12:2–5	274

NEW TESTAMENT
Matthew
1:21	147
1:23	147
3:17	147
4:23	66, 156
5:1—7:29	156
5:3–12	153
5:10–12	162
5:19	162
5:21–24	153, 159
5:22	162
5:24	161
5:25–26	153
5:38–42	161
5:40	161
5:42	161
6:1–18	164
6:2	66, 156
6:5	66, 156
7:1–5	161
7:29	162
9:35	66, 156
10:2	162
10:5–6	150
10:16–23	150
10:17–25	150
10:17	66, 151, 156, 159
10:18	151
10:21	150
10:25	150
10:32–33	150
10:35–36	150
10:36	150
10:40–42	162
11:9	162
11:25–27	147
12:9	66, 156
13:53—17:27	146
13:3–9	147
13:52	162
13:54	66, 156
13:57	162

Matthew (continued)

16:7	148
16:13–20	146
16:16	149
16:17–19	148
16:17	146, 149
16:18	65, 66, 146, 148, 154, 156
16:19	146, 162
17:22—18:35	156
17:1–8	147
17:5	147
18:1–5	160
18:6–9	160
18:10–14	160
18:15–22	156
18:15–17	140, 160
18:17	65, 154
18:18	162
18:20	147
18:21–35	151
18:22	157, 161
21:11	162
21:23–27	162
23:6–12	75
23:8–10	162
23:11–12	164
23:13–26	66, 156
23:29–36	162
23:34	66, 156, 162
24:9–14	150
24:9–13	160
24:9–12	151
24:9–10	151
24:14	165
26:26–30	87
27:2	151
27:18	151
27:26	151
28:19–20	165
28:20	162

Mark

1:39	156
3:16	147
10:41–45	331
13:9–13	150
13:12	150
13:22–26	87

Luke

1:3	330
6:1–5	271
6:29–30	161
6:37–38	161
6:41–42	161
7:1–10	330
7:36–47	271
8:1–3	330
11:37–40	271
12:8–12	320
12:8–19	150
12:10	320
12:12	330
12:33–34	332
12:58–59	159
16:40	330
18:22	332
19:1–10	331
19:8	331
22:3	321
22:17–20	87
22:19–20	271
22:24–27	330
22:25	330–31
22:27	331
22:28–30	331

Acts

2:14–16	123
2:41–47	319
2:42	87
2:44	326, 331
2:46	87
4:9	330
4:32–35	319
4:32	323, 326, 331
4:36–37	319
5:1–11	319, 321, 324
5:2–3	321
5:2	321
5:3	320
5:4	321
5:5	319
5:9	320
5:11	319
6:1–2	87
9:27	323

Index of Ancient Sources 375

9:35	134	16:25	186
10:1–8	330		
10:31	330	## 1 Corinthians	
10:38	330		
10:44–48	330	1–4	76
11:22–26	323	1:2	65, 102, 104
11:27–30	319	1:10–17	101
13:1	323	1:12	10
15:5	269	3:5	69
15:10	261	3:16	134
15:19	269–70	4:12	125
15:20	262, 271, 273–74, 275	4:16	178, 205
15:29	262, 271	4:17	103
17:1–9	122, 124	5:2	316
17:1–4	123	5:4–5	311–12
18:3	126	5:9	311–12
19:32	30, 66	5:11	311–12
19:39	66	5:13	312
19:41	66	6:1–11	76
20:28	69	7:17	65, 102, 103
21:25	262	7:39	293
23:26	330	8:1–11:1	300
24:3	330	8–10	76, 78, 81
26:25	330	8:1–13	100
		8:10	78
		9:2	103
## Romans		10:14	78
		10:32	102
1:8	184	10:23–11:1	100
2:6	186	11–14	76
7:4	293	11:1	178, 205
8:13	293	11:16	65, 102, 103
8:36	293	11:17–34	76
11:13	124	11:17–22	300
13	81	11:18	65, 102
13:4	69	11:23–26	87, 299
13:8–10	300	11:30	293
13:10	313	15:6	293
13:13	303	15:9	102
14:1	313	15:12–19	300
14:17	300, 313–14, 314	15:18	293
15:5–12	50	15:20	293
15:7	313	15:21–22	292
15:8	69	15:26	292
15:26	186	15:29	294, 300
16:1	65, 69, 102	15:51	293
16:5	65	15:54–55	292
16:13	100	16:5	186
16:16	65, 102	16:19	65, 102
16:23	78		

2 Corinthians

1:15—2:13	103
1:16	186
2:13	186
3:6	69
4:3–5	186
4:11	300
6:4	69
6:9	293
7:5	186
8	103
8:1–15	101
1–7	186
1–3	292
1	65, 102
9:1–5	101, 186
10–13	103
11:3	85
11:9	101, 186
11:15	69
11:23	69
11:28	65, 102

Galatians

1:13	65, 102
1:22	102
2:11–13	300
2:12	311
2:14	312
2:17	69
4:9	134
4:12	205

Ephesians

3:7	69
5:14	300
6:5	85
6:21	69

Philippians

1:1	69, 70, 72
1:7	205
1:21–23	300
3:2–21	204
3:2–3	204

3:2	204
3:3–19	205
3:3	204
3:4–5	204
3:4	204
3:5	204
3:6	65, 102
3:10	205
3:15	204–5
3:16	205
3:17	205
3:18–21	205
3:20	206
3:21	205
4:14–16	101
4:15	65

Colossians

1:7	69
1:23	69
1:25	69
3:22	85

1 Thessalonians

1:1	65
1:2–10	169, 171, 174, 184, 186, 189
1:3	169, 171, 185–86
1:4–6a	185
1:5–8	172
1:5	124–25, 169, 176, 179, 185, 186
1:6–10	169, 170
1:6	185, 186, 205
1:7–9	135
1:7	172, 185, 188, 307
1:8–9	171
1:8	171, 173, 182, 184, 185, 187, 188
1:9–10	175, 176, 184
1:9	123, 133, 134, 176, 179, 186, 188, 189, 291, 303
1:10	176, 180, 292
2:1–12	125, 292
2:1	182
2:5	182
2:6	182, 190
2:8	180, 182
2:9	125, 128, 176, 180, 182, 303

2:11	182
2:13	182
2:14–16	123
2:14	102, 182
2:19–20	182, 289
2:20	125
3:2	69
3:5	128
3:6	182
4:1–12	288
4:1–8	288–89
4:1	125
4:3	137
4:4–6	136
4:4	303
4:6	85
4:7	137
4:9–12	128, 288–89
4:9–11	292–93
4:9	293
4:10	11, 305
4:11	125, 129, 132, 133, 302, 310
4:13–18	11, 288–89, 289, 292–93, 293, 300, 305
4:13	288, 289, 291, 292, 293
4:14	293
4:15	293, 294
4:16–17	11, 294
4:18	298
4:19	11
4:13—5:11	303
5:1–11	130, 288–89, 292–93
5:1	293
5:5b–8	303
15:2–22	130
5:12–13	128, 178, 302
5:13b–14	302
5:14–15	310
5:14	129, 130, 308, 309
5:16–22	130

2 Thessalonians

2:1–12	309
2:14	186
2:13–3:5	309
3:6–16	308
3:6–15	130, 309
3:6–12	308, 314
3:6–11	129
3:6	308–10, 310–11, 312
3:7	308
3:10	308–10, 312, 314–16
3:11	308, 309
3:12	309
3:14–15	312
3:14	311, 312

1 Timothy

1:3	186
2:1–2	81
3:2	69
3:8	69
3:12	69
4:6	69

Titus

1:7	69
3:1	81

James

2:15–16	300

1 Peter

2:9	75
2:11–17	81
2:25	69

2 Peter

1:14	300

Jude

12	300

DEAD SEA SCROLLS

1QS

6	323
6.12–20	70
6.24—7.24	315
7.6–8	324

CD

13.7–9	70

RABBINIC WRITINGS

t.Hul. 2.3	100

GRECO-ROMAN WRITINGS

Aelius Aristides

Orationes 45.27–28	242

Apuleius

Metam. 18	25, 96–97

Aristotle

Rhet.

1.5.5	198
1.9.2	196
1.9.35	196
1.9.36	196
1.9.38–41	204
1.9.38	199–200
1.9.39	201

Athenaeus

Deipn. 420	258

Cassius Dio

60.6.6–7	42

Cicero

De Nat. 3.5	272
On Goals 1.65	22

Digest

47.22.1.2	77–78

Dio Chrysostom

Orations 3.97	272–73

Diogenes Laertius

8.10	20

Iamblichus

Life of Pythagoras

6	20
17	20
18	21

Josephus

Ant.

14.213–216	39, 40, 53
14.235	39, 53
14.259–260	39
16.6.160–165	195
18.3.5	42

Lucian

Pergr. mort. 11	104

Lucretius

De rerum natura	296

Pausanias

Descr.

4.33.3–6	26
4.33.3–6	26

Philo

Contempl.

40	40
64	40
83–89	40

Ebr.

14	100
20–21	40

20	100	Seneca	
23	40	*Ep.* 25.5	23
Flacc.		Strabo	
4	233	*Geog.* 18.1.8	35
4–5	40		
4.1.36	78	Suetonius	
10.311–312	260, 268	*Aug.* 32.1	40, 265
135–137	40		
136	259, 268	*Claud.* 25.4	42
Legat.		*Jul.* 42.3	40, 49
281–283	124		
311–316	40	*Tib.* 36	42
311–313	39		
316	39	Tacitus	
Praem. Poen.		*Ann.* 2.85	42
20	131	Varro	
Spec. Laws		*Rust.* 3.2.16	258
4.23.122	23		

EARLY CHRISTIAN WRITINGS

Pliny		1 Clement	
Ep.		60–61	81
10.33–34	152		
10.92	152	Didache	
10.96	104, 152	9–10	87
		12.4–5	308
Pliny the Elder			
Nat.		Eusebius	
7.16.73	295–96	*Hist. eccl.*	
21.10	280		6.19
33.138	280	6.16	104
		7.32	104
Plutarch		7.27	104
Def. Orac. 424A	131	10.1	104
Porphyry			
De Antro 15	86		
Quintilian			
Inst. 3.7.28	196		

Praep. Ev.
14.5 — 22

Ignatius

Magn. 6.1 — 160

Phld. 8.1 — 160

Smyrn.
7.1 — 87
8.9 — 87

Polycarp

Mart. Pol. 10.2 — 81

Phil. 12.3 — 81

Origen

Cels.
1.1 — 59
3.2.3 — 104
8.17 — 59
8.47 — 59

Philocal.
24.1 — 131

Tertullian

Apol.
21.1 — 51
38–39 — 59
38.1.5 — 35
39 — 104, 205–6

INSCRIPTIONS AND PAPYRI

AGRW

2	174
5	181
6	183
7	43, 175, 183
9	183
10	174
12	174
16	183
18	43, 174, 183
20	174, 183
21	174, 177–78, 183
22	178
24	177
28	249
36	175
38	175
39	53, 183
45	53, 175
47	174–75, 177
49	53
50	174
51	174
52	181–82
53	177
54	64
63	53, 56
64	42, 53
65	175
71	42
74	43
77	42
78	42
80	175
82	42
85	175
95	53
108	43
109	43
110	175, 254–55
115	175
116	175
123	183
125	183
138	183

139	183	327	175
148	175	B6	253
160	183	B14	253
162	43	B23	253
164	183	L8	40
165	183	L9	40
168	183	L10	40
170	183	L25	42
174	42	L26	42
184	183	L28	42
188	183	L32	40, 49
193	175	L33	39
198	183	L34	40
212	183	L36	40
218	175	L37	39
221	42, 183		
223	42, 179	**BE**	
224	42, 181		
229	42	(1972) 263	300
230	42		
231	42	**Bloch**	
232	42		
235	183	42	222
237	42		
238	42	**CBP**	
239	42		
240	183	455	328
243	183		
247	183	**CIG**	
248	183		
251	175	1793b	72
252	177	1800	72
257	177	2007f	64, 279–80
258	175	3037	72
273	42	3540	128
281	183	5853	82, 95
284	183		
283	183	**CIJ**	
295	175		
298	183	694	328, 332
304	183	1401	328
306	183	1432	328
310	47		
312	42	**CIL**	
319	42		
317	42	III 633	64, 328
322	41	III 656	240, 281, 282
325	183	III 659	328
		III 703	64, 281

CIL (cont.)

III 704	64, 281
III 707	281
III 870	96, 302
III 6150	41
V 2283	290
V 7906	241
VI 22	201
VI 253	241
VI 2193	152
VI 10234	238, 251
VI 17985a	290
VI 26003	290
VI 30983	259
VI 31615	283
VIII	41
IX 1837	290
IX 5177	241
X 1786	201
XI 1230	201
XI 3711	290
XI 5047	282
XIV 250	222, 223
XIV 251	81, 222, 223
XIV 1900	81
XIV 2112	32, 47, 61, 114, 132, 140, 158, 238, 239, 251, 256, 280, 328
XIV 4567	222
XIV 4568	222
XIV 4570	259

DFSJ

33	328

GRA

I 21	183
I 24	175
I 26	175
I 27	175, 183
I 28	183
I 29	183
I 32	183
I 33	175, 183
I 36	175
I 44	41
I 45	41
I 48	179, 183
I 54	175
I 58	175
I 72	64
I 73	54
I 75	64
I 82	54
I 86	56
II 95	54
II 106	54
II 113	54
II 139	54
II 150	54

I.Alex.

98	35

IBeroea

1	64
371	64

IDelos

1519	155, 328
1520	243, 328
1521	328
1522	71

IEph

22	98
1503	219
2212	328
3216	241
3801	242
3803	240

IFayum

2 122	234, 252

IG

II2 337	94
II2 1177	94
II2 1263	32, 133, 164, 327–28

Index of Ancient Sources   383

II² 1275	251
II² 1283	94
II² 1314	132
II² 1327	286, 327
II² 1343	86
II² 1361	158
II² 1366	31, 85, 149, 238, 252
II² 1368	33, 131, 140–41, 157, 199–200, 202, 238, 251
II² 1369	33, 34, 133, 327
II² 2345	215
IV 774	72
IV 824	72
V/1 1390	131–32, 158
VII 33	94
IX/1 486	72
X/2.1 58	64, 72, 128, 301, 307
X/2.1 60	306
X/2.1 65	128
X/2.1 68	64, 307
X/2.1 185	218
X/2.1 192	64, 301
X/2.1 220	64, 128, 301
X/2.1 244	128, 301, 306
X/2.1 255	34, 97, 135
X/2.1 259	64, 281, 304, 306, 328
X/2.1 260	33, 64, 281–82, 304
X/2.1 288	64, 128, 279, 301, 304, 305
X/2.1 289	128, 279, 304, 305
X/2.1 291	64, 127, 279, 300, 304
X/2.1 309	42, 53, 64, 96, 279, 300, 302, 304
X/2.1 403	128
X/2.1 406	64
X/2.1 480	42, 279, 300, 302, 304
X/2.1 503	279, 304
X/2.1 506	301
X/2.1 821	279, 304
X/2.1 824	285
X/2.1 860	64
X/2.1 933	64
XI/1 1327	77
XI/1 1328	77
XI/2 1325	77
XI/2 1326	77
XI/2 2948	77
XI/4 1299	96, 148–49, 216
XII/1 127	63
XII/1 155	215–16
XII/1 736	328
XII/1 937	328, 328–29
XII/3 329	70
XII/3 330	244
XII/3 1098	63
XII/7 58	329
XII/7 506	82, 96

IGL

1989	70
1990	70
2298	70

IGLAM

1381	155
1382	155

IGR

IV 386	218

IHierapP

305	241

IIasos

245	241
246	241

IJO

I Arh. 41	53
II Nysa 26	53

IKnidos

23	329

IKyme

30	63

IMagMai

99	97
109	72
117	328
215	96
217	72

IMakedD

284	64
920	64, 281
1104	64

IPerg

222	218
319	218
320	218
485	218
486	218
487	218
488	218

IPerinthos

59	53

IPontEux

II 449	288
II 450	288
II 451	288
II 452	288
II 456	288

IPriene

111	244
112	244
118	244
195	96

ISardBR

22	79–80

ISide

102	201

IStratonikeia

309	244
684	244
685	244

ITralleis

1	296

Jaccottet

94	218
95	218
96	218
97	218

LSAM

9	158, 328

MAMA

6 239	328

Μουσῖον

93	72
100	72

Nigdelis

II.9	304
II.10	300, 304
II.11	300–301

OGIS

50	68
51	68
488	155
611	71
614	71

P.Cairo.dem

30605	158
30606	158

P.Enteuxeis

20	280–81
21	281

Pilhofer

029	281
095	64
133	281
209	64
338	64
339	64
697/2	64

P.Kar.

575	32

P.Lond.

2193	34, 81, 238, 251–52
2710	158

P.Mich

V 243	85, 88, 132, 158–59, 236, 259, 280
V 244	158, 236

Poland, *Geschichte des griechischen Vereinswesens*

B 79	71
B 186	71

P.Paris

42	68, 160

Rhomiopoulou 1981

6	300, 302

RIG

1226	72
1307	94

SEG

37 (1987) 559	64, 279–80
40 (1990) 524	132
42 (1992) 625	304
45 (1995) 2074	35

SIG^3

694	98
965	83
985	29, 33, 83, 84, 91, 135, 148, 273
1108	32
1140	64

SIRIS

122	64
123	64
124	64

TAMSuppl

III 201	68

Index of Modern Authors

Adkins, A. W. H., 83
Allison, Dale C., 146, 147, 148, 154, 160
Applebaum, Shimon, 40
Arnaoutoglou, Ilias N., 35, 74, 236–37
Ausbüttel, Frank M., 116

Bagnall, Roger S., 250
Balch, David L., 258
Barclay, John M. G., 54, 310
Barrett, C. K., 275
Bartchy, S. Scott, 324
Barton, Stephen C., 63, 75, 83, 86–87, 91–92, 144, 156, 161, 166
Bassler, Jouette M., 136
Batten, Alicia, 83, 84, 85, 86
Baumgarten, Albert, 44
Beard, Mary, 285
Beare, Francis W., 280
Beck, Roger, 227
Belayche, Nicole, 113
Bendlin, Andreas, 188, 248, 265–66
Bertram, Georg, 134
Best, Ernest, 128, 133, 134, 171
Bloch, Herbert, 222
Bock, Darrell L., 271, 274
Bollmann, Beate, 116, 181, 252, 254
Bömer, Franz, 301
Boring, M. Eugene, 144
Brady, Thomas A., 96
Brashaer, William, 249
Brawley, Robert L., 271
Bruce, F. F., 171, 324
Bryant, Joseph M., 197–98
Burke, Trevor J., 180

Burkert, Walter, 24, 26
Burtchaell, James Tunstead, 48

Cameron, Ron, 111, 118
Campbell, J. Y., 65
Cancik, Hubert, 295, 296
Capper, Brian J., 322–23, 326, 330, 331
Carter, Warren, 148, 153, 162–63, 166
Cassidy, Richard J., 321
Castells, Manuel, 192, 193–94, 195
Champion, Craige B., 257
Chester, Stephen J., 212–13
Clarke, Andrew D., 62
Claussen, Carsten, 48–49
Collart, Paul, 64, 329
Collins, John N., 69, 72, 125
Collins, Raymond F., 65, 123, 125–26, 129, 134, 136–37, 308
Constantakoupoulou, Christy, 187
Corley, Kathleen E., 163
Cormack, James M. R., 132
Cotter, Wendy J., 42, 50, 152, 155, 206
Coulot, Claude, 173
Countryman, L. William, 91, 103
Crosby, Michael H., 142
Crossley, James, 110
Crossan, John Dominic, 257–58
Culpepper, R. Alan, 18–19, 22, 23

Danker, Frederick W., 331
D'Arms, John H., 225, 226
Davies, W. D., 146, 147, 148, 154, 160
Derrett, J. Duncan M., 322
De Vos, Craig Steven, 131, 135
DeWitt, Norman, 23

Index of Modern Authors

Dibelius, Martin, 70, 71
Dickson, J. P., 172, 173
Dill, Samuel, 247, 268
Donahue, John R., 234, 235, 236, 237, 238, 239, 241, 242, 244, 246, 247, 251, 252, 256, 269
Donfried, Karl Paul, 137, 308
Doublet, Georges, 288
Douglas, Mary, 250, 274
Dow, Sterling, 102
Downing, F. Gerald, 295, 296
Duff, P. W., 266
Duling, Dennis C., 65-66, 140-41, 155, 160, 161, 162, 165, 324
Dunbabin, Katherine M. D., 234, 239, 240, 247, 251, 252, 253, 254, 269

Edson, Charles, 282, 301, 302, 307
Edwards, Douglas R., 80
Ehrman, Bart D., 47-48, 61-62
Elliott, John H., 325
Ernst, Josef, 75
Esler, Philip F., 263, 275
Evans, Craig A., 294

Fatum, Lone, 138
Fee, Gordon D., 73, 75, 175, 176, 184, 185, 186
Ferguson, Everett, 25
Ferguson, William Scott, 94
Fisher, Nicholas R. E., 92, 245-46
Fitzpatrick-McKinley, Anne, 46
Forkman, Goran, 320
Fotopoulos, John, 273
Foucart, Paul, 71, 328
Fox, W. S., 329
Fraikin, Daniel, 97
Frame, James E., 171, 189
Frankfurter, David, 273
Fraser, Peter M., 286

Gabrielsen, Vincent, 188, 216
Garnsey, Peter, 325
Gaventa, Beverly Roberts, 274, 308
Gehring, Roger W., 51, 53
Gennep, Arnold van, 288
Georgi, Dieter, 66-67
Goodman, Martin, 135, 202, 210-11, 211-12

Gordon, R. L., 226
Gordon, Richard, 285
Greenfield, Jonas, 99
Grignon, Charles, 235, 237, 238, 239, 242, 243, 244-5, 246, 250, 251, 252, 256
Gruen, Erich, 7
Gschnitzer, F., 80
Gundry, Robert H., 147, 154
Guterman, Simeon L., 40-41, 43, 50-51
Gutsfeld, Andreas, 266

Habinek, Thomas, 196
Haenchen, Ernst, 320, 321
Hainz, Joseph, 65, 128
Hardy, E. G., 90, 102, 266, 268
Harland, Philip A., 39, 77, 82, 116, 201-02, 203, 224, 256, 267-68, 286
Harnack, Adolf von, 209-10
Harrington, Daniel J., 146, 155
Hatch, Edwin, 73, 90
Heinrici, Georg, 268
Hengel, Martin, 43-44, 295
Herz, Peter, 224
Heyob, Sharon Kelly, 97
Hill, Judith L., 292
Hill, Shaun, 316
Hock, Ronald F., 125, 126
Hoey, A. S., 240, 282
Holtz, Traugott, 123, 134
Hopkins, Keith, 283, 284, 290
Horsley, G. H. R., 63, 75, 79, 80, 83, 85, 86-87, 91-92, 97, 241, 279

Jaccottet, Anne-Françoise, 218, 219
Jeffers, James S., 82
Jeremias, Joachim, 322
Jewett, Robert, 128, 130, 300, 303, 309, 312, 313, 314, 315, 316, 317
Johnson, Luke Timothy, 270, 273, 274, 321
Judge, E. A., 60, 90-91, 122
Juster, Jean, 40, 43

Kahl, Brigitte, 263, 264, 276
Karner, Christian, 110
Kim, Seyoon, 180, 182

Index of Modern Authors 389

Klauck, Hans-Josef, 67, 78, 87, 304
Klinghardt, Matthias, 268, 323–24, 326
Kloppenborg, John S., 2, 36, 38, 51–52, 53–54, 63, 66, 68, 74, 76, 77, 82, 87, 92, 101, 102, 102–03, 116, 127, 134, 155, 157–58, 160, 163, 266, 278, 279, 295, 325–26
Koester, Helmut, 204
Kolb, Anne, 259–60
Kraabel, A. Thomas, 80
Kreitzer, L. Joseph, 294
Krentz, Edgar, 162, 163

Lambert, Stephen D., 215
Lampe, Peter, 316
La Piana, George, 49, 95, 96, 99, 100–01, 104
Laub, Franz, 129, 171
LaVerdiere, E. A., 165
Leiwo, Martti, 248
Lemerle, Paul, 64
Levine, Lee I., 40–41
Levinskaya, Irina, 124
Liebenam, W., 102
Lietzmann, Hans, 67, 70
Lightfoot, J. B., 70, 73, 317
Lincoln, Bruce, 107, 108, 110
Linderski, J., 117
Liu, Jinyu, 116–17, 248, 249, 254, 255, 269
Lolos, Yannis, 187
Longaker, Mark Garrett, 197
Lüdemann, Gerd, 126, 319, 320
Luz, Ulrich, 155, 157, 161

Mack, Burton L., 277, 288, 289, 291, 297
MacMullen, Ramsay, 247, 278
Malherbe, Abraham J., 104, 171, 291, 292, 297, 309
Malina, Bruce J., 107, 143, 144, 145, 150, 153, 164–65, 166, 186, 201, 324
Malkin, Irad, 187
Mantel, Hugo, 44
Marshall, Peter, 204, 310, 324
Martin, Dale B., 137, 138
Marxsen, Willi, 130

Masuzawa, Tomoko, 108, 109, 110, 110–11
Matson, David Lertis, 262, 270
McCready, Wayne O., 43, 155
McLean, Bradley H., 2, 71, 74, 77, 96, 224, 225
Meeks, Wayne A., 7, 8, 36–37, 38, 60, 63, 67, 68, 75, 77, 78, 92, 101, 103, 104, 163, 164, 174, 293, 297
Meiggs, Russell, 77, 222
Merkelbach, Reinhold, 304
Metzger, Bruce M., 69
Miller, Merrill P., 111, 118
Milligan, G., 68, 69, 72
Milner, Vincent L., 108
Mommsen, Theodor, 90, 114
Moulton, J. H., 68, 69, 72
Moxnes, Halvor, 324, 325, 326, 331, 332
Murphy-O'Connor, Jerome, 137

Nanos, Mark D., 49–50, 56
Neil, William, 210
Neill, Stephen, 210
Neumann, K. J., 67
Neyrey, Jerome H., 201, 243
Nicholl, Colin R., 314–15, 316
Nigdelis, Pantelis M., 177, 301, 306, 317
Nijf, Onno M. van, 200–01, 222, 229, 240, 241, 244, 252, 267, 279, 282, 283, 284, 285, 286, 304
Nilsson, Martin P., 220, 225
Nock, A. D., 81, 149, 210
North, John A., 117
Northcut, Kathryn, 197

O'Brien, Peter T., 204
Öhler, Markus, 5, 7, 116, 264–65
Olbrechts-Tyteca, Lucie, 196
Overman, J. Andrew, 147–48, 148, 151, 151–52, 153, 162

Panagopoulou, Katerina, 187
Pandermalis, D., 304, 305
Papazoglou, Fanoula, 305
Paton, W. R., 279
Patte, Daniel, 151
Patterson, John R., 287, 288
Peerbolte, L. J. Lietaert, 211

Perdrizet, Paul, 282
Perelman, Chaïm, 196
Perkins, Pheme, 134, 165
Perry, Jonathan S., 47, 113–14, 114–15, 116, 304
Pesch, Rudolf, 321
Peterlin, Davorin, 69
Phillips, C. Robert, 281
Piccottini, Gernot, 227
Pickard-Cambridge, Arthur W., 98
Pilch, John J., 186
Pilhofer, Peter, 217, 218–19
Plummer, Alfred, 67–68, 130, 154
Pomeroy, Sarah B., 135
Poland, Franz, 71, 72, 86, 98, 102, 281
Poole, Fitz John Porter, 106, 119
Psoma, Selene, 188

Rackham, Richard B., 324
Radin, Max, 90
Radt, Wolfgang, 217, 218, 253
Rajak, Tessa, 54–55
Rathbone, Dominic, 186
Rauh, Nicholas K., 283, 286
Reicke, Bo, 132, 303, 312
Reed, Jonathan L., 257–58
Reinmuth, Eckart, 173
Reumann, John, 69, 70, 71, 73
Richard, Earl J., 134, 171–72, 291, 310
Richardson, Peter, 41, 44, 45, 195
Rigaux, Béda, 128
Rives, James B., 111–12, 113, 116, 245
Roberts, Colin, 81
Robinson, David M., 305
Rossi, Giovanni Battista de, 90, 114
Roth, Roman, 257
Rowlandson, Jane, 250
Roueché, Charlotte, 285
Royden, Halsey L., 222, 223
Runesson, Anders, 45, 46, 49, 51
Rüpke, Jörg, 247, 256, 258, 265, 268, 269
Russell, Ronald, 309

Saldarini, Anthony J., 141–42, 143, 144, 154, 155, 156–56, 161, 163, 164
Saller, Richard, 325
San Nicolò, Mariano, 267

Savelle, Charles H., 270, 274
Scheid, John, 229, 272
Schenk, Wolfgang, 69
Scherrer, Peter, 221
Schmeller, Thomas, 75
Schmidt, Karl L., 66, 67, 102
Schulz-Falkenthal, Heinz, 267
Scullion, Scott, 112
Segal, Alan F., 7
Seland, Torrey, 259
Sirks, Boudewijn, 117
Skeat, T. C., 81
Slater, William J., 229, 254
Smallwood, E. Mary, 40, 41
Smit, Peter-Ben, 313–14
Smith, Dennis E., 252, 253, 254
Smith, Jonathan Z., 8–9, 52, 55, 57, 58, 59, 106–107, 107, 108, 117, 118–19, 120, 121, 277, 286–87, 295
Sokolowski, Franciszek, 97, 148–49
Stanton, Graham N., 145, 160, 162, 163, 166
Stegemann, Wolfgang, 191–92

Takács, Sarolta, 220
Talbert, Charles H., 321, 322
Tellbe, Mikael, 50
Thompson, William G., 156, 160–61, 165
Tinh, Tran Tam, 97
Tod, Marcus N., 83, 89, 92, 93, 94, 98
Townsend, John T., 101, 103
Tykwer, Tom, 106

Ulhorn, Gerhard, 329

Vaage, Leif E., 209, 212
Vermes, Geza, 99
Vincent, M. R., 73
Vom Brocke, Christoph, 187, 302–03, 306–07

Wainwright, Elaine Mary, 163
Walaskay, Paul, 270
Walters, James, 219–20
Waltzing, Jean-Pierre, 115, 135, 272
Wanamaker, Charles A., 136, 137, 184, 185, 289

Ware, James, 172
Warrior, Valerie M., 272
Weinfeld, Moshe, 70
White, L. Michael, 37, 156, 209, 214, 216, 226–27, 228–29
Wild, Robert A., 96
Wilken, Robert L., 63, 91, 93
Wilkins, John M., 316
Williams, David John, 134
Williams, Margaret H., 40
Williams, Rowan, 192
Wilson, Stephen G., 146, 162, 208–09
Winter, Bruce W., 180, 310
Witherington, Ben III, 262–63, 271–72, 273, 274, 321–22
Woodward, A. M., 279

Youtie, Herbert Chayyim, 249

Ziebarth, Erich Gustav Ludwig, 155

Index of Subjects

abortion, 85
abuse, 33, 34, 131, 132, 157, 158, 159, 267, 310
accounts, 27, 198
adoption, 288
adultery, 162
album. *See* membership lists
altar, 183, 218, 250, 272, 274n49, 296
Andania, 7, 26–28, 29, 131, 158,
archive, 178
artisan, 9, 10, 30, 62, 94, 127, 170, 180, 182, 184, 186, 187, 286
association names,
  collegium, 4, 38, 40–46, 49, 51, 53, 64, 89n1, 90, 91, 95, 114, 115, 200, 223, 225, 226, 234, 236, 238, 239, 240, 242, 254, 255, 256, 265, 267, 282, 295n85
  corpus, 36, 41, 64, 104n87, 201, 226
  cultores, 64
  curia, 206
  eranos, 53, 89n1, 316n82, 329
  familia, 224, 225
  hetaireia, 35
  koinon, 33, 34, 40n19, 53, 68, 70, 72, 81, 133n53, 155, 177, 179, 181, 216, 244n62, 286, 327, 329
  mystai, 64, 77, 306
  orgeōnes, 41, 77, 89n1, 94n27, 177
  sodales, 234
  symmystai, 64
  synagōgē, 49, 53n74, 65, 66, 155, 156
  synedrion, 30, 155, 159, 160, 162
  synklitai, 64, 177, 307
  synodos, 30, 34, 53n74, 71, 81, 155, 177, 179, 181, 183, 243
  systēma, 155
  therapeutai, 55, 79, 203, 316
  thiasos, 35, 39, 40n19, 41, 45, 53, 64, 67, 71, 79, 80n1, 94, 96n42, 99n58, 104, 215, 248, 282, 295n85, 301, 202, 304, 327, 328, 329
  thiasus, 64
association size, 173, 215–16, 218, 223
association types, 4, 18, 34–35, 49, 52–59, 60, 62, 81, 116, 126–27, 139, 140, 142n9, 163n100, 206, 248, 249, 278
attendance, 32, 158, 159, 236, 243, 251, 280, 306
autonomy, 267n16
awning maker. *See* tentmaker

Bacchanalia, 203
baker, 29
banker, 181, 243
banquet. *See* meal
baptism, 87, 90n4, 147
barber, 56n82
bath, bathing, 21, 25, 226, 258
belonging, 38, 46n47, 252, 260, 277, 284–91, 293, 316n83

Index of Subjects

benefaction, benefactor, 1, 10, 27, 21, 32, 71, 83n141, 88, 132n52, 133, 164, 170, 175, 176–78, 181, 182–83, 184, 190, 225, 228, 234, 238, 240, 241–44, 255, 256, 268, 269, 282, 310n53, 324–33, *see also* patron, patronage
benefits of associations, 25, 77, 92n22, 127n27, 145, 183, 189, 225, 239, 243, 260, 267
bequest, 33, 239, 241, 281, 304, *see also* endowment
birthday, 23, 235, 238, 239, 241, 281, 304
bishop. *See* episkopos
bouncer, 31, 33, 131, 157
bread, 21, 271n33, 307, 329
brother, *adelphos*, 6, 26, 33, 34, 66, 68, 81, 85, 136, 138, 140, 150, 153, 159, 160n84, 161, 229, 280, 285, 286, 288, 292, 311, 317
brotherly love, *philadelphia*, 292, 317n84, 314
building, 5, 10, 28, 30, 33, 97, 116n66, 174, 183, 214–22, 225n96, 233–34, 238, 243, 245, 251–55, 260, 264n6, 266, 312n82, 328, 329. *See also proseuchē*
burial, 11, 33, 43, 46, 89n1, 114, 127, 198, 199, 239, 241, 277–88, 291, 292, 298, 304, 329
businessmen, 201
bylaw, 1, 47, 198–99, 238, 248, 251, 254, 255, 269

carpenter, 29, 253
catacomb, 114
cemetery, 234
charity, 90n5, 115, 329
child, children, 20, 25, 27, 29, 38, 52, 84, 136, 150, 162, 178, 204, 226n102, 249n11, 304n26, 329
Christ adherent, 12, 42, 50, 176n29, 186
citizenship, 30, 40n15, 95n33, 206, 287
clothing, 20
collection, 31, 101, 164, 186n48, 262, 319n1, 322n24, 327,

collegia domestica, 49, 325
collegia funeraticia, 47, 61, 114, 115, 278, 280n15, 285, 304
collegia illicita, 266
collegia tenuiorum. *See collegia funeraticia*
columbarium, 285, 287, 288
common chest, 292n77
commensality, segregative, 10, 235–39, 240, 246, 251, 256, 269
commensality, transgressive, 10, 235–37, 242–46, 256, 257, 269
common fund, 33, 101, 323, 327, 328
communal meals. *See* meal(s)
comparison, 5, 7, 9, 12, 38, 102n71, 110, 117–20, 201, 235, 259, 300, 322
contract, 43, 157n77, 281
contributions, 46, 79, 83n141, 100, 181, 186n48, 199, 266, 283, 329
coppersmith, 127n31
costs, 25, 32, 333
court of law, 76, 151, 153, 157, 159n80, 160n82, 206, 280
cowheards, 29, 217, 218, 253
crown, 27, 80, 132n52, 164, 179, 182, 182, 282, 305, 327, 328, *see also* wreath

dancing, 279, 304n26, 249, 255, 306n37
daughter, 290, 328
deacon, *diakonos*, 69n61, 73n90
Dead Sea Scrolls, 60, 99, 322, 323
death. *See* funeral
decree, 1, 31, 39, 94, 152, 174, 177, 178, 179, 183
dedication, 1, 174, 177, 179, 218, 241, 300, 301, 302, 329
dendrophori, 200, 201, 229
dining couch, *klinē*, 249
dining room, 234n4, 252n33, 253, 255, *see also triclinium*
Dionysiac artists, 29, 68, 82, 97, 98, 244
disorderly, 27, 33, 129, 131–32, 157, 158, 303, 308–12, 316
disruptive behavior, 238, 256, 269, 311

divine patron. *See* patron deity
donkey driver, 64, 127n31, 279, 300, 304
dream, 84, 97, 148, 149, 181
drink, drinking, 20, 34, 56n82, 81, 99n58, 132n51, 158, 203, 205, 206, 217, 233n1, 234, 236, 237, 250, 251, 253, 255n44, 259n24, 271n33, 290, 303, 306
drunkenness, 39, 55, 56, 78, 202, 203, 233n1, 236, 259, 268n24, 303, 311, 314
dues, 23, 32–33, 79, 198, 199, 278, 283, 292n77

elder, *presbyteros*, 72, 73, 74n94, 160n82, 183
election, 21, 26, 27, 32, 40n15, 42, 43
Eleusis, 7, 24, 25–26
emperor cult, 194
equality, 20, 75, 163, 255, 266
Essene, 43, 44n35, 45, 326n45
exemption, 20, 40n15, 42, 44, 114, 152n53
expulsion, 28, 33, 42, 157, 159, 160, 161, 268n22, 270, 312, 315, 316, 327

fabri, 200, 229, 253
family, 12, 20, 23, 51, 135, 149, 178, 188, 192, 224, 235, 240, 250, 281, 283, 284, 287, 291, 321, 325, 328
father, *pater*, 6, 23, 33, 35, 150, 162, 223, 224, 290, 296
fellow members, *synthiasōtai*, 32, 64, 158, 280
festival, 25, 27, 29, 32, 33, 43, 158, 164, 181, 240, 244, 248, 258, 281, 286
fighting, 132, 159, 263, 310
finances, 88, 213, 248, 280, 331
fine, 28, 33, 85, 131, 133, 153, 157, 158, 159, 236, 259, 270, 280, 285n45, 310, 315, 327
fire, 86, 268n22, 290
firefighter, 152, 267n18
fishing, 219, 238n24
flute player, 27

founder, 6, 10, 18, 19, 21, 23, 27, 30, 32, 63, 71, 84, 147, 148, 149, 163, 165, 170, 174, 176–78, 179, 182, 184, 186, 187, 189, 190, 198, 205n49, 289, 301
fraternal love. *See* brotherly love
freedperson, 28, 30, 74, 224, 225, 226n102, 245, 258, 301, 302
friends, *philoi*, 20, 22, 23, 33, 126, 133, 187, 188, 229, 250, 251, 272n42, 286, 325, 326, 327
friendship, 6, 20, 22, 265, 286, 326, 327
funerary bequest, 33, 239, 241, 281, 304, 306
funeral, 23, 31, 236, 266, 279, 280, 281–88, 304, 306

garden, 22, 284, 288, 322, 329
gardeners, 29, 286n45
garlic, 85
gender, 28–30, 118, 138
gladiator, 29, 266
god-fearer, 41, 46n47, 122, 123, 124n13
gods and heroes:
 Agdistis, 79, 80
 Aphroditē, 94, 175, 264n6, 301n5, 305
 Demeter, 24, 27, 29, 94
 Diana and Antinoüs, 47, 114, 238n24, 239
 Dionysos, 12, 24, 26, 29, 33, 54, 64, 68n54, 74, 77 96n42, 104, 152, 173, 174, 175, 178, 199, 217, 218, 219, 221, 225, 278, 279, 303, 304, 305n32, 306
 Great Mother, 27, 72
 Herakles, 215, 279, 301n5, 304, 305n31
 Hygia, 238, 251
 Isis, 9, 12, 17, 24, 25, 26, 95, 96, 97, 104, 148, 173, 181, 219, 220, 266, 301n5, 307
 Mēn Tyrannos, 85, 178, 238, 252
 Mithras, 24, 26, 86, 226, 227
 Poseidon, 29, 88n158, 243, 296
 Sabazios, 79, 80

Sarapis, 88n158, 95, 96, 97, 104, 132, 148, 149, 181, 216, 220, 241, 242, 249, 301n5, 307n41
Theos Hypsistos, 174, 301n5, 307
Zeus, 9, 12, 30, 54, 56n82, 79, 80, 83n142, 84, 148, 174, 255, 296, 306
Zeus Hypsistos, 34, 175, 238, 251, 254, 301n5
guest, 242, 243, 245, 250, 258, 259, 272n42

honor, 1, 9, 10, 12, 23, 27, 31, 32, 35, 48, 62, 76, 79, 81, 88, 98, 126, 132, 133, 135n65, 160, 161–64, 170, 174 – 78, 180 n, 36, 181 – 90, 196n24, 197, 198, 199, 200, 205, 215, 216, 218, 226, 240–44, 248, 250, 254–59, 268, 282, 284–89, 301, 302, 304, 324-33
hospitality, 76, 91, 181, 182, 184, 185
house, *oikos*, 10, 22, 24, 45, 55, 73n90, 74, 148, 220–21, 224, 228, 234n3, 252n33, 258, 270, 312n59, 329, 330, 332
house church, 48, 51, 66, 142, 155, 213
household, 7, 22, 37, 38, 49, 51, 60, 62, 74, 84, 114, 116, 142, 150, 163, 181, 182, 199, 216, 224, 244, 281n21, 287, 312n59
hymn, 25, 86, 87, 88n158
hymn-singer, 242

idol food, idol meat. *See* sacrificial meat
immigrant, 39n13, 41n23, 42, 177, 178, 181, 224
impoverished, 32, 319n1, 320
initiate, 26, 27, 86, 87, 174, 203, 219, 227, 306, 323
initiation, 20, 25, 26, 30, 34, 86, 96, 97n44
initiation fee, 32, 198, 199
insult, 33, 131, 157, 158, 159, 160, 204n45
integration into the *polis*, 266, 284
invite, 181, 244, 245, 273, 316n83
invitation, 241, 243, 245, 270, 332

Iobacchoi, 33, 131, 199, 200, 238, 251, 252

Jesus, 9, 65, 66n47, 87, 104, 135, 142, 144n20, 145–53, 157, 160, 162, 169, 171, 175, 182, 184, 210, 212, 213, 271, 289, 291n74, 292, 293, 294, 298, 299, 305, 330, 331, 332

koinōnia, 18, 19, 20, 307, 314, 321

lawsuit, 199
lazy, 129, 132n51, 309
letter, 24, 32, 39, 69, 95, 104, 124, 181, 200, 210, 280
libation, 21, 34, 55, 183, 244n62
liberti, freed slaves. *See* freedperson
linen worker, 240n37
lists. *See* album
litigation. *See* court of law
loan, 183

maenad, 96n42, 304n26
manager, 31
market supervisor, 27
marzeaḥ, 99n58
meal, 6, 7, 10, 11, 19, 20, 21, 27, 38, 39, 43, 44, 45, 46, 56n82, 76, 81, 86, 87, 100n62, 119, 120, 213, 233–46, 247–60, 262, 265, 268, 269, 271, 273, 274, 275, 288, 299–300, 303, 306, 307–18, 323
membership list, 1, 10, 81n131, 222–29, 301, 306n38
menstruation, 85
merchants, 62, 64, 94, 95, 104, 127, 180, 181, 186, 187, 189, 190, 229n126, 243, 286, 300
miscarriage, 85
monotheism, 108, 109, 112, 134, 135, 175, 176, 210, 297
mother, *mater*, 31, 33, 67
multiple membership, 77, 216n39
music. *See* hymn
mystai, 77, 306, *see also* initiate
mysteries, 3, 7, 18, 24, 25, 28, 29, 35, 37, 58, 60n16, 79, 80, 86, 131–32, 148, 158, 203, 210, 213, 220n64, 226

Index of Subjects   397

networks, 10, 82, 107n4, 120, 121, 170, 180, 181, 186n49, 187–90, 192, 225, 227, 236, 245, 248, 307, 317, 325
nocturnal rite, 25
nomos. See bylaws

oath, 23, 27, 28, 158, 306
offices, 48, 69, 72, 74, 74, 162, 248
oracle, 148, 149, 178, 296
ordo, 225n94, 256, 276

parentalia, 281, 282n21
paterfamilias, 73n90, 224
patron, *prostatēs*, 1, 9, 10, 12, 30–33, 43, 75, 79, 91, 101, 128n33, 134, 135, 178, 184, 186, 189, 199, 235, 238, 239, 242, 243, 248, 256, 272, 281, 287, 301, 312, 316n81, 324, 325, 327, 330, 331n71, 333
patron deity, 9, 63, 84n142, 134, 174, 175, 291, 293, 298
patronage, 6, 23, 29, 20, 32, 33, 46, 128n33, 213, 214, 216, 219, 225, 228, 310n53, 326n44, 330, 331, *see* also benefaction
payment, 32, 100, 308n45, 315
peristyle, 221
persecution, 50, 123n6, 150, 151, 153, 165, 169
Pharisee, 44n35, 45, 146, 269
philosophical school, 18–24
phratras, 81
piety, *eusebeia*, 80, 83n141, 130, 164, 177, 251
pious, 34, 206, 327
plebs, 223, 267
polis, city, 24, 43, 45, 199, 200, 240, 283
politeuma. See citizenship
prayer house, *proseuchē*, 40n17, 49, 67n47, 329
president, 32, 34, 75, 81, 164, 307
priest, 26, 27, 31, 32, 72, 75, 77, 79n116, 86, 96, 97, 104, 136, 149, 157, 164, 179, 193, 199, 200, 216, 218, 244, 274, 301, 302
priestess, 26, 27, 31, 33, 34, 72, 75, 164, 224, 281, 282, 304

procession, 25, 26, 27, 158, 183, 243, 264n6, 310
patron, *prostatēs*,
punishment, 11, 27, 28, 33, 131, 158, 159, 263, 268, 309, 310, 311, 314, 315, 320, 324, 327
purity, 19, 20, 25, 27, 28, 83, 85, 86, 87, 110, 148, 275
purple-dyers, 29, 64, 127n31 241, 279, 285n45, 300, 304

recruitment, 7, 9, 10, 118, 152 n, 51, 170, 171, 176, 183, 189, 190, 192, 193, 195, 197, 198, 201, 203, 204, 206, 207, 209–15, 223, 224, 229
religio licita, 50, 51n68
religion, religions, 39n13, 59, 101, 104, 108–12, 115, 120, 191–92, 203, 209–10, 220n64, 249, 264, 276n56, 287, 317
resignation, 32
rites, 7, 20, 25, 27, 31, 34, 87, 96, 99n58, 174n26, 273, 279, 283, 302
ritual, 6, 11, 19, 25, 26, 28, 29, 33, 83–87, 100, 111, 112, 118, 119, 153, 161, 173, 185, 195, 197, 214, 236, 241, 243n56, 248, 249, 261, 271–75, 280, 293, 299, 306, 316, 317, 318
rivalry, 7, 78, 97, 132, 146, 181, 201, 237
rosalia, 281–82, 304
roster. *See* album
rotating leaders, 302

sacred object bearer, 175, 177
sacrifice, 11 25, 26, 27, 30, 78, 86, 100, 131, 158, 163, 164, 178, 181, 241, 243, 24n62, 249, 262, 272 273, 274, 310, 327
sacrificial meat, 271, 273–75, 317
Sadducee, 44n35, 45
Samaritan, 45
scribe, 27, 141 nn. 4, 5, 146n31, 162, 228
seat-stealing, 33, 131, 157, 259
Senate, 152, 265
senatus consultum, 199, 266n11

sexuality, 11, 33, 84, 85, 87n157, 136–38, 250, 273, 275, 311
shippers, 29, 81, 243
shit, 283n32
shrine, 97n44, 111, 181, 306
silversmith, 29, 31, 64, 128n31, 285n45
skeuos, vessel, penis, 136–38, 303
slave, 17, 24, 28, 29, 30, 62, 74, 76, 84n144, 85, 95, 148, 163, 178, 258, 287, 301
sleep, 148, 181, 293, 306
soldier, 30, 132n50, 151n49, 228, 257
Solon, 17
sportula, 246, 248, 272, 329
statue, 33, 35, 72, 80, 133, 164, 177, 178, 181, 183, 219, 224, 225, 243, 258, 328
statute, 32, 43, 158n78, 199, 200, 268, 326n45
strikes, 92–93n22
student, 19, 21, 26, 60n18, 235
synagogue, 3, 7, 8, 12, 28, 34, 36–56, 60, 62, 65, 66, 67, 73, 82, 99, 107n5, 119, 122, 123, 127, 135n62, 141n5, 144, 145, 146, 151, 155, 156 n, 73, 159n79, 160n82, 162, 202, 203, 228, 295n85, 326n45, 332

taberna, 116n66, 234, 252, 254
tanner, 29
teacher, 74n94, 162, 235
technitai. See artisan
temple, 6, 10, 26, 34, 70, 71, 78, 79, 80, 81, 94, 96, 97, 100n62, 116n66, 149, 177, 183, 193, 194, 218, 219, 220, 234n5, 254, 257, 264n6, 272n36, 273, 281n21
temple in Jerusalem, 38, 39, 44, 46, 263
temple warden, 79–80
tenement, 50, 312, 316
tentmaker, *skēnopoios*, 126, 135
textile dealers, *centonarii*, 4, 200, 229

thanks, 30, 32, 71n78, 72, 133, 164, 169, 183, 188, 237, 296, 309, 328
theater, 43n29
tomb, 20, 68, 86, 239–41, 279, 281–87, 290, 304, 305n33, 327, 328n53
topos inscription, 43, 45, 66, 67, 183
Torah, 40n15, 45–46, 204, 261, 269, 270, 275
translocal, 8, 46, 48, 82 83, 89–105, 145n27, 188n54, 215n38, 299n1
treasurer, 27, 31, 32, 75, 78, 100n62, 132n52, 164, 179, 286, 327
treasury, 43
triclinium, 234, 240, 245, 253

veteran, 257
vineyard, 239, 240n37, 281, 304, 306
vice, 33, 83, 180n36
virtue, 39, 40, 83, 128n33, 166, 180
vote, voting, 158, 183, 199, 200, 227n102
vow, 288, 322

warehouses, 226
warehousemen, 243
water, 20, 25, 86, 87, 96n39, 253
water bearer, 31
wine, 32, 78, 85, 198, 203, 218, 219, 255, 258, 271n33, 290, 306n37, 329
woman, women, 24, 25, 27, 29, 30, 33, 36, 59n9, 64, 65, 69, 74, 84, 85, 126, 135–38, 144, 148, 162, 163, 194, 203, 226, 241, 247, 249, 256, 257, 280, 296, 317n86, 330
workshop, 126n25, 129, 217, 222, 284
wreath, 86, 179, 243, 300, *see also* crown

youths, 4, 22, 305n34

zeal, zealous, 32, 133, 164, 179, 194, 284, 327, 328
zeal for honor, *philotimia*, 132, 133, 164, 179n32, 328

www.ingramcontent.com/pod-product-compliance
Lightning Source LLC
Chambersburg PA
CBHW020604300426
44113CB00007B/505